THE EUROPEAN SOCIAL CHARTER AND THE EMPLOYMENT RELATION

This collection addresses the potential of the European Social Charter to promote and safeguard social rights in Europe as a whole and, in particular, in the European Union. Drawing on the expertise of Transnational Trade Union Rights experts network from across Europe, it provides a comprehensive commentary on these fundamental rights. Taking a two-part approach, it offers an in-depth legal analysis of the European Social Charter as a new social constitution for Europe, investigating first the potential of the general framework in which the Charter is embedded. In a second phase, a series of social rights are examined in light of the case law of the European Committee of Social Rights, to demonstrate the crucial but difficult role of the Charter's supervisory bodies to secure the respect and promotion of social and workers' rights at national level, bearing in mind the reciprocal influence of other international social rights instruments. This examination is timely, given the pressure exerted on those rights during the recent period of economic and financial crisis. Furthermore, in the light of the predominantly economic vision of Europe, such analysis is crucial. The collection will stimulate academic scrutiny and raise awareness amongst practitioners and trade unions about the necessary anchor of the social dimension of the European Union in legal and political practice.

The European Social Charter and the Employment Relation

Edited by
Niklas Bruun
Klaus Lörcher
Isabelle Schömann
and
Stefan Clauwaert

etui.
european trade union institute

•HART•
PUBLISHING
OXFORD AND PORTLAND, OREGON
2017

Hart Publishing
An imprint of Bloomsbury Publishing Plc

Hart Publishing Ltd
Kemp House
Chawley Park
Cumnor Hill
Oxford OX2 9PH
UK

Bloomsbury Publishing Plc
50 Bedford Square
London
WC1B 3DP
UK

www.hartpub.co.uk
www.bloomsbury.com

Published in North America (US and Canada) by
Hart Publishing
c/o International Specialized Book Services
920 NE 58th Avenue, Suite 300
Portland, OR 97213-3786
USA

www.isbs.com

First published 2017

British Library Cataloguing-in-Publication Data
A catalogue record for this book is available from the British Library.

ISBNs: HB: 978-1-50990-632-1
ePDF: 978-1-50990-635-2
ePub: 978-1-50990-633-8

Library of Congress Cataloging-in-Publication Data

Names: Bruun, Niklas, editor. | Lörcher, Klaus, editor. | Schömann, Isabelle, editor. | Clauwaert, Stefan, editor.

Title: The European Social Charter and the employment relation / edited by Niklas Bruun, Klaus Lörcher, Isabelle Schömann and Stefan Clauwaert.

Description: Oxford ; Portland, Oregon : Hart Publishing, an imprint of Bloomsbury Publishing Plc, 2016. | Includes bibliographical references and index.

Identifiers: LCCN 2016034349 (print) | LCCN 2016034953 (ebook) | ISBN 9781509906321 (hardback : alk. paper) | ISBN 9781509906338 (Epub)

Subjects: LCSH: European Social Charter (1961 October 18) | Labor laws and legislation—Europe.

Classification: LCC KJC2839 .E925 2017 (print) | LCC KJC2839 (ebook) | DDC 344.401—dc23

LC record available at https://lccn.loc.gov/2016034349

Typeset by Compuscript Ltd, Shannon
Printed and bound in Great Britain by
CPI UK (Group) Ltd, Croydon CR0 4YY

Preface

The European Social Charter has emerged as 'a real counterpart to the European Convention on Human Rights (ECHR) and as an instrument with the capacity to advance social justice even in times of profound economic change', said Ms Maud de Boer-Buquicchio, then Deputy Secretary General of the Council of Europe, in her welcome address at a conference on the Reform of the European Social Charter organised at the House of the Estates and the University of Helsinki in 2011.

Today, the Charter has developed into a successful European human rights instrument that gives social and economic rights a similar wingspan and nearly the same footing as civil and political rights.

As the most developed human rights instrument in the social field at European level, it is essential for academics, but also for (legal) practitioners (judges, ombudspersons, national human rights institutions, civil servants, lawyers), trade unions and NGOs to obtain ownership of the Charter to better defend social and labour rights, and in particular the rights attached to the individual and collective employment relations, so badly hit in times of crisis.

Against this background, the ETUI Transnational Trade Union Rights Experts Network (TTUR) felt the need to enrich the ongoing academic and political debate and stimulate recourse to the Charter by providing an in-depth analysis of the role and impact of the Charter on rights in the employment relation. This volume on 'The European Social Charter and the Employment Relation' is the result of an ambitious two-year research project of the TTUR network. As an independent expert research network attached to the European Trade Union Institute (ETUI),[1] the TTUR was founded in 1999 by the late Brian Bercusson and brings together leading labour law professors from eight member states with an active interest in the development of EU labour law, and ETUI researchers: Niklas Bruun (universities of Stockholm and Helsinki), Klaus Lörcher (former legal secretary of the European Union Civil Service Tribunal and legal adviser to ETUC), Simon Deakin (Cambridge University), Filip Dorssemont (Catholic University of Louvain), Antoine Jacobs (Tilburg University), Csilla Kollonay-Lehoczky (Central European University and Eötvös Loránd University, Budapest, Hungary), Aristea Koukiadaki (University of Manchester, UK), Barbara

[1] See: www.etui.org/Networks/The-Transnational-Trade-Union-Rights-Experts-Network-TTUR.

Kresal (University of Ljubljana, Slovenia), Mélanie Schmitt (University of Strasbourg), Bruno Veneziani (University of Bari), Stefan Clauwaert and Isabelle Schömann (both senior researchers at the ETUI).

On the occasion of this publication, several external leading experts have joined this project with much valuable contribution. We would like to thank particularly: Régis Brillat, Head of the Department of the European Social Charter and Executive Secretary of the European Committee of Social Rights of the Council of Europe; Teun Jaspers of Utrecht University School of Law, International and European Law; Olivier De Schutter of the University of Louvain Centre for Philosophy of Law (CPDR); the Institute for Interdisciplinary Research in Legal Sciences (JUR-I); and Zoe Adams of Cambridge University for their most valuable contributions.

This book was preceded by related scientific projects conducted by the TTUR network aimed at strengthening awareness of and recourse to international and European legal sources of social and labour rights:

B Bercusson, *European Labour Law and the EU Charter of Fundamental Rights* (Baden-Baden, Nomos, 2006).

N Bruun, K Lörcher and I Schömann, *The Lisbon Treaty and Social Europe* (Oxford, Hart Publishing, 2012).

F Dorssemont, K Lörcher and I Schömann, *The European Convention on Human Rights and the Employment Relation* (Oxford, Hart Publishing, 2013).

N Bruun, K Lörcher and I Schömann, *The Economic and Financial Crisis and Collective Labour Law in Europe* (Oxford, Hart Publishing, 2014).

The present volume endorses the conceptual approach developed in particular in the 2013 publication and forms, together with the 2006 publication, a trilogy on the European legal instruments involved in promoting fundamental social rights as a lever for social justice and progress. It highlights the potential of the Charter as the European legal source of social rights, together with the dynamic case law of the European Committee of Social Rights. Part I looks at the general framework in which the Charter should be interpreted, implemented and monitored, while Part II thoroughly examines individual and collective labour rights, combining the international and European context in which they have developed, together with a thorough analysis of their current interpretation and finally their impact on other prominent European and national sources of social rights.

The book strongly emphasises the striking added value of the Charter in legal proceedings, and also as a source of proactive interpretation of social and labour rights. It is also aimed at encouraging academics and legal practitioners to take up the Charter as a vivid instrument for protecting and promoting social rights in Europe.

The ETUI would like to express its gratitude to the authors for their comprehensive and forward-looking analyses, which show how a systematic examination of fundamental social rights—and in particular those anchored in the Charter and its case law—can help to achieve a more social Europe.

Maria Jepsen
Director of the Research Department
ETUI

Contents

List of Contributors

Zoe Adams is a PhD student at the University of Cambridge, UK.

Régis Brillat is Head of the Department of the European Social Charter and Executive Secretary of the European Committee of Social Rights.

Niklas Bruun is Professor of Private Law at the University of Helsinki, Finland. He is leader of the research programme ReMarkLab, Stockholm University, and member of the research team of the Centre of Excellence in the Foundations of European Law and Polity, University of Helsinki.

Stefan Clauwaert is Senior Researcher at the European Trade Union Institute, (ETUI), Belgium and since 2000 representative of the European Trade Union Confederation (ETUC) in the European Social Charter Governmental Committee.

Simon Deakin is Professor of Law at the University of Cambridge, UK.

Olivier De Schutter is Professor at the University of Louvain (Belgium) and Member of the UN Committee on Economic, Social and Cultural Rights.

Filip Dorssemont is Professor of Law at the Catholic University of Louvain, Belgium.

Antoine Jacobs is Emeritus Professor of Law at the University of Tilburg, The Netherlands.

Teun Jaspers is Emeritus Professor at the Utrecht University, School of Law, The Netherlands.

Csilla Kollonay-Lehoczky is Professor of Law, Eötvös Lóránd University, Faculty of Law and Central European University, Legal Studies Department, Budapest, Hungary.

Aristea Koukiadaki is Senior Lecturer in Employment Law at the University of Manchester, UK.

Klaus Lörcher is former Legal Adviser to the European Trade Union Confederation (ETUC) and former Legal Secretary to the Civil Service Tribunal of the European Union, Germany.

Mélanie Schmitt is Maître de conférences HDR, Université of Strasbourg, Faculté de droit—UMR DRES—équipe Droit social, France.

Isabelle Schömann is Senior Researcher at the European Trade Union Institute (ETUI), Belgium.

Bruno Veneziani is Emeritus Professor of Labour Law and Comparative Trade Union Law, University of Bari, Italy.

Foreword

The European Committee of Social Rights and the Employment Relation: Strengths and Future Prospects

RÉGIS BRILLAT, HEAD OF THE DEPARTMENT OF THE EUROPEAN SOCIAL CHARTER AND EXECUTIVE SECRETARY OF THE EUROPEAN COMMITTEE OF SOCIAL RIGHTS

The European Social Charter ('the Charter')[1] is the result of a long negotiation process, which began as early as 1949, when the Council of Europe's ambition was to draft a comprehensive human rights treaty that would embody all the rights included in the Universal Declaration of Human Rights adopted by the United Nations in 1948: civil, political, economic, social and cultural rights. At the end of this process, the member states decided to adopt a treaty, only proclaiming civil and political rights: the European Convention on Human Rights ('the Convention').

During the negotiations that followed the adoption of the Convention, there were constant shifts between two possibilities: the first one was to draft another human rights treaty dedicated to social and economic rights, at the same level as the Convention; the second was to draft a European treaty that would serve as a framework for social policies and would allow Council of Europe member states to coordinate and/or harmonise their social policies.

The Charter adopted in 1961 and opened for signature on 18 October 1961 constitutes, in several respects, a compromise between the two options.

Today, however, after more than 50 years of practice and after its revision in 1996, the Charter is, beyond doubt, a true human rights instrument, and the strategy of developing the Charter as a human rights treaty can be seen to have been successful.

The 'employment' concept under the Charter is governed by several provisions, with a holistic approach.

[1] The term 'Charter', as well as any Article without further indication, refers to the Revised European Social Charter of 1996, unless it is otherwise specified (see the Introduction for more details).

The Charter rests on the principle of full employment based on the following principal characteristics:

(i) employment must be freely entered upon;
(ii) employment must be exercised without any type of discrimination;
(iii) employment must respect fair conditions;
(iv) the employment relationship under the Charter has a collective dimension.

In addition, the employment relationship constitutes a basis for access to many of the other Charter rights.

Indeed, the European Committee of Social Rights ('the Committee'), through its interpretation of the Charter within the reporting system and the collective complaints procedure, has continuously insisted on the importance of the employment relationship as a right and a source of rights.

The general principles of interpretation enunciated by the Committee have shaped the reality of the employment relationship.

The Committee maintains that the Charter is a human rights instrument. The main values underpinning the Charter are: solidarity, non-discrimination and participation.

In addition, the Charter's rights should be concrete and effective: the implementation of the Charter requires the state parties to take not merely legal action but also practical action to give full effect to the rights recognised in the Charter, and also to make available the resources and introduce the operational procedures necessary to give full effect to the rights specified therein. The implementation of the Charter must also be accompanied by effective and rigorous control at domestic level (for example, through the labour inspectorate).

Today, the Charter's approach to the employment relationship faces numerous challenges, both technical and political.

The first challenge is the level of unemployment in State Parties, which leads to a great part of the population being denied its rights under the Charter. This applies to the right to work, but also to all the rights that are dependent on being employed or in employment.

Second, the notion of employment has been totally transformed since 1961. The deterioration of the employment relationship is not only quantitative, but also qualitative, which puts the heart of the Charter at stake.

The third challenge concerns the efficacy of rights. In many European countries, rights are proclaimed through legislation, through compulsory texts of a binding nature and, prima facie, this corresponds to the guaranties enshrined in the Charter. But rights are not always implemented in practice. There is an extraordinary gap between what is proclaimed by constitutions, statutory law or case law, and the practical reality.

The growing complexity of the ways in which the employment relationship functions in practice makes the monitoring procedure of the Charter complex, and the Committee faces difficulties when it has to assess whether domestic legislation is implemented in practice.

Another challenge concerns the relationship between EU law and the Charter. Indeed, there are situations in which the Committee has found situations not in conformity with the Charter as a result of the implementation or effect of European Union law. Examples of discrepancies between the two legal orders concern the Working Time Directive, the Posted Workers Directive, the Directive on the right to family reunion, and the impact of 'austerity' measures on the rights guaranteed by the Charter.

With a view to overcoming all these difficulties, the Council of Europe has engaged in the 'Turin process', following the High-level Conference organised in Turin on 17–18 October 2014 by the Italian Presidency of the European Union, together with the Council of Europe. Its aim is to revitalise the Charter and to make the commitments accepted by the State Parties a reality. It is an ambitious process, placing the Charter at the heart of the European human rights strategy: in this framework, it aims at strengthening the treaty system of the Charter within the Council of Europe and in its relationship with the law of the European Union. The key objective of the Turin process is to improve the implementation of social rights at national level in order to reduce economic and social tensions, promote political consensus and, where appropriate, draw on this agreement to facilitate the adoption of the necessary reforms.

> From a historical standpoint, there is no declaration of rights or constitutional charter whose authors did not draft it with breaches of human dignity in mind and with the desire to remedy them. To understand the Declaration of 1948 and the Convention of 1950 we must bear in mind the fact that those who drew them up had before their eyes not only the appalling violations of freedoms perpetrated by totalitarianism, but also the tragedy of the poverty resulting from the ravages of war.
>
> A citation by Altiero Spinelli, that great Europeist, was selected for inclusion in the introduction to the programme of this Conference, and if we re-read his extraordinary 'Ventotene Manifesto' today, we can see that its central focus is concern about social issues, or as Spinelli put it 'for social reform', central to which was the duty to afford young people equal opportunities to work and to realise their potential. Many pro-Europeans perceived the failure to resolve major social questions as the origin of the nationalist and racist follies in so many countries. The Social Charter of 1961 therefore partakes of this concern for human suffering and of the conviction that social and democratic issues are closely linked and that the efforts to rebuild Europe from the ruins—yesterday and today—cannot be founded on indifference, which is the enemy of the protection of fundamental rights.
>
> The crisis has revealed the deficiencies of the legal arsenal available to European countries for safeguarding fundamental rights. ... The European welfare model can be saved only at the supranational level. The negative context of the economic

crisis has itself enabled us to rediscover those supranational instruments, like the Social Charter, which, as someone said, seemed to have been put in cold storage and which, with the crisis, instead revealed their key characteristic as treaties that unite States, individuals, international organisations, workers' organisations and NGOs, laying the foundations for a reconstruction of the Europe of values and rights. The crisis highlighted, if there were any need to do so, the fundamental relevance of social rights. And for European societies it constituted an opportunity to grasp the importance of implementing those rights.[2]

[2] 'General Report on the High-level Conference on the European Social Charter (Turin, 17–18 October 2014)', statement by Michele Nicoletti, Vice-president of the Parliamentary Assembly of the Council of Europe (Appendix 2t), available at www.coe.int/en/web/turin-european-social-charter/turin-process.

Introduction

NIKLAS BRUUN, KLAUS LÖRCHER, ISABELLE SCHÖMANN AND STEFAN CLAUWAERT

I. THE CHARTER AS THE MOST IMPORTANT HUMAN RIGHTS INSTRUMENT GUARANTEEING FUNDAMENTAL SOCIAL RIGHTS IN EUROPE

FUNDAMENTAL SOCIAL RIGHTS form an indivisible part of human rights. In accordance with this Council of Europe credo, the separation of human rights into first-class (civil and political) and second-class (economic, social and cultural) rights has been terminated, and both categories should be considered as having equal moral and legal value.

Against this background it is perhaps surprising that the European Convention on Human Rights (ECHR), which mainly guarantees civil and political rights, remains so much better known and legally recognised than its counterpart, the Charter,[1] notwithstanding that this is also often considered to be weak and/or only programmatic. Such an approach could arguably be defended when looking only at Part I of the Charter. Indeed, by this part the contracting parties 'accept as the aim of their policy to be pursued by all appropriate means both national and international in character, the attainment of conditions in which the following rights and principles may be effectively realised', a political obligation which relates to the following 31 points, including, in principle, the rights contained in the Charter in a summary way. However, Part II of the Charter further specifies those political principles and clarifies that the contracting parties undertake 'to consider themselves bound by the obligations in the following articles and paragraphs'. It is therefore obvious that Part I of the Charter addresses the political aims to be pursued, whereas the 31 Articles of Part II all contain legal obligations.

[1] The term 'Charter' is used throughout this volume for the 1996 Revised European Social Charter unless otherwise specified (for example, Art 8 of the 1961 Charter or ESC). However, there is a specific problem in relation to Article C of the Charter, which states that 'The implementation of the legal obligations contained in this Charter shall be submitted to the same supervision as the European Social Charter'. It thus refers to Part IV of the 1961 Charter, which in practice has been amended by the Turin Amending Protocol (although it has not entered into force legally, because it still lacks ratification by four states) (for more details, see the contribution by S Clauwaert in this volume).

While the history and development of social rights at international level in general and at European level in particular can be characterised by a general reluctance to consider them justiciable rights, increasingly they are being recognised as justiciable rights. This is true of the jurisprudence of the ECtHR and also at national level. It is also true, at national level, of the recognition of self-executing provisions of the Charter (in particular, Article 6§4 and Article 12).

The Charter is becoming more and more important. The latest decisions of the European Committee of Social Rights (ECSR) on the crisis, the consequences of the *Laval* judgment and the extension (to the police) of the right to strike demonstrate increasing awareness.

II. THE AIM OF THE PUBLICATION

The idea for this publication stems from Filip Dorssemont, who was already actively engaged in the project that culminated in the prior ECHR publication, *The European Convention on Human Rights and the Employment Relation*. Indeed, that book is the point of reference for the present publication in several respects. First and most obviously, in relation to the title; second, concerning the general concept of analysing a European human rights instrument in relation to employment; and last but not least, the ECtHR's jurisprudence, taking international (labour) standards into account when interpreting the relevant articles based on the *Demir and Baykara* judgment.[2]

In general, this publication aims at providing judges, legal experts, trade union lawyers and other persons interested in fundamental social rights with a framework for the comprehension of this European instrument, and tries to provide a certain orientation by referring to relevant international material. More particularly, the publication aims to:

- make the Charter more widely known in legal circles, and also show the interaction between the provisions of the Charter and other human rights instruments at the European level (within the Council of Europe and the European Union), as well as at the global level (within the ILO and UN);
- be part of a development giving the Charter more visibility by contributing to the increasing (legal) debate, in particular the so-called 'Turin process';[3]
- contribute to strengthen the impact of the Charter in itself but also in respect of Europe's fundamental rights architecture, in particular the

[2] See for more details F Dorssemont, K Lörcher and I Schömann (eds), *The European Convention on Human Rights in the Employment Relation* (Oxford, Hart Publishing, 2013).

[3] See in particular the contribution by S Clauwaert in this volume.

EU Treaty provisions (TEU and TFEU) referring to fundamental social rights (instruments) and the ECHR, as well as the Charter of Fundamental Rights in the European Union (CFREU);[4]

— provide guidance to trade unions, NGOs and others on how to make use of the Charter in order to defend and promote social rights in the world of work.

III. STRUCTURE

The two substantive parts are framed by introductory contributions at the beginning of the publication, and a conclusion at the end.

Part I of the publication addresses general overarching questions,[5] whereas the chapters in Part II deal with specific articles and provisions that address the employment relation. Therefore, a choice had to be made. We chose to include articles that deal directly with employment issues in their more individual (Articles 1 to 4, 24 and 26) or more collective dimensions (Articles 5 and 6, 21, 22, 28 and 29), protection of specific groups in employment in relation to young people, maternity, disabilities and migrant workers (Articles 7, 8, 15 and 19§4, respectively), as well as related discrimination problems (Articles 20, 27 and E). On the other hand, articles and provisions that address labour market policy (Article 9 and 25), education (Article 10), social security (Article 12), social protection (Articles 13 and 14) and social policy (Articles 11, 16, 17, 30 and 31) were not examined.

In order to facilitate understanding of the relevant provisions, the contributions in Part II start by reproducing the authoritative texts of articles contained in Part II of the Charter, together with the respective formulations in the Appendix to Part II. The contributions begin by analysing the framework (section I), describing the context and main content of the respective article (section I.A), followed by the sources and relations to other international instruments (section I.B); for example, whether there is an indication (for example, in the Explanatory Report for the RESC) of a reference to ILO or EU instruments. In order to clarify the role of the respective article in the Charter system, its relationship to other relevant Charter articles is examined (section I.C).

[4] See in particular the contribution by O de Schutter in this volume.

[5] Part I does not contain a general overview of the content of the Charter, as it is focused on the employment relation and also because a number of recent publications follow such a general approach (see, for example, M Mikkola, *Social Human Right of Europe* (Porvoo, Karelatico, 2010), and Council of Europe (ed), *European Social Charter—Collected texts*, 7th edn, 1 January 2015, available at: http://rm.coe.int/CoERMPublicCommonSearchServices/DisplayDCTMContent?documentId=090000168048b059, compiling all relevant official documents.

The main analysis focuses on the content of the respective article (section II), describing and exploring the substance of protection based on the case law of the ECSR, with special emphasis on its latest Conclusions or decisions. If there are specific paragraphs, they are dealt with individually (sections II.A, II.B, II.C).

Finally, the actual or potential impact of the respective provisions on other human rights instruments (section III), in particular the ECHR (section III.A) and the Charter of Fundamental Rights of the European Union (CFREU, section III.B) is explored. This analysis may be complemented by references to further EU (mainly secondary) legislative provisions and important examples at national level. A novelty in dealing with the Charter, it is obvious that such an influence has often not yet emerged and therefore can be considered only as a starting point that might have to be further developed.

Against this background, the contributions in Part II are, in principle, structured as follows:

I. Introduction
   A. Context and Main Content
   B. International Sources
   C. Relationship to Other Provisions of the Charter
II. Content (as appropriate:
   A. Para 1
   B. Para 2 …)
III. Impact on Human Rights Instruments
   A. European Convention on Human Rights (ECHR)
   B. EU Charter of Fundamental Rights (CFREU)
   C. National Level (where applicable)

Although all the contributions have been extensively discussed in the TTUR (Transnational Trade Union Rights Experts network), the individual authors bear sole responsibility for their own contributions, which do not necessarily reflect the views of the other authors of this volume.

Part I

General Part*

* Throughout Part I and Part II, the term 'Charter', as well as any Article without further indication, refers to the Revised European Social Charter of 1996, unless it is otherwise specified (see the Introduction for more details).

The European Social Charter as the Social Constitution of Europe[*]

OLIVIER DE SCHUTTER

I. INTRODUCTION

BY COMPARISON WITH the attention given to the European Convention on Human Rights (ECHR), both in the case law of the Court of Justice of the European Union (CJEU) and in the treaties establishing the European Union (EU), the Council of Europe's Social Charter is a relatively neglected instrument: a reference to the Charter appeared for the first time in the Treaty of Rome in 1987 and the CJEU refers to it sparingly, while the question of the EU's accession to the Charter has been referred to only on rare occasions and its implications hardly studied in detail, except in academic writings.[1] It is perhaps ironic therefore that the Charter, at a time when it was still under negotiation, had an impact on the architecture of the Treaty establishing the European Economic Community (EEC) in 1957.[2]

Indeed, when the creation of an EEC was being considered, the question arose of whether the Treaty establishing it should also include social

[*] This chapter is based on a study commissioned, overseen and published by the European Parliament's Policy Department for Citizens' Rights and Constitutional Affairs at the request of the European Parliament's Committee on Constitutional Affairs. It is republished here in an amended form with the kind permission of the European Parliament. The author expresses his gratitude to Klaus Loercher for the very useful feedback provided on an initial draft of this chapter.

[1] See, for studies on the status of the Charter in EU law, O De Schutter, 'Le statut de la Charte sociale européenne dans le droit de l'Union européenne', in *Mélanges en hommage à Jean-Paul Jacqué* (Paris, Dalloz, 2010) 217–61; U Khaliq, 'The European Union and the European Social Charter: Never the twain shall meet?' (2014) 15 *Cambridge Yearbook of European Legal Studies* 169.

[2] See, *inter alia*, S Deakin, 'Labour Law as Market Regulation: the Economic Foundations of European Social Policy', in P Davies, A Lyon-Caen, S Sciarra and S Simitis (eds), *European Community Labour Law: Principles and Perspectives* (Oxford, Clarendon Press, 1996) 62–93; J Kenner, *EU Employment Law: From Rome to Amsterdam and Beyond* (Oxford, Hart, 2003) 1–21.

provisions: should the common market, based on the free movement of workers and the freedom of companies to provide services and to establish themselves across the EEC member states, go hand in hand with harmonisation of social protection and workers' rights? That was the main question discussed by a group of experts chaired by the Swedish economist Bertil Ohlin when, acting at the request of the Governing Body of the International Labour Office (ILO), they ventured to examine the 'Social Aspects of European Economic Co-Operation'. The Ohlin Report concluded that improvements in living standards and labour conditions in the common market should essentially result from the functioning of the market itself.[3] The experts acknowledged, however, that these results held only 'when account is taken of the strength of the trade union movement in European countries and of the sympathy of European governments for social aspirations, to ensure that labour conditions would improve and would not deteriorate',[4] and that their conclusion depended on the strength of the ability of both workers' and employers' organisations to organise at transnational level.[5] Most importantly, they emphasised that this 'equalisation in an upward direction' of labour standards could be facilitated if all European countries joined the international conventions adopted by the ILO or the Charter, then under negotiation within the Council of Europe. The experts considered that it would be useful

> to consider what steps might be taken to promote the more widespread application of the provisions of these Conventions by European countries and thus add to their effectiveness as instruments for solving certain of the social problems connected with closer European economic co-operation.[6]

One might have thought, therefore, that links would have been established between the integration of the economies of the EEC member states and the Charter, after this instrument was signed in Turin on 18 October 1961—at a minimum, by encouraging the countries concerned to ratify the Charter and perhaps to agree on a core set of provisions of the Charter that they should all accept under the original 'à la carte' system of commitments it inaugurated;[7] or perhaps even by establishing a mechanism through which

[3] Report by a Group of Experts, *Social Aspects of European Economic Co-Operation* (Geneva, International Labour Office, 1956) (reproduced in (1956) 74 *International Labour Review* 99).

[4] ibid §210.

[5] ibid §215.

[6] ibid §273, (vi).

[7] Under the system of the Charter, states are allowed to select, within limits, the undertakings by which they will be bound. For a full description of the system of the Charter, see O De Schutter and M Sant'Ana, 'The European Social Charter', in G de Beco (ed), *Human Rights Monitoring Mechanisms of the Council of Europe* (London and New York, Routledge, 2012) 71–99.

the EEC itself would align its secondary law with the requirements of the Charter.

This did not happen. Only with the adoption of the Single European Act (SEA), signed in Luxembourg on 17 February 1986 before entering into force on 1 July 1987, did the Charter make its first and timid appearance in the Treaties establishing the European Communities (EC).[8] The SEA put in place the mechanisms designed to ensure that the internal market would be established progressively over a period expiring on 31 December 1992, but at the same time strengthening the ability of the EEC to adopt provisions in the social policy area. In the Preamble, the Heads of State and Government expressed their determination to 'promote democracy on the basis of fundamental rights recognised in the constitutions and laws of the member states, in the [ECHR] and the Charter, notably freedom, equality and social justice'. Yet in 1989, when the President of the European Commission, Jacques Delors, insisted that the EEC commit to providing the internal market with a strong social dimension, he encouraged the adoption of a Community Charter on the Fundamental Social Rights of Workers (CCFSRW).[9] This was proclaimed at the Strasbourg European Summit of 9–10 December 1989, in the form of a political declaration adopted by 11 of the 12 EEC member states.[10] The signal was clear: the CCFSRW resulted from a deliberate choice to adopt a catalogue of social rights specific to the EEC, rather than to seek to implement the *acquis* of the Council of Europe in this regard. Thus, just as 'social Europe' was emerging as part of the objective of completing the internal market, the Charter was increasingly marginalised.

In 1992, the Treaty on the European Union (TEU)[11] assigned to the EC, *inter alia*, the objective of achieving 'a high level of employment and of social protection',[12] and under the Protocol on Social Policy, 11 member states agreed to rely on the institutions, procedures and mechanisms of the EC Treaty to implement an Agreement on Social Policy (the United Kingdom again declining to join). However, confirming the separation between the construction of 'social Europe' within the EU and the Council of Europe, the TEU makes reference not to the Charter, but instead to the 1989 CCFSRW. Only in 1997, with the adoption of the Treaty of Amsterdam and the repatriation, within the EC Treaty, of the Agreement on Social Policy, was the Charter again referred to. Here again, however, the references were rather discrete. In addition to the 1961 Charter being mentioned in the Preamble,

[8] [1987] OJ L169.

[9] COM(89) 471 final.

[10] The United Kingdom, at the time under a Conservative government led by Prime Minister Margaret Thatcher, did not join.

[11] [1992] OJ C191.

[12] Art 2 of the EC Treaty, as amended by Art G of the TEU.

the new Article 117 inserted into the EEC Treaty (later Article 136 EC, now Article 151 TFEU) mentioned the Charter as a source of inspiration for the European legislator in the social policy field. It was not a binding reference, however, nor did it instruct the CJEU to uphold the Charter in the implementation of EU law.[13]

The relative invisibility of the Charter during this period stood in sharp contrast to the attention paid to the ECHR. While emphasising the 'special significance' of the ECHR as a source of inspiration for the development of the general principles of law which it sought to ensure respect for[14]—a position endorsed in the Treaty of Maastricht, which referred to the ECHR in Article F (later Article 6 TEU)—the CJEU refused to elevate the Charter to the same status. In 1999, one Advocate General of the CJEU explained that, because the Charter allowed the Contracting Parties to choose at the moment of ratification which provisions of the instrument they would be bound by, the rights listed in the Charter could not be considered fundamental rights that were generally recognised and thus worthy of being included among the general principles of EU law.[15]

II. THE EU CHARTER OF FUNDAMENTAL RIGHTS (CFREU)

The launch of the negotiations on a CFREU presented the EU with an opportunity to bridge that gap and to align the status of the rights and freedoms of the Charter with that of those listed in the ECHR. However, the difference in treatment between the two Council of Europe instruments was made, if anything, even more visible. The Cologne European Council of 3–4 June 1999, which launched the process that would lead to the adoption of the CFREU,

[13] The objectives of social policy as set forth in Art 117 EEC Treaty (Art 136 EC, now Art 151 TFEU) have been considered by the CJEU as programmatic, and as lacking any direct effect: see, eg, Case 149/77, *Defrenne v Sabena*, judgment of 15 June 1978 [1978] ECR 1365, and Case 170/84, *Bilka-Kaufhaus v Weber van Hartz* [1986] ECR 1607. In Case 126/86, *Giménez Zaera*, judgment of 29 September 1987 [1987] ECR 3712, the CJEU noted that such social policy objectives could serve as a means of interpretation of Community law: 'The fact that the objectives of social policy laid down in Article 117 are in the nature of a programme does not mean that they are deprived of any legal effect. They constitute an important aid, in particular for the interpretation of other provisions of the Treaty and of secondary Community legislation in the social field.' Nevertheless, it added, '[the] attainment of those objectives must ... be the result of a social policy which must be defined by the competent authorities' (para 14). See section II.C below, for more recent examples.

[14] Joined Cases 46/87 and 227/88, *Hoechst AG v Commission of the European Communities*, judgment of 21 September 1989 (ECLI:EU:C:1989:337), para 13. The ECHR was initially referred to in Case 4/73, *Nold v Commission*, judgment of 14 May 1974, [1974] ECR 491).

[15] See the opinion of AG Francis G Jacobs delivered in the *Albany International* case (Case C-67/96, judgment of 21 September 1999, ECR I-5751), para 146. The CJEU does not get to the question of the status of the right to bargain collectively in the judgment of 21 September 1999 it delivered in this case.

instructed that 'In drawing up such a Charter account should ... be taken of economic and social rights as contained in the European Social Charter and the Community Charter of the Fundamental Social Rights of Workers (Article 136 TEC), insofar as they do not merely establish objectives for action by the Union'.[16] Trench warfare was fought for months about the significance of these words. It was finally won at the end of the summer of 2000 by the partisans of inserting social provisions in the CFREU, led by the representative of the French government, Guy Braibant. By then, however, it had become clear that the CFREU would not be legally binding, at least at an initial stage: what may have been impossible to obtain from the British delegate, Lord Goldsmith, in a binding text, probably had become easier to achieve in what was going to be (according to the consensus that had been reached by then) a mere political declaration.[17]

A. Social 'Rights' or 'Principles'?

Moreover, the victory was only partial.[18] As part of the compromise reached in July 2000, when the drafters of the CFREU finally struck an agreement on the inclusion of social provisions in the CFREU under discussion, it was understood that some of these provisions to be listed in the CFREU would only be justiciable in combination with legislative or other measures adopted at EU or member state level, and as a means to interpret such acts, or to assess their validity: in other words, such social guarantees were not to be invoked as free-standing 'subjective rights' that the individual could claim, unless some measure had been adopted to implement the said guarantee.[19] It is this understanding that came to be codified in Article 52(5)

[16] Conclusions of the Cologne European Council, 3–4 June 1999, Annex IV.

[17] On the drafting of the Charter, see G de Búrca, 'The drafting of the European Union Charter of Fundamental Rights' (2001) *European Law Review* 126; and Lord Goldsmith QC, 'A Charter of Rights, Freedoms and Principles' (2001) 38 *Common Market Law Review* 1201. According to the report published by the United Kingdom House of Lords Select Committee on the European Union on the incorporation of the CFREU in the EU Treaties: 'The need to maintain this "important" distinction [between "rights" and "principles"] and the lack of precision of the December 2000 Charter's wording were reasons why Lord Goldsmith opposed the Charter becoming legally binding' (Tenth Report, session 2007–2008 (February 2008), para 5.18).

[18] See generally, on the status of social rights in the CFREU, 'Les droits et principes sociaux dans la Charte des droits fondamentaux de l'Union européenne', in J-Y Carlier and O De Schutter (eds), *La Charte des droits fondamentaux de l'Union européenne* (Bruxelles, Bruylant, 2002) 117–48; T Hervey and J Kenner (eds), *Economic and Social Rights under the EU Charter of Fundamental Rights. A Legal Perspective* (Oxford, Hart, 2003).

[19] See especially in this regard the two contributions presented by G Braibant, representative of the French Executive, respectively, on 2 May 2000 (CHARTE 4280/00, CONTRIB 153) and on 19 May 2000 (CHARTE 4322/00, CONTRIB 188).

of the CFREU when, with the adoption of the Treaty of Lisbon in 2007, it was agreed to integrate the CFREU in the Treaties.[20] Article 52(5) states:

> The provisions of this Charter which contain principles may be implemented by legislative and executive acts taken by institutions, bodies, offices and agencies of the Union, and by acts of Member States when they are implementing Union law, in the exercise of their respective powers. They shall be judicially cognisable only in the interpretation of such acts and in the ruling on their legality.

While it may not have been easy to anticipate how the CJEU would read this restriction on its ability to enforce the social provisions of the CFREU, the developments since the entry into force of the Treaty of Lisbon illustrate its reluctance to move beyond this narrowly defined mandate in order to strengthen the protection of social rights. Social rights as 'principles' have occasionally been relied upon as a means of interpretation of EU law. In the case of *Kamberaj*, for instance, the CJEU relied on Article 34 CFREU in support of its view that the notion of 'core benefits', for which the 2003 Directive on the status of third-country nationals who are long-term residents imposes a requirement of equal treatment with citizens of the Union, necessarily should include housing benefits.[21] According to Article 34 CFREU, the European Union recognises and respects the right to social and housing assistance so as to ensure a decent existence for all those who lack sufficient resources. The CJEU considered that 'in so far as the [housing] benefit in question in the main proceedings fulfils the purpose set out in that article of the Charter, it cannot be considered, under European Union law, as not being part of core benefits within the meaning of Article 11(4) of Directive 2003/109'.[22]

The CJEU was far less generous in other cases, however. In *Association de Médiation Sociale*, which it decided two years later, it was asked whether Article 27 CFREU, which recognises the fundamental right of workers to information and consultation, could be invoked in proceedings between private parties in order to disallow the application of a national measure adopted in violation of Directive 2002/14/EC establishing a general

[20] The wording of this provision was initially proposed by the European Convention, which submitted the Draft Treaty establishing a Constitution for Europe to the European Council on 18 July 2003 (see Art II-52(5) of the Draft Treaty). For the revised version of the EU Charter of Fundamental Rights, see [2007] OJ C303/1.

[21] According to Art 11(1) of Council Directive 2003/109/EC of 25 November 2003 concerning the status of third-country nationals who are long-term residents [2004] OJ L16/44, 'Long-term residents shall enjoy equal treatment with nationals as regards: ... (d) social security, social assistance and social protection as defined by national law; ... (f) access to goods and services and the supply of goods and services made available to the public and to procedures for obtaining housing'. Under Art 11(4) of Directive 2003/109, however, 'member states may limit equal treatment in respect of social assistance and social protection to core benefits'.

[22] Case C-571/10, *Kamberaj*, judgment of 24 April 2012 § 92.

framework for informing and consulting employees in the EC.[23] The CJEU answered in the negative. It took the view that, in order for Article 27 CFREU to be fully effective, 'it must be given more specific expression in European Union or national law', and that this provision therefore cannot 'be invoked in a dispute ... in order to conclude that the national provision which is not in conformity with Directive 2002/14 should not be applied'.[24] The CJEU reached this conclusion although the right of workers to information and consultation had been invoked not as a right to be granted independently of any implementing measure, but simply as a tool to support a generous reading of the 2002 directive on the same subject, in order to allow that directive to be invoked in 'horizontal' relationships (that is, in a dispute between private persons).

A few months later, in *Glatzel*, the CJEU refused to conclude that a 2006 directive on driving licences was discriminatory against persons with a (visual) disability. By imposing certain minimum standards as regards visual acuity relating to physical fitness to drive a motor vehicle, the directive had led in the main proceedings to the applicant being denied a driving licence for heavy vehicles because he was able to detect hand movements with his right eye only, despite the fact that the central visual acuity in his left eye was 1.0 and therefore he had full visual acuity.[25] Faced with the argument that denying Mr Glatzel a driver's licence could be contrary to the requirements of Article 26 CFREU, which requires the EU to respect and recognise the right of persons with disabilities to benefit from integration measures, the CJEU answered that 'the principle enshrined by that article does not require the EU legislature to adopt any specific measure. In order for that article to be fully effective, it must be given more specific expression in EU or national law'.[26] This again is a surprising conclusion, because the 2006 directive in question did, in fact, affect persons with visual impairments, and the 'principle' according to which the EU should respect and recognise the right of persons with disabilities to benefit from integration measures was not invoked as a self-standing right: instead, its invocation by Glatzel seemed perfectly in line with the kind of situation envisaged under Article 52(5) CFREU in its 2007 (revised) form.[27]

[23] Directive 2002/14/EC of the European Parliament and of the Council of 11 March 2002 establishing a general framework for informing and consulting employees in the European Community [2002] OJ L 80/29.

[24] Case C-176/12, *Association de Médiation Sociale*, judgment of 15 January 2014 §§ 45 and 48.

[25] Directive 2006/126/EC of the European Parliament and of the Council of 20 December 2006 on driving licences [2006] OJ L403/18 and corrigendum [2009] OJ L19/67, as amended by Commission Directive 2009/113/EC of 25 August 2009 [2009] OJ L223.

[26] Case C-356/12, *Glatzel*, judgment of 22 May 2014 §78.

[27] Consistent with the idea of 'normative justiciability' referred to above, the 'principles' listed by the CFREU in the social field should be 'observed', which means that they may be

Social provisions were included in the CFREU, therefore, but this came at a price: some of them were to be treated as embodying 'principles', rather than self-standing 'rights' or 'freedoms', and the conditions under which they shall be justiciable appear to have been defined quite restrictively by the CJEU. Moreover, although most social provisions include at least some components that are fully justiciable—indeed, part of the compromise struck in 2000 was to leave it open to the courts to identify those elements—there is a real risk that all social provisions listed in title IV of the CFREU ('Solidarity') shall be considered mere 'principles'. Such a development would be damaging to the credibility of the CFREU, and unfaithful to the intention of its drafters.[28] It would be particularly difficult to explain as regards the provisions of title IV that relate to employment. Unfortunately, however, it cannot be excluded.[29]

relied on to challenge Union or national legislation that violates them (J-P Jacqué, 'The Explanations Relating to the Charter of Fundamental Rights of the European Union', in S Peers, T Hervey, J Kenner and A Ward (eds), *The EU Charter of Fundamental Rights* (CH Beck/Hart/Nomos, Oxford and Portland, 2014) 1715–24, 1720). Whereas Directive 2006/14/EC obviously did not have as its primary aim implementation of the rights of persons with disabilities, or to favour their integration, it undoubtedly had the potential of affecting such rights or of having an impact on such integration, as illustrated by the individual situation of Mr Glatzel.

[28] The Explanations Relating to the Charter of Fundamental Rights themselves acknowledge that the distinction between 'principles' and 'rights' is not a clear-cut one: 'For illustration, examples for principles, recognised in the Charter include eg Articles 25, 26 and 37. In some cases, an Article of the Charter may contain both elements of a right and of a principle, eg Articles 23, 33 and 34'. Arts 33 and 34, which refer to 'Family and professional life' and to 'Social security and social assistance', respectively, are both located in Title IV of the CFREU. As noted by the UK House of Lords in the reports cited above, 'there is obscurity about how and where the distinction is to be drawn, and, in particular, a failure in the Charter and its Explanations to spell out clearly which of the Charter articles involve rights and which principles. The distinction will in practice have to be worked out in future cases before the ECJ' (§5.22).

[29] Indeed, the Protocol (No 30) on the Application of the Charter of Fundamental Rights of the European Union to Poland and the United Kingdom, appended to the Treaty of Lisbon (OJ C306/157), may have introduced confusion in this regard. At the request of the United Kingdom, the chief author of the Protocol (compare with Declaration No 62 by Poland concerning the Protocol, in which the Polish government 'declares that, having regard to the tradition of the social movement of "Solidarity" and its significant contribution to the struggle for social and labour rights, it fully respects social and labour rights, as established by European Union law, and in particular those reaffirmed in Title IV of the Charter'), the Protocol (No 30) states that '*for the avoidance of doubt*, nothing in Title IV of the Charter creates justiciable rights applicable to Poland or the United Kingdom except in so far as Poland or the United Kingdom has provided for such rights in its national law' (Art 1(2)). This formulation is deeply problematic, since, as it presents itself as a mere restatement of what the CFREU requires, it creates the impression that none of the provisions of Title IV include justiciable rights. Though this is entirely implausible, it cannot be excluded that British and Polish national courts, at least, will refrain from addressing a referral to the CJEU when questions of interpretation or of validity of EU law shall be raised on the basis of Title IV of the CFREU.

B. Selectivity in the Choice of Social Provisions

A second limitation is that the list of social rights, freedoms and principles of the EU Charter of Fundamental Rights paled in comparison with the full list of the 1961 and 1996 versions of the European Social Charter. There are certain areas, of course, in which the EU Charter of Fundamental Rights goes beyond the European Social Charter: this is the case, for instance, insofar as the EU Charter refers in Article 36 to services of general economic interest, or insofar as it provides for environmental protection and for consumer protection. These are areas about which the European Social Charter is silent, although the case law of the European Committee of Social Rights has, to some extent, compensated for this.[30] In general, however, the EU Charter of Fundamental Rights presents significant omissions when compared with the protection of social rights by the successive versions of the European Social Charter.

These gaps are not limited to the choice of wording, in the EU Charter of Fundamental Rights, which is more concise and general than that found in the detailed prescriptions of the Council of Europe Charter. Nor do the gaps identified result merely from the fact that the EU has not been attributed competences in the area concerned: as regards the right to health care, to social assistance as a means to combat social exclusion, or the right to housing, although they are all mentioned in the EU Charter of Fundamental Rights, it is clear from the wording chosen that the drafters of these provisions were uncomfortable with the idea of guaranteeing certain entitlements in the field of application of EU law (the only field in which the EU Charter of Fundamental Rights applies, in accordance with Article 51) where the subject-matter is be to regulated by the member states.[31] Similarly, the EU Charter is entirely silent about the right to a fair remuneration, which Article 4 of the European Social Charter aims to guarantee, except for one dimension of this right, which concerns the right to equal remuneration for women and men.[32] It says nothing about the right to childcare

[30] For instance, taking into account 'the growing link that states party to the Charter and other international bodies ... make between the protection of health and a healthy environment', the ECSR has interpreted Art 11 CFREU (right to protection of health) as including the right to a healthy environment (ECSR, Decision on the merits, 6 December 2006, Complaint No 30/2005, *Marangopoulos Foundation for Human Rights v Greece* §195).

[31] Although Art 153(1)(j) TFEU does mention the 'combating of social exclusion' among the fields in which the action of the EU may complement and support that of the member states, this is an area in which the treaties have not provided for the adoption of EU legislation (see Art 153(2) TFEU).

[32] However, a level of remuneration that would be below the poverty rate and thus would not allow the worker to live a decent life, may be considered to be contrary to human dignity, or to constitute inhuman or degrading treatment, in violation of Arts 1 and 4 of the CFREU respectively (see, in support of that interpretation, *MSS v Belgium and Greece* App no 30696/09 (ECtHR(GC), 21 January 2011) §263.

services, mentioned in Article 17 of the European Social Charter (which guarantees the right of mothers and children to social and economic protection), although the 'legal, economic and social protection' of the family stipulated in Article 33§1 of the EU Charter of Fundamental Rights partly compensates for this. The same is true for the right to social welfare services, referred to in Article 14 of the European Social Charter. This cautious approach is largely based on a misunderstanding. It is premised on the idea that to guarantee a right is necessarily to have the power to take measures that will implement it, whereas in fact stipulating such a guarantee could mean, more modestly but at the same time importantly, that the Union commits not to restrict the ability of the member states, which are competent in this regard, to adopt such measures aiming at the realisation of the right in question. Yet, it is this idea that explains many of the silences, or the hesitant formulations ('the Union recognises and respects the right X, in accordance with the rules laid down by Union law and national laws and practices') adopted by the drafters of the CFREU in these areas.

In other cases, the gaps stem from a deliberate choice not to define as a fundamental right a guarantee that is protected under EU law only through secondary legislation. This is the case, in particular, as regards some provisions of the 1996 Charter that were directly inspired by EU legislation: thus, Article 8 of the Charter, in its revised version from 1996, to a large extent summarises what the 1992 directive on safety and health at work of pregnant workers and workers who have recently given birth or are breastfeeding.[33] Article 25 of the 1996 Charter recognises the right of workers to the protection of their claims in the event of the insolvency of their employer: although, again, the CFREU does not include a similar provision, this is an area in which EU legislation has existed since 1980,[34] and it is this legislative framework that directly influenced the revision of the Charter in 1996.

Finally, some omissions of the CFREU in the area of fundamental social rights stem from a narrow understanding of what constitutes social rights, as opposed to mere 'objectives for action by the Union', to reiterate the distinction used by the 3–4 June 1999 Cologne European Council's conclusions.[35]

[33] Council Directive 92/85/EEC of 19 October 1992 on the introduction of measures to encourage improvements in the safety and health at work of pregnant workers and workers who have recently given birth or are breastfeeding [1992] OJ L348/1–7.

[34] See Council Directive 80/987/EEC of 20 October 1980 on the protection of employees in the event of the insolvency of their employer [1980] OJ L283/23. This directive was subsequently amended by Council Directive 87/164/EEC [1987] OJ L66/11 and by Directive 2002/74/EC of the European Parliament and of the Council [2002] OJ L270/10. These successive changes were consolidated in Directive 2008/94/EC of the European Parliament and of the Council of 22 October 2008 on the protection of employees in the event of the insolvency of their employer [2008] OJ L283/36–42.

[35] Conclusions of the Cologne European Council, 3–4 June 1999, Annex IV.

The most notorious example is the right to work. The EU Treaty lists 'full employment' as one of the objectives of the Union, and Article 9 TFEU provides that the Union shall take into account requirements linked to the promotion of a 'high level of employment' in defining and implementing its policies and activities. Nevertheless, whereas Article 1 of the Charter commits state parties to achieve and maintain 'as high and stable a level of employment as possible, with a view to the attainment of full employment', the equivalent provision in the CFREU only refers in fact to the freedom of everyone to engage in work (replicating Article 1 para 2 of the Charter), without implying a duty of the state to aim to provide employment to all; although provisions of the CFREU do refer to the right of access to placement services free of charge (Article 29) or to the protection against unjustified dismissal (Article 30), these are only some dimensions of the duties that correspond to the fulfilment of the right to work as a human right.[36]

C. The Absence of any Explicit Link to the ECSR

There is finally a last indication of the unwillingness of the drafters of the CFREU clearly to align the status of the Charter with that of the ECHR. In order to promote consistency between the approaches of, respectively, the CJEU and the ECtHR, they sought to ensure that the rights and freedoms of the CFREU that correspond to rights and freedoms listed in the ECHR would be interpreted in accordance with the case law of the ECtHR. This of course was the intention of Article 52§3 CFREU. In contrast, no such reference was made to the provisions of the Charter, let alone to the jurisprudence of the ECSR.

This is perhaps unsurprising, taking into account both the privileged position of the ECHR in the case law of the CJEU, and the suspicion of the CJEU towards the views adopted by non-judicial bodies tasked with the interpretation of other international human rights instruments.[37] At the same time, it is far from inevitable. A number of provisions of the CFREU are inspired by the Charter, and it would serve legal certainty—as well as acknowledging the role assigned to the ECSR under this instrument—to read the provisions of the CFREU in light of the approach followed by the ECSR. Moreover,

[36] The right of access to placement services free of charge reflects Art 1§3 of the Charter, which commits state parties to 'establish or maintain free employment services for all workers'; the protection against unjustified dismissal is considered by the UN Committee on Economic, Social and Cultural Rights as part of the right to work mentioned in Art 6 of the International Covenant on Economic, Social and Cultural Rights (see General Comment No 18: The right to work (Art 6 of the Covenant), UN doc E/C12/GC/18 (6 February 2006) §§34–35).

[37] See, in particular, *Case C-249/96*, Lisa Jacqueline Grant v South-West Trains Ltd [1998] ECR I-621 *(judgment of 17 February 1998) §46.*

the CJEU has occasionally referred to international human rights instruments other than the ECHR: it relied on the International Covenant on Civil and Political Rights in areas where the ECHR was insufficiently comprehensive or the case law of the ECtHR was unclear;[38] it relied on the 1989 Convention on the Rights of the Child in *Parliament v Council*,[39] when the European Parliament sought to annul the 2003 Family Reunification Directive,[40] explaining in this regard that, just like the ICCPR, the Convention on the Rights of the Child 'binds each of the member states'.[41]

The Charter is mentioned in Article 151 TFEU (formerly Article 136 of the EC Treaty), and the CJEU has occasionally acknowledged that it therefore could be relied upon in order to guide the interpretation of EU law. In the case of *Kiiski*,[42] the CJEU relied on the Charter in order to support its interpretation of the requirements of Council Directive 92/85/EEC on the improvement of the safety and health at work of pregnant workers and workers who have recently given birth or are breastfeeding.[43] The CJEU adopted a generous reading of the protection afforded by the directive, noting in this regard that

> Article 136 [of the EC Treaty] refers to the European Social Charter signed at Turin on 18 October 1961 and revised at Strasbourg on 3 May 1996, to which in its original or revised version or both, all Member States are parties. Article 8 of the European Social Charter concerning the right of employed women to protection of maternity, aims to provide them with a right to maternity leave of at least 12 weeks (original version) or at least 14 weeks (revised version) … In those circumstances, the right to maternity leave granted to pregnant workers must be regarded as a particularly important mechanism of protection under employment law.[44]

Similarly, in the *Impact* case,[45] the CJEU was requested to provide an interpretation, in particular, of Clause 4 of the framework agreement on fixed-term work concluded on 18 March 1999 between the social partners at the Union level.[46] Clause 4 imposes a principle of non-discrimination between

[38] See, eg, *Case 374/87*, Orkem v Commission *[1989] ECR 3283, para 31, and Joined Cases C-297/88 and C-197/89*, Dzodzi v Belgian State *[1990] ECR I-3763 §68.*

[39] Case C-540/03, *European Parliament v Council of the European Union*, judgment of 27 June 2006 §37.

[40] Council Directive 2003/86/EC of 22 September 2003 on the right to family reunification [2003] OJ L251/12.

[41] *European Parliament v Council of the European Union* (n 39) §37.

[42] Case C-116/06, *Sari Kiiski*, judgment of 20 September 2007.

[43] Council Directive 92/85/EEC of 19 October 1992 on the introduction of measures to encourage improvements in the safety and health at work of pregnant workers and workers who have recently given birth or are breastfeeding (10th individual Directive within the meaning of Art 16§1 of Directive 89/391/EEC) [1992] OJ L348/1.

[44] *Kiiski* (n 42) §§48–49.

[45] Case C-268/06, *Impact*, judgment of 15 April 2008.

[46] The framework agreement is annexed to Council Directive 1999/70/EC of 28 June 1999 concerning the framework agreement on fixed-term work concluded by ETUC, UNICE and CEEP [1999] OJ L175/43.

fixed-term workers and permanent workers 'in respect of employment conditions': the referring court asked whether this expression included conditions of an employment contract relating to remuneration and pensions. The CJEU took the view that, at the very least, it would be unjustified to exclude entirely financial conditions such as those relating to remuneration and pensions from the notion of 'employment conditions'. Indeed, the CJEU noted, the Charter includes among the objectives that its Contracting Parties have undertaken to achieve the right for all workers to a 'fair remuneration sufficient for a decent standard of living for themselves and their families': the non-discrimination principle contained in Clause 4 of the framework agreement on fixed-term work therefore 'must be interpreted as articulating a principle of Community social law which cannot be interpreted restrictively'.[47]

Cases such as *Kiiski* or *Impact* illustrate how the Charter can operate as a guide for the interpretation of EU law, so as to encourage a reading of EU law that will, to the fullest extent possible, facilitate attainment of the objectives the Contracting Parties have set for themselves. Indeed, the CJEU has occasionally found that the General Court of the European Union is under a duty to interpret EU law in light of the CFREU, as well as in light of the Charter as regards those provisions of the Charter that correspond to rights listed in the CFREU.[48] However, the Charter still is not recognised as having a status similar to that of the Convention on the Rights of the Child or the International Covenant on Civil and Political Rights: the use of expressions such as 'particularly important principle of European Union social law' to designate social rights listed in the Charter betrays the unease of the CJEU in this regard.[49] The reason for this is probably that, in the eyes of the CJEU, the undertakings of the EU member states in the à la carte system of the Charter are too varied for this instrument to provide an authoritative source of inspiration for the development of fundamental social rights in the EU legal order. The adoption of the CFREU did not bring about any change in this regard. Whereas, in a number of cases, the CJEU did refer to the Charter as a source of interpretation of the rights or principles listed in the CFREU, such a reference remains selective, because it is only where a social right has been identified by the CFREU as establishing more than an 'objective for action by the Union'—to paraphrase the conclusions of the Cologne European Council—that a reference to the Charter shall be deemed fitting.[50]

[47] See §§113 and 114 of the judgment.

[48] See, eg, Case C-579/12 RX-II, *European Commission v Strack*, judgment of 19 September 2013.

[49] See S Robin-Olivier, 'The contribution of the Charter of Fundamental Rights to the protection of social rights in the European Union: a first assessment after Lisbon' (2013) 1 *European Journal of Human Rights* 109 (in French).

[50] Conclusions of the Cologne European Council, 3–4 June 1999, Annex IV.

As to the interpretation given to that instrument by the ECSR, it is hardly relevant at all, even in those instances where a provision of the Charter has inspired the drafting of the CFREU.

D. Fundamental Social Rights in Impact Assessments

The adoption of the CFREU may be seen, therefore, as a missed opportunity. It could have led to a strengthening of the relationship between the EU and the Charter, and overcome the tendency to prioritise the protection of civil and political rights over that of economic and social rights in the integration of the EU: instead, the implicit hierarchy between the two sets of rights was largely confirmed. Following the proclamation of the CFREU on 7 December 2000, the European Commission could have sought to bridge this gap. It refrained from doing so: during the following decade, it gradually improved the methodology through which it would verify the compatibility of its legislative proposals with the CFREU at an early stage,[51] but in none of the documents by which it describes this methodology does the Commission pledge to ensure that its reading of the CFREU would comply with the Charter.

Similarly, whereas the practice of impact assessments was also improved during this period in order to better take into account the requirements of fundamental rights, the references to the CFREU seemed to operate as a screen—shielding, in effect, the choices proposed by the European Commission from being assessed against the requirements of the Charter, even as such choices were being scrutinised on the basis of their economic, social and environmental impacts. The preparation of such impact assessments has become standard practice since 2002.[52] When they were revised in 2005, the guidelines for the preparation of impact assessments paid greater attention to the potential effects of different policy options on the guarantees listed in the CFREU,[53] an option that has been further strengthened since then.[54] The Commission pledged, in its 'smart regulation' communication of 2010, to take more steps in this direction.[55] However, the current guidelines provided to the European Commission services as part of the 'better regulation' approach still refer exclusively to the CFREU, compliance with which must be examined to assess the 'regulatory fitness' of the

[51] See Communication from the Commission, 'Compliance with the Charter of Fundamental Rights in Commission legislative proposals. Methodology for systematic and rigorous monitoring' COM (2005) 172 final.

[52] Communication of 5 June 2002 on Impact Assessment COM (2002) 276.

[53] See SEC (2005) 791.

[54] SEC (2009) 92.

[55] See COM (2010) 543 final, 7.

proposals made by the Commission. Except for a reference to Council of Europe instruments (including the European Social Charter) in the list of 'online sources of information on fundamental rights relevant to Commission Impact Assessments' appended to a 2011 Staff Working Document on this issue,[56] nowhere are the Commission services encouraged to look beyond the CFREU.

III. THE COSTS OF NON-COOPERATION

As we saw in the previous section, the status of the Charter in EU law remains unsatisfactory. It would be incorrect to state that the Charter is ignored: it has been referred to on many occasions. However, such references are not systematic. They are also indirect: the Charter is not seen as providing an authoritative source of inspiration for the gradual development by the CJEU of fundamental rights as part of the general principles of Union law, both because of the lack of uniformity of the EU member states' undertakings in the à la carte system of the Charter, and because the CJEU appears to have doubts as to the justiciable nature of the guarantees listed in the Charter.

The Charter is referred to in Article 151 TFEU (ex-Article 136 of the EC Treaty), and certain of its provisions inspired the wording of the CFREU. This allowed the Charter to serve as a means of interpretation of EU law in general, as well as of the CFREU in particular. This is insufficient, however, to ensure that EU law shall always be consistent with the requirements of the Charter. It was therefore almost inevitable that conflicts would occur between the consequences flowing from membership in the EU and the undertakings of the EU member states under the Charter. Such conflicts may occur in two rather different sets of situations. First, in certain instances, direct conflicts may arise between requirements imposed respectively under EU law and under the Charter. Second, the governance of the eurozone, which leads to the imposition on the EU member states of certain forms of pressure in the adoption of macroeconomic policies, particularly when they are under financial assistance, may create a tension with the Charter.

A. The Risks of Conflict between the Charter and EU Law

In sharp contrast to the Charter's provisions, the rights and freedoms listed in the ECHR have been de facto incorporated as part of the general

[56] Commission Staff Working Paper, 'Operational Guidance in taking account of Fundamental Rights in Commission Impact Assessments' SEC (2011) 567 final, p 25.

principles of EU law,[57] and they also have been taken into account systematically in the drafting of the CFREU. This led the ECtHR to express its trust in the fact that the EU guarantees a level of protection of fundamental rights equivalent to what the ECHR provides itself: in the well-known *Bosphorus* case of 2005, the ECtHR therefore established a presumption that any measure adopted by an EU member state in fulfilment of its obligations under EU law, under the supervision of the CJEU, is compatible with the ECHR's requirements unless a 'manifest deficiency' is apparent.[58]

This the ECSR explicitly refused to do. Instead, the ECSR took the view in *Confédération Générale du Travail (CGT) v France* that 'neither the situation of social rights in the European Union legal order nor the process of elaboration of secondary legislation would justify a similar presumption—even rebuttable—of conformity of legal texts of the European Union with the European Social Charter'.[59] France argued in the *Confédération Générale du Travail (CGT)* case that, because the contested measures (reforms to working time regulations) were in conformity with EU law (in particular, with the 2003 Working Time Directive)[60], they therefore should be treated as consistent with the requirements of the Charter (specifically, of the right to reasonable working hours provided by Articles 2§1 and 4§2 of the 1996 Charter, and of the right to rest periods provided by Article 2§5). The ECSR explicitly refused to endorse that view. Instead, it insisted on the duty of the EU member states, when they 'agree on binding measures in the form of directives which relate to matters within the remit of the European Social Charter', to 'take full account of the commitments they have taken upon ratifying the European Social Charter', 'both when preparing the text in question and when transposing it into national law'.[61] Although the ECSR did not exclude that, in the future, it may be led to establish a *Bosphorus*-like presumption of compatibility with the Charter of measures adopted by the EU member states in compliance with obligations imposed under EU law,[62] it considered that this would be premature.

In *Confédération Générale du Travail (CGT) v France*, the ECSR thus concluded that, although the French legislation was not incompatible with the 2003 Working Time Directive, France had violated a number of provisions of the Charter. Those violations were not *directly* attributable to EU law, however: whereas the Working Time Directive included a number of

[57] See Art 6(3) of the Treaty on the European Union, which codifies this jurisprudence.

[58] *Bosphorus Hava Yolları Turizm ve Ticaret Anonim Şirketi v Ireland* App no 45036/98 (ECtHR(GC), 30 June 2005) §§155–56.

[59] ECSR, Decision on the merits, 23 June 2010, *Confédération Générale du Travail (CGT) v France*, Complaint No 55/2009 §35.

[60] Directive 2003/88/EC of the European Parliament and of the Council of 4 November 2003 concerning certain aspects of the organisation of working time [2003] OL L299.

[61] *CGT v France* (n 59) §33.

[62] ibid §37.

exceptions or derogations that could be misused by the EU member states (as they may rely on such exceptions or derogations without taking into account the requirements of the Charter), the directive as such did not *oblige* the EU member states to take measures in violation of their undertakings under the Charter.

In contrast, a direct conflict with EU law arose in the so-called '*Lex Laval*' case. The background was the following. In its well-known *Laval* judgment of 2007, the CJEU had taken the view that it was in violation of Article 49 of the EC Treaty (guaranteeing the freedom to provide services) and the 1996 Posted Workers Directive[63] to allow Swedish unions to pressure a service provider from another member state to enter into negotiations with local unions with a view to concluding a collective agreement, where the collective action resorted to by unions (in that case, a blockade of the site where the service was to be provided by a building contractor, which finally led the service provider to bankruptcy) goes beyond the aim of ensuring an acceptable level of social protection for workers.[64] Specifically, the CJEU considered that allowing trade unions of a member state to resort to collective action in order to force undertakings established in other member states to sign the collective agreement 'is liable to make it less attractive, or more difficult', for such undertakings to exercise their freedom to provide services by posting workers in another member state, and therefore would constitute a restriction on this fundamental economic freedom.[65]

The CJEU acknowledged that the right to take collective action is a fundamental right recognised under Community law, and it cited the Charter to that effect.[66] It also acknowledged that respect for the right to collective action may constitute an overriding reason of public interest justifying, in principle, a restriction of one of the fundamental freedoms guaranteed by the Treaty.[67] It continued, however, by noting that this right may be

[63] Directive 96/71/EC of the European Parliament and of the Council of 16 December 1996 concerning the posting of workers in the framework of the provision of services [1997] OJ L18/1.

[64] Case C-341/05, *Laval un Partneri Ltd* [2007] ECR I-11767. For useful commentaries, see ACL Davies, 'One Step Forward, Two Steps Back? The Viking and Laval Cases in the ECJ' (2008) 37 *Industrial Law Journal* 126; AR Ganesh, 'Appointing Foxes to Guard Henhouses: The European Posted Workers' Directive' (2008) 15 *Columbia Journal of European Law* 123; S Deakin, 'Regulatory competition after *Laval*' (2009) 10 *Cambridge Yearbook of European Legal Studies* 581; J Malmberg and T Sigeman, 'Industrial Action and EU Economic Freedoms: The Autonomous Collective Bargaining Model Curtailed by the European Court of Justice' (2008) 45 *Common Market Law Review* 1115.

[65] *Laval* (n 64) § 99.

[66] ibid §90.

[67] ibid §103. The CJEU has routinely considered that compliance with fundamental rights may justify restrictions on the fundamental economic freedoms recognised under the Treaties, provided such restrictions are proportionate and do not lead to discrimination. See, eg, Joined Cases C-369/96 and C-376/96, *Arblade and Others* [1999] ECR I-8453 §36; Case C-165/98 *Mazzoleni and ISA* [2001] ECR I-2189 §27; Joined Cases C-49/98, C-50/98, C-52/98 to

subject to certain restrictions, and must be exercised in accordance with national and Community law. In the case at hand, the obstacle to the freedom to provide services caused by the blockade launched by the Swedish unions could not be justified with regard to the objective of improving social protection, because this objective had already been achieved by the Posted Workers Directive: 'with regard to workers posted in the framework of a transnational provision of services, their employer is required, as a result of the coordination achieved by Directive 96/71, to observe a nucleus of mandatory rules for minimum protection in the host member state'.[68] In other words, collective action cannot seek to impose obligations on employers beyond the obligations which the host state must in any case impose in accordance with Article 3§1(a) to (g) of the Posted Workers Directive. The CJEU thus concluded that the blockade imposed by the Swedish unions on the construction site of the company's subsidiary violated Community law and should not be allowed: Article 49 EC and Directive 96/71 preclude a trade union from resorting to collective action in order to force a service provider established in another member state to enter into negotiations with it on the rates of pay for posted workers and to sign a collective agreement the terms of which lay down, as regards some of the matters referred to in Article 3§1(a) to (g) of the said directive, more favourable conditions than those resulting from the relevant legislative provisions in the state concerned, while other terms relate to matters not referred to in Article 3 of the directive. One important element that led the CJEU to take this position has to do with the uncertainty, for a service provider posting workers in that country, arising from the decentralised nature of Sweden's system of collective bargaining: in the absence of 'sufficiently precise and accessible' provisions in Swedish law allowing such a service provider to know which obligations it must comply with, the possibility for unions to resort to industrial action in order to force the conclusion of a collective agreement could make it in practice very difficult or impossible for the service provider to enter the Swedish market.[69]

The *Laval* decision of the CJEU also addressed the Codetermination Act initially adopted in Sweden in 1976.[70] Section 42 of this Act prohibited collective action taken with the aim of obtaining the repeal of or amendment to a collective agreement between other parties. In 1989, in a dispute

C-54/98 and C-68/98 to C-71/98, *Finalarte and Others* [2001] ECR I-7831; Case C-36/02, *Omega* [2004] ECR I-9609 §35.

[68] *Laval* (n 64) §108. Art 3§1(a) to (g) of the Posted Workers Directive lists the core areas in which, in a transnational posting of workers, the host member state is bound to ensure at a minimum that service providers established in another member state comply with the rules stipulated in the legislation of the host state.

[69] *Laval* (n 64) §110.

[70] Lagen (1976: 580) om medbestämmande i arbetslivet ou medbestämmandelagen.

concerning working conditions for the crew of a container ship, *Britannia*, flying a foreign flag, the Swedish courts held that the prohibition stipulated in section 42 of the Codetermination Act extended to collective action undertaken in Sweden in order to obtain the repeal of or amendment to a collective agreement concluded between foreign parties, in a workplace abroad, if such collective action is prohibited by the foreign law applicable to the signatories to that collective agreement. In reaction, and with the clear intention of combating what they saw as a risk of social dumping, the Swedish legislature adopted the '*Lex Britannia*', limiting the scope of the principle expounded in the *Britannia* judgment. The '*Lex Britannia*' entered into force in 1991. It provided, *inter alia*, that the prohibition of collective action to undo an existing collective agreement shall apply only if an organisation commences collective action by reason of employment relationships falling directly within the scope of the Swedish law. In practice, the '*Lex Britannia*' thus authorised collective action against foreign service providers only temporarily active in Sweden, even in circumstances where such service providers had concluded a collective agreement in their home state.

Perhaps predictably, the CJEU took the view that the '*Lex Britannia*' introduced a discriminatory obstacle to the provision of services. It held that

> national rules, such as [the '*Lex Britannia*'], which fail to take into account, irrespective of their content, collective agreements to which undertakings that post workers to Sweden are already bound in the Member State in which they are established, give rise to discrimination against such undertakings, in so far as under those national rules they are treated in the same way as national undertakings which have not concluded a collective agreement. (§116)

Such discrimination, the CJEU reasoned, could not be justified under the EC Treaty. The CJEU acknowledged that the '*Lex Britannia*' was intended to combat 'social dumping'. This objective, however, did not appear to the CJEU to correspond to the grounds of public policy, public security or public health which are limitatively enumerated in Article 46 EC, applied in conjunction with Article 55 EC, as justifying derogations from the freedom to provide services guaranteed in Article 49 EC. The '*Lex Britannia*' thus was incompatible with Community law.

Following the answer of the CJEU, the Swedish Labour Court decided to impose on the Swedish unions a penalty of 342,000 euros in damages to Laval's Latvian trustee in bankruptcy, to compensate for the industrial action they had taken.[71] The Swedish legislature also drew the consequences from the judgment.[72] In 2010, legislative amendments known colloquially

[71] Decision 89 of 2 December 2009 (Case No A 268/04).

[72] For a comprehensive assessment, see N Bruun and J Malmberg, '*Lex Laval*: Collective Actions and Posted Workers in Sweden', in R Blanpain and F Hendrickx (eds), *Labour Law Between Change and Tradition, Liber Amicorum Antoine Jacobs* (Alphen aan den Rijn, Kluwer, 2011) 21–33.

as the '*Lex Laval*' brought changes to the Codetermination Act (1976: 580) and the Foreign Posting of Employees Act (1999: 678). In particular, section 5a of the latter Act imposed strict limitations on the exercise of collective action by unions. It provided that

> industrial action against an employer for the purpose of regulating conditions for posted workers through a collective bargaining agreement may [in principle] only be taken if the conditions demanded:
>
> 1. correspond to the conditions contained in a collective bargaining agreement concluded at central level that are generally applied throughout Sweden to corresponding workers within the sector in question;
> 2. relate only to a minimum rate of pay or other minimum conditions [as limitatively enumerated in section 5 of the Act]; and
> 3. are more favourable for the workers than those prescribed by Section 5.

Moreover, such industrial action 'may not be taken if the employer shows that the workers, as regards pay or within the areas referred to in Section 5, have conditions that in all essential respects are at least as favourable as the minimum conditions in such a central collective bargaining agreement'. In order to rely on this protection from industrial action, the employer therefore does not need to be bound by a collective agreement with a trade union in its own country, nor must it prove that it is legally required to comply with the minimum conditions concerned: it is sufficient that the employer prove that such conditions in fact benefit the workers employed.[73]

The riposte came in two phases. First, the ILO's Committee of Experts on the Application of Conventions and Recommendations (CEACR) took the view that the decision adopted by the Swedish courts, which followed receipt of the CJEU's answer in the *Laval* case, raised serious concerns under the 1948 ILO Convention (No 87) concerning Freedom of Association and Protection of the Right to Organise and under the 1949 ILO Convention (No 98) concerning the Right to Organise and to Collective Bargaining.[74] The most important concern of the CEACR was that, as a result of the legislative changes made in Sweden, unions have been put off from exercising the right to call for industrial action.[75] As regards the damages imposed on the Swedish unions, the CEACR noted that 'the union in question has been held liable for an action that was lawful under national law and for which it could not have been reasonably presumed that the action would be found to be in violation of European Law'. It underlined that, when

[73] See ECSR, *Swedish Trade Union Confederation (LO) and Swedish Confederation of Professional Employees (TCO) v Sweden*, Complaint No 85/2012 §91.

[74] International Labour Conference, 102nd Session, 2013 Report of the Committee of Experts on the Application of Conventions and Recommendations (Sweden), ILC 102/III(1A), p 176.

[75] ibid.

examining the permissible restrictions to the right to strike, it had never in the past 'included the need to assess the proportionality of interests bearing in mind a notion of freedom of establishment or freedom to provide services': in fact, CEACR was challenging the very idea that the right to take collective action could be balanced against the fundamental economic freedoms as stipulated under the EU treaties. Moreover, while expressing its agnosticism as regards the abolition of the '*Lex Britannia*', it remarked that the new version of the Foreign Posting of Employees Act in fact denied posted workers the choice of which union should defend their interests, because the amendments to the Act not only restrict the possibility of recourse to collective action to cases where the minimum conditions of the 1996 Posted Workers Directive are at stake, but also 'bar unions from taking industrial action even if they have members working in the enterprise concerned and regardless of whether a collective agreement covers the workers concerned, provided that the employer can show that the employees' terms and conditions are as favourable as the minimum conditions in the central collective agreement'.[76] In other words, the foreign nationality of the company as such could be an obstacle to the industrial action, even though the workers posted in Sweden by that foreign company might have preferred to join a Swedish union and to have that union call for industrial action against the company concerned.

The second riposte originated with the filing by the Swedish unions of a complaint to the ECSR. The complaint alleged that the amendments to its labour legislation were in violation of Sweden's undertakings under Article 6§§2 and 4 of the Charter, concerning, respectively, the duty to promote collective bargaining and the right of workers and employers to resort to collective action. Invoking Article 19§4 of the Charter, it also alleged a violation of the right of migrant workers to equal treatment as regards remuneration and other employment and working conditions, as well as with regard to membership of trade unions and the benefits of collective bargaining. Finally, the Swedish unions questioned the amendments introduced in 2009 to the Foreign Branch Offices Act (1992: 160) and the Foreign Branch Offices Ordinance (1992: 308). In effect, these legislative changes removed the obligation of companies within the European Economic Area to have a legal representative in Sweden when they conduct economic activities there. This was required under Directive 2006/123/EC on services in the internal market.[77] The result, however, the Swedish unions alleged, was that henceforth, 'when Swedish trade unions want to engage in collective bargaining, they could be forced to try to get in touch with the employer abroad', which would create another serious obstacle to the exercise of the right to collective

[76] ibid, p 177.
[77] [2006] OJ L376/36.

bargaining stipulated in Article 6§2 of the Charter.[78] (After the complaint was filed, the Swedish legislation was amended in this regard: since 1 July 2013, the foreign employer is obliged to appoint a contact person in Sweden and notify the Swedish Work Environment Authority accordingly. However, although this makes it easier for Swedish unions to enter into contact with the employer, the obstacle is only partly removed, because the said contact person has no authority to conclude a collective agreement.)[79]

In its decision of 3 July 2013, the ECSR found that the restrictions to the conclusion of collective agreements were such that the situation in Sweden was not in conformity with Article 6§2 of the Charter.[80] It also considered that, whereas the right to resort to collective action is not absolute, and may be limited, for instance, to protect public order or the rights and freedoms of others (such as the right of co-workers to work, or the right of employers to engage in a gainful occupation),

> national legislation which prevents *a priori* the exercise of the right to collective action, or permits the exercise of this right only in so far as it is necessary to obtain given minimum working standards would not be in conformity with Article 6§4 of the Charter, as it would infringe the fundamental right of workers and trade unions to engage in collective action for the protection of economic and social interests of the workers.[81]

In a thinly veiled allusion to the balancing exercise achieved by the CJEU between the freedom to provide services and the right to resort to collective action, the ECSR adds:

> [T]he facilitation of free cross-border movement of services and the promotion of the freedom of an employer or undertaking to provide services in the territory of other States—which constitute important and valuable economic freedoms within the framework of EU law—cannot be treated, from the point of view of the system of values, principles and fundamental rights embodied in the Charter, as having a greater *a priori* value than core labour rights, including the right to make use of collective action to demand further and better protection of the economic and social rights and interests of workers.[82]

The statement is of course in part disingenuous, because however much there is to criticise in the *Laval* judgment of the CJEU, at least it cannot be said that it treats economic freedoms as having 'a greater *a priori* value than core labour rights'. However, what the ECSR does correctly identify is that,

[78] ECSR, Decision (admissibility and merits), 3 July 2013, Complaint No 85/2012, *Swedish Trade Union Confederation (LO) and Swedish Confederation of Professional Employees (TCO) v Sweden* §96.
[79] ibid §114.
[80] ibid §116.
[81] ibid §120.
[82] ibid §122.

due to the respective positions of the CJEU, on one hand, and of the ECSR itself, on the other hand, the balancing exercise proceeds rather differently in the two instances: whereas, for the CJEU, the resort by unions to industrial action imposes a restriction on the freedom to provide services (or, at least, to the attractiveness of exercising such freedom), so that collective action is seen as allowable only to the extent it is not disproportionate, the ECSR assesses whether the restriction imposed on collective action in the name of complying with EU law can indeed be justified. In theory, 'balancing' should erase such differences in framing. In practice, however, the framing does matter: it is telling, for instance, that the CJEU would never ask whether the freedom to provide services has disproportionately affected the right of unions to resort to collective action.

Finally, the ECSR considered that posted workers, although they are only temporarily in the host state and are not expected to remain present in that state, may nevertheless be considered 'migrant workers' for the purposes of the Charter. This qualification was not necessarily obvious. In EU law, the status of posted workers is markedly different from that of foreign workers employed by an employer established in the host state. Moreover, ILO Convention (No 143) (the Migrant Workers (Supplementary Provisions) Convention, 1975) explicitly excludes the extension of the right to equality of opportunity and treatment, which is otherwise recognised for migrant workers, to

> employees of organisations or undertakings operating within the territory of a country who have been admitted temporarily to that country at the request of their employer to undertake specific duties or assignments, for a limited and defined period of time, and who are required to leave that country on the completion of their duties or assignments.[83]

The employers' organisations that invoked that instrument in their observations submitted to the ECSR perhaps omitted to take into account the fact that Article 19§8 of the ILO Constitution (Effect of Convention or Recommendations on More Favourable Existing Provisions) excludes such reliance on ILO instruments.

The immediate implication of the ECSR's choice to treat posted workers as 'migrant workers' was that, in accordance with Article 6§4 of the Charter, these workers had a right to equality of treatment with the workers employed in the host state, in respect of remuneration, other employment and working conditions, and enjoyment of the benefits of collective bargaining. Of course, it follows from the Posted Workers Directive that workers posted in Sweden by an employer established in another state are protected under the Swedish legislation or through central collective agreements, in all the areas covered by Article 3§1(a) to (g) of the

[83] Art 11§2(e) of the Migrant Workers (Supplementary Provisions) Convention, 1975.

directive. Beyond that minimum, however, they would only be protected to the extent that their employer voluntarily concludes a collective agreement with Swedish unions, without it being possible for these unions to force the employer to consider concluding such an agreement. This puts these workers at risk, because in Sweden 'collective agreements do not very often provide for rules concerning minimum wages, and ... the minimum wage [as defined in central collective agreements for the protection of workers without qualification, such as young workers] can be considerably lower than the normal rate of pay generally applied throughout the country to Swedish workers (working in the same professional sector)'.[84] The ECSR concluded that the situation in Sweden was not in conformity with the requirements of Article 6§4 of the Charter:

> excluding or limiting the right to collective bargaining or action with respect to foreign undertakings, for the sake of enhancing free cross-border movement of services and advantages in terms of competition within a common market zone, constitutes, according to the Charter, discriminatory treatment on the ground of nationality of the workers, on the basis that it determines, in the host State, lower protection and more limited economic and social rights for posted foreign workers, in comparison with the protection and rights guaranteed to all other workers.[85]

It would be incorrect to state that the ECSR was thus contradicting the CJEU: it was, after all, assessing the situation on the basis of a different set of norms. But the conflict is nevertheless real, and difficult to ignore.[86] Indeed, the *Laval* episode shows the perils of ignoring the requirements of the Charter in the implementation of EU law by the EU member states to whom it is addressed. It also suggests that, in order to avoid potential situations of conflict, such requirements should be taken into account in the design of EU legislative measures.

B. The Risks of Conflict between the Charter and the Requirements Linked to Membership of the Euro Area

Nor can the Charter be ignored in the imposition of macroeconomic disciplines on the member states of the euro area. This was explicitly confirmed by the ECSR, acting under the 1961 Charter, in a series of cases

[84] ECSR, *Swedish Trade Union Confederation (LO) and Swedish Confederation of Professional Employees (TCO) v Sweden* (n 78) §135.

[85] ibid §141.

[86] On the resulting conflict, see, *inter alia*, M Rocca, 'A clash of kings—The European Committee of Social Rights on the "Lex Laval" ... and on the EU framework for the posting of workers' (2013) 3 *European Journal of Social Law* 217.

concerning the implementation by Greece of austerity measures which it committed to adopt in successive loan agreements, concluded in 2010 and 2012.

The circumstances are sufficiently well known to be only briefly summarised here.[87] After the Greek government had revealed, in October 2009, that Greece's public deficit had been grossly underestimated by previous governments, the country faced speculation on the financial markets that significantly raised Greece's costs of borrowing, to the point that the situation became unsustainable. Greece called for financial assistance on 23 April 2010. In response, the representatives of the euro area member states other than Greece decided on 2 May 2010 to provide stability support to Greece through a Loan Facility Agreement: in effect, an intergovernmental framework that allowed the pooling of bilateral loans in the form of an international contract. Represented by the European Commission, which was in charge of negotiating on their behalf a Memorandum of Understanding with Greece, the euro area member states provided Greece through this channel with a total of 80 billion euros in loans on the understanding that the International Monetary Fund (IMF), to which Greece had also turned for assistance, would provide another 30 billion euros.[88] The disbursements, however, were conditional on the adoption of fiscal consolidation measures by Greece, entailing 30 billion euros' worth of spending cuts for the period 2010–14. The 'Economic Adjustment Programme for Greece' included so-called 'austerity' measures purportedly to restore Greece's fiscal balance: the privatisation of state assets, in the amount of 50 billion euros; and 'structural measures', involving in particular the 'flexibilisation' of the labour market, as a means to restore the competitiveness of the Greek economy.[89] In June 2011, after this first set of measures appeared insufficient, the eurozone member states granted a second loan for an amount of 130 billion euros for the years 2012–14. This second bail-out was effected through the European Financial Stabilisation Mechanism (EFSM) and the European Financial Stability Facility (EFSF). It was officially launched in March 2012.

[87] For an excellent summary, see L Papadopoulou, 'Can Constitutional Rules, even if "Golden", Tame Greek Public Debt?', in M Adams, F Fabbrini and P Larouche (eds), *The Constitutionalization of European Budget Constraints* (Oxford, Hart, 2014) 223–47.

[88] Loan Facility Agreement (2010), preambular §3.

[89] See European Parliament Report 2009–14 on the inquiry on the role and operations of the Troika (ECB, Commission and IMF) with regard to the euro area programme countries (2013/2277 (INI)), A7-0149/2014, 28.2.2014; Report of the Independent Expert on the effects of foreign debt and other related international financial obligations of states on the full enjoyment of all human rights, particularly economic, social and cultural rights, Mission to Greece (22–26 April 2013), UN doc A/HRC/50/15/Add 1 (27 March 2014).

Although various human rights bodies expressed serious concern at the impact of the austerity measures adopted under these programmes,[90] the clearest condemnation came from the ECSR. The first wave of fiscal consolidation measures, adopted following the conclusion of the 2010 Memorandum of Understanding between Greece and its creditors, led to a total of seven decisions of the ECSR. In Complaint No 65/2011, the ECSR found that, by amending its labour legislation in December 2010 in order to provide that, during the probationary period, a permanent contract may be terminated without notice and with no severance pay, Greece had created a situation that was not in conformity with the right of workers to a reasonable period of notice for termination, which forms part of the right to a fair remuneration under Article 4§4 of the Charter.[91] Complaint No 66/2011, which was filed by the same public sector unions,[92] again led to findings of non-conformity, resulting from the introduction in July 2010 of 'special apprenticeship contracts' between employers and individuals aged 15 to 18, without regard for the main safeguards provided for by labour and social security law, and of a provision allowing employers to pay new entrants in the labour market aged under 25 a rate of 84 per cent of the minimum wage or daily wage.

Although, in its responses to complaints 65 and 66, the Greek government did mention the constraints imposed by the economic crisis it was facing, there was no explicit discussion in these proceedings of the fact that the measures under scrutiny had been imposed on Greece by its creditors. By contrast, that issue came to the fore in the five decisions the ECSR adopted on 7 December 2012, following complaints filed by public sector pensioners' unions.[93] At issue were significant reductions in pensioners' social protection. The Greek government asserted that these changes

> have been approved by the national parliament, are necessary for the protection of public interests, having resulted from Greece's grave financial situation, and,

[90] See, eg, Committee on the Elimination of Discrimination against Women, Concluding Observations on the seventh periodic report of Greece, UN doc CEDAW/C/GRC/CO/7 (1 March 2013); Committee on the Rights of the Child, Concluding Observations on the combined second and third periodic reports of Greece, UN doc CRC/C/GRC/CO/2–3 (13 August 2012).

[91] ECSR, Decision on the merits, 23 May 2012, Complaint No 65/2011, *General Federation of Employees of the National Electric Power Corporation (GENOP-DEI) and Confederation of Greek Civil Servants' Trade Unions (ADEDY) v Greece.*

[92] ECSR, Decision on the merits, 23 May 2012, Complaint No 66/2011, *General Federation of Employees of the National Electric Power Corporation (GENOP-DEI) and Confederation of Greek Civil Servants' Trade Unions (ADEDY) v Greece.*

[93] ECSR, *Federation of Employed Pensioners of Greece (IKA-ETAM) v Greece*, Complaint No 76/2012; *Panhellenic Federation of Public Service Pensioners v Greece*, Complaint No 77/2012; *Pensioners' Union of the Athens–Piraeus Electric Railways (ISAP) v Greece*, Complaint No 78/2012; *Panhellenic Federation of Pensioners of the Public Electricity Corporation (PAS-DEI) v Greece*, Complaint No 79/2012; *Pensioners' Union of the Agricultural Bank of Greece (ATE) v Greece*, Complaint No 80/2012. The decisions on the merits

> in addition, result from the Government's other international obligations, namely those deriving from a financial support mechanism agreed upon by the Government together with the European Commission, the European Central Bank and the International Monetary Fund ('the Troika') in 2010.[94]

The argument was swiftly dismissed by the ECSR, which took the view that 'the fact that the contested provisions of domestic law seek to fulfil the requirements of other legal obligations does not remove them from the ambit of the Charter'.[95] Instead, recalling its previous case law in which it refused to remove from the ambit of the Charter national legislation adopted by a EU member state in order to comply with prescriptions of EU law—for instance, implementing an EU directive—the ECSR noted that: '[W]hen States Parties agree on binding measures, which relate to matters within the remit of the Charter, they should—both when preparing the text in question and when implementing it into national law—take full account of the commitments they have taken upon ratifying the European Social Charter.'[96]

Though this statement is of course correct as a matter of international law—a state cannot escape its international obligations by concluding subsequently a separate agreement with other parties[97]—it begs the question of whether the eurozone member states other than Greece, if not the EU itself, might also bear a responsibility in the situation resulting from the implementation of the adjustment programme imposed on Greece. The Loan Facility Agreement through which the 2010 bail-out was implemented makes explicit the link between the provision of financial assistance, on one hand, and compliance by Greece with the macroeconomic adjustment measures prescribed, on the other hand.[98] Moreover, while the European Commission signed the 2010 MoU, this was 'after approval by all Euro Area member states (except Greece), by the borrower and the Bank of Greece',[99] and each disbursement following the first loan has been preceded by a presentation of a report to the lending parties by the European Commission, in liaison with the European Central Bank (ECB), confirming that Greece has complied with the terms and the conditions set out in the MoU and in the Council Decision.

This raises the question of whether, in addition to Greece itself, the violations of the Charter should not be attributed to the other euro area member

of all five complaints were adopted on 7 December 2012. Though these complaints were filed by different organisations, they all raise the same issues of substance and may thus be considered together.

[94] Complaint No 76/2012, Decision on the merits of 7 December 2012 §10.

[95] ibid §50.

[96] ibid §51.

[97] Art 30(4) of the Vienna Convention on the Law of Treaties, signed on 23 May 1969, in force since 27 January 1980 (UNTS, vol 1155, p 331).

[98] Loan Facility Agreement, preambular para 6.

[99] ibid, preambular para 6.

states, who might be said to have coerced Greece into disregarding its obligations under the Charter.[100] It is telling in this regard that, in its discussions with the ILO's High-Level Mission to Greece, which visited the country in September 2011 at the request of the Greek government, Greece clearly noted that it had been unable to raise the question of the social impacts of the austerity measures with the Troika, and therefore expressed its hopes that the ILO would be acting as a counterweight to the impositions of the European Commission, the ECB and the IMF.[101] It also encourages us to ask whether the EU as such, acting through its institutions, should not take into account the Charter in negotiating memoranda of understanding defining the fiscal consolidation measures that should be adopted by the eurozone member states receiving financial assistance.

The latest reforms to the governance of the eurozone only raise the urgency of these questions. On 21 May 2013, the European Parliament and the Council adopted two regulations forming the 'Two-Pack' combination of measures placing the eurozone member states under surveillance in order to safeguard the eurozone's overall stability. Regulation 473/2013, the first component of the 'Two-Pack', governs the so-called 'European semester' for the monitoring of national budgets.[102] It strengthens the surveillance of budgetary and economic policies in euro area member states, with closer monitoring of member states that are subject to an excessive deficit procedure under Article 126 TFEU.[103] Though the Regulation refers to Article 28 CFREU, as well as to various social objectives of the EU,[104] neither in the assessment of the draft budgetary plans that eurozone member states should submit annually to the Commission and to the Euro-group, nor in the preparation of the economic partnership programmes by states placed under an excessive deficit procedure, is there any reference to an assessment of the social impacts, let alone to the requirement than any measure to maintain a sound fiscal balance or to correct an excessive deficit should comply with fundamental social rights.

The second component of the 'Two-Pack' defines the conditions applying to countries of the eurozone placed under 'enhanced surveillance'. These are countries experiencing or threatened with serious financial difficulties,

[100] This is the hypothesis envisaged under Art 18 of the International Law Commission's Arts on Responsibility of States for Internationally Wrongful Acts (annex to General Assembly Resolution No 56/83 of 12 December 2001, and corrected by document A/56/49(Vol I)/Corr 4), under the heading 'Coercion of another State'.

[101] See International Labour Office, *Report on the High Level Mission to Greece (19–23 September 2011)* (Geneva, ILO, 2011), para 88.

[102] Regulation (EU) 473/2013 of the European Parliament and of the Council on common provisions for monitoring and assessing draft budgetary plans and ensuring the correction of excessive deficit of the member states in the euro area [2013] OJ L140/11.

[103] ibid, preambular para 9.

[104] ibid, preambular paras 7–8.

and which have therefore asked for financial assistance from either one or several other member states or third countries, the EFSM, ESM, EFSF, or another relevant international financial institution, such as the IMF.[105] Regulation (EU) 472/2013[106] places such countries under closer monitoring than that provided normally under the 'European semester' for economic policy coordination. Like its sister regulation mentioned in the previous paragraph, Regulation 472/2013 requires that any measures adopted as part of economic adjustment programmes comply with the right of collective bargaining and action recognised in Article 28 CFREU; but also like that other regulation, it is otherwise silent on the need to ensure that fundamental social rights are taken into account in the preparation of such programmes.

Of course, one of the implications of important reforms in the governance of the eurozone is that the EU member states are implementing EU law when taking measures that are adopted under Article 136 TFEU (the legal basis of the 'Two-Pack' regulations) and Regulations 472 and 473/2013 themselves. Such measures thus drawn into the ambit of EU law include the memoranda of understanding concluded with the member states concerned, as well as the Council decision approving the macroeconomic adjustment programme: this decision 'may be challenged (either directly before the EU courts or indirectly before the national courts on the ground that it is incompatible with the CFREU).'[107] Although the case law of the CJEU has cast doubt on this issue,[108] it is at least arguable that the domestic measures adopted in order to fulfil such a programme also could be considered to fall within the scope of application of EU law, and thus have to comply with the CFREU, under the supervision of the CJEU. However, it is doubtful that such judicial supervision on the basis of the CFREU, should it take place at all, would result in a robust protection of fundamental social rights: the relative timidity of the CFREU in the area of social rights in general, as well as the reluctance of the CJEU to recognise the justiciability of such rights in

[105] The Regulation applies to Greece, as a country in receipt of financial assistance from the EFSF on the date of 30 May 2013: see Art 16 of Regulation (EU) 472/2013.

[106] Regulation (EU) 472/2013 of the European Parliament and of the Council on the strengthening of economic and budgetary surveillance of member states in the euro area experiencing or threatened with serious difficulties with respect to their financial stability [2013] OJ L140/1.

[107] K Lenaerts, 'EMU and the EU's Constitutional Framework' (2014) 39 *European Law Review* 753.

[108] See Case C-665/13, *Sindicato Nacional dos Profissionais de Seguros e Afins*, Order of the Court (Sixth Chamber), 21 October 2014 (CJEU lacking jurisdiction to assess compliance with the CFREU of Portuguese Law No 64-B/2011 of 31 Dec 2011 approving the State Budget for 2012, which resulted in salary reductions for certain public sector employees, although the budgetary measures involved were explicitly stated in Art 21(1) of the 2012 Budget Law to be linked to the Economic and Financial Assistance Programme (EFAP) applied to Portugal). Judge Lenaerts, now the President of the CJEU, was not a member of the three-judge chamber that adopted this Order.

similar circumstances, should warn us not to place too high hopes on such a mechanism.

A preventive approach, in which any impacts on social rights are assessed before the adoption of fiscal consolidation measures, therefore seems required, as the only effective means to avoid potential conflicts between the disciplines imposed on the eurozone member states and the requirements of the Charter. Consistent with President Juncker's July 2014 Political Guidelines for the next European Commission, in which he committed to ensuring that future support and reform programmes would be subjected to social impact assessments to feed into the public discussion,[109] the European Commission has announced its intention to pay greater attention to 'the social fairness of new macroeconomic adjustment programmes to ensure that the adjustment is spread equitably and to protect the most vulnerable in society', and it has proposed a number of improvements in this regard.[110] The preparation of such social impact assessments would seem to constitute an obvious first step towards ensuring compliance with fundamental rights, and the implications of this new approach are already visible: for instance, after Greece was granted a new package of financial assistance in August 2015—the third 'bail-out' in a row—this was accompanied by a social impact assessment showing 'how the design of the stability support programme has taken social factors into account'.[111] Social impact assessments could, moreover, relatively easily be built into existing procedures under the 'European budgetary semester' and the enhanced monitoring to which states under financial assistance are subject.[112] They would also appear to be in line with the position of the European Commission, according to which it is 'important that member states comply with the European Social Charter also when implementing reform measures'.[113]

While these are promising signs, there remains a gap between the shift towards 'social fairness' considerations being included in reform programmes, and a social rights-based assessment of their impacts. Grounding reform programmes in fundamental social rights would require (i) basing

[109] *A New Start for Europe: My Agenda for Jobs, Growth, Fairness and Democratic Change, Political Guidelines for the next European Commission*, 15 July 2014.

[110] European Commission, Communication from the Commission to the European Parliament, the Council and the European Central Bank: 'On Steps Towards Completing Economic and Monetary Union' COM (2015) 600 final, p 5. See also European Commission, Commission Work Programme 2016, COM (2015) 610 final, p 9.

[111] Commission Staff Working Document, Assessment of the Social Impact of the New Stability Support Programme for Greece, SWD (2015) 162 final.

[112] For instance, Regulation (EU) 472/2013 already establishes certain procedural requirements linked to the assessment of the impacts of the measures to be adopted (see especially Arts 6 and 8).

[113] Statement made by Commissioner M Thijssen on behalf of the European Commission on 30 April 2015, in response to a parliamentary question on the social rights impacts of reform programmes (more specifically, on wage decline in Spain) (question from P Iglesias (GUE/NGL) of 6 March 2015, P-003762-15).

the assessments explicitly on the normative components of social rights, (ii) moving beyond references to the CFREU, to integrate the full range of social rights guaranteed in the Charter, and (iii) ensuring that procedures are established to allow for participation of unions and other components of civil society in the design and implementation of such programmes, and for re-examination of the draft programmes if negative impacts on social rights are found to occur.[114]

IV. MOVING FORWARD: FOUR DIRECTIONS

The status of the Charter in the law- and policy-making of the EU remains deeply unsatisfactory, and the risk of tensions will increase in the future. It is necessary to move beyond the current status quo, not simply in order to avoid situations in which the EU member states will face potentially conflicting obligations, imposed respectively under the EU legal order and under the Charter, but also in order to improve the legitimacy of the EU, particularly as regards the adoption of national reform programmes within the euro area or the adoption of structural adjustment programmes for states receiving financial assistance from the European Stability Mechanism. Improvements could be made in four directions.

A. The Charter as a Source of EU Law

At the very least, it can be expected from the CJEU that, when interpreting the CFREU, it shall take into account the interpretation given to the Charter by the ECSR. A number of provisions of the CFREU were directly inspired by the Charter, the corresponding provisions of which are referred to by the Explanations of the CFREU.[115] As recognised by the European Court of Human Rights,

> the ECSR's competence [as stipulated in the Protocol Amending the European Social Charter (also known as the 'Turin Protocol', Council of Europe Treaty Series No 142) is] to 'assess from a legal standpoint the compliance of national law and practice with the obligations arising from the Charter' …[The] interpretative value of the ECSR appears to be generally accepted by States and by the Committee of Ministers [of the Council of Europe].[116]

[114] It is to be welcomed in this regard that the Proposal for a Council Regulation on the establishment of the Structural Reform Support Programme for the period 2017 to 2020 (COM (2015) 701 final) makes explicit reference to its potential impact on fundamental rights (see p 9).

[115] [2007] OJ C303/17.

[116] *Case of the National Union of Railroad, Marine and Transport Workers v the United Kingdom* App no 31045/10 (ECtHR (4th section), 8 April 2014) §94.

The ECSR is therefore 'particularly qualified' to provide an authoritative interpretation of the Charter's provisions.[117]

The CJEU could be beyond this, however. It could align the status of the Charter with that of the ECHR, and seek inspiration from the Charter to develop the fundamental rights that are included among the general principles of EU law. After all, the Charter has been ratified by all EU member states (whether in its original version of 1961 or in its revised form of 1996), and although the range of commitments is uneven, they all therefore have pledged to 'accept as the aim of their policy, to be pursued by all appropriate means both national and international in character, the attainment of conditions in which the ... rights and principles [listed in Part II of the European Social Charter] may be effectively realised'.[118] The EU member states have 'confirm[ed] their attachment to fundamental social rights as defined in the European Social Charter' in the Preamble of the Treaty on the European Union,[119] and they further pledged to build on the Charter in Article 151 TFEU, as well as in the Preamble of the CFREU.

Far from subverting EU law, such a shift in the attitude of the CJEU towards the Charter and the body of case law developed by the ECSR would constitute four major advantages. First, it would overcome the tensions resulting from the selectivity of the CFREU as regards the social rights listed (more extensively, and in greater detail) in the Charter. Second, it would dispel the suspicion that the CJEU pays greater attention to civil and political rights as enumerated in the ECHR than to social rights as listed in the Charter, or that it tends to prioritise the protection of economic freedoms over that of social guarantees. Third, it would favour the uniform application of EU law, because EU member states would have to take into account the Charter in the implementation of all EU secondary legislation: in other words, they would not be allowed to use loopholes or exceptions carved into regulations or directives in violation of the requirements of the Charter. This would mean that the implementation of EU law would be more uniform across the member states, and the 'social dumping' that the economic freedoms of the internal market have sometimes been accused of encouraging, would be much less likely. Fourth, aligning the status of the Charter with that of the ECHR may lead the ECSR to establish a presumption according to which measures adopted by EU member states in fulfilment of their obligations under EU law shall be treated as in principle compatible with the requirements of the Charter, unless the CJEU does not have an opportunity to assess the compatibility with fundamental rights

[117] *Tüm Haber Sen and Çınar v Turkey* App no 28602/95 (ECtHR (2nd section), 21 February 2006) §39, ECHR 2006-II.

[118] This is the definition of the undertaking of state parties under both the 1961 and the 1996 Charters.

[119] See 5th preambular paragraph of the EU Treaty [2010] OJ C83/13.

of the said measures (including their compatibility with the requirements of the Charter, understood 'within the framework of the structure and the objectives of the European Union')[120] or unless a 'manifest deficiency' is apparent in the protection of fundamental social rights.[121]

B. Improving Impact Assessments

However much we can expect from the CJEU, the other EU institutions should also move towards strengthening the implementation of the Charter in the EU. A first step could consist of including explicit references to the Charter in the guidelines for impact assessments of legislative proposals prepared by the European Commission, as recommended by the European Parliament.[122] Expanding the list of fundamental rights on which impact assessments are based in order to include the Charter, or at least the provisions of the Charter that were a source of inspiration for the drafting of the CFREU, would go a long way to ensuring that EU law would be fully consistent with the obligations of the member states under international law, thus reducing the risk that they might be faced with conflicting international obligations.[123]

This would fulfil the mandate of the Treaty on the Functioning of the European Union, which commits the EU to 'take into account requirements linked to the promotion of a high level of employment, the guarantee of adequate social protection, the fight against social exclusion, and a high level of education, training and protection of human health' in defining and implementing its policies and activities.[124] It could also lead to shifting the fundamental rights policy of the EU from being *reactive* to becoming *proactive*. Unless they are more or less equated with assessments of compatibility with fundamental rights and conceived therefore as purely negative, impact assessments could ensure that fundamental rights are mainstreamed in all legislative proposals of the European Commission.[125] In its resolution

[120] See Case 11/70, *Internationale Handelsgesellschaft mbH v Einfuhr-und Vorratsstelle für Getreide und Futtermittel* [1970] ECR 1125 §4.

[121] See above, text corresponding to nn 58–61.

[122] European Parliament resolution of 12 December 2012 on the situation of fundamental rights in the European Union (2010–2011) (2011/2069 (INI)), doc P7_TA(2012)0500, op §3.

[123] For an in-depth discussion, see O De Schutter and I de J Butler, 'Binding the EU to International Human Rights Law' (2008) 27 *Yearbook of European Law* 277.

[124] Art 9 TFEU. See also Art 3§3 TEU, listing among the objectives of the EU the establishment of 'a highly competitive social market economy, aiming at full employment and social progress', the combating of social exclusion and the promotion of social justice and protection, as well as of equality between men and women.

[125] See O De Schutter, 'Les droits fondamentaux dans le projet européen. Des limites à l'action des institutions à une politique des droits fondamentaux', in O De Schutter and P Nihoul (eds), *Une Constitution pour l'Europe. Réflexions sur les transformations du droit de l'Union européenne* (Bruxelles, Larcier, 2004) 81–117.

of 12 December 2012, the European Parliament notes that 'observing the duty to protect, promote and fulfil does not require new competences for the EU but rather proactive institutional engagement with human rights, developing and reinforcing a genuine culture of fundamental rights in the institutions of the Union and in member states'.[126] It appears from the 2006 *Parliament v Council* case that the EU legislator is not considered to have acted in violation of fundamental rights simply because it leaves to the EU member states a freedom to act in certain areas (for instance, the implementation of directives), even in situations in which the member states might be tempted to exercise such freedom in violation of fundamental rights. But this is precisely the point at which fundamental rights impact assessments should be seen as an opportunity to move beyond verifying the compatibility of legislative proposals with the requirements of the CFREU, in order to ensure that the European legislator not only does not violate fundamental rights (a merely negative requirement), but in addition exercises its competences in order to contribute to the full realisation of fundamental rights (which amounts to a positive duty). This is of particular importance for the realisation of social rights, which require the adoption of measures across time in order to become truly effective.

C. Defining a Common Approach towards the Charter

One major obstacle to relying on the Charter as a source of inspiration for the development of fundamental rights as general principles of EU law, thereby allowing it to complement the CFREU, is that, in the à la carte system on which the Charter is built, the undertakings of the EU member states under the Charter are widely variable. The CJEU is therefore understandably hesitant to derive from this instrument social rights that it can consider to be sufficiently consensual due to the wide recognition they benefit from.

It is against this background that one should consider the proposals presented by the ECSR to the High-Level Conference on the European Social Charter, which the Council of Europe convened in Turin (Italy) on 17 and 18 October 2014.[127] The ECSR suggests that the EU could encourage its member states to

> harmonise their commitments, in particular by all ratifying the revised Charter and all accepting all the provisions in the Charter which are most directly related in terms of substance to the provisions of EU law and the competences of the EU [such as] Articles 4§3 (equal pay for women and men) and 2§1 (reasonable

[126] Preamble §F.

[127] ECSR, *The relationship between European Union law and the European Social Charter*, Working document, 15 July 2014.

> working hours). It would be useful for a definition of a kind of 'Community core' within the Charter to be drawn up so as to give EU member states clear indications in this respect.[128]

Implementing such a proposal would favour the uniform application of EU law. The case of working time is typical in this regard. Although it makes no reference to the Charter, the 2003 Working Time Directive[129] does seek to contribute, in the EU, to the same objectives as those of Article 2§1 of the Charter. At the request in particular of the United Kingdom, however, the directive includes a number of exceptions and exemptions that the EU member states may rely on in order to reduce the level of their commitments. However, because relying on such exceptions or exemptions may be in violation of the requirements of Article 2§1 of the Charter, only the EU member states that have not accepted this provision[130] upon ratifying the Charter shall be able to make use of this possibility without violating their other international obligations. This is anomalous: it means, in effect, that not all EU member states are equal before the flexibilities built into the Working Time Directive, and that those states that have chosen to limit the level of their commitments under the Charter are rewarded within intra-Community competition. Instead, were all EU member states encouraged to accept at least a core set of provisions of the Charter that correspond to legislative instruments adopted by the EU, the implementation of such instruments would be more consistent across the EU.

Quite apart from such immediate benefits in terms of what the ECSR calls 'consistency', ensuring that the EU member states' undertakings under the Charter are aligned would encourage the CJEU to include the fundamental social rights thus identified as part of the general principles of law it ensures respect for: once such rights are identified on a consensual basis, they will be much more difficult for the CJEU to ignore.

D. Launching the Process for the Accession of the EU to the Charter

Finally, a third option may be to launch the process for the accession of the EU to the Charter.[131] The idea is less novel, and less radical, than it

[128] ibid §§83–84.

[129] Directive 2003/88/EC of the European Parliament and of the Council of 4 November 2003 concerning certain aspects of the organisation of working time.

[130] These are Austria, Bulgaria and Sweden, which are parties to the 1996 Charter; and Denmark and the United Kingdom, which are parties to the 1961 Charter.

[131] See O De Schutter, 'L'adhésion de l'Union européenne à la Charte sociale européenne' (2015) 105 *Revue trimestrielle des droits de l'homme* 259; and O De Schutter, 'Anchoring the European Union to the European Social Charter: The Case for Accession', in G de Búrca and B de Witte (eds), *Social Rights in Europe* (Oxford University Press, 2005) 111–52.

might seem. Already in 1984, when the European Parliament symbolically adopted a Treaty on the European Union—the so-called 'Spinelli Treaty'—the document included a reference to the possibility of the EU joining the Charter.[132] This was again suggested in 1989, when the European Commission was preparing the document that was to become the CCF-SRW: both the Parliamentary Assembly of the Council of Europe and the European Economic and Social Committee declared that acceding to the Charter could be more economical, and perhaps more effective, than to reinvent a social rights catalogue for the EU.[133] Finally, when the Charter was revised, the draft that was presented to the Committee of Ministers in October 1994 included a provision allowing for the accession of the EC to the new instrument:[134] although the Ministers did not finally adopt this proposal, this was a clear signal that, within the Council of Europe at least, this option remained very much alive. More recently, the European Trade Union Confederation (ETUC) mentioned this objective as part of its 2012 'Social Compact for Europe'.[135] And the European Parliament itself, in its resolution of 27 February 2014 on the situation of fundamental rights in the European Union (2012), mentioned the need to move towards accession of the EU to the Charter.[136]

In response to a parliamentary question on EU accession to Charter, the European Commission stated that it 'is in dialogue with the Council of Europe on the interplay between the EC law and the Charter as well as on ratification and better application of the latter by EU member states', and that the legal context is not favourable because 'there is currently no accession clause in the Charter and such a clause would need to be introduced to allow for accession by the EU'.[137] That is, of course, not satisfactory: the question is precisely whether the legal context should be amended in order to allow for such accession. Launching a political process in favour of accession

[132] Art 4(2) of the draft Treaty on the European Union of 14 February 1984, *Bull EC*, February 1984, No 2, p 8.

[133] Parliamentary Assembly of the Council of Europe, Res. 915 (1989) on the future role of the European Social Charter, adopted on 9 May 1989 on the basis of the report of the Committee on Social, Health and Family Affairs (doc 6031, rapporteur M Forschi); European Economic and Social Committee, Opinion on Community Fundamental Social Rights, doc CES 270/89 of 22 February 1989.

[134] Charte/Rel (84)23, 14 October 1994 (see Art L of the draft).

[135] The 'Social Compact for Europe' was adopted by the ETUC Executive Committee on 5–6 June 2012: see ETUC position on the social dimension of the European Union (Brussels, 23 April 2013), Annex, available at: www.etuc.org/a/11136.

[136] European Parliament resolution of 27 February 2014 on the situation of fundamental rights in the European Union (2012) (2013/2078 (INI)), doc P7_TA-PROV(2014)0173 para 8(a).

[137] Answer given by Ms Thijssen on behalf of the European Commission on 8 July 2015 to a parliamentary question raised by Ms Paloma López Bermejo (GUE/NGL) on 28 April 2015 (E-006720-15).

would send a powerful signal to European public opinion: it would provide a clear indication that the EU is committed not only to the establishment of the internal market and to the creation of an area of freedom, security and justice, but also to social justice—and that it pays equal attention to both civil and political rights and to economic and social rights. The indivisibility, interdependence and equal importance of all human rights—which the CFREU partly embodies by bringing together, in a single instrument, different categories of rights—would be reaffirmed. Beyond these symbolic gains, however, more concrete advantages would follow from accession. The risk of conflicts would be minimised. It would, of course, remain possible that, in concrete cases, the balancing of interests as performed by the CJEU might arrive at a different result from the balancing performed by the ECSR.[138] But if the EU were formally bound to comply with the Charter, such conflicts would remain temporary: it would be necessary to arrive at a common position—not, it should be emphasised, on the basis of some hierarchy between different monitoring bodies, but on the basis of a judicial dialogue respectful of the various positions expressed.

From the point of view of EU law, the question of accession raises two questions. The first is whether the EU has a competence to accede to the Charter. Such a competence need not be explicitly attributed in the EU Treaties: according to Article 216§1 TFEU, the Union may conclude an international agreement also 'where the conclusion of an agreement is necessary in order to achieve, within the framework of the Union's policies, one of the objectives referred to in the Treaties, or is provided for in a legally binding Union act or is likely to affect common rules or alter their scope'.

This wording is inspired in part, interestingly, by Opinion 2/91 of the CJEU on the compatibility with the EEC Treaty of ILO Convention No 170 concerning safety in the use of chemicals at work.[139] The CJEU concluded that the EC could join the ILO Convention concerning safety in the use of chemicals at work, although not all fields covered by the said convention had yet been covered by secondary legislation adopted by the EC. The CJEU simply noted that under the social provisions of the Treaty of Rome, the Community 'enjoys an internal legislative competence in the area of social policy. Consequently, Convention No 170, whose subject matter coincides, moreover, with that of several directives adopted under Article 118a, falls within the Community's area of competence'.[140] Later opinions make it clear that when assessing whether, given the existing allocation of competences between the EU and the member states in a particular area, the EU may have the authority to conclude an international agreement, not only the

[138] See also U Khaliq, 'The European Union and the European Social Charter: Never the twain shall meet?' (n 1) 182–83.

[139] [1993] ECR I-01061.

[140] ibid §17.

scope of the rules in question should be taken into account, but also their nature and content. Moreover, one should take into account 'not only the current state of Community law in the area in question but also its future development, insofar as that is foreseeable at the time of that analysis'.[141]

It is not possible here to provide a full analysis of the international competence of the EU. It seems clear, however, considering the large number of areas covered by the Charter in which the EU has been attributed certain powers by the member states, as well as the potential for further legislative instruments to be adopted in these areas, that the EU could accede to the Charter on the basis of Article 216§1 TFEU. Indeed, the relationship of the EU to this instrument would be very similar to the one it has developed with the UN Convention on the Rights of Persons with Disabilities, which the EU acceded to in 2009: both the EU member states and the EU itself have certain competences to implement the provisions of the international instrument concerned, and it is therefore by their joint action that they can fully discharge their international obligations.[142]

The other question that shall arise if the accession of the EU to the Charter is considered is whether such accession respects the autonomy of EU law and takes into account its specific characteristics. These concerns, as is well known, were at the heart of Opinion 2/13 delivered by the CJEU on 18 December 2014, in which it concluded that the EU could not accede to the ECHR. Would the same objections apply to accession to the Charter?

In order to answer this question, it is important to distinguish between accession to the Charter and accession to the Optional Protocol providing for a system of collective complaints. By acceding to the Charter, the EU would be committing to present reports to the ECSR, on the basis of which the ECSR would adopt conclusions, expressing its views, in effect, as to whether or not the EU's legislation is, or is not, in conformity with the requirements of the Charter. The monitoring mechanism would not differ substantially from that in which the EU already participates within the framework of the UN Convention on the Rights of Persons with Disabilities. It would not seem that, under such a scenario, questions arise as to the need to respect the autonomy or the specific characteristics of the EU legal order. The CJEU has consistently agreed that 'competence of the EU in the field of international relations and its capacity to conclude international agreements necessarily entail the power to submit to the decisions of a court which is created or designated by such agreements as regards the interpretation and

[141] Opinion 1/03, Competence of the Community to conclude the new Lugano Convention on jurisdiction and the recognition and enforcement of judgments in civil and commercial matters, 7 February 2006 §126 (referring to Opinion 2/91 §25).

[142] Council decision of 26 November 2009 concerning the conclusion, by the European Community, of the United Nations Convention on the Rights of Persons with Disabilities (2010/48/EC) [2010] OJ L23/35. The EU signed the Convention on 30 March 2007; it entered into force vis-à-vis the EU on 22 January 2011.

application of their provisions':[143] in this case, the monitoring system to which the EU would submit would remain very light indeed.

The question becomes far more complex once accession to the Collective Complaints mechanism is envisaged. A number of objections raised by the CJEU against the draft agreement providing for EU accession to the ECHR are irrelevant, because they concern features of the ECHR that are not replicated in the system of control established, under the Charter, by the Collective Complaints Protocol. In particular, the ECSR is not competent to deliver advisory opinions at the request of domestic courts, and the Charter does not allow for inter-state applications: therefore, the risks of circumvention of the referral procedure (Article 267 TFEU) through the request for advisory opinions,[144] as well as the risk that states would derogate from the monopoly that Article 344 TFEU reserves to the CJEU for the adjudication of disputes between EU member states concerning the interpretation of application of the EU Treaties,[145] are absent. Other objections of the CJEU are essentially technical in nature (which is not to say that they are minor), and could be easily met by carefully drafting the Accession Protocol. For instance, such an Accession Protocol should ensure that, when a complaint is filed against an EU member state or the EU, the EU or any EU member state, respectively, should be allowed to join *ex officio* and be treated as a co-respondent, without the ECSR having to authorise this.[146]

Two issues are perhaps more delicate. First, in the course of the negotiation of the draft agreement providing for the accession of the EU to the ECHR, the CJEU obtained the establishment of a specific mechanism, allowing for its prior involvement in the exceptional cases where an application would have been filed before the ECtHR without the CJEU (as the judicature of the EU) having been given an opportunity to pronounce itself on the interpretation of the provision of EU law concerned or its compatibility with fundamental rights. This procedure, according to the CJEU, is 'necessary for the purpose of ensuring the proper functioning of the judicial system of the EU'.[147] A similar procedure would presumably have to be established if the EU were to consider acceding to the Collective Complaints Protocol. Indeed, such prior involvement of the CJEU would play a far more significant role in this framework, because the Collective Complaints Protocol does not require that unions or non-governmental organisations

[143] Opinion 2/13 §182 (the Court refers to Opinions 1/91, EU:C:1991:490 §§40 and 70, and 1/09, EU:C:2011:123 §74).

[144] Opinion 2/13 §§196–199 (where the CJEU finds that Protocol No 16 to the ECHR, allowing the ECtHR to deliver advisory opinions on the interpretation or application of the rights and freedoms guaranteed by the ECHR, would threaten the autonomy and effectiveness of the referral procedure established by Art 267 TFEU).

[145] See on Art 344 TFEU Opinion 2/13 §§201–14.

[146] Opinion 2/13 §§215–35.

[147] ibid §236.

use domestic remedies prior to filing a complaint with the ECSR: in order to preserve the role of the CJEU, the Accession Protocol would have to provide that the CJEU will be given an opportunity to pronounce itself on any question of interpretation or validity of EU law prior to such question being examined by the ECSR.

Second, in what is clearly the most sensitive part of Opinion 2/13, the CJEU insists on the need to ensure that the EU member states may establish between themselves rules that should not be obstructed by requirements imposed on the EU by instruments external to the EU legal order: although this is not quite how the CJEU expresses itself, it is this idea that explains its comments on the need to ensure some form of coordination between Article 53 ECHR (which allows state parties to the ECHR to provide for a higher level of protection of rights and freedoms than the minimum standard imposed under the ECHR) and Article 53 CFREU,[148] as well as its insistence on the possibility to rely on mutual trust, a principle which 'requires … each of [the EU member states], save in exceptional circumstances, to consider all the other member states to be complying with EU law and particularly with the fundamental rights recognised by EU law'.[149] In effect, the CJEU appears to make any subordination of the EU to an external control mechanism conditional upon a provision allowing this process of integration to continue, by disconnecting the relationships established between the EU member states under EU law from the commitments of the EU or its member states under another international instrument.[150]

This concern of the CJEU is particularly relevant to the establishment of the area of freedom, security and justice, a domain that is hardly relevant to the Charter. The implication may be, however, that any rule of the Charter that could result in creating obstacles to the ability of the EU member states to pursue the process of integration within the EU should be disregarded where the relationships between the member states are concerned. In particular, workers that are posted by a company established in one EU member state in order to provide a service in another member state, may have to be considered not as 'migrant workers', as did the ECSR (with the implication that, in accordance with Article 6§4 of the Charter, these workers have a right to equality of treatment with the workers employed in the host state), but rather as workers with a specific status linked to the temporary nature of their stay, as provided in the Migrant Workers (Supplementary Provisions)

[148] ibid §189.

[149] ibid §191.

[150] On this feature of integration within the EU, see O De Schutter, 'The Two Europes of Human Rights. The Emerging Division of Tasks Between the Council of Europe and the European Union in Promoting Human Rights in Europe' (Summer 2008) 14 *Columbia Journal of European Law* 509, esp pp 536–42; see also O De Schutter and F Tulkens, 'Confiance mutuelle et droits de l'homme. La Convention européenne des droits de l'homme et la transformation de l'intégration européenne', in *Mélanges en hommage à Michel Melchior* (Bruxelles, Anthemis, 2010) 939–60.

Convention (ILO Convention No 143 of 1975). If that were the only price to pay for the EU acceding to the Charter and joining the Collective Complaints Protocol, it is one that many would be glad to accept. However, a more systematic study should be prepared to identify any other rules of the Charter that could pose a similar problem, by creating obstacles to the deepening of economic integration in the EU through the full implementation of EU rules, to the exclusion of requirements imposed by the Charter.

V. CONCLUSION

In the present situation, the EU member states may face conflicting international obligations, under EU law and under the Charter, respectively. It is also a situation in which the uniformity of application of EU law is impeded by the uneven commitments of the EU member states under the à la carte system of the Charter. And it is one in which the CJEU is perceived as protecting economic freedoms at the expense of social rights, in situations where the two have to be balanced against one another. There is nothing inevitable in this situation. The CJEU would be fully consistent with its approach towards other instruments of international human rights law, that have inspired the development of fundamental rights in the EU legal order, by acknowledging the Charter, and treating it for what it is: the most mature and the most detailed expression of the consensus of the EU member states in the area of fundamental social rights. Even if the CJEU is reluctant to take such a step, the other EU institutions could contribute, by systematically aligning law- and policy-making in the EU with the requirements of the Charter, and by denying those EU member states that have been the least eager to accept the provisions of the Charter a privileged position, as a result of that choice, in the implementation of EU law itself.

As stated by Jean-Claude Juncker, in a 2006 report he prepared in a personal capacity at the request of the Heads of State and Government of the Council of Europe, the final objective should remain that the EU join the Council of Europe as a member.[151] But the accession of the EU to the Charter should be seen as a priority on its own merits: in addition to bringing about a significant improvement in the protection of social rights in Europe, this would clearly express that the EU has reached its age of majority and can now relate to international instruments in the field of human rights in accordance with the degree of integration it has achieved. Only then will the Charter be able to fully play its role as the Social Constitution for Europe.

[151] See report by Jean-Claude Juncker to the Heads of State and government of the member states of the Council of Europe, *Council of Europe—European Union. A sole ambition for the European continent*, 11 April 2006 (recommending that the EU accede to the Council of Europe by 2010 (p 29)).

Interpretation

KLAUS LÖRCHER

I. INTRODUCTION

INTERPRETATION OF LEGAL texts can be considered to be one of the core tasks of legal work, perhaps *the* core task. This is all the more so in relation to international treaties.[1] The Charter is no different. The following contribution will describe the approach taken by the European Committee of Social Rights (ECSR) and analyse whether it is sufficient to fulfil the interpretative function fully and consistently. Although the question of interpretation of the Charter constitutes more of a work in progress than a completed framework, certain elements have been defined and form a sound basis. However, other elements, which should have a more substantial impact on the ECSR's practice, are still missing.

Historically, the ECSR's interpretative function was not undisputed. Indeed, the Governmental Committee (GC)[2] also 'interpreted' the Charter, in particular concerning probably the most disputed issue (at least at that time), namely the right to strike (Article 6§4).[3] As one example of conflicting interpretations, the ECSR had found since Conclusions II that 'the prohibition ... of all strikes which are not ... led by a trade union [is] inconsistent with the Charter',[4] whereas the majority of the GC decided otherwise.[5]

The conflicting interpretations were one reason for the ineffectiveness of the Charter, leading to the 'new impetus' at the beginning of the 1990s and, finally, to the adoption of the Amending (Turin) Protocol providing in its Article 2 (as a new formulation for Article 24§2 ESC) that the ECSR

[1] See eg N Gardiner, *Treaty Interpretation* (Oxford, The Oxford International Law Library, 2008); H Senden, *Interpretation of Fundamental Rights in a Multilevel Legal System—An analysis of the European Court of Human Rights and the Court of Justice of the European Union* (Cambridge, Intersentia, 2011); for the Charter see in particular M Mikkola, *Social Human Rights of Europe* (Helsinki, Karelactio, 2010) 646 et seq.

[2] See for more details Clauwaert in this volume.

[3] Council of Europe, Governmental Committee, 10th report (I), Strasbourg 1988 §66 ('The Committee devoted one session to the interpretation of Article 6 paragraph 4').

[4] Conclusions II (1971), Art 6§4, Germany.

[5] Council of Europe, Governmental Committee, 10th report (I), Strasbourg 1988 §75.

'shall assess from a legal standpoint the compliance of national law and practice with the obligations arising from the Charter', whereas the Governmental Committee's role was limited to 'social, economic and other policy considerations' (Article 4 of the Turin Protocol, as the new formulation of Article 27§3 ESC).

This clear attribution of the legal assessment attributed the exclusive interpretative and in this respect authoritative role to the ECSR.

II. THE ECSR'S APPROACH[6]

Over a number of decades the ECSR has developed a framework for interpretation of the Charter. However, a clearer definition has emerged only since the development of its new quasi-judicial function by means of the Collective Complaints Procedure Protocol (CCPP). Within the framework of this function the need for specific justification arose mainly when particularly fundamental issues were at stake. The most prominent example is the widening of the personal scope of the Charter by interpreting the wording of the Appendix, as some say, '*contra legem*'.[7]

Generally speaking, as an interpretative rule the ECSR stresses the importance of Article 31 of the Vienna Convention on the Law of Treaties (VCLT), stating that the Charter

> should be interpreted—as is generally the case for any provision of an international treaty—in the light of the object and purpose of the treaty concerned and in harmony with other relevant and applicable rules of international law. (Vienna Convention on the Law of Treaties, 23 May 1969, Article 31, paragraphs 1 and 3)[8]

A. Interpretation in Harmony with Its Context, Object and Purpose: The Charter as a Human Rights Instrument (Article 31§1 VCLT)

(i) General Principles

First and foremost, the ECSR has stated that 'the Charter must be interpreted so as to give life and meaning to fundamental social rights', referring, among

[6] This part builds on and further develops: K Lörcher, 'Legal and Judicial Avenues: The (Revised) European Social Charter', in N Bruun, K Lörcher and I Schömann (eds), *The Economic and Financial Crisis and Collective Labour Law in Europe* (Oxford, Hart Publishing, 2014) 265 et seq (under II.A, pp 267 et seq).

[7] Appendix to Resolution CM/ResChS(2015)5, Address by the Representative of the Netherlands at the GR-SOC meeting of 16 September 2014 (ECSR Decision on the merits, 1 July 2014, *Conference of European Churches (CEC) v The Netherlands*, Complaint No 90/2013): 'The decisions by the ECSR do not merely contain an extensive interpretation of the treaty provisions; they contain an interpretation which is simply *contra legem*' (author's emphasis).

[8] ECSR Decision on the merits, 23 October 2012, *Defence for Children International (DCI) v Belgium*, Complaint No 69/2011 §29.

other things, to its well-known counterpart, the European Convention on Human Rights (ECHR):

> 27. The Charter was envisaged as a human rights instrument to complement the European Convention on Human Rights. It is a living instrument dedicated to certain values which inspired it: dignity, autonomy, equality and solidarity. The rights guaranteed are not ends in themselves but they complete the rights enshrined in the European Convention on Human Rights.
>
> 28. Indeed, according to the Vienna Declaration of 1993, all human rights are 'universal, indivisible and interdependent and interrelated' (paragraph 5). The Committee is therefore mindful of the complex interaction between both sets of rights.
>
> 29. Thus, the Charter must be interpreted so as to give life and meaning to fundamental social rights. It follows inter alia that restrictions on rights are to be read restrictively, ie understood in such a manner as to preserve intact the essence of the right and to achieve the overall purpose of the Charter.[9]

More specifically, the ECSR has stressed the 'human rights' character of the social rights enshrined in the Charter.[10] On the basis of Article 31§1 VCLT ('in the light of its object and purpose'), it has furthermore recognised the 'teleological approach' as an important interpretative tool.[11]

Although these principles have been developed and applied with regard to a number of different specific rights (especially the right to social protection,[12] the right of children for protection and schooling and so on), it is in this spirit that all rights at work guaranteed by the Charter—in particular the 'hard-core' trade union rights enshrined in Articles 5 and 6—have to be interpreted.

(ii) Application

These principles have been developed in cases in which the ECSR felt the necessity to justify the result it achieved in more detail. The most prominent example is the extension of the personal scope of the Charter. According to the Appendix,[13] it is limited to 'nationals of other Contracting Parties lawfully resident or working regularly within the territory of the Contracting

[9] ECSR Decision on the merits, 8 September 2004, *FIDH v France*, Complaint No 14/2003.
[10] ECSR Decision on the merits, 20 October 2009, *DCI v The Netherlands*, Complaint No 47/2008 §34.
[11] ibid §36.
[12] *FIDH v France* (n 9).
[13] Scope of the Social Charter in terms of persons protected, para 1 (subject to some exceptions).

Party concerned'. By referring to the principles mentioned (see above (i)), the ECSR found that

> legislation or practice which denies entitlement to medical assistance to foreign nationals, within the territory of a State Party, *even if they are there illegally*, is contrary to the Charter.[14] (author's emphasis)

Another field of application is the approach to be taken concerning permissible restrictions (Article G).[15] The ECSR 'considers that any restrictions on this right must not be interpreted in such a way as to impede the effective exercise by these groups of the right to protection of health'.[16]

B. Interpretation in Harmony with Other Rules of International Law

The relationship to international (social) standards is of the utmost importance for the interpretation process.

(i) General Principles of International (Human Rights) Law

Generally speaking, Article 31§3(c) VCLT requires an interpretation in harmony with other rules of international law.[17] It thus follows the line of interpretation developed by the European Court of Human Rights (ECtHR)[18] and reconfirmed more recently by the ECtHR's Grand Chamber.[19]

Consequently, and as an example, the ECSR referred to international and European human rights standards and the relevant case law in its *Laval* decision on the rights to collective bargaining and collective action:

> [T]he Committee notes that the right to collective bargaining and action receives constitutional recognition at national level in the vast majority of the Council of Europe's member states, as well as in a significant number of *binding legal instruments at the United Nations and EU level.* In this respect, reference is made inter alia to Article 8 of the International Covenant on Economic, Social and Cultural Rights ... the relevant provisions of the ILO Conventions Nos 87, 98 and 154 ... as well as the EU Charter of Fundamental Rights, Directive 2006/123/EC on services in the internal market (cf Article 1§7) and the Directive 2008/104/EC on temporary agency work—recital 19. (emphasis added)[20]

[14] *FIDH v France* (n 9) §32.

[15] For more details, see chapter on 'Restrictions—Article G' by A Koukiadaki' in this volume.

[16] Conclusions 2005, Interpretive Statement on Art 11.

[17] *DCI v The Netherlands* (n 10) §35.

[18] For the background and consequences of the ECtHR's jurisprudence see F Dorssemont, K Lörcher and I Schömann, *The European Convention on Human Rights and the Employment Relation* (Oxford, Hart Publishing, 2013).

[19] *Catan and others v Moldova and Russia* App nos 43370/04, 8252/05 and 18454/06 (ECtHR (GC), 19 October 2012) §136.

[20] ECSR Decision on admissibility and the merits, *LO and TCO v Sweden*, Complaint No 85/2012 §110 (*Laval* decision) (author's emphasis).

(ii) The Council of Europe Instruments, in Particular the ECHR and the Case Law of the ECtHR

At Council of Europe level, the two human rights instruments (the ECHR and the Charter) exist in a close relationship. It will be recalled that the ECtHR has interpreted the human right of freedom of association (Article 11 ECHR)[21] consistently by referring in particular to Articles 5 and 6 of the Charter.[22] The complementary and mutually reinforcing relationship between the ECHR and the Charter[23] has been expressed by the ECSR several times.[24] This specific relationship has often led the ECSR to refer to ECtHR judgments.[25]

However, the references are not limited to the ECHR and ECtHR rulings. They include also other Council of Europe instruments such as the Convention on Action against Trafficking in Human Beings,[26] or the European Code of Social Security (1964, ETS No 48).[27]

(iii) ILO Instruments and the Case Law of the Supervisory Bodies

There is also a specific and close link to the ILO and its standards.[28] It is expressed in various ways by the Charter itself and by the case law of the ECSR. By incorporating the ILO in the supervisory procedure of the Charter[29] the latter recognises this relationship.[30] Moreover, many

[21] See for the evaluation of austerity measures against the background of Art 11 ECHR: KD Ewing, 'Austerity and the Importance of ILO and the ECHR for the Progressive Development of European Labour Law: A Case Study from Greece', in W Däubler and R Zimmer (eds), *Arbeitsvölkerrecht. FS für Klaus Lörcher* (Baden-Baden, Nomos, 2013) 366.

[22] In *Demir and Baykara* App no 34503/97, (ECtHR (GC), 12 November 2008) eg §§45, 49, 77, 103 and 149; in *Enerji Yapi-Yol Sen v Turkey* App no 68959/01 (ECtHR, 21 April 2009) §24.

[23] See for the references of the ECtHR to the Charters, eg ECtHR (Research Division) *The use of Council of Europe Treaties in the case law of the European Court of Human Rights* (Strasbourg, Council of Europe/European Court of Human Rights, 2011) ('The European Social Charter of 1961, revised in 1996, is the treaty that has been the most referred to', 1; see the specific references in nos 035 (ESC), 14 et seq, and 163 (RESC) 35 et seq).

[24] See in particular section II.A.

[25] See, eg *DCI v The Netherlands* (n 10) §73.

[26] ECSR Decision on the merits, 12 September 2014, *FAFCE v Ireland*, Complaint No 89/2013 §19.

[27] ECSR Decision on the merits, 9 September 2014: *Finnish Society of Social Rights v Finland*, Complaint No 88/2012 §17.

[28] See S Evju, 'The European Social Charter and the International Labour Organization—Interlinks Past and Present', in W Däubler and R Zimmer (eds), *Arbeitsvölkerrecht. FS für Klaus Lörcher* (Baden-Baden, Nomos, 2013) 146, see also P O'Higgins, The interaction of the ILO, the Council of Europe and European Union labour standards, in B Hepple (ed) *Social and labour rights in a global context -- international and comparative perspectives* (Cambridge, Cambridge University Press, 2002) 55-69.

[29] See Art 26 of the 1961 Charter (Participation of the ILO), referred to in Art C of the RESC.

[30] Expressed also by the obligation to notify the ILO Director General of any ratification, declaration and so on (see Arts 34–37 of the 1961 Charter and Art O of the 1996 Charter).

(if not most) of the provisions of the 1961[31] and 1996[32] Charters are based on or at least 'inspired' by ILO instruments in force at that time. This is particularly demonstrated by the references to the two trade union rights Conventions (Nos 87 and 98)[33] being categorised as 'core conventions'.[34] Finally, the ECSR has referred to case law mainly of the Committee of Experts on the Application of Conventions and Recommendations (CEACR)[35] or has adopted the same approach as ILO supervisory bodies such as the Committee on Freedom of Association (CFA).[36] Whereas the relationship to the ECHR is linked mainly to the human rights character, the relationship to ILO standards strengthens also the social aspect.

(iv) UN Instruments and the Case Law of the Supervisory Bodies

The practice of the ECSR referring to UN instruments should start with the Universal Declaration of Human Rights (UDHR).[37] Indeed, on the occasion of the tenth anniversary of the RESC the ECSR stated in 2006 that the Charter's 'purpose is to apply the Universal Declaration of Human Rights

[31] See [H Wiebringhaus], 'The European Social Charter and international labour standards' (1961) 84 *International Labour Review* 354 and the 1958 ILO Tripartite Conference that led to the adoption of the text.

[32] The clear references to ILO Conventions are included directly in the Explanatory Report (references in brackets refer to this report) as the source of 'inspiration': Art 8 (new) §4a—ILO Convention No 171 (§49); Art 24—ILO Convention No 158 (§84); Art 25—ILO Convention No 173 (§§91 and 95); Art 27—ILO Convention No 156 (§§102 and 105); Art 28—ILO Convention No 135 (§§106 and 108); Art 29 –ILO Convention No 158 (§109). See also F Vandamme, 'The Revision of the European Social Charter' (1994) (5–6) 133 *International Labour Review* 635.

[33] ECSR Decision on admissibility and the merits, 2 December 2013, *EuroCOP v Ireland*, Complaint No 83/2012 §§28 and 29; ECSR Decision on admissibility and the merits, 3 July 2013, *LO/TCO v Sweden* §38.

[34] *EuroCOP v Ireland* (n 33) §30 'The Committee observes that the above Conventions belong to the eight "core Conventions" of the ILO, setting out the most fundamental principles and rights at work.'

[35] ECSR Decision on the merits, 13 September 2011, *European Trade Union Confederation (ETUC)/Centrale Générale des Syndicats Libéraux de Belgique (CGSLB)/Confédération des Syndicats Chrétiens de Belgique (CSC)/Fédération Générale du Travail de Belgique (FGTB) v Belgium*, Complaint No 59/2009 §19 (reference to CEACR Report 2006 on ILO C 87, Belgium); ECSR Decision on admissibility and the merits, 3 July 2013, *LO/TCO v Sweden* (n 20) §§54–56 (reference to CEACR Report 2013 on ILO C. 87, Sweden) §59 (reference to CEACR Report 2013 on ILO C 98, Sweden) and §§60–63 (reference to CEACR Report 2010 on ILO C 87, UK).

[36] *Digest* of the Freedom of Association Committee of the Governing Body of the ILO, 5th (rev edn) 2006, para 1051. Interpretative statement on Art 6§2 (Conclusions XIX-3 and 2010); see also Conclusions XV-1 vol 2, Art 6§2 (Spain) concerning the CFA: 'The Committee shares the concern of the ILO Committee'.

[37] Referring both to Art 25(1) UDHR: *Finnish Society of Social Rights v Finland* (n 27) §19; ECSR Decision on the Merits, 2 July 2014, *FEANTSA v The Netherlands*, Collective Complaint No 86/2012 §29.

within Europe'.[38] Accordingly, it attributed great importance to 'the rights guaranteed to all human beings by the Universal Declaration of Human Rights of 1948' in widening the personal scope of the Charter.[39]

Having the same position as the Charter (vis-à-vis the ECHR) at international level the most important example is obviously the International Covenant on Economic Social and Cultural Rights (ICESCR vis-à-vis the International Covenant on Civil and Political Rights—ICCPR). In particular in its decisions on the merits the ECSR refers to specific Articles of the ICESCR,[40] as well as to the case law of the Committee on Economic Social and Cultural Rights (CESCR), especially to its General Comments.[41] These references also relate to (collective) labour rights,[42] even in the Concluding Observations.[43] The range of instruments mentioned also includes the Convention on the Elimination of All Forms of Racial Discrimination (CERD)[44] and the Convention on the Rights of the Child (CRC).[45]

[38] See Interpretative Statement (2006), '*Comments of a general nature*'.

[39] *DCI v Belgium* (n 8) §30.

[40] ECSR Decisions: References to Art 11 ICESCR: *FEANTSA v The Netherlands* (n 37) §30; Decision on the merits, 28 June 2011, *COHRE v France*, Collective Complaint No 63/2010 §17; Decision on the merits, 30 June 2011, *ERRC v Portugal*, Collective Complaint No 61/2010 §11; Decision on the merits, 25 June 1010, *Centre on Housing Rights and Evictions (COHRE) v Italy*, Collective Complaint No 58/2009 §20; *DCI v The Netherlands* (n 10) §18; Decision on the merits, 8 August 2009 *FEANTSA v Slovenia*, Collective Complaint No 53/2008—08.08.2009 §36; to Art 12 ICESCR: Decision on the merits, 10 September 2013: *IPPF EN v Italy*, Complaint No 87/2012 §37; Decision on the merits, 6 December 2013, *FIDH v Greece*, Complaint No 72/2011 §13; ECSR Conclusions: reference to Art 12 ICESCR: Conclusions XX-2—Spain—Art 11§1—06.12.2013.

[41] ECSR Decisions: reference to General Comment No 4: *FEANTSA v The Netherlands* (n 37) §30; Decision on the merits *MDAC v Bulgaria*, Complaint No 41/2007—03.06.2008 §37; *COHRE v France* (n 40) §18; *COHRE v Italy* (n 40) §21; Decision on the merits *FEANTSA v Slovenia*, Collective Complaint No 53—08.08.2009 §37; to General Comment No 7: *COHRE v France* (n 40) §18; *COHRE v Italy* (n 40) §21; *FEANTSA v Slovenia* (n 40) §37; to General Comment No 13: Decision on the merits Mental Disability Advocacy Centre (MDAC) v Bulgaria, Collective Complaint No 41/2007—03.06.2008 §37; to General Comment No 14: *FEANTSA v The Netherlands* (n 37) §32; Decision on the merits *IPPF EN v Italy* (n 40) §38; *FIDH v Greece* (n 40) §13; to General Comment No 15: *FIDH v Greece* (n 40) §13; ECSR Conclusions: Conclusions XX-2—Spain—Art 11§1 ESC—06.12.2013 (reference to General Comment No 14).

[42] References to Art 8 ICESCR: Decision on admissibility and the merits: *EuroCOP v Ireland* (n 33) §31; *LO/TCO v Sweden* (n 20) §37; *ETUC/CGSLB/CSC/FGTB v Belgium* (n 35) §17.

[43] ECSR Decision on the merits in *ETUC/CGSLB/CSC/FGTB v Belgium* (n 35) §8 (reference to 'Observations of the UN Committee on Economic, Social and Cultural Rights on the third Report submitted by the Belgian Government on the application of the International Covenant on Economic, Social and Cultural Rights' concerning Art 8 ICESR).

[44] See, eg, the several references to UN instruments and documents in *COHRE v France* (n 40) §§16–18 (Art 2). It is interesting to note, however, that the Committee was not satisfied with references to international obligations for demonstrating compliance with the Charter's standards (see, eg: Conclusions XVII-2, Netherlands Antilles, Art 20 RESC (Art 1 Protocol No 1).

[45] ECSR Decision on the merits, 5 December 2014, *APPROACH v Italy*, Complaint 94/2013 §16 (with references to relevant General Comments Nos 6 and 13 and in §§17 and 18 respectively).

(v) *Further Pertinent International Material*

It is interesting to note that in practice the ECSR not only refers to further international (law) instruments or those of the World Health Organization (WHO),[46] but also takes into account other relevant international documents, issued by, for example, national human rights bodies. It appears to follow in this respect the approach used by the ECtHR, which often refers to material of a non-binding character (particularly coming from the Council of Europe's institutions, such as Recommendations of the Committee of Ministers or the Parliamentary Assembly). An important further example is that of the Greek National Commission for Human Rights.[47]

(vi) *Interim Conclusions: Relations between the Charter and International Agreements (Article H)*

Given the wide range of social human rights guaranteed by the Charter, it is not surprising that many of them are seen in the context of other international standards. This is particularly true of ILO and UN Conventions at international level, on one hand, and at European level the ECHR, on the other. As already outlined, according to the ECSR's case law the Charter is to be interpreted in line with those international standards, as well as the respective case law of the competent bodies, thus providing a minimum level of protection.[48] Therefore, nothing should and, indeed, nothing does prevent the ECSR from going beyond this minimum level.[49] Indeed, European standards should in principle be considered to guarantee a higher level of protection than international standards, which have to take into account different levels of development.[50]

This is confirmed by the basic human rights rule contained in Article H (and Article 32 ESC) defining the 'Relations between the Charter and domestic law or international agreements' in the sense of a 'most favourable clause'. This approach is consistent with, and indeed indispensable

[46] Eg 'World Health Organization's Guidelines for drinking-water quality' in ECSR Decision on the merits, 23 January 2013, *FIDH v Greece* (n 40) §§42 and 143, for the purpose of interpreting Art 11 of the Charter; ECSR Decision on the merits, 4 November 2002, *International Association Autism-Europe v France*, Complaint No 13/2002 §54 (definition of 'autism').

[47] See, as a recent example, the reference to the 'NCHR [Greek National Commission for Human Rights] Recommendation: On the imperative need to reverse the sharp decline in civil liberties and social rights' (8 December 2011) in the ECSR Decision on the Merits, 7 December 2012, *IKA–ETAM v Greece*, Complaint No 76/2012 §38.

[48] Expressly recognised, eg, in Art 12§2 ESC ('at least equal to that required for the ratification of International Labour Convention (No 102)') and in particular in combination with §3 ('raise progressively'). This principle is even confirmed by the new Art 12§3 RESC referring to the higher standard of the European Code of Social Security.

[49] M Mikkola, *Social Human Rights of Europe* (Helsinki, Karelactio, 2010) 75.

[50] See, eg, Art 19(3) ILO Constitution ('imperfect development of industrial organization').

for international human rights standards. Otherwise they would endanger the human rights protection achieved elsewhere. Thus, similar provisions are to be found in practically all international human rights instruments.[51] The ECSR referred to Article H when defining the relationship between the Charter and EU law.[52] More explicitly, this was expressed in two Dissenting Opinions in the sense that 'it needs to be borne in mind that, in accordance with Article H of the revised Charter, the Charter is only a minimum standard and should in any case aim to secure a higher level'[53] and that the majority's interpretation (of Article 5) 'means a restrictive systematic interpretation which is not in the line of the most favourable standard imposed by Article H'.[54]

III. EVALUATION OF THE ECSR'S APPROACH

A. Does the ECSR Apply Its Interpretative Approach?

(i) Dissenting Opinions

It might first be interesting to look at the dissenting opinions that are often related to interpretative questions. The (internal) critics sometimes go too far: from 'sheer treaty-making',[55] 'form of arbitrariness but also, and no less seriously, to implicitly subverting fundamental traits of national industrial relations systems',[56] to 'unseemly concern for the interests of governments at the expense of individuals'.[57] But rarely do dissenters refer to fundamental interpretation rules such as Article 31 VCLT,[58] or criticise the majority's

[51] See Arts 5(2) ICESCR and ICCPR, Art 19(8) ILO Constitution, Arts 53 ECHR and CFREU.

[52] ECSR Decision on the merits, 12 September 2012, *Syndicat de Défense des Fonctionnaires v France*, Complaint No 73/2011 §29 ('This interpretation by the Committee is consistent with Art H of the Charter on the relations between the Charter and the domestic law or international agreements').

[53] ECSR Decision on the merits, 9 September 2009, *CFDT v France*, Collective Complaint No 50/2008, Dissenting Opinion Jimena Quesada §19.

[54] *EuroCOP v Ireland* (n 33) Partly Dissenting Opinion Jimena Quesada §3.2.

[55] Dissenting opinion Evju and Schlachter (Conclusions (2007) on Art 26): 'An assessment to that effect by the Committee does not justify what cannot be even thinly disguised as dynamic interpretation but amounts to sheer treaty-making').

[56] Dissenting opinion on Art 6§4 Evju, Birk and Mikkola (Conclusions XVIII-1: 'conclusion ... amounts not merely to a form of arbitrariness but also, and no less seriously, to implicitly subverting fundamental traits of national industrial relations systems').

[57] Dissenting opinion on Art 12§4 Belorgey, Aliprantis, Kollonay-Lehoczky and Francois (Conclusions XVIII-1).

[58] See eg Dissenting opinion Evju, Koncar and François in *FIDH v France* (n 9): 'Due regard being had to the relevant provisions of the 1969 Vienna Convention on the Law of Treaties, and in particular its Article 31§1, in my opinion they do not offer support for the interpretation of the Charter'.

view as 'insufficiently reasoned'.[59] On the other hand, 'Concurring opinions'[60] providing for more interpretative clarity do not appear to be used frequently.

(ii) Analysis of Case Law

The ECSR's case law comes in a number of varieties, mainly Decisions, Conclusions and Statements of Interpretation. Concerning the latter two it would appear that the ECSR rarely refers to interpretation rules[61] in the sense of Article 31 VCLT.

Concentrating therefore on the decision, and in order to evaluate the real impact of the ECSR's interpretative approach, we have to distinguish between the description of the legal framework for which the ECSR uses different words[62] and the real impact in the reasoning of the Committee. For the first category one can sometimes find an extensive description of international standards and even of other international material containing from time to time very specific statements. On the other hand, the real impact on the interpretation process is often very limited. Even when revising its case law it did not rely for the new interpretation on Article 31 VCLT.[63] Further systematic implementation of this approach in the ECSR's case law would be desirable.

B. Is There a Need for Interpretation in Harmony with Principles Specifically Related to the Charter?

Looking at the concept of the Charter, it is characterised by a positive tendency towards the effective enjoyment of social rights, in both its original and revised versions. This is expressed mainly in an impressive catalogue of originally 19 (later extended to 31) fundamental social rights. Of the 47 Council of Europe member states, only four have not yet ratified

[59] Dissenting Opinion Evju and Schlachter on Art 4§3 (Conclusions XVIII-2).

[60] Explicitly permitted by r 22(3) for conclusions, r 30(2) for admissibility of complaints and r 35(1) on the merit decisions.

[61] See as a general reference to the ECtHR's jurisprudence Statement of Interpretation on Art 16 (2006): 'With a view to interpreting states' obligations in this field, the Committee refers to the European Court of Human Rights ... judgment *X and Y v The Netherlands* of 26 March 1985'.

[62] Usually 'Relevant International Materials' but also (Relevant) 'International Law', (Relevant) 'International Conventions', 'Relevant Law ... International Level', 'International Sources,' etc.

[63] See, for example, the 'Observation' concerning Art 10 (Interpretive Statement, Conclusions XIV-2). The most recent example of the 'Statement of interpretation on the rights of refugees under the European Social Charter' (5 October 2015) with wide interpretative arguments has the potential to mark a general shift.

the Charter. The number of accepted provisions is still increasing, not decreasing. These positive trends clearly contrast more and more with the social reality characterised by drastic reductions in social rights and cuts in social benefits. The ECSR has responded in general that the crisis as such cannot be used as justification.[64] However, this approach does not appear to be sufficient for the safeguarding of all rights concerned, as well as for all negative impacts on law and practice. Therefore, the ECSR should, in harmony with Article 5 VCLT providing for the priority of the practice of international organisations, apply at least the following principles.

The Preamble refers to the aim of the Council of Europe to facilitate 'economic and social progress, in particular by the maintenance and further realisation of human rights and fundamental freedoms' (1st Recital). Moreover, the governments declare themselves 'resolved to make every effort in common to improve the standard of living and to promote the social well-being of both their urban and rural populations by means of appropriate institutions and action' (4th Recital). This general framework may be summarised as a principle obliging them to 'social progress'. This principle should directly imply the general prohibition of reducing existing rights.[65]

Moreover, particular attention is required in respect of the 'effective exercise' of the Charter rights at stake.[66] Therefore the full implementation 'in law and practice' has to be ensured.

[64] K Lörcher, 'Legal and Judicial Avenues: The (Revised) European Social Charter', in N Bruun, K Lörcher and I Schömann (eds), *The Economic and Financial Crisis and Collective Labour Law in Europe* (Oxford, Hart, 2014) 265 et seq (under II.C., pp 276 et seq.).

[65] For more details, see 'Restrictions—Article G' by A Koukiadaki in this volume.

[66] See the introductory words in nearly every Article of the Charter, in particular the two main Articles (6 and 19) at stake in this Complaint ('With a view to ensuring the effective exercise of the right'). In this respect, reference should also be made to Art A§4 of the Charter requiring a 'system of labour inspection', thus aimed at strengthening practical application.

Implementation

Article I

TEUN JASPERS

Article I—Implementation of the undertakings given

1. Without prejudice to the methods of implementation foreseen in these articles the relevant provisions of Articles 1 to 31 of Part II of this Charter shall be implemented by:
   a. laws or regulations;
   b. agreements between employers or employers' organisations and workers' organisations;
   c. a combination of those two methods;
   d. other appropriate means.
2. Compliance with the undertakings deriving from the provisions of paragraphs 1, 2, 3, 4, 5 and 7 of Article 2, paragraphs 4, 6 and 7 of Article 7, paragraphs 1, 2, 3 and 5 of Article 10 and Articles 21 and 22 of Part II of this Charter shall be regarded as effective if the provisions are applied, in accordance with paragraph 1 of this article, to the great majority of the workers concerned.

Appendix Part V

Article I

It is understood that workers excluded in accordance with the appendix to Articles 21 and 22 are not taken into account in establishing the number of workers concerned.

I. INTRODUCTION

APPLICATION OF THE Charter, whether in its original 1961 or revised 1996 version in the various States Parties,[1] is connected directly to implementation of the Charter provisions not only in national law (although that is usually considered the main option) but also in practice. In official documents of the various bodies of the Council of Europe, and also of other international institutions dealing with (fundamental) social rights, such as the United Nations[2] and the International Labour Organization, not to mention in the literature, it is stressed that the rights and duties contained in the treaties have to be implemented *effectively*. The introductory words of each of the Charter provisions—'with a view to ensuring the effective exercise of the right to…'—express this objective.[3] The emphasis on effectiveness can be understood when taking into account the mostly weak nature of the rights and duties and the lack of supervisory mechanisms that can effectively enforce (correct) implementation and, consequently, the application of the provisions. It makes sense that such emphasis is laid on the supervisory mechanisms and the remedies provided against violations. Enforcement is therefore a crucial issue, if not the most important.[4]

Implementation of the Charter provisions can be done by various means. Usually the national legislators or governments are the main actors; but not exclusively. Courts can be involved in implementation by applying the provisions in domestic cases. But application in practice is accepted also. This approach is quite common in the field of international socio-economic rights.[5] The ECSR looks at actual application, even when a legal source is lacking.[6] Assessment of the correct implementation of the Charter provisions

[1] The term 'state parties' indicates which national states are covered, although the official term is 'Contracting Parties'. References to state parties are restricted to the countries bound by the Charter. References to other countries shall be clearly indicated.

[2] I refer to the International Covenant on Economic, Social and Cultural Rights and the institutions supervising its (correct) application.

[3] Cf Declaration of the Committee of Ministers of 12 May 2004: 'Ensuring the effectiveness of the implementation of the ECHR at national and European levels, Guaranteeing the effectiveness of the European Convention on Human Rights', *Collected texts* (Council of Europe, 2004) 5–7, and the documents attached. *Effective* exercise of the rights laid down in the Charter is one of the main requirements the ECSR uses when controlling application. Cf also the Limburg Principles on the Implementation of the International Covenant on Economic, Social and Cultural Rights, 2006. See also M Mikkola, *Social Human Rights of Europe* (Porvoo, Karelactio, 2010) 650; and G Staberock, *Human Rights, Domestic Implementation* (Max Planck Encyclopedia of Public International Law, 2011).

[4] The issue of enforcement will only be touched upon when it is necessary for elaborating the subject of implementation.

[5] Compare the ICESCR as well as other UN Treaties in this field and the ILO conventions. The bodies supervising these treaties take this approach. Cf J-M Servais, *International Labour Law* (Wolters Kluwer, 2014), Pt III, ch 1.

[6] See the chapter on the Charter's supervisory procedures by S Clauwaert in this volume.

is therefore somewhat complicated because, apart from national legislation, decisions of domestic courts and application in practice also have to be taken into account.

To give a comprehensive picture of the various ways and methods of implementation of the Charter in national law and practice, the focus will be on three topics related to the main theme. The first topic (section II) will be the two general issues concerning implementation: the form of implementation and the methods used. The form of implementation is closely connected to the (legal) nature of the provisions. For that reason a distinction has to be made between directly applicable subjective rights and programmatic rights; for the application of the latter, additional regulatory measures are needed. The methods the Charter provides for vary, as Article I shows. Apart from legislation—the Charter speaks of laws and regulations—implementation is also possible by agreements between social partners or by other appropriate means.[7] It should be noted that actual implementation is or can be influenced when state parties exercise the option of making reservations to articles or parts of them. This possibility is disputed because the Charter itself does not create that possibility. Section II.B will deal with this. A separate issue of the general subject of *effective implementation* is the obligation of providing for effective remedies, a subject that has been dealt with by Clauwaert in this volume.

Another subject we shall touch on—in section III—is the use and meaning of general terms in the Charter, and the way they have to be understood. This question is related to the room state parties have or can take to implement obligations according to their own wishes and needs by using *their own* definitions. The room for this is restricted when the Charter uses a term that has to be understood and interpreted as a general Charter term.

A last subject that needs to be tackled in this context is the relation between the way in which the rights the Charter provides for are applied and actually exercised, and the economic situation a State Party is facing. Because the actual application of important parts of the Charter can be connected to economic situations—in particular when programmatic rights of a progressive nature are at stake—it is necessary to look at whether the content and meaning of provisions fluctuates and may fluctuate with economic ups and downs.[8] That is called the dynamic approach. It is dynamic in two respects: the first is directly related to, but can go beyond some Charter provisions in which the term 'progressive' is used.[9] In the literature the concept of *progressive realisation* of rights is often used. Application of Charter provisions in a progressive way by raising standards in favour of the persons

[7] Art I, previously Art 7 of the Additional Protocol to the European Social Charter 1988.

[8] We return to the discussion in section IV.

[9] See, for instance, Art 12§3.

to be protected is not a disputed issue. The contrary, the second way, is lowering standards and norms—temporarily or permanently—for economic or other (external) reasons, often described as 'adaptation to economic reality'. This will be examined in section IV.

II. IMPLEMENTATION, METHODS AND WAYS

The Charter can be implemented in various ways, as Article I indicates. Generally speaking, implementation is an obligation imposed on the state—the State Party has to take action in order to ensure that the provisions are implemented in domestic law and practice. Legislation is the most usual way, but not the only one. It might be termed the 'royal way', and implies that state intervention is needed or even required by the Charter itself (see section B). This way of implementation is not necessarily required if direct effect is assigned to the Charter provision, of which horizontal direct effect is the most effective (see section A). Implementation by collective agreements is another way of implementing Charter provisions, recognising the important role social partners can play. In section C, an overview is given of the conditions under which the instrument can be used effectively. A separate issue is the use of reservations with the objective of evading obligations if state parties are not willing or perhaps—in their view—not capable of implementing certain obligations. In the past, some countries exercised this option. This issue will be discussed in section II.D.

Enumerating explicitly the range of means that can be used in order to give effect to the rights is common to international treaties in this field, although not always in the same wording. The International Covenant on Economic, Social and Cultural Rights refers simply to all appropriate measures, including in particular the adoption of legislative measures.[10] ILO conventions take a different approach. Several conventions do not have a particular implementation provision. They simply stipulate that the countries that have ratified the convention have to promote, ensure exercise of the right or pursue a certain policy aimed at achieving the goals of the convention. Some conventions state that the provisions shall be implemented by means of laws and regulations, collective agreements, arbitration awards or in any other appropriate manner.[11]

The wording of Article I of the Charter assumes that any form of implementation is acceptable as long as the objectives are achieved. Practice counts, it seems to say. As the Explanatory Report to the 1996 Charter

[10] Art 2 ICESCR.

[11] Cf Art 5 ILO Convention No 177 (homework) and Art 18 ILO Convention No 189 (domestic workers). See also ILO Convention No 140 (paid educational leave) Art 5.

emphasises, the term 'shall' indicates that the method chosen must be effective. Implementation must also be adequate.[12] It is again the ECSR that assesses whether the method used is effective, in the sense that the goals are attained. In accordance with its conclusions, the ECSR forms the opinion that a certain way of implementation can be required. In particular the ECSR points explicitly to legislation. The Explanatory Report is aware of that, stating that the composition of the means (in Article I of Part V) has been chosen:

> The model for this provision has been Article 7 of the Additional Protocol to the Charter of 1988. The first paragraph provides that without prejudice to the methods of implementation foreseen in Articles 1 to 31 of Part II of the Revised Charter, this provision may be implemented by any of the means enumerated in the paragraph. This composition has been chosen so as not to interfere with the case law of the Committee of Independent Experts according to which a certain form of implementation, such as legislation, is sometimes required. The word 'shall' indicates that the method chosen must be efficient.[13]

From an analysis of the case law on this point it can be deduced that for some provisions the ECSR requires implementation by legislation. When a kind of discrimination is at stake the ECSR is very clear about it.[14]

A. Direct Effect

In some cases it is not necessary for the state to take action apart from going through the whole ratification procedure. When a Charter provision has direct effect, or in other words, when a provision is self-executing, no further implementation action by the state—beyond ratification—is needed, provided all the criteria for direct effect are fulfilled. In that case the provision can be invoked directly by the person[15] on whom the right is conferred. Whether that is the case depends on the national constitutional system and on the wording of the provision. This requirement is met when a constitution explicitly stipulates that the international norm has priority over the domestic law on condition that the international treaty provides for a subjective right. That is—anyhow—the case in countries with monist (constitutional) systems, but also in countries in which the international norm, fulfilling the necessary requirements, has priority over conflicting national

[12] Explanatory Report to the Additional Protocol 1988 §32.

[13] Explanatory Report §139.

[14] See the conclusions on Art 1§2 in combination with the Appendix to the Charter, Arts 4§3, 15§1, 20 and 23. Cf Digest 2008, pp 20, 45, 112, 139 and 147, and the there-quoted conclusions of the ECSR. Another example is the protection of pregnant women against dismissal in Art 8§2 in combination with the Appendix; cf Digest 2008, p 68.

[15] An individual person, but also a legal person, such as a trade union or an enterprise.

norms.[16] But apart from that the provision has also to meet the criteria for direct effect: the provision has to be clear, unambiguous, unconditional and not subject to further regulation. If both requirements—the nature of the constitutional system and clarity—are fulfilled, no implementation act by the state is needed. And the individual can invoke that right before a national court, provided it has granted a subjective right to the individual. By implication, for all provisions of the Charter that do not have direct effect, implementation by state action is required. The number of provisions that meet the direct effect requirements is low. However, it is interesting to note that the number of provisions that have direct effect in several countries is increasing. That is due to the fact that national judges—in those countries with monist systems—are attributing direct effect to provisions that in their opinion meet the criteria.[17] For this kind of provision, effective implementation is guaranteed without any additional act.

B. Implementation by State Action

For all other norms of international law, implementation has to be realised by their transposition into national law. The manner of transposition can differ state by state.[18] The latitude that is given to states when transposing a (fundamental) social right into national law can be less wide than is supposed to be the case. An example is the obligation to ensure rights without discrimination. In the case law of supervisory bodies, the freedom of a country with regard to transposition of this type of provision has been restricted. They argue that the obligation carries an immediate obligation: an obligation to take steps to ensure the right, and to respect the 'minimum core' content of the right.[19] That does not imply that the right can be invoked

[16] Countries with a monist system include Belgium, the Netherlands, France and some central and eastern European countries. In countries with a mixed system, such as Italy, Austria and Germany, international norms can have direct effect. In countries with a clear dualist system (United Kingdom and the Scandinavian countries), full transposition of the international norm into their own body of law is necessary. Cf HD Jarass, B Pieroth, *Grundgesetz, Kommentar* (München, 2011) 600 and 762–63. See also D Van Eeckhoutte and A Vandaele, 'Doorwerking van internationale normen in de Belgische rechtsorde' (Instituut voor Internationaal Recht, Working Paper No 33, October 2002).

[17] A well-known example is Art 6§4. In several countries—such as The Netherlands and some countries in central and eastern Europe—domestic judges have attributed direct effect to this provision. See also the chapter on Art 6 by F Dorssemont in this volume. A recent example is the direct application of Art 12§4, also in the Netherlands.

[18] In some countries, ratification of the treaty is sufficient; in others, additional legal acts are required.

[19] Committee on Economic, Social and Cultural Rights (CESCR), General Comment No 3: 'The Nature of the General Legal Obligation Imposed on States Parties to the Covenant' (29 March 2004) GAOR 59th Session Supp 40, vol 1, 175. The ECSR uses the same approach;

directly, but the state is not free to choose its own ways of guaranteeing the full exercise of the right.[20]

As already mentioned, the majority of the Charter provisions have to be implemented by a regulatory action of the state, be it legislation or administrative measures.[21] A usual method of doing so is the incorporation of Charter provisions in the national body of laws. That can involve transposition of the substance of the Charter provision into national law in such a way that it at least complies with the Charter obligations. It is argued that treaties tend to have the greatest impact if they have been made part of domestic law. Far from being indifferent as to the mode of implementation, it is recommended that states incorporate the respective treaty provisions into domestic law and provide them with appropriate status. It has been argued that this practice is an expression of a duty of incorporation. Incorporation is considered the preferred option to ensure the full realisation of the rights contained in the respective treaties.[22] The objective is *effective* implementation.[23] States that do not directly incorporate or transform the treaty have the burden of showing that they are able to ensure the rights under the treaty effectively through other means. Similarly, the CESCR considers that incorporation in domestic law is desirable, although not legally required. However, incorporation of the provisions in domestic law is not sufficient to ensure full realisation, as supervisory committees and scholars have emphasised. It has to be combined with effective remedies for their enforcement.[24]

Regarding implementation of Charter provisions, a distinction has to be made as to the nature of the respective provisions, as already mentioned. Incorporation is the preferred way if the provision contains a subjective

cf Conclusions XIII-5. Cf D Harris and J Darcy, *The European Social Charter* (New York, International Publishers, 2001) 239–43.

[20] As long since formulated by the ECSR: 'any restrictions on rights are to be read restrictively, ie understood in such a manner as to preserve intact the essence of the right and to achieve the overall purpose of the Charter'; cf the chapter on 'Article G Restrictions' by A Koukiadaki in this volume. See also Decision on the merits, *International Federation of Human Rights Leagues (FIDH) v France*, Collective Complaint No 14/2003 §29.

[21] Regularly applied (social) policy is also an accepted method, but may be not fully in conformity—literally—with the Charter. But if the practice is in conformity with the obligations set out in the Charter and the ECSR and the Committee of Ministers are satisfied, still the government concerned is asked to guarantee the continuation of this practice, preferably by adopting legal rules, if possible.

[22] See Human Rights Committee of the ICCPR in its General Comment No 31 para 13, UN Doc CCPR/C/21/Rev 1/Add 13 (2004); see also the supervising Committee of ICESCR (CESCR) in its General Comment No 9: 'The Domestic Application of the Covenant', E/C12/1998/24 para 8.

[23] In that sense see the Explanatory Report to Protocol 1988 §32. Apart from being effective, implementation has to be adequate.

[24] C Heyns and F Viljoen, *The Impact of the United Nations Human Rights Treaties on the Domestic Level* (The Hague, Kluwer, 2002) 5.

right; namely a right conferred on an individual person or a *collective person*, a trade union or an enterprise, for instance.[25] Implementing programmatic rights usually requires a different method of transposing the obligation into national law. Room is left to the state parties to choose the means that best suit them, provided effective application of the rights enshrined in the Charter is ensured. Because a major part of the provisions of the Charter have a programmatic nature, different methods of implementation are used. The room left to State Parties when implementing these rights can nevertheless be limited because the ECSR has given a specific content to some Charter provisions. In consequence, such provisions provide for a specific level of protection, provided a State Party takes the conclusions of the ECSR seriously. A striking example (there are more) is Article 4§1: the right to a decent remuneration.[26]

The case law of the ECSR also indicates that implementation by legislative measures or other state regulations is not sufficient. The ECSR not only looks at the written laws and/or regulations; it also investigates whether the practice is in conformity with the Charter's obligations.[27] If the obligation is actually put into practice—which apart from state regulation can be done by all kinds of measures, including the application of *regularly deployed policy measures*—the ECSR concludes that the country is acting in conformity with the Charter.[28] That is particularly true when programmatic rights are at stake, such as the right of Article 1§1: the right to work can be complied with if the national government pursues an active employment policy by taking effective employment measures. In the context of Article 1§1, measures aiming at and resulting in a reduction of unemployment, or measures to create jobs or effectively facilitating job creation, can prove that a country is complying with that obligation. Legal measures can assist and support this policy, but may not be the most effective means.[29] Legislation is not required, as the Appendix to the Revised European Social Charter under Article 26 states.[30] In other cases legislation or other types of

[25] Legal personality per se is not required. Contrary to an enterprise that has legal personality, a trade union or a works council does not need to have legal personality. Works councils usually do not have this. In some countries, for instance Belgium, even trade unions are lacking legal personality.

[26] See hereafter the chapter on Art 4 by K Lörcher in this volume.

[27] Explicitly in decisions on the merits, Collective Complaint 1/1998, International Commission of Jurists ICJ and *Autism Europe v France,* Collective Complaint No 13/2002.

[28] Examples can be found in the chapters of this book dealing with the substantive rights and duties of the Charter, in particular the Chapters on Art 1, Art 3, Art 7 and Art 15.

[29] Employment policy is mostly embedded in legal rules laying down the conditions of and funds for employment in general and more particularly for (vulnerable) groups of people. Cf the chapter on Art 1 by S Deakin in this volume. See also Mikkola (n 3) 144 et seq.

[30] Cf Appendix to the Revised European Social Charter, Part II, p 28. *A contrario* it can be argued that if it is stated expressly in the Appendix for a specific article that, at least in principle, other articles require legislation. In its case law the ECSR seems not to support this approach.

written regulations are considered appropriate means. In relation to some subjects it is required that a common policy of a State Party has to be based on a precise legal framework concerning certain elements.[31]

C. Implementation by (Collective) Agreements between Social Partners

As explained above, it is supposed that national legislation and regulations comprise a reliable tool when guaranteeing the rights of the persons to whom the provisions extend.[32] However, if other instruments are used, it has to be certain that all persons who are addressed in the Charter provision are covered, unless the Charter provides for exceptions. A specific exception to the overall personal coverage is found in Article 1§2 of Part V of the Charter;[33] according to this Article, for a particular group of rights enshrined in the Charter coverage of the majority of the workers concerned is sufficient to qualify for compliance. That is the case, for example, when a provision is implemented by collective agreement between social partners and when they are carried out 'otherwise than by law'. A state is complying with that provision if it is *applied to the great majority of the workers concerned.* The exception applies to a number of provisions all related to workers: Article 2§1, 2§2, 2§3, 2§4, 2§5 and 2§7 (conditions of work), Article 7§4, 7§6 and 7§7 (working conditions of young workers), Article 10§1, 10§2, 10§3 and 10§5 (vocational training) and Articles 21 (information and consultation of workers) and 22 (workers' involvement in working conditions). By implication it can be stated that, as to the other provisions when a collective agreement or another instrument (other than law) is used as a means of implementation, it has be sure that the instrument used applies to all persons addressed.

The use of collective agreements as an instrument for implementation of a Charter provision is restricted in that the substance of such an agreement may not run counter to obligations of the Charter. The state has to ensure that this does not take place and has to intervene either to bring about the repeal of the agreements concerned, or to rule out their implementation.[34] This situation cannot be covered by Article I of Part V of the Charter if the provision concerned is not mentioned in that Article. The case concerned

[31] As an example I refer to Art 3§2. The ECSR is quite clear about this requirement. Cf K Lörcher in this volume.

[32] Provided of course the relevant provision does not exclude people from application who are the addressees of the right.

[33] Formerly Art 33§1 ESC.

[34] Decision on the merits, *Confederation of Swedish Enterprise v Sweden*, Collective Complaint No 12/2002. The issue at stake was a kind of pre-entry closed shop in Sweden, laid down in collective agreements.

the negative freedom of association, a provision Sweden was alleged to be violating. It is obvious that such a case falls under the general obligation resting on the state to ensure full exercise of the right.[35]

Regarding the possibility of implementing Charter provisions by collective agreements, two issues have to be addressed. The first is what can be considered a collective agreement between social partners. The second is the great majority rule.

(i) Meaning of 'Collective Agreement'

Article I of the Charter speaks of *agreements between employers or employers' organisations and workers' organisations*. The collective agreement is in many provisions proposed as an appropriate means of implementing Charter provisions.[36] The Charter does not give a definition of 'collective agreement'. The ECSR does not do so, either. It must be noted that the Appendix to the RESC extends the possibility of regulating collectively by allowing that some matters can be regulated collectively also by *other agreements between employers and workers' representatives*. It concerns Articles 21 and 22. The extension fits well with the content of these provisions. They all are about the involvement of workers or their representatives in business affairs or directly related to workers' rights to protection. The Charter by itself defines the term 'workers' representatives': persons who are recognised as such under national legislation or practice.[37]

Because the RESC does not provide for a definition, or refers to national law (and practice), the national law determines what is understood by collective agreements, and which bodies are capable of concluding such agreements. This implies that regarding the *ordinary* collective agreements—that is, agreements concluded between social partners, understood as organisations of employers and employees—the laws of the various countries set the requirements for qualifying an arrangement as a collective agreement according to provisions of the Charter referring to them. That fits with the general approach of the RESC: it is left to the states to choose—under conditions—how they wish to implement the Charter provisions securing the full exercise of the rights conferred. Thus if the route of collective agreements has been chosen, the national law determines the conditions under which a collective agreement can be concluded with the binding effect

[35] B Veneziani points to another field in which a collective agreement plays an important role: the implementation of Art 21 RESC by collective agreements. See the chapter on Art 21 by B Veneziani in this volume.

[36] Arts 4§5 and final sentence, 6§§2 and 4, and 27§2. In the Appendix to RESC the collective agreement turns up as a tool to implement or to specify how a provision could be implemented. See Appendix, Part II as to Arts 3, 4, 5, 4; 21 and 22, and finally Art 24§4.

[37] Appendix to the RESC as to Arts 21 and 22.

that national law attributes to it. The effectiveness of this implementation method thus depends on the legal system, including the legal effect of such agreements. The same is true when the Charter delegates regulatory power to *other agreements between employers and workers' representatives*. The national law has to give effect to these agreements. In fact, that is hardly ever the case.[38]

(ii) Great Majority Rule

As mentioned above, for some explicitly enumerated provisions, coverage does not necessarily have to be general. That is the case when a provision is implemented by collective agreement between social partners[39] and when they are carried out 'otherwise than by law'. A state is in compliance with that provision if it is *applied to the great majority of the workers concerned*.

It is consistent case law of the ECSR that 'great majority' means at least 80 per cent of the workers.[40] Does that mean that only workers can be counted, or is it possible that all persons that, according to national law, can be covered by a collective agreement, may be taken into account? If in the past this was a more academic question, because the definition of worker has been changed and some legal systems have widened the scope of those who can be covered by collective agreements, this question cannot be overlooked. The answer varies country by country, depending on the definition of personal scope in the relevant legislation. A question that could arise in this respect is whether *quasi self-employed* persons can be counted as meeting the (great) majority requirement, subject to the fact that they can be covered by collective agreements.[41] Another problem can be that in some countries, certain atypical workers are not covered by collective agreements and therefore do not count, whereas in other countries they do. A possible difference between countries has not been taken into consideration by the ECSR because it assesses conformity with Charter provisions by country.

For counting the 'great majority', the number of workers has to be taken as a whole. It therefore does not matter whether the collective agreement

[38] Under conditions that may be possible in countries such as Germany, France, the Netherlands, Spain (since the reform of 2012), as well as Italy (also since the Italian (collective) labour law was amended). It has to be taken into account that a certain hierarchy exists between these types of agreements.

[39] This method is frequently used in ILO conventions. The involvement of social partners in social policy measures, including legislative actions, is well known in continental Europe. It is institutionalised in the European Union (see Art 154 TFEU).

[40] Conclusions XIII-5, Finland; Conclusions XIII-5, Portugal. For the particular questions raised concerning the application of the great majority rule when Art 21 has been implemented by a collective agreement, see the chapter on Art 21 by B Veneziani in this volume.

[41] That is dependent on national law. The issue has come to the fore since a recent decision of the CJEU in the FNV *Kunsten Informatie en Media v Staat der Nederlanden*; cf CJEU of 4 December 2014, C-413/13. This question has not (yet) been raised before the ECSR.

is applied to the great majority of a *particular* group of workers—be it a group of workers in a certain industry or branch, or workers in a particular region—provided it is being applied to the great majority of the workers overall.[42] As long as categories of workers who are excluded from a collective agreement account for less than 20 per cent overall, there is no problem of conformity with the Charter.[43] However, when evidence is lacking that the great majority of (young) workers—in accordance with Article 7§6—have a right to remuneration for time spent on vocational training, the situation is not in conformity with the Charter: 'it has not been established that the great majority of young workers have a right to remuneration for time spent on vocational training'.[44] The importance of keeping the 'great majority rule' can be derived from the ECSR's case law in its conclusion that a country is violating Article 2§2 when information that demonstrates that 'the great majority of workers were entitled to paid public holidays through collective agreements or otherwise' is lacking.[45] Another example is the decision of the ECSR in a collective complaint procedure when assessing whether a working time regulation by collective agreement complied with the obligation of the Charter. The ECSR considers that the guarantees afforded by collective bargaining are not sufficient to comply with Article 2 paragraph 1.[46]

In this case another issue was raised: is it possible to regulate under Article 2§1 an issue established by an agreement at enterprise level? The ECSR feels that the possibility to do so is not in conformity with Article 2§1 unless specific guarantees are provided for, which is not the case in the view of the ECSR.[47] This decision can be doubted, because Article I does not exclude that. If in a particular country the legislator allows the social partners to regulate an issue within the scope of the Charter (in particular on the subjects mentioned in Article I) and social partners are doing so, this regulation could be in conformity with the Charter provisions, provided the collective agreement covers the great majority of the workers concerned. That seems to be so in the French case of 2000. The two dissenting members seem to share this view.

[42] Conclusions II, Germany and Conclusions III, Sweden, both on Art 2§3.

[43] Conclusions XIV-2, Belgium. It was about the application of Art 2§1 (working time). In the opposite direction, ECSR, Conclusions XX-3, United Kingdom on Art 2§2.

[44] Conclusions 2011, Netherlands (Art 7§6). In quite a number of conclusions the ECSR came to a similar judgment; see eg Conclusions 2011, Ireland (Art 7§4) and Conclusions 2010, France (Art 2§3).

[45] Conclusions 2010, United Kingdom (Art 2§2).

[46] Decision on the merits, *Confédération Française de l'Encadrement CFE-CGC v France*, Collective Complaint No 9/2000 §§32–34. The managerial staff were totally excluded from the working time regulation of the collective agreement. The decision was not unanimous. Stein Evju and Rolf Birk had a different opinion.

[47] The same question was put forward in Collective Complaint No 56/2009 also on the application of Art 2§1. The ECSR reached the same conclusion on this point.

This leads to the question of what steps a government has to take if Article I§2 Part V RESC is not respected in the sense that the great majority of the workers are not protected. Harris has pointed out that from the history of Article 33 ESC—the equivalent of Article I§2 Part V RESC—it can be learned that a country must legitimate, take administrative measures or persuade the social partners to regulate, but within the borders set out in the system of industrial relations. That is the ambit. The country cannot be forced to go beyond it.[48] The Committee of Ministers has the same opinion: 'the state cannot be required to attempt to exercise some influence on the labour market partners in order to have the provisions complied with'.[49] By analogy, one can say that if an issue is not regulated in accordance with Article I§2 Part V, the state is obliged to ensure that the worker can benefit fully from the right conferred on him or her. Implementation is sufficient when a country deals with a matter by legislation for a part of the workers and by collective agreement for the others. It has to be ensured that the great majority of the workers concerned are protected either by legislation or by collective agreement—or even by other means. As the explanatory Report to the RESC explains: the means employed must be effective. That may imply that a certain form of implementation, such as legislation, might sometimes be required. The word 'shall' in Article I§1 indicates that the method chosen must be efficient. The assessment has to be done by the ECSR. It allows the ECSR to conclude that a particular form of implementation—for instance legislation—has to be seen as the only 'appropriate' means. The choice of means the state has at its disposal may be limited. The ECSR uses this approach if it concludes non-conformity because the legislation of the state is insufficient.

D. Reservations

A possibility to evade the obligation of implementing Charter provisions is to make reservations with regard to specific Charter provisions. The Charter does not contain any rule admitting the use of this instrument. The ECSR, faced with this issue, took the view that reservations were not permitted. As a consequence of an obligation in the Charter for state parties to implement at least a minimum number of provisions[50] the ECSR argued:

> the Charter's very structure compelling as it does every Contracting Party ratifying the Charter to accept the obligations laid down in a certain number of paragraphs,

[48] Cf Harris and Darcy (n 19), p 383. He is referring to the opinion of the Legal Adviser to the TC, Rec Proc TC 238.

[49] CMSC 6th Session, 20 December 1957.

[50] Art A Pt III RESC. A similar provision in the ESC: Art 20 Pt III.

necessarily implies that acceptance of a particular paragraph extends to all the obligations embodied therein so that none of them may be evaded by means of reservation or otherwise.[51]

The practice has differed from that. Some countries have made reservations: Norway as to Article 12§4, and the Netherlands as to Article 6§4 (excluding civil servants), followed by other state parties.[52] None of the other countries have reacted, which has been taken to mean that they were not opposed. The ECSR changed its position and accepts reservations, provided that the minimum number of provisions is fully accepted and the object and purpose of the Charter is otherwise not infringed.[53]

Another way of escaping certain obligations is a practice introduced by Germany, although not in the form of a reservation. Before the Charter was opened for signature Germany declared that it would not—and could not—apply Article 6§4 to civil servants (*Beamten*).[54] This approach raised the problem of whether the 1961 Charter allows state parties to make reservations.[55] The 1961 Charter did not provide for this; nor do additional protocols or the 1996 Charter. Apart from the issue of the form—a declaration made by Germany—the ECSR initially rejected this escape route by arguing that because the Charter's very structure (which compels every Contracting Party ratifying the Charter to accept the obligations laid down in a certain number of paragraphs) necessarily implies that acceptance of a particular paragraph extends to all the obligations, that further implies that none of them may be evaded by means of a reservation or otherwise.[56] The discretion given to state parties under Article 20 of the 1961 Charter was considered to be sufficient.[57] Later the ECSR's opinion changed because other state parties[58] made reservations to particular provisions of the Charter which were not contested by the other state parties.[59] In the Dutch case of a reservation to Article 6§4 regarding civil servants, the possibility

[51] Conclusions IV, Germany. In the *Travaux Preparatoires* one can find arguments that suggest that reservations were not possible. See about the issue of reservations, Harris and Darcy (n 19), p 392.

[52] Cf Harris and Darcy (n 19), p 392.

[53] Conclusions VII. The last addition could imply that reservations that could result in an infringement of the prohibition of discrimination are not acceptable.

[54] See on this issue L Samuel, *Fundamental Social Rights. Case Law on the European Social Charter*, 2nd edn Council of Europe Publishing 2002 p 157. The ground for it was the specific relationship of civil servants to the state, characterised as 'loyalty to the state'.

[55] Contrary to the ECHR in Art 57.

[56] Conclusions IV, Germany (Art 6§4). The ECSR reiterated the non-compliance of Germany with Art 6§4 in Conclusions I and repeatedly in Conclusions III.

[57] See Harris and Darcy (n 19), pp 391–93.

[58] The Netherlands made a reservation similar to Germany (on Art 6§4 regarding civil servants). The other country was Norway on Art 12§4. Cf Harris and Darcy (n 19), p 392.

[59] The reservations were communicated to the state parties and no one protested against them.

of making reservations was accepted, not expressly but by implication.[60] This has changed the position concerning the German situation.[61] Although there can still be a discussion of the acceptability of the instrument of the reservation,[62] in practice the problem is solved by assessing reservations such as that of Article 6§4 by Germany as a problem under Article G.

III. USE AND MEANING OF GENERAL NOTIONS AND TERMS

The RESC uses several general notions or terms. For effective application of the rights that are conferred on various addressees, it is crucial that there be a clear meaning of these general notions. That does not imply per se that the Charter provides a sharp and univocal definition of these terms. Interpretation of these terms is necessary. Apart from the task the ECSR has in this respect, the national authorities are equally important when transposing the Charter provisions into national law. The way they 'translate' the terms of the Charter can be subject to the control mechanisms of the Charter, among which the ECSR plays an important role. In particular, decisions of national courts when they apply rights with direct effect provide good examples.[63] How far the influence of a national court can go in this respect is demonstrated by a remarkable decision of a Dutch court on the denial of emergency social assistance to migrants by Dutch authorities.[64] Referring to the decision on collective complaints of the ECSR[65] the Dutch court imposed on the (local) authorities the duty to provide these services, at least for a certain period of time. Recognising that a decision of the ECSR (as well as the CMSC) lacks direct applicability, the court felt that the decision of the ECSR *cannot be without effect*. The national court must seriously take this decision into account.

[60] The ECSR repeatedly asked the Dutch government to withdraw the reservation. See Conclusions VIII. In Conclusions 2010 the ECSR stated that since the RESC has been ratified by the Netherlands the reservation has been lifted.

[61] Conclusions VII. Cf L Samuel (n 54), pp 156–57. Now the ECSR is assessing the German situation under Art G. A complete strike ban for civil servants is not in conformity with the Charter. See also the chapter on Article G: Restrictions by A Koukiadaki in this volume.

[62] The Committee of Ministers took the view that it would not exclude the possibility of making reservations. Cf L Betten, *The Right to Strike in Community Law* (The Hague, TMC Asser Institute, 1985) 195–96; Harris and Darcy (n 19), p 392; and T Novitz, *International and European Protection of the Right to Strike* (Oxford University Press 2003), p 308. In Germany the issue is still under discussion.

[63] Examples of decisions of national courts have been mentioned in the chapters of this book dealing with specific rights.

[64] CRvB 17 December 2014 ECLI:NL:CRVB:2014:4178 *X, Y a.o. v het college van burgemeester en wethouders van Amsterdam*. The case was about the supply of 'bed, bread and bath' to migrants who were illegally on the territory but not (yet) expelled. See hereafter.

[65] Decisions on the merits, *CEC v The Netherlands*, Collective Complaint No 90/2013 and *FEANTSA v The Netherlands*, Collective Complaint No 86/2012.

When defining the personal scope of Charter provisions the ECSR has played an important role. The developments in that area are worth following (section E).

General terms often used in the Charter are 'worker', 'employer' and 'workers' representatives'. The Charter does not define these terms in a univocal way; nor do other international treaties. The Council of Europe, like other international organisations, has deliberately opted for the general terms. That implies that the Charter applies to all workers, including therefore part-time workers, workers on a temporary basis—including temporary agency workers and workers on contracts on call—as well as workers in some specific industries such as agriculture. Seamen are mainly covered by the Charter provisions. Domestic or homeworkers are protected by most of the provisions dealing with employment issues. Self-employed 'workers' are often included in the protective regulations unless the nature of the provision prohibits it, such as rules on safe and healthy working conditions (Article 3§3), and termination of employment in Article 4§4 and Article 24.[66] Even unemployed or retired workers are included in some rights, such as those of Article 5.

A similar approach is taken with regard to the notion of 'employer'. Employers are apparently simply persons who employ people in their enterprise, including self-employed persons.

The notion of 'workers' representatives'[67] is explained in the Appendix, which states that 'for the purpose of the application of these articles, the term "workers' representatives" means persons who are recognised as such under national legislation or practice'.[68] According to the case law of the ECSR such representatives can be trade union representatives, designated or elected by trade unions or by members of such unions, or representatives who are freely elected by the workers of the undertaking. This implies that states are free to decide who can operate as workers' representatives.[69]

A. Addressees

An issue that might raise questions is the determination of those who are addressed by Charter provisions. To determine the identity of the addressees is therefore important. The addressees of rights and duties vary and are not always clearly expressed in the RESC. Most of the provisions address

[66] See, respectively, the chapters by K Lörcher, S Deakin and M Schmitt in this volume.

[67] In Arts 28 and 29 explicitly and in Arts 21 and 22 in the wording of 'workers and their representatives'.

[68] See also B Veneziani in this volume.

[69] Conclusions 2003, Sweden.

the state that has to implement the Charter provisions, in particular when it concerns so-called programmatic rights. But even in most of these cases the Charter grants a right to a worker, his/her family, employers, employers' and employees' associations, young people, elderly people, (pregnant) women, migrants and even 'everyone' (Articles 30 and 31). Some provisions do not grant a right to someone, but contain a duty for the state to act on the subject mentioned. Article 1 of the Charter is a striking example; but there are more.[70] The personal scope of these provisions is general. Apart from the nationals of the countries party to the Charter, the Appendix to the Charter extends the personal scope to *nationals of other countries* lawfully resident or working regularly within the territory of the countries concerned. According to the ECSR that is also the case when the state of the individual concerned has not accepted that particular provision.[71] 'Lawfully resident' implies that tourists and persons on family or business visit do not fall within the extension. A permit to settle on the territory of a country is not a condition to be protected. The requirement of 'regularly working' has been added by the ECSR in order to cover persons working across borders between countries, as well as seamen under certain conditions, and seasonal workers, mainly in the agricultural industry. That is also the case for businessmen regularly visiting another country or countries. It can be argued that a person temporarily working in another country—in a single job—might also be covered. A remarkable extension of the scope has taken place since 2004 with regard to to undocumented migrants.[72] In four cases the ECSR decided that some specific rights of the Charter may apply to them even when they are living in an irregular situation in a State Party. The extension is limited to specific rights such as the most basic rights enshrined in the Charter; fundamental rights, such as the right to life or to physical integrity or to human dignity.[73] The extension by the ECSR can also be characterised as an example of its dynamic approach.[74]

[70] Such as Arts 11 to 17, 23, 30 and 31.

[71] Conclusions VII. Statement of Interpretation on Art 13§4. Cf Harris and Darcy (n 19), p 385.

[72] Sometimes also indicated by the unofficial term *irregular*, or even *illegal*, which are certainly not the correct legal terms.

[73] The ECSR refers to cases where such rights were at stake: Decisions on the merits, *FIDH v France*, Collective Complaint No 14/2003 about *medical assistance*; *DCI v The Netherlands*, Collective Complaint No 47/2008 about *shelter*; *DCI v Belgium*, Collective Complaint No 69/2011 about *medical assistance, shelter and social, legal and economic protection*; *CEC v The Netherlands*, Collective Complaint No 90/2013 about *bed, board and bath*, and *FEANTSA v The Netherlands*, Collective Complaint No 86/2012 about *social medical assistance, social and economic protection of family and children, poverty and social exclusion and shelter.*

[74] See section IV.

IV. DYNAMIC IMPLEMENTATION/PROGRESSIVE REALISATION

From the perspective of the effectiveness of the Charter, it is pertinent to ask about the impact of changes made by the ECSR interpreting provisions of the Charter on implementation. This is covered by the general terms 'dynamic implementation' or 'progressive realisation'. The term is also well-known in other international treaties.[75] The term was developed and used by the ECSR, when it stated that

> [the] realisation of the fundamental social rights recognised by the Revised Charter is guided by the principle of progressiveness, which is explicitly established in the Preamble and more specifically in the aims to facilitate the 'economic and social progress' of States Parties and to secure to their populations 'the social rights specified therein in order to improve their standard of living and their social well-being'.[76]

In the Charter itself the concept itself is also used in some provisions.[77] The practice of the ECSR is more far-reaching, although tempered with caution when using this method.

More recently the ECSR has followed this interpretation in specific situations connected to the migration of people from outside Europe to state parties. The ECSR developed the reasoning in the *FIDH* complaint.[78] In short, (i) the Charter has to be interpreted, according to the 1969 Vienna Convention on the Laws of Treaties, *in light of its object and purpose*; (ii) the ESC's purpose is to protect human rights, which are all *universal, indivisible, interdependent and interrelated* (1993 Vienna Declaration); (iii) the Charter complements the ECHR and is first and foremost a value-oriented *living instrument*, devoted to human dignity, autonomy, equality and solidarity; and (iv) its provisions must be read as designed to give *full life and meaning* to the rights embodied therein, or quoting the ECSR 'understood in such a manner as to preserve intact the essence of the right and to achieve the overall purpose of the Charter'.[79]

From a conceptual point of view, the way in which the concept of dynamic implementation or progressive realisation has been developed by the ECSR is most interesting. The way in which the ECSR has extended personal scope in relation to foreigners is another good example.[80]

[75] Art 2§1 ICESCR speaks of aiming at 'achieving progressively the full realization of the rights'. Cf E Riedel, *International Covenant on Economic, Social and Cultural Rights* (Oxford, Oxford Public International Law, 2011).

[76] Decision on the merits, *COHRE v Italy*, Collective Complaint No 58/2009.

[77] Art 2 (reducing working time). See the chapter on Art 2 by K Lörcher in this volume; Art 3§4 (occupational health services); Art 12§3 (social security).

[78] Decision on the merits, *FIDH v France*, Collective Complaint No 14/2003.

[79] See *FIDH v France*, Collective Complaint No 14/20038 September 2004 §§26–29.

[80] This issue has been dealt with under the heading of 'Addressees'. It is argued that the approach of the ECSR may go beyond the competence of the ECSR. Cf C Panzera, 'The

A. Provisions Dynamic by Nature

Assessing the impact of the 'judgments' of the ECSR, a distinction has to be made between the kinds of provision. Some provisions are dynamic in themselves, as the ECSR has pointed out explicitly. That is the case with regard to Articles 1§1, 2§1,[81] 12§3, 14, 18 and 26 of the Charter.[82] In its Statement of Interpretation with regard to Articles 1, 2, 12 and 14, the ECSR recognises their dynamic character:

> The Committee interpreted this provision as imposing an obligation as to means rather than an obligation as to results. It recognised that in order to decide whether a country is really fulfilling this obligation, it is necessary to adopt a dynamic standpoint, to assess the situation existing at a given moment, having regard to the continuous action pursued.[83]

On the basis of the information requested, the ECSR assesses and monitors the way a country is implementing its obligations. The ECSR is prudent, requiring that governments take severe measures. Apart from the lack of 'decisive' (legally binding) power on the part of the ECSR,[84] it recognises the discretionary power of states when deploying a certain policy aimed at achieving the objectives of the Charter. It also is sensitive as to the way governments are operating under given economic and political circumstances. It emphasises that the Charter imposes obligations on the country more as to *means* rather than to *results,* unless a core right is seriously infringed: 'if a State at any time abandoned the objective of full employment (Article 1 issue) in favour of an economic system providing for a permanent pool of unemployed'.

The ECSR necessarily adopts a dynamic standpoint on these provisions to assess the situation existing at a given moment, having regard to the continuous action being pursued.[85] When a crucial right is at stake, such as the right to equality of opportunity and equal treatment in the field of employment and occupation—prohibition of discrimination based on sex (Article 20)—the ECSR can be severe when requiring the state to remedy

Personal Scope of the European Social Charter: Questioning Equality' (presented at *Europe Restarts in Turin*, high-level conference on the European Social Charter, 17–18 October 2014).

[81] The statement dates from the first cycle (1971) Conclusions I, Art 2§1.

[82] See S Deakin and K Lörcher in this volume.

[83] Conclusions III, Statement of Interpretation on Art 1§1. In its Conclusion V on Art 14§1 the ECSR requested the Italian government to produce for each supervisory period new elements in order to show that progress is continually being made in implementing this provision.

[84] It has to be emphasised that the ECSR is the authoritative organ in establishing the content of Charter provisions (see the chapter on Interpretation by K Lörcher in this volume). National governments as well as national courts (can and will) take the conclusions and decisions of the ECSR seriously.

[85] Statement of Interpretation on Art 1§1.

the situation.[86] For instance, when collective agreements (or individual contracts) are infringing the principle of equality of Article 20 by providing neither for adequate appeal procedures in case the right has been violated nor for the effective protection of workers against any retaliatory measures (such as dismissal), the state has to take measures to ensure workers benefit from the right. In these cases the ECSR insists that 'the reports go further than merely describing the applicable texts, but explain in detail the practical situation and the case law dealing with the protection of the rights guaranteed by this provision'.[87] Taking into account the dynamic nature of some of the provisions and allowing states a wide margin of appreciation in these Articles the ECSR holds states to be in non-conformity with Article 1.[88] Continuous improvement is not always required, given the concrete economic and social circumstances in a country.

An example of how the ECSR is dealing with the issue of 'progressive realisation' is the decision in the French *Autism* case about the protection of children and young persons by ensuring the care, assistance, education and training they need (Article 7). Although this provision as such does not have a typical dynamic nature, also in these cases the ECSR applies this doctrine. The ECSR took the view that even in the case of an exceptionally complex and particularly expensive situation, a state has to achieve the objectives laid down in the provision concerned by taking measures 'within a reasonable time' ensuring 'measurable progress' in the application of the right and using 'maximally the available resources'.[89]

B. Explicitly Progressive

The Charter also contains provisions that require an approach involving progressive adaptation of rights, such as Article 12§3. The ECSR follows the prudent way of assessing conformity with the Charter's obligations when typical dynamic provisions are at stake. In its Statement of Interpretation the committee requires that states *make a continuous effort to bring their social security systems progressively to a higher level and to inform the Council of Europe regularly of any new steps taken.* However, in the event of a long-term economic slowdown the ECSR accepted that changes to social security could be made accordingly, but only when the viability of the system is secured, discrimination against any group is avoided and the basic

[86] See the contribution of C Kollonay-Lehoczky in this volume.

[87] Interpretative statement, Conclusions XIII-3.

[88] Cf S Deakin in this volume.

[89] Decision on the merits, *ICJ v Portugal*, Collective Complaint No 1/1998 §32 and *International Association Autism v France*, Collective Complaint No 13/2002 §53.

subsistence level is ensured.[90] The means used by a state are assessed with regard to whether they are appropriate and reasonable to achieve the aims. That means whether the reforms are necessary to achieve the desired results and therefore proportional.[91] The argument that, due to the economic burdens it is facing, a state cannot afford the required (better) standard of protection, given the resources that are available, is generally not acceptable. The ECSR understands that states may feel a need for (more) flexibility when implementing fundamental social rights. It also takes into account that opinions in a country may change or in respect of the extent of social protection, but infringing of rights in their core content cannot be justified. The ECSR draws some dividing lines and at the same time offers a way out. On one hand, it does not admit changes in pejus for benefits and wage levels and on the other hand it promotes gradual implementation.[92] According to the ECSR, 'measures aimed at dismantling social security schemes and arrangements designed solely to help to preserve a social security system that meets the Social Charter requirements, so that the system may resume its progress as soon as economic conditions permit' can be accepted.[93]

C. Barrier to Regression

One may wonder whether the ECSR changes its approach when states argue that the economic crisis has forced them to take measures that could be qualified as a regression. Faced with this situation in the mid-1970s the ECSR took the view that a regression was permissible, but only if (i) the plausible intent was to secure the viability of the system, (ii) it was not discriminatory with regard to any group of people and (iii) the regression was not below the minimum.[94] According to the ECSR the pursuit of economic goals is not per se incompatible with Charter provisions, such as Article 12. But on the other hand the state has the obligation to pursue by all appropriate means the attainment of the conditions to ensure the effective realisation of the rights. Faced with the economic crisis of 2007 and thereafter, the committee repeated its opinion that an economic crisis should not have as a consequence a reduction of the protection of the rights of the Charter.

[90] Conclusions XIII-4 and XVI-2 Introduction. For the assessment the ECSR has developed six criteria. Conclusions XVI-1, Statement of Interpretation on Art 12. See also Digest 2008, p 86.

[91] Cf M Mikkola (n 3), pp 322–23. See also Harris and Darcy (n 19), pp 159–61.

[92] States, when confronted with these challenges, can make use of the assistance the Council of Europe offers—in general—such as consultations and advice 'on the spot'.

[93] Conclusions IX-2, General introduction.

[94] Conclusions XIII-4 and XVI-2.

Therefore governments are bound to take all necessary steps to ensure that rights are effectively guaranteed.[95]

The anti-crisis measures in Greece affecting the labour and social rights of various groups have challenged the ECSR to reconsider its approach.[96] The collective complaints filed to the ECSR by Greek persons and organisations offered a good opportunity for fine-tuning. While understanding the needs of the state to cope with it, the ECSR found that what applies to the right to health and social protection should apply equally to labour law, and

> that while it may be reasonable for the crisis to prompt changes in current legislation and practices in one or other of these areas to restrict certain items of public spending or relieve constraints on businesses, these changes should not excessively destabilise the situation of those who enjoy the rights enshrined in the Charter.[97]

Increasing employment 'flexibility' in order to combat unemployment and encourage employers to take on staff should not result in depriving broad categories of employees—particularly vulnerable people who do not benefit from a stable job for long—of the fundamental labour rights that protect them from arbitrary decisions by their employers or from economic fluctuations. Establishment and maintenance of such rights are the main aims of the Charter. And additionally, as the Committee points out, 'doing away with such guarantees would force employees to shoulder an excessively large share of the consequences of the crisis'.[98]

In the other Greek case the ECSR reconfirmed its position. It emphasised that when restrictive measures have a cumulative effect, they cause a significant degradation of the standard of living and the living conditions of many of the persons concerned. Even when urgent decisions had to be taken by the government due to the economic crisis—and the conditions imposed by others, namely the Troika—the government had to 'conduct a minimum level

[95] Opinion on the repercussions of the economic crisis on social rights, see the General introduction to Conclusions XIX-2.

[96] Greece is not the only state to have been heavily affected by the crisis—Cyprus, Ireland, Portugal and Spain have also suffered. The measures imposed by the Troika were more beneficial to employers aiming at reducing labour costs by all kind of measures affecting employment and social rights for which workers 'paid the bill'. In his contribution Luis Jimena Quesada (former president of the ECSR) elaborates on this aspect. Luis Jimena Quesada, 'Adoption and Rejection of Austerity Measures: Current Controversies under European Law (Focus on the Role of the European Committee of Social Rights)' (December 2014) 49 *Revista catalana de dret public* 41.

[97] Complaint No 65/2011 §17.

[98] The ECSR has even taken a stand in an economic debate when adding that by doing so it accepts that pro-cyclical effects are liable to make the crisis worse and to increase the burden on welfare systems, particularly social assistance. The only way out would be a decision *to stop fulfilling the obligations of the Charter in the area of social protection.* Decision on the merits, *General Federation of Employees of the National Electric Power Corporation (GENOP-DEI) and Confederation of Greek Civil Servants' Trade Unions (ADEDY) v Greece*, Collective Complaint No 65/2011 §§17–18.

of research and analysis into the effects of such far-reaching measures that is necessary to assess in a meaningful manner their full impact on vulnerable groups in society'. The state is also to blame if it neglects consultations with relevant organisations, such as trade unions and other representative organisations. Furthermore, the fact that the government has not reconciled the general interest of the state with the interests of the individuals affected implies a shortcoming in decision-making procedures.[99] And finally—using part of the proportionality test—the state did not investigate whether other measures could have been put in place that had less cumulative effects.

In a third case, also concerning Greece,[100] the ECSR used the proportionality test when assessing whether an infringement of the Charter could by justified by urgent reasons. The case was about discrimination on the basis of age by introducing fixed-term 'special apprenticeship contracts' for individuals aged 15 to 18, depriving them of protective measures applied to other workers affecting employment, employment conditions and training opportunities for young people. The ECSR declared that it is up to a state to demonstrate objective justification for differential treatment of young employees; for example, the state has to prove that the measures are furthering a legitimate aim of employment policy and are proportionate to achieve that aim. Similar to the approach taken by other 'judges', the ECSR does not impose high barriers with regard to the legitimate aim. The aim as put forward by the state—integrating younger workers into the labour market in a time of serious economic crisis as part of employment policy—was accepted by the ECSR. With regard to political aims, the ECSR, like the ECtHR and the CJEU,[101] leaves states a lot of room, refraining from interfering in the autonomy of the state when developing and pursuing its own (economic and social) policy. In assessing the criterion of proportionality, however, the ECSR is the most severe of the three. The extent of the reduction of the minimum wage and the manner in which it is applied to all workers under the age of 25 was judged to be disproportionate, even when taking into account the particular economic circumstances.[102]

[99] Decision on the merits, *Federation of Employed Pensioners of Greece (IKA-ETAM) v Greece*, Collective Complaint No 76/2012 §§78–81. The ECSR takes also into account that the state did not respect the legitimate expectations that individuals may have in respect of the stability of the rules applicable to social security benefits (*in casu* pensions) §82).

[100] Decision on the merits, *GENOP-DEI and ADEDY v Greece*, Collective Complaint No 66/2011.

[101] The ECtHR allows states a fairly wide margin of appreciation. Illustrative examples of the CJEU's manner of reasoning in age discrimination cases include Case C-341/08 *Petersen* (CJEU, 12 January 2010), Case C-45/09 *Rosenbladt* (CJEU, 12 October 2010) and Case C-88/08 *Hütter* (CJEU, 28 June 2009).

[102] Decision on the merits, Collective Complaint No 66/2011 §68.

V. CONCLUDING REMARKS

According to the objective as expressed in all provisions of the Charter—'ensuring the effective exercise of the right to …'—effective implementation is the crucial instrument to guarantee or at least increase the impact of the Charter. Because the Charter is directed towards member states to take the necessary measures, implementation by legislative action is the main route, but not the only one. The supervisory body, the ECSR, emphasises that application in practice is just as important. For that reason, consistent policy measures by governments also meet the requirements set out in the Charter. It is also clear that with regard to some provisions, policy measures are even more appropriate for attaining the objective. That is particularly true of so-called programmatic rights. In that respect the role of the supervisory system is crucial. If the opinions and decisions of the ECSR get an increasing added value, the impact of the Charter can grow further. Although the current supervisory system has its deficiencies—as pointed out in the chapter on the Charter's supervisory procedures by S Clauwaert in this volume[103]—that does not imply that the ECSR is ineffective. The collective complaints procedure seems to be paying off. The possibility of implementing Charter provisions by collective agreements can contribute here—in theory—in the event that a member state does not act as it is supposed to do. In practice there seem to be few examples of such agreements implementing Charter provisions.[104] A third way of increasing the impact is the application of provisions in a directly binding way by court decisions. In this area, too, there have been few examples to date, but the number seems to be growing, albeit very slowly.

A final concluding remark concerns the application by the ECSR of the principle of dynamic implementation or progressive realisation. It can be considered a contribution to more effective application of Charter provisions. We have examined a number of examples of this. Even in the recent period of economic and financial crisis, it turned out that it can function as a barrier against regression. The ECSR is not deaf to the needs of states when facing economic difficulties, but they are not permitted to use—or misuse—it as a means of 'getting rid' of their obligations to respect fundamental social rights. 'Prompt changes in current legislation and practices in (some) areas to restrict certain items of public spending or relieve constraints on businesses' can be acceptable but 'these changes should not excessively destabilise the situation of those who enjoy the rights enshrined in the Charter'.[105] The ECSR consistently requires that the *essence of the right must be respected.*

[103] Cf the chapter on the Charters' supervisory procedures by S Clauwaert in this volume. One is the lack of power to pursue its findings, conclusions and decisions. It remains dependent on the willingness of the member states.

[104] It is more successful in countries in which national collective agreements exist, for instance Belgium. Data on implementation by collective agreements at a lower level are scarce.

[105] See n 97 above.

Restrictions

Article G

ARISTEA KOUKIADAKI

Article G—Restrictions

1. The rights and principles set forth in Part I when effectively realised, and their effective exercise as provided for in Part II, shall not be subject to any restrictions or limitations not specified in those parts, except such as are prescribed by law and are necessary in a democratic society for the protection of the rights and freedoms of others or for the protection of public interest, national security, public health, or morals.
2. The restrictions permitted under this Charter to the rights and obligations set forth herein shall not be applied for any purpose other than that for which they have been prescribed.

I. INTRODUCTION

HUMAN RIGHTS HAVE to be protected and guaranteed effectively. Having said that, only a few of the rights and freedoms laid down in international human rights documents are absolute. A number of them can lawfully be limited for specific reasons.[1] The rationale for permitting such limitations is twofold: 'first, limitations highlight that human rights are rarely absolute or unconditional rights, which makes the human rights framework manageable ... Second, limitation clauses mirror the

[1] See, for instance, Arts 12, 18, 19, 21 and 22 of the International Covenant on Civil and Political Rights (ICCRR) 1966; and Art 8 of the International Covenant on Economic, Social and Cultural Rights 1966 (ICESCR). On these, see Lockwood, Finn and Jubinsky, 'Working Paper for the Committee of Experts on Limitation Provisions' (1985) 7 *Human Rights Quarterly* 35.

necessity to solve conflicts between rights.'[2] In a similar manner, the Charter regulates the admissibility of excluding and limiting the rights within.[3] It distinguishes between derogations and restrictions: the former are subject to Article F; the latter—which constitute the focus of this chapter—are regulated by Article G.[4]

Article G of the 1996 Charter, which corresponds, *mutatis mutandis*, to the provisions of Article 31 of Part V of the ESC, provides:

1. The rights and principles set forth in Part I when effectively realised, and their effective exercise as provided for in Part II, shall not be subject to any restrictions or limitations not specified in those parts, except such as are prescribed by law and are necessary in a democratic society for the protection of the rights and freedoms of others or for the protection of public interest, national security, public health, or morals.
2. The restrictions permitted under this Charter to the rights and obligations set forth herein shall not be applied for any purpose other than that for which they have been prescribed.

Procedurally, Article G of the Charter cannot be directly invoked as such, but only provides a reference for the interpretation of the substantive rights provisions of the Charter which are at stake in a given complaint.[5]

II. CONTENT

A restriction on or limitation of a right is in conformity with the Charter only if it satisfies the conditions laid down in Article G. Importantly, the ECSR has held that 'any restrictions on rights are to be read restrictively, i.e. understood in such a manner as to preserve intact the essence of the right and to achieve the overall purpose of the Charter.'[6] However, an examination of the ECSR's assessments in its conclusions reveals that it rarely analyses all elements of Article G in detail.[7]

[2] A Müller, 'Limitations to and Derogations from Economic, Social and Cultural Rights' (2009) 9 *Human Rights Law Review* 4, 557, 557 and 560.

[3] The chapter discusses the European Social Charter (ESC) only insofar as it is necessary to clarify the historic developments and the similarities and differences between the two. All references made in the analysis to Art G also apply to Art 31, unless stated otherwise.

[4] See also Art A under which contracting parties may refuse to accept some of the Charter provisions. A related and highly disputed issue here concerns the possibility of contracting states including reservations regarding the application of Charter rights (see Jaspers in this volume).

[5] The ECSR justifies this by reference to the European Convention of Human Rights (ECHR) (Decision on the Merits, 15 June 2005, *Syndicat des Agrégés de l'Enseignement Supérieur (SAGES) v France*, Collective Complaint No 26/2004 §31).

[6] Decision on the merits, 8 September 2004, *International Federation of Human Rights Leagues (FIDH) v France*, 12/2005 §29. On this basis, the personal scope of the Charter has been expanded in some cases (see K Lörcher in this volume).

[7] Observations by the European Trade Union Confederation (ETUC), *Greek General Confederation of Labour (GSEE) v Greece*, Collective Complaint No 111/2014.

A. 'Prescribed by Law'

First, a restriction or limitation has to be prescribed by law. In line with the principle of legality, the objective here is the prevention of arbitrary restrictions on human rights by requiring that all limitations be established by general rule.[8] The Charter does not require that restrictions must necessarily be imposed solely through provisions of statutory law.[9] Instead, the case law of domestic courts should also comply with this requirement, provided that 'it is sufficiently stable and foreseeable to provide sufficient legal certainty for the parties concerned'.[10] The requirement that fair procedures exist also applies here,[11] reflecting more abstract or general assumptions about the requirements of the 'rule of law', a basic Council of Europe ideal.[12]

B. 'Legitimate Aim'

State parties are empowered to limit Charter rights only where a legitimate purpose is pursued.[13] The ECSR tends to be 'relatively deferential to state arguments in relation to the question of whether a limitation serves a legitimate aim, but often subsequently finds the limitation to be disproportionate.'[14] Restrictions are permitted on one of five grounds: protection of the rights and freedoms of others, public interest, national security, public health or morals.[15] In this respect, the scope of limitations under the Charter is wider than that of the ICESCR and the Charter of Fundamental

[8] Garibaldi, 'General Limitations on Human Rights: The Principle of Legality' (1976) 17 *Harvard International Law Journal* 503.

[9] Conclusion XVII-2, Hungary.

[10] The ECSR has found that inconsistencies of approach appear to exist as between similar cases, and the case law lacks sufficient precision and consistency so as to enable parties wishing to engage in picketing activity to foresee whether their actions will be subject to legal restraint: Decision on the merits, 13 September 2011, *Centrale Générale des Syndicats Libéraux de Belgique* (CGSLB)/*Confédération des Syndicats Chrétiens de Belgique* (CSC)/*Fédération Générale du Travail de Belgique (FGTB) v Belgium*, Collective Complaint No 59/2009 §§43–44).

[11] Collective Complaint No 59/2009, n 10 above.

[12] S Greer, *The Exceptions to Arts 8 to 11 of the European Convention of Human Rights*, Human Rights Files No 15 (Strasbourg, Council of Europe Publishing, 1997) 9.

[13] Decision on admissibility and the merits, 2 December 2013, *European Confederation of Police (EuroCOP) v Ireland*, Collective Complaint No 83/2012; Decision on the merits, 2 July 2013, *Fellesforbundet for Sjøfolk (FFFS) v Norway*, Collective Complaint No 74/2011; Decision on the merits, 16 October 2006, *Confederation of Independent Trade Unions in Bulgaria, Confederation of Labour 'Podkrepa' and European Trade Union Confederation (ETUC) v Bulgaria*, Collective Complaint No 32/2005.

[14] H Cullen, 'The Collective Complaints System of the European Social Charter: Interpretative Methods of the European Committee of Social Rights' (2009) 9 *Human Rights Law Review* 61, 85.

[15] The list of legitimate aims in Art 31 ESC/Art G Revised ESC is exhaustive (Cullen, n 14 above).

Rights of the European Union (CFREU).[16] The European Convention of Human Rights (ECHR) does not include a general clause on restrictions of ECHR rights; instead, tailor-made restriction clauses outlining a wide range of grounds are inserted in particular articles, where appropriate.[17] The rather wide scope of limitations under the Charter is balanced to some extent by the prohibition, in principle, of the notion of 'progressive realisation'.[18] The latter has been accepted by the ECSR only when the achievement of a right is 'exceptionally complex and particularly expensive to resolve'.[19] In allowing for this, the ECSR has stressed that the measures taken to implement the Charter must meet three criteria: '(i) a reasonable timeframe, (ii) measurable progress and (iii) financing consistent with the maximum use of available resources'.[20] Particular attention should be paid to 'groups with heightened vulnerabilities'.[21] Attention is paid here not only to the legal action required on the part of the contracting states for ensuring steady progress towards achieving the goals laid down by the Charter, but also to ensuring the availability of resources and introducing 'the operational procedures necessary to give full effect to the rights specified therein'.[22]

A related issue here concerns the scope for regression.[23] The emphasis in Article G on the effectiveness of the rights under the Charter (that is, 'when effectively realised', 'effective exercise') implies that once a right has

[16] Under Art 4 of the ICESCR, limitations may be placed on the Covenant rights only if compatible with the nature of these rights and solely for the purpose of promoting the general welfare in a democratic society. Under the CFREU, a general rule on limitations of rights is applicable but this is limited to grounds of general interest or the need to protect the rights and freedoms of others (Art 52§1).

[17] See, among others, Art 10§2 on freedom of expression, where the exercise of the right may be subject to restrictions in the interests of national security, territorial integrity or public safety, for the prevention of disorder or crime, for the protection of health or morals, for the protection of the reputation or rights of others, for preventing the disclosure of information received in confidence, or for maintaining the authority and impartiality of the judiciary; Art 11§2 on freedom of association provides for restrictions in the interests of national security or public safety, for the prevention of disorder or crime, for the protection of health or morals or for the protection of the rights and freedoms of others.

[18] See, for instance, Arts 2§1 and 12§3. But note here the freedom of the states to choose 'á la carte those statutory provisions they accept', a technique that may be seen as an obstacle to the 'legal homogenisation and harmonisation that the creation of a common legal space entails' (J Bonet Pérez, 'The European Social Charter', in G Gómez Isa and K de Feyter (eds), *International Human Rights Law in a Global Context* (Bilbao University of Deusto, 2009).

[19] Decision on the merits, 4 November 2003, *Autism-Europe v France*, Collective Complaint No 13/2002 §53. See, more generally, the case law involving Arts 2§1, 3, 4 and 12.

[20] Collective Complaint 13/2002, n 19 above §53.

[21] ibid §53.

[22] ibid §53. See also Decision on the Merits, 10 September 2013, *International Planned Parenthood Federation—European Network (IPPF EN) v Italy*, Collective Complaint No 87/2012 §162.

[23] On the principle of regression, see O De Schutter, 'Les Générations des Droits de l'Homme et l'Interaction des Systèmes de Protection: Les Scénarios du Système européen de Protection des Droits Fondamentaux', in *Juger les Droits Sociaux*, Actes du colloque organise par ADEAGE, 19 October 2001, Les Chroniques de l'OMIJ, PULIM (2004) 13.

been 'effectively realised', any reduction requires specific justification to prove that Article G is satisfied.[24] Since the 1990s, some states have adopted 'regressive' measures in the area of social security, the professed grounds for which have included 'demographic change' and 'reducing the budget deficit'.[25] In such cases, the ECSR has recognised that 'in view of the close relationship between the economy and social rights, the pursuit of economic goals is not necessarily incompatible' with the progressive obligation.[26] In this context, the recent case law dealing with crisis-related austerity measures in health and safety and social security in Greece points to the complexities in the relationship between the rights guaranteed under the Charter and the principle of non-regression.[27] The decisions could be seen as legitimising the replacement of a 'ratchet effect' (*effet cliquet*) under the non-regression principle with a 'floor effect' (*effet plancher*) maintaining the core minimum of rights.[28]

(i) 'Rights and Freedoms of Others'

The 'rights and freedoms of others' is a concept that has no specific or predictable limits.[29] So far, the ground of 'rights and freedoms of others' has often been invoked regarding limitations on the right to organise and the right to bargain collectively.[30] With regard to the right to organise, the ECSR has referred to the 'rights and freedoms of others' in order to stress that the restrictions relating to members of the police and armed forces will be justified as long as there is a reasonable relationship of proportionality between the restrictions and the legitimate aim of protecting the rights and freedoms of others.[31] In complaints regarding restrictions on duration and measures

[24] Observations by the European Trade Union Confederation (ETUC), n 7 above.

[25] See, for instance, Conclusions XIII-4 (1996).

[26] Conclusions XIV-1, General introduction.

[27] Decisions on the merits, 7 December 2012, *Federation of Employed Pensioners of Greece (IKA-ETAM) v Greece*; Collective Complaint No 76/2012; *Panhellenic Federation of Public Service Pensioners (POPS) v Greece*, Collective Complaint No 77/2012; *Panhellenic Federation of Pensioners of the Public Electricity Corporation (POS-DEI) v Greece*, Collective Complaint No 78/2012; *Pensioners' Union of the Athens-Piraeus Electric Railways (ISAP) v Greece*, Collective Complaint No 79/2012; *Pensioners' Union of the Agricultural Bank of Greece (ATE) v Greece*, Collective Complaint No 80/2012.

[28] JP Marguénaud and J Mouly, 'Le Comité européen des droits sociaux face au principe de non-régression en temps de crise économique' (2013) 4 *Droit Social* 339.

[29] D Harris, *The European Social Charter* (Charlottesville, University Press of Virginia, 1984).

[30] See the contributions of A Jacobs and F Dorssemont in this volume for an analysis of Arts 5 and 6, respectively.

[31] See, among others, Conclusions 2014, Andorra (Art 5); Conclusions 2014, Bosnia and Herzegovina (Art 5); Conclusions 2014, Serbia (Art 5). See also Collective Complaint No 32/2005, n 13 above.

of collective action, it has been held that protection of economic interests of third parties can be taken into consideration only in exceptional cases.[32]

(ii) 'Public Interest'

The 'public interest' ground reads '*pour proteger l'ordre public*' in the French text, which incorporates the concept of '*ordre public*' in civil law systems.[33] The difference in the interpretation of the term is illustrated in *European Confederation of Police (EuroCOP) v Ireland*:[34] the French version of the decision read '*proteger l'ordre public*', while the English version mentions only 'public safety'.[35] 'Public interest' has been the basis for a number of limitations on the right to engage in voluntary arbitration procedures,[36] the right to strike[37] and the right of migrant workers and their families to protection and assistance.[38] Economic or financial aims are not listed in Article G as grounds for legitimately limiting rights under the Charter. Despite this, they have been brought up fairly frequently in conjunction with 'public interest' goals, leading to the imposition of restrictions in respect of rights guaranteed under the Charter.[39] But in light of the incorporation of the notion of 'ordre public' in the definition of 'public interest', the state's economic or legal system as a whole should be taken into account, and not just financial aims.[40]

(iii) 'National Security'

National security is frequently used in conjunction with other words of limitation, including public interest.[41] Among others, 'national security' has been relied upon by the ECSR when permitting the implementation of restrictions on Article 5.[42] The ECSR has also drawn on the notion of

[32] Conclusion XIV-1, Netherlands (Art 6).

[33] D Harris and J D'Arcy, *The European Social Charter* (New York: Transnational Publishers, 2001) 381.

[34] Collective Complaint No 83/2012, n 13 above.

[35] The German translation refers to '*öffentliche Sicherheit und Ordnung*', which translates as 'public safety and order' in English.

[36] Conclusions XIV-1, Ireland (Art 6§3).

[37] Conclusions XIV-1, Norway (Art 6§4); Conclusions 2014, Azerbaijan (Art 6§4).

[38] Conclusions 2011, Poland (Art 19§6).

[39] Harris and D'Arcy, n 33 above, p 381.

[40] M Schlachter, 'Social Rights for Europe: Can the European Social Charter further alternatives to Austerity?' (2015) 4 *Delavci in Delodajalci* 453, 468.

[41] AM Swiatkowski, *Charter of Social Rights of the Council of Europe* (The Netherlands, Kluwer Law International, 2007). See, *inter alia*, Conclusions 2004, Estonia (Art 6§4), where it is stated that the right to strike of civil servants may only be restricted on the ground that they perform duties affecting public interest or national security.

[42] Among others, see Conclusions XI-1, United Kingdom (Art 5); cf the ILO FAC and the Committee of Experts on the Application of Conventions and Recommendations (CEACR) and the plenary session of the ILO's conference (F Dorssemont, 'The Right to Take Collective

'national security' to hold that the only jobs from which foreigners may be banned are those that are inherently connected with the protection of the public interest or national security and involve the exercise of public authority.[43] Exclusion of individuals from functions, either in the form of refusal to recruit or dismissal, on grounds of previous political activities, is also prohibited when it is not necessary within the meaning of Article G.[44] Finally, restrictions can be permissible if allowing free emigration ran against the public interest or posed a threat to national security.[45]

(iv) 'Public Health or Morals'

Contracting states have drawn on the concept of 'public health' to justify the exclusion of family members of migrant workers who have contagious diseases[46] and to end a hospital strike.[47] 'Morals' are principles that are acceptable to the vast majority of citizens as basic guidelines for their individual and collective conduct, but which are not necessarily legally enforceable.[48] States have attempted to suggest that restrictions on the right to organise of the police force may be justified on the basis that they maintain public morals, as they serve to maintain the perception of the impartiality of the police force. However, the ECSR has found that the impartiality of the police force would be unlikely to be affected by their membership of a national umbrella organisation alongside with other civil servants, who are likewise required to fulfil public service obligations in a strictly impartial manner.[49]

C. 'Necessary in a Democratic Society'

The requirement that the restriction or limitation be 'necessary in a democratic society' narrows the scope of the provision considerably and the concept, in particular, of 'necessity'[50] includes a requirement of proportionality: the limitation of rights must be proportional in its scope and intensity to the purpose being sought.

Action under Article 11 ECHR', in F Dorssemont, K Lörcher and I Schömann (eds), *The European Convention on Human Rights and the Employment Relation* (Oxford, Hart, 2013).

[43] AM Swiatkowski, n 41 above; Conclusions 2006, Albania (Art 1§2).

[44] AM Swiatkowski, n 41 above; Conclusions 2006, Lithuania (Art 1§2).

[45] AM Swiatkowski, n 41 above; Conclusions 2005, Cyprus (Art 18§4).

[46] Conclusions III, Austria (Art 19§6).

[47] Conclusions XIV-1, Norway (Art 6§4). See AM Swiatkowski, n 41 above.

[48] AC Kiss, 'Permissible Limitations on Rights', in L Henkin (ed), *The International Bill of Rights: The Covenant on Civil and Political Rights* (New York, Columbia University Press, 1981) 291.

[49] Collective Complaint No 83/2012 (n 13 above) §§ 117–18.

[50] See definition of 'necessary' in *Silver v United Kingdom* (1983) 5 EHRR 347 §97.

(i) The Notion of a 'Democratic Society'

The ECSR has to date not interpreted the term 'democratic society'. Similar to the ECHR, it can be taken to be a political society of the type required for the membership of the Council of Europe.[51] In its early case law, if a contracting party had a restriction that other contracting parties—who were necessarily members of the Council of Europe—lacked, this was strong evidence that the restriction was not 'necessary' in a democratic society.[52] This approach is no longer followed.[53] In this respect, the ECSR has stated recently with regard to the right to collective bargaining and action that it 'receives constitutional recognition at national level in the vast majority of the Council of Europe's member States'.[54]

(ii) The Principle of Proportionality and the Doctrine of 'Margin of Appreciation'

The principle of proportionality plays a vital role in assessing the necessity of restrictions on rights.[55] The ECSR makes a distinction between two aspects: on one hand, the procedural arrangements, and on the other, the substance of the restrictions.[56] With regard to the former, the ECSR has emphasised that restrictions to Charter rights have to be complemented by, among other things, procedural safeguards. With regard to, for example, limits on collective bargaining, the ECSR has accepted that these can be introduced to remedy a particularly serious economic situation, but compliance should be sought with a set of conditions:

> such restrictions should be imposed only after extensive consultation of all the parties concerned, notably trade unions and employers' associations and that they should be of an exceptional kind and limited duration. Furthermore, they should not be imposed unless it has been proved that no other measures can produce the same effects without recourse to such government intervention.[57]

[51] Harris, n 29 above. Similarly, in the ECHR, the models of a 'democratic society' are the member states themselves and the ECtHR compares the law and practices of the member states when considering a restriction (Lockwood, Finn and Jubinsky, n 1 above p 50).

[52] Conclusion IV, Germany (Art 6§4).

[53] Harris, n 29 above. *Swedish Trade Union Confederation (LO) and Swedish Confederation of Professional Employees (TCO) v Sweden*, Collective Complaint No 85/2012 §110.

[54] Collective Complaint No 85/2012, n 53 above §110. See also Conclusion XV-2, Cyprus (Art 11§1), concerning the accessibility of health care systems, where it was stated that in the vast majority of contracting parties to the Charter, 98–100% of the population were covered by the health care system.

[55] On this see Steiner, Alston and Goodman (eds), *International Human rights in Context: Law, Politics, Morals* (Oxford, Oxford University Press, 2008) 385.

[56] Decision on admissibility and the merits, 19 March 2013, *European Committee for Home-Based Priority Action for the Child and the Family (EUROCEF) v France*, Collective Complaint No 82/2012.

[57] Conclusions IX-1, Netherlands (Art 6§2). See also Conclusions XV-1, Iceland (Art 6§4), where it was stated that Iceland was consistent with Art 6§4 in accordance with Art 31§1 when

With regard to the substance of restrictions, an important consideration here is the scope of the restriction. The ECSR has attempted to narrow down the scope in a number of ways. With regard to discrimination in employment, for instance, the ECSR has held that

> even where restrictions are prescribed by law within the meaning of Article G and serve one of the purposes therein, namely the protection of national security, they will not be necessary and proportionate if they apply to a large range of different jobs, and not solely to those services which had responsibilities in the field of law and order and national security or to functions involving such responsibilities.[58]

Similarly, the ECSR has held on the right to strike that there is no reasonable relationship of proportionality between prohibiting all civil servants from exercising the right to strike, irrespective of their duties and function and the legitimate aims pursued.[59] As such, only a restriction can be justified, and not an absolute ban.[60] Another way of limiting the scope for restrictions or limitations to Charter rights has been by taking into account the cumulative effect of the measures in question. Even though certain of the restrictions introduced by governments do not, in themselves, amount to a violation of the Charter, 'the cumulative effect of the restrictions is bound to bring about a significant degradation of the standard of living and the living conditions of many of the pensioners concerned'[61] and as such lead to a finding of violation of Charter rights.

On the other hand, contracting states have on numerous occasions relied on the 'margin of appreciation' doctrine to justify restrictions on Charter rights. A first justification for the use of the doctrine is that it may provide states with a certain level of discretion in choosing the means for complying with the Charter rights.[62] Indeed, the ECSR has accepted the use of the

they drew up a list of all public sector workers deprived of the right to organise strikes. The ECSR demanded, however, that the information concerning the criteria on which this list was dependent should be produced.

[58] Conclusions 2006, Lithuania (Art 1§2).

[59] Collective Complaint No 32/2005, n 13 above §§44–46; Conclusions I, Statement of Interpretation on Art 6§4.

[60] Conclusions XVII-1, Germany.

[61] Collective Complaint No 76/2012 §78.

[62] Decision on the merits, 3 December 2007, *European Council of Police Trade Unions (CESP) v Portugal*, Collective Complaint No 37/2006 §14. See also Decision on the merits, 9 September 2009, *Confédération Française Démocratique du Travail (CFDT) v France*, Collective Complaint No 50/2008, para 39, where the ECSR recalled that states enjoy a certain margin of appreciation in assessing whether and to what extent differences in otherwise similar situations justify a different treatment in law, but it is ultimately for the ECSR to decide whether the difference lies within this margin. But, as Harris notes, the use of the doctrine is not as regular as that by the ECtHR (D Harris, 'Collective Complaints under the European Social Charter: Encouraging Progress?', in KH Kaikobad and M Bohlander (eds), *International Law and Power: Perspectives on Legal Order and Justice, Essays in Honour of Colin Warbrick* (Leiden, Martinus Nijhoff Publishers, 2009) 9.

doctrine in cases related to the manner in which an objective required by the Charter is realised. Among other things, it has held that whereas the right to form and join a trade union in Article 5 includes for unions the possibility of membership of consultation bodies established by the government that are relevant to the protection of their members' interests, states had a 'margin of appreciation' in determining the composition of such bodies, so that a trade union could not, as was argued in the case, insist upon a particular election procedure.[63] Furthermore, the doctrine has sometimes been brought up, albeit unsuccessfully, in cases involving significant variation in the rights themselves of various member states of the Council of Europe. For instance, in *European Confederation of Police (EuroCOP) v Ireland*, which involved the right to strike of members of the Irish police force, the ECSR noted that:

> The effects of granting the right to strike to the police upon the public interest may equally vary according to the internal legal systems. For these reasons, it falls to states, within their margin of appreciation, to decide, in light of the circumstances of a given national system, whether a restriction upon the right to strike of the police for a certain part of the police force is truly necessary with a view to achieving the legitimate objective pursued...[64]

It is the case that states' defence based on the margin of appreciation plays a more minor role in the ECSR's assessment than in this of the ECtHR.[65] This is illustrated when comparing the ECSR's and the ECtHR's case law related to the crisis-related austerity measures. In this respect, the ECtHR has recently accorded member states broad leverage when setting the legitimate aims to be pursued during an economic crisis, and interference with the applicants' rights is accepted, unless the applicants are totally deprived of the rights at issue.[66] Importantly, the ECtHR's crisis-related approach has been directly related to state budget issues (pensions provided to civil servants). In contrast, the majority of the measures challenged before the ECSR concern (private) labour law issues. It is true that the ECSR has not strictly adhered to the 'ratchet effect' of the rights guaranteed under the Charter.[67]

[63] Collective Complaint No 26/2004, n 5 above.

[64] Collective Complaint No 83/2012, n 13 above §207. See also Collective Complaint No 74/2011, n 13 above, where Norway was unsuccessful in persuading the ECSR that a lower retirement age-limit for seamen was in line with the Charter.

[65] L Mola, 'The Margin of Appreciation accorded to States in Times of Economic Crisis: An Analysis of the Decision by the European ECSR of Social Rights and by the European Court of Human Rights on National Austerity Measures' (2015) *Lex Social: Rivista Juridica de los Derechos Sociales* 5, 174.

[66] *Koufaki and ADEDY v Greece* Apps nos 57665/12 and 57657/12; *Antonio Augusto Da Conceicao Mateus against Portugal and Lino Jesus Santos Januario v Portugal* Apps nos 62235/12 and 57725/12. Previous case law includes *Stec and Others v the United Kingdom* Apps nos 65731/01 and 65900/01.

[67] Marguénaud and Mouly, n 28 above.

But in reserving the possibility of assessing whether the methods chosen by the contracting parties to achieve these objectives are appropriate, and in assessing the effective realisation of the Charter rights with reference to the reasonableness of the changes and the proportionality of the burden suffered by individuals, the ECSR has attempted to narrow to some extent the margin of appreciation that state parties have in such cases.[68]

D. Article G§2

Article G§2 incorporates the doctrine of 'abuse of power' that is usually found in the law of the contracting parties[69] and points to 'one of the general principles of treaty construction, that an instrument will be construed in consonance with its dominant purpose.'[70] 'Restrictions' meant restrictions allowed by Article G§1 and those allowed by particular paragraphs of Part I or provisions of Part II. The ECSR has emphasised the duty of state parties to submit a range of information, including, among others, the nature of the changes, the reasons given for the changes and outcomes of the changes introduced.[71] The scope of limitations may change over time in line with developments in the society or changes of circumstances that make them no longer 'necessary'.[72] In this respect, the ECSR has stressed that the Charter is 'a living instrument dedicated to certain values which inspired it: dignity, autonomy, equality and solidarity.'[73]

III. CONCLUSION

As Lockwood, Finn and Jubinsky have noted, 'if the legislature is given an unrestricted grant of power to restrict human rights and freedoms generally, the rights and freedoms are simply made subject to the laws. The lack of protection afforded the rights and freedoms renders them valueless.'[74] It cannot be overstated that the Charter 'was envisaged as a human rights

[68] Mola, n 65 above.

[69] Harris and D'Arcy, n 33 above, p 382.

[70] Lockwood, Finn and Jubinsky, n 1 above, p 36.

[71] Conclusions 2002, Interpretative Statement on Art 12§1, 2 and 3.

[72] A. Müller, Limitations to and Derogations from Economic, Social and Cultural Rights (2009) 9 *Human Rights Law Review*, 4, 557–601, p 560.

[73] Decision on the merits, 8 September 2004, *International Federation of Human Rights Leagues v France*, Collective Complaint No 14/2003. The Preamble's reference to 'social progress' could be seen as providing greater scope for interpreting the Charter in a more dynamic way than is considered by the ECSR at present.

[74] Lockwood, Finn and Jubinsky, n 1 above, p 46.

instrument'.[75] In light of this, Article G should be read as an attempt to limit the extent to which state parties can restrict or limit the rights recognised in the Charter. While the scope for restrictions under Article G is greater than the one provided under ILO Conventions,[76] it still goes further than regional international human rights, most notably the ECHR and EU law, in recognising the need for guaranteeing social rights effectively. This is all the more important at present, as human rights vigilance should be heightened in difficult times.[77]

[75] Decision on the merits, 20 October 2009, *Defence for Children International (DCI) v The Netherlands*, Collective Complaint No 47 §34.

[76] At the time of the adoption of the 1961 ESC, there were no similar provisions in ILO Conventions. The only case of an express stipulation of this kind was in the Freedom of Association and Protection of the Right to Organise Convention, 1948 (No 87).

[77] G Katrougalos, 'The Greek Austerity Measures: Remedies under International Law', *International Journal of Constitutional Law* Blog, 30 January 2013.

The Charter's Supervisory Procedures

STEFAN CLAUWAERT

I. INTRODUCTION

THE FACT THAT various scholars have referred to the Charter in very flattering and/or ambitious terms as, for example, 'one of the cornerstones of European social justice',[1] 'the backbone of the European system for the protection of fundamental social rights in Europe'[2] or 'the North star for our social policies',[3] only underlines the fundamental and far-reaching role this instrument has had in the protection of fundamental (social) rights.[4] But as with every fundamental rights instrument, its added

[1] T Halonen, Opening words, in N Johanson and M Mikkola, *Reform of the European social charter, seminar presentations delivered on 8 and 9 February 2011 at the House of the Estates and the University of Helsinki* (Porvoo, Bookwell, 2011) 2; Coyer calls 'La Charte sociale européenne: Un instrument au service de la cohesion sociale en Europe' or 'La Charte: un instrument de progrès social' (X Coyer, 'La Charte sociale européenne: Un instrument au service de la cohesion sociale en Europe' in Ministère de l'emploi et de la solidarité (1999) 'Le Conseil de l'Europe. 50 ans au service de l'homme et du progrès social' (June 1999) 94 *Echanges santé-social* 38, 34–39); for S Evju the Charter 'is the sole international legal instrument at European level which guarantees a comparatively wide and comprehensive set of social and economic rights' (S Evju, 'The European Social Charter and the International Labour Organization—interlinks past and present', in W Däubler and R Zimmer (eds), *Arbeitsvölkerrecht (Festschrift Lörcher)* (Baden-Baden, Nomos-Verlag, 2014) 147).

[2] M Faruggia, in M Nicoletti, 'General Report High-Level Conference on the European Social Charter', Turin, 17–18 October 2014, Strasbourg: European Social Charter, 2014, Appendix 2n.

[3] A Tajani (First Vice-President of the European Parliament) at the High-Level Conference on the European Social Charter, Turin, 17–18 October 2014; oral translation (from Italian to English) of presentation at conference but not as such recorded in Nicoletti (n 2) 14, Appendix 2f.

[4] Others were/are less positive, however, referring mainly to the rather weak 1961 Charter and in particular its à la carte acceptance of provisions, its restrictions on personal scope and its rather weak supervisory system. See, for instance, M de Boer-Buquicchio, former Deputy Secretary General of the Council of Europe, who described the ESC as the 'proverbial "sleeping

value stands or falls with the adequate implementation of the obligations undertaken by—in the case of the Charter—mainly governments and the effectiveness of the applicable monitoring and enforcement procedures. As in the case of many other international human rights instruments, the sole monitoring procedure under the 1961 Charter consisted of a reporting procedure, which will be looked at more closely in section III. After serious deficiencies were detected in this system, and with a view to 'revitalising' the 1961 Charter, important changes were made in the 1991 Amending Protocol reforming the supervisory system (the so-called 'Turin Protocol', whose main changes will be highlighted in sections II, III, IV and V) and the establishment of a new monitoring system in 1995 via the so-called Collective Complaints Procedure Protocol (CCPP), which will be analysed more in detail in section IV. But before looking into both procedures, section II goes into the different institutional bodies that are involved (or not yet) in both procedures, in particular as their composition, mandate, working methods and interrelations might also influence the effectiveness of the monitoring

beauty" compared to the ECHR' (M De Boer-Buquicchio, 'Welcome address', in N Johanson and M Mikkola, *Reform of the European social charter. Seminar presentations delivered 8 and 9 February 2011 at the House of the Estates and the University of Helsinki* (Porvoo, Bookwell, 2011) 5; also, O Kahn-Freund, who called the Charter 'a big footnote' to the ECHR: O Kahn-Freund, 'The European Social Charter', in A Jacobs (ed), *European Law and the Individual* (Amsterdam, North-Holland Publishing Company, 1976) 172; and Harris, who considered that the Charter led a 'twilight existence' compared with the ECHR, the 'jewel in the Council of Europe crown': D Harris, 'A Fresh impetus for the European Social Charter' (1992) 41 ICLQ 659. Prouvez described it as having been for many years the 'poor relative' of the ECHR: N Prouvez, 'The European social charter, an instrument for the protection of human rights in the 21st century?', in International Commission of Jurists, Review No 58–59/1997, December 1997 30–44; and Petman who 'would rather, with notable chagrin, draw a picture of a "low-profile", "bureaucratized", "invisible" instrument': J Petman, 'Final remarks and conclusions', in N Johanson and M Mikkola, *Reform of the European social charter. Seminar presentations delivered 8 and 9 February 2011 at the House of the Estates and the University of Helsinki* (Porvoo, Bookwell, 2011) 41–44. Quin, in the same vein, referred to the Charter as 'a Complex Web of Human Rights Treaties', as the Charter is actually an amalgam of five separate treaties (1961 ESC, 1988 Additional Protocol, 1991 Turin Protocol, 1995 Collective Complaints Procedure Protocol (CCPP) and 1996 ESC) leading to the confusing situation of the continued legal coexistence of two Charters and the monitoring of two separate but related instruments by the ECSR: G Quin, 'The legal status of the European Social Charter taking interdependence and indivisibility of human rights seriously', Report for the UNIDEM Seminar on *The status of international treaties on human rights*, Coimbra (Portugal), 7–8 October 2005 (organised by the European Commission for Democracy through law (Venice Commission) in the framework of the activities of the Portuguese Chairmanship of the Committee of Ministers of the Council of Europe in cooperation with the University of Coimbra (IUS Gentium Conimbrigae Centre, Faculty of Law) and the International Association of Constitutional Law (IACL)), CDL-UD(2005) 021 rep, Strasbourg, 28 September 2005, p 12). The latter led Brillat to the view that when thinking of the Charter 'venait immédiatement l'image d'un vide ou d'un trop-plein', because 'pas d'organe de contrôle ou bien trop d'organes concurrents, de sorte que le fonctionnement de mécanisme était brouillé': R Brillat, 'La Charte sociale européenne et le contrôle de son application', in N Aliprantis (ed), *Les droits sociaux dans les instruments européens et internationaux—défis à l'échelle mondiale* (Bruxelles, Bruylant, 2009) 44.

and enforcement procedures as a whole. Finally in this chapter we will also look at the strength and weaknesses of the different procedures (as well as proposals on how to further strengthen them—section V).

II. THE MONITORING BODIES

In the monitoring process, four bodies play an important role: the European Committee of Social Rights (ECSR), the Governmental Committee (GC), the Parliamentary Assembly (PACE) and finally the Committee of Ministers (CM).[5]

A. The European Committee of Social Rights (ECSR)

The main supervisory body within the framework of both the reporting and the Collective Complaints Procedure (CCP) is the ECSR, formerly known as the Committee of Independent Experts,[6] which assesses from a legal standpoint the compliance of national law and practice with the obligations arising from the Charter for the Contracting Parties concerned. Its main mission is to judge whether state parties are in conformity in law and in practice with the provisions of the Charter, and this in the form of 'conclusions' within the framework of the reporting procedure and 'decisions' under the collective complaint procedure.[7] The rules relating the ECSR's organisation and functioning are established in the 1961 Charter, the Turin Protocol and supplemented by the ECSR's own Rules of Procedure.[8]

Currently, the ECSR is composed of 15 members[9] who have to 'perform their duties in conformity with the requirements of independence, impartiality

[5] Evju highlights that 'at an early stage in the drafting process of the 1961 ESC it was rejected to employ a judicial procedure in any way similar to that under the ECHR. Subsequent proposals ranged from establishing a large scale, tripartite European Economic and Social Council to involving the European Commission for Human Rights or to vest supervisory tasks with the ILO's Committee of Experts on the Application of Conventions and Recommendations (CEACR). Suffice it here to say, first, that whichever the alternative, throughout the process the need to ensure links and collaboration with the ILO was emphasised. Secondly, the structure of the supervisory mechanism that was finally adopted was to a large extent modelled on that of the ILO' (Evju (n 1) 150–51).

[6] According to Harris and Darcy, it was decided to change its name in 1998 to better reflect its human rights character (D Harris and J Darcy, 'The system of supervision' in D Harris and J Darcy, *The European Social Charter*, 2nd edn, The Procedural Aspects of International Law Book Series, Vol 25 (Ardsley, NY, Transnational Publishers, 2001) 293–376).

[7] r 2 of the ECSR Rules of Procedure 2004. All conclusions and decisions of the ECSR can be found on the Charter website.

[8] The initial Rules of Procedure of the ECSR were adopted on 9 September 1999 but subsequently were amended several times. The currently applicable rules were adopted during the 273rd ECSR session on 9 September 2014.

[9] r 1, the original Art 25§1 provided that the ECSR shall consist of not more than seven members. This was changed in the Protocol to 'at least nine members', and 'the exact number

and availability inherent in their office'[10] and elected by the Committee of Ministers for a six-year term of office, renewable once.[11] Currently, elections takes place every second year, with a third of the seats (that is, five) being up for election. To enhance the requirements of independence, impartiality and availability, the ECSR members sit in their individual capacity and shall throughout their term of office not perform any function incompatible with the requirements of independence, impartiality and availability inherent in their office.[12,13] Apart from a working knowledge of one of the official languages of the Council of Europe (English and French),[14] there exist no further conditions of (legal) qualification and nationality. However, the

of members shall be determined by the Committee of Ministers'. The ECSR is thus still smaller than the number of Contracting Parties to the Charter. This might indeed, as Harris and Davis note, on the one hand be considered a weakness, as the ECSR is unlikely to have expert knowledge of the law and practice of all Contracting Parties (and this will only increase with further ratifications by other states of both the ESC and the CCP), although a widening of the ECSR to one member per Contracting Party, might render the work more complex and less collegial. To partially overcome this lack of complete coverage, the members are now being divided into four working groups. See below.

[10] r 2 ECSR Rules of Procedure.

[11] The Turin Protocol stipulates that members of the ECSR are to be elected by the Parliamentary Assembly, but this is the only provision of the Turin Protocol which is still not being applied. Initially, the number of terms was unlimited, but this was altered by the Turin Protocol, which furthermore states that a member who is elected to replace a member whose term of office has not expired shall hold office for the remainder of his or her predecessor's term. For the election, all Contracting Parties are distributed over five groups (for more information on the distribution of the Contracting Parties over the five groups see Committee of Ministers Decision (2014) 1198/4.3 of 5 May 2014. Three seats are allocated to each group. When (a) seat(s) become available in a certain group, the other Contracting Parties in that group can put forward the name of a candidate. The Secretary General will then forward the list of nominations to the Committee of Ministers, which will hold an election by secret ballot. These groups might possibly change in the future in the context of proposals emerging from the Turin process (eg on increasing the number of ECSR members, possible involvement of the Parliamentary Assembly in the election procedure, etc), also because in the past the 'appropriateness' of the groups in their current composition has sometimes been questioned, but the problem has always been to come up with a better arrangement.

[12] Art 25§4 1991 Turin Protocol. According to Harris and Darcy (n 6), this has never really been an issue as such and former members of the ECSR formerly held office in a national government or have even been civil servants who represented their governments in the GC to the Charter (see below). It is clear, however, that appointing candidates who, at the time of their election to the ECSR, are members of a government is contrary to the requirement of independence and even membership of the ECSR; appointment of a person currently holding office as a civil servant is also questionable. The latter occurred, among other examples, at the elections of December 2014, when two candidates, civil servants who had even represented their government in the GC, were called into question.

[13] As this status apparently was not always respected and there were 'more or less explicit attempts by certain political, institutional or administrative players both inside and outside the Council of Europe to interfere with or exert undue pressure on the ECSR and its secretariat', the ECSR considered it necessary to make public in its General Introduction to the Conclusions 2013/XX-2 a 'Declaration on protecting the independent status of the members of the ECSR', asking all institutions and bodies both inside and outside the Council of Europe to make sure that this independence is preserved.

[14] ECSR Rules of Procedure, r 18.

Committee of Ministers tries to observe a wide geographic representation when electing its members, and has agreed that nationals of all of the member states of the Council of Europe, whether Parties to the Charter or not, are eligible for membership (meaning thus that a national of a non-member state is not eligible) and that no member state shall have more than one national on the ECSR. Also within the ECSR it tries to have participation of men and women in an equitable proportion.[15] Furthermore, both the Charter and the ECSR Procedures provide for the participation of a senior official of the ILO—in a consultative capacity—in the deliberations of the ECSR to ensure consistency with ILO norms and case law.

The ECSR meets on average for seven sessions lasting one week, in principle in Strasbourg.[16] Meetings are held in private, ECSR deliberations shall be kept secret and working documents relating to them are confidential (with the exception of course of the final conclusions reached, which are publicly available online).[17] Although in principle, decisions are taken by consensus, in case of an eventual vote, with each member having one vote (and the President having an eventual casting vote), decisions are adopted by simple majority.[18]

B. The Governmental Committee (GC)

This Committee, which in the initial Article 27§1 ESC was referred to as 'a sub-committee of the Governmental Social Committee of the Council of Europe', is currently officially known as the 'Governmental Committee of the European Social Charter and the European Code of Social Security' (GC), following an internal Council of Europe restructuring in 2012, merging the former GC with the committee monitoring compliance with the European Code of Social Security. The rules relating to the GC's organisation and functioning are established in the 1961 Charter, the Turin Protocol and supplemented by the GC's own Rules of Procedure.[19]

The GC is composed of a representative of each Contracting Party to the Charter and to the European Code of Social Security.[20] Members are

[15] In line with CM Recommendation Rec(81)6 of 30 April 1981.

[16] Overview of the calendar of the meeting sessions and related documents (agendas, short reports, etc) can be found on the Charter website, www.coe.int/en/web/turin-european-social-charter/sessions.

[17] ECSR Rules of Procedure, r 15.

[18] ibid, r 16.

[19] The currently applicable Rules of Procedures were adopted by the Committee at its 125th meeting in March 2012 and are available on the ESC website.

[20] Art 1 GC's Rules of Procedure. States that have so far only signed but not yet ratified the Charter or the Code are also invited, but in an observer capacity. The idea behind this is mainly to allow those states to get better acquainted with the ESC, its content and case law and thus

mainly civil servants from relevant government departments nominated by their governments; each government can nominate only one member, but can change them at any time.[21] From among its members, the GC elects a Bureau, for a two-year period (but eligible for re-election), composed of a chair, a first and second deputy chair and at least two other members. One of the two deputy chairs must be an expert in the field of the European Code of Social Security. The chair directs the work and chairs sessions of the GC; he/she participates in votes as a representative; if a situation under examination concerns the Party represented by the chair, the chair is replaced by the deputy chair.[22]

Furthermore, the GC shall invite no more than two international organisations of employers and two international trade union organisations to send observers in a consultative capacity (that is, with full speaking rights but no right to vote) to its meetings.[23] Currently, the employers' side is represented by the International Employers' Organisation (IOE) and BUSINESSEUROPE, whereas on the trade union side only the ETUC sits in the GC.[24] Moreover, the GC may consult representatives of international non-governmental organisations which have participatory status with the Council of Europe and have particular competence in the matters governed by the present Charter.[25]

prepare better for ratification. To be noted also is that at the invitation of the Committee of Ministers, states enjoying observer status with the Council of Europe, as well as other non-member states, may send a representative to attend the meetings dealing with the Code as an observer (that is, without voting rights or defrayal of expenses).

[21] In recent years, the GC has seen an enormous turnover of delegates, with many long-standing and experienced national delegates being replaced by new colleagues. In addition, and with the increased number of ratifications, in particular by central and eastern European countries, many new delegates have joined the GC. Both latter factors have certainly had an impact on the continuity of (firm) decision-making within the GC and general respect for the working methods of the GC in general.

[22] Art 3 GC Rules of Procedure.

[23] Art C referring to Art 27§2 ESC as amended by the Turin Protocol. In practice this means that they receive all documentation relating to the GC's meetings, are allowed to circulate their own documents/positions, can play a full part in all the discussions at the meetings (including on cases of alleged violations of the ESC) and have their observations annexed to the meeting reports. They have, however, no right to vote on eventual warnings and recommendations adopted by the GC for violations of the Charter. According to the GC Rules of Procedure, the invitation to international organisations of employers and trade unions is valid for four years; unless it is expressly withdrawn by the GC at the end of this period, it shall be considered to have been tacitly renewed. These organisations are also invited to take part in the work of working groups and any other GC activities, and the travel and subsistence expenses of one representative of the ETUC and of IOE/BUSINESSEUROPE is borne by the Council of Europe budget.

[24] The fact that only the ETUC represents—since 1974—the trade union side is the result of a political agreement between the ICFTU (now ITUC) and the ETUC, whereby the ITUC would mainly represent the trade union world in international bodies, whereas the ETUC would focus on EU and Council of Europe bodies.

[25] Art 27 of the Charter provides for an obligation to invite the social partners, whereas it only entails a possibility for consultation of the INGOs and this 'in respect of questions with

The main mandate of the GC is to prepare the decisions of the Committee of Ministers. Based on the conclusions of the ECSR, it shall select, giving reasons for its choice, on the basis of social, economic and other policy considerations the situations that should be the subject of recommendations to each Contracting Party concerned.[26] It shall thus not make legal interpretations of the provisions of the Charter and can certainly not act as a kind of appeal instance on the conclusions/decisions of the ECSR.[27]

The notion that the GC should judge alleged violations of the Charter on the 'basis of social, economic and other policy considerations' was an important change made under the revitalisation process in the Turin Protocol, whereby after 30 years of experience it was considered that there was a need for a clearer distinction between the mandates (and status) of the ECSR and the GC. Indeed, over time the diverging interpretation seriously undermined the credibility of the supervisory system.[28] According to Article 14 GC Rules of Procedures the GC shall not carry out legal interpretations of the provisions of the Charter (based, among other things, on the Turin Protocol, which has not legally entered into force because four states have not ratified it).[29] It is now also accepted practice that it is the ECSR that makes a legal assessment of a possible violation of the Charter, whereby the GC on the basis of social, economic and other policy considerations subsequently deals with the situation. It might, on this basis, adopt a sanction (in the form of a recommendation or a warning) or refrain from voting on such a sanction and urge the government to remedy the situation as soon as possible and await the next assessment of the situation by the ECSR.

Following another change to the Turin Protocol, it is also in the GC's remit, next to dealing with the ECSR conclusions, to submit 'on the basis of its findings on the implementation of the Charter in general, proposals to the CM aiming at studies to be carried out on social issues and on articles

which the organisations are particularly qualified to deal, such as social welfare, and the economic and social protection of the family'. Under the 1991 Turin Protocol the language was made slightly less strict by referring to INGOs that 'have particular competence in the matters governed by the present Charter' (Art 4). The GC has now developed an approach whereby a delegation of the Conference of INGOs with participatory status in the Council of Europe are invited at the beginning of each supervisory cycle to express their particular observations on the Charter articles under scrutiny in that cycle. Up till now, both government representatives as well as the represented social partners have not been favourable to a more formal role for INGOs in the work of the GC (eg same observer status as the social partners), for various reasons. More information on the participation of civil society in the work of the Council of Europe is available on the Council of Europe website. Under the umbrella of a so-called standing committee on 'Human Rights Committee' the INGOs also established a working group on the European Social Charter.

[26] Art C referring to Art 27§2 ESC as amended by the Turin Protocol.

[27] Art 14 GC Rules of Procedure; Coyer (n 1) confirms that 'le CG doit formellement s'abstenir de jouer le rôle d'instance d'appel du CEDS' (p 37).

[28] See the contribution by K Lörcher on 'interpretation' in this volume.

[29] Denmark, Germany, Luxembourg and the United Kingdom.

of the Charter which possibly might be updated'.[30] Although not provided for by the Charter, the GC has always considered it an aspect of its role and competence to make proposals to the CM for Charter amendments,[31] or proposals for changes in the operation of the monitoring system, in particular the reporting system.

Whereas in the past, the GC met four times a year for a full week, currently and despite the considerable increase in ratifying countries (and thus an increased number of ECSR negative conclusions), the GC meets only twice a year. The considerable decrease of meeting days has surely not enhanced the effectiveness of the GC's work (in particular in relation to adopting warnings and recommendations –see also below section III.A.iv) and has also even obliged the GC to change its working methods, making them less stringent. Given that the GC is now also responsible for monitoring the follow-up provided by states on cases of non-compliance within the framework of the European Code of Social Security within those two weeks, and whereby in principle the first two days of the first meeting week in the year are devoted to discussions of that Code, this leaves the GC only eight working days a year to discuss (the increased number of) cases of violations of the Charter.[32]

Finally, and unlike the ECSR, with the exception of the limited possibility of being consulted by the CM in accordance with Article 9§2 CCPP (see below, section IV), the GC plays no role in the collective complaints procedure. This is mainly because this procedure is considered a quasi-judicial process, leaving no room for social, economic or other policy considerations. However, the GC increasingly is being confronted—in its debates within the framework of the reporting procedure—with cases of non-conformity based on decisions of the ECSR taken within the collective complaints procedure and which have not yet been rectified by the concerned government, and thus are considered to represent (repeated) non-conformity in respect of the Charter. A solution for this 'blending of both procedures' was recently adopted and endorsed by the CM (see below).

[30] Art 27§4 ESC (as amended by the 1991 Turin Protocol). The author is, however, not aware of any such studies being requested or conducted.

[31] See, for example, the proposal by the GC to set up the so-called Charte-Rel Committee, which led to the elaboration and adoption of both the 1991 Turin Protocol as well as the 1995 CCPP.

[32] In practical terms, it is additionally problematic, in particular for the week in which the GC also discusses cases related to the Code, that states often have to send two experts (one for the Code and one for the Charter), knowing that due to budgetary constraints only one of them is reimbursed.

C. The Committee of Ministers (CM)

The CM intervenes only in the last stage of the supervisory process of both the reporting procedure and the collective complaints procedure.

In the reporting procedure, the CM adopts, by a majority of two-thirds of those voting (entitlement to voting being limited to the Contracting Parties), on the basis of the report of the GC, first, a resolution covering the entire supervision cycle and second, where relevant, individual recommendations to the Contracting Parties concerned.[33]

As for the collective complaints, Article 9 CCPP provides that the CM shall adopt a resolution closing the procedure on the basis of the report of the ECSR and, where the ECSR has found a violation of the Charter, it shall adopt a recommendation addressed to the State Party concerned. However, hitherto, with one exception,[34] the CM has not adopted such recommendations but mere resolutions, which is to be deplored as it weakens even more the (quasi-legal) value and potential impact of the ECSR decisions.

D. The Parliamentary Assembly (PACE)

As mentioned before, the PACE[35] no longer plays a formal role in the monitoring system.[36] The only role conferred upon it is in the 1991 Turin

[33] Art 28§1 of the Charter, as amended by the Turin Protocol. One of the reasons why the supervisory system of the Charter needed to be revitalised was because the CM did not use its powers as foreseen in Art 29 of the 1961 Charter, whereby at the end of each supervisory cycle the CM could make, by a majority of two-thirds of the members sitting on the CM, any necessary recommendations to each Contracting Party. In practice, however, the CM, over a period of more than 20 years, made no individual recommendations and 'limited' its resolutions to 'drawing the attention' of states to the ECSR's conclusions, and recommended that the governments concerned should take account in an appropriate manner of the various observations made in the reports. With the 1991 amendments, the voting rules were improved: now only the CM members of states that have ratified the Charter take part in the vote. Harris and Darcy (n 6), however, regret that the two-thirds majority was upheld and that simple majority voting was not introduced, as foreseen in the drafting process of the 1991 Amending Protocol (ibid p 350). This is indeed deplorable, as even in the framework of the ECtHR proceedings, Art 46§2 ECHR does not formally require such a two-thirds majority (unless in specific cases mentioned in §§ 3 to 5 of this provision).

[34] Recommendation R ChS (2001)1 in relation to *Syndicat national des Professions du tourisme v France*, Collective Complaint No 6/1999.

[35] The PACE is composed of representatives of each member state, who are also members of the national parliaments of the member states.

[36] Although Art 28 of the 1961 Charter foresaw that 'the Secretary General of the Council of Europe shall transmit to the Consultative Assembly [now Parliamentary Assembly] the conclusions of the Committee of Experts' and the 'Consultative Assembly shall communicate its views on these Conclusions to the Committee of Ministers' and that the PACE did indeed express such views repeatedly, it was at the request of the PACE itself to change its role in the 1991 Turin Protocol (Art 29) as it had noted that their 'views' had little or no impact and their intervention only lengthened and rendered more complex the supervisory system.

Protocol, where it was foreseen that the PACE would elect the members of the ECSR, instead of the Committee of Ministers; however, this is the sole article of the Protocol that has not yet been put into practice.

Furthermore, Article 29 of the Charter foresees that 'the Secretary General of the Council of Europe shall transmit to the Parliamentary Assembly, with a view to the holding of periodical plenary debates, the reports of the Committee of Independent Experts [now the ECSR] and of the Governmental Committee, as well as the resolutions of the Committee of Ministers.' It is in the latter capacity that the PACE has over time devoted particular attention and importance to the (effectiveness of the) Charter and its monitoring and enforcement procedures in several important recommendations.[37] It has even established a specific 'Sub-Committee on the European Social Charter', currently hosted by the Assembly Committee on Social Affairs, Health and Sustainable Development.[38]

III. THE REPORTING PROCEDURE(S)[39]

As already mentioned, and before the entry into force of the 1995 Collective Complaints Procedure Protocol, the only monitoring procedure under the 1961 Charter, but also applicable to the 1996 Charter (Article C), consisted of a reporting procedure.

There are two kinds of report. Under Article 21 of the Charter, 'Contracting Parties shall send to the Secretary General of the Council of Europe a report at two-yearly intervals, in a form to be determined by the Committee of Ministers, concerning the application of such provisions of Part II of the Charter as they have accepted.'

By virtue of Article 22,

> Contracting Parties shall send to the Secretary General, at appropriate intervals as requested by the Committee of Ministers, reports relating to the provisions of Part II of the Charter which they did not accept at the time of their ratification or approval or in a subsequent notification. The Committee of Ministers shall

[37] For example, PACE Recommendation 1354 (1998) on 'The Future of the European Social Charter' in which the PACE suggested, among other things, the establishment of a European Court of Social Rights, the introduction of a right of individual complaints and making acceptance of all hard-core provisions compulsory. Or, PACE Recommendation 1415 (1999), in which it proposed an additional protocol to the ECHR concerning fundamental social rights.

[38] This subcommittee has also been very active in formulating proposals to enhance the effectiveness of the Charter's monitoring system. See, for instance, the Declaration by the Sub-Committee participating in the High-level Conference on the European Social Charter on behalf of the PACE (AS/Soc/ESC (2014) 03rev, 17 October 2014).

[39] It is to be noted that this section describes the current system (2015); where relevant and appropriate, references will be made to previous features of the system and how they were amended over time.

determine from time to time in respect of which provisions such reports shall be requested and the form of the reports to be provided.

Both reporting obligations extend to the 1998 Additional Protocol and the 1996 Charter (Article C).

Despite its deficiencies (see below), the reporting system remains of the utmost importance for the effective supervision of the Charter, in particular for as long as not all states have ratified the Collective Complaints Procedure Protocol.

A. Reports on Accepted Provisions

(i) Calendar of Reporting

Under the currently applicable system,[40] and following a decision of the Committee of Ministers of May 2006,[41] the provisions of the Charter have been divided into four thematic groups. States present a report on the provisions relating to one of the four thematic groups on an annual basis. Consequently, each provision of the Charter is reported on only once every four years. The four thematic groups are:

Group 1 'Employment, training and equal opportunities' (Articles 1, 9, 10, 15, 18, 20, 24 and 25).

Group 2 'Health, social security and social protection' (Articles 3, 11, 12, 13, 14, 23 and 30).

[40] The reporting system has indeed been changed several times—mainly to accommodate the increasing workload of the monitoring bodies due to increased ratifications of the Charter. During the first 12 reporting cycles (1965–89) all Contracting Parties submitted biennial reports, whereby at first they all reported all at the same time, submitting a report every other year, but from 1984 onwards the countries were divided into two groups, with one group reporting in the even years and the other group in the odd years, the reports thus covering the preceding two years. Again, due to an increase in ratifications, the CM decided on a trial period of four years during which the governments could report on a less frequent basis, which led to a system whereby governments reported on so-called 'hard-core' articles of the Charter every two years, and on the other provisions once every four years. In 1996, the CM then decided that as from the 14th supervisory cycle (1997), all Contracting Parties had to report biennially on their performance in respect of the hard-core articles during a reference period of the previous years and on their performance over a reference period of the previous four years in relation to half of the non-hard-core provisions. This system was heavily criticised by the ETUC as not allowing sufficiently frequent monitoring of non-hard-core articles, in particular if the ECSR had to defer its conclusion of non-conformity due to lack of or insufficient information provided by the Contracting Party and thus the application of the provision would only happen after eight (or even more) years, not four.

[41] CM (2006) 53, European Social Charter—Governmental Committee of the European Social Charter—New system for the presentation of reports on the application of the European Social Charter—Proposal of the Governmental Committee, adopted at its 963rd meeting, 3 May 2006.

Group 3 'Labour rights' (Articles 2, 4, 5, 6, 21, 22, 26, 28 and 29).
Group 4 'Children, family, migrants' (Articles 7, 8, 16, 17, 19, 27 and 31).

Following a CM decision in 2014,[42] national reports should focus on ECSR conclusions of non-conformity from the previous cycle, as well as on questions raised by the ECSR. In any case, additional information should be provided on changes that have occurred since the preceding report. In the event of a lack of information after examination of Group 1 'Employment, training and equal opportunities', the state concerned must submit the requested information when reporting on Group 3 'Labour', and vice versa. In the event of a lack of information after examination of Group 2 'Health, social security and social protection', the state concerned must submit the requested information when reporting on Group 4 'Children, families, migrants', and vice versa. Consequently, the requested additional information is to be submitted within two years. If not, the situation will be discussed by the GC.

Due to the 'blending or melting of the two procedures',[43] whereby cases of non-conformity found under the collective complaints procedure are also reiterated as a case of (repeated) non-conformity under the reporting system, it was agreed via CM Decision (2014) 26 that the burden of reporting for those Contracting Parties that have ratified the CCPP had to be simplified. The system currently is that states that have accepted the collective complaints procedure will submit a simplified report every two years. To prevent this simplification from causing excessive fluctuations in the workload of the ECSR and the GC from year to year, the current 15 states that have accepted the collective complaints procedure are divided into two groups, according to the number of complaints registered against them (from the highest to the lowest), as follows: Group A, made up of eight states (France, Greece, Portugal, Italy, Belgium, Bulgaria, Ireland, and Finland), and Group B, made up of seven states (the Netherlands, Sweden, Croatia, Norway, Slovenia, Cyprus and the Czech Republic). As new states accept the collective complaints procedure, they will be assigned on an alternating basis to Group B, then Group A, then to Group B again, and so on. States that have to submit a simplified report are required to declare what

[42] CM (2014) 26, European Social Charter—Governmental Committee of the European Social Charter and the European Code of Social Security—Ways of streamlining and improving the reporting and monitoring system of the European Social Charter, adopted at its 1196th meeting, 2–3 April 2014.

[43] This 'blending' is a consequence of Art 10 CCPP, which provides that states should provide information on the measures it has taken to give effect to the CMs' recommendation taken in relation to the collective complaint in the next report that it submits to the Secretary General under Art 21 of the Charter. And although the decisions of the ECSR also appear in the reporting system as a case of (repeated) non-conformity, often within a very short time after the ECSR decision, this is not necessarily to be deplored, as the follow-up of CM resolutions within the framework of the CCPP is far from effective.

follow-up action has been taken in response to the decisions of the ECSR on collective complaints, and to reply to any questions put in the event of deferrals for the relevant provisions.[44,45]

(ii) Form

National reports have to be submitted in one of the two official languages of the Council of Europe (English or French)[46] and have to be prepared along the lines of a pre-prepared 'report form' adopted by the CM.[47] Unfortunately, it has been noticed that more and more states are submitting their reports with a (considerable) delay, which creates—as argued many times by ETUC delegates in the GC—an unacceptable situation as it hampers a serious and qualitative assessment of the reports by the ECSR and even creates discriminatory situations between those countries that make the effort to submit their reports on time and those that do not. Although the GC at one time adopted an informal approach of addressing an automatic warning or even recommendation (in case of recidivism) to states that submitted their reports too late, it seems, unfortunately, to have abandoned this approach in recent times.

(iii) Comments on the National Reports by Social Partners and NGOs

According to Article 23 of the Charter (as amended by the 1991 Turin Protocol), each Contracting Party shall communicate copies of its national reports (on both accepted and non-accepted provisions) to the mem-

[44] A calendar for submission of the full as well as simplified reports can be found on the Charter website.

[45] It is, however, still disputed whether this new dimension in the reporting system is indeed 'simplified' and lessens the reporting burden of states concerned. (See GC (2015) 17 final, 18 December 2015, pp 69–70.)

[46] This language regime has in recent years (in particular with the ratification of the Charter by states from central and eastern Europe, the Balkans and beyond) led to more and more problems with submission of reports on time. In these countries the reports are often prepared in the national language (which then needs to be translated—in times of crisis this is also very expensive) and also according to the internal legal proceedings formally adopted by government and/or parliament (whereby the latter, in less stable political regimes, often creates additional delays due to more frequent government or parliamentary elections).

[47] The original Report Form was adopted by the CM on 26 January 1968, but has been amended several times. The Report Form(s) (different forms exist for those countries that ratified the 1961 or 1996 Charter) currently used were adopted by the CM on 26 March 2008 and can be found on the Charter website. See also Harris and Darcy (n 6) on the weaknesses of allowing states to use other sources, such as the reports to the ILO supervisory cycle, statistics, etc for the reports (ibid 307–14). Whereas the 1961 Charter contained no provision for the publication of the national reports submitted under Art 21 (and 22) and for a long time they were indeed treated as confidential within the Council of Europe, this was changed in the 1991 Turin Protocol, following which the reports are to be made available to the public on request. In the meantime, most national reports are available on the Charter website.

bers of the international organisations of employers (currently IOE and Businesseurope) and of trade unions (currently ETUC) represented in the GC. Those national organisations are invited to make comments and observations on these reports (Article 27§2), which they have to send to the Secretary General, who in turn will send a copy of those comments to the Contracting Parties concerned, who might wish to respond. The comments are also communicated to the ECSR, which takes them into consideration in its examination of the national reports.

To date, and although over time the number of comments received has increased, unfortunately only a few national employer and trade union organisations (affiliated to the ETUC) have made a habit of such observations, although they are a valuable way of correcting and/or clarifying information, in particular for the ECSR in its assessment of situations of (non-)conformity.

Under Article 23§2 of the 1961 Charter, the Contracting Parties were not obliged to send the reports for comments to any other organisations. This was amended by the Turin Protocol, and the Secretary General of the Council of Europe is now obliged to forward a copy of the national reports to the international NGOs that have consultative (participatory) status with the Council of Europe and have particular competence in the matters governed by the Charter. Although the reports are in principle forwarded for information (and thus not with the express competence to make comments), several international NGOs have used this opportunity to submit their observations.[48]

(iv) Examination of the Reports by the Different Supervisory Bodies (ECSR, GC and CM)

(a) ECSR

Having received the national reports, the ECSR assesses, from a legal standpoint, the compliance of national law and practice with the obligations arising from the Charter (Article 24).[49]

In deciding whether situations are in conformity with the Charter, the ECSR first checks whether existing laws and regulations are consistent with

[48] All observations made by the affected social partners and INGOs can be found—ordered by supervisory cycle/year since 2007—on the Charter website. As there is also no provision in the Charter obliging the Council of Europe to make the replies of governments public, they also do not appear -unfortunately—on its website.

[49] In order to conduct this work efficiently, the ECSR Rules of Procedures provide several working methods, such as the designation of a General Rapporteur for each supervisory cycle who has to ensure the consistency of the conclusions and decisions on the various articles (r 10), participation of a senior official of the ILO—in a consultative capacity—to ensure consistency with ILO norms and case law (r 12 and Art 25), the designation of a rapporteur for each article (r 19) and the formation of sub-committees (r 20). In practice, each member of

the Charter rights and do not impede their application. If this first 'test' is passed, it then goes on to ensure that the law is properly applied in practice. A situation is 'not in conformity' if the relevant legislation is incompatible with the Charter requirements, or if compatible legislation is incorrectly or not fully applied. Although the ECSR makes its assessment in relation to a given 'reference period', it may occur that the ECSR comes across information that a situation during the reference period which it decides is not in conformity has changed (but due to changes in law or practice taking place outside the reference period). The ECSR then maintains its decision of non-conformity, but the fact that the changes took place outside the reference period will be duly reflected in the ECSR conclusions.[50]

For its assessment, the ECSR increasingly also relies for its conclusions, next to the information provided in the national report, on reports by academic institutions, other international/European institutions (EU, ILO, UN bodies, or other Council of Europe reports on other treaties), INGOs, statistical offices (for example, Eurostat) and so on.[51] This approach is not always appreciated, and even sometimes heavily contested by government representatives in the GC as this 'external' information can contradict information provided in the national reports, or bring to light further possible situations of non-conformity in the state concerned.

As already mentioned, the ECSR assesses, from a legal standpoint, the compliance of national law and practice with the obligations under the Charter. This underlines that the ECSR has, as an independent and impartial body, the exclusive competence to interpret and determine compliance with the Charter. It is also consistent with the *travaux préparatoires*, which made it clear that the ECSR is intended to exercise a similar role to that of the ILO Committee of Experts. The latter is also one of the reasons, besides ensuring consistency with the ILO norms, why according to the Charter and the ECSR rules of procedure an official of the ILO is invited to participate in a consultative capacity in the deliberations of the ECSR, although this seems in practice to occur less and less and one could thus question the compatibility of current practice with the Charter and the ECSR Rules of Procedure. But although this exclusive 'legal assessment' competence thus stems from

the ESCR is, given the number of Charter provisions, specifically appointed as rapporteur for several articles and examines all provisions allocated to him/her for all states concerned. Since 1995, there have been two such sub-committees, each responsible for a certain number of provisions; however, difficult points may be referred back to the ECSR plenary, whose work is prepared by the sub-committees. During the whole process, all comments submitted by the social partners and (international) NGOs are available to the ECSR members.

[50] It is then in practice up to the GC members to consider whether these new developments, which occurred outside the reference period, are sufficient to give the government concerned 'the benefit of the doubt' and decide to await a new assessment by the ECSR in the following reporting/supervisory cycle on the article concerned.

[51] On the use of these external sources see also Harris and Darcy (n 6) 324.

a longstanding practice, it was only 'written in stone' in the 1991 Turin Protocol to overcome the manifold situations in which the GC was contesting this exclusive competence.[52]

The ECSR does not regard itself as bound by previous interpretations of the Charter and thus might alter, adjust and/or complement its interpretations (or case law) over time. Although in general the ECSR has not drastically overruled its own interpretations, it has over time at least further developed and clarified its interpretations, in particular when confronted for instance with new developments in society in general or in the world of work in particular. Such changes/complements to its interpretations are reflected in its so-called 'statements of interpretation'.[53]

The ECSR adopts its conclusions and decisions by vote. In most cases, voting is unanimous. Occasionally, though, the ECSR decides by majority vote. The ECSR's Rules of Procedure allow any member who has voted against a conclusion or a decision to present a dissenting opinion, which is published at the same time as the conclusion or decision.[54]

If considered appropriate, the ECSR may address requests for additional information and clarification directly to Contracting Parties and might even hold, if necessary, a meeting with the representatives of a Contracting Party, either on its own initiative or at the request of the Contracting Party concerned.[55] In that sense, it should also be noted that the GC, in particular for very long-standing cases of non-conformity, urges the state concerned to contact the ECSR directly to hold such a meeting in order to rectify the situation or at least better understand the ECSR conclusions.

At the end of its examination, the ECSR submits a report containing its so-called 'conclusions' to all Contracting Parties and the GC and makes it available on the Charter website. The report encompasses, besides a general introduction (with its 'statement of interpretation') a detailed over-

[52] Council of Europe (1991) Explanatory Report to the Protocol amending the European Social Charter, Turin, 21.10.1991.

[53] See also the chapter on 'Interpretation' by K Lörcher in this volume.

[54] r 22 ESCR Rules of Procedure.

[55] This is also reiterated in r 21 ECSR Rules of Procedure. Under the 1961 Charter, such an opportunity for dialogue between the ECSR and governments was not foreseen and the supervisory procedure was entirely in writing. In order to overcome this weakness, this possibility for dialogue was introduced. According to Harris and Darcy (n 6), from the drafting history of the 1991 Turin Protocol there seems to be no legal obligation on a government to participate in such a meeting, nor is the ECSR legally bound to hold a meeting if a state requests it. In case the ECSR holds such meetings the international organisations of employers (IOE and BUSINESSEUROPE) and trade unions (ETUC) shall be informed and will, in certain cases, be invited to participate. They are then invited to inform their national member organisations, which could then be invited to participate in these meetings but only on the condition that the state concerned agrees. According to Harris and Darcy (n 6), the ETUC participated in meetings in relation to Finland (1997) and Portugal (1997) (the invited employers' organisations did not accept the invitation) and the FNV was represented at the meeting for the Netherlands held in 1999—ibid 320–21). The (summary) records of these meetings are private.

view of both the cases of conformity (Part I of the report), and the cases of non-conformity, as well as cases of deferral due to lack of (sufficient) information (Part II of the report).[56]

(b) Governmental Committee (GC)

Based on the ECSR conclusions, the GC then deals with cases of non-conformity based on social, economic and other policy considerations (Article 27§3 Charter) and to see whether they should be the subject of recommendations to the Contracting Party concerned.

Originally, the GC discussed and decided upon each situation of non-conformity identified by the ECSR, irrespective of whether it concerned a so-called 'first time negative conclusion' or situations of repeated negative conclusions over several supervisory cycles.[57] Given the greater workload due to the increased number of ratifications and thus the number of eventual situations of non-conformity, the GC changed its Rules of Procedures and (informal) working methods in treating the different cases of non-conformity.

The most recent changes introduced, via CM Decision (2014) 26 (see also section III.A above), entailed a further but important shift in the way the GC handles the different situations at its meetings. From 2015, the ECSR selects from the cases of non-conformity and only those that are selected will be discussed orally by the GC. Situations of non-conformity that are not discussed will be dealt with in the next national report on the relevant group of Articles. In practice, this means now that irrespective of whether it concerns a situation of first-time or renewed non-conformity, the GC will only discuss it if the ECSR has listed the situation in its report on the conclusions at the beginning of the supervisory cycle in a pre-established list of situations to be handled by the GC. For situations not enlisted and thus not to be discussed by the GC, it suffices to provide written information to the Secretariat by the end of July, and this information will then be incorporated in the GC meeting report for that cycle, as well as the GC

[56] These Conclusions are published each year according to the following referencing system: for the 1961 Charter, the Conclusions are numbered with a roman numeral (I, II, III, etc), whereas those relating to the 1996 Charter are numbered according to the year of publication (2005, 2006, 2007, etc). Until 1997, the conclusions were presented article by article and the statements appeared at the start of each chapter. Since 1998, conclusions have been published country by country, with statements of interpretation repeated in each country chapter. To avoid such repetition, as of 2006 these statements appear in the general introduction to the conclusions. All this information can also be accessed via the HUDOC ESC database available on the Charter website.

[57] Thus in line with Art 16A(a) of the GC Rules of Procedure which states that 'The Committee shall consider the non-conformity conclusions of the European Committee of Social Rights provision by provision'.

report to the CM.[58] However, states may always request that non-selected cases might nevertheless be orally discussed. In addition, following a rather weak discussion at its 130th meeting, and in order to enable the GC to hold a focused discussion on particular situations of non-conformity, the GC asked the ECSR to limit the number of cases selected for discussion. Ten situations of non-conformity for discussion per meeting day was considered an appropriate number. Given that the GC had eight meeting days per year to dedicate to Charter matters, the number of situations of non-conformity to be discussed by the GC should not exceed 80.

In any case, these new formal and informal working methods can be considered a further weakening of the supervisory system because now, situations of renewed non-conformity also might be passed on to the next assessment by the ECSR (that is, four years later) without discussion in the GC.

Formally, and according to Article 16A(c–g) GC Rules of Procedure, when examining cases of non-conformity, and following deliberations within the GC, the GC shall vote on each non-conformity conclusion of the ECSR,[59] unless it decides by consensus not to proceed to a vote. The first vote shall be on whether to make a recommendation to the Party concerned; the GC shall then observe the same voting rules as the CM, namely a two-thirds majority of votes cast[60] and a simple majority of the Parties. Where there is no majority in favour of a recommendation, the GC shall then vote on whether to address a warning to the Party concerned (two-thirds majority of votes cast).[61]

A 'warning', which has been introduced into the system without a respective reference in the Charter's text, serves as an indication to the Party

[58] This new procedure thus (partially) overrules what is stipulated in Art 16A(b) of the currently applicable GC Rules of Procedure.

[59] As for situations of which the conclusion has been deferred because of lack of information, and according to Art 17A GC Rules of Procedure, the GC shall not examine at meetings national situations on which a conclusion has been deferred for the first time, unless a representative expressly requests it. These situations shall nevertheless be referred to in the working document and the report to the CM, for information. The representatives concerned may, however, submit written information to the Secretariat that they would like to be included in the GC report. The GC should vote on each situation on which the ECSR has repeatedly had to defer a conclusion for lack of information; this is not always done in practice. Art 17B provides a list of selection criteria which the GC can take into consideration in its examination and decision to vote. Concerning the voting on cases of non-conformity, this procedure is in practice not followed strictly, to say the least.

[60] According to Art 13§3 GC Rules of Procedure, 'votes cast' means the votes of representatives voting for or against; representatives abstaining are considered not to have cast a vote. Representatives in the GC with observer status (such as states that have only signed but not ratified the Charter, as well as the representatives of ETUC, Businesseurope and IOE) have no right to vote.

[61] If a recommendation has already been adopted against a state on the situation of non-conformity, and the ESCR finds in a following assessment that the situation has not (sufficiently) been remedied and confirms its finding of non-conformity, the GC can vote on a renewal of the recommendation whereby the same voting rules (and selection criteria) apply as for the first recommendation.

concerned that, unless it takes steps to comply with its obligations under the Charter, the GC may propose a recommendation the next time this provision is examined.[62] Where the GC does not propose a recommendation or a warning in response to a non-conformity conclusion, it may consider it necessary to express an opinion on the relevant national situation or conclusion in its report to the CM. Insofar as the examination concerns a Party submitting its first report, which is the subject of a first set of conclusions of the ECSR, the GC shall issue a warning rather than a recommendation in the case of non-conformity conclusions.

In order to conduct such an examination and come to a decision, the GC Rules of Procedure also list in Article 16(B) a number of (non-exhaustive) selection criteria, such as (a) does the provision in question belong to the hard-core of the Charter or the revised Charter?, (b) in which cycle was the situation first criticised? and (c) have the social partners expressed an opinion on the seriousness of this type of breach?[63]

In practice now, the GC assesses each case based on the additional information given orally by the government representative of the state concerned at the GC meeting (for example, announcing new legislation, new policy measures or other developments that could remedy the situation). Depending on this additional information, and taking into account the criteria mentioned above, the GC decides on the eventual message or 'sanction' it will give to the government concerned.

This has led, however, to the situation that if a government is able to provide convincing evidence of new legislation or policies being in place, or their adoption is well advanced, the GC will ask the government to provide detailed information on these new developments in its next report on the article concerned and await the next ECSR assessment. Also if the representative is able to show that the negative conclusion is based on inaccurate or incomplete information (even though this resulted from a deficiency of information in the national report), this will in practice preclude the GC from voting, and it must instead ask the government to provide all necessary information in the next report. If it concerns a renewed situation of non-conformity and the evidence provided to the GC seems unconvincing, the GC might send what is known as a 'strong or very strong message' urging the government to remedy the situation as soon as possible.

[62] Indeed, in the text of the Charter and the 1991 Turin Protocol, there is no mention of 'warnings'. The GC itself introduced the system of warnings when it had to establish its new working methods following its new role as defined in the 1991 Turin Protocol. According to Harris and Darcy, the lack of legal base and thus the legality of a system of warnings has only been questioned once in the first cycle when the new system was applied (13th cycle) by one country, Iceland (Harris and Darcy (n 6) 344).

[63] Each of these criteria has different weight and some are considered more serious than others. Criteria that (used to have) most weight are for instance (a) and (c). However, everything depends on the article and specific situation at stake. See also on this Harris and Darcy (n 6) 338–39.

Unfortunately, as a result of this the GC goes to a vote on particular cases less and less frequently (and often at the (indirect) request of the ETUC delegate).[64] Furthermore, over recent years, in particular with the participation of many new members (see above), most votes do not obtain the required quorum, mainly due to manifold abstentions by those new representatives.[65] All this has seriously undermined the 'striking force' of the GC and thus its role, credibility and effectiveness have increasingly come into question (in particular in combination with the growing importance of the collective complaints procedure).[66]

At the end of its two meetings a year, the GC presents a report to the CM. According to Article 19 GC Rules of Procedure, the report describes developments since the previous supervision cycle, showing positive and negative changes in national situations and includes general observations on the measures taken by Parties to comply with CM recommendations and proposals for individual recommendations to be addressed to Parties. Only proposals for first recommendations shall be appended to the draft resolution ending the supervision cycle; the renewal of recommendations still to be acted on shall simply be mentioned in the draft resolution.

Observations made by the international social partners represented in the GC and made orally at the various meetings shall be appended to the GC's report. However, since 2001 only the GC report has been submitted, and as foreseen in Article 19§6 GC Rules of Procedure, in an abridged version containing a general part and an extract from the detailed report on the national situations concerning which it is proposed to ask the CM to adopt or renew recommendations. Following CM decision (2014) 26, and to enhance visibility at the CM level, the abridged annual report should also include more information on the discussion held at GC level during the previous year. Positive developments since the previous examination by the ECSR may also be included.

(c) Committee of Ministers (CM)

Following the GC's submission of the report, the CM shall vote on adopting a resolution covering the entire supervision cycle and containing individual

[64] Indeed implicit as in principle the ETUC cannot ask for a vote. This is a prerogative of the states. The informal rules applied foresee that a vote will only be taken if one government representative asks for the vote and/or supports the implicit call of the ETUC delegate.

[65] In practice, and again depending on the case, the most likely chance to get a warning or recommendation adopted is in (longstanding) cases of renewed non-conformity, whereby the government representative announced no new (legal) measures and confirms that there is no will on the part of the government to change the situation (in the short term).

[66] See also Harris and Darcy (n 6) 341–46 on the (reasons for) decreasing numbers of recommendations and warnings.

recommendations to the Contracting Parties concerned. A two-thirds majority of those voting (entitlement to voting being limited to the Contracting Parties to the Charter) is required.[67] The CM recommendations give more political weight to the conclusions of non-conformity of the ECSR, but also represents a clear (political) obligation/signal for governments to look more quickly for effective implementation and to ensure conformity with the Charter obligations.

B. Reports on Non-accepted Provisions

Bearing in mind the list of principles enshrined in Part I of the Charter, on one side, and the possibility of selecting only a limited number of articles/ provisions on the other side, there was a need to foresee a mechanism which made it possible to monitor the state of play in both law and practice regarding both accepted and non-accepted provisions.

Article 22 of the Charter therefore provides that Contracting Parties must make reports on the Charter provisions that they have not accepted 'at appropriate intervals as requested by the Committee of Ministers'.[68] Initially, the CM thereby acts on the advice of the GC when deciding to call for reports under Article 22, but the ECSR also has a right to take the initiative by making suggestions to the GC.[69]

However, in order to make the 'Article 22 reporting procedure' more effective, in particular due to the growing number of ratifications (and Contracting Parties preparing for ratification) of the 1996 Charter, the CM, upon a proposal of the ECSR, adopted Decision CM (2002) 184 on 13 November 2002, whereby only Contracting Parties that have ratified the 1996 Charter are to report on all non-accepted provisions every five years after the date of ratification. The reporting is thus no longer done following certain articles but by states every five years on all non-accepted provisions. The practical details surrounding the submission of national reports are agreed between

[67] Art 28§1 Charter (as amended by the 1991 Turin Protocol). This voting rule was applied as from the 12th supervisory cycle (1993). However, following a CM Decision of June 1995 adopted at its 541st Meeting, the CM made it more difficult to adopt recommendations by deciding that recommendations had to be adopted by a majority of two-thirds of the Contracting Parties to the Charter casting a vote (with abstentions not counting as a vote cast) and a majority of the Contracting Parties to the Charter.

[68] A procedure which is based on Art 19§5 (e) ILO Constitution which requires an ILO member state that is not a party to an ILO Convention to report 'at appropriate intervals as requested by the Governing Body' on 'the position of its law and practice in regard to matters dealt with by the Convention, showing the extent to which effect has been given, or is proposed to be given' to it and 'stating the difficulties which prevent or delay' the ratification of the Convention concerned.

[69] Over time, the CM has called for such reports in, among others, 1978, 1981, 1986, 1993 and 1995 in relation to Arts 2§1, 2§4, 4§§3–4, 5, 7§1, 7§§4–7, 7§9, 8§§1–2, 8§4 and 19§4.

the ECSR and the states concerned, so that it is no longer necessary for the CM to adopt a form for reports. As for states that have not ratified the 1996 Charter, the CM reserves the possibility to make proposals for the application of Article 22 ESC, as before.[70,71]

The purpose of the ECSR examining these reports is to better understand the different reasons for non-acceptance, to draw conclusions and eventually to make general suggestions on developing social legislation and institutions in the contracting states. It is also a means of getting a more complete picture of the legal and practical situations existing in the Contracting Parties in relation to those non-accepted provisions, but also in more general terms—in particular when the provision is not accepted by a large number of states—to be able to provide a more comprehensive statement of its interpretation on the given provision.

Following Article 27§1, the national reports on non-accepted provisions and the ECSR's reports on them are to be submitted to the GC, which adopts its own report, mainly consisting of a record of its discussions, and provides the basis for the CM resolution that closes the procedure for the consideration of Article 22 reports.

IV. THE COLLECTIVE COMPLAINTS PROCEDURE (CCP)

A. General

Besides the Turin Protocol (and a change to the reporting system via a CM decision of September 1992, 479th meeting—see above), the Charter revitalisation process resulted in another major breakthrough to improve the supervisory machinery, namely the Additional Protocol providing for a system of collective complaints (Collective Complaints Procedure Protocol—CCPP) which was opened for signature on 9 November 1995 and entered into force on 1 July 1998.[72]

[70] According to the Report of the 102nd meeting of the GC (Strasbourg, 14–18 October 2002), 'the ETUC representative wished the examination under Article 22 to be tripartite in nature. A period of five years appeared very long and he would prefer examinations to take place every two years. In addition, he feared that the new procedure could lead to a loss of coherence and a lack of comparison between states. Consequently, he requested that the Secretariat make a special effort to ensure fairness and equal treatment of states. Finally, he recalled that ETUC attached particular importance to states accepting all provisions of the hard-core, which should be made mandatory. In this respect, it might be appropriate to introduce a procedure calling on those states that had not yet ratified to explain the reasons and encouraging them to ratify as soon as possible.' (§12)

[71] All reports submitted under the current system are available on the Charter website.

[72] For a historical overview of the work of so-called 'Committee on the European Social Charter (Charte-Rel)' set up by the CM in December 1990 to draw up proposals for reforming the Charter, see L Samuel, 'The long way towards more social rights in Europe', in W Däubler

The major objective of this new system was to increase the efficiency of supervisory machinery based solely on the submission of government reports and thus to complement the examination of such reports, which still constitutes the basic mechanism for supervision of the Charter's application.

The system is quite closely modelled on the complaints system pertaining to the ILO Committee of Freedom of Association, with the very significant difference that whereas the ILO complaints procedure is limited to matters of freedom of association, the CCP covers all substantive provisions of the Charter. Within the Council of Europe framework, the CCP also forms a parallel protection system which complements the judicial protection system provided under the ECHR. In contrast to the latter, which is based on individual applications (and can be brought only after having exhausted all domestic remedies), the 'collective nature' of these complaints lies in the fact that (i) they can only be filed by privileged international organisations of employers and trade unions, as well as by certain pre-listed non-governmental organisations (so not by individuals), and (ii) they can only raise questions concerning non-compliance of a state's law or practice with one of the (accepted) provisions of the Charter (so no individual situations). In addition, collective complaints can be filed without having exhausted all domestic remedies and without the requirement that the claimant organisation is a victim of the alleged violation.

To date (18 August 2016), of the 43 Contracting Parties that have ratified either the 1961 or the 1996 Charter, only 15 have ratified the CCPP, and 121 collective complaints have been registered.[73]

B. Organisations that May Bring a Complaint

In respect of its collective nature, only (collective) organisations have the right to submit complaints. According to Articles 1 and 2 of the CCPP, this right is attributed to the following organisations.

(i) International Organisations of Employers and Trade Unions Referred to in Article 27§2 Charter (Article 1(a) CCPP)

At present this concerns ETUC, Businesseurope and IOE—the same organisations that are represented as observers in the GC (see above).

and R Zimmer (eds), *Arbeitsvölkerrecht (Festschrift Lörcher)* (Baden-Baden, Nomos-Verlag, 2013) 138 et seq.

[73] Belgium, Bulgaria, Croatia, Cyprus, Czech Republic, Finland, France, Greece, Ireland, Italy, the Netherlands, Norway, Portugal, Slovenia and Sweden.

(ii) International Non-Governmental Organisations having Consultative[74] *Status with the Council of Europe and Having been put on a List Established for this Purpose by the GC (Article 1(b) CCPP)*

To date (December 2015), more than 300 international non-governmental organisations have participatory status with the Council of Europe.[75] Only an INGO that has such participatory status and considers itself particularly competent in any matters governed by the Charter can, if it so wishes, apply to be put on a specific list of INGOs admitted to lodge collective complaints. This list is drawn up by the GC.

All applications are transmitted to the GC, accompanied by an opinion of the Secretary General that reflects the degree of interest and participation shown by the INGO in its relationship with the Council of Europe. An application is considered accepted by the GC unless it is rejected in a ballot by a simple majority of votes cast. To date, this acceptance within the GC has been a rather pro-forma process (hardly any debate, no need to vote so far) and only a few applicants have been refused, mainly because of doubts concerning the relevant link between the INGOs' mandate/activities and the (articles of the) Charter.

Inclusion on the special list is valid for a period of four years and revised at four-yearly intervals, but any INGO can apply at any time, not just when it expires. To date, around 70 INGOs have been included in this special list.[76]

However, the inclusion of an INGO on this list does not relieve the ECSR, when examining admissibility, from the obligation to ascertain whether the complaint actually falls within a field in which the INGO concerned has been recognised to be particularly competent (Article 3 CCPP).[77]

(iii) Representative national organisations of employers and trade unions within the jurisdiction of the Contracting Party against which they have lodged a complaint (Article 1(c) CCPP)

Following the requirement in the reporting procedure (see above, section III.A) that governments must submit a copy of their report to certain of their national organisations of employers and trade unions, it was

[74] Recognising the increasingly active role played by INGOs, the Council of Europe decided via the CM Resolution (2003) 8 of 19 November 2003 to change the former consultative status to participatory status.

[75] The full list of INGOs can be consulted in the INGO database on the Council of Europe website.

[76] The list of complaints can be consulted on the Charter website.

[77] Note that the particular competence is related to the matter raised in the complaint, and thus not restricted to certain concrete article(s) of the Charter.

considered only normal that organisations of this type should be entitled to submit complaints as well. This is the main reason why it was considered also wrong if this right were be restricted to member organisations of the international organisations ETUC, Businesseurope and IOE. So, according to the Explanatory Report to the CCPP, it is clear that the member organisations of ETUC, being representative trade unions in the national framework, are also considered representative under the CCPP, but, however, not exclusively. On the employers' side, and given that it is required to be an 'organisation', individual employers can thus not lodge complaints.[78]

As for non-member organisations on both sides, the requirement of 'representative' organisation is examined by the ECSR on a case-by-case basis in the admissibility phase of the complaints procedure, and this also in light of information and observations submitted by the state and the organisation concerned. As possible selection criteria, the Explanatory Report to the CCPP states only that 'in the absence of any criteria on a national level, factors such as the number of members and the organisation's actual role in national negotiations should be taken into account'. Over time, the ECSR has adopted a fairly wide approach (and for ETUC, at least, too wide an approach) to the criterion of representativeness in such cases.[79]

Unlike the international social partners and the INGOs, these representative national organisations can only bring complaints against the state within whose jurisdiction they operate.

(iv) Any other representative national non-governmental organisation with the jurisdiction of a Contracting Party (Article 2 CCPP)

Although the Charter does not refer specifically to these national NGOs, for the same reasons as those invoked in respect of international NGOs and national organisations of employers and trade unions, it was thought that these national NGOs should also be entitled to submit complaints. However, recognition of this right is not mandatory for parties to the Protocol: NGOs may only submit a complaint against a state if the state in question has previously issued a declaration recognising that NGOs are entitled to do so. Such declarations may be made for a specific period.

[78] para 22 states: 'As laid down in paragraph 1 of Article 23 of the Charter, each Contracting Party must forward a copy of its report to certain of its national organisations of employers and trade unions. It is *only normal* that *organisations of this type should be entitled to submit complaints*, because they are very well informed of the situation in their country. For this reason those who drafted the Protocol considered that *it would be wrong to restrict this right to the national organisations mentioned in Article 23 (that is those which are members of the international organisations referred to in paragraph 2 of Article 27*) (emphasis added).

[79] For example, Decision on Admissibility and the merits, 2 December 2013, *Union syndicale des magistrats administratifs (USMA) v France*, Collective Complaint No 84/2012 §28.

When a state makes such a declaration, it recognises the right of all 'representative' NGOs within its jurisdiction to submit complaints without, for example, drawing up a national list, and it may not restrict this right to certain articles or paragraphs of the Charter. It will again be for the ECSR to decide within the framework of the admissibility phase and based on the information then submitted by the NGO and the state whether the NGO can be considered a representative national NGO, as well as to decide, in accordance with Article 3 CCPP, whether the NGO has a particular competence in the matter (and thus not concrete articles) it raises in the complaint.[80] As for national employers' and trade union organisations, these NGOs can lodge complaints only against states within whose jurisdiction they operate.

To date, only Finland has made such a declaration.[81] Of the eight collective complaints made as of December 2015 against Finland, one was lodged by a national trade union organisation (complaint 10/2000), one by a national employer organisation (complaint 35/2006) and six by two different national NGOs (namely the Central Association of Carers in Finland, Complaints 70–71/2011, and the Finnish Society for Social Rights, Complaints 88/2012 and 106–108/2014).[82]

C. The Procedure of Collective Complaints

(i) Lodging the Complaint

To lodge a complaint, and according to the CCPP and the ECSR Rules of Procedure, the following requirements must be fulfilled. The complaint must be:

— lodged by an organisation falling within one of the four categories entitled to lodge a complaint mentioned above (Articles 1 and 2 CCPP);
— in writing, clearly indicating the name and contact details of the complainant organisation(s) and be signed by the person(s) entitled

[80] On the strengths and weaknesses of allowing national NGOs to submit collective complaints see Prouvez (n 4) 38–39; O Cullen, 'The Collective Complaints Mechanism of the European Social Charter' (2000) 25 *European Law Review* HR/18, HR/22R and RR Churchill and U Khaliq, 'The Collective Complaints System of the European Social Charter: An Effective Mechanism for Ensuring Compliance with Economic and Social Rights?' (2004) 15 *European Journal of International Law* 426.

[81] For reasons why other states have not yet made such a declaration, see for instance Coyer in relation to France, which has not done so yet because, first, it wanted to see how the system would actually work, second, it feared an avalanche of complaints submitted by national NGOs (whose representativeness would be difficult to identify) and third, because—at least in France—most NGOs in the social field are members of a European or international NGO that figures on the list of INGOs entitled to submit complaints (Coyer (n 1) 38).

[82] For more information on the complaints and the decisions of the ECSR, see the Charter website.

to represent the complainant organisation and provide proof that the person(s) submitting and signing the complaint are entitled to represent the organisation(s) (Article 4 CCPP and rule 23§2 ECSR Rules of Procedure);

— (when lodged by international social partners or an admitted INGO) drafted in one of the Council of Europe's official languages (English or French); complaints by national organisations may be drafted in (one of) the official languages of the state concerned (rule 24 ECSR Rules of Procedure);

— lodged against a state that has ratified the Charter and the CCPP (Article 4 CCPP);

— related to one or more provision(s) of the Charter,[83] possibly in combination, and accepted by the Contracting Party concerned, indicating in what respect the latter has not ensured the satisfactory application of the provisions concerned (Article 4 CCPP).[84]

In practice, complaints are now usually directly addressed to the Executive Secretary of the ECSR who acts on behalf of the Secretary General of the Council of Europe.[85] Complaints are registered in the order in which they are received.[86] Complaints registered are immediately published on the Council of Europe website.[87]

(ii) Examination of the Complaint by the ECSR

First, it needs to be highlighted that during all proceedings under the CCPP, the ECSR acts in its composition as foreseen by Articles 25 and 26 of the Charter, namely with the participation of an ILO representative.[88]

[83] In concrete terms this means: Arts 1–19 of Pt II 1961 Charter, Arts 1–4 of Pt II 1988 Additional Protocol and Arts 1–31 of Pt II and Art E (on non-discrimination) of Pt V 1996 RESC. If further protocols to the Charter should be adopted in future, they must contain a provision specifying that the CCPP also applies to the articles of those further protocols that have been accepted.

[84] According to Quin (n 4), a state that was Party to the 1961 Charter and which has ratified the CCPP and which later proceeds to ratify the 1996 Charter is considered bound by the CCPP with respect to the obligations it undertakes under the 1996 Charter. A state that had not previously ratified the CCPP might make a declaration upon the ratification of the 1996 Charter that it will be also bound by the CCPP with respect to the 1996 Charter.

[85] r 23 ECSR Rules of Procedure. According to Art 5 CCPP, the complaint shall be addressed to the Secretary General who shall acknowledge receipt of it, notify it to the Contracting Party concerned and immediately transmit it to the ECSR.

[86] r 26 ECSR Rules of Procedure.

[87] The use of the adverb 'immediately' underlines one of the advantages of the new procedure, which is its rapidity. During the whole procedure, and to ensure the timely handling of the complaint, it is the role of the ECSR President to set time limits to provide observations and additional information by the different parties involved in the complaint procedure. He/she may even—especially in order to ensure that complaints are dealt with within a reasonable time—decide to convene additional sessions of the ECSR (r 28 ECSR Rules of Procedure).

[88] Explanatory report to Art 5 CCPP.

The examination of the complaint by the ECSR consists of a two-stage procedure, whereby the ECSR will first judge on the admissibility of the complaint and second, if found admissible, on the merits of the complaint. But the ECSR may also decide to join both stages for a decision on the admissibility and the merits at the same time (see below).[89] The ECSR will deal with the complaints in the order in which they become ready for examination, although it may decide to give precedence to a particular complaint.[90]

(iii) Decision on Admissibility

Before the ECSR decides on admissibility, the President may ask the respondent state for written observations, within a time limit that he or she decides, on the admissibility of the complaint. If the President considers it appropriate, to ensure that complaints are processed within a reasonable time, he or she may, on the Rapporteur's proposal, ask the respondent state to make written submissions on the merits of the case, on the assumption that the complaint will be declared admissible, at the same time as it makes its observations on the admissibility of the complaint. The President may also ask the organisation that lodged the complaint to respond, on the same conditions, to the observations made by the respondent state.[91]

Next to all requirements mentioned above, the ECSR will also assess, if the complainant is a national trade union or employer organisation, whether the organisation is representative within the meaning of the collective complaints procedure and, if the complainant is an international or national NGO, whether the NGO has a particular competence in relation to the matter at stake in the complaint. It must furthermore take account of the fact that in the course of the negotiations on the CCP within the Charte-Rel Committee the following was agreed: (i) a complaint may be declared admissible even if a similar case has already been submitted to another national or international body; (ii) the fact that the substance of a complaint has been examined as part of the 'normal' government reports procedure does not in itself constitute an impediment to the complaint's admissibility;[92] and (iii) because of their 'collective' nature, complaints may only raise questions concerning non-compliance of a state's law or practice with one of the provisions of the Charter. Individual situations may not be submitted.[93] Also, the fact that a complaint relates to a claim already

[89] See eg ECSR, Decision on admissibility and the merits, 3 July 2013, *Swedish Trade Union Confederation (LO) and Swedish Confederation of Professional Employees (TCO) v Sweden*, Collective Complaint No 85/2012.

[90] r 26 ECSR Rules of Procedure.

[91] r 29§1 ECSR Rules of Procedure.

[92] See reasoning in the decision on admissibility in *ICJ v Portugal*, Collective Complaint No 1/1999 and Harris and Darcy (n 6) 363.

[93] Explanatory report ECSR Rules of Procedure, §31.

examined in the context of a previous complaint is not in itself a reason for inadmissibility, as the submission of new evidence during the examination of a complaint may prompt the ECSR to reassess a situation it has already examined in the context of previous complaints and, where appropriate, take decisions which may differ from the conclusions/decisions it adopted previously.

The ECSR may declare any complaint either admissible or inadmissible, without having invited the government concerned to submit observations, where it considers that the admissibility conditions are either manifestly fulfilled or manifestly unfulfilled.[94] Although nothing is provided in the CCPP or ECSR Rules of Procedure, nothing hinders the ECSR from deciding in one go both the admissibility and the merits of the complaint.

The ECSR's decision on the admissibility of the complaint shall be accompanied by reasons and be signed by the President, the Rapporteur and the Executive Secretary. Each member of the ECSR may express a separate opinion, concurring or dissenting, which shall be joined to the ECSR's decision. The ECSR's decision on the admissibility of the complaint shall be notified to the complainant organisation and to the respondent state and will be transmitted to the Contracting Parties that have ratified the CCPP. The decision shall be made public via the website of the Council of Europe. The publication of the decision on the website of the Council of Europe will be regarded as the notification of other state parties to the ESC who have not accepted the collective complaints procedure. In respect of complaints lodged by national organisations of employers, national trade unions or non-governmental organisations, the publication of the decision on the website of the Council of Europe will be regarded as notification of the international organisations of employers or trade unions.[95] Case documents are also published on this website. Appendices that are not in electronic format may be consulted at the Secretariat.[96]

If a complaint has been found admissible but the conditions for upholding it are no longer met, the ECSR may decide to strike it from the list of pending complaints.[97]

(iv) Decision on the Merits of the Complaint

If a complaint is declared admissible, the ECSR asks the respondent state to make written submissions on the merits of the complaint within a time

[94] r 29§4 ECSR Rules of Procedure.

[95] This is in essence somewhat problematic: if state parties are informed individually, why not the international social partners? Practice, fortunately, goes rather in the other direction, as the Charter secretariat informs the international social partners as well.

[96] r 30 ECSR Rules of Procedure.

[97] r 39 ECSR Rules of Procedure.

limit that it fixes and invites the organisation that lodged the complaint to submit, on the same conditions, a response to these submissions. In the latter case, the ECSR may then invite the respondent state to submit a further response.[98]

As a form of (privileged) third-party intervention, all other state parties that have ratified the CCPP, as well as the states that have ratified the 1996 Charter and made a declaration under Article D§2, shall be invited to make comments within the same time limit to all complaints found admissible. Taking into account the key role played by the international organisations of employers and trade unions in the supervisory system, they also have the right to make observations on all collective complaints, irrespective of the complainant organisation lodging the complaint and the country it is submitted against. All observations/comments received are transmitted to the organisation that lodged the complaint and to the respondent state, which then again have a right to react.[99] Furthermore, and upon a proposal by the Rapporteur, the ECSR may invite any organisation, institution or person to submit observations, which shall be transmitted to the respondent state and to the organisation that lodged the complaint.[100]

It is up to the ECSR President, when he considers this appropriate and after consultation with the Rapporteur, to decide whether the written procedure shall be closed. Following this decision, the parties may only submit further documents with good reason.[101]

Although the procedure is, in principle, considered to be a written procedure, a hearing may be held at the request of one of the parties or on the ECSR's initiative, whereby it is up to the ECSR itself to decide whether or not to act upon a request made by one of the parties.[102] The respondent state

[98] r 31 ECSR Rules of Procedure.

[99] Art 7 CCPP and r 32 ECSR Rules of Procedure.

[100] r 32A ECSR Rules of Procedure. This occurred for the first time in *Confederazione Generale Italiana del Lavoro (CGIL) v Italy*, Collective Complaint No 91/2013 and appears to be somewhat problematic as this new rule figures in the ECSR Rules of Procedure but has no legal basis in the CCPP itself. Prouvez regretted that the possibility of providing observations is not offered to international and national NGOs when the complaint is presented by international or national organisations of employees or employers, and hoped that the ECSR would nevertheless accept observations from such NGOs that take the initiative. For her, this would thus be in line with the considerable evolution over the years of the ECtHR's receptiveness to third-party interventions whereby the ECtHR accepts submissions from individuals or groups able to show that they have a discernible interest in the case and that their intervention is in the interest of the proper administration of justice (Prouvez (n 4) 39). Although in principle one could agree with this reasoning, it might also make the procedure more complex and longer and thus undermine some of the main advantages of the CCPP.

[101] r 31 ECSR Rules of Procedure.

[102] Most of the hearings organised so far took place in the phase of the decision of the merits. Although nothing is foreseen in either the CCPP or the ECSR Rules of Procedure, nothing hampers the ECSR from organising a hearing when deciding on admissibility, if considered necessary and appropriate.

and the organisation that lodged the complaint are invited to the hearing, as well as the international social partners, but only if the latter made written observations on the particular complaint. The hearing is public unless the President decides otherwise. Only the states and organisations that submitted observations in the course of the procedure (in support of the complaint or for its rejection) are invited to take part in the hearing.[103]

Following the closure of the written procedure (and the eventually hearing), the ECSR will deliberate on the decision on the merits and whether—from a legal point of view—the state concerned is considered to have committed a violation of the ESC or not.[104] The whole procedure of deliberation is confidential.[105] The ECSR's decision shall be accompanied by reasons and be signed by the President, the Rapporteur and the Executive Secretary. Any separate opinions by an ECSR member is appended to the ECSR's decision. The report containing the decision on the merits is transmitted to the parties to the procedure, who may not publish it before the expiry of a time limit of four months, and also to the CM.

On the basis of the ECSR's report, the CM shall adopt a resolution by a majority of those voting. This resolution takes account of the respondent state's declared intention to take appropriate measures to bring the situation into conformity. If the state does not indicate its intention to bring the situation into conformity, the CM shall also adopt, by a majority of two-thirds of those voting, a recommendation addressed to the state concerned.[106] The CM cannot reverse the legal assessment made by the ECSR. However, its decision (resolution or recommendation) may be based on social and economic policy considerations. In both cases, entitlement to voting shall be limited to the Contracting Parties to the Charter. At the request of the Contracting Party concerned, the CM may decide, where the report of the ECSR raises new issues, by a two-thirds majority of the Contracting Parties to the Charter (as opposed to two-thirds of the Contracting Parties that vote), to consult the GC.[107]

The ECSR's decision on the merits of the complaint shall be made public at the moment of the adoption of a resolution by the CM or, at the latest,

[103] Art 7§4 CCPP and r 33 ECSR Rules of Procedure.

[104] It is to be noted that any ESCR member who was not present at the hearing cannot participate in the deliberations on the merits of the complaint and any member who has not participated in the essential parts of the deliberations cannot vote on the decision on the merits (r 34 ECSR Rules of Procedure).

[105] r 38 ECSR Rules of Procedure and except if the ECSR President decides otherwise following r 15 ECSR Rules of Procedure.

[106] Although the wording of Art 9§1 CCPP is 'shall' and not 'may', the fact the CM has so far, with only one exception, adopted resolutions and not recommendations, can be criticised.

[107] Art 9 CCPP. On the vagueness of what is meant by 'new issues', see Harris and Darcy (n 6) 367–68. Although the Charte-Rel Committee had foreseen that the GC would not be involved in the procedure for examining complaints, the CM decided before adopting the CCPP this possibility of involving the GC. When the draft text of the CCPP was discussed

four months after the report was transmitted to the CM. This prolongation of the period of confidentiality after the adoption of the final report does not appear to be in conformity with basic requirements of 'equality of arms' (Article 6 ECHR), as it puts the government in a far better situation of political influence than that complainant organisation.[108] The decision is also published on the internet site of the Council of Europe and this will be regarded as transmission to the PACE.[109]

All documents (complaints, appendices, submissions by states and so on) are made public unless the ECSR decides otherwise, on a case-by-case basis.

(v) Follow-Up of the ECSR's Decision

In the event that the ECSR concludes that the state concerned has violated one or more provisions of the Charter, and the CM has adopted its resolution, appropriate follow-up must be ensured. ECSR decisions must be respected but are not enforceable as such in the domestic legal system, although domestic courts can abide by such a decision and even, independently, declare it invalid, or set aside domestic legislation if the ECSR has ruled that it is not in compliance with the ESC.

In line with the practice adopted for other international supervisory machinery (ECtHR, ILO supervisory bodies and so on), the state concerned is required to provide information on the measures it has taken or planned to bring the situation in conformity. This information should be included in the next report the state concerned submits under Article 21.[110] It will thus ultimately be up to the ECSR (under the reporting procedure) to determine whether the situation has been brought into compliance with the ESC or not.

(vi) Immediate Measures

Following a change in the ECSR Rules of Procedure in 2011, it is provided that as from the adoption of the decision on the admissibility of a collective complaint, or at any subsequent time during the proceedings before or after

at the CM meeting of June 1995, the UK delegation regretted this minor role for the GC and even suggested replacement of the two-thirds majority by a simple majority. To date, no such consultation has taken place. On the (envisaged) role of the GC in the CCP, see also Churchill and Khaliq (n 80) 440.

[108] On this prolongation, see also below section V.

[109] Arts 8 and 9 CCP and r 35 ECSR Rules of Procedure.

[110] The state thus may not wait until the time it would normally submit a report on the provision(s) in the complaint. However, r 40 ECSR Rules of Procedure both strengthens and weakens this requirement by declaring that the state should present in every subsequent report on the provisions concerned in the complaint the measures taken to bring the situation into conformity.

the adoption of the decision on the merits, the ECSR may, at the request of a party, or on its own initiative, indicate to the Parties any immediate measure the adoption of which seems necessary with a view to avoiding the risk of a serious irreparable injury and to ensuring effective respect for Charter rights.[111] In case of a request for immediate measures made by a complainant organisation, the request shall specify the reasons for it, the possible consequences if it is not granted, and the measures requested. The ECSR's decision on immediate measures shall be accompanied by reasons and be signed by the President, the Rapporteur and the Executive Secretary. It shall be notified to the Parties. The ECSR may request information from the respondent state on the implementation of the immediate measures.[112]

D. Strengthening the Charter and Its Supervisory Procedures/Bodies: Suggestions for the Way Forward

As with any other human rights instruments, the impact of the Charter depends mainly on two things: first, the rights it entails and that need to be protected/implemented, and secondly, the way in which implementation is monitored by the respective bodies/procedures.

As for the rights entailed in the Charter, over time several initiatives have been taken to increase the number of rights and/or enlarge/adapt the language and coverage of the rights as enshrined in the 1961 Charter. Particular reference can be made to the additional/adapted rights integrated in the 1988 Additional Protocol and the 1996 Charter.[113] Although the Charter already forms the most comprehensive compilation of fundamental social rights, at least within the European context, any 'Charter relaunch process' should grasp the opportunity to add and/or adapt existing rights to the (rapidly) changing world of work in particular and societal developments

[111] See, for instance, ECSR Decisions on immediate measures, 25 October 2013 in relation to *European Federation of National Organisations working with the Homeless (FEANTSA) v The Netherlands*, Collective Complaint No 86/2012 and *Conference of European Churches (CEC) v The Netherlands*, Collective Complaint No 90/2013.

[112] r 36 ECSR Rules of Procedure. For examples of ECSR decisions on immediate measures, see decisions on immediate measures of 25 October 2013 in relation to Collective Complaints No 86/2012 and No 90/2013, both against the Netherlands.

[113] The Additional Protocol of 1998 extended the social and economic rights guaranteed by the European Social Charter which were later incorporated in the 1996 Charter (Arts 20–23). These were later complemented by seven new rights (Arts 24–31), such as protection in case of termination of employment and against sexual harassment in the workplace and other forms of harassment; and rights of workers' representatives in undertakings (see the respective contributions in this volume).

in general.[114] Recognising, however, that such integration of new/adapted rights into a human rights instrument is often a long and politically sensitive process (especially in times of economic crisis),[115] an intermediate solution is of course that at least the main monitoring bodies, like the ECSR, take these societal developments into consideration ('living instrument' doctrine) in the establishment or fine-tuning of their case law.

As for the second strand—the reform of monitoring procedures/bodies—the 1991 Turin Protocol and the 1995 CCPP are milestone attempts to increase their effectiveness and enhance the Charter's impact and visibility. In addition, as already described, over time several formal and informal changes have been introduced in the working methods of the main supervisory bodies, such as the ECSR and GC, in order to render their work and impact more efficient and effective. Although in particular both protocols led to significant progress in this regard, experience shows there is still room for improvement.

With the twentieth anniversary of the 1996 Charter in 2016 on our doorstep, the strengthening of the Charter (monitoring procedures) is thus rightly a key concern and priority in both the second mandate of the Council of Europe's Secretary General Thorbjørn Jagland and the derived 'Turin Process', started by a high-level conference on the European Social Charter in Turin on 17–18 October 2014.[116]

[114] Over time the ETUC has also made proposals not only to extend the ECHR by one or more protocols dealing with social rights, but also to:

- extend the coverage of the Charter to all nationals of third countries that are not members of the Council of Europe (or have not yet ratified the Charter) provided they are legally residing in one of the member states of the Council of Europe;
- introduce progressively a series of new rights, such as (1) entitlement to time off for continuing vocational training throughout working life, (2) consumer rights, (3) a quality environment and (4) non-discriminatory access to essential services (distribution of water, gas, electricity etc); and
- endow some rights with a transnational character, in particular (1) the right of association and collective action, (2) information and consultation rights of workers in multinational groups, (3) rights of consumers in relation to health and safety and (4) right to a quality environment. (G Fonteneau, 'European trade unionism and the European social charter', in R Blanpain (ed), *The Council of Europe and the social challenges of the XXIst Century* (Deventer, Kluwer, 2001) 245; E Gabaglio, G Fonteneau and K Lörcher, 'Der Europäische Gewerkschaftsbund zu Europäischen Sozialcharta: Errungenschaften, Defizite und Vorschläge zur Verbesserung' (September 1997) XLV *Arbeit und Recht* 345).

On the extension of the ECHR with certain fundamental social rights, see also PACE Recommendation 1415 (1999), adopted on 23 June 1999.

[115] See for instance the two (failed) attempts in 2004 and 2005 to add an Art 32 on health care and to have an Additional Protocol to the Charter on the right to higher education.

[116] See Nicoletti (n 2) for the deliberations and interventions at this conference, which was followed up by a second so-called 'Brussels Conference' on the future of the protection of social rights in Europe, 12–13 February 2015 in Brussels (Belgian Chairmanship of the Council of Europe, Turin Process, Brussels Document on the Future of the Protection of Social Rights in Europe, 12–13 February 2015. All relevant documents relating to both conferences can be

As a (small) contribution to this important exercise, an overview of the panoply of ideas on improving the system proposed over time by key stakeholders (for example, Council of Europe (Charter) bodies, social partners), as well as academics, is provided below, structured around the bodies and procedures as already described. Whereas some of these ideas are relatively easy to implement (and mainly depend on political will rather than intrusive treaty reforms), others may seem more utopian. However, they are no less valuable in light of current ongoing reform debates.

(i) (A la Carte) Ratification of Instruments

The impact of the Charter stands or falls with ratification. A key demand/priority, repeatedly raised or supported also by the ETUC, thus remains to increase ratification.[117]

This demand includes in particular:

— the four countries that have not ratified either the 1961 or 1996 Charter and those countries that have ratified the 1961 Charter but not yet the 1996 Charter should ratify the 1996 Charter as soon as possible, thereby accepting the highest proportion of provisions;[118]

found on the Charter website.) In the meantime, a so-called 'Turin Conference 2' took place 17–18 March 2016. The Turin process has four main axes: (i) promotion of ratification of the Charter (provisions) and the CCPP, (ii) upgrading the Charter inside the Council of Europe, (iii) enhancing parliamentary input (both national parliaments and the PACE) and (iv) creating more synergies between EU and Charter law. 'Turin Conference 2' focused mainly on the parliamentary dimension.

[117] Concerning appeals from various stakeholders or academics see, among others: several interventions at the high-level conference in Turin in Nicoletti (n 2), Brussels Document (n 116) 6–7; PACE Resolution 1792 (2011) §§4.1–4.2 and Recommendation 1958 (2011) of 28 January 2011 §§4.3–4.4. As for ETUC texts, see eg ETUC Statement on the occasion of the 3rd Summit of Heads of State and Government, Brussels, 15–16 March 2005; ETUC press release, 'ETUC congratulates the Council of Europe on the 10th anniversary of the Revised Social Charter', Brussels, 4 May 2006; ETUC press release, 'The ETUC calls for effective recognition within the Council of Europe', Brussels, 30 March 2012; and ETUC Declaration on the 50th anniversary of the European Social Charter, Brussels, adopted by the ETUC Executive Committee on 19–20 October 2011. On the academic side, see eg Churchill and Khaliq (n 80) 451–52; L Jimena-Quesada (2011) 'The European Committee of Social Rights and the collective complaints procedure: present and future', in N Johanson and M Mikkola (eds), *Reform of the European social charter. Seminar presentations delivered 8 and 9 February 2011 at the House of the Estates and the University of Helsinki* (Porvoo, Bookwell, 2011) 12; and Samuel (n 72) 144.

[118] In any case, although legally still possible, the system should no longer allow ratification of the 1961 Charter and the 1998 Additional Protocol, but only the 1996 Charter (M Mikkola, "Need to strengthen the monitoring mechanisms of social human rights, in Johanson and Mikkola, (n 1) 32.

— the many countries that have not yet accepted all provisions of the 1996 Charter should accept as many provisions as possible;[119]
— the four countries that have still not ratified the 1991 Turin Protocol should do so as soon as possible in order to allow its full implementation;
— the many countries that have not yet ratified the CCPP should do so as soon as possible.

In that sense—but often forgotten in this framework, particularly given the recent reforms whereby the GC is now also monitoring application of the European Code of Social Security—increased ratification of the (revised) Code should also be ensured because there is a close relationship between the (more detailed and explicit) rights in the Code and several articles of the Charter.

Another reason why the Charter is considered to be 'a faint shadow' of the ECHR is its 'à la carte acceptance' of provisions.[120] Several scholars consider this 'cherry-picking' of rights by governments to be unreasonable and unacceptable, and that it should be abolished.[121] Others, such as De Schutter, are more doubtful whether the à la carte approach has been an obstacle to the adequate functioning of the system, and propose, as a transition to full acceptance, a more systematic use of Article 22 reports, which could attenuate the difference between the accepted and non-accepted provisions and lead to more ratification.[122] Another alternative, if full abolition of the à la carte system is not possible in the short term, has been suggested by the ETUC, and involves making binding at least all hard-core Articles of the Charter.[123]

[119] This includes lifting any national reservations and opt-outs concerning specific articles of the Charter (see Committee on Social Affairs, Health and Sustainable Development, Sub-Committee on the European Social Charter, Declaration in the High-level Conference on the European Social Charter on behalf of the Parliamentary Assembly of the Council of Europe, Turin, 17–18 October 2014, in M Nicoletti (n 2) Appendix 3a).

[120] De Boer-Buquicchio (n 4) 5.

[121] For example, Mikkola (n 118) 32; C Mac Amhlaigh and M Nedelka, 'Forty Years of the European Social Charter: Celebration or Commiseration?' (2001) 1 *University College Dublin Labour Review* 76 (who call it 'an idiosyncrasy' of the Charter); V Mantouvalou and P Voyatzis, 'The Council of Europe and the protection of Human Rights: a system in need of reform', in Joseph and McBeth (eds), *Research Handbook on International Human Rights Law* (Cheltenham, Edward Elgar, 2010) 326–52; and M Schlachter, 'The European Social Charter: could it contribute to a more Social Europe?', in N Countouris and M Freedland, *Resocialising Europe in a time of crisis* (Cambridge, CUP, 2013) 105–17, who refers to a 'cafeteria system of rights'.

[122] O De Schutter, 'Chapter 1. The two lives of the European Social Charter', in O De Schutter, *La Charte sociale européenne: une constitution sociale pour l'Europe* (Bruxelles, Bruylant, 2010) 116–17.

[123] G Fonteneau, 'European trade unionism and the European social charter', in Blanpain (n 114) 244; and E Gabaglio et al (n 114) 346, who went even further, requiring that any new state joining the Council of Europe should automatically be bound not only by the ECHR but also by the Charter.

All this leaves aside the question of EU accession to the Charter subsequent to its adhesion to the ECHR.[124]

(ii) ECSR

Although the ECSR is now acting as a quasi-judicial body judging the conformity of national law and practice and thereby using increasingly judicial methods,[125] several proposals might further enhance its judicial status and visibility and the impact of its conclusions/decisions.

In the first instance there is implementing the only provision of the 1991 Turin Protocol that is still not being applied in practice, namely the election of ECSR members by the PACE, as is the case for the judges of the ECtHR.[126] Mikkola also suggests ensuring the impartiality of choice of ECSR members by means of a hearing process, whereby selection could be by an independent expert panel, as is often done for selection of judges.[127] As long as the Turin Protocol is not in force, one could also consider alternatives, such as the PACE proposal that the CM should adopt, as on previous occasions to ensure application of other provisions of the Protocol, a unanimous decision to ensure that the PACE can fully discharge its appointed function in the Charter's monitoring machinery;[128] or from the ECSR that the CM and PACE 'could initiate a dialogue with a view to developing a procedure which would involve the two organs of the Council of Europe jointly in the process of electing members of the ECSR'.[129] Moving on to

[124] On how this could enhance the legitimacy of the Charter, see eg T Aubert-Monpeyssen, 'Une justicibilité accrue de la Charte sociale européene' (2011) *Journal de Droit Européen* 166. See also O De Schutter in this volume.

[125] Jimena-Quesada (n 117) confirms that the ECSR has constantly tried to reinforce its judicial profile by its interpretative methods and techniques and align them with those of the ECtHR and by basing its case law on that of the ECtHR (ibid 10). See also on this L Jimena-Quesada, 'Chapitre 1: Profils juridictionnels et effectivité des decisions du Comité Européen des Droits Sociaux', in D Roman, *La justicibilité des droits sociaux: vecteurs et résistances, Actes du colloque tenu au Collège de France, Paris, 25–26 May 2011* (Paris, Editions A Pedone, 2011) 165–77.

[126] De Boer-Buquicchio (n 4) 6; Jimena-Quesada (n 117) 12; JP Marguenaud and J Mouly, 'Le Comité européen des droits sociaux, un laboratoire d'idées sociales méconnu' (2011) 3 *Revue du Droit Public* 685; Samuel (n 72) 144 and several interventions at the high-level conference in Turin in October 2014 (see Nicoletti (n 2)).

[127] Mikkola (n 118) 32; also note regarding 'selection' PACE Recommendation 2012 (2013) and Resolution 1923 (2013) on 'reinforcing the selection processes for experts of key Council of Europe Human Rights monitoring mechanisms'. In its comments to this recommendations, the ECSR argued that, while welcoming the general aims and objectives of these texts, it might be sufficient if the CM apply the provisions of the Turin Protocol. (Appendix 8 Observations by the Committee on texts submitted by the Committee of Ministers, in ECSR (2014) Activity Report 2013, Strasbourg: Council of Europe, pp 183–84.)

[128] PACE Recommendation 1958 (2011) of 28 January 2011, §4.5.

[129] ECSR (2014, n 127), pp 183–84.

election and selection, the idea has been raised of increasing the number of ECSR members.[130]

Other proposals regarding the working methods and status of the ECSR, such as providing the members (or at least those of the ECSR Bureau) permanent or semi-permanent status, might be worth considering.[131] Also, one could envisage the possibility of replacing the system of a six-year term, renewable once, by a nine-year non-renewable term, similar to that established by Protocol No 14 to the ECtHR.[132]

Another solution to upgrade the judicial status of the ECSR would be to change its name to the 'Social Rights Court' or the 'European Social Rights Chamber',[133] which brings us to the debate on the merger or at least creation of links or 'passerelles' between the ECSR (and in particular the collective complaints procedure) and the ECtHR. Whereas some people, based on the indivisibility of rights, consider the best solution to be that, ultimately, all violations of fundamental rights, including social rights, should be dealt with by a single supervisory body, namely the ECtHR,[134] we tend to agree with M Pellonpää that, for various reasons, it would not be a good idea to entrust social rights protection entirely to the ECtHR, for instance by merging the Charter into the ECHR structure.[135] Nevertheless it should be explored how institutional and procedural reforms could, on one hand, enhance judicial treatment of Charter rights (by the (reformed) ECSR) and on the other hand, alleviate the workload of the ECtHR in particular when it deals with social rights.[136]

[130] ECSR, 'Some proposals concerning the role and status of the European Committee of Social Rights on the occasion of the High-level Conference in Turin, Italy, 17–18 Turin 2014', in Nicoletti (n 2), Appendix 3c and ANESC, 'Positions and Proposals of the Academic Network on the European Social Charter and Social Rights, High-level Conference on the European Social Charter, Turin, 17–18 October 2014', in Nicoletti (n 2) Appendix 3d and e, and Brussels Document (n 116) 8.

[131] Jimena-Quesada (n 117) 9; J Petman (n 4) 42.

[132] Jimena-Quesada (n 117) 12.

[133] Marguenaud and Mouly (n 126) 685.

[134] Mikkola (n 118) 31.

[135] M Pellonpää, 'Social Rights and the European Court of Human Rights', in N Johanson and M Mikkola, *Reform of the European social charter. Seminar presentations delivered 8 and 9 February 2011 at the House of the Estates and the University of Helsinki* (Porvoo, Bookwell, 2011) 53–54.

[136] For ideas and proposals, see eg de Boer-Buquicchio (n 4) 6; F Kandji-Kombé, 'Chapitre 6 Charte sociale européene et Convention Européenne des droits de l'homme: quelles perspective pour les 10 prochaines années?', in O De Schutter, *The European Social Charter: a social constitution for Europe = La Charte sociale européenne: une constitution sociale pour l'Europe* (Bruxelles, Bruylant, 2010) 147–65; PACE Recommendation 1354 (1998); Harris and Darcy (n 6) 373–74; T Novitz, 'Remedies for Violation of Social Rights within the Council of Europe: The significant Absence of a Court', in C Kilpatrick, T Novitz and P Skidmore (eds), *The Future of Remedies in Europe* (Oxford, Hart Publishing, 2002) and Nicoletti (n 2), eg p 20 §52.

Whereas these institutional and procedural reforms might necessitate long and politically sensitive discussions, intermediate solutions—at least to enhance the authoritative status of the ECSR in dealing with fundamental social rights violations—might include allowing the Commissioner of Human Rights to refer questions to the ECSR or to seek advisory opinions,[137] or, in a similar vein, to provide the same possibility to national (or even European) judges and legislators. Another option would be to allow the redirection of cases concerning social rights that have been declared inadmissible by the ECtHR to the ECSR, for example, by suggesting to the applicants that their application could be transformed into a collective complaint.[138]

(iii) The Governmental Committee

Although the GC over time has, via its rules of procedures, introduced the possibility of voting on warnings and even recommendations for states in non-conformity with a Charter article (not being 'treaty-based', however, sanctions would not be binding, which represents a weakness), it has become increasingly reluctant to apply its own working methods and has preferred to send '(very) strong messages' to such states, even in cases of long-standing non-conformity, lasting 20 years or more (see above). This has increasingly diminished the credibility of GC decisions in particular, and of the GC in general. Re-establishing the voting system and having the GC vote automatically when certain criteria are met (for example, repeated conclusion of non-conformity, clearly no change during reference period and/or willingness to change in future) might already be helpful.

In that sense, and given the very much appreciated role of the social partners (in particular the ETUC) in driving the GC debates and decisions,[139] their lack of voting rights in the GC might also be something to reconsider. This might overcome the many situations in which for instance the ETUC called for a vote on a warning or recommendation, but no vote took place because their call was not supported by at least one governmental delegate.

It might also be worth reviving the 'old' idea, raised when drafting the 1991 Turin Protocol, to provide a full tripartite element in the GC (similar to ILO committees); amendments were made in that sense, but not adopted.[140]

(iv) PACE

Although it attaches great importance to the Charter, the role of PACE should be enhanced as it is indeed 'an ideal forum to raise awareness and

[137] C O'Cinneide, 'Chapter 7 social rights and the European Social Charter—new challenges and fresh opportunities', in De Schutter (n 136).

[138] For example, Mikkola (n 134).

[139] Coyer (n 1), p 36.

[140] Harris and Darcy (n 6).

debate on social rights, [and] could intensify its considerations of the Charter and the ECSR case law when adopting recommendations or organising promotional activities of the Charter'. PACE could even provide a route whereby members could follow up ECSR decisions through the Assembly's monitoring procedures and parliamentary questions.[141]

In any case, the fact that enhancing the parliamentary dimension (be it national parliaments and/or PACE itself and directly or indirectly via the) forms one of the priority strands of the Turin process can only be welcomed.

(v) The Committee of Ministers

Although several scholars consider it undesirable that a political body should be involved in an independent quasi-judicial process,[142] others consider that the CM should play a more active political role in the monitoring system by supervising the implementation of the ECSR decisions and this preferably in a manner that approaches the role the CM plays within the framework of implementing ECtHR judgments.[143]

Suggestions to bar the CM completely from (some) supervisory mechanisms may (at least for the moment) be going too far,[144] but it would be a step forward if the CM played its role at the fullest at the end of both procedures. In that sense, some 'practical' deficiencies might need to be overcome. For instance, to bar the defendant state from taking part in the CM's proceedings and voting (which makes it party and judge in its own case), as well as to require a simple majority (as foreseen at one point in the drafting of the 1991 Protocol) rather than a two-thirds majority in a vote on non-conformity.[145] Also the fact that, according to the explanatory report to the CCPP, the CM can base its decision on considerations of social and economic policy (and even consult the GC in certain cases) should be revisited, if only because the possibility of taking into account social and economic policy considerations is not provided for in the Protocol.[146] It also

[141] Gabaglio et al (n 114) 349; Jimena-Quesada (n 117) 13; and O'Cinneide (n 137) 177.

[142] For example, Mikkola (n 118) 42; Harris and Darcy (n 6) 375; Churchill and Khaliq (n 80) 447.

[143] Jimena-Quesada (n 117) 13.

[144] For example, Churchill and Khaliq (n 80) 452, who seem to suggest removal of the CM from the CCPP, as they consider the CM's role one of the 'most obvious defects' of the latter.

[145] For example, Harris and Darcy (n 6) 350, who also regret that the CM Decision of June 1995, adopted at its 541st Meeting, made it more difficult to adopt recommendations by deciding that it had to be done by a two-thirds majority of the Contracting Parties casting a vote (with abstentions not counting as a vote cast) and a majority of the Contracting Parties to the Charter. In a similar sense see also Prouvez (n 4) 41: in particular the CM Decision of June 1995 suggests to her 'that an unwelcome distinction persists between on the one hand civil and political rights and economic and social rights on the other hand'. See also Gabaglio et al (n 114) 346.

[146] Prouvez (n 4) 41 and, in a similar vein, T Novitz, 'Are social rights necessarily collective rights? A critical analysis of the Collective Complaints Protocol to the European Social Charter' (2002) 1 *European Human Rights Law Review* 50.

seems a little makeshift that the procedures do not foresee a right for the ECSR to be heard in the proceedings before the CM.[147]

Another serious weaknesses in the mechanism that needs remedying is the fact that CM decisions are not legally binding and, for instance, states that are not in conformity cannot be fined or otherwise forced to comply and are not even contractually obliged to change national legislation following a recommendation.[148]

One can thus agree with Petman that better working relationships with and working methods in the CM need to be found, so that, for instance, the important ECSR decisions that, in principle, the CM has to voice to the general public are properly channelled and at least not 'muffled', as the case may be.[149] Also the relationship with the social partners should be revisited by re-establishing the previous Liaison Committee between the CM and social partners (which stopped meeting in 2002).

In any case the CM should ensure the raising of the political profile of the Charter in its activities and campaign for further ratification (but also monitor such campaigns at regular intervals).[150]

(vi) Reporting

On the positive side, one might agree with O De Schutter that the current system of thematic reporting brings a welcome clarity and has the additional advantage that by the comparison of all reports covering the same areas, the ECSR gains a better understanding of emerging problems and tendencies and is able to compare states' approaches to new problems in a much more systematic way.[151]

However, even under this new approach, many weaknesses already existing under the 'old reporting system' persist, and need to be remedied. First, there is the problem of states submitting their reports with a serious delay, or even not at all, which makes it difficult for the ECSR to draw conclusions from them. At least the GC could consider re-establishing the informal working method it applied previously and vote automatically in such cases on (preferably) a recommendation to such states (as a kind of sanction for 'obstruction of justice). Second, when submitting their reports, states should be reminded to improve their quality and to reply more specifically to the questions and cases of non-conformity raised by the ECSR in its conclusions rather than providing masses of information, which rather confuses than

[147] Cullen (n 80) 6.

[148] For example, Harris and Darcy (n 6) 376; Mac Amhlaigh and Nedelka (n 121) 90; Novitz (n 146) 105–17 and Schlachter (n 121) 109.

[149] Petman (n 4), p 42.

[150] ETUC (2011, n 117).

[151] De Schutter (n 136) 18–19.

clarifies the situation.[152] It might thus be helpful if the ECSR, in turn, could also provide more detail and rigorous justification for its decisions in its conclusions, also because the rigour of its deliberations is not always apparent in the text of conclusions (although this is often due to the the Secretariat's lack of sufficient resources).[153] It would thus make sense to have more intermediary meetings between the ECSR and governments and social partners, in particular on longstanding cases of non-conformity, to clarify the situation and problems on both sides (on top of the ECSR's meetings with governments within the framework of Article 22 reports on non-accepted provisions).

Finally, there is still the problem of the intervals of reporting. Although the new thematic reporting takes place basically every four years, but allows for simplified reports every two years (see above), the situation is probably not in conformity with Article 21 and, in any event, far from ideal. This is because of the new working methods between ECSR and the GC, whereby the latter only orally discusses cases of non-conformity selected by the ECSR. This thus still allows for certain cases to be discussed at the earliest opportunity only after four years, or even later. This situation is not acceptable, and needs to be remedied. This more targeted or concentrated examination of cases appears so far not to have led to politically more incisive conclusions or a more rational use of the limited resources of the ECSR and its Secretariat, as some had hoped.[154] And although the simplified reports were construed as a kind of concession to those countries that have adopted the CCPP, it has apparently not (yet) diminished the workload of such countries (see also above).

Whereas some are calling strongly for a transition from reporting to a complaints procedure,[155] we are more inclined to the reasoning of M Pellonpää that such a replacement would not necessarily promote the development of social rights in Europe in the most desirable manner, also because the Charter has a kind of 'promotional' aspect, for which reporting and ensuing dialogue are an appropriate method of supervision.[156] This transition would also run counter to the spirit of both mechanisms. The Explanatory Report to the CCPP states that the reporting system is to remain the 'basic mechanism' for enforcement, whereas the CCPP is designed to 'increase the efficiency of the existing machinery' and to be seen

[152] Gabaglio et al (n 114) 347; ETUC (2011, n 117).

[153] Gabaglio et al (n 114) 347–48; O'Cinneide (n 137) 175–76.

[154] De Boer-Buquicchio (n 4) 6.

[155] Mikkola (n 134) 31–32; he in particular considers that if individual complaints were admissible under the CCPP, the reporting system could even be given up altogether.

[156] M Pellonpää, 'Social Rights and the European Court of Human Rights', in N Johanson and M Mikkola, *Reform of the European social charter. Seminar presentations delivered 8 and 9 February 2011 at the House of the Estates and the University of Helsinki* (Porvoo, Bookwell, 2011) 53–54.

as a complement to the pre-existing system.[157] It would be better to try to find ways of making the systems mutually reinforcing.[158]

One should also reflect, within this framework, on how to enhance the role of the social partners (and in particular the trade unions) in this reporting procedure. There is definitely a need for this because, to date, observations by trade unions have been limited. (Renewed) trade union interest in this procedure and thus the Charter could be triggered by considering the provision of (i) (active) participation of national social partners in meetings with states on non-accepted provisions, and/or (ii) the introduction/revival of the participation of national and European social partners in meetings between ECSR and governments, held within the framework of the normal reporting procedure if the ECSR needs more clarification on reports. Moreover, the interpretative and guiding role of the ECSR could be much strengthened if it adopted systematic 'General comments' on Charter provisions instead of (more dispersed) 'Statements of interpretation', which would also be in line with the practice of relevant UN Committees (and—at least to a certain extent—with the General Surveys of the ILO CEACR).

(vii) CCPP

The first key priority is to improve the visibility of the collective complaints mechanism, particularly in terms of better publicity and execution of the decisions adopted by the ECSR. This may be achieved, first, by abolishing the deadline of four months to make public an ECSR decision on the merits,[159] and second by having the CM play a more active political role in the monitoring system through supervising the implementation of ECSR decisions, preferably in a similar manner to the role the CM plays in the execution of ECtHR judgments.[160]

Other proposals to enhance the use and effectiveness of the CCPP include ensuring an increase in the number of states that allow national NGOs to submit a complaint,[161] to give to complainants in national organisations the possibility of compensation for their legal costs.[162]

157 Explanatory Report to the CCPP §§1–2.

158 It might be worth looking at UN practices in relation to reporting systems in the Covenants/Conventions, supplemented by Optional Protocols for complaints/representations/communications.

159 Jimena-Quesada considers this term unreasonable, in particular when considering that all documents constituting the file of each case are almost immediately published on the Charter website (Jimena-Quesada (n 117) 13). See also the proposal by the ECSR itself in M Nicoletti, 'Appendix 3c and ANESC', in Nicoletti (n 2) Appendix 3d and e.

160 ibid.

161 Churchill and Khaliq (n 80) 435; ANESC in Nicoletti (n 2) Appendix 3d and e.

162 Mikkola (n 134) 32.

Other interesting proposals to consider include allowing for third-party interventions (*amicus curia*), in particular by important Council of Europe players, such as PACE or the Commissioner for Human Rights,[163] or for instance UN bodies (for example, Office of the High Commissioner for Refugees).[164] In principle, such third-party intervention is possible as it was introduced in 2010 in the ECSR Rules of Procedures via rule 32A 'Requests for observations'. However, this option is not yet widely used.

Another frequently recurring proposal is to consider allowing for individual applications also because allowing such individual applications on social rights might avoid a multitude of individual applications to the ECtHR.[165]

(viii) The Secretariat

Over the years, the quality and quantity of ECSR conclusions and decisions would have not been so impressive if crucial work had not been done by the members of the so-called 'Secretariat', the administration responsible for all work on the Charter. Distilling the enormous volume of information received from states in reporting into (working) documents for the ECSR, GC and CM is very time-consuming and meticulous work.

There have thus rightly been repeated calls to improve the status of the staff of the Secretariat, in both qualitative and quantitative terms, as well as to ensure an appropriate budget.[166]

(ix) Promotion and Capacity-Building

As many have already pointed out, ensuring the effectiveness of the social rights laid down in the Charter is a genuine shared responsibility of players at the Council of Europe level and at national level (such as judges, MPs, government officials, local and regional authorities, social partners and civil society organisations, mediators, labour inspectors, national human rights institutions and structures, academics and higher education institutions—for example, by encouraging students to write PhDs on the Charter—legal practitioners, journalists and the public at large). Their call for (increased)

[163] PACE Resolution 1792 (2011) §6.4 and Recommendation 1958(2011) of 28 January 2011 §4.6.

[164] Jimena-Quesada (n 117) 8.

[165] For example, Jimena-Quesada (n 117) 12–13; Mikkola (n 134) 31–32; Novitz (n 146) and Marguenaud and Mouly (n 126).

[166] Gabaglio et al (n 114) 348–49; Jimena-Quesada (n 117) 11; Mikkola (n 134) 31; Petman (n 4) 42; L Jimena-Quesada (2011, n 117), 9; Nicoletti (n 2) 11; and Brussels Document (n 116) 8.

promotion of and capacity-building with regard to the Charter and the (use of the) monitoring procedures can only be underlined and fully supported.[167]

Particular attention should thereby be given to initiatives that can enhance the use of the Charter by judges (to ensure more references to the Charter in their judgments),[168] national legislators (to ensure that when drafting national or regional legislation, principles and rights enshrined in the Charter are taken into consideration) and national social partners and NGOs (as they also have a particular role in the monitoring system).[169] But trade unions also can make legal use of the Charter and its monitoring procedures, which also clearly needs to be enhanced.[170]

V. CONCLUSIONS

Although one might indeed partially agree with O'Cinneide that 'it would be artificial, distorted and erroneous to present the Charter process as an example of a great triumph for human rights mechanisms and it would be a considerable exaggeration to describe the revitalisation process as an unqualified success',[171] this chapter has tried to show that, nevertheless, considerable progress has been made—albeit on a trial and error basis—to render the Charter and its supervisory mechanisms more effective and efficient. Many challenges remain, but proposals have been made to overcome them and it is welcome that many are included in the 'Action Plan for the Turin Process'.[172]

[167] CM Declaration on the 50th anniversary of the European Social Charter, adopted on 12 October 2011 at the 1123rd meeting of the Ministers' Deputies; PACE Resolution 1792 (2011) §§5–6; Brillat (n 4) 46–52; Jimena-Quesada (n 117) 7; Petman (n 4), p 43; Samuel (n 72) 144; and Nicoletti (n 2), eg p 27, §75; ETUC (2005, n 117) §5.

[168] See in that sense, ETUC (2005, n 117) §5, ANESC, in Nicoletti (n 2) Annex 3d and e; and Brussels Document (n 116) 7 (where the call is even extended to ensure better use of the Charter (case law) by the CJEU).

[169] See on the latter, Fonteneau, who proposed the setting up at national level of a concertation structure involving economic and social players and the relevant NGOs in active monitoring of the Charter. This should cover in particular (1) drawing up national reports to serve as a basis for the monitoring, (2) follow-up on the assessments by the monitoring bodies (conclusions, decisions, warnings, recommendations) and (3) regular examination of the pertinence of exemption from certain articles. This structure could also encompass monitoring of ILO standards and EU Directives (Fonteneau (n 114) 247). This proposal extending it to NGOs was based on an earlier ETUC proposal which limited it to a pure tripartite forum, see Gabaglio et al (n 114) 347). For different ideas on increasing national forums and debates at national level, see also Nicoletti (n 2) Appendix 2t, p 4 and Appendix 3d and e.

[170] K Lörcher, 'Chapter 10 Legal and Judicial International Avenues: The (Revised) European Social Charter', in N Bruun, K Lörcher and I Schömann (eds), *The Economic and Financial Crisis and Collective Labour Law in Europe* (Oxford, Hart Publishing, 2014) 265–94.

[171] O'Cinneide (n 137) 173.

[172] Nicoletti (n 2) 45–51.

In any case, overcoming the remaining challenges will require a major change in political opinion and a rejuvenation of political will to put—in accordance with the principle of indivisibility—social rights on the same level as civil and political rights, so that the Charter becomes more effective and has an impact comparable with that of the ECHR.[173]

Second, and again along the lines of O'Cinneide, it is not the dry text of a human rights instrument that is ultimately decisive in its success or failure, but whether it is in fact taken up and used by the various stakeholders.[174] What is required to bring this human rights instrument to life, as suggested by Anne Brasseur, President of the PACE, at the opening of the high-level conference in Turin in October 2014, is to adopt the spirit of Robert Frost's famous lines: 'Two roads diverged in a wood, and I—I took the one less travelled by, and that made all the difference'.[175]

Finally, everybody should be reminded of the words once expressed by current Secretary General of the Council of Europe Thorbjørn Jagland: 'irrespective of whether budgets are austere or not, protecting social rights is not a policy choice. It is a moral obligation.'[176] Let it be added and not forgotten that it is also a legal obligation!

[173] Mac Amlaigh and Nedelka (n 121) 82.

[174] O'Cinneide (n 137) 182–83.

[175] M Nicoletti (n 2) Appendix 2k, p 4.

[176] Appendix 10a. Speech by the Secretary General of the Council of Europe Thorbjørn Jagland at the ceremony on the occasion of the 50th anniversary of the Charter, 18 October 2011, in ECSR (2012) "European Committee of Social Rights—Activity Report 2011", Strasbourg, Council of Europe, May 2012, 111–13.

Part II*

Specific Articles

* Throughout Part II, the term 'Charter', as well as any Article without further indication, refers to the Revised European Social Charter of 1996, unless it is otherwise specified (see the Introduction for more details).

Article 1

The Right to Work

SIMON DEAKIN

Article 1—The right to work

With a view to ensuring the effective exercise of the right to work, the Parties undertake:

1. to accept as one of their primary aims and responsibilities the achievement and maintenance of as high and stable a level of employment as possible with a view to the attainment of full employment;
2. to protect effectively the right of the worker to earn his living in an occupation freely entered upon;
3. to establish or maintain free employment services for all workers;
4. to provide or promote appropriate vocational guidance, training and rehabilitation.

Appendix Part II

Article 1, paragraph 2

This provision shall not be interpreted as prohibiting or authorising any union security clause or practice.

I. INTRODUCTION

A. Context and Main Content

Can there be a legal right to work in a market economy? Many have doubted it.[1] Nevertheless, the right to work contained in Article 1 of the European Social Charter (ESC) 'protects and gives expression to the human interest

[1] See BA Hepple, 'A right work?' (1981) 10 *Industrial Law Journal* 65, 81 ('in our type of market economy, a "right to work", enforceable against the state, would be meaningless'); O O'Neill, 'The dark side of human rights' (2005) 82 *International Affairs* 427 (the 'noble lie' of social rights); J Nickel, 'Giving up on the human right to work', in V Mantouvalou, *The Right to Work* (Oxford, Hart, 2015) ch 8 (compare his earlier and more optimistic analysis,

in engaging in productive labour'.[2] Article 1 is a core right, binding on all signatory states. It is moreover, the 'cornerstone' of the Charter, a 'foundational' right which other social rights 'follow and build upon'.[3]

Even so, the content of Article 1 is not easily delineated. It is a complex provision, within which a number of different individual rights are present. These include the right to practise a freely chosen occupation or profession; the right to protection against forced labour; the right to vocational training; and the right to assistance in finding work. Article 1 also entails an acceptance by the state of responsibility for maintaining a high and stable level of employment.

Looking at these provisions as a whole, and considering how they are related to each other, it can be argued that the unifying idea in Article 1 is that of *a right to access the labour market*. This right may be distinguished from other possible meanings attributable to the right to work, such as a right to a particular job or employment, or a right to access decent work.[4] Article 1 does not go so far as protecting the right to work in either of these senses. However, it does go significantly further than simply guaranteeing the right to access the market in the minimal sense of being able to enter a chosen profession or trade, or being free to contract for the sale of labour services.

The first sense in which Article 1 goes beyond protecting the bare right to contract for work is that it protects the property right, *labour capacity*, which is at the core of the employment relationship in a market economy.[5] There cannot be a meaningful right of labour market access if the commodity, labour power, which is exchanged in the labour market setting, is not first identified and protected by the legal system. Thus the 'work' protected in Article 1 is work in the context of the wage–work bargain, in which labour power is exchanged for remuneration, broadly defined to include relationships coming under the category of independent or professional

'Is there a human right to employment?' (1980) 10 *Philosophical Forum* 149); A Bogg, 'Only fools and horses: some sceptical reflections on the right to work', in Mantouvalou, *The Right to Work* ch 9.

[2] C O'Cinneide, 'The right to work in international human rights law', in Mantouvalou (n 1) ch 6, p 99.

[3] ibid.

[4] On whether the right to work can extend to the right to a particular job, see Hepple (n 1) 76–78; J Howe, 'Why do so few employees return to their jobs? In pursuit of a right to work following unfair dismissal', in Mantouvalou (n 1) ch 14.

[5] On the idea that the employment contract consists of the sale, not of finished labour but of the labour power or capacity to work of the individual, see K Marx, *Capital*, Vol I trans E Moore and G Aveling (London, Lawrence and Wishart, 1975) ch 7; RH Coase, 'The nature of the firm' (1937) 16 *Economica* (NS) 386; H Braverman, *Labor and Monopoly Capital: The Degradation of Work in the Twentieth Century* (New York, Monthly Review Press, 1974); A Supiot, *Critique du droit du travail* (Paris, PUF, 1994) ch 1.

work involving some element of personal or economic dependence on another.[6]

Article 1 acknowledges that, in a market economy, labour power is a commodity, but in so doing it also insists that the physical person of the worker is not, hence the idea that the right to work also entails a prohibition on slavery or forced labour.[7] If labour power is to be exchanged, it must be for value; and the exchange does not entail alienation of the physical person of the worker, as opposed to the fruits of their labour. Thus, to say that Article 1 is concerned with commodification is only half the story, as it also sets a limit on what may be commodified.

A second sense in which Article 1 goes beyond a mere right to contract is that it articulates and defends a particular conception of the labour market. This is that the labour market is not a natural order that pre-exists the state, but a social institution, constituted and regulated by the legal system and other instruments of the state, including the instruments of active labour market policy and vocational training and education policy, which are referred to in the text of Article 1.[8]

A third aspect of the wide extent of Article 1 can be understood by reference to the normative goals that it expresses. Article 1 assumes that the state and the legal system constitute the labour market not in an abstract sense, but with a particular instrumental goal in mind: this is the goal of protecting and enhancing the capabilities of market actors.[9] The market is not an end in itself, but a means to an end, that is, human well-being, broadly understood. To protect and enhance human capabilities in this sense entails not

[6] This is not to suggest that Art 1 should be confined in its effects to the protection of the right to work in the context of the 'contract of employment' or other legal definition of the employment relationship, narrowly conceived. In its approach to the interpretation of Art 1, the ECSR has taken a broad view of the personal scope of the right to work, to include relationships of intermittent, precarious and highly exploitative work (see below, section II.B), and it is clear more generally that the principal beneficiaries of the obligations undertaken by states under Art 1 will often be jobseekers and applicants for work, along with others lacking regular employment (see section II.A, below). If, as suggested in the text, Art 1 applies to situations where there is some element of personal *or* economic dependence, it could in principle cover situations in which the worker provides labour services under the control of another but does not receive payment, as in the case of the volunteer worker in *X v Mid-Sussex CAB* [2012] UKSC 59. However, subject to these caveats, the view that 'work' in Art 1 refers, in its core meaning, to work in a market setting, in the context of a relationship of employment or akin to employment, seems justified in light of the content of the Article. This point is important because if 'work' is defined in this specific sense, some of the legal and philosophical objections to the coherence of the concept of the right to work—in particular, that it is not compatible with the logic of a market economy (see references in n 1 above)—lose much of their force.

[7] This is the focus of the prohibition on forced labour in Art 1§2 see below, section II.B.

[8] On the idea that the labour market is, at least in part, constituted by the state and, more specifically, by the legal system, see S Deakin and F Wilkinson, *The Law of the Labour Market: Industrialization, Employment, and Legal Evolution* (Oxford, OUP, 2005) ch 1.

[9] S Deakin and A Supiot (eds), *Capacitas; Contract Law and the Institutional Preconditions of a Market Economy* (Oxford, Hart, 2009).

just removing discrimination and other formal barriers to market access, but also ensuring that, once in employment, individuals are not subjected to conditions of employment that undermine their capacity to work, broadly understood to include their physical and mental capabilities and also their skills, vocational and educational qualifications, and professional status.[10]

Thus Article 1 assumes that work should not just be *accessible* via the labour market, but should also be *acceptable*,[11] as defined by reference to notions of what constitutes a living wage or income, or of conventional limits on the exploitation of the physical person of the worker, as expressed in health and safety laws or working time legislation. This is the sense in which Article 1 is intrinsically linked to other provisions of the ESC that set out substantive social rights in the context of the employment relationship. Article 1 also sets limits on conditionality in the payment of social security benefits that are intended as replacements for wage income during periods of sickness or unemployment: requiring benefit recipients to take up offers of employment that do not meet certain minimum standards in relation to wages and working conditions can be seen as undermining the property rights that workers have in their labour capacity. Article 1 is thereby linked to the provisions of the Charter governing the right to social security.[12]

A controversial question, which applies to discussions of the right to work in general, as well as to the specific interpretation of Article 1, is how far a right to work implies a duty to work, understood as a duty to take up paid employment or otherwise enter into commodified work relations through the exercise of a profession or trade.[13] A number of national constitutions explicitly link the right to work to the duty to work, although these references to the duty to work appear to have little practical significance at the level of justiciable legal rights in the countries concerned.[14] There is no reference to the duty to work in Article 1. This omission is not accidental. As Bob Hepple notes, the type of legal duty to work contained in Soviet-era constitutions 'does not—indeed cannot—form part of the legal system of a

[10] S Deakin, '*Capacitas*: contract law, capabilities, and the legal foundations of the market', in Deakin and Supiot (n 10) ch 1.

[11] O'Cinneide (n 2) 100.

[12] See below, section II.B.

[13] For discussion, see V Mantouvalou, 'Introduction', in Mantouvalou (n 1) 9 ('Is there a hidden agenda, namely a duty to work in disguise, because of the need for productive labour in a market economy?'); G Mundlak, 'The right to work—the value of work', in D Barak-Erez and A Gross (eds), *Exploring Social Rights—Between Theory and Practice* (Oxford, Hart, 2007); A Paz Fuchs, 'The right to work and the duty to work', in Mantouvalou (n 1) ch 10.

[14] These include the current versions of the French and Japanese constitutions. See, respectively, S Robin-Olivier, 'The French approach to the right to work: the potential of a constitutional right in ordinary courts', in Mantouvalou (n 1) ch 11; K Arita, 'The development of right to work theories of labour law in Japan: a comparative perspective', in Mantouvalou (n 1) ch 12.

"capitalist" market economy except in times of war and emergency when the state assumes the role of directing labour'.[15] The content of Article 1 reflects the Cold War logic of the Charter: it was initially drafted in the late 1950s in large part as a response of the market-based systems of western Europe to those of the Soviet bloc.[16] In the same way that the Charter avoids equating the right to work with a duty to work, it also stops some way short of imposing on states an obligation to provide work for all their citizens, of the kind found in constitutions of the socialist states in the decades following the Second World War.[17]

However, it could be argued that explicit legal articulation of a duty to work is strictly unnecessary in the context of a market economy, in which workers have no direct access to the means of production and depend on the sale of labour power for subsistence. Under such conditions, the duty to work takes a concrete form in the legal rules that determine entitlements to social security in situations in which individuals cannot access the labour market by reason, for example, of unemployment, illness, age, or family responsibilities.[18]

If the right to work is understood as a right to access the labour market *under particular conditions*, the limits of that right, as expressed by reference to the nature of those conditions, in effect define the content of the duty to work in a market economy. This is exactly how Article 1 operates: it defines how far states can go in requiring individuals to work, on pain of losing access to social security benefits that are intended as a replacement for wages or other income from work.[19] More generally, the ESC as a whole defines the minimum contents of acceptable work by reference to Articles of the Charter setting basic labour standards in the areas of pay, health and safety and working time, among others.[20] There can be no duty to work under circumstances in which conditionality in social security goes beyond what is compatible with the idea of 'acceptable' work.[21] Thus in giving a concrete meaning to the right to work, Article 1—and the Charter more generally—acknowledge, but also confine, the duty to work.

[15] Hepple (n 1) 69.

[16] ibid.

[17] Hepple (n 1), referring to Arts 40 and 60 of the USSR Constitution of 1977. The former set out a right to work which was qualified by the 'needs of society', while the latter proscribed 'evasion of socially useful work' as 'incompatible with the principles of socialist society'.

[18] Deakin and Wilkinson (n 8) ch 3; Paz-Fuchs, (n 13).

[19] Under Art 1§2: see below, section II.B.

[20] These include Art 2 on just conditions of work, Art 3 on health and safety, and Art 4 on fair remuneration. See the chapters on Arts 2, 3 and 4 by, respectively, K Lörcher, and Z Adams and S Deakin, in this volume.

[21] O'Cinneide (n 2).

B. Relationship to International Sources

Article 1 is linked, through a common approach to interpretation, to a number of other provisions of international human rights instruments that refer to the right to work. According to Article 23(1) of the Universal Declaration of Human Rights (UDHR), 'Everyone has the right to work, to free choice of employment, to just and favourable conditions of work and to protection against unemployment'. Article 6 of the International Covenant on Economic, Social and Cultural Rights (ICESR) provides that the right to work includes 'the right of everyone to gain his living by work which he freely chooses and accepts' and which entails steps to be taken by states in the areas of 'technical and vocational guidance and training programmes, policies and techniques to achieve steady economic, social and cultural development and full and productive employment under conditions safeguarding fundamental economic and political freedoms to the individual'. According to Comment No 18 on the right to work, which was issued in 2005 by the UN Committee on Economic, Social and Cultural Rights (CESCR), the right contained in Article 6 'is essential for realising other human rights and forms an inseparable and inherent part of human dignity', as well as contributing to the 'survival of the individual and to that of his/her family, and in so far as work is freely chosen and accepted, to his/her development and recognition within the community'.[22] Other provisions referring to the right to work include Article 15 of the Charter of Fundamental Rights of the European (CFREU);[23] Article 11(1)(a) of the Convention on the Elimination of All Forms of Discrimination against Women; Article 15 of the African Charter on Human and People's Rights;[24] and Article 6 of the American Convention on Human Rights in the Area of Economic, Social and Cultural Rights (the San Salvador Convention).[25] Several ILO Conventions also make reference to the right to work.[26]

According to Colm O'Cinneide, a common approach to interpreting right to work provisions in international human rights instruments has emerged by virtue of convergence between the interpretations given to Article 6 ICESR and Article 1 ESC by the CESCR and ECSR, respectively. This common interpretative approach, while 'not without its flaws', has been 'generally acknowledged to be highly authoritative' in the sense of serving as a 'significant point of reference for national governments, courts, civil

[22] General Comment No 18 §7.

[23] 'Everyone has the right to engage in work and to pursue a freely chosen or accepted occupation'.

[24] 'Every individual shall have the right to work under equitable and satisfactory conditions, and shall receive equal pay for equal work'.

[25] 'Everyone has the right to work, which includes the opportunity to secure the means for living a dignified and decent existence by performing a freely elected or accepted lawful activity'.

[26] These include the ILO Employment Policy Convention, No 122 of 1964.

society, and other international bodies'.[27] Article 6 ICESR has been interpreted as providing for non-discrimination in access to employment, freedom of choice in how individuals dispose of their labour, and an obligation on the part of states to direct policy towards ensuring full employment and dignified working conditions. Article 6 has not been read as guaranteeing just and favourable conditions of work as set out in Article 7 ICESR, but it is understood that Article 6 'should be applied in a manner that harmonises with the guarantees of dignity at work and other fundamental socio-economic rights set out in the Covenant'. In Comment No 18, the CESCR took the view that 'work' in the context of Article 6 means 'decent work', which implies a living wage ('an income allowing workers to support themselves and their families') and working conditions compatible with the preservation of the individual workers' 'physical and mental integrity'. Thus according to the CESCR, Article 6 is 'best viewed as obliging States to take action to secure access to "decent work"', so defined.[28]

C. Relationship to Other Provisions of the Charter

Article 1 ESC is linked to the substantive work-related rights set out in the Charter, in the sense that the right it protects is a right to access work that is compatible with the rights (among others) to just conditions of work (Article 2), safe and healthy working conditions (Article 3) and fair remuneration (Article 4). However, the jurisprudence of the ECSR had not made the link between Article 1 and these other rights in the same explicit way as the CESCR has done in the context of Article 6 ICESR. As a result, the question of the acceptability of work, as opposed to its accessibility, has been dealt with under the rubric of other provisions of the ESC. It is nevertheless the case that:

> the Committee's reading of the other labour rights contained in the Social Charter, which set out strong standards relating to decent work conditions, forms part of the general interpretative backdrop that it takes into account when interpreting and applying the provisions of Article 1,

making the differences in the approaches of the CESCR and ECSR 'more apparent than real'.[29]

Certain specific connections have been made between Article 1 and other provisions of the Charter in the case law of the ECSR. Article 1§2, in so far as it contains a prohibition on forced labour, falls to be interpreted by

[27] O'Cinneide (n 2) 115. See also the reference to the authoritative status of ECSR interpretations in the ECtHR's judgment in *RMT v UK* App no 31045/10 (ECtHR, 8 April 2014).
[28] See O'Cinneide (n 2).
[29] ibid.

reference to Article 12 on the right to social security.[30] Article 1§2, which prohibits all forms of discrimination in employment, has been interpreted as linked to Article 20 on the right of equal treatment and non-discrimination, and to Article 15§2 on the right of persons with disabilities to employment.[31] Article 1§4, on the provision by states of vocational guidance, training and rehabilitation, is interpreted by the ECSR as complemented by the right to vocational guidance in Article 9, the right to continuing vocational training of adult workers in Article 10§3, and the right of persons with disabilities to guidance, education, and vocational training under Article 15§1. Where states have not accepted these provisions of the Charter, which are optional, the ECSR is nevertheless able to consider the issue of conformity with Article 1§4.[32]

The Appendix to the ESC states that Article 1§2 on the right of an individual to earn their living in an occupation freely entered into shall not be interpreted as 'prohibiting or authorising any union security clause or practice'. In this way, the possibility of an unwelcome link between Article 1§2 and the provisions of the Charter governing freedom of association and the right to collective bargaining (including Articles 5 and 6) is avoided, as is the use of Article 1 to justify restraints on union security arrangements in the name of the right to work, of the kind found in some common law jurisdictions.[33]

II. CONTENT

A. Paragraph 1: The Maintenance of a High and Stable Level of Employment

Under Article 1§1 of the Charter, states accept as one of their 'primary aims and responsibilities' the achievement and maintenance of 'as high and stable a level of employment as possible'. According to the ECSR, this means that states must, first, adopt and follow an economic policy that is conducive to creating and preserving jobs, and second, take adequate measures to assist the unemployed in finding or qualifying for a job. This implies an obligation as to means rather than ends, so that the failure to achieve a high level of employment does not in itself justify a conclusion of non-conformity. The ECSR takes into account constraints on state policy arising from 'international economic trends' and 'the complexity of effectively combating unemployment'.

30 Conclusions 2012, Statement of Interpretation on Art 1§2.
31 Conclusions XVIII-I, Iceland; Conclusions 2006, Albania.
32 Conclusions 2003, Bulgaria.
33 On this aspect of the right to work, see Hepple (n 1) 78–81.

To facilitate the task of reviewing states' conformity with Article 1§1, the ECSR has developed detailed indicators. These refer, in the first instance, to the components of states' policies and include the existence of a legal or other declaratory commitment to full employment; levels of expenditure on employment measures (such as expenditure as a share of GDP); the numbers of unemployed persons accessing relevant schemes and the normal duration of unemployment prior to participating in a given programme; and the balance between active measures (such as work experience schemes) and passive ones (unemployment compensation or social assistance). The ECSR has also evaluated outcomes, including the impact of programmes on overall employment and the quality of jobs created through such interventions. In addition, the ECSR has indicators related to features of the national economic situation in signatory states, including GDP growth, employment growth and inflation, and to the structure of the labour market, including the use of different forms of employment, overall employment rate and labour market participation rates for minorities and workers with disabilities.

In practice, the ECSR allows states a wide margin of appreciation under this provision. However, it has held states to be in non-conformity with Article 1§1 on a number of occasions. Examples of non-conformity in the mid-2000s included the absence of a clear public commitment to full employment;[34] high levels of youth and long-term unemployment in a context where the state concerned had low numbers of participants in active labour market programmes;[35] and a failure to increase expenditure on active programmes, from a low base, at a time of increasing unemployment.[36]

In 2012 the ECSR conducted a general review of states' compliance with Article 1. It identified non-conformity with the duty set out in Article 1§1 on grounds that included a failure to include a sufficiently high number of persons in active measures;[37] a very low level of expenditure on active programmes, coupled with a failure on the part of the state in question to monitor outcomes;[38] inadequacy of employment policy efforts in a context in which economic growth was relatively good but unemployment remained high;[39] and, in several cases, failure of the state concerned to establish that labour market interventions were effective.[40] In a significant number of instances, member states were found to be in breach of their obligations

[34] Conclusions XVI–I, Netherlands (Netherlands Antilles and Aruba).
[35] Conclusions 2004-1, Bulgaria.
[36] Conclusions XVI-1, Poland.
[37] Conclusions 2012, Albania.
[38] Conclusions 2012, Armenia.
[39] Conclusions 2012, Slovakia.
[40] Conclusions 2012, Bosnia and Herzegovina; Bulgaria; Georgia; Italy; Moldova; and Turkey.

under Article 1§1 by failing to provide sufficient information on policies and outcomes. Only a minority of states were found to be in conformity with Article 1§1.

Article 1§1 reflects the origins of the Charter in the period of Keynesian influence over economic policymaking in the 1950s, a period when states believed in the power of macroeconomic policy to reduce unemployment, but the interventionist approach taken by the ECSR to assessing conformity with this aspect of the right to work is consistent with the more recent emphasis within EU law and policy from the late 1990s on raising employment rates. The ECSR's focus on active labour market measures in interpreting Article 1§1 may nevertheless be contrasted with the wider range of measures, many deregulatory, adopted by the European Union institutions and member states in the context of the European Employment Strategy.[41]

A further deregulatory influence on EU member states has been the so-called 'new economic governance', which has been imposed in response to the sovereign debt crisis that began in Greece in 2009 and then spread to several other countries. The policy embedded in the Euro Plus Pact of 2011 and the Treaty on Stability, Coordination and Governance of 2012, in insisting on budgetary stability across the economic cycle, is at odds with the Keynesian approach of the immediate post-1945 period, when states were more willing to run fiscal deficits in times of recession.[42] It is unlikely that a policy of fiscal stability as such could be found to give rise to non-conformity with Article 1§1, but some of its effects, in terms of rising unemployment, could be seen as infringing the duty to maintain a high and stable level of employment. Thus it is possible that Article 1§1 will provide scope in future to challenge 'austerity' policies if, as seems likely on the basis of recent experience, they not only fail to alleviate unemployment, but make it worse.

B. Paragraph 2: The Right to Earn a Living in an Occupation Freely Entered Upon

Under Article 1§2, states must 'protect effectively' the right earn a living in a freely chosen occupation. This provision has been given a broad interpretation to include a prohibition of all forms of discrimination in employment and a prohibition of forced or compulsory labour.

[41] For a discussion of the European Employment Strategy from the viewpoint of the right to work, see M Freedland and N Countouris, 'The right to (decent) work in a European comparative perspective', in Mantavoulou (n 1).

[42] See S Deakin, 'Social policy, economic governance and EMU: alternatives to austerity', in N Bruun, K Lörcher and I Schömann (eds), *The Economic and Financial Crisis and Collective Labour Law in Europe* (Oxford, Hart, 2014).

(i) Prohibition of All Forms of Discrimination in Employment

Article 1§2 has been interpreted by the ECSR as entailing a prohibition of discrimination in employment on any unjustified grounds, which include sex, race, ethnic origin, religion, disability, age, sexual orientation, and political opinion.[43] Article 1§2 thereby overlaps with the right to equal treatment in Article 20 and the protection of people with disabilities in Article 15§2. Discrimination issues are normally dealt with under these provisions, but if a state has not accepted them, a complaint may lie under Article 1§2. Article 1§2 has also been interpreted as requiring states to enact adequate legal protections against discrimination in relation to part-time work.[44]

Article 1§2 extends to the protection of the rights of foreign nationals seeking employment. It does not bar states from making access to their territory subject to the possession of a work permit, and so does not mandate freedom of movement, but they may not otherwise bar nationals of state parties from occupying particular jobs, except on the grounds set out in Article G. In effect, this limits the exclusion of foreign nationals to jobs connected with the protection of the public interest or national security, or which involve the exercise of public authority. The scope of Article G also sets limits on the exclusion of individuals from state functions on the grounds of previous political activities.[45]

The ECSR has determined that the prohibition on employment discrimination in Article 1§2 extends to both direct and indirect discrimination,[46] the former referring to a difference in treatment between persons in comparable situations that does not pursue a legitimate aim,[47] and the latter to a measure or practice that applies to all persons equally, but which, without a legitimate aim, disproportionately affects those having a particular protected characteristic. The question of what constitutes a legitimate aim and whether a difference is proportionate is considered by reference to Article G of the Charter.[48] The ECSR has also ruled that discrimination can result from failing to take account of relevant differences, and failing to ensure that rights and advantages that are intended to be generally available are genuinely accessible and open to all.[49]

The prohibition on discrimination extends to all aspects of recruitment, employment conditions and benefits, and dismissal.[50] Specific cases of

[43] Conclusions XVIII-1, Iceland; Conclusions 2006, Albania; Conclusions 2006, Lithuania.

[44] Conclusions XVI-1, Austria.

[45] Conclusions 2006, Albania.

[46] Conclusions XVIII-1, Austria.

[47] *Syndicat national des professions du tourism v France*, Collective Complaint No 6/1999, ECSR Decision on the merits of 10 October 2000 §§24–25.

[48] Conclusions XVI-1, Greece.

[49] *Association Internationale Autisme-Europe (AIAE) v France*, Collective Complaint No 13/2000, ECSR Decision on the merits of 4 November 2003 §52.

[50] Conclusions XVI-1, Austria.

non-conformity with the obligation to make the prohibition of discrimination effective include a failure to provide for a legal power to set aside discriminatory provisions in collective agreements, employment contracts or company regulations;[51] failure to provide for protection against retaliatory dismissal;[52] limitations on the remedies available to the victims of discrimination, including statutory caps on compensation claims; failure to provide for reversal of the burden of proof;[53] and failure to allow trade unions to pursue claims on behalf of the victims of employment discrimination.[54]

(ii) Prohibition of Forced or Compulsory Labour

Article 1§2 requires states to prohibit all forms of 'forced or compulsory labour', which for this purpose means 'all work or service which is exacted from any person under the menace of any penalty and for which the said person has not offered himself voluntarily', following the definition given in Article 4 ECHR and in ILO Convention No 29 on Forced Labour. A case of non-conformity with the Charter may be established where legislation prohibiting forced labour is not enforced in practice.[55]

(a) Forced Labour

Cases of non-conformity with this aspect of Article 1§2 include provisions authorising criminal sanctions against seamen abandoning their posts, which extended to situations in which the safety of people on board the ship was not at stake,[56] and the practice of imposing lengthy terms (up to 25 years) of military service on army officers following the completion of their training, subject only to the repayment to the state of the costs of their education and training.[57] Article 1§2 has also been held to cover cases of excessive periods of conscriptive service for those wishing to avoid compulsory military service.[58]

The ECSR's approach to the definition of forced labour has recently seen it extend the ambit of Article 1§2 to cover situations of precarious and

[51] Conclusions XVI-1, Iceland.

[52] ibid.

[53] Conclusions 2006, Albania.

[54] Conclusions, XVI-1, Iceland.

[55] Conclusions XIII-3, Ireland.

[56] *International Federation of Human Rights Leagues (FIDH) v Greece*, Collective Complaint No 7/2000, ECSR Decision on the merits of 2 December 2000 §22.

[57] *FIDH v Greece*, Collective Complaint No 7/2000, ECSR Decision on the merits of 2 December 2000 §21; Conclusions 2004, Ireland.

[58] *Quaker Council for European Affairs (QCEA) v Greece*, Collective Complaint No 8/2000, ECSR Decision on the merits of 25 April 2001 §§23–25; Conclusions 2012, Statement of Interpretation on Art 1§2.

exploitative work, in effect building on the ruling of the European Court of Human Rights in the *Siliadin*[59] case. The ECSR's 2012 Conclusions point to several cases of non-conformity arising from the failure of states to ensure adequate protection for domestic workers and those working in family enterprises.[60]

(b) Prison Work

Article 1§2 does not prohibit prison work, but it does regulate its commercial application, and so can be understood as limiting the use of prison labour to undercut other forms of employment. Where prisoners work for private firms, their consent is required, and their pay and terms and conditions of employment must be as 'similar as possible' to those applying to regular, waged employment.[61]

(c) Conditionality in Social Security

The attachment of conditions to the receipt of social security benefits—in particular unemployment compensation or social assistance connected to unemployment—generally falls under Article 12 ESC, but the imposition of excessively strict conditions can also give rise to an issue of non-conformity with Article 1§2. Article 1§2 has been used to question the practice of requiring unemployed persons to take up offers of employment involving wages and terms and conditions below those normally applicable to such work, or which do not allow them to pursue their chosen profession or occupation. The ECSR's review of State Parties' practices under Article 1 in 2012 revealed several such cases.[62] These include situations in which the job in question required skills or qualifications significantly below those of the individual concerned, or physical or mental requirements that the individual did not possess; jobs which posed physical threats or that were otherwise incompatible with the dignity or integrity of the person of the worker; jobs that imposed unreasonable travelling requirements; or jobs below the relevant regional or national minimum wage or generally applicable wage. Thus the ECSR treats excessive conditionality in social security law as a form of compulsion that is compatible with Article 1§2 only if the resulting employment is 'consistent with the dignity of the individual concerned and [their] family responsibilities' or, more generally, can be regarded as 'non-exploitative'.[63]

[59] *Siliadin v France* App no 73316/01 (ECtHR, 26 July 2005). See V Mantouvalou, 'The right to non-exploitative work', in Mantouvalou (n 1).

[60] Conclusions 2012 and XX-I.

[61] Conclusions XVI-1, Germany; Conclusions 2012, Statement of Interpretation on Art 1§2.

[62] Conclusions 2012, Statement of Interpretation on Art 1§2.

[63] ibid.

(iii) An Emerging Area: The Right to Privacy

A developing area of the ECSR's jurisprudence is based on the idea that 'the right to undertake work freely includes the right to be protected against interferences with the right to privacy'. In its 2006 Conclusions, the ECSR pointed to the need to ensure that individuals be protected against interference in their private or personal lives arising from employers' uses of 'modern electronic communication and data collection techniques'.[64] Its 2012 Conclusions refer to new technologies that have 'permitted employers to organise a continuous supervision of employees ... at any time and in any place', with the result that 'the frontier between professional and private life has been weakened'. The ECSR has stressed the importance in this context of asserting 'the fundamental right of workers to privacy'.

C. Paragraph 3: The Provision of a Free Employment Service

Under Article 1§3, states commit to providing, free of charge, a service for placing the unemployed and other job seekers in employment, and for employed workers seeking a new job. The state is under an obligation to provide a placement service free of charge to both employers and employees, and which comes up to certain minimum standards of effectiveness. Article 1§3 thereby illustrates the aspect of the right to work that is concerned with what some commentators have called the 'right to pursue a livelihood' and which dovetails with the idea that the state should support labour market 'transitions' at different stages of an individual's employment history.[65]

The ECSR has held that it is a contravention of Article 1§3 for states to charge employers for the notification of vacancies, even where the fee covers basic administrative costs.[66] Laws permitting private employment agencies to operate on a fee-charging basis are not contrary to Article 1§3 if the state also provides a placement service free of charge that operates in all geographical regions and industrial sectors of the country concerned.[67]

The ECSR has developed indicators for assessing the extent of compliance with Article 1§3. These include the ratio between the number of placements made by public employment services and the total of notified vacancies (the placement rate) and the market shares of public and private services.[68] The ECSR has also held that trade unions and employers' associations should be given a role in organising and running employment services.[69]

[64] Conclusions 2006, Statement of Interpretation on Art 1§2.
[65] Conclusions 2012, Statement of Interpretation on Art 1§2.
[66] Conclusions XIV-1, Statement of Interpretation on Art 1§3.
[67] Conclusions XIV-1, Turkey.
[68] Conclusions XIV-1, Greece.
[69] Conclusions XV-1, Poland.

D. Paragraph 4: The Provision of Vocational Guidance, Training and Rehabilitation

Under Article 1§4, states undertake to provide vocational guidance, continuing vocational training for the employed and unemployed, and specialised guidance for persons with disabilities. States must provide these services equally to their own nationals and nationals of other states that are party to the Charter.[70] As noted above, this part of Article 1 overlaps with substantive provisions of the Charter (Articles 9 on vocational guidance, 10§3 on vocational training and 15§1 on rights of persons with disabilities), and it is in the context of these provisions that the ECSR has mostly decided issues of conformity with the Charter.

III. IMPACT ON EUROPEAN HUMAN RIGHTS INSTRUMENTS

A. European Convention on Human Rights

The European Court of Human Rights has held on a number of occasions that 'workfare'—the practice of requiring unemployed persons to undertake work for the public authorities or for a private employer as a condition of receiving social security benefits—does not infringe the prohibition on forced labour in Article 4 ECHR.[71] This was also the approach taken by the UK Supreme Court in the *Poundland* case.[72]

However, it is arguable that Article 1 ESC could be used to give a wider reading to Article 4 ECHR. Reading Article 1§2 in such a way as to regulate workfare would fulfil a number of linked objectives: protecting the individual worker's property right in their labour power; protecting regular, waged employment from being undercut by forms of work in which the employer obtains labour services without paying for them; and protecting the labour market more generally from being undermined by alternative forms of work not based on the exchange principle.

Viewed from this perspective, workfare raises similar issues to prison labour: as such, it should be subject to review under Article 1§2, in cases where it is effectively competing with, or substitutes for, normal employment. This should include situations in which unemployed persons are required, by the rules or practice of the social security system, to undertake work for employers that would normally attract a regular wage. In addition, requiring unemployed persons to undertake labour that has no educational

[70] Conclusions XII-1, Statement of Interpretation on Art 1§4.
[71] *X v Netherlands* (1976) 7 DR 161; *Talmon v Netherlands* [1997] EHRLR 448.
[72] *R (Reilly) v Secretary of State for Work and Pensions* [2013] UKSC.

or vocational value for them can be seen as undermining their right to pursue their chosen profession, and so as devaluing their labour capacity. In this respect, workfare is similar to the practice of requiring excessively long service for conscientious objectors, which the ECSR has held to be in breach of Article 1§2. It remains to be seen how far the broad view taken of Article 1§2 by the ECSR is capable of influencing the future interpretation of Article 4 ECHR.

B. Charter of Fundamental Rights of the European Union

Article 15 CFREU is directly drawn from Article 1 ESC, although it stops short of endorsing a 'right to work' in clear terms, referring instead to 'a right to engage in work and to pursue a freely chosen or accepted occupation', a reading that perhaps stresses the 'accessibility' of work rather than its 'acceptability'. The link between the two provisions nevertheless poses the question of how far the concept of the right to work could be used to inform debates over the limits of austerity policy in the context of the EU's 'new economic governance'. States pursuing austerity policies today have the imprimatur of the EU's economic and monetary policy, as expressed through the 'new economic governance'. In certain cases they have been required to implement austerity policies, for example as a condition of financial assistance under the Memoranda of Understanding agreed between the Troika of the European Commission, the European Central Bank and the IMF, on one hand, and debtor states, on the other, between 2009 and 2011. The Treaty on Stability, Coordination and Governance and the Euro Plus Pact may in the future make austerity policies a matter of legal obligation for certain EU member states.[73]

To date, the European Court of Justice has shown little enthusiasm for allowing social rights arguments to be weighed in the balance against elements of austerity policy, including the terms of the Memoranda of Understanding agreed between the Troika and the debtor states.[74] Can Article 1 be invoked to counter this pressure? Defenders of austerity policies argue that they are necessary for job creation, but empirical evidence suggests that there is no clear link in practice between cuts to social security benefits and deregulation of labour laws, on one hand, and economic growth and productivity improvements, on the other.[75]

[73] See Deakin (n 42).

[74] ibid.

[75] Z Adams and S Deakin, 'Structural adjustment, economic governance and social policy in a regional context: the case of the Eurozone crisis', in A Blackett and A Trebilcock (eds), *Research Handbook on Transnational Labour Law* (Cheltenham, Edward Elgar, 2015).

Even where such policies are demonstrably failing to restore full employment, a state will not necessarily be in breach of Article 1 if it has used what the ECSR regards as appropriate means to achieve the goal of a high and stable employment rate. So far, the ECSR has focused on labour market activation measures narrowly conceived, rather than addressing broader issues of policy. There may, however, be scope to challenge some of the means used to implement austerity policy under Article 1§2, if they are clearly counterproductive. Excessive conditionality in social security law has already been the subject of ECSR rulings on non-conformity under Article 1§2. Thus there is scope for Article 1 to be invoked in the continuing debate over austerity in Europe, and for this to feed into the interpretation of Article 15 CFREU.

IV. CONCLUSION

A number of different rights are intertwined in Article 1: the right to practise a freely chosen occupation or profession; the right to protection against forced labour; the right to vocational training; and the right to assistance in finding work, which is coupled with an undertaking by the State to take steps to maintain full employment. These rights can be thought of as rights to access the labour market, understood in a specific sense as a labour market constituted and regulated by the legal system and other instruments of the State, with a view to enhancing the capabilities of market actors. Article 1 expresses these rights in a series of steps or stages that mirror the evolution of labour law itself, which is a movement from formal to substantive market access.

In classical private law, the right to access the labour market was simply a right to enter into a contract to provide personal services in return for remuneration. The law protected such a right by specifying property rights and enforcing agreements. It did not specify a minimum content to the parties' property rights, nor did it impose mandatory terms (*ordre public social*) for the protection of the weaker party. It did not proscribe discrimination.

The right to practise an occupation that has been freely chosen is one step up from this liberal conception of a right to market access: it affirms that the right to contract is insufficient, in and of itself, to prevent forms of social discrimination that have the effect of barring individuals from trading. This aspect of the right to work protects the dignity of the worker, but it also protects the market from social forces that would limit its scope and extent.

A further step is for the law to constitute the labour market by protecting the property rights that are at stake in the exchange of work for wages. This is one of the functions of the prohibition on forced labour. This prohibition protects the dignity of the worker by preventing their physical person being the object of the exchange: labour is not a commodity. However, it is also making an affirmative statement about the nature of the wage–work bargain. The object of the exchange is the worker's labour power or capacity to work. The worker is at the employer's disposal, in a position of formal and economic subordination, for the limited time and space indicated by the employment contract. Although labour is not a commodity, labour power is. The prohibition on forced labour is there to ensure precisely that labour power is commodified in this sense: to allow forced exchanges to take place would undermine the market and limit its extent. The right to work protects the worker's property in their human capital.

It is for this reason that Article 1 regulates the *commercial* exploitation of prison labour. It does not prevent prisoners being subject to the duty to work, but it does limit the involvement of private enterprise in the organisation of prison labour. Prison work must be demarcated from work in a commercial setting, and must not compete with, or undercut it. Thus the market is protected, and along with it private enterprise. The same idea underlies the logic of placing limits on the duration of civilian work where it substitutes for military service.

Having identified the basic property right—labour capacity—that is at stake in the wage–work bargain, Article 1 then goes to a further stage, which is to protect this right in various ways that go beyond merely defending the principle that it has a commercial value. The right to vocational training and the right to access employment services free at the point of supply are rights that enable workers more fully to realise the value of their labour capacity. They can be thought of, conversely, as requiring states to take positive steps to enhance the human capital of market actors. Again, in asserting a social right that is based on the idea of the dignity of the individual, Article 1 also extends the scope of the market and deepens the division of labour on which it depends.

Does Article 1 go further and provide a right to be provided with decent work? The Charter falls short of ensuring access to decent work for all. State parties to the Charter do not undertake to find well-remunerated and meaningful employment for all their citizens. However, Article 1 does require signatory states to adopt certain *means* to this *end*. There is no breach of Article 1 if the state fails to achieve the goal of full employment, but states have in numerous instances been found to be in breach of Article 1 where the means of achieving full employment are inadequate, in particular where they have devoted insufficient resources to active labour market measures.

There is a strong case for regarding workfare schemes as a form of compulsory labour in breach of Article 1, in light of the growing use of Article 1 to scrutinise conditionality in the operation of the law of social security. More generally, there is scope to use Article 1 to mount a critique of labour market policies, sometimes referred to as 'activation policies', which aim to increase the labour supply without putting in place certain basic social guarantees in respect of offers of employment made to those entering or re-entering the labour market.

It might be thought that the potential of Article 1 is limited in what it can achieve by the Charter's overall commitment to a market-orientated framework for social rights. The Charter is the product of a Cold War logic, as part of which European democracies sought to articulate their commitment to social rights in a market setting, as a response to the Soviet bloc. The Charter was drafted in opposition to a state socialist model in which the means of production were vested in the state, and private property was suppressed, or at least much reduced. Can the Charter be invoked today to defend the model of the social market economy against its new opponent, namely the libertarian model of a minimalist state, which is nothing more or less than an attempt to restore the 'private law society' of the nineteenth century? The private law society is a myth, an invention of the 1960s, a feature, like the Charter, of the Cold War logic of that period. But it is a myth with the power to influence contemporary events.

Since the onset of the sovereign debt crisis in 2009, the ordoliberal and neoliberal elements of European institutions have come to the fore, and the crisis has been used to justify deregulatory policies that take the private law society as their inspiration. This represents a great leap backwards for the European Union and for the goal of economic integration within a framework of respect of human rights and social cohesion. Against this background, the Charter might seem to be something of a relic, expressing social market principles that are out of time. Yet, as we have seen, the ECSR has used Article 1 to mount a sustained examination and critique of states' active labour market policies in the current crisis. This is a debate that will continue.

Article 2

The Right to Just Conditions of Work

KLAUS LÖRCHER

Article 2—The right to just conditions of work

With a view to ensuring the effective exercise of the right to just conditions of work, the Parties undertake:

1. to provide for reasonable daily and weekly working hours, the working week to be progressively reduced to the extent that the increase of productivity and other relevant factors permit;
2. to provide for public holidays with pay;
3. to provide for a minimum of four weeks' annual holiday with pay;
4. to eliminate risks in inherently dangerous or unhealthy occupations, and where it has not yet been possible to eliminate or reduce sufficiently these risks, to provide for either a reduction of working hours or additional paid holidays for workers engaged in such occupations;
5. to ensure a weekly rest period which shall, as far as possible, coincide with the day recognised by tradition or custom in the country or region concerned as a day of rest;
6. to ensure that workers are informed in written form, as soon as possible, and in any event not later than two months after the date of commencing their employment, of the essential aspects of the contract or employment relationship;
7. to ensure that workers performing night work benefit from measures which take account of the special nature of the work.

Article I Implementation of the undertakings given

2. Compliance with the undertakings deriving from the provisions of paragraphs 1, 2, 3, 4, 5 and 7 of Article 2 … shall be regarded as effective if the provisions are applied, in accordance with paragraph 1 of this article, to the great majority of the workers concerned.

Appendix Part II

Article 2, paragraph 6

Parties may provide that this provision shall not apply:

a. to workers having a contract or employment relationship with a total duration not exceeding one month and/or with a working week not exceeding eight hours;
b. where the contract or employment relationship is of a casual and/or specific nature, provided, in these cases, that its non-application is justified by objective considerations.

I. INTRODUCTION

A. Context and Main Content

The 'right to just conditions of work' (Article 2) is an important social right as it covers the main aspects of working time, which has a great impact on (the time available for) private and family life. Together with the right to safe and healthy working conditions (Article 3), the right to fair remuneration (Article 4) and the right to protection in cases of termination of employment, it forms the essence of the individual employment relationship.[1] Nevertheless, it has not acquired the status of a 'hard-core' right (Article A§1b).

In relation to working time Article 2 regulates many elements. Most importantly, §1 defines the general limits of working time, even requiring its reduction under certain conditions. Paragraph 2 provides for public holidays with pay and §3 defines the minimum length of annual paid holidays (four weeks). Specific protection of workers in dangerous workplaces is contained in §4. Under §5, even a cultural element of working time is included, in the obligation for the weekly rest period to be aligned with 'tradition or custom'. Newly introduced by the RESC and of a quite different character from the other paragraphs—but still in line with the wider heading of this article ('just conditions of work')—§6 requires the provision of information on essential working conditions. Again related to working time the last paragraph, 7—also newly introduced in the RESC—obliges contracting parties to protect night workers. Finally, it should be noted that the RESC amended two existing paragraphs (3 and 4), improving their content.[2]

[1] See on 'conditions of employment', M Mikkola *Social Human Right of Europe* (Porvoo, Karelatico, 2010), 167 et seq, M Mine, *Le droit du temps de travail à la lumière de la Charte sociale européenne* (2011) Semaine sociale Lamy, (1475), 17 janvier, 7–11.

[2] Council of Europe (1996) *Explanatory Report to the European Social Charter* (Revised), paras 21 et seq.

B. International Sources

Generally speaking, a significant number of international instruments formed the basis for this article. Moreover, many instruments have been developed since the adoption of the ESC and also the RESC.[3] The ILO Conventions are particularly important sources, forming the foundation of several provisions,[4] as follows:

— §1: Convention No 1, the Hours of Work (Industry) Convention 1919, although the eight-hour day and 48-hour week principles have not been retained;[5]
— §3: Holidays with Pay Recommendation 1954 (two weeks);[6] followed by Convention No 132, the Holidays with Pay Convention (Revised) 1970 (three weeks, Article 3(3) of the Convention);
— §4: Convention No 43, the Sheet-Glass Works Convention 1934; Convention No 46, the Hours of Work (Coal Mines) Convention (Revised) 1935; Convention No 49, the Reduction of Hours of Work (Glass-Bottle Works) Convention 1935;[7]
— §5: Convention No 14, the Weekly Rest (Industry) Convention 1921 (No 14); Convention No 106, the Weekly Rest (Commerce and Offices) Convention 1957.[8]

As regards §7, ILO Convention No 171—the Night Work Convention 1990—is not mentioned in the Explanatory Report. However, it did form the background to it.[9] Beyond these instruments a significant number of international standards have been developed in the mean time,[10] in particular concerning hours of work, weekly rest and paid leave.[11]

Without being directly expressed in the Explanatory Report of the RESC, the extension of annual paid leave from two to four weeks in §3 and the reference to prevention obligations with regard to safety and health in §4 are based on EU secondary legislation.[12] Instead, the Explanatory Report

[3] See Council of Europe (ed), *Conditions of employment in the European Social Charter*, Human Rights—Social Charter monographs—No 6, Strasbourg 1999, Appendix VII, pp 123 et seq.

[4] 'European Social Charter and International Labour Standards' (1961) 84 *International Labour Review* 354.

[5] ibid 359.

[6] ibid 359.

[7] ibid 360.

[8] ibid 360.

[9] Decision on the merits 7 December 2004, *Confédération Générale du Travail (CGT) v France*, Collective Complaint No 22/2003 §34.

[10] For an overview of all ILO instruments related to working time, see the ILO website, section on 'International Labour Standards'.

[11] ibid.

[12] Art 7, Working Time Directive 2003/88/EC.

expressly mentions Council Directive 91/533/EEC of 14 October 1991 on an employer's obligation to inform employees of the conditions applicable to the contract or employment relationship[13] for the purpose of clarifying the sources of §6.[14]

More generally, Article 7(d) ICESCR protects workers in relation to working time, stating that 'States Parties to the present Covenant recognize the right of everyone to the enjoyment of just and favourable conditions of work which ensure, in particular ... (d) Rest, leisure and reasonable limitation of working hours and periodic holidays with pay, as well as remuneration for public holidays.'[15]

C. Relationship to Other Provisions of the Charter

The relationship of working time provisions as guaranteed in Article 2 to safety and health at the workplace as enshrined in Article 3 is obvious and has also been explicitly recognised by the ECSR, stressing that 'the provisions of the Revised Charter concerning working time are intended to protect workers' safety and health in an effective manner'.[16] Even more directly, §4 provides for compensation in case of certain unhealthy work, thus showing the close interrelationship between the two articles. However, §2, providing for public holidays with pay, and certain aspects of §5 (weekly rest period according to customs) may be considered not to be directly related to safety and health.[17] However, there is also a close relationship to Article 4, as several provisions require payment as part of the (fair) remuneration. Besides this more technical relationship, working time in general is closely linked to remuneration as the latter forms the financial 'compensation' for the former.

By referring to the 'working environment' and to 'working conditions' Article 22(a) offers the necessary collective protection by providing for consultation of workers' representatives.[18] Article 20 leads to the conclusion that male and female workers are now equally protected in respect

[13] [1991] OJ L288/32–35.

[14] '... reference as to the minimum requirements in this respect may be found in European Community Directive (91/533)', Explanatory Report to the European Social Charter (Revised) §26.

[15] See for more details General Comment No 23 (2016).

[16] Decision on the merits 23 June 2010, *CFE-CGC v France*, Collective Complaint No 56/2009 §69; see J Akandji-Kombé, *Réflexions sur l'efficacité de la Charte sociale européenne: à propos de la décision du Comité européen des droits sociaux du 23 juin 2010*, (2011) Revue de droit du travail, Vol 4, 233–240, M Morand, *Les forfaits-jours et la Charte sociale européenne* (2011) La Semaine Juridique—Edition sociale, (19), 10 mai, 10–13.

[17] See CJEU 12 November 1996, Case C-84/94 *UK v Council* [1996] ECR I-5755 para 37.

[18] See the chapter on Art 22 by N Bruun in this volume.

of all working conditions; nevertheless, a gender mainstreaming approach will require a close look at the consequences of legislation and practice for each of them.[19] This is all the more important, as working time is increasingly becoming one of the core issues of reconciliation of work and family obligations.

II. CONTENT

A. Paragraph 1: Working Time

This provision plays a central role in defining most important working conditions. It has a dynamic character.

Article 2§1 guarantees workers the right to reasonable limits on daily and weekly working hours, including overtime. This right must be guaranteed through legislation, regulations, collective agreements or any other binding means. In order to ensure that the limits are respected in practice, an appropriate authority must supervise whether the limits are being respected.[20]

(i) Definition of and Limits to Daily and Weekly Working Time

The Charter does not expressly define what constitute reasonable working hours. The ECSR therefore assesses situations on a case-by-case basis: extremely long working hours—for example, those of up to 16 hours on any one day[21] or, under certain conditions, more than 60 hours in one week[22]—are unreasonable and therefore contrary to the Charter.

Working overtime must not simply be left to the discretion of the employer or the employee. The reasons for overtime work and its duration must be subject to regulation.[23]

The ECSR considers that periods of on-call duty (*'périodes d'astreinte'*) during which the employee has not been required to perform work for the employer, although they do not constitute effective working time, cannot be regarded as a rest period within the meaning of Article 2 of the Charter, except within the framework of certain occupations or particular circumstances and pursuant to appropriate procedures. The absence of effective work cannot constitute an adequate criterion for regarding such a period as a rest period.[24]

[19] See the chapter on Art 20 by C Kollonay-Lehoczky in this volume.
[20] Conclusions I, Statement of Interpretation on Art 2§1.
[21] Conclusions XIV-2, Norway.
[22] Conclusions XIV-2, Netherlands.
[23] Conclusions XIV-2, Statement of Interpretation on Art 2§1.
[24] Decision on the merits of 12 October 2004, *Confédération Française de l'Encadrement CFE-CGC v France*, Collective Complaint No 16/2003 §§50–53.

Concerning the ECSR's approach to defining the limitations of daily and weekly working time, it does not appear sufficient to fulfil the Charter's requirements of reasonableness. The first step is the maximum daily working hours. The ECSR has considered that if the 'staff concerned cannot work for more than 13 hours on any day worked over the year, whatever the circumstances' this daily limit would be 'in conformity with Article 2§1'.[25] But it does not justify why such an enormously long working day would be in line with the requirement of reasonableness.

Obviously, the background is the EU legislation setting an 11-hour minimum daily rest period in Article 3 of Directive 2003/88/EC, thereby (indirectly) permitting the remaining 13 hours for working purposes. But this approach is not in harmony with Article 2§1 of the Charter. Indeed, the EU secondary legislation does not define daily maximum working hours. It follows a limited concept by only regulating 'certain aspects'. In contrast to this legislation, Article 2§1 of the Charter expressly requires 'reasonable daily … working hours'. Therefore, an autonomous interpretation is needed.

Basing the interpretation on international standards, the normal maximum for daily working hours would be eight hours.[26] In this context the (historical) argument that the drafters of the Charter did not, in the end, refer to this principle enshrined in ILO Convention No 1 is not convincing. First, this is only an ancillary means of interpretation (Article 32 VCLT). Second, references to international standards for interpretation purposes have been recognised by the ECSR. Third, excessive daily working hours are harmful to the health of workers.

In conclusion, the ECSR should abandon its case law on a permitted maximum 13 daily working hours. Instead, it should limit them to eight hours per day, with certain limited exceptions.

As regards the permitted 60 weekly working hours[27] the same principle should apply to further limit them to 48 hours per week, in line with Article 2 of ILO Convention No 1.

[25] Decision on the merits of 23 June 2010, *Confédération Française de' l'Encadrement CFE-CGC v France*, Collective Complaint No 56/2009 §58.

[26] 'The working hours of persons employed in any public or private industrial undertaking or in any branch thereof … shall not exceed eight in the day', Art 2 ILO Convention No 1, the Hours of Work (Industry) Convention, 1919 (providing for certain strictly defined exceptions).

[27] Only in cases such as 78 working hours per week has the ECSR considered that they were 'manifestly excessive and therefore cannot be considered reasonable within the meaning of Article 2§1' of the Charter. See Decision on the merits of 23 June 2010, *Confédération Française de l'Encadrement CFE-CGC v France*, Collective Complaint No 56/2009 para 59, and see also Decision on the merits of 23 June 2010, *Confédération Générale du Travail (CGT) v France*, Collective Complaint No 55/2009 §52.

(ii) Progressive Reduction

Article 2§1 also provides for the progressive reduction of weekly working hours, to the extent permitted by productivity increases and other relevant factors. These 'other factors' may be the nature of the work and the safety and health risks to which workers are exposed. This obligation is closely related to the reasonable nature or otherwise of working time. The widespread introduction of a working week of less than 40 hours has greatly reduced the need to shorten the working week.[28]

This approach by the ECSR appears to empty this part of the provision of real content (at least for the present situation). The (previous) trend of reduction to 40 hours a week might turn out to be an accurate description of previous situations. But even if this is the case, it would be all the more important that the obligation of 'progressive reduction' has not come to an end, but still requires effective implementation under the specific conditions referred to in §1.

This is the dynamic element in Article 2§1. Unlike most of the Charter's provisions[29] it is not a certain level of protection that once achieved, would as such allow for assessing conformity at this level for the future. Therefore there is a continuing obligation to seek further reductions if the conditions laid down in this paragraph are fulfilled. The dynamic character also sets barriers to regression, in other words, increasing working time instead of reducing it.

(iii) Flexibility?

The ECSR considers that flexibility arrangements regarding working time are not as such in breach of the Charter. In order to be in conformity with the Charter, national laws or regulations must fulfil three criteria:[30]

(i) They must prevent unreasonable daily and weekly working time. The maximum daily and weekly hours referred to above must not be exceeded in any case.
(ii) They must operate within a legal framework providing adequate guarantees. A flexible working time system must operate within a precise legal framework that clearly circumscribes the discretion left to employers and employees to vary, by means of a collective agreement, working time.
(iii) They must provide for reasonable reference periods for the calculation of average working time. The reference periods must not exceed six

[28] Conclusions XIV-2, Statement of Interpretation on Art 2§1.
[29] See as another example of a 'dynamic' provision Art 12§3 of the Charter.
[30] Decision on the merits of 16 October 2001, *Confédération Française de l'Encadrement CFE-CGC v France*, Collective Complaint No 9/2000 §§29–38.

months. They may be extended to a maximum of one year in exceptional circumstances.

This framework could appear acceptable if the limits defined above were accepted by the ECSR for the purposes of definition (i). In case of flexibility arrangements the wishes of the workers (within the given limits) should be taken into account more seriously, for example, by referring to working time arrangements in order to (better) cope with family responsibilities (Article 27 of the Charter).

(iv) New Challenges

It is becoming more and more obvious that working time protection is under increasing threat. This is true in relation to changing legislation in times of crisis[31] and globalisation (in the direction of a '24-hour economy').[32] But it is also the case in relation to all sorts of non-standard employment, for example in the form of freelancing, work in the so-called 'sharing economy' or, increasingly, online 'crowdsourcing' platforms. Developments in relation to 'digitalisation' appear to render separation between working and (private) rest time increasingly difficult. Increasingly, workers are expected to be available at all times (for example, on their mobile telephones, which are often provided by employers), for example in the evenings, at weekends and also during their paid leave. Moreover, work at home or at any other place (outside working premises) is becoming increasingly common (often in order to cope with the tasks given to the worker within a given timeframe), thus also making it difficult to control the distinction between work and leisure time.

These challenges require additional answers on at least two levels. They relate to the prevention of violation and to the monitoring of the legal limits of working time. In providing answers, due account must be taken of the necessity not to undermine safety and health at work in relation to preventing more stress. As it will be difficult to require a one-size-fits-all solution, contracting parties must at least be required to ensure the effective exercise of the right to just working conditions also under these changing circumstances.

[31] C Lang, S Clauwaert and I Schömann, *Working time reforms in times of crisis*, Working Paper 2013.03, ETUI, Brussels, 2013; as to permissible restrictions, see the chapter on 'Article G—Restrictions' by A Koukiadaki in this volume.

[32] WL Roozendaal and RF Hoekstra, *Working Hours and Overtime: Balancing Economic Interests and Fundamental Rights in a Globalized Economy* (forthcoming).

(v) Conclusions

There is a need for new reflection on the reasonableness of maximum daily and weekly working hours by the ECSR. It should base its (new) case law on the principles developed in the first international labour standards, nearly a century ago, namely ILO Convention No 1, 1919, providing for eight hours per day and 48 hours per week as normal limits. Moreover, specific attention should be attached to the 'dynamic' nature of the provision requiring continuous efforts for the reduction of working time. Furthermore, flexibility should not lead to any weakening of protection. Instead, workers' interests with regard to flexibility (for example in cases of family responsibilities) should be taken into account. Finally, effective safeguards are needed, in particular in a period in which working life is being subjected to 'digitalisation'.

B. Paragraph 2: Public Holidays with Pay

Article 2§2 guarantees the right to public holidays with pay, in addition to weekly rest periods and annual leave. Public holidays may be specified in law or in collective agreements.

The Charter does not stipulate the number of public holidays. Currently, this varies from six to 17 days per year. There has been no finding of non-conformity with this provision because of states' granting too few public holidays.

Work should be prohibited during public holidays. However, working on public holidays may be carried out in special cases; the conditions governing weekly rest periods apply (see Article 2§5 below).

The compensatory rest period may be replaced by monetary compensation. The ECSR considers that work performed on a public holiday requires a constraint on the part of the worker, who should be compensated with a higher remuneration than that usually paid. Accordingly, in addition to the paid public holiday, work carried out on that holiday must be paid at least double the usual wage. The remuneration may also be provided as compensatory time-off, in which case it should be at least double the days worked.[33]

This protection assumes the existence of public holidays, which can be considered as quite normal in Europe. However, the extent to which national legislation provides for such free days in addition to annual holidays with pay varies greatly from one country to another (and in federal states it can even vary within the country concerned). The ECSR is right in linking this

[33] Conclusions 2010, Statement of Interpretation on Art 2§2; Conclusions XIX-3, Statement of Interpretation on Art 2§2.

protection to the weekly rest period requirements in §5. But specific attention is required to prevent the undermining of this protection, in particular by reducing the number of public holidays.

C. Paragraph 3: Annual Holiday with Pay

Whereas the 1961 Charter provided for a minimum of two weeks, Article 2§3 guarantees the right to a minimum of four weeks (or 20 calendar days) of annual holiday with pay. Annual leave may not be replaced by financial compensation, and employees must not have the option of giving up their annual leave.[34]

A worker must take at least two weeks' uninterrupted annual holidays during the year the holidays were due. Annual holidays exceeding two weeks may be postponed in particular circumstances defined by domestic law, the nature of which should justify the postponement.[35] Workers may be required to have been employed for 12 months before they become eligible for annual paid leave.[36] Workers who suffer from illness or injury during their annual leave are entitled to take the days lost at another time, so that they receive the four-week annual holiday provided for under this paragraph, possibly on the condition of producing a medical certificate.[37]

There is ample case law by the CJEU on Article 7 of the Working Time Directive 2008/33, which provides for four weeks' paid annual leave. This jurisprudence should form the minimum level of protection provided for under this paragraph.

D. Paragraph 4: Unhealthy Occupations

The 1961 Charter was drafted at a time when working hours were longer and the main aim of occupational health and safety policies was not to prevent and eliminate risks, but to compensate for them. Since then, daily and weekly working hours have generally decreased and, above all, prevention has become the priority, most often taking the form of the reduction of exposure times to the minimum length considered not to present a threat to workers' health. The 1996 Charter takes account of this development by dividing Article 2§4 into two parts: the first requires states to take the necessary measures to eliminate risks, and the second requires them to provide

[34] Conclusions I, Ireland.
[35] Conclusions 2007, Statement of Interpretation on Art 2§3.
[36] Conclusions I, Norway, Sweden.
[37] Conclusions XII-2, Statement of Interpretation on Art 2§3.

for compensation in the event of residual risks. This change ensures consistency with Articles 3 (right to safe and healthy working conditions) and 11 (right to protection of health).[38]

It is to be noted specifically that when interpreting Article 2§4 of the 1961 Charter, the ECSR takes into consideration the new wording of Article 2§4 in the 1996 Charter.[39]

(i) Elimination or Reduction of Risks

The first part of Article 2§4 requires states to eliminate risks in inherently dangerous or unhealthy occupations. This part is closely linked to Article 3 of the Charter (right to safe and healthy working conditions, see Article 3). It requires states to introduce policies and measures aimed at improving health and safety at work, and at preventing accidents and threats to health, particularly by reducing to a minimum risk factors in the working environment. In assessing compliance with Article 2§4, the ECSR therefore refers to its conclusions related to the right to safe and healthy working conditions in general.[40]

Accordingly, this provision should be interpreted as requiring an ongoing evaluation and assessment of whether, in particular, risks connected with certain sectors and risks connected with psychological factors related to specific professions have to be considered 'unhealthy occupations'.

(ii) Measures in Response to Residual Risks

The second part requires states to ensure that some form of compensation is received by workers exposed to risks where it has not yet been possible to eliminate or sufficiently reduce these risks, despite application of the aforementioned preventive measures or in the absence of their application.[41] This interpretation relates to the 1961 Charter and is valid a fortiori for the Revised Charter.

States have a certain discretion to determine the activities and risks concerned, but the ECSR monitors their decisions.[42] They must at least consider sectors and occupations that are manifestly dangerous or unhealthy, such as mining, quarrying, steel making and shipbuilding, as well as occupations exposing employees to ionising radiation,[43] extreme temperatures and

[38] Decision on the merits of 6 December 2006, *Marangopoulos Foundation for Human Rights (MFHR) v Greece*, Collective Complaint No 30/2005 §§232–36.

[39] Conclusions XVIII-2, Statement of Interpretation on Art 2§4 of the 1961 Charter.

[40] Conclusions 2005, Statement of Interpretation on Art 2§4.

[41] Conclusions XII-1, United Kingdom.

[42] Conclusions II, Statement of Interpretation on Art 2§4.

[43] Decision on the merits of 17 October 2001, *STTK ry and Tehy ry v Finland*, Collective Complaint No 10/2000 §27.

noise.[44] For the definition of unhealthy work, it is important that the ECSR take a specific look at new dangers coming from stress or other factors that have a negative impact on the psychological situation of workers.

The aim of the compensation must be to offer those concerned sufficient and regular time[45] to recover from the associated stress and fatigue, and thus to maintain their vigilance.[46]

Article 2§4 mentions two forms of compensation: reduced working hours and additional paid holidays. In view of the emphasis in this provision on health and safety objectives, the ECSR considers that other approaches to reducing exposure to risks may also be in conformity with the Charter.[47] It does not consider early retirement to be 'a relevant and appropriate measure to achieve the aims of Article 2§4'. Under no circumstances can financial compensation be considered an appropriate response under Article 2§4. Apart from this particular situation, the ECSR rules on the suitability of other approaches not in the abstract, but case-by-case.[48] For example, in a situation in which a measure of this type was contemplated as a general solution, making no distinction according to the type and nature of the risk involved, it deemed that a reduction in the number of years of exposure was not an appropriate measure in all cases.[49]

E. Paragraph 5: Weekly Rest Period

Article 2§5 guarantees a weekly rest period, which insofar as possible shall coincide with the day traditionally or normally recognised as a day of rest in the country or region concerned, which is Sunday in all the states that have ratified the Charter. Weekly rest periods may not be replaced by compensation, and workers may not be permitted to give them up. Although the rest period should be 'weekly', it may be deferred to the following week, as long as no worker works for more than 12 days consecutively before being granted a two-day rest period. Working on a Sunday is permitted in certain circumstances: the persons concerned must receive a compensatory rest period of at least equal duration.[50]

[44] Conclusions XIV-2, Norway.
[45] Conclusions V, Statement of Interpretation on Art 2§4.
[46] Conclusions III, Ireland.
[47] Conclusions 2005, Statement of Interpretation on Art 2§4.
[48] Decision on the merits of 6 December 2006, *Marangopoulos Foundation for Human Rights (MFHR) v Greece*, Collective Complaint No 30/2005 §416.
[49] Conclusions 2003, Bulgaria.
[50] Conclusions XIV-2, Statement of Interpretation on Art 2§5.

If on-call periods—wrongly regarded as rest periods—occur on Sundays, the ECSR is of the opinion that the situation is in breach of Article 2§5.[51]

F. Paragraph 6: Information on Essential Aspects of Contract

Although Article 2§6—newly introduced by the 1996 Charter—guaranteeing the right of workers to written information when starting employment[52] is not best placed within working time obligations (and would probably have been better placed at least at the end of the article), this opens up a new dimension of the Charter. Indeed, it deals with the individual employment relationship in a transversal manner. It requires that the information for the individual worker must at least cover essential aspects of the employment relationship or contract, namely the following:

— the identities of the parties;
— the place of work;
— the date of commencement of the contract or employment relationship;
— in the case of a temporary contract or employment relationship, the expected duration thereof;
— the amount of paid leave;
— the length of the period of notice in case of termination of the contract or the employment relationship;
— the remuneration;
— the length of the employee's normal working day or week;
— where appropriate, a reference to the collective agreements governing the employee's conditions of work.[53]

The ECSR acknowledges the reference to Directive 91/533/EEC in the Explanatory Report.[54] However, it only refers to the 'initial obligation to provide information', and appears to neglect the important requirement in case of changes of essential working conditions.[55] Indeed, Article 5 of that Directive puts modification of aspects of the contract or employment relationship within the same framework as the initial obligation (and in respect of time, an even tighter requirement of one month). As the ECSR has not only to examine the conformity of the legislation with the requirements of

[51] Decision on the merits of 23 June2010, *Confédération Générale du Travail (CGT) v France*, Collective Complaint No 55/2009 §66 (referring to Decision on the merits of 712. 2004 *CGT v France*, Collective Complaint No 22/2003 §39) and §67.

[52] See the possible exceptions provided for in the Appendix to Art 2§6 (see above).

[53] Conclusions 2003, Bulgaria.

[54] Decision on the merits of 9 December 2012, *Syndicat de Défense des Fonctionnaires v France*, Collective Complaint No 73/2011 §18.

[55] ibid.

Article 2§6, it will have to deal also with practice, for example, the question of appropriate sanctions in case of non-compliance with existing legal requirements.

G. Paragraph 7: Night Work

Inserted also by the RESC, Article 2§7 guarantees compensatory measures for persons performing night work. National law or practice must define 'night' within the context of this provision.

Measures that take account of the special nature of the work must at least include the following:

— regular medical examinations, including a check prior to employment in night work;
— the provision of possibilities for transfer to daytime work;
— continuous consultation with workers' representatives on the introduction of night work, on night work conditions and on measures taken to reconcile the needs of workers with the special nature of night work.[56]

Night work might amount to an unhealthy occupation, protection against which is provided for in Article 2§4 and will, accordingly, have to be taken into account.

III. IMPACT ON EUROPEAN HUMAN RIGHTS INSTRUMENTS

A. European Convention on Human Rights

The case law of the ECtHR is not rich in dealing with social rights in general (besides Article 11 ECHR), and in relation to working conditions is even less so. However, the ECtHR has laid down foundations for an increasing role of Article 8 ECHR as regards working conditions.[57] This might lead to some (probably only extreme) cases in which private or family life is endangered by working conditions. At least one example dealing with excessive working hours is under examination by the ECtHR,[58] which should take due account of the ECSR's case law.

[56] Conclusions 2003, Romania.

[57] For more details, see, for example, under Arts 3 and 24 RESC. See also N Bruun and K Lörcher, 'Social innovation: the new ECHR jurisprudence and its impact on fundamental social rights in labour law', in I Schömann (ed), *Mélanges à la mémoire de Yota Kravaritou: a trilingual tribute* (Brussels, ETUI, 2011) 353, 367 et seq.

[58] *Menteş ea v Turkey* App no 57818/10 ea (ECtHR, communicated to the Government on 26 May 2014).

B. Charter of Fundamental Rights of the European Union

Article 31 CFREU guarantees the right to 'fair and just working conditions'. Its second paragraph provides for the right to reasonable working time. According to the respective Explanations[59] this provision is, among other things, based on Article 2 ESC.[60] An increasing number of judgments by the CJEU deal with several aspects of working time, in particular holidays with pay, some of which also refer to the ESC, such as *Strack*.[61] The CJEU should also put human rights protection at the centre of its 'normal' jurisprudence and thus take into account the protection provided for in Article 2 as a minimum level when dealing with working time issues.

[59] Explanations Relating to the Charter of Fundamental Rights of the European Union [2007] OJ C303/17.

[60] ibid. 'Paragraph 2 is based on Directive 93/104/EC concerning certain aspects of the organisation of working time, Article 2 of the European Social Charter and point 8 of the Community Charter on the rights of workers.'

[61] Case C-579/12 RX-II *Strack* (CJEU 19 September 2013). In para 27 the CJEU refers to the Explanations quoted in n 32.

Article 3

The Right to Safe and Healthy Working Conditions

KLAUS LÖRCHER

Article 3—The right to safe and healthy working conditions

With a view to ensuring the effective exercise of the right to safe and healthy working conditions, the Parties undertake, in consultation with employers' and workers' organisations:

1. to formulate, implement and periodically review a coherent national policy on occupational safety, occupational health and the working environment. The primary aim of this policy shall be to improve occupational safety and health and to prevent accidents and injury to health arising out of, linked with or occurring in the course of work, particularly by minimising the causes of hazards inherent in the working environment;
2. to issue safety and health regulations;
3. to provide for the enforcement of such regulations by measures of supervision;
4. to promote the progressive development of occupational health services for all workers with essentially preventive and advisory functions.

Appendix Part II

Article 3, paragraph 4

It is understood that for the purposes of this provision the functions, organisation and conditions of operation of these services shall be determined by national laws or regulations, collective agreements or other means appropriate to national conditions.

I. INTRODUCTION

A. Context and Main Content

Closely linked to the 'right to just conditions of work' (Article 2), the right to safe and healthy working conditions (Article 3) is an important fundamental social right forming a sort of umbrella right for the former.[1] However, it has not acquired the status of a 'hard-core' right (Article A§1b). It has undergone a substantial improvement in the modernising process leading to the RESC.

Article 3 is based on the principles of improvement of occupational safety and health and the prevention of associated risks. It mainly regulates safety and health requirements from different angles. The overall consultation obligation is enshrined in its introductory part. The necessary political framework is defined in its §1, whereas §2 requires a specific legal framework. The latter cannot be effective if it is not adequately enforced (§3). Finally, supportive institutions are necessary to ensure effective implementation (§4).

Whereas two paragraphs (§§1 and 4) were newly introduced by the 1996 Charter, §3 ESC on consultation was removed to the Preamble, thus forming an overall obligation concerning all four paragraphs. In order to clarify the relationship between the old and new versions for ratification purposes (non-regression principle in Article B§1) the Appendix to Article B§2 defines that Article 3§2 RESC corresponds to Article 3§1 and §3 ESC, and Article 3§3 RESC corresponds to Article 3§2 and §3 ESC. The logic behind this complicated definition is that the consultation requirements that were included in §3 ESC are still relevant.

Nearly all contracting parties to the Charter have accepted Article 3 (exceptions being Azerbaijan, Bosnia and Herzegovina, Georgia and Croatia).[2] Some countries, however, have not accepted all provisions.[3]

B. International Sources

A set of important international instruments formed the basis for the content of this article. Moreover, many instruments have been developed after the adoption of the ESC and also the RESC.[4] Concerning more precisely the ILO Conventions, which formed the basis of several provisions,[5] the article

[1] See on 'working environment' M Mikkola *Social Human Right of Europe* (Porvoo, Karelatico, 2010) 193 et seq, with special emphasis on 'Protection of health and safety' 196 et seq. See also K Lasak, *Health and safety in the European social charter*, [2010] International Journal of Comparative Labour Law and Industrial Relations, 215 (2) 109–122, M Trilsch, *European Committee of Social Rights: the right to a healthy environment* [2009] International Journal of Constitutional Law, 7 (3) 529–538.

[2] This non-acceptance appears surprising, at least for the time after its accession to the EU.

[3] Obviously, the countries that have still only ratified the ESC are deprived of the possibility to accept the newly introduced §§1 and 4 by the RESC; as a further example concerning the RESC, seven states have not accepted §4 on occupational health services.

[4] See Council of Europe (ed), *Conditions of employment in the European Social Charter*, Human Rights, Social Charter monographs, No 6 (Strasbourg, 1999), Appendix VII, pp 123 et seq.

[5] [H Wiebringhaus], 'European Social Charter and International Labour Standards' (1961) 84 *International Labour Review* 354.

referred to 'some ten international labour Conventions each dealing with specific categories of workers'.[6]

In the meantime, the number of ILO Conventions has more than doubled and their scope has also been enlarged, in particular by the two fundamental Conventions No 155 on occupational safety and health (1981)[7] and No 187 on the promotional framework for occupational safety and health (2006).[8] Further conventions will be taken into account in dealing with specific paragraphs.[9]

Concerning EU law, several developments should be taken into account. First, the Community Charter of the Fundamental Social Rights of Workers (CCFSR), adopted in 1989[10] and referred to in the fifth recital of the TEU and Article 151§1 TFEU, contains a separate chapter on 'Health protection and safety at the workplace'.[11] Although adopted some months earlier, the so-called 'Framework Directive' on safety and health[12] has made this provision operational. It has been supplemented in the meantime by about 20 individual directives regulating specific aspects.[13] Even more importantly, in its Article 31 the EU Charter of Fundamental Rights has explicitly recognised the right to just working conditions (see below).

Finally, it should be noted that Article 7(b) ICESCR refers to this right in a general way.[14]

C. Relationship to Other Provisions of the Charter

The relationship of Article 3 on safety and health at the workplace to working time provisions, as guaranteed in Article 2, is obvious and has also

[6] ibid 361.

[7] See also Protocol of 2002 to the Occupational Safety and Health Convention, 1981.

[8] For an overview of all ILO instruments relating to occupational safety and health working time, see the ILO website, section on 'International Labour Standards'.

[9] See eg the reference in Conclusions 2013—Article 3§2 on Moldova—to the non-ratification of ILO Convention No 115 on Radiation Protection (1960).

[10] Commission of the European Communities (ed), *Community Charter of the Fundamental Social Rights of Workers* (Luxembourg, 1990); B Bercusson, 'The European Community's Charter of Fundamental Social Rights of Workers' (1990) 53 *The Modern Law Review, New Perspectives on European Law* 624, reprinted in: ETUI (ed), *Labour Law and Social Europe—Selected writings of Brian Bercusson* (Brussels, 2009) 55 et seq.

[11] Para 19§1: 'Every worker must enjoy satisfactory health and safety conditions in his working environment. Appropriate measures must be taken in order to achieve further harmonization of conditions in this area while maintaining the improvements made.'

[12] Council Directive 89/391/EEC of 12 June 1989 on the introduction of measures to encourage improvements in the safety and health of workers at work [1989] OJ L183/1.

[13] For an overview of these directives, see the website of the European Agency for Safety and Health at Work (EU-OHSA), in particular in the section on 'legislation'.

[14] 'The States Parties to the present Covenant recognize the right of everyone to the enjoyment of just and favourable conditions of work which ensure, in particular: ... (b) Safe and healthy working conditions', see General Comment No 23 (2016).

been explicitly recognised by the ECSR, which stressed that 'the provisions of the Revised Charter concerning working time are intended to protect workers' safety and health in an effective manner'.[15] However, Article 2§2 and §6—providing, respectively, for public holidays with pay and for information on essential aspects of the employment relationship—may be considered not directly related to safety and health.[16] Conversely, Article 2§4 and §7—providing, respectively, for compensation in cases of certain unhealthy work and for protection in the case of night work (see also Articles 7§8 for young workers and 8§4 for pregnant workers)—show the close relationship between the two articles. However, the ECSR excludes risks related to work organisation, in particular working time, and concludes that this does not come within the scope of Article 3.[17]

In contrast, the ECSR is more open in relation to Article 11. Indeed, it considered that its findings in connection with Article 11 applied mutatis mutandis to Article 3.[18] Importantly, the ECSR noted that the right to protection of health guaranteed in Article 11 of the Charter complemented Articles 2 and 3 ECHR—as interpreted by the ECtHR—by imposing a range of positive obligations designed to secure its effective exercise.

Regarding the relationship to the right to social security (Article 12) concerning arrangements for compensating for occupational diseases and accidents, the ECSR noted that the majority of States Parties to the Charter had introduced specific insurance for occupational risks, which generally offer more generous benefits than those paid by sickness and invalidity insurance schemes. It did not, however, consider that states were required to introduce such insurance to comply with Article 3§1.[19]

There is a very close link to Article 22 containing the right to take part in the determination and improvement of working conditions and the working environment.[20] Article 20 leads to the conclusion that male and female workers are now equally protected even when working under hard, unusual or strenuous conditions; nevertheless, a gender mainstreaming approach will require a close look at the consequences of legislation and practice for each of them.[21]

[15] Decision on the merits of 7 December 2004, *Confédération Générale du Travail (CGT) v France*, Collective Complaint No 22/2003 §34.

[16] See CJEU Judgment 12 November 1996, Case C-84/94 *United Kingdom of Great Britain and Northern Ireland v Council of the European Union* [1996] ECR I–5755 §37.

[17] Decision on the merits of 23 June 2010, *Confédération française de l'encadrement CFE-CGC v France*, Collective Complaint No 56/2009 §§69 and 71.

[18] Decision on the merits 12 June 2006, *Marangopoulos Foundation for Human Rights (MFHR) v Greece*, Collective Complaint No 30/2005, §222.

[19] Decision on the merits of 12 June 2006, *MFHR v Greece*, Collective Complaint No 30/2005, §226.

[20] For more detail. see the chapter on Art 22 by B Veneziani in this volume.

[21] See the chapter on Art 20 by C Kollonay-Lehoczky in this volume.

II. CONTENT

The right of every worker to a safe and healthy working environment is a 'widely recognised principle, stemming directly from the right to personal integrity, one of the fundamental principles of human rights'.[22] The purpose of Article 3 is thus directly related to that of Article 2 ECHR, which recognises the right to life.[23] It applies to the whole economy, covering both the public and private sectors[24] and to all workers, including the self-employed, especially as the latter are often employed in high-risk sectors.[25] States' first obligation under Article 3 is to ensure the right to safe and healthy working standards at the highest possible level.[26]

Assessment of the conformity of national situations with Article 3 is taken into account under Article 2§4, which requires provision for reduced working hours or additional paid holidays in dangerous and unhealthy occupations where it has not yet been possible to eliminate or reduce risks sufficiently.[27]

The ECSR's general approach of examining conformity by a means-oriented rather than result-oriented method has been criticised.[28] Indeed, looking for (positive or negative) 'trends' does not appear sufficient.

The Explanatory Report explains that the requirement of consultation with employers' and workers' organisations contained in Article 3§3 ESC has been included in the introductory part of Article 3 RESC and consequently applies to all four paragraphs contained in Article 3 of this instrument.[29] This aspect will therefore be dealt with under each paragraph.

A. Paragraph 1—Policy Requirements

This new provision was not included in the 1961 Charter. In contrast, the duty to consult employers' and workers' organisations on occupational health and safety was already contained in Article 3(3) ESC.

The Explanatory Report states that this paragraph obliges the Parties to formulate, implement and periodically review a coherent national policy on occupational safety, occupational health and the working environment.

[22] Conclusions I, Statement of Interpretation on Art 3.
[23] Conclusions XIV-2, Statement of Interpretation on Art 3.
[24] Conclusions II, Statement of Interpretation on Art 3.
[25] Conclusions 2005, Estonia.
[26] Decision on the merits of 12 June 2006, *MFHR v Greece*, Collective Complaint No 30/2005 §§223 and 224.
[27] Conclusions 2005, Statement of Interpretation on Art 2§4; see in particular Conclusions 2005, Lithuania.
[28] Mikkola (n 1) 196.
[29] Council of Europe (1996), Explanatory Report to the European Social Charter (Revised) §30.

It emphasises that the aim of this policy shall be to improve occupational safety and health and to prevent accidents and injury to health, inter alia, by minimising risks.[30]

Generally speaking, Article 3§1 requires states to formulate, implement and periodically review a coherent policy on occupational health and safety in consultation with social partners, that is, employers' organisations and trade unions.[31]

(i) General Objective of National Policy

According to the ECSR's case law[32] the main policy objective must be to foster and preserve a culture of prevention in the areas of health and safety at national level. Occupational risk prevention must be a priority. It must be incorporated into the public authorities' activities at all levels and form part of other public policies (on employment, persons with disabilities, equal opportunities and so on).[33]

The policy and strategies adopted must be regularly assessed and reviewed, particularly in light of changing risks.

In its most recent Statement of Interpretation concerning Article 3§1 the ECSR indicated that it would include work-related stress, aggression and violence when examining whether policies are regularly assessed or reviewed in light of emerging risks.[34]

In Conclusions 2013[35] the ECSR found that Italy was lacking a functioning overall policy for occupational health and safety; it also referred to an infringement procedure against Italy for not transposing Council Directive 89/391/EEC on the introduction of measures to encourage improvements in the safety and health of workers at work.[36]

In assessing the interpretation and application of Article 3§1 it is noteworthy that the ECSR takes note of the (non-)ratification of relevant ILO Conventions.[37] But harmony with the substantial requirements could be improved by referring, among other things, to the relevant General Survey

[30] ibid §31.

[31] Conclusions 2003, Statement of Interpretation on Art 3§1; see in particular Conclusions 2003, Bulgaria.

[32] The respective descriptions of the ECSR's case law have been taken from the Digest of the Case Law of the European Committee of Social Rights (1 September 2008).

[33] Conclusions 2005, Lithuania.

[34] Conclusions 2013, General Introduction, Statement of Interpretation on Art 3.

[35] ECSR, 15 January 2013, Press Briefing Elements, Conclusions 2013/XX-2 (Brussels, 29 January 2014).

[36] It would appear that the infringement procedure referred to in the Conclusions (No 2010/4227 of 21 November 2012) had not at that stage led to an action against Italy by the Commission.

[37] For example, non-ratification of ILO Conventions 155 and 187: Andorra, Armenia, Estonia and Malta.

compiling the case law of the CEACR on Convention No 155.[38] Moreover, the place of preventive policy in the overall political sphere and the issue of periodic reviews should be given more relevance. In particular, in times of deregulation and of economic and financial crisis prevention, costs run the risk of being considered less relevant compared with 'competitiveness' and budgetary restraints.[39]

(ii) Organisation of Occupational Risk Prevention

The ECSR's case law stresses the need for a culture of prevention, which implies that all the partners—authorities, employers and workers—will be actively involved in occupational risk prevention, working within a well-defined framework of rights and duties and predetermined structures.

The main aspects are:

— *at company level*: besides compliance with protective rules, the assessment of work-related risks and the adoption of preventive measures geared to the nature of risks, as well as information and training for workers. Employers and/or users are required to provide appropriate information, training and medical supervision for temporary workers and employees on fixed-term contracts, that is, taking account of accumulated periods of exposure to dangerous substances while working for different employers;

— *at government level*: the development of an appropriate system of public prevention and supervision, which is generally the task of the labour inspectorate. The only responsibility of inspectors covered by Article 3§1 is their duty to share the knowledge about risks and risk prevention they have acquired during their inspections and investigations conducted as part of their preventive activities (information, education, prevention). Their duty to ensure compliance with the rules comes under the rights guaranteed by Article 3§3 (right to occupational health and safety—supervisory measures).[40]

In any event, new challenges and dangers for workers' health coming from, among other causes, globalisation or digitalisation (for example,

[38] ILO, International Labour Conference, 98th Session, 2009 Report III (Part 1B) General Survey concerning the Occupational Safety and Health Convention, 1981 (No 155), the Occupational Safety and Health Recommendation,1981 (No 164), and the Protocol of 2002 to the Occupational Safety and Health Convention 1981, Geneva (General Survey 2009), see paras 53 et seq on principles of national policy for prevention and paras 76 et seq on the review process.

[39] See in relation to further problems such as short-term profit seeking, Mikkola (n 1) 194.

[40] Conclusions 2005, Lithuania.

cloud-working) require specific measures at the political and also legislative levels.[41]

(iii) *Improvement of Occupational Health and Safety (Research and Training)*

According to the ECSR's case law, the methods used to increase general awareness, knowledge and understanding of the concepts of danger and risk and of ways of preventing and managing them must include:[42]

— training (qualified staff);
— information (statistical systems and dissemination of knowledge);
— quality assurance (professional qualifications, certification systems for facilities and equipment);
— research (scientific and technical expertise).

In its most recent Statement of Interpretation on Article 3§1, the ECSR indicated that it would examine research, knowledge and communication activities on psychosocial risks, when examining the involvement of public authorities in the improvement of occupational health and safety.[43]

(iv) *Consultation with Employers' and Workers' Organisations*

The ECSR's case law stresses that when devising and implementing national policies and strategies, the relevant authorities must consult trade unions and employers' organisations at national, sectoral and company level.

Consultation between the relevant authorities and employers' and workers' organisations on measures to improve occupational health and safety was already required under Article 3§3 ESC. Therefore the ECSR's case law with regard to Article 3§3 ESC applies mutatis mutandis also to Article 3§1 RESC.[44] However, Article 3§1 RESC requires broader consultation in that it calls not only for tripartite cooperation between authorities, employers and workers to seek ways of improving their working conditions and working environment but also for the coordination of their activities and cooperation on key safety and prevention issues.

Consultation mechanisms and procedures must be set up. At national and sectoral level, this requirement is satisfied where there are specialised bodies made up of government, employers' and workers' representatives, which

[41] See, for example, W Kohte, 'Arbeitsschutz in der digitalen Arbeitswelt' (2015) *Neue Zeitschrift für Arbeitsrecht* 1417.
[42] Conclusions 2003, Statement of Interpretation on Art 3§1; see in particular Conclusions 2003, Bulgaria.
[43] Conclusions 2013 General Introduction, Statement of Interpretation on Art 3.
[44] Conclusions 2003, Sweden.

are consulted by the public authorities. These bodies may be permanent or ad hoc consultation forums. At company level, the employer's duty to consult trade unions forms part of the 'right of workers to take part in the determination and improvement of the working conditions and working environment in the undertaking' guaranteed by Article 22 of the Charter. Consultation at company level in states that have accepted both Article 3§1 and Article 22 is examined only under Article 22.[45]

B. Paragraph 2—Legal Requirements (Safety and Health Regulations)

Besides the general political framework defined in §1, the most important aspect is the adoption of a comprehensive legal framework, as required by §2. According to the ECSR's case law the determination and implementation of an occupational health and safety policy must be based on a precise legal framework concerning the following elements:

(i) Risks that Must be Regulated[46]

States' first obligation under Article 3 is to ensure the right to safe and healthy working standards of the highest possible level. Under §2, this obligation entails issuing health and safety regulations providing for preventive and protective measures against workplace risks recognised by the scientific community and laid down in Community and international regulations and standards.[47]

The Charter does not actually define the risks to be regulated. Supervision takes an indirect form, referring to international technical occupational health and safety standards, such as the ILO Conventions[48] and EU Directives on health and safety at work.[49]

Domestic law must include framework legislation—often the Labour Code—setting out employers' responsibilities and workers' rights and duties, as well as specific regulations. In view of the particularly variable nature of the subject matter in light of technological, ergonomic and medical advances, existing regulations must be geared to new circumstances when the rules prove to be no longer appropriate to the situation. Depending on such changes, the ECSR states, where necessary, which new risks it is referring to. The risks to which the ECSR currently refers are as follows.

[45] Conclusions 2005, Lithuania; Conclusions 2003, Statement of Interpretation on Art 3§2; see, for example, Conclusions 2003, Bulgaria.

[46] Conclusions XIV-2, Statement of Interpretation on Art 3§1 of the 1961 Charter (ie on Art 3§2 of the Revised Charter).

[47] Decision on the merits of 6 December 2006, *MFHR v Greece*, Collective Complaint No 30/2005 §224.

[48] See the references in n 8.

[49] See the references in n 13.

(a) Establishment, Alteration and Upkeep of Workplaces—Work Equipment

- Workplaces and equipment, particularly the protection of machines, manual handling of loads, work with display screen equipment.
- Hygiene (shops and offices).
- Maximum weight.
- Air pollution, noise and vibration; personal protective equipment; safety and/or health signs at work.

(b) Hazardous Agents and Substances

- Chemical, physical and biological agents, particularly carcinogens, including: white lead (in paint), benzene, asbestos, vinyl chloride monomer, metallic lead and its ionic compounds and ionising radiation.
- Control of major accident hazards involving dangerous substances.

(c) Risks Connected with Certain Sectors

- Indication of weight on packages to be transported by boat.
- Protection of dockers against accidents.
- Dock handling.
- Building safety rules, temporary or mobile construction sites.
- Mines, extractive industries using drilling and opencast or underground mining.
- Ships and fishing vessels.
- Prevention of major industrial accidents.
- Risks connected with agriculture and transport must also be controlled.

(d) Risks Connected with Psychological Factors

In its most recent Statement of Interpretation[50] the ECSR added to the list set out above risks connected with psychological factors. It therefore will:

- include work-related stress, aggression and violence when examining the risks covered by occupational health and safety regulations;
- examine measures taken by public authorities to protect workers against work-related stress, aggression and violence specific to work performed under atypical working relationships, in examining the personal scope of occupational health and safety regulations.

[50] Conclusions 2013 General Introduction, Statement of Interpretation on Art 3.

(e) Further Developments

According to Conclusions 2013[51] the ECSR proceeds from the presumption that the requirements of the Charter are met if the Union *acquis* in this field is implemented, which means that the EU member states' record of compliance with the Charter is high. However, residual problems remain: in some countries, for example, self-employed workers are excluded from the scope of otherwise satisfactory regulations (Andorra, Austria, France, the United Kingdom). In other countries domestic workers are not covered (Hungary, Romania).

(ii) Levels of Prevention and Protection

In its case law the ECSR requires that most of the risks listed above have to be covered by a specific regulation. Regulations must set out rules in sufficient detail for them to be applied properly and efficiently.[52] Accordingly, the ECSR does not consider that states are required to introduce specific insurance for occupational diseases and accidents to comply with Article 3§2.[53] Limits must be aligned with those adopted in the above-mentioned international reference standards,[54] for example, in respect of benzene.[55]

A state is considered to have satisfied this general requirement if it has transposed most of the *acquis communautaire* (now *acquis de l'Union*) on occupational health and safety into its domestic legislation.[56]

The control carried out by the ECSR is also affected by the relative size of the sectors of activity of the country's economy, and hence the number of workers involved, the degree of danger of the activities and trends in the situation with regard to employment injuries and occupational diseases.[57]

States are required to pay particular attention with regard to asbestos and ionising radiation, producing evidence that workers are protected to a level at least equivalent to that set by international reference standards.[58] With regard to asbestos, the ECSR refers to international standards such as Council Directive 83/477/EEC on the protection of workers from risks related to exposure to asbestos at work,[59] as amended by Directive

[51] ECSR, 15 January 2013, Press Briefing Elements, Conclusions 2013/XX-2 (Brussels, 29 January 2014).

[52] Conclusions XIV-2, Norway.

[53] Decision on the merits of 6 December 2006, *MFHR v Greece*, Collective Complaint No 30/2005 §226.

[54] Conclusions XIV-2, Italy; Conclusions XIV-2, Spain.

[55] Conclusions XIV-2, Spain.

[56] Conclusions 2005, Cyprus.

[57] Conclusions XIV-2, Portugal.

[58] To ensure that this was indeed the case, the ECSR put general questions on the subject to the states in Conclusions XIII-4.

[59] Council Directive 83/477/EEC of 19 September 1983 on the protection of workers from the risks related to exposure to asbestos at work, [1983] OJ L263/25.

2003/18/EC.[60] ILO Convention No 162 on asbestos of 1986 stresses the need for exposure limits to be equal to or lower than those laid down by these international instruments; it adds more elements that must be fulfilled in order to be in conformity with Article 3§2 in relation to the use of asbestos.

National standards with regard to ionising radiation must take account of the recommendations made in 1990 by the International Commission on Radiological Protection,[61] relating in particular to maximum doses of exposure in the workplace but also to persons who, although not directly assigned to work in a radioactive environment, may be exposed to radiation occasionally. The transposition into domestic law of Council Directive 96/29/Euratom of 13 May 1996, laying down basic safety standards for the protection of the health of workers and the general public against the dangers arising from ionising radiation,[62] is sufficient, as this Directive takes up the International Commission for Radiation Protection (ICRP) recommendations.[63]

In assessing this approach the references to relevant international and European standards ensure an important level of protection. However, to be generally satisfied whether a particular country has transposed most of the *acquis de l'Union* on occupational health and safety into its domestic legislation would appear to be problematic. It is high time that the higher RESC standards were interpreted as prohibiting exclusions from personal or material scope, comprising an overall prohibition of asbestos or any other level required to effectively ensure the health of workers in their workplaces.

(iii) Consultation with Employers' and Workers' Organisations

Regulations must be drawn up in consultation with employers' and workers' organisations (on the scope of this consultation, see above under Article 3§1).

Consultation between the relevant authorities and employers' and workers' organisations on measures to improve occupational health and safety was already required under Article 3§3 ESC. The requirement in Article 3§2 RESC is the same, mutatis mutandis, as that in Article 3§3 ESC.[64]

[60] Directive 2003/18/EC of the European Parliament and of the Council of 27 March 2003 amending Council Directive 83/477/EEC on the protection of workers from the risks related to exposure to asbestos at work [2003] OJ L97/48.

[61] ICRP (1991) 1990 Recommendations of the International Commission on Radiological Protection, ICRP, publication No 60 (and superseded by ICRP publication No 103); available on the ICRP website.

[62] Directive 2013/59/Euratom will repeal the Directive by 6 February 2018.

[63] Conclusions XVI–2, Netherlands.

[64] Conclusions 2005, Norway.

C. Paragraph 3—Enforcement Requirements

More concretely than the general obligation to maintain a system of labour inspection (Articles 20§5 ESC, and A§4 RESC), Article 3§3 3 RESC (and Article 3§2 ESC) oblige contracting parties to implement effective enforcement mechanisms. Based on the lack of effective supervision of health and safety regulations, the ECSR recalls that compliance with the Charter 'cannot be ensured solely by the operation of legislation if this is not effectively applied and rigorously supervised'.[65] The enforcement of health and safety regulations required by Article 3§2 is therefore essential if the right embodied in Article 3 is to be effective.[66] Whereas the ECSR allows a measure of discretion regarding not only how they organise their inspection services, but also what resources they allocate to them under Article 20§5 ESC, it is strict on services under Article 3 as they are the main safeguard of health and safety in the workplace: 'there must be a minimum number of regular inspections to ensure that the largest possible number of workers benefit from the right enshrined in Article 3'[67] and that the risk of accidents is reduced to a minimum.[68]

In its most recent Statement of Interpretation on Article 3§3, the ECSR announced that it would examine measures taken by public authorities to:

— address increasingly complex and multidimensional demands on the competence, resources and institutional capacity of labour inspection systems;
— focus labour inspection on small and medium-sized enterprises (SMEs).[69]

Generally speaking, the important case law of the ILO on labour inspection should be taken into account, in the sense that it should form a minimum level of protection for the interpretation of Article 3§3.[70]

According to the ECSR's case law, the aim of Article 3§3 is to guarantee the effective implementation of the right to safety and health at work. It thus

[65] Decision on the merits of 9 September 1999, *International Commission of Jurists v Portugal*, Collective Complaint No 1/1998 §33.

[66] Decision on the merits of 12 June 2006, *MFHR v Greece*, Collective Complaint No 30/2005 §228.

[67] Conclusions XIV-2, Belgium.

[68] See Decision on the merits of 12 June 2006, *MFHR v Greece*, Collective Complaint No 30/2005 §229.

[69] Conclusions 2013, General Introduction, Statement of Interpretation on Art 3.

[70] ILO (ed), International Labour Conference 95th Session, 2006, Report III (Part 1B)—General Survey of the reports concerning the Labour Inspection Convention, 1947 (No 81), and the Protocol of 1995 to the Labour Inspection Convention, 1947, and the Labour Inspection Recommendation, 1947 (No 81), the Labour Inspection (Mining and Transport) Recommendation, 1947 (No 82), the Labour Inspection (Agriculture) Convention, 1969 (No 129), and the Labour Inspection (Agriculture) Recommendation, 1969 (No 133), Geneva 2006 (General Survey 2006).

goes beyond the general obligations deriving from Article A§4 concerning the maintenance of a system of labour inspection.

(i) Employment Injuries and Occupational Diseases[71]

Monitoring trends in the relationship between the number of accidents and the total number of workers makes it possible to determine the frequency of injuries (number per hundred workers). A situation is considered incompatible with the Charter in which, for several years, this frequency is clearly too high for it to be maintained that the right to health and safety at work is being effectively secured. This assessment can be made on the basis of absolute figures[72] or in relation to the average in the state parties to the Charter.[73] It relates to total injuries in all sectors or in one sector in particular. The same approach is applied to the relationship between the number of fatal accidents and total injuries.

The criteria for the assessment of trends in occupational diseases have not yet been established by the ECSR. The problem stems primarily from the time lag between the emergence of the risk, its identification and the notification or even the recognition of the illness.

In its Conclusions 2013[74] the ECSR held that a fatal accident rate which is more than twice as high as the European average constitutes evidence that measures taken to reduce such accidents are inadequate. On this basis the ECSR found the situation in Bulgaria, Lithuania, Republic of Moldova, Romania, the Russian Federation, Turkey and Ukraine to be in breach of the Charter. The ECSR also found fault with the systems for reporting accidents and occupational injuries in certain countries (Albania, Republic of Moldova), with indications of widespread underreporting and even concealment of workplace accidents and injuries. In some countries (Albania, Republic of Moldova, Ukraine) the ECSR found the entire labour inspection system to be inefficient, including, due to insufficient resources, low numbers of inspection visits or ineffective fines and sanctions.

(ii) Workers and Sectors Covered by the Regulations

All workers, all workplaces and all sectors of activity must be covered by occupational health and safety regulations.[75]

[71] Conclusions XIV-2, Statement of Interpretation on Art 3§2 of the 1961 Charter [ie Art 3§3 of the Revised Charter].

[72] Conclusions 2003, Slovenia.

[73] Conclusions XIV-2, Portugal.

[74] ECSR, 15 January 2013, Press Briefing Elements, Conclusions 2013/XX-2 (Brussels, 29 January 2014).

[75] Conclusions II, Statement of Interpretation on Art 3§1 of the 1961 Charter [ie on Art 3§2 of the Revised Charter].

The term 'workers' used in Article 3 covers both employed and self-employed persons, especially as the latter are often employed in high-risk sectors.[76] The aim is to ensure that the working environment is safe and healthy for all operators, where necessary by adopting rules adapted to the operators' specific situation.[77]

All economic sectors must be covered by the regulations.[78] It is not necessary for a specific text to be adopted for each activity or sector, but the wording of texts should be sufficiently precise to allow their effective application in all sectors, taking particular account of the scale or degree of danger in each sector. Sectors must be covered in their entirety, and all companies must be covered, regardless of the number of employees.[79]

No workplace, even if inhabited, can be 'exempted' from the application of health and safety rules. Workers employed on residential premises—domestic staff and home workers—must therefore be covered, but the rules may be adapted to the type of activity and the relatively risk-free nature of these workers' occupations, and be worded in general terms.[80]

(iii) Consultation with Employers' and Workers' Organisations

Regulations must be drawn up in consultation with employers' and workers' organisations (on the scope of this consultation, see above under Article 3§1).

Consultation between the relevant authorities and employers' and workers' organisations on measures to improve occupational health and safety was already required under Article 3§3 ESC. The requirement in Article 3§2 RESC is the same, mutatis mutandis, as that in Article 3§3 ESC.[81]

D. Paragraph 4—Occupational Health Services

Concerning this new paragraph introduced by the RESC, the Explanatory Report stresses that this provision provides that the Parties shall promote the progressive development of occupational health services for all workers with essentially preventive and advisory functions. In the appendix it is provided that for the purposes of this provision the function, organisation and conditions of operation of occupational health services shall be

[76] Conclusions 2005, Estonia.

[77] Conclusions III, Statement of Interpretation on Art 3§1 of the ESC (ie on Art 3§2 RESC); Conclusions IV, Statement of Interpretation on Art 3§1 of the ESC [ie on Art 3§2 RESC]; Conclusions XIII-4, Belgium.

[78] Conclusions I, Statement of Interpretation on Art 3.

[79] Conclusions XIII-1, Greece.

[80] Conclusions XIV-2, Belgium.

[81] Conclusions 2005, Norway.

determined by national laws or regulations, collective agreements or other means appropriate to national conditions.[82]

According to its case law, the ECSR requires that all workers in all branches of economic activity and all companies must have access to occupational health services. These services may be run jointly by several companies.[83]

State parties are required to promote the progressive development of such services. This means that 'a State Party must take measures that allow it to achieve the objectives of the Charter within a reasonable time, with measurable progress and to an extent consistent with the maximum use of available resources'.[84] Therefore, if occupational health services are not established for all enterprises, the authorities must develop a strategy, in consultation with employers' and employees' organisations, for that purpose.[85]

III. IMPACT ON EUROPEAN HUMAN RIGHTS INSTRUMENTS

A. European Convention on Human Rights (ECHR)

As might appear normal, the case law of the ECtHR is not rich in dealing with social rights in general (besides on Article 11 ECHR), and as regards working conditions even less. However, starting from the right to life in Article 2 of the Convention, in cases of fatal work accidents the ECtHR has developed an increasing role for Article 8 ECHR[86] in relation to health and safety. Indeed it recognised a close relationship between Article 2 and the right to private life under Article 8 of the Convention in the judgment in *Vilnes v Norway*,[87] when the ECtHR examined Articles 2 and 8 of the Convention at the same time. In *Binişan v Romania*[88] the ECtHR found a violation of the responding state in relation to negligence on the part of a national railway company, with no effective investigation into who

[82] §§34 and 36 (§35 clarifies that the term 'occupational health services' shall include the French concept of *médecine du travail*).

[83] Conclusions 2003, Statement of Interpretation on Art 3§4, see eg Conclusions 2003, Bulgaria.

[84] Decision on the merits of 4 November 2003, *Association Internationale Autisme-Europe (AIAE) v France*, Collective Complaint No 13/2002 §53.

[85] Conclusions 2003, Statement of Interpretation on Art 3§4.

[86] For more details, see eg under Arts 3 and 24 RESC. See also N Bruun and K Lörcher, 'Social innovation: the new ECHR jurisprudence and its impact on fundamental social rights in labour law', in I Schömann (ed), *Mélanges à la mémoire de Yota Kravaritou: a trilingual tribute* (Brussels, ETUI, 2011) 353, 367 et seq.

[87] *Vilnes ea v Norway* App nos 52806/09 and 22703/10 (ECtHR, 5 December 2013) (see for the general principles paras 219 and 220).

[88] *Binişan v Romania* App no 39438/05 (ECtHR, 20 May 2014).

was liable for the accident.[89] A similar approach is found in *Kosamata v Ukraine*[90] and in *Pop v Romania*.[91]

Importantly, the ECSR noted that the right to protection of health guaranteed in Article 11 of the Charter complemented Articles 2 and 3 of the European Convention on Human Rights—as interpreted by the European Court of Human Rights—by imposing a range of positive obligations designed to secure its effective exercise. This normative partnership between the two instruments is underscored by the ECSR's emphasis on human dignity. In Collective Complaint *FIDH v France* (No 14/2003), it stated that 'human dignity is the fundamental value and indeed the core of positive European human rights law—whether under the European Social Charter or under the European Convention of Human Rights and [that] health care is a prerequisite for the preservation of human dignity'.

B. Charter of Fundamental Rights of the European Union (CFREU)

Article 31 CFREU guarantees the right to 'Fair and just working conditions'. Under this heading, §1 provides for safe and healthy working conditions.[92] According to the respective Explanations[93] this provision is drawn, inter alia, from Article 3 ESC.[94] Together with all the other links between EU law and the Charter[95] this close relationship leads to the conclusion that the CJEU should take account of the case law of the ECSR as a minimum level of protection as regards the interpretation of Article 31§1 CFREU.

[89] In describing the 'Relevant Domestic Law' the Court refers to the material national legislation on safety and health, see paras 44 to 46, referring to Order No 26 of 11 January 2000 which sets out 'the health and safety regulations for the rail transport industry'.

[90] *Kosmata v Ukraine* App nos 10558/11 and 28218/11 (ECtHR, 5 January 2015).

[91] *Pop v Romania* App no 43885/13 (19 July 2016).

[92] See T Blanke, 'Fair and just working conditions (Article 31)', in B Bercusson (ed), *European Labour Law and the EU Charter of Fundamental Rights* (Baden-Baden, Nomos, 2006) 357 et seq; K Lörcher, 'Das soziale Grundrecht auf gesunde, sichere und würdige Arbeitsbedingungen', in W Kohte/K Feldhoff/U Faber (eds), *Gesamtes Arbeitsschutzrecht* (Baden-Baden, Nomos, 2014) 27 et seq (with specific reference to the Charter in paras 18 et seq).

[93] Explanations Relating to the Charter of Fundamental Rights [2007] OJ C303/17.

[94] ibid, 'Paragraph 1 of this Article is based on Directive 89/391/EEC on the introduction of measures to encourage improvements in the safety and health of workers at work. It also draws on Article 3 of the Social Charter and point 19 of the Community Charter on the rights of workers' (for the purpose of the working conditions which require respect of dignity, the Explanation also refers to Art 26 RESC).

[95] For more details see the chapter by O de Schutter in this volume.

Article 4

The Right to a Fair Remuneration

ZOE ADAMS AND SIMON DEAKIN

Article 4—The right to a fair remuneration

With a view to ensuring the effective exercise of the right to a fair remuneration, the Parties undertake:

1. to recognise the right of workers to a remuneration such as will give them and their families a decent standard of living;
2. to recognise the right of workers to an increased rate of remuneration for overtime work, subject to exceptions in particular cases;
3. to recognise the right of men and women workers to equal pay for work of equal value;
4. to recognise the right of all workers to a reasonable period of notice for termination of employment;
5. to permit deductions from wages only under conditions and to the extent prescribed by national laws or regulations or fixed by collective agreements or arbitration awards.

The exercise of these rights shall be achieved by freely concluded collective agreements, by statutory wage-fixing machinery, or by other means appropriate to national conditions.

Appendix:

Article 4, paragraph 4

This provision shall be so understood as not to prohibit immediate dismissal for any serious offence.

Article 4, paragraph 5

It is understood that a Contracting Party may give the undertaking required in this paragraph if the great majority of workers are not permitted to suffer deductions from wages either by law or through collective agreements or arbitration awards, the exceptions being those persons not so covered.

I. INTRODUCTION

A. Context and Main Content

Article 4 is a rare example of an international human rights standard that addresses the core right to a decent minimum level of remuneration. The Article protects a number of complementary aspects of this right: the right to a wage that will provide workers and their families with a 'decent standard of living'; the right to additional pay for overtime; the right for male and female workers to equal pay on the basis of work of equal value; the right to reasonable notice prior to termination; and the right to protection against arbitrary deductions from pay. The core right is the first, from which the others are in essence derived. However, and despite its crucial importance in practice for all wage and salary earners, this right has proved to be controversial throughout its history.[1] This is for several reasons, but above all because the right is defined in instrumental terms: the wage must be such as to bring about a result: access of workers and their families to a 'decent standard of living', which is itself not clearly defined.

Numerous issues arise from this approach. It is necessary to arrive at a view not just on what a 'decent' standard of living is, but also to consider the relationship between wages and living standards, as they are not the same thing. Thus a critical issue is to what extent account should be taken of the operation of the tax and benefit system, which may lead to significant divergences between gross and net wages. There are additional problems. For example, should attention be focused on the minimum rates of pay set by law or by collective agreements in a given country, or on wages actually received by low income earners in a given country? When choosing an average wage against which to benchmark minimum wages, how should the average be calculated? The answers to these questions depend in part on the detail of statistical categories and definitions and on the nature and quality of available data on wages and incomes in different member states, but they are also framed by normative considerations. Is Article 4 intended to ensure proportionality of effort and reward; to reduce poverty; to promote social cohesion; or some combination of all of these aims?

In its first Conclusions on the 1961 Charter, published in 1969, the Committee of Independent Experts, the forerunner of the ECSR, took the view that Article 4§1 'obliges contracting states to take appropriate measures to ensure a decent standard of living for workers and their families' and that their efforts had to be 'continuous', taking account of 'the fact that the socio-economic status of the worker and his family changes and that his

[1] Conclusions XIV-2: 'the interpretation of Art 4§1 has proved difficult through the history of the supervision of the Charter'.

[*sic*] basic needs, which at first are centred on the provision of purely basic material necessities such as food and housing, subsequently move towards concerns of a more advanced and complex nature, such as educational facilities and cultural and social benefits'.[2] This then was a recognition that the right contained in Article 4§1 was not simply concerned with fair pay, in the sense of a wage that reflected the individual worker's efforts and inputs. The wage had a wider social function, which was to ensure access on the part of earners and their dependants to an income that met certain needs. These were needs that went beyond the physical requirements of existence, and which could be expected to change over time according to the rate of material, social and cultural progress in a given country. This approach is broadly consistent with the concept of the minimum wage as a device for reducing or alleviating poverty, defined as a state of affairs in which individuals and households cannot access a standard of living that permits them to participate at a basic level in society.[3]

In its fifth Conclusions, which appeared in 1977,[4] the ECSR went further in defining the right in Article 4§1 in terms consistent with the objective of promoting social cohesion through the reduction of earnings inequalities.[5] Adopting an 'assessment method based on statistical studies carried out by the OECD and the Council of Europe'[6] the ECSR arrived at a 'so-called decency threshold' for defining the lowest wage compatible with Article 4§1. The premise of this methodology was that 'wages which fall markedly below those of the community in general could not be considered decent or fair'.[7] This was translated into a benchmark that defined a decent wage as at least equivalent to 68 per cent of the national average wage, although if wages fell below that level, the ECSR would also consider the role of

[2] Conclusions I (1969).

[3] On this, widely adopted, definition of poverty, see P Townsend, *Poverty in the United Kingdom* (London, Allen Lane, 1979) 312: 'Individuals, families and groups in the population can be said to be in poverty when they lack the resources to obtain the types of diet, participate in the activities and have the living conditions and amenities which are customary, or are at least widely encouraged or approved, in the societies to which they belong. Their resources are so seriously below those commanded by the average individual or family that they are, in effect, excluded from ordinary living patterns, customs and activities'.

[4] Conclusions V (1977).

[5] Inequality and poverty are related, because as Townsend pointed out, 'poverty can be defined and applied consistently only in terms of the concept of relative deprivation' (Townsend (n 3) 31). However, a broader case can be made for the reduction of income inequality on grounds that include health effects (R Wilkinson and K Pickett, *The Spirit Level: Why More Equal Societies Almost Always Do Better* (London, Allen Lane, 2009)), promotion of individual opportunity (A Sen, *Development as Freedom* (Oxford, OUP, 1999)) and the use of society's productive resources (A Atkinson, *Inequality: What Can Be Done?* (Cambridge, MA, Harvard University Press, 2015)).

[6] See Conclusions XIV-2 (1998).

[7] ibid.

'compensatory factors', including taxes and family and housing benefits, in offsetting the effects of low pay in a given member state.[8]

The concept of the decency threshold was widely adopted from this point on to frame national debates, and it was prominently used by the UK Low Pay Unit in its long-running campaign for the introduction of a legally binding national minimum wage in Britain.[9] However, in the late 1990s the ESCR abandoned the 68 per cent benchmark, as well as the methodology that had informed the original decency threshold. In its 13th reporting cycle the ECSR came to the view that it was not in a position to assess compliance with Article 4§1, 'both because of increasing doubts as to whether the method applied was appropriate considering the social and economic developments which had taken place since the Charter entered into force and because the data furnished by governments in many cases simply did not enable it to assess the situation with any degree of validity'.[10] In the 14th cycle, in 1998, it adopted a new benchmark of 60 per cent of the average *net* national wage.

Two main reasons were given for the change. The first was that there had been 'developments in the earnings patterns of families since the 68% threshold was introduced [that] make it untenable to maintain a general requirement that a single wage income must give a decent living standard to a whole family'. The previous reading of Article 4§1 had, it was suggested, privileged a male breadwinner model of the household, which was not 'conducive to promoting equal opportunities of women in the labour market'.[11]

The second reason given by the ECSR was the increasing heterogeneity of the group of states making up the contracting parties, following the ratification of the ESC by 'new democracies of Central and Eastern Europe' in which 'the wage structure is different and dispersion greater' than had been the case in the Charter's original signatory states. Taking these factors into account, the ECSR took the view that the 60 per cent threshold, calculated net of social transfers and taxes, would in general be sufficient to provide an individual wage earner, although 'not the family', with a 'decent living standard' that was 'clearly above the poverty line for a given country'.[12]

The UK Low Pay Unit criticised the change, arguing that it 'has served to obscure both the general effectiveness of the Decency Threshold as a means for poorer European citizens to hold their governments to account, and

[8] ibid.

[9] See Low Pay Forum, *Why Britain Needs a National Minimum Wage* (London, Low Pay Unit, 1988).

[10] Conclusions XIV-2.

[11] ibid.

[12] ibid.

has buried its value as a tool of analysis with unnecessary complications that only the statisticians in the service of the member states can hope to unravel'.[13] The reference to the male breadwinner model did 'not address the sad reality that women workers across Europe still earn less than male counterparts' and could not explain the shift from a calculation based on gross earnings to one based on net income.[14]

In addition, the ECSR's new definition was, the UK Low Pay Unit suggested, opaque. The concept of net wages referred to income from earnings after deductions for income tax and social security contributions. According to the ECSR's secretariat, 'States should not be punished for large wage differences measured gross, if they pursue an efficient redistribution policy through a progressive tax system that serves to even out, at least to some extent, differences when looked at "net"'.[15] However, this position left unclear how far the ECSR would take into account in-work benefits in the form of tax credits, which have formed a significant part of UK labour market policy since the 1980s.[16] The ECSR stated in its 14th Conclusions that it would not take into account 'minimum guaranteed income' schemes and social transfers 'not directly linked to wages' when assessing compliance with the threshold.[17] This left open the question of how far systems of tax credits, which in the United Kingdom are payable in proportion to the extent to which income from wages falls below certain thresholds,[18] could offset the effects of a low minimum wage. More generally, the shift from gross to net earnings complicated the task of determining whether the new benchmark had been met: 'the effectiveness of the Decency Threshold as a valid measure would too easily become lost in arguments over how the calculation was made, the reliability of data, and so on'.[19] As a result of these considerations, the UK Low Pay Unit announced in 2003 that it would be abandoning the use of the Council of Europe threshold as a campaigning and research tool.[20] According to a briefing note issued by the Scottish Low Pay Unit in 2004, the episode highlighted the dangers of expressing a human rights standard in terms of quantitative measures that 'fail to stand up to scrutiny'.[21]

[13] Low Pay Unit, 'Council of Europe Decency Threshold' (2003).

[14] ibid.

[15] Correspondence between the Secretariat of the ECSR and the Scottish Low Pay Unit, reproduced in C Murray, 'The definition of "adequate remuneration"' (2004) 85 *Radical Statistics*.

[16] See S Deakin and F Wilkinson, *The Law of the Labour Market: Industrialization, Employment, and Legal Evolution* (Oxford, OUP, 2005) 185–95.

[17] Conclusions XIV-2.

[18] Deakin and Wilkinson (n 16) 188–89.

[19] Low Pay Unit (n 13).

[20] ibid. The UK Low Pay Unit was wound up shortly afterwards.

[21] Murray (n 15).

Despite these misgivings, the ECSR has gone on to make active use of Article 4§1, clarifying its position on the meaning of net income and applying a layered approach to judging compliance, in which states with minimum wages below 50 per cent of the average wage are generally held to be in breach of the Charter, while those in the 50–60 per cent range have some leeway to defend their position on the basis of the offsetting effects of taxes and social transfers.[22] In 2014 the ECSR reported that, of the contracting parties ratifying Article 4§1, 'most' failed to comply with it, as a result of a number of factors, including statutory minimum or actual wages that were too low in relation to the average wage, and gaps in coverage.[23] The ECSR has relied extensively on Article 4§1 in its assessment of austerity measures, in the course of which it has emphasised that the 'economic crisis should not have as a consequence the reduction of the protection of the rights recognised by the Charter' and that 'governments should take all necessary steps to ensure that the rights of the Charter are effectively guaranteed at a period of time when citizens need it most'.[24] The ECSR has found a number of recent violations of Article 4 and related provisions of the Charter in Greece,[25] but the impact of these determinations has been limited in light of rulings of the ECtHR and CJEU that have rejected arguments that austerity measures were contrary to the ECHR and CFREU, respectively.[26] The ECSR has recently identified numerous other breaches of provisions of Article 4, arising from failures to provide for time off in lieu of overtime (Article 4§2), the persistence of a substantial gender pay-gap (Article 4§3), notice periods of insufficient duration (Article 4§3), and ineffective protection against arbitrary deductions from pay (Article 4§5).[27]

B. Relationship to International Sources

The ILO Constitution refers in its Preamble to 'the provision of an adequate living wage' as one of the conditions for 'universal and lasting peace ... based on social justice', and ILO Conventions on minimum wages[28] and protection of wages[29] are among the most widely ratified. The ILO Decent Work Agenda does not refer to a living or minimum wage among its four 'pillars', and the right to a fair remuneration is not one of the four core

[22] For further details see section II, below.
[23] ECSR, *Activity Report 2014* pp 20–21.
[24] Conclusions XIX-2 (2009).
[25] See below, section II.
[26] See below, section III.
[27] See ECSR, *Activity Report 2014*, pp 22–24, and section II, below.
[28] In particular Convention No 26 concerning the Creation of a Minimum Wage-Fixing Machinery, 1928.
[29] Convention No 95 concerning the Protection of Wages, 1949.

labour rights referred to in the ILO's 1998 Declaration on Fundamental Principles and Rights at Work, but it can be argued that the right to protection against forced labour, which is one of those listed in the Declaration, entails recognition of a right of access to a wage that can support a worker and the members of their family or household.[30] The ILO's Declaration on Social Justice for a Fair Globalisation, adopted in 2008, refers to the ILO's commitment to 'pursue policies with regard to wages and earnings designed to ensure a just share of the fruits of progress to all'.[31]

The Universal Declaration of Human Rights (UDHR) addresses the question of just remuneration sufficient to ensure the dignity of a worker and of his or her family in the context of the right to work (Article 23), which also refers to a right to equal pay for equal work. Article 23 is linked to other rights contained in the UDHR, including the right to a reasonable limit to hours of work (Article 24), the right to an adequate standard of living (Article 25), and the right to social security (Article 22). The International Covenant on Economic, Social and Cultural Rights (ICESR) refers to the right to fair wages (Article 7(a)(i)) and the right to an adequate standard of living (Article 11(1), while the right to work under the Covenant is understood to encompass the right to a decent income that allows 'workers to support themselves and their families'.[32]

C. Relationship to Other Provisions of the Charter

By virtue of its teleological approach to the interpretation of the Charter, the ECSR regards Article 4 as complementary to the protection offered by several other Articles, in particular Article 1 on the right to work, Article 2 on the right to just conditions of work and Article 3 on the right to health and safety.[33] Articles 4 and 2 overlap on the issues of paid annual leave and regulation of overtime. Article 4§3 on the right to equal pay for equal work overlaps with the right to equal opportunities in employment. Article 16 on the right of the family to social, legal and economic protection entails an obligation on the part of member states to create the living conditions under which this right can be realised; this has been held to be linked to the aim of Article 4§1 in ensuring access to a decent standard of living for workers and

[30] G Macnaghten and D Frey, 'Decent work for all: a holistic human rights approach' (2011) 26 *American University International Law Review* 446, 467.

[31] ILO, Declaration on Social Justice for a Fair Globalisation (Geneva, International Labour Office, 2008).

[32] Committee on Economic, Social and Cultural Rights, General Comment 18.

[33] See *European Council of Policy for Trade Unions v Portugal*, Collective Complaint No 37/2006, Decision on the merits of 03.12.2007; S Sanz Caballero, 'The European Social Charter as an instrument to eradicate poverty: failure or success?' (2008) 64 *Cuadernos Constitucionales de la Cádedra Fadrique Furió Ceriol* 166.

their families.[34] There is also a link between Articles 4§1 and 30, inserted on the revision of the Charter in 1998, which defines poverty as a 'lack of resources'[35] of a kind that is seen to 'violate human dignity'.[36] The ECSR has emphasised that the provision of adequate resources in this sense should be regarded as part of strategies to counter social exclusion.[37]

II. CONTENT

A. Paragraph 1: The Right to a Fair Remuneration Sufficient for a Decent Standard of Living

Under the methodology adopted by the ECSR in the late 1990s,[38] compliance with Article 4§1 is determined by the relationship between the net statutory minimum wage or its equivalent, on one hand, and the net average wage of a full-time wage-earner, on the other.[39] To be more precise, the net statutory minimum wage is calculated by taking the minimum rate set by law and then making deductions for income tax and social security contributions. It is generally expressed as an annual sum. If there is no statutory minimum wage, the ECSR will look to relevant collective agreements in representative sectors, and if these do not exist or have no binding force, it will take into account levels of wages actually paid. It takes the same approach when defining the reference wage: this, too, is calculated net of tax and social security contributions, and will be based on collective bargaining or wages in payment if there is no statutory minimum wage.

As we have seen, the initial threshold with which the member state must comply is the 60 per cent figure, which replaced the 68 per cent decency threshold in 1998. In practice, very few contracting parties have been able to meet this standard on a consistent basis. France has a minimum wage system that is generally regarded as being at the more protective end of the spectrum. Under legislation governing the definition of the *salaire minimum interprofessionnel de croissance* ('SMIC'), the minimum wage should, in principle, be uprated or increased on a yearly basis so that it keeps up not just with prices but also with at least half the increase in the purchasing

[34] ibid 167.

[35] Conclusions 2003, France.

[36] Conclusions 2005, France.

[37] Conclusions 2005, Slovenia. Relevant links to other Charter provisions also include those to Art 7§5 (recognising 'the right of young workers and apprentices to a fair wage or other appropriate allowances'), Art 12 (aimed at establishing the 'effective exercise of the right to social security'), and Art 24(b) (referring to 'the right of workers whose employment is terminated without a valid reason to adequate compensation or other appropriate relief').

[38] See above, section I.A.

[39] Conclusions XIV-2

power of the average wage.[40] Thus in contrast to the position in the majority of countries that have a statutory minimum wage, the SMIC is tied to average wages in a way that is intended to ensure that low-waged workers do not lose out on social and economic gains made in the wider working population. Despite this, the SMIC has not generally met the 60 per cent threshold.[41]

If a member state fails the 60 per cent benchmark, it is not necessarily in breach of Article 4§1. If the minimum wage is below 60 per cent, but above 50 per cent of the reference wage, the ECSR's view is that the state concerned can demonstrate compliance by producing 'detailed evidence that the lowest wage is sufficient to give the worker a decent standard of living', for the purpose of which 'consideration will be given to the cost of having health care, education, transport, etc'.[42] This option is not available if the lowest wage is less than half the average wage; in that event, the ECSR will find a breach of the Charter.

The ECSR's approach has the effect that even member states with more protective minimum wage systems, such as France, tend to find themselves required to demonstrate compliance with the Charter by presenting evidence on the effects of taxes and social transfers. Having found the SMIC to be below the 60 per cent threshold in its 2003 Conclusions, the ECSR asked the French government for more complete information on the operation of the tax and benefit systems in future reports on Article 4§1.[43] In its 2007 Conclusions it found that in the year to which the French government's report relates (2005), the annual net value of the SMIC for a single worker was 56 per cent of the annual net average wage. Once a statutory wage bonus (*restitution de prime pour l'emploi*) and housing allocation paid to single workers receiving the SMIC were taken into account, the deemed net minimum wage rose to 66 per cent of the net reference wage. On this basis the ECSR found that France was in conformity with the Charter.[44]

The French experience of compliance with Article 4§1 can be compared with that of the United Kingdom. Up to the 1980s UK policy had been to support a selective but nonetheless legally binding minimum wage that applied in low-wage sectors where collective bargaining was weak. In most other sectors the minimum terms set by sector-level agreements could be made binding on non-unionised employers through an

40 Code du travail, Art L 3231-1 et seq.

41 See Conclusions 2003-I and Conclusions XX-I (2014), France.

42 Conclusions XIV-2 (1998).

43 Conclusions 2003-I, France.

44 Conclusions XVIII-I (2007), France. By contrast, in its 2014 Conclusions, the ECSR came to the view that it had insufficient information to establish whether France was in conformity with Art 4§1. At this point the annual net value of the SMIC was 51% of the reference wage, and with the addition of the *restitution de prime pour l'emploi* was 53%. See Conclusions XX-I (2014), France.

arbitration mechanism.[45] The latter was repealed with effect from 1980 and in 1988 the powers of the wages councils to set legally binding minima in low-paying sectors were scaled back, before being repealed with effect from 1993. From that year until 1999 there was no legally binding minimum wage of any kind. A system of tax credits filled the gap, providing social transfers to low-waged earners with dependent children. Although a legally binding minimum wage was restored with effect from 1999, this time with national coverage, it was set below the level deemed necessary for basic subsistence, and tax credits continued to play a significant role in maintaining household incomes.[46] From 2003, when the tax credit system for households with children was expanded and single earners became eligible for this kind of fiscal transfer for the first time, the effects of fiscal transfers operating in conjunction with the statutory minimum wage was that average net household incomes for the lowest wage-earners generally did not fall below 60 per cent of the median level.[47]

Since the early 1990s the ECSR has consistently found the United Kingdom to be in breach of Article 4§1. In 1991, at a point when legally binding minima were in still force in selected sectors, it found minimum wage arrangements in the United Kingdom to be 'manifestly unfair', on the grounds that the net minimum failed to reach the 50 per cent benchmark. In its 2003 Conclusions it considered the effects of the introduction of the national minimum wage from 1999. It received information from the UK Low Pay Commission, the statutory body charged with advising ministers on the rate at which the minimum wage should be set, that the hourly rate for adult workers was 46 per cent of median full-time earnings. The development rate, paid to younger workers, was below 40 per cent. In the absence of information on monthly or annual earnings, the ECSR relied on Eurostat figures, which indicated that the gross full-time minimum wage amounted to less than 50 per cent of the net average wage in the manufacturing sector. The ECSR's Conclusions indicate that no information was received from the UK government on the extent of social transfers, beyond an observation to the effect that the income taxes levied on low-wage earners had been reduced.[48] On this basis the ECSR concluded that the United Kingdom was

[45] Deakin and Wilkinson (n 16) ch 4.

[46] ibid.

[47] See S Deakin, 'Droit social et travailleurs pauvres dans la Grande-Bretagne: une perspective historique', in P Auvergnon (ed), *Droit social et travailleurs pauvres* (Brussels, Bruylant, 2013). The annual Households Below Average Income (HBAI) Survey takes 60% of median household income to be equivalent to poverty, and this 'UK Poverty Line' has been used by government and NGOs since the late 1990s to benchmark child poverty rates. See Department of Work and Pensions, *Child Poverty Transitions: Exploring the Routes Into and Out of Poverty 2009–2012* (London, DWP, 2015).

[48] 'While indicating that measures have been taken to reduce the tax burden on the lowest wages, the report does not contain the requested information on the value of the minimum wage as well as that of the national average wage after deduction of taxes and social security contributions': Conclusions XVI-2 (2003), United Kingdom.

in breach of Article 4§1: 'the ECSR does not consider that the introduction of the statutory national minimum wage has improved the situation sufficiently to alter its previous assessment'.[49]

In the next reporting cycle, the UK government presented evidence on the operation of its tax credit system, and noted in particular the introduction from 2003 of working tax credits, which were payable to individual earners.[50] This was presumably done in an attempt to demonstrate that working tax credits, because they were explicitly linked to the wage received by a single earner, qualified as transfers 'directly linked to the wage' within the terms of the methodology adopted by the ECSR for assessing compliance with Article 4§1.[51] The ECSR '[took] note of the reforms to the tax and benefit system implemented by the Government with a view to reducing the burden of taxation on the lowest paid workers', but concluded that in light of information to the effect that the minimum monthly wage represented less than 34 per cent of gross average monthly earnings in manufacturing and services, the United Kingdom had failed to demonstrate compliance.[52]

In 2014 the UK government again attempted to invoke the tax credit system, stating that 'the Government sought to ensure that the [national minimum wage] remained around 51% of gross median earnings and that, as it was not designed as a living wage, it had to be considered in the context of the state benefits available'.[53] It also argued that account should be taken of changes to income tax allowances that had had the effect of ensuring that workers receiving the minimum wage would not start to pay tax until they worked 28 or more hours per week. The ECSR, however, having determined that Eurostat data placed the gross minimum wage at 39.4 per cent of gross average earnings, found the United Kingdom to be in breach once again.[54]

The ECSR's contrasting treatment of the French and British situations highlights some of the difficulties inherent in its use of numerical benchmarks to judge compliance with Article 4§1. The adoption of a new methodology in the early 1990s was justified by the need to take into account changing patterns of male and female labour market participation, as well as the role of taxes and social transfers in augmenting household incomes.[55] However, it is not immediately obvious that the revised method meets these objectives.

[49] ibid.
[50] Conclusions XVIII-2 (2007), United Kingdom.
[51] Conclusions XIV-2 (1998), United Kingdom.
[52] Conclusions XVIII-2 (2007), United Kingdom.
[53] Conclusions XX-3 (2014) United Kingdom.
[54] ibid.
[55] See above, section I.A.

The text of Article 4§1 defines decent remuneration in terms of the relationship between the minimum wage and a decent standard of living for workers 'and their families'. When introducing its new methodology, on the other hand, the ECSR took the view that the new 60 per cent threshold would be sufficient to ensure that an individual salary earner but 'not the family' would have access to a decent living standard.[56] As a reason for reducing the threshold from the original benchmark of 68 per cent this seems less than adequate, given the explicit reference to family subsistence in Article 4§1.

At the time of the ECSR's change of view, virtually none of the contracting parties was in a position to meet the 68 per cent threshold. However, a practice of non-conformity with an international standard can hardly be considered, in itself, to be a good reason to modify or relax that standard. For the same reason, the ECSR does not appear to have been on strong ground when invoking, as a basis for the change, the accession to the Council of Europe of states with high levels of earnings inequality. Even now, over a decade after the ECSR adopted the 60 per cent figure, minimum wages in Europe mostly fall in a range between 40 and 60 per cent of the median.[57] The difficulties some contracting parties face in complying with Article 4§1 are increased by the ECSR's practice of using the mean rather than the median as the reference wage.[58]

It is by permitting member states to show compliance by reference to the operation of the tax and benefit system if the minimum wage falls between 50 and 60 per cent of the reference wage that the ECSR allows for flexibility in the assessment of compliance with Article 4§1. This also has the effect of bringing family subsistence back into the picture, because social transfers are largely designed with the income of the household, rather than that of the individual earners, in mind. The ECSR's approach can be rationalised in the following way: as long as the minimum wage reaches at least 50 per cent of the average wage and is combined with the relevant fiscal and

[56] Conclusions XIV-2.

[57] According to the *ILO Global Wage Report 2012–13*, France had the highest minimum wage of all OECD countries, but it was still below 60% of the median wage. The United Kingdom stood at 47% and was in the middle of the range for OECD countries. These data calculate the minimum wage on the basis of real average monthly wages of all employees, including those not working full-time. The UK Low Pay Commission uses a different method of calculation, which refers to the hourly rate of the adult minimum wage and uses the hourly median wage as a reference. On this basis the UK national minimum wage was 52.4% of the median wage in 2013, slightly below its peak of 52.6% in 2012. Since its introduction in 1999 the UK national minimum wage has been increased by approximately 75%, a faster rate of increase than average prices and wages. See Low Pay Commission, *Work That Pays: The Final Report of the Low Pay Commission* (London, Low Pay Commission, 2014).

[58] This is a particular problem for states with a significant number of very high earners, which has the effect of taking the arithmetical mean above the level of the median (or 50th percentile) wage. On the UK case, see Deakin (n 47).

social transfers, access to a decent standard of living is sufficiently protected, whether the individual is a sole earner or part of a multi-member household, with the tax and benefit system, rather than the wage itself, adjusting for differences in household circumstances.

If this is the philosophy underlying the ECSR's approach to Article 4§1, why has it repeatedly found the United Kingdom to be breach of Article 4§1 when the effect of the tax credit system is to bring net household incomes for lowest earners up to 60 per cent of the median level for households, again calculated net? One reason, stressed by the ECSR in successive assessments of the UK position, is that the data made available by the British government have been insufficient to allow for a nuanced evaluation of this kind. Translating the hourly rate of the UK national minimum wage into an annual figure, which is then adjusted to take into account the operation of taxes and benefits, is not straightforward. In the absence of the data needed to make this calculation the ECSR has fallen back on Eurostat figures that show the UK minimum wage to be below the 50 per cent benchmark, and so automatically in breach of Article 4§1.[59]

In both Britain and France, the combined effect of wages and transfers is to bring the incomes of households with low earners to about the same level of 60 per cent of the median household income.[60] The difference between the two countries is that in Britain the role of the minimum wage in ensuring access to this level of income is relatively less important, and the role of transfers correspondingly more important, than is the case in France. This is the reason for the United Kingdom's failure to comply with Article 4§1, and for France's relatively better record of compliance.

In effect, the ECSR's methodology privileges an approach to poverty alleviation that is based on the wage as the main source of household subsistence, with taxes and transfers playing a secondary role, an approach that reflects Article 4's explicit reference to 'remuneration' as opposed to 'income'.[61] If a

[59] See Conclusions XVIII-2 (2007) and Conclusions XX-3 (2014), United Kingdom.

[60] See S Deakin (n 47).

[61] Even so, by defining its approach to Art 4 at least partially by reference to household income and net remuneration as opposed to gross wages paid by the employer, the Committee has opened itself up to the charge that it has shifted 'the responsibility to pay a decent wage from the employer to the state': *ETUC Action Programme 2015–19*, para 175, fn 6 (adopted at the European Trade Union Confederation 13th Congress, September 2015). See also para 176, ibid, referring to the need to explore 'other possible definitions and targets besides the standard of the Council of Europe, such as for example the Living Wage approach as practised in the UK'. More generally, it could be argued that the Committee has not sufficiently taken into account the need to interpret Art 4 in a way that does not undermine the effective exercise of the right to social security under Art 12, given the potentially negative consequences for the financial basis of social security systems associated with the use of in-work benefits to subsidise employment, and the negative incentive effects of high marginal tax rates associated with tax credits (see Deakin and Wilkinson (n 16) ch 3).

member state chooses, as the United Kingdom did in the 1990s and 2000s, to downplay the role of wage regulation and to extend the system of fiscal transfers, it may take itself outside the range of compliance with Article 4§1. This result is to some degree independent of the results achieved by income transfers in narrowing the gap between the poorest households and those in the middle range of the income scale; as we have seen, in net terms low-income households in Britain and France are not far apart. Conversely, the United Kingdom's recent decision to reduce the extent of transfers through the tax credit system, while raising the level of the statutory minimum wage, may bring it into the range of outcomes that is consistent with Article 4§1, as currently interpreted by the ECSR, although this may be open to question given that the net effect of the proposed changes will be negative for the high proportion of low-income households that will be affected by cuts to tax credits.[62] The United Kingdom's decision to strengthen its minimum wage protection was influenced by the high cost of fiscal transfers and by the need to provide an alternative to collective bargaining in sectors without effective collective bargaining arrangements, and in these respects reflects a wider international trend, with Germany introducing a statutory minimum wage with effect from 2015 for similar reasons.[63]

The practice of paying a lower minimum wage to younger workers is not in principle incompatible with Article 4§1, but the reduction must be shown to be in furtherance of a legitimate aim and must be a proportionate means of achieving that aim.[64] In its 2014 Conclusions the ECSR determined that the reduction in the minimum wage in Ireland for adult workers in their first employment and for those following a course of study, which were implemented as part of the Memorandum of Understanding (MoU) agreed with the Troika in July 2011, resulted in minimum wage levels that were below the minimum threshold. The ECSR called for a report on the impact of the Irish MoU on pay in light of this finding.[65]

[62] The 2015 UK July Budget contained an announcement indicating the government's intention to introduce a 'national living wage' (NLW) for workers over the age of 25, with effect from April 2016, which would reach the level of 60% of median earnings by 2020. This would place the United Kingdom near the top of the OECD group of countries. The NLW (which was subsequently introduced via amendments to the National Minimum Wage Act 1998) is legally binding in contrast to the advisory 'Living Wage' which, in a variety of forms, has been set by a consortium of NGOs, local government bodies and research organisations since the early 2000s. The projected cuts to tax credits were set out in the Welfare Reform and Work Bill 2015, but amendments to this measure limited the scope of the planned reductions. On the NLW and its relationship to tax credits and the Living Wage see Resolution Foundation, *Analysing the National Living Wage: Impact and Implications for Britain's Low Pay Challenge* (July 2015).

[63] See T Schulten and T Müller, 'Back on the agenda? A European minimum wage standard', ETUI Policy Brief, No 8/2014.

[64] *General Federation of Employees of the National Electric Power Corp and Confederation of Greek Civil Servants' Trade Unions v Greece*, Collective Complaint No 65/2011, ECSR Decision on the merits of 23.05.2012 §60.

[65] Conclusions XX-1 (2014), Ireland.

B. Paragraph 2: Increased Remuneration for Overtime

The principle underlying Article 4§2 is that work performed outside normal working hours requires an increased effort on the part of the worker, with the result that the worker must not only receive payment for overtime, but payment at a *higher* rate than that applicable to normal working time.[66] Where remuneration is entirely given in the form of time off, this must be longer than the additional hours worked.[67]

In the context of recognising that many states have adopted schemes providing for flexible working hours, the ECSR has adopted the position that the definition of overtime as hours exceeding normal working hours or hours of service may be applied differently depending on the type of responsibility exercised and the nature of the activity, the way in which the work is organised, and the mode of calculation of the wage. The ECSR has acknowledged widespread use of averaging periods and has ruled that in principle they are not in breach of the Charter.[68]

As regards on-call work, the ECSR has adopted the position that employees on call or standby but not actually working must be compensated for this time.[69] Once a situation arises in which employees have to give up any private activity that would prevent them from responding immediately to a request from their employer, the only acceptable remuneration is one which is based on a variable percentage according to the amount of time spent on call. It is a breach of the Charter for employees on call to be paid at a lower rate than for other working time.[70] However, an on-call allowance that forms part of basic pay may be compatible with the Charter.[71]

There are exceptions to the obligation to grant entitlement to increased remuneration for overtime work in 'particular' or 'special cases'. These cover state employees and management executives. In respect of executives, the ECSR has confirmed that the exception applies to all senior managers, but has ruled that limits must apply, particularly on the number of hours of overtime not paid at a higher rate.[72] In respect of state employees, by

[66] Conclusions I (1969), Statement of Interpretation of Art 4§2. It is insufficient for the overtime pay to be the same as ordinary pay: Conclusions XVII-2, Czech Republic.

[67] *European Council of Police Trade Unions (CESP) v France*, Collective Complaint No 57/2009, ECSR decision on the merits of 01.12.2010 §31.

[68] General Introduction to Conclusions XIV-2, Portugal.

[69] *CESP v Portugal*, Collective Complaint No 37/2006, ECSR Decision on the merits of 03.12.2007 §33.

[70] *CESP v France*, Collective Complaint No 57/2009, ECSR Decision on the merits of 01.12.2010.

[71] *CESP v Portugal*, Collective Complaint No 37/2006, ECSR Decision on the merits of 03.12.2007 §33.

[72] *Confédération Française de L'Encadrement CFE-CGC v France*, Collective Complaint No 9/2000, ECSR Decision on the merits of 16.10.2001 §45.

contrast, the ECSR has recently emphasised that the categories of exceptions must be few in number.[73] This led to the conclusion that the range of employees covered by a flexible working system in France, the 'annual working days system', was too wide to constitute a valid exception.[74] In 2010 the ECSR confirmed that senior police officers must be distinguished from police commissioners for this purpose, and that only the latter could be considered to fall within the category of exceptions provided for in the Charter.[75]

In 2010 the ECSR affirmed that it is not required to rule on the level of flat-rate overtime payments, nor their effects on the worker's purchasing power, but was merely required to determine whether those affected by a particular national measure received adequate remuneration for overtime worked, and whether this was at a higher rate than normal hourly pay. Failure to take account of actual remuneration according to a worker's grade, on the other hand, constitutes a violation if, irrespective of the nature of the grade in question, in practice the level is set at a flat rate.[76]

While systems adopting a flexible working system, calculating working time on the basis of an 'averaging' calculation, are not necessarily contrary to Article 4§2, the conditions set out in Article 2§1 of the Charter must be respected. This means that overtime work must be subject to statutory or collective regulation, and not left to individual contracting.[77] In addition, all flexible working systems must prevent unreasonable daily and weekly working time, operate within a legal framework providing adequate guarantees clearly circumscribing the discretion left to the parties, and must provide for reasonable reference periods, which in principle means not exceeding six months, extendable to one year only in exceptional circumstances.[78]

C. Paragraph 3: Equal Pay for Work of Equal Value

Article 4§3 guarantees the right to equal pay without discrimination on grounds of sex.[79] It overlaps with Article 20 and as such is regarded as an aspect of the right to equal opportunities in employment. The Article 20 case law applies, mutatis mutandis, to Article 4§3.

[73] Conclusions IX-2, France.

[74] *Confédération Générale du Travail (CGT) v France*, Collective Complaint No 55/2009, ECSR Decision on the merits of 23.06.2010 §75. Here, a reference period of one year was found to be excessive and hence contrary to Art 4§2.

[75] *CESP v France*, Collective Complaint No 57/2009, ECSR Decision on the merits of 01.12.2010 §45.

[76] ibid §35.

[77] Conclusions XIV-2, Statement of Interpretation on Article 2(1).

[78] *Confédération Française de l'Encadrement CFE-CGC v France*, Collective Complaint No 9/2000, ECSR Decision on the merits of 16.11.2001 §§29–38.

[79] See the chapter on Art 20 by C Kollonay-Lehoczky in this volume.

The principle of equality applies to all elements of remuneration, including benefits in kind,[80] and applies as between full-time and part-time workers.[81] The right to equal pay must be set out in legislation and effective sanctions must be supplied.[82] While member states have discretion to determine how wages in general are to be set, they are required to lay down a framework for the negotiation of equal pay through collective bargaining, and to supply legal wage-fixing mechanisms if equality cannot be achieved through collective agreements. Employees must have the option of taking an equal pay claim to a tribunal or court[83] and should have the benefit of the normal burden of proof being reversed in their favour. The victim of discrimination should receive compensation that makes good their loss[84] and serves as a deterrent.[85] The principal remedy for retaliatory dismissal should be reinstatement,[86] and if compensation is paid there should no cap on the amount.[87] States must provide for appropriate mechanisms of classification to enable jobs to be compared[88] and should allow for comparisons beyond single employment units, where differences can be attributed to a single source.[89] The ECSR has also ruled that states are under a positive obligation to take steps to narrow the gender pay gap, including the publication of relevant statistical data.[90]

D. Paragraph 4: Reasonable Notice for Termination of Employment

According to the ECSR, the purpose of Article 4§4 is to ensure that the employee can look for work and continue to be paid while looking for alternative employment, hence its inclusion in a provision governing the right to remuneration, although the practice of paying wages in lieu of dismissal is not contrary to the Charter.[91] The 'reasonableness' of the notice period is determined mainly by reference to the employee's length of service. Through a series of decisions, it has become clear which periods the ECSR considers to be reasonable: notice of two months for 15 years of service was recently held to be insufficient,[92] as was notice of two weeks beyond

[80] Conclusions I (1969), Statement of Interpretation on Art 4§3.
[81] Conclusions XVI-2, Portugal.
[82] Conclusions XV-2, Slovakia.
[83] Conclusions I (1969), Statement of Interpretation on Art 4§3.
[84] Conclusions XVI-2, Malta.
[85] Conclusions XIII-5, Statement of Interpretation on Art 1 of the Additional Protocol.
[86] Conclusions XX-3 (2014), Iceland.
[87] Conclusions XX-3 (2014), Germany.
[88] Conclusions XVI-2, Portugal.
[89] Conclusions XX-3 (2014), Greece.
[90] Conclusions XVII-2, Czech Republic.
[91] Conclusions XIII-1, Greece, p 124; Conclusions XIII-3, Greece.
[92] Conclusions XX-3 (2014), Czech Republic.

six months of service for manual and skilled workers,[93] and one week per year of service below three years.[94] In providing for only two weeks' notice for fixed term workers, Polish legislation implementing EU Directive 1999/70/EC was in breach of Article 4§4, while Spanish legislation providing for no notice period where a fixed-term contract lasted less than one year was also not in conformity with this provision.[95]

The ECSR has ruled that all workers, in principle, are protected by Article 4§4,[96] including those working under probation.[97] It has also determined that Article 4§4 applies irrespective of the grounds of termination of employment.[98]

E. Paragraph 5: Deductions from Wages

The purpose of Article 4§5 is to ensure that deductions from wages are not capable of undermining the role of the wage as a means of access to a decent standard of living.[99] The ECSR has recently held that where, after deductions are made for maintenance payments and other authorised deductions, workers on low pay were left with between 50 and 70 per cent of their gross wages, a breach of the Charter had occurred.[100] The ECSR has ruled that an absolute limit to deductions should in principle be respected, and that laws allowing for 'fair and reasonable' deductions are too loosely framed to be in compliance with Article 4§5.[101] While in principle a 'proportionality' test may be compatible with the Charter, a state must be able to show that this principle is capable of being applied in practice.[102]

The ECSR has determined that it is contrary to the Charter for the law to allow workers to waive their right to protection against arbitrary or excessive deductions, and that the determination of what is an appropriate deduction may not be left to the discretion of the individual parties.[103]

[93] Conclusions XX-3 (2014), Iceland.
[94] Conclusions XX-3 (2014), United Kingdom.
[95] Conclusions XIX-3 (2010), Spain.
[96] Conclusions XIII-4 (1996), Belgium.
[97] *General Federation of Employees of the National Electric Power Corp (GENOP-DEI) and Confederation of Greek Civil Servants' Trade Unions (ADEDY) v Greece*, Collective Complaint No 65/2011, ECSR Decision on the merits of 23.05.2012 §§ 26 and 28: the concept of probationary period should not be so long that guarantees concerning notice and severance pay were rendered ineffective. In this case failure to provide for notice or severance pay during an extended probationary period constituted a violation of Art 4§4.
[98] Conclusions XIV-2 (1998), Spain.
[99] Conclusions XVIII-2 (2007), Poland.
[100] Conclusions XX-3 (2014), Iceland.
[101] Conclusions XX-3 (2014), Ireland.
[102] Conclusions XX-3, United Kingdom.
[103] Conclusions XVI-2 (2004) and XVIII-2 (2007), United Kingdom.

Individual negotiations are not completely prohibited, but must be subject to rules established by statutory provisions, case law, regulations or collective agreement.[104] In principle, national laws or regulations, collective agreements or arbitration awards should define the ground for deductions from wages in a clear and precise manner and the protection must cover all forms of deductions, including trade union subscriptions, criminal fines, deductions for reductions in output, assignment or attachment of wages, and the payment of tax debts or maintenance claims.[105]

III. IMPACT ON EUROPEAN HUMAN RIGHTS INSTRUMENTS

A. European Convention on Human Rights

The European Court of Human Rights (ECtHR) has ruled that the Convention guarantees neither a right to work nor a right to a salary or pension of a particular amount, as long as the scheme or provision in question is compatible with the non-discrimination principle contained in Article 14.[106] It is possible that state measures imposing reductions in salaries or social security benefits could amount to a breach of the right to peaceful possession under Article 1 of Protocol 1 of the Charter, but here the ECtHR has accorded member states a wide margin of appreciation, in particular in light of the austerity crisis.[107] The ECtHR has said that it will generally not intervene on matters of social and economic policy that lie within the allocation of limited public resources.[108] A near-total deprivation of wages or social security entitlements could result in a breach of Article 1 of Protocol 1,[109] but a 'reasonable and commensurate reduction' would not. It has been suggested that the ECtHR's recent assessments in this line of cases have not been 'untouched by the dominant austerity discourse'.[110]

[104] Conclusions XIV-2 (1998), United Kingdom.

[105] Conclusions (2014), Ireland.

[106] *De Conceição Mateus v Portugal* App nos 62235/12 and 57725/12 (ECtHR, 31 October 2013) §18.

[107] *Koufaki and ADEDY v Greece* App nos 57665/12 and 57657/12 (ECtHR, 7 May 2013).

[108] *Asmundsson v Iceland* App no 606669/00 (ECtHR, 12 October 2004) §§ 39–45; *Pentiacova v Moldova* App no 14462/03 (ECtHR, 4 January 2005); *De Conceição Mateus v Portugal* App nos 62235/12 and 57725/12 (ECtHR, 31 October 2013) §24.

[109] *NKM v Hungary* App no 66529/11 (ECtHR, 14 May 2013) (98% tax on severance pay); see also *Larioshina v Russia* App no 56969/00 (ECtHR, 22 April 2002), in which the ECtHR indicated that 'a complaint about a wholly inadequate amount of pension and other social benefits may, in principle, raise an issue under Article 3 of the Convention' on the prohibition on inhuman or degrading treatment. The general view on Art 3 is that it does not provide a right to a given level of economic or social support: see C Warbrick, 'Economic and social interests and the European Convention on Human Rights', in M Baderin and R McCorquodale (eds), *Economic, Social and Cultural Rights in Action* (Oxford, OUP, 2007).

[110] F Tulkens, 'The European Convention on Human Rights and the economic crisis: the issue of poverty', Distinguished Lecture delivered on the occasion of the XXIV Human Rights

In *Koufaki and ADEDY v Greece*[111] a challenge was mounted to austerity measures that included reductions imposed in the remuneration, benefits, bonuses and retirement pensions of public servants, with a view to reducing public expenditure. The ECtHR found that the applications were unfounded, on the grounds that the pay-cuts imposed did not amount to a deprivation of possessions sufficient to trigger Article 1 of Protocol 1, and that the removal of the 13th and 14th months of pensions had been offset by a one-off bonus payment. The ECtHR was not in a position, it ruled, to determine whether the Greek government had chosen the best means of addressing the problem. Similarly, in *De Conceição Mateus v Portugal*[112] the ECtHR ruled that an application arising from cuts to public sector pensions was unfounded under Article 1 of Protocol 1, as restrictions on the right to property in this case were proportionate in light of the 'exceptional financial problems facing the country'. By contrast, the ECSR has found several Council of Europe member states implementing austerity programmes to be in violation of Article 4 of the Charter, on issues including cuts to minimum wages in Ireland[113] and Greece,[114] and reductions in notice and severance pay entitlements in Greece.[115] Under the 'dynamic' approach to the interpretation of the Convention set out by the ECtHR in the *Demir and Baykara* case,[116] these rulings of the ECSR could yet prove significant in the continuing debate over how far international human rights instruments can be used to challenge policies of austerity.

B. Charter of Fundamental Rights of the European Union

There is no competence under Article 157 TFEU to adopt a directive on the issue of pay as this was one of the areas explicitly excluded from the scope of the Social Policy title under the Treaty of Maastricht in 1991. There is no reference to a right to a minimum wage in the CFREU, and the CJEU

Law course of the Academy of European Law on 24 June 2013. See also C Kilpatrick and B De Witte, 'A comparative framing of fundamental rights challenges to social crisis measures in the Eurozone' (2014) 7 *Sieps European Policy Analysis* 1; L Mola, 'The margin of appreciation accorded to states in times of economic crisis' (2015) 5 *Lex Social Revista de Derechos Sociales* 191.

111 *Koufaki and ADEDY v Greece* App nos 57665/12 and 57657/12 (ECtHR, 7 May 2013).

112 *De Conceição Mateus v Portugal* App nos 62235/12 and 57725/12 (ECtHR, 31 October 2013).

113 Conclusions XX-1 (2014), Ireland.

114 *General Federation of Employees of the National Electric Power Corp and Confederation of Greek Civil Servants' Trade Unions v Greece*, Collective Complaints No 65/2011 and 66/2011, ECSR Decision on the merits of 23.05.2012.

115 ibid.

116 *Demir and Baykara v Turkey* [2008] ECHR 1345. See the chapter by K Lörcher in this volume.

has refused to consider claims under Article 263 TFEU arising from salary reductions and related austerity measures in Portugal.[117]

The Commission adopted, in the early 1990s, a non-binding opinion arguing for 'appropriate measures to ensure that the right to an equitable wage is protected' at member state level,[118] and there may be scope for the member states to coordinate minimum wage policies through open coordination methods under what is now the European Semester process,[119] but there are no signs yet of a concerted effort in favour of such an initiative. By contrast, economic governance procedures established since the start of the crisis define wages as one of the economic adjustment variables that should be used to overcome economic imbalances and improve competitiveness,[120] and several of the MoUs agreed between the Troika and debtor states have made provision for minimum wage cuts, including reductions of over 30 per cent for young workers in Greece.[121]

IV. CONCLUSION

The right to fair remuneration has proved to be one of the more controversial measures of the Charter, but it has arguably stood the test of time. The abandonment of the original 68 per cent 'decency threshold' in the late 1990s appeared to signal a dilution of the Charter's commitment to the minimum wage as a core labour standard, but the more flexible methodology that it went on to adopt has enabled Article 4 to play a role in countering pressures for labour market deregulation. At no point has the ECSR accepted arguments to the effect that wages should simply reflect differences in productivity; on the contrary, it has consistently applied the philosophy, inherent in the Charter, that in a market economy wages are the principal means of subsistence for workers and their families and should be protected

[117] Case C-127/12 *Sindicato dos Bancários do Norte*, Order of 7 March 2013; Case C-264/12 *Sindacato Nacional dos Profissionais de Seguro v Fidelidade Mundial*, Order of 26 June 2014.

[118] Commission, 'Opinion on an Equitable Wage', COM (93) 388 final. See also Art 5 of the (non-binding) Community Charter of Social Rights of 1989, which states that 'All employment shall be fairly remunerated'. The exclusion of 'pay' from the competence to adopt a directive under the Social Policy Title, now contained in TFEU Art 153(5), goes back to the Treaty of Maastricht: see J Kenner, *EU Employment Law: From Rome to Amsterdam and Beyond* (Oxford, Hart, 2003). On the relationship between the ESC and the Community Charter, see chapter by O de Schutter in this volume.

[119] T Schulten, 'Towards a European minimum wage policy? Fair wages and social Europe' (2008) 14 *European Journal of Industrial Relations* 421.

[120] C Barnard, 'The financial crisis and the Euro Plus Pact: a labour lawyer's perspective' (2012) 41 *Industrial Law Journal* 98.

[121] T Schulten and T Müller, 'A new European interventionism? The impact of the new European governance on wages and collective bargaining', in B Natali and B Vanhercke (eds), *Social Developments in the EU* (Brussels, ETUI, 2012).

as such. It follows that while the tax and benefit system has a role in adjusting household incomes according to circumstances, this role is secondary to that of minimum wage regulation in establishing a floor to the labour market. The ECSR's practice of ruling states to be in breach of the Charter if they do not provide for at least a net minimum wage of 50 per cent of the average reference wage, while allowing states to justify their arrangements by reference to the role of fiscal and social transfers if the minimum falls between 50 and 60 per cent of the average, has proved to be a durable and pragmatic solution to the complex problem of defining fair remuneration for a range of different settings. In the recent austerity crisis, the ECSR has used Article 4 to call into question measures at state level that have reduced the effectiveness of wage protection for disadvantaged groups. Although this approach stands in contrast to those of the ECtHR and CJEU in their responses to the crisis, it is not obvious that the ECSR is out of line with emerging state practice, with several member states, including the United Kingdom and Germany, having recently taken steps to strengthen minimum wage protection. Moreover, the possibility exists that, in due course, the ECSR's interpretation of the Charter will be used to give a more expansive scope to other instruments, including the ECHR and the CFREU.[122] Thus the development, under Article 4, of a sophisticated jurisprudence on the meaning of decent remuneration, may come to have wider significance for international human rights law.

[122] See the chapters by O de Schutter and K Lörcher in this volume.

Article 5

The Right to Organise

ANTOINE JACOBS

Article 5—The right to organise

With a view to ensuring or promoting the freedom of workers and employers to form local, national or international organisations for the protection of their economic and social interests and to join these organisations, the Contracting Parties undertake that national law shall not be such as to impair, nor shall it be so implied as to impair, this freedom. The extent to which the guarantees provided for in this article shall apply to the police shall be determined by national laws or regulations. The principle governing the application to the members of the armed forces of these guarantees and the extent to which they shall apply to persons in this category shall equally be determined by national laws or regulations.

I. INTRODUCTION

A. Context and Main Content

The right to organise, or the freedom of association, is a classic element of fundamental human rights. It emerged as such in the mid-nineteenth century,[1] was destroyed by fascism, Nazism and communism, but was confirmed in the mid-twentieth century in Western Europe as one of the cornerstones of a free democratic society. No wonder it was reserved a prominent place in the European Social Charter of 1961, and again in the Revised European Social Charter of 1996. One can debate the extent of the coverage of this fundamental right. Does it also embrace the right to bargain collectively? Does it embrace the right to strike? These questions are dealt with in the contribution on Article 6 to this volume by F Dorssemont. It is, however, up to me to deal with the right to organise in the narrower

[1] ATJM Jacobs, 'Collective Self-Regulation', in BA Hepple (ed), *The Making of Labour Law in Europe* (Oxford, Hart, 2010) 193–241.

sense of the term, as formulated in Article 5 of the Charter. The wording of Article 5 was included unchanged in the 1996 Charter, so for this chapter it is not important to differentiate between the interpretation of the texts of the two Charter versions.

B. International Sources

A large range of international, as well as regional sources on the freedom of association remind us of the long battle for this tool for workers' protection. Sources prior to the 1961 Charter clearly influenced the way the Council of Europe drafted the freedom of association. First was the Preamble to the Constitution of the International Labour Organization (1919), its Declaration of Philadelphia (1944) and Convention No 87 on freedom of association and protection of the right to organise (1948), Article 23§4 of the UN Universal Declaration of Human Rights (1948) and finally Article 11 of the European Convention on Human Rights of the Council of Europe (1950). After 1961 the Freedom of Association was recognised in Article 22 of the UN International Covenant on Civil and Political Rights and Article 8 of the UN International Covenant on Economic, Social and Cultural Rights (both 1966) and moreover in Article 11 of the Community Charter of Workers Rights (1989) and in the Charter of Fundamental Rights of the European Union (2000), in which Article 12 on the Freedom of Assembly and Association is said to imply 'the right of every person to form and to join trade unions for the protection of his or her interests'. Finally, there is the identification of ILO Convention No 87 as one of the eight core conventions of the ILO in the Declaration of the Fundamental Principles and Rights at Work (1998).

C. Relationship to Other Provisions of the Charter

Article 5 belongs to the 'hard-core' of the rights contained in both Charter versions. It means that—although the contracting parties are not obliged to ratify Article 5—the possibilities for avoiding ratification of this Article are more restricted than with regard to the articles of the Charters that do not belong to the 'hard-core' (see Part III, Article A§1b). In fact, of all the member states of the Council of Europe, only Turkey and Greece have not ratified Article 5.[2]

[2] However, this point seems to have lost most of its relevance now that the ECtHR has established violations of Art 11 ECHR with regard to rules and facts that impair the freedom recognised under Art 5. See *Ismail SeZer v Turkey* (ECtHR, 24 March 2015, def 24 June 2015).

The freedom to organise has two social and therefore two legal functions. It is a civil liberty, a human right, an aspect of freedom of association. Its existence and adequate guarantees of its exercise are, however, also indispensable for the operation of collective labour relations.[3] Given the importance of the right of trade union association the ECSR has established that this right must be protected by national law; any gap in legislation or case law cannot be made good simply by practice.[4]

The wording of this Article has been the subject of debate in the legal literature. Some scholars have noticed that the more common name, 'trade union', is not used. Others have observed that the text ignores various more concrete aspects of this fundamental right, such as that individuals, both workers and employers, without distinction whatsoever, shall have the right to establish and to join organisations of their own choosing without previous authorisation, and that the organisations themselves shall enjoy certain rights and guarantees, including the right to draw up their constitutions and rules to elect their representatives, to organise their administration and activities to formulate their programmes, to establish and join federations and confederations at both the national and international level and to enjoy protection against dissolution or suspension by administrative authority and so on.[5] All these aspects are indeed not in the text of Article 5; but are they implicit?

In the study that follows I shall examine the interpretation that Article 5 has received from its monitoring bodies during the various stages of the supervisory cycles since the 1960s.[6] In fact, there are three monitoring bodies: the ECSR,[7] the Governmental Committee and the Committee of Ministers. The harvest of interpretations obtained from the ECSR is by far the richest. However, the authority of these interpretations is greater the more explicitly they have been reinforced by the other monitoring bodies. As such, notably the Recommendations of the Committee of Ministers are to be taken into account and also 'warnings' from the Governmental Committee. I shall further mention the decisions made by the Committee

[3] O Kahn-Freund, 'Labour Relations and International Standards: Some Reflections on the European Social Charter', in: *Miscellanea* (Brussels, WJ Ganshof van der Meersch, 1972) 134, 138.

[4] Conclusions XI-1, Iceland; see D Harris and J Darcy, *The European Social Charter* (New York, Ardsley, 2001) 88.

[5] See Anon, 'The European Social Charter and International Labour Standards' I, (1961) LXXIV-5 *International Law Review* 16–17.

[6] L Samuel, *Fundamental social rights. Case law of the European Social Charter*, 2nd edn (Strasbourg, Council of Europe Publishing, 2000); M Schlachter, 'Der Schutz der Vereinigungsfreiheit durch die Europäische Sozialcharta' (2013) 3 *Soziales Recht* 77.

[7] I shall mention all the decisions of this monitoring body under the indication 'ECSR', irrespective of whether they have been made by the Committee of Independent Experts or by the European Committee on Social Rights.

in the various complaints regarding Article 5, made under the collective complaints procedure.

The ECSR has emphasised that two obligations were embodied in Article 5, which have a negative and a positive aspect, respectively. The implementation of the first obligation requires the absence, in the municipal law of each contracting party, of any legislation or regulation or any administrative practice such as to impair the freedom of employers and workers to form and join their respective organisations. By virtue of the second obligation, the contracting state is obliged to take adequate legislative or other measures to guarantee the exercise of the right to organise and, in particular, to protect workers' organisations from any interference on the part of employers.[8]

Almost all the case law concerns trade unions as, in practice, the freedom of employers has not caused any problems,[9] apart from the question of the negative freedom of association.

The ECSR judges all the decisions on restrictions and limitations of the rights guaranteed by Article 5 of the Charter in light of Article 31 of the Charter (Article G of the Revised Charter).[10]

II. CONTENTS

A. The Freedom to Form Trade Unions

Trade unions and employers' organisations must be free to organise without prior authorisation, and initial formalities, such as declaration and registration, must be simple and easy to apply.[11]

The ECSR requires that national law be applied in such a way that it does not impair the freedom to register a trade union.[12] The principle of compulsory registration is not incompatible with Article 5, so long as the persons concerned have adequate administrative and jurisdictional protection against abuse of the power to refuse to register a trade union.[13] If fees are charged for the registration or establishment of an organisation, they must be reasonable and designed only to cover strictly necessary administrative costs.[14] The ECSR, after initial hesitation, accepted that the

[8] Conclusions I, State of Interpretation of Art 5.

[9] Samuel (n 7) 103; Harris and Darcy (n 5) 89.

[10] Samuel (n 7) 103.

[11] Conclusions 2014, Hungary.

[12] Conclusions 2014, Moldova.

[13] Conclusions II.

[14] Conclusions IV; Conclusions XII-2; Conclusions XV-1, United Kingdom; Conclusions 2014, Ukraine.

United Kingdom charges £3,891 for the certification of the independence of a trade union by its certification officer.[15]

The ECSR established that requirements concerning the minimum number of members comply with Article 5 if the number is reasonable and presents no obstacle to the founding of organisations.[16] It ruled that Portugal was violating Article 5 by requiring a minimum of 10 per cent of the total or 2,000 workers[17] and that Georgia was violating Article 5 by requiring a minimum of hundred members, to form a trade union. This is excessive and undermines the freedom to organise enshrined in Article 5.[18] The ECSR came to the same verdict as regards Latvia, which required a minimum of 50 members.[19] Also a minimum threshold of 5 per cent of the total number of employees in a given bargaining unit was considered an obstacle to the freedom to organise,[20] but the ECSR accepted a Polish minimum of 10 members[21] and that of Lithuania of 20 members.[22] For the ECSR's criticism of this element in the Irish system of a negotiation licence, see paragraph IIF.

Trade unions must be able to apply for and be recognised as having legal personality. Of course this may be subject to reasonable requirements, the principles for which have been set out in a complaint case.[23] The ECSR considered not to be in conformity with Article 5 a statutory provision that made belonging to a national, sectoral or intersectoral trade union a prerequisite for local and company-level trade unions to acquire legal personality and thus to fully defend their members' interests.[24]

On the other hand, trade unions must be free to form federations and join similar national and international organisations,[25] and so a State Party may not limit the degree to which they are authorised to organise.

Trade unions and employers' organisations must be largely autonomous where anything to do with their infrastructure or functioning is concerned. They are entitled to perform their activities effectively and devise a work programme.[26] Consequently, any excessive state interference constitutes a violation of Article 5.

The following examples also constitute infringements of Article 5: prohibiting the election or appointment of foreign trade union representatives;

[15] Conclusions XVI-1, United Kingdom; Conclusions 2014, Bosnia and Herzegovina; Conclusions 2014, Georgia.

[16] Conclusions XIII-5, Portugal.

[17] Conclusions XIII-3; Conclusions XIV-1; Conclusions XV-1.

[18] Conclusions 2010, Georgia; Conclusions 2014, Georgia.

[19] Conclusions 2014, Latvia.

[20] Conclusions 2014, Russia.

[21] Conclusions XV-1, Poland.

[22] Conclusions 2004, Lithuania; Conclusions 2010, Lithuania; Conclusions 2014, Lithuania.

[23] *European Council of Police Trade Unions v Portugal*, Collective Complaint No 11/2000, 21.05.2000; Conclusions 2004, Slovenia.

[24] Conclusions 2010, Moldova; Conclusions 2014, Moldova.

[25] Conclusions I, Statement of Interpretation of Art 5.

[26] Conclusions XII-2, Germany; Conclusions 2010, Georgia.

substantially limiting the use that a trade union can make of its assets; and substantially limiting the reasons for which a trade union is entitled to take disciplinary action against its members.[27]

The ECSR also does not accept unjustified incursions into the autonomy of the trade union. In the 1980s and 1990s the ECSR had noted an increase, in a number of countries, of government interference with the exercise of the rights guaranteed by Article 5.[28] Notably in the United Kingdom there had been amendments to the legislation such that the provisions of the law amounted to an interference with the right of trade unions to manage their own internal affairs. Later the ECSR renounced its earlier criticism of several aspects of the trade union laws of the UK Conservative government (1979–96),[29] but it continued to identify other aspects of this legislation as constituting an unacceptable interference with the autonomy of trade unions.

Excessive restrictions on the reasons for which a trade union may take disciplinary action against a member constitute an unwarranted interference in the autonomy of trade unions inherent in Article 5.[30] The ECSR does not accept excessive restrictions on the right of a trade union to determine its conditions for membership and goes beyond what is required to secure the individual right to join a union. Therefore it censured statutory provisions in the United Kingdom that limited the grounds on which a person may be refused admission to or expelled from a trade union,[31] that made it unlawful for a trade union to indemnify an individual trade union member for a penalty imposed for an offence or contempt of court, or that severely restricted the grounds on which a trade union may lawfully discipline members.[32] The Committee of Ministers endorsed the negative conclusions of the ECSR as regards these provisions in a Recommendation.[33]

The ECSR requires that grants to trade unions are only made for the financing of activities for social and trade union training purposes and that financing facilities are not granted to trade unions for other purposes.[34]

[27] Conclusions XIII-1; Conclusions XIV-1.

[28] Council of Europe, *The right to organize and to bargain collectively*, 2nd edn (Strasbourg, 2001) 11.

[29] Conclusions XIII-1, United Kingdom; D Harris and J Darcy (n 5) 95.

[30] Conclusions XVII, United Kingdom; Conclusions 2010, Georgia.

[31] Conclusions 2002, United Kingdom. Later this was endorsed by the ECtHR (*ASLEF v United Kingdom*, 27 February 2007) and the United Kingdom changed its legislation, see Conclusions 2010, United Kingdom.

[32] Conclusions XIII-3; Conclusions XIV-1; Conclusions XIV-2, United Kingdom; Conclusions XV-1; Conclusions 2002, United Kingdom; Conclusions 2006, United Kingdom; Conclusions 2010, United Kingdom; Conclusions 2014, United Kingdom; Conclusions 2014, Andorra.

[33] R Chs (97)3 of 15 January 1997.

[34] Conclusions 2004, France.

The ECSR emphasises that domestic law must provide a right of appeal to a court to ensure that the right to form trade unions and employers associations is upheld.[35]

B. Freedom to Join a Trade Union

The ECSR requires that national law guarantee the right of workers to join a trade union.[36] It referred to the case of *Danilenkov and Others v Russia*, in which the ECtHR ruled that 'the State had failed to fulfil its positive obligations to afford effective and clear judicial protection against discrimination on the ground of trade union membership'.[37]

Initially the ECSR was critical of Cyprus, where the right of workers to freely join and form organisations of their own choosing was not secured, but it later reconsidered its position.[38]

According to the ECSR a provision in domestic law that an employee's right to organise may be restricted by the employer in the employment contract restricts unduly the enjoyment of trade union rights by workers, as they may be forced to accept restrictions on their right to establish to join or not to join a trade union in order to obtain employment.[39]

The freedom to join must be a concrete freedom in practice. The ECSR took note from other sources that in Bulgaria,[40] Estonia,[41] Georgia[42] and Bosnia and Herzegovina[43] there have been repeated allegations of anti-union behaviour and harassment. Sometimes this was a reason for the ECSR to defer its conclusion on whether the situation was in conformity with Article 5. Sometimes—as in the case of Azerbaijan, where the right to organise in multinational companies is problematic, and in only a few of them have workers been able to establish trade unions—it straightforwardly concluded that the situation was not in conformity with Article 5 on the ground that it has not been established that, in practice, the free exercise of the right to form trade unions is ensured in multinational companies.[44]

[35] Conclusions 2010, Macedonia; Conclusions 2010, Georgia.

[36] Conclusions 2014, Russia.

[37] *Danilenkov and Others v Russia* (ECtHR, 30 July 2009).

[38] Conclusions II; Conclusions XI-2; Conclusions XII-2; Conclusions XIII-1; Conclusions XIII-3; L Samuel (n 7) 105.

[39] Conclusions 2010, Georgia; Conclusions 2014, Georgia.

[40] Conclusions 2010, Bulgaria.

[41] Conclusions 2010, Estonia; Conclusions 2014, Estonia.

[42] Conclusions 2010, Georgia; Conclusions 2014, Georgia.

[43] Conclusions 2014, Bosnia and Herzegovina.

[44] Conclusions 2010, Azerbaijan; Conclusions 2014, Azerbaijan.

C. Freedom Not to Join a Trade Union

According to the ECSR, workers must be free not only to join but also not to join a trade union.[45] No worker may be forced to join a trade union or to remain a union member. The ECSR stated that any form of compulsory trade union membership imposed by national law must be considered incompatible with the obligation arising under this article of the Charter.[46] The freedom guaranteed by Article 5 implies that the exercise of a worker's right to join a trade union is the result of a choice and that, consequently, it is not to be decided by the worker under the influence of constraints that rule out the exercise of this freedom.[47] This freedom necessarily implies the absence of any sort of obligation to become or remain a member of a trade union.[48] Consequently, clauses in collective agreements or legally authorised arrangements whereby jobs are reserved in practice for members of a specific trade union are in breach of the freedom guaranteed by Article 5.[49]

To secure this freedom, domestic law must clearly prohibit all pre-entry or post-entry closed-shop clauses and all union security clauses (automatic deductions from the wages of all workers, whether union members or not, to finance the trade union acting within the company).[50] Article 5 requires an adequate protection of such freedom in national law either through statute or case law.[51] No contracting party can fail to provide legal remedies or sanctions for practices that unduly obstruct the freedom to form or join trade union organisations.[52] The ECSR wants to read Article 5 in light of Article I. The commitment made by the Parties to the Charter not to infringe employers' and workers' freedom to establish organisations may be implemented by domestic legislation or by other means under Article I, according to national traditions. This implies that, in the event of contractual provisions likely to lead to a violation of this freedom, the relevant national authority, whether legislative, regulatory or judicial, should intervene, either to bring about their repeal or to rule out their implementation.[53] The ECSR also stated that depriving workers of their right to economic protection in

[45] Conclusions I, Statement of Interpretation of Art 5.

[46] Conclusions III, Statement of Interpretation of Art 5.

[47] *Confederation of Swedish Enterprise v Sweden*, Collective Complaint No 12/2002, Decision on the merits of 15.05.2003 §29.

[48] Conclusions XI-1; Conclusions XV-1, Denmark.

[49] Conclusions XV-1, Denmark; Conclusions 2010, Georgia; Conclusions XIX (2010), Macedonia; Conclusions 2014, Bosnia and Herzegovina.

[50] Conclusions VIII, Statement of Interpretation of Art 5; Conclusions 2010, Albania.

[51] Conclusions XI-1; Conclusions XIV-1, Iceland.

[52] Conclusions VIII.

[53] *Confederation of Swedish Enterprise v Sweden*, Collective Complaint No 12/2002, Decision on the merits of 23.05.2003 §29.

the event of unemployment represents an inadmissible measure to exert pressure on them to become or remain a member of a trade union.[54]

The same attitude towards the right not to join apply to the freedom to organise of employers.[55] This was the position of the ECtHR in the *Sigurjonsson* case about mandatory membership of a business organisation.[56]

The inflexible position of the ECSR in this field was supported by the Parliamentary Assembly of the Council of Europe, which on 24 September 1991 unanimously adopted a recommendation, among other things, to insert a sentence to this effect into Article 5 of the 1961 Charter.[57] Even in the absence of an express provision, the ECSR considers that a negative right is covered by this instrument and it has in several instances disapproved of closed-shop practices found in certain state parties.

The Irish system of pre- and post-entry closed shop arrangements was seen as a violation of Article 5.[58] The Committee of Ministers endorsed the negative conclusions of the ECSR as regards the law of Ireland on this point in a Recommendation.[59] The situation in Sweden also was, in the eyes of the ECSR, not in conformity with Article 5 because pre-entry closed shops are permitted in law and occur in practice.[60] The same went for Finland[61] and also for Iceland, as in this last country, too, closed shop clauses and priority clauses were permitted in law and common in practice.[62] Following this, the Governmental Committee issued a warning to Iceland.[63] Iceland subsequently changed the law prohibiting closed shop clauses, but still considering legal priority clauses agreed by trade unions and employers as part of collective bargaining. Such clauses mean that the employer undertakes to accept union members in preference to non-unionised workers as long as they are available. However, the ECSR considers that also such priority clauses constitute a serious interference with the right not to join trade unions as non-unionised workers find themselves in a clearly disadvantageous position on the labour market compared with workers belonging to

[54] Conclusions XI-1.

[55] Conclusions XII-1.

[56] ECtHR 30 June 1993, Application No 16130/90 (*Sigurdur A Sigurjonsson v Iceland*).

[57] See Parliamentary Assembly, Forty-third Ordinary Session (second part), 18–25 September 1991: Official Report of Debates, Vol II 502, and Texts adopted by the Assembly, Appendix to Recommendation 1168 (1991) 5.

[58] Conclusions XIII-1, Ireland; Conclusions XIV-1, Ireland; Conclusions XV-1, Ireland; Conclusions 2004, Ireland; Conclusions 2014, Ireland.

[59] RChs (99)2 of 4 March 1999.

[60] Conclusions XIII-3; Conclusions XIV-1; Conclusions XV-1; Conclusions 2000, Sweden; Conclusions 2004, Sweden; Conclusions 2006.

[61] Conclusions XIII-5.

[62] Conclusions X-1, Iceland; Conclusions XI-1, Iceland; Conclusions XII-1; Conclusions XIII-3; Conclusions XIV-1, Iceland; Conclusions XV-1; Conclusions 2000, Iceland; Conclusions 2002, Iceland; Conclusions 2006, Iceland.

[63] See the Governmental Committee's 12th report to the Committee of Ministers of 22 March 1993 §113.

trade unions with negotiated priority clauses for their members.[64] Among other things because of the pressure of the ECSR, Norway changed its law in 2003 and therefore was no longer considered to be in violation on this point.[65] However, a pending collective complaint[66] has given rise to fresh doubts.[67] Also Denmark, which previously[68] was castigated by the ECSR for not respecting the freedom not to join trade unions, amended its legislation in 2006 in order to protect the right not to be a member of a union, including during recruitment. Closed shop agreements have therefore been prohibited on the Danish labour market.[69] However, the ECSR put new questions to the Danish government after it had been informed that there are in practice serious allegations of pressure and discrimination on the part of one of the three main trade unions in the areas of careers and promotion, particularly in the public sector. The situation in the Netherlands was only judged to be in harmony with Article 5 after the government had given assurances that the closed shop in the printing industry had been removed from the collective agreement.[70] The ECSR several times ruled France to be in violation of Article 5 because, although closed shops are statutorily prohibited in that country, de facto the monopoly of certain trade unions in certain sectors of the economy persisted, notably in dock work and book publishing.[71]

The ECSR also holds a critical view on clauses in collective agreements that authorise deductions to the wages of all employees, both unionised and non-unionised, to pay the trade unions. Do they amount to compulsory unionism, or to strong pressure to join the trade union? When collective agreements apply to all workers in an enterprise, irrespective of their length of service or trade union membership, the imposition of a fee on workers who are not members of a trade union constitutes a union security practice that is contrary to the right to organise.

When the ECSR was first confronted with the Romanian version of such a fee it considered this a violation of Article 5.[72] However, it later revised its position, considering that the Romanian version of such a fee cannot in itself be regarded as an infringement of employees' right to join or not to join a

[64] Conclusions XIX-3, Iceland; Conclusions 2014, Iceland.

[65] Conclusions 2004, Norway.

[66] Collective Complaint No 103/2013.

[67] Conclusions 2014, Norway.

[68] Conclusions VIII; Conclusions IX-1; Conclusions X-1; Conclusions XI-1; Conclusions XII-1, Denmark; Conclusions XIII-1, Denmark; Conclusions XIV-1; Conclusions XV-1; Conclusions XVIII-1, Denmark.

[69] Conclusions XIX-3, Denmark; Conclusions XIV-1; Conclusions XV-1.

[70] Conclusions 2002, the Netherlands.

[71] Conclusions XII-1, France; Conclusions XIII-3, France; Conclusions XIV-1; Conclusions XV-1; Conclusions 2002, France; Conclusions 2004, France; Conclusions 2010, France; Conclusions 2014, France.

[72] Conclusions 2002, Romania; however, see the dissenting opinion of Mr Akillioglu.

trade union.[73] In Sweden, for the activity of monitoring the correctness of wages, which is carried out by trade unions according to certain collective agreements, the union is entitled to a wage-monitoring fee. The fee constitutes a percentage of each worker's wage (for example, 1.5 per cent), which is deducted by the employer from the wages of the workers, trade union members and non-members alike. The ECSR considers that the system of wage monitoring may, based upon national traditions, be assumed by either public authorities, professional association or trade unions.[74] In the latter case[75] the ECSR found that this could legitimately require the payment of a fee, and thus cannot be regarded as an interference with the freedom of a worker to join a trade union as the payment of the fee does not automatically lead to membership of the trade union. However, if the fees were to finance activities other than wage monitoring, this would be in violation of Article 5, but in the present case the ECSR was not in a position to verify the extent to which the fees are proportional to the services carried out. The ECSR considers that it is for the national courts to decide the matter in light of the principles it has laid down or, as the case may be, for the legislator to enable the courts to draw consequences as regards conformity with the Charter and the legality of the provisions at issue.

However, when the point arose of a statutory obligation on an employer to pay an industry charge the ECSR found[76] that this too amounted to an interference with the right not to join an association, pointing to the judgment of the ECtHR in the case *Ólafsson v Iceland*.[77]

For further debate on these issues I refer to section II.I(1).

D. Trade Union Activities

Article 5 protects not only the right of workers to join or not to join a trade union, but also the right of trade unions to organise freely and to perform their activities effectively, which is essential for 'the protection of workers' economic and social interests'.[78] According to the ECSR, trade unions and employers' organisations must be largely independent where anything to do with their functioning is concerned. They are entitled to perform their activities effectively and to devise a work programme.[79]

[73] Conclusions 2004, Romania.
[74] Conclusions 2002, Sweden.
[75] *Confederation of Swedish Enterprise v Sweden*, Collective Complaint No 12/2002, Decision on the merits of 23.05.2003. See for a Danish case in this field, Conclusions XV-1, Denmark.
[76] Conclusions 2014, Iceland.
[77] *Vörður Ólafsson v Iceland* (ECtHR, 27 July 2010).
[78] Conclusions XII-2, Germany.
[79] Conclusions VIII, Statement of Interpretation on Art 5.

These activities must include the access of trade union representatives to the workplace and union members must be able to hold meetings at work in so far as employers' interests and company requirements permit.[80]

Employers must guarantee facilities for selected union representatives, and union representatives must be allowed to enter workplaces, take part in union activities, hold meetings and distribute documents and should not be discriminated against by reason of their trade union activities.[81]

As mentioned in the Introduction there is a question of whether the protection of the right to trade union association of Article 5 also embraces the right to bargain collectively and to strike. These aspects are specifically dealt with in Article 6, but for contracting parties that have not ratified Article 6 in full, the question may arise as to whether these rights can also find their basis in Article 5 if they have ratified Article 5. According to D Harris and J Darcy, based on the *travaux préparatoires*, the taking of industrial action does not come within the scope of Article 5,[82] but it is unlikely that the ECSR will share this opinion, in light of the recent case law of the ECtHR.[83] For the various aspects of the right to collective bargaining and the right to strike I may refer to the contribution on Article 6 of F Dorssemont in this volume.

E. Protection of (the Activities of) Trade Union Members

Not only employee representatives but also ordinary trade union members should be fully protected against any harm that their trade union membership or their activities may have on their employment.[84] This embraces dismissal on the ground of trade union membership and activities, as well as lesser forms of detriment than dismissal.[85]

The forms of discrimination that are prohibited under Article 5 are all those that may occur in connection with recruitment and with employment conditions in general (mainly remuneration, training, promotion, transfer, dismissal and other detrimental action).[86]

[80] Conclusions XII-2, Germany; Conclusions X-III-2, Germany; Conclusions XV-1, Germany; Conclusions XV-1, France; Conclusions 2010, Macedonia; Conclusions 2010, Armenia; Conclusions 2014, Bosnia and Herzegovina; Conclusions XIII-5, Portugal; Conclusions 2010, Georgia.

[81] Conclusions 2006; Conclusions 2010, Albania.

[82] Harris and Darcy (n 5) 97.

[83] *Demir and Baykara v Turkey* [GC] App no 34503/97 (ECtHR, 12 November 2008) §§45, 64, 103 and 149.

[84] Conclusions 2010, Albania; see *Ismail Sezer v Turkey* (ECtHR, 24 March 2015, def 24 June 2015) and *Dogan Altun v Turkey* (ECtHR, 26 May 2015).

[85] Conclusions 2002, Ireland; Conclusions 2004, Ireland.

[86] Conclusions 2004, Bulgaria; Conclusions, 2010, Moldova.

The ECSR therefore criticised Austria, where workers in enterprises with fewer than five employees were not protected against dismissal on grounds of trade union activities.[87] The Committee of Ministers endorsed the negative conclusions of the ECSR as regards this omission twice in a Recommendation.[88] The ECSR also considers Ireland in breach of Article 5, as only workers who are member of trade unions holding a negotiation licence are entitled to dismissal protection on the ground of trade union membership and activities.[89]

Domestic law should provide effective sanctions and remedies in cases of discrimination and reprisals based on trade union membership and activities.[90] The ECSR criticised UK law that permitted employers to persuade employees to relinquish union representation and collective bargaining, for example by awarding preferential remuneration.[91]

The ECSR established that where such discrimination has occurred, there must be adequate compensation proportionate to the harm suffered by the victim.[92] In the particular case of termination of employment on the ground of trade union activities, it considers—in accordance with its ruling under Article 24 of the Charter, which prohibits termination of employment without valid reasons—that the compensation must at least correspond to the wage that would have been payable between the date of the dismissal and the date of the court decision or reinstatement.[93] As Bulgarian lawmakers failed to correct this situation,[94] the Governmental Committee issued a warning urging the government to take all adequate measures to bring the situation into conformity with the Charter.[95]

Consequently, the ECSR was also critical of Belgium, where blue-collar workers could only obtain a lump-sum payment of six months' pay in the event of a discriminatory dismissal, and were not entitled to compensation proportional to the real damage, if this was higher than the lump sum.[96]

The protection under this heading is not only applicable to ordinary trade union members, but—as A Swiatkowski has emphasised[97]—it is especially

[87] Conclusions XI-2; Conclusions XII-2; Conclusions XIII-1, Austria; Conclusions XIII-3; Conclusions XIV-1; Conclusions XV-1; Conclusions 2000, Austria.

[88] R Chs (94)1 of 8 April 1994; R Chs (95)1 of 22 June 1995.

[89] Conclusions XV-1, Ireland; Conclusions 2014, Ireland.

[90] Conclusions 2014, Ukraine.

[91] Conclusions XIII-3; Conclusions XIV-1; Conclusions XV-1.

[92] Conclusions XVI-1, Turkey; Conclusions 2004, Bulgaria; Conclusions 2014, Armenia; Conclusions 2014, Moldova.

[93] Conclusions 2004, Bulgaria; Conclusions 2010, Bulgaria.

[94] See the Report of the Governmental Committee concerning Conclusions (2010) p 61.

[95] Conclusions 2014, Bulgaria.

[96] Conclusions 2010, Belgium.

[97] AM Swiatkowski, 'Protection of employee rights in the case of restructuring of their employer and other cases', in AM Swiatkowski (ed), *European Social Charter, Towards common application of the Revised Charter* (Warszawa, Beck, 2005) 45–91.

relevant for the protection of employees' representatives. Article 5 is interpreted by the ECSR as a standard that ensures effective protection of the employment relationship of the trade unions' functionaries, and which imposes on the state authorities the obligation to enable them to carry out their functions.[98] Moreover, such protection should also be granted to employees active in bodies representing employees other than trade unions (for instance, job safety committees).[99]

F. Representativeness

Many countries have developed practices for differentiating between trade unions. The ECSR recognised that in order for trade union participation in various procedures of consultation and collective bargaining to be rendered efficacious, it is open to state parties to require them to meet an obligation of representativeness subject to certain general conditions. However, with regard to Article 5, any requirement of representativeness must not amount, directly or indirectly, to a hindrance to the formation of trade unions. In order to determine whether the requirements of representativeness have this effect, the ECSR holds that domestic law may restrict participation in various consultation and collective bargaining procedures to representative trade unions alone. For the situation to comply with Article 5, the following conditions must be met: (a) decisions on representativeness must not present a direct or indirect obstacle to the founding of trade unions; (b) with regard to Article 6§1, any requirement of representativeness must not excessively limit the possibility of trade unions to participate effectively in consultation; (c) a trade union that is not representative should nevertheless enjoy certain key trade union prerogatives, for example: they may approach the authorities in the individual interest of an employee; they may assist an employee who is required to justify his or her action to the administrative authority; they may display notices on the premises of services; and they must receive documentation of a general nature concerning the management of the staff they represent;[100] (d) at company level trade unions that did not fulfil statutory representativeness criteria could still take part in collective bargaining; (e) the statutory employment protection for trade union officials should not be restricted to representative trade unions;[101] (f) criteria used to determine representativeness must be reasonable, clear, predetermined,

[98] See also Samuel (n 7) 118–19.

[99] Conclusions 2003, Romania.

[100] Conclusions VI; Conclusions XV-1, Belgium; Conclusions 2010, Georgia; Conclusions 2014, Romania.

[101] Conclusions 2004, Slovenia.

objective, prescribed by law and open to judicial review[102] or by a body independent from the deciding body.[103] Finally the ECSR seems to require that a 'plurality of trade unions' be assured.[104]

The ECSR has accepted as not inconsistent with Article 5 the various criteria applied in Slovenia,[105] but it considered the situation in Spain not to be in conformity with Article 5, as it had not been established that representatives of trade unions other than the most representative had access to workplaces.[106] Portugal also did not meet the criteria of the ECSR.[107] The ECSR initially assessed the criteria in the French legislation on representativeness as reasonable, objective and subject to judicial review.[108] Even if the procedure puts trade unions under constraints of urgency, such constraints are justified by the deadlines of the electoral process. Although the appeals against administrative court judgments do not have suspensive effect, it is not considered a right of appeal to be necessary for the situation to be in conformity with the Charter. Given the safeguards referred to, the criteria of representativeness that must be met for the trade unions to be eligible to take part in elections to public service consultative bodies are not in breach of Articles 5 and 6§1. Later, the ECSR took note of new criticism of the 2008 reform of the French system of representativeness, and in 2010 and 2014 it was still uncertain whether the 2008 reform of this system was acceptable.[109]

Being or seeking to be represented on public law bodies, whether consultative, judicial or administrative, may be an additional means among many for the pursuit by a trade union of the protection of the interests of its members. Consequently, according to the ECSR, the issue of trade union participation in such bodies falls within the scope of Article 5 when read in conjunction with Article 6§1 (joint consultation). However, where state parties establish various consultation bodies that are not directly concerned with the essential trade union prerogatives, such as collective bargaining, they have a wide margin of appreciation in determining the composition of the bodies in question. This applies a fortiori to any modalities, such as elections, which may be used to determine the composition of these bodies as long as said modalities do not arbitrarily benefit certain trade unions at the

[102] Conclusion XIII-2, Belgium; Conclusions XV-1, France; Conclusions XV-1, Belgium; Conclusions 2010, Malta; Conclusions 2010, Andorra; Conclusions 2014, Andorra; Conclusions Georgia, 2010; Conclusions 2014, Macedonia.

[103] Conclusions 2010, Albania.

[104] Conclusions 2014, Moldova.

[105] Conclusions 2002, Slovenia; Conclusions 2004, Slovenia.

[106] Conclusions 2010, Spain.

[107] Conclusions 2014, Portugal.

[108] Conclusions VI, France.

[109] Conclusions 2010, France; Conclusions 2014, France; see also Arrêt 889 of 14 April 2010 (09-60.426; 09-60.429) French Cour de Cassation–Chambre sociale.

expense of others or effectively prevent certain trade unions from enjoying the essential trade union prerogatives.[110]

The ECSR has consistently criticised the Irish system of negotiation licences, as this system impairs the right of freedom of association because the criteria for obtaining a licence (among other things, requiring at least 1,000 members resident in Ireland, as well as a substantial amount of money) are excessive, and trade unions that are unable to fulfil them suffer very significant limitations to the scope of their activities.[111] The Committee of Ministers endorsed the negative conclusions of the ECSR as regards the Irish system of negotiation licences in a Recommendation.[112]

For further debate on the issues here I refer to section II.I(ii).

G. Coverage/Personal Scope

According to the ECSR, Article 5 not only covers workers in activity, but also persons who exercise rights resulting from work (pensioners, unemployed persons).[113] Consequently, the ECSR considered Polish provisions granting a separate legal regime for the right to organise to retired persons, homeworkers and to the unemployed to be not in conformity with the Charter.[114] In 2010 the ECSR issued a Statement of Interpretation of Article 5 emphasising that unemployed and retired workers may join and remain in trade unions. However, states are not required to allow them to form trade unions, as long as they are entitled to form organisations which can take part in consultation processes that may impact on their rights and interests.[115] Organisations of retired and unemployed workers, irrespective of their status, should have access to consultation procedures open to trade unions in which they are formally consulted on public policies or legislative developments that may affect retired or unemployed workers.[116]

Whether professional organisations of doctors and dentists constitute trade unions within the meaning of Article 5 ESC depends of whether such organisations are empowered to negotiate employment conditions, including remuneration of doctors and dentists.[117]

110 *SAGES v France*, Collective Complaint No 26/2004, Decision on the merits of 15.6.2005.

111 Conclusions I; Conclusions II; Conclusions III; Conclusions IV; Conclusions IV, Ireland; Conclusions VII, Ireland; Conclusions XIII-1; Conclusions XIII-3, Ireland; Conclusions XIV-1, Ireland; Conclusions XV-1, Ireland; Conclusions 2002, Ireland; Conclusions 2004, Ireland.

112 R Chs (99)2 of 4 March 1999.

113 Conclusions XVII-1, Poland; Conclusions 2014, Montenegro.

114 Conclusions XVII-1, Poland; Conclusions, Poland; Conclusions 2010, Poland; Conclusions 2014, Poland.

115 Conclusions 2010, Statement on Interpretation of Art 5; Conclusions 2014, Russian Federation.

116 Conclusions 2014, Serbia.

117 Conclusions 2004, Bulgaria.

Article 5 applies to nationals and to foreigners, within the meaning of the Appendix to the Revised Charter. According to this Appendix the general principle of equality of treatment between nationals and nationals of other contracting parties applies to all the rights protected by the Charter.[118] This provision is backed up by Article 19§4b of the Charter, which requires the contracting parties to secure for nationals of other Parties treatment not less favourable than that of their own nationals in respect of membership of trade unions and enjoyment of the benefits of collective bargaining.[119] If the state has accepted both Article 5 and Article 19§4b, then the ECSR's conclusion is negative if this principle of equal treatment is not respected, because it prevents non-national workers from enjoying full trade union membership rights (including the right to become a founding member of a trade union).[120] Moreover it impairs the freedom that this provision guarantees to trade unions whose members must be free to elect persons of their choice to be their representatives.[121] Quite early on, France was held to be in violation of the Charter on this point, but in 1982 the situation was remedied.[122] Also other nations had provided that only their own nationals (eventually also EU nationals) were eligible as trade union representatives, or to stand as candidates for works councils.[123] Therefore Bulgaria, where foreign workers' right to form or to participate in the formation of trade unions is subject to prior authorisation, is violating Article 5.[124] Also on that ground, the ECSR considered nationality criteria for the membership of works councils as not in conformity with Article 5.[125] This opinion was reinforced by the Committee of Ministers in a Recommendation.[126] Moreover the ECSR, too, does not accept nationality criteria for the membership of representatives of management and labour in public bodies like a Social and Economic Council,[127] but it accepts a restriction on foreign nationals becoming trade union representatives, which makes them ineligible for election to employment tribunals, to be compatible with Article 5.[128]

[118] Samuel (n 7) 103.

[119] Conclusions 2006; Conclusions 2010, Armenia; Conclusions 2014, Bulgaria; Conclusions 2014, Ukraine.

[120] Conclusions XIII-3, Turkey; Conclusions XIV-1.

[121] Conclusions 2002, Romania; Conclusions XIV-1; Conclusions XV-1; Conclusions 2002, Finland.

[122] Conclusions VI; Conclusions VII; Conclusions VIII; Samuel (n 7) 104.

[123] Conclusions XIV-2, Luxembourg; Conclusions XV-1, Luxembourg; Conclusions 2002, Luxemburg; Conclusions 2006, Luxembourg; Conclusions 2014, Luxembourg; Conclusions XIV-1, Austria; Conclusions 2000, Austria; Conclusions 2002, Austria; Conclusions XIV-1; Conclusions XV-1; Conclusions 2000, Finland.

[124] Conclusions 2014, Bulgaria.

[125] Conclusions 2000, Austria.

[126] R Chs (99)1 of 4 March 1999.

[127] Conclusions 2002, Romania; Conclusions 2010, Romania; Conclusions 2014, Romania.

[128] Conclusions XV-1, France; See also Addendum to Conclusions XV-1, Germany.

The ECSR considers provisions that collective agreements on wages and working conditions are only applicable to workers residing in the country to be a violation of the right of non-resident workers to be fully represented by their trade union and the right of trade unions to protect effectively the social and economic interests of such workers. Denmark has been condemned by the ECSR because of provisions in the Danish International Ships Register on a second Register, excluding non-resident seafarers from the coverage of the collective agreement.[129] The Committee of Ministers endorsed the negative conclusions of the ECSR as regards the Danish legislation in this field in a Recommendation.[130] The Danish item was a reason for the ECSR in 1992[131] to explicitly ask all other states to provide information on any regulations on a second ships' register applicable in their territories. It was able to note,[132] from the reports under Articles 5 and 6, that no such register existed in most of the states reporting. In France there existed a second ships' register for the registration of vessels in the French Southern and Antarctic Territories (TAAF), the crews of vessels covered by this register being subject to the terms of an Act of 15 December 1952 establishing the Labour Code for the Overseas Territories. Apparently this model was acceptable to the ECSR.[133] In Austria the only exception to the general application of collective agreements concerned the Collective Agreement for Danube River Traffic Employees, which does not apply to employees of foreign enterprises who work on ships belonging to these enterprises or who work temporarily (for up to six months) in Austria. The ECSR considered[134] that this did not constitute a breach of Article 5 because in this case the labour relationship is subject to the law of the country of the enterprise, and, in any event, there was no distinction between Austrian and foreign nationals.

For further debate on the issues here I refer to section II.I(iii).

H. Civil Servants

According to the ECSR Article 5 applies to both the public and the private sector. All classes of employers and workers, including public servants, subject to the exceptions mentioned below, are in principle fully entitled to the right to organise in accordance with the Charter.[135] The ECSR

[129] Conclusions XII-1; Conclusions XIII-1, Denmark; Conclusions XIII-3; Conclusions XIV-1; Conclusions XIV-1; Conclusions XV-1; Conclusions 2000, Denmark; Conclusions XIX-3, Denmark; Conclusions 2014, Denmark.

[130] R Chs (95)2 of 22 June 1995.

[131] Conclusions XII-1 and XII-2.

[132] Conclusions XIV-1.

[133] Conclusions XIII.

[134] Conclusions XIII-1.

[135] Conclusions I, Statement of Interpretation of Art 5; Conclusions II.

highlighted that consultation should take place also in the public sector, including the civil service.[136] While some restrictions may apply to certain categories of civil servants, by reason of their specific status or responsibilities (see below), if too many categories of senior civil servants are prevented from enjoying the right to form trade unions, this will not be in conformity with Article 5.[137]

The Committee considers that Article 5 authorises restrictions on or the removal of the right to organise for two categories of employees, namely members of the police and the armed forces. Any other measures aimed at restricting or abolishing the right to organise of other employees are only permissible to the extent that they are in accordance with the provisions of Article 31 of the 1961 Charter or Article G of the 1996 Charter. That Article provides that a restriction must be prescribed by law, pursue a legitimate aim and be necessary in a democratic society for the achievement of that aim. In the case under consideration here, this means that there must be a reasonable relationship of proportionality between the restrictions imposed on the freedom to organise and the legitimate aim of protecting the rights and freedoms of others.

On the basis of that criterion, the ECSR has ruled that restrictions on the right to organise can be prescribed by law for members of national security bodies and the Prosecutor's Office, as well as for judges and members of the Constitutional Court.[138] The restrictions on the right of association of the employees of the British Intelligence Service (CGHQ) at Cheltenham did not exceed the terms of Article 31.[139] The ECSR recalled that it had admitted that some restrictions might be imposed on certain categories of civil servants with reference to Article 31 as long as judges have the right to join professional associations in order to be able to defend and protect their interests.[140] The ECSR recently requested information from Andorra on the reasons and the aim of the prohibition of trade union membership for judges and prosecutors.[141]

Conversely, the ECSR determined that the law in various countries violated the Charter.[142] For example, Poland was judged in violation because the freedom of appointed civil servants to organise was impaired by the statutory prohibition on their performing trade union functions.[143] Polish

[136] Conclusions III, Denmark; Conclusions 2010, Macedonia.

[137] Conclusions 2010, Albania.

[138] Conclusions 2010, Armenia.

[139] Conclusions X-1; Conclusions XI-2, United Kingdom; see Council of Europe (n 29) 38–39.

[140] Conclusions XI-1, United Kingdom; Conclusions XVI-1, Poland and Conclusions XVIII-1, Spain; Conclusions 2014, Ukraine.

[141] Conclusions 2014, Andorra.

[142] Conclusions 2002, Romania; Conclusions 2004, Romania.

[143] Conclusions 2002, Poland; Conclusions 2006, Poland.

law was later amended, but the ECSR still considered the denial of the right of a number of civil servants in the veterinarian field, among others, to join trade unions not to be in conformity with Article 5.[144] In another Polish case the ECSR considered that simply removing the right to organise of the personnel of the Internal Security Agency cannot be deemed proportionate to the legitimate aim pursued, and therefore cannot be considered necessary in a democratic society.[145]

Additional restrictions on the right to organise are, however, permissible under the terms of the two last sentences of Article 5 in respect of members of the police and armed forces.[146]

With regard to the police, the ECSR has held that it is clear, in fact, from the second sentence of Article 5 and from the 'travaux préparatoires' on this clause, that while a state may be permitted to limit the freedom of organisation of the members of the police, it is not justified in depriving them of all the guarantees provided for in the Article.[147] Initially, the ECSR stated that regulations that (i) forbid policemen to set up their own trade union or to join a trade union of their own choice and (ii) oblige policemen to join a trade union imposed by statute are contrary to the Charter because they effectively completely suppress the freedom to organise.[148] In accordance with these criteria the United Kingdom was initially held to be in violation of the Charter, but later the ECSR withdrew this criticism.[149] Later the ECSR also reformulated its standards. Police personnel must be able to form or join genuine organisations for the protection of their material and moral interests and secondly, such organisations must be able to benefit from most trade union prerogatives. In other words, police officers must enjoy the main trade union rights, which are the right to negotiate their salaries and working conditions, and freedom of association.[150] Or, again in other words, the situation is in conformity with Article 5 even if police members do not have the right to form 'trade unions' as long as they are given the right to establish 'professional associations' having similar characteristics and competences as trade unions.[151] It is not in conformity

[144] Conclusions 2010, Poland; Conclusions 2014, Poland.

[145] Conclusions XVIII-1, Poland; Conclusions 2006; Conclusions 2010, Poland.

[146] Conclusions I, Statement of Interpretation of Art 5.

[147] Conclusions I, Statement of Interpretation of Art 5; Conclusions 2010, Armenia.

[148] Conclusions III, United Kingdom.

[149] Conclusions IX-1, United Kingdom; Conclusions X-1, United Kingdom; Harris and Darcy (n 5) 91.

[150] *European Council of Police Trade Unions (CESP) v Portugal*, Collective Complaint No 11/2001, Decision on the merits of 22.05.2002 §§25–26; Conclusions X-2; Conclusions XIII-3; Conclusions XIV-1; Conclusions 2004, Romania; Conclusions 2002, Romania; Conclusions 2004, France; Conclusions 2014, Armenia.

[151] *European Confederation of Police (EuroCOP) v Ireland*, Collective Complaint No 83/2012 § 77.

with Article 5 if such organisations are simply lacking.[152] It is permissible under Article 5 for a contracting party to restrict members of the police to joining or forming organisations composed exclusively of their own members.[153] However, to offer the police only one monopolistic trade union, as is the case in Malta[154] and Albania,[155] violates Article 5. The Committee of Ministers twice endorsed the negative conclusion of the ECSR on Malta on this point in a Recommendation.[156] Also, compulsory membership of police staff organisations constitutes a breach of Article 5.[157] In a Collective Complaint[158] the ECSR ruled that the requirement of registration of a police union is not contrary to Article 5, if the persons concerned have adequate administrative and jurisdictional protection against abusive power to refuse to register a trade union, and that a threshold of 10 per cent of the vote at national professional elections in order for a police trade union representative to enjoy specific protection is in conformity with Article 5. In another Collective Complaint[159] the ECSR ruled that there is no violation of Article 5 on the ground of the prohibition to establish trade unions by the police, as the ECSR considers that the police representative associations enjoy the basic trade union rights within the meaning of Article 5; there is however a violation of Article 5 on the ground of the prohibition to join national employees' organisations by police representative associations. The ECSR considered that, evaluated within the framework of trade union rights applicable to the Irish *Gardaí*, the contested restriction is not proportionate as it exploits in an undue manner the difference between police associations and trade unions established under national legislation. The restriction has the factual effect of depriving the representative associations of the most effective means of negotiating conditions of employment on behalf of their members. The ECSR further recalls that the right of police members to affiliate to national employees' organisations shall not be restricted if this has the consequence of disallowing them from negotiating on pay, pensions and service conditions represented by these national organisations. Only the right to affiliate to international trade union confederations may be restricted in the case of police unions.[160]

[152] Conclusions 2014, Azerbaijan.
[153] Conclusions X-2; Conclusions XIII-3, Spain.
[154] Conclusions, II; Conclusions III; Conclusions XII-2, Malta; Conclusions XIV-1, Malta; Conclusions XIV-2, Malta; Conclusions 2000, Malta; Conclusions 2014, Malta.
[155] Conclusions 2010, Albania.
[156] R Chs (97)1 of 15 January 1997; R Chs 2001/3 of 7 February 2001.
[157] Conclusions I, Statement of Interpretation of Art 5.
[158] *CESP v Portugal*, Collective Complaint No 11/2001, Decision on the merits of 22.05.2002 §§25–26; Conclusions 2010, Malta.
[159] *European Confederation of Police (EuroCOP) v Ireland*, Collective Complaint No 83/2012, Decision on the admissibility and merits of 02.12.2013 §§119 and 121.
[160] Conclusions IX-1, United Kingdom; Conclusions XIII-3, Spain; Schlachter (n 7) 85.

As regards the armed forces, the ECSR has also consistently held that it follows from the final wording of Article 5 that states are permitted to limit in any way and even to suppress entirely the freedom to organise.[161] However, the ECSR checks that bodies defined in national law as belonging to the armed forces do indeed perform military functions.[162]

With regard to *gendarmes* in France, the ECSR has found that they can be equated with military personnel in light of their duties, and therefore are excluded from the right to organise.[163] In a case regarding the Czech Republic, however, the ECSR considered that even where considerations of national security are at stake, the complete suppression of the right to organise would not be in conformity with the Charter.[164]

I. Items for Debate

For too long the conclusions of the ECSR have received little academic attention. However, in recent years the interest in this quasi case law has increased substantially, although it has not yet generated much debate. In the following paragraphs I shall do my best to stimulate this debate as far as it concerns Article 5.

Under various headings I researched the case law of the ECSR and the Committee of Ministers requiring that trade unions and employer organisations must be free to organise without undue incursions on their autonomy and independence; that there be no obstacles either in law or in practice for workers to join the trade union of their choice; that there be no obstacles either in law or in practice for trade unions to deploy their most essential types of activities, such as holding meetings at the premises of the employer; that every trade union member should be protected against disadvantages because of his membership of or activities for his trade union; and that the freedom of trade union association under municipal law not be unduly limited by restrictions on its coverage or scope. It is submitted that the overwhelming majority of the decisions of the ECSR in all these fields are lily-white in their blamelessness. Three issues, however, deserve more debate.

[161] Conclusions I; Conclusions 2002, Romania; Conclusions 2004, France; see also *EUROFEDOP v France/Greece/Italy/Portugal*, Collective Complaints Nos 2-5/1999, Decision on the merits of 04.12.2000 §27.

[162] Conclusions XVIII-1 (2006), Poland.

[163] Conclusions 2006, France.

[164] Conclusions X-1; Conclusions 2002, Czech Republic; Conclusions 2014, Czech Republic.

(i) The Right Not to Join Trade Unions

Under this heading I researched the case law of the ECSR requiring that there shall be no pressure whatsoever either in law or in practice on workers to join a trade union.

There was a cautious beginning in 1969 when the ECSR, on one hand, judged that any form of compulsory unionism was incompatible with Article 5, but on the other hand stated that 'Article 5 does not rule on the admissibility of union security clauses.'[165] In those years labour lawyers all over the Western world and also in the framework of the Council of Europe were still very much divided about the legality of the various forms of union security clauses and practices.[166] My opinion in those years was that 'the present system of industrial relations cannot function without a strong trade union movement with a large membership. On the other hand, putting a strong obligation to organise does not fit in with our concepts of liberty. Between this Scylla and Charybdis ambiguous compromises will be inevitable.'[167] This is still my personal conviction. However in the wake of the judgment of the ECtHR in the case of *Young, James and Webster v United Kingdom*, 1983,[168] the ECSR clearly went beyond that case[169] Since 1985 it has consistently considered that Article 5 guarantees both the negative and the positive aspect of the right to organise, and that therefore no one should be compelled to join a trade union or a specific trade union. Initially not every member state was convinced that the Charter implied such a distinct right not to join trade unions. Denmark for instance once referred to the—until 2006 more nuanced—ECtHR case law which considered Denmark to be in conformity with Article 11 ECHR. The ECSR replied however,[170] 'that the European Convention on Human Rights and the Social Charter are two separate instruments; according to Article 5 of the Charter there can be no sort of obligation to become or remain a member of a trade union.'

Often, attention was drawn to the fact that in the Appendix to Article 1§2 of both the 1961 and 1996 Charter the following restriction is made: 'This

[165] Conclusions I; Harris and Darcy (n 5) 95.

[166] L Betten, *International Labour Law* (Deventer, Kluwer, 1993) 75–82.

[167] A Jacobs, *Het Recht op Collectief Onderhandelen in rechtsvergelijkend en Europees perspectief* (Alphen aan den Rijn, Samsom h.d. Tjeenk Willink, 1986) 111.

[168] See for the case law of the ECtHR on the negative freedom of trade union association I van Hiel, 'The Right to Form and Join Trade Unions Protected by Article 11 ECHR', in F Dorssemont et al (eds), *The European Convention on Human Rights and the Employment Relation* (Oxford, Hart, 2013) 289, 300.

[169] H Kristensen, 'The European Committee of Social Rights and its case law on the negative freedom of association' in *Studia z zakresu prawa pracy I polityki społecznej* (*Studies in labour law and social policy*) Liber Amicorum Prof Dr habil Andrzej Marian Świątkowski (Kraków, Rocznik, 2009) 275–84.

[170] Conclusions XIV-1, Denmark.

provision shall not be interpreted as prohibiting or authorising any union security clause or practice.'[171] Although this restriction is not formulated as regards Article 5, should it not have mitigated the inflexible position of the ECSR about union security clauses and practices?[172] However, the ECSR considers in view of the clear wording of Article 5, that no contracting party can fail to provide legal remedies or sanctions for practices which unduly obstruct the freedom to form or join trade union organisations, for otherwise the scope of the aforementioned provision of the Appendix would be excessively widened and situations incompatible with the fundamental freedom secured by Article 5 would be considered lawful.[173]

It should be open for debate whether the ECSR has not gone somewhat too far. Since the 1980s the trade unions in most European countries have lost much of their countervailing power; their membership has decreased. The ban on union security clauses and practices may have been one of the reasons for that development.

In the same vein there is the case law about clauses in collective agreements authorising deductions from the wages of all employees, both unionised and non-unionised, to pay the trade unions. The ECSR has taken a hostile position to such clauses, yet has accepted them in some specific cases.

And what about clauses in collective agreements offering trade union members a bonus to compensate for their trade union contributions? Such clauses are flourishing in Belgium, but are illegal in Germany. In my opinion such positive incentives to become and remain a trade union member should be allowed. I prefer them above the Dutch method of employers financing the trade unions in order to avoid calls for a closed shop and differentiation in employment conditions.

In the Netherlands, employers substantially finance the activities of trade unions (usually 10 euros or more a year for each member) with the official purpose of defraying the costs of their participation in the process of collective bargaining. However, a union that does not sign a new collective agreement loses this contribution for the period covered by the new collective agreement. Another part of the finances of trade unions comes from compensation for their functionaries serving on public bodies, such as pension funds. Does not all this impair the independence of the unions? Do comparable subsidies exist in other member states? In my opinion it should be a task for the ECSR to oversee the financial independence of trade unions and employers' associations. However, on the other side of this coin the ECSR should allow differentiation with regard to working conditions in favour of trade union members.

[171] On the genesis of this provision see Kristensen (n 170) 278; Harris and Darcy (n 5) 95.

[172] Schlachter (n 7) 86 mentions the connection between Art 1 and Art 5.

[173] Conclusions VIII, Statement of Interpretation of Art 5.

(ii) Representativeness

Under this heading I researched the case law of the ECSR accepting national rules and practices to differentiate between trade unions on the criterion of representativeness, but under certain conditions.

In the course of its monitoring job the ECSR had observed that in certain contracting parties, 'representative' trade unions (or the 'most representative' trade union) enjoy special privileges. Is that acceptable? In order to obtain the necessary wisdom in this matter the ECSR has requested the contracting parties for detailed information on this subject,[174] on various points. I do not know what the ECSR has done with the outcome of this research, but until today the ECSR has not clearly determined the extent to which such arrangements may be considered compatible with Article 5 of the Charter, although a certain direction can be distilled from its case law, as mentioned above.

It is submitted that the ECSR has done a good job by informing itself well about all background factors and aspects of the representativeness question, and its first case law does not give reason for serious criticism. Nevertheless, it should be emphasised that in this field, as in the former (the negative right to organise), the contracting parties should be left a wide margin of appreciation, because this item touches the very heart of the balance of power between the management and labour in the contracting parties. In particular, the situation in France traditionally shows how delicate this problem is and how wary international organisations must be in order not to upset a tottery equilibrium.

In this context perhaps the ECSR's negative stand on the Irish system of negotiation licences could be nuanced. The Irish government has justified that country's system by stating that it is necessary in order to reduce the number of trade unions so as to improve their bargaining power.[175] Cannot this system be accepted as a typical Irish way to differentiate between trade unions on the basis of representativeness, possibly after certain adaptations have been made?

(iii) Coverage/Scope

Until now, the ECSR has not had to pass judgment on the right to trade union association of workers who are not working under a formal contract of employment, but as this section of the labour market is steadily growing, this may come in due course. I would welcome an extension of the Charter to cover such workers, who are in reality economically dependent workers.

[174] Conclusions XIV-1.

[175] See Council of Europe (n 29) 30.

Over the years the ECSR has been very critical of every differentiation between national and non-national workers, as they may prevent non-national workers from enjoying full trade union membership rights. Moreover, it impairs the freedom that this provision guarantees to trade unions whose members must be free to elect the persons of their choice to be their representatives.[176] Therefore the ECSR has become keen to check the eligibility of non-nationals for works councils and other official bodies in which management and labour in the state concerned participate, such as employment tribunals, social security institutions and public bodies representing trades and professions.

It is submitted that this interpretation of the right to association of non-national workers may be too broad. The membership of works councils (unless they are part of the trade union movement or established by collective agreement) and of 'other official bodies in which management and labour participate' is somewhat broader than 'the membership of trade unions and the benefits of collective bargaining', mentioned in Article 19§4b of the Charter, and the concept of 'non-national workers' is broader than the concept of 'foreigners only insofar as they are nationals of other contracting parties legally resident or working regularly within the territory of the Contracting Party concerned', mentioned in point 1 of the Appendix to the Charter.

Another aspect of this matter is the application of collective agreements to foreign workers. The ECSR considers provisions that specify that collective agreements on wages and working conditions are only applicable to workers residing in the country as a violation of the right of non-resident workers to be fully represented by their trade union and the right of trade unions to protect effectively the social and economic interests of such workers. The ECSR was apparently alarmed by the Danish International Ships Register, which excluded non-resident seafarers from the coverage of the collective agreement.[177] Many Western nations are confronted with the phenomenon of the 'flagging out' of their merchant marine, as labour costs in Third World countries are much lower than in Western Europe. Apparently countries with overseas territories can solve this problem legally by a second ships' register for the registration of vessels, as France has done in the French Southern and Antarctic Territories (TAAF). This model was acceptable to the ECSR.[178] Why is such a model acceptable, but not the Danish model? What are the essential differences between the French and the Danish models? This is not clear to me. Anyway, these cases focus our

[176] Conclusions 2002, Romania; Conclusions 2002, Finland.

[177] Conclusions XIII-1, Denmark; Conclusions 2000, Denmark; Conclusions XIX-3, Denmark.

[178] Conclusions XIII.

attention on the more general problem of the enforceability and sustainability of the social rights contained in the Charter in trades that operate in global markets.

III. IMPACT ON OTHER EUROPEAN HUMAN RIGHTS INSTRUMENTS

A. European Convention on Human Rights

From the case law of the ECtHR it has become clear that the Charter and its interpretation by the ECSR has had a major impact on the interpretation of Article 11 ECHR.[179] Article 5 and the case law of the ECSR on it have been cited, largely with approbation, in cases such as *Sigurjonsson*,[180] *Tüm Haber Sen*,[181] *Sorensen and Rasmussen*,[182] *ASLEF*,[183] *Demir and Baykara*,[184] *Danilenkov*,[185] *Olaffson*[186] and *SeZer*.[187]

B. Charter of Fundamental Rights of the European Union

The impact of the Charter on the primary and secondary law of the European Union is best demonstrated by the fact that the Charter is recognised as one of the sources for the determination and interpretation of the CFREU, in particular in its preamble and in the Explanations to Article 12 CFREU on the freedom of association. However, until now there has been scant primary and secondary EU law on the freedom of association, in the narrow sense of the concept, which is the subject of this paragraph. EU legislation on this topic can hardly be expected, as it is excluded in Article 153 TFEU. However, CJEU case law is imaginable on the right of association of migrant workers (cf the *Rutili* case)[188] and in matters of representativeness (cf the *UEAPME* case).[189] In such cases the CJEU may in future be inspired by the case law on Article 5.

[179] See Council of Europe, 'The use of Council of Europe Treaties in the Case Law of the European Court of Human Rights', Research Paper, Strasbourg, 2011.

[180] *Sigurjonsson* App no 16130/90 (ECtHR, 30 June 1993) §35.

[181] *Tüm Haber Sen* App no 28602/95 (ECtHR, 21 February 2006) §39.

[182] *Sorensen and Rasmussen* App no 52562/99 (ECtHR, 11 January 2006) §§35–36 and 72.

[183] *ASLEF* App no 11002/05 (ECtHR, 27 February 2007) §§22–24.

[184] *Demir and Baykara* App no 34503/97 (ECtHR, 12 November 2008) §§45, 64, 103 and 149.

[185] *Danilenkov* App no 67336/01 (ECtHR, 30 July 2009) §§102–104.

[186] *Olaffson* App no 20161/06 (ECtHR, 27 April 2010) §§22 and 53.

[187] *SeZer* App no 36807/07 (ECtHR, 24 March 2015) §§20–21.

[188] Case 36–75 *Rutili* (ECJ, 28 October 1975).

[189] Case T-135/96 *UEAPME* (CFI, 17 June 1998).

C. National Case Law

Several cases have been highlighted in this chapter in which national law has been amended after criticism of the ECSR and the Committee of Ministers.

IV. CONCLUSIONS

If one looks at the various decisions of the ECSR on Article 5, it is interesting to note that until the mid-1990s they almost exclusively concerned the states of Western Europe. This is not surprising because membership of the Council of Europe was until that time more or less limited to the states of Western Europe. After the fall of the Berlin Wall, however, the states of Central and Eastern Europe also became members of the Council of Europe and ratified the Charter. Ever since, the overwhelming part of the critical decisions of the ECSR on Article 5 has concerned the states in Central and Eastern Europe. Criticism of states in Western Europe has faded away. Is that because the states in Western Europe now more obediently follow the views of the ECSR?

One also may note that the Committee of Ministers, after a certain prolific period in the 1990s, has almost stopped reinforcing the decisions of the ECSR by Recommendations. Why? Because it does not agree with the decisions? If this is the case, it should express that opinion. If it is not the case, the Committee of Ministers should enforce the decisions of the ECSR by issuing Recommendations. However, perhaps the silence of the Committee of Ministers has something to do with the former point, namely that most criticism of the ECSR is nowadays focused on the new democracies. These states have much less historical experience of the freedom to organise. Its roots there are still weak. It may, indeed, be wise to be patient with developments in these states, and not immediately put them under the same detailed scrutiny as the old democracies in Europe.

It is good to note that the ECSR is not naive in the justification of its conclusions. It not only founds its conclusions on the information it received from the reporting governments of the member states. If it has received information from serious sources about the situation that contradicts the situation in the law or in practice as reported by the government, it confronts the government with such contradictions and often defers its judgment until it has received responses on that. Those other sources are often cases brought before the Committee on Freedom of Association of the ILO or from international or national trade union (con)federations. And the ECSR even takes note of critical books and articles. However all this still appears to be an 'ivory tower' approach. Fortunately, in recent years the

ECSR has seemed willing to descend from this 'ivory tower' and to meet in a contracting party the representatives of the government, parliament, the social partners and other NGOs to obtain a proper understanding of the national complications in complying with the judgments of the ECSR, also in the field of freedom of association in that country. A delegation of the ECSR did so, for instance, in a visit to Denmark on 23 September 2014. In my view, such exchanges of views may also be helpful in solving outstanding disagreements, for instance that between the ECSR and Ireland on the 'negotiation licence'.

Article 6

The Right to Bargain Collectively

A Matrix for Industrial Relations

FILIP DORSSEMONT

Article 6—The right to bargain collectively

With a view to ensuring the effective exercise of the right to bargain collectively, the Parties undertake:

1. to promote joint consultation between workers and employers;
2. to promote, where necessary and appropriate, machinery for voluntary negotiations between employers or employers' organisations and workers' organisations, with a view to the regulation of terms and conditions of employment by means of collective agreements;
3. to promote the establishment and use of appropriate machinery for conciliation and voluntary arbitration for the settlement of labour disputes; and recognise:
4. the right of workers and employers to collective action in cases of conflicts of interest, including the right to strike, subject to obligations that might arise out of collective agreements previously entered into.

Appendix:

Article 6, paragraph 4

It is understood that each Party may, insofar as it is concerned, regulate the exercise of the right to strike by law, provided that any further restriction that this might place on the right can be justified under the terms of Article G.

I. INTRODUCTION

A. Context and Main Content

Article 6 dates back to 1961 and has never been revised. The ESC tends to juxtapose the right to organise (Article 5) and the right to bargain collectively (Article 6). The right to bargain collectively is construed as a matrix shaping a catalogue of procedures and/or practices that are crucial for a system of industrial relations. They range from joint consultation, voluntary negotiation, conciliation, voluntary arbitration to collective action. Some of these procedures and practices can be related to fundamental workers' rights.

However, Article 6 only refers to two rights explicitly: the aforementioned right to bargain collectively and the right to collective action. Whereas the Charter refers to an obligation to promote machinery for voluntary negotiations, as well as machinery for voluntary mediation and arbitration, it refers to an obligation to ensure the effective exercise of the right to bargain collectively and to an obligation to recognise the right to take collective action.

The use of the word 'negotiation' in the English language version of the Charter is helpful to distinguish the comprehensive right to bargain collectively, *sensu lato*, from a right to negotiation *sensu stricto*. The French language version, however, does not make such a distinction. It refers to negotiation in a generic as well in a specific way.

Whether Article 6 allows for the construction of a *right* to joint consultation is a more troublesome issue. In the same vein, it is questionable to refer to a right to conciliation or arbitration under Article 6.

B. International Sources

This approach is significantly different from the way in which fundamental rights related to industrial relations have been fleshed out in other fundamental rights instruments.

As far as the European Convention on Human Rights (ECHR) and the International Covenant on Civil and Political Rights (ICCPR) are concerned, the matrix for the progressive development of fundamental rights shaping systems of industrial relations has definitely not been the right to bargain collectively. Indeed, both instruments are mute on the existence of such a right. The only right relevant for industrial relations that is mentioned is the right of individuals to form and join trade unions for the protection of their interests. This rather individualistic approach to the right to organise has not prevented the ECtHR from recognising that the wording 'for the protection of his interests' is not redundant.[1] This formula entails an obligation incumbent on member states to ensure that trade unions are granted the means to protect these interests. Some of these means have been underpinned as essential, although non-essential means will come under the

[1] *National Union of Belgian Police* App no 4464/70 (ECtHR, 27 October 1975).

scrutiny of the Court as well.[2] The Court has recognised the right to be heard, the right to collective bargaining and the freedom of trade union expression as such essential means.[3] The ECtHR has consistently qualified the right to strike as merely an important means.[4]

To some extent, the Declaration of Philadelphia (1944) constitutes a prefiguration of such a juxtaposition of the freedom of association and the right to bargain collectively. In its Article 1, freedom of association is recognised as a fundamental principle on which the International Labour Organization is based. In its Article 3 the effective exercise of the freedom of collective bargaining is highlighted. This juxtaposition, which is mute on the existence of a right to strike or to take collective action, has also been reiterated in the ILO Declaration on Fundamental Principles and Rights at Work (1998).

Such a juxtaposition of the right to organise and the right to collective bargaining is also apparent in instruments that have been adopted in the aftermath of the (R)ESC. Thus, the Community Charter of Fundamental Workers' Rights of the European Union,[5] as well as the Charter of fundamental rights of the European Union (CFREU) recognise the freedom of association in a provision which is separated from the one recognising the freedom of collective bargaining. Fortunately, the latter are not mute on the existence of a right to take collective action.

In sum, the way in which the right to organise and the right to bargain collectively are juxtaposed is reminiscent of the approach of the ILO's Declaration. Both rights had been fleshed out previously by ILO Conventions No 87 (1948) and No 98 (1949), which pre-date the adoption of the Charter. Furthermore, some prior ILO recommendations can also be

[2] *Unison v UK* App no 53574/99 (ECtHR, 10 January 2002).

[3] In *Adefdromil v France* App no 32191/09 (ECtHR, 2 October 2010) §§58 and 60 the Court furthermore seems to indicate that the right for a trade union to have access to justice concerning matters related to the right to organise also affects that essential hard-core.

[4] In *RMT v UK* App no 31045/10 (ECtHR, 8 April 2014) the Court overtly refused to take an explicit stance on this issue, despite a request to do so from the plaintiff. In a recent Croatian case, *Hrvatski Lijecnicki Sindikat v Croatia* App no 36701/09 (ECtHR, 27 November 2014), the Court took a more courageous and less ambiguous stance. It qualified the right to strike as the 'most powerful instrument of trade unions to protect the occupational interests of their members'. The concurring opinion explicitly qualifies the right to strike as an essential means.

[5] '11. Employers and workers of the European Community shall have the right of association in order to constitute professional organisations or trade unions of their choice for the defence of their economic and social interests. Every employer and every worker shall have the freedom to join or not to join such organisations without any personal or occupational damage being thereby suffered by him.

12. Employers or employers' organisations, on the one hand, and workers' organisations, on the other, shall have the right to negotiate and conclude collective agreements under the conditions laid down by national legislation and practice.'

mentioned as sources of inspiration.[6] Thus, Article 6§2 is extremely reminiscent of Article 4 ILO Convention No 98.[7]

Although both ILO Conventions No 87 and No 98 are mute on the existence of a right to strike, the Freedom of Association Committee (CFA) had already developed the idea that the right to strike is embedded in the right to organise as early as 1952, stating that 'the right to strike and the organisation of trade union meetings are *essential* elements of trade union freedoms'.[8] At the time of the adoption of the Charter, the CEACR[9] had not yet produced a General Survey that clearly embraced the position of the CFA. The latter would occur only as late as 1983.[10]

Although Article 6 contains no safeguard clause referring explicitly to Convention No 87 precluding state parties to that convention from taking 'legislative measures which would prejudice, or apply the law in such a manner as would prejudice the guarantees provided for in that Convention',[11] the inspiration of Article 6 is clear. It stems from both ILO Conventions, No 87 and No 98, as well as from the case law of the monitoring bodies.[12] The only international instrument to integrate the right to organise and the right to strike into one provision is the ICESCR. Unfortunately, it is mute on the issue of collective bargaining.[13]

C. Relationship to Other Provisions of the Charter

This contribution will focus on the relationship between the various paragraphs of Article 6. Another issue concerns the relationship between Article 6 and other Articles of the Charter. The first relevant relationship is that between Article 5 (the right to organise) and Article 6 (the right to collective bargaining). Insofar as Article 6 deals with essential aspects of the

[6] See in this respect the Collective Agreement Recommendations (1951) and the Voluntary Conciliation and Arbitration Recommendation (1951). See also 'The European Social Charter and International Labour Standards' (1961) LXXXIV *International Labour Review* 364.

[7] 'Measures appropriate to national conditions shall be taken, where necessary, to encourage and promote the full development and utilisation of machinery for voluntary negotiation between employers or employers' organisations and workers' organisations, with a view to the regulation of terms and conditions of employment by means of collective agreements.'

[8] T Novitz, *International and European Protection of the Right to Strike* (Oxford, Oxford University Press, 2003) 192.

[9] ILO Committee of Experts on the Application of Conventions and Recommendations.

[10] Novitz (n 8) 200.

[11] Such a clause appears in Art 8§3 ICESCR.

[12] Novitz (n 8) 140.

[13] See M Craven, *The International Covenant on Economic, Social and Cultural Rights* (Oxford, Clarendon Press, 1995) 275–77 and B Saul, D Kinley and J Mowbray, *The International Covenant on Economic, Social and Cultural Rights* (Oxford, Oxford University Press, 2014) 543.

right to organise, a violation of these aspects protected under Article 6 will entail a violation of Article 5.[14]

Another issue is the use of the notion of consultation, which is not restricted to Article 6. It is crucial to distinguish between a process that can be qualified as negotiation and another process that could be described as consultation. In this respect, negotiations could amount to collective agreements, whereas joint consultations could amount to joined opinions.

'Consultation' figures at least eight times in the Charter. For this reason, it seems necessary to distinguish the scope of these various provisions. If a contracting party has accepted several provisions related to 'consultation', it is crucial to distinguish the exact scope of each provision by avoiding any overlap between them, in order not to complicate the monitoring procedure. If a contracting party has only accepted a part of the provisions related to consultation, the relationship between the various provisions is different. They can operate as communicating vessels by virtue of a more systematic interpretation. In this respect, it is worth recalling that a Recommendation adopted in 1952 dealing with consultation at the level of the undertaking has been identified as a source of inspiration.[15]

As far as the interpretation of the various paragraphs of Article 6 is concerned, it is crucial to avoid any overlap between these subsequent parts. According to Article A (Third Part) of the Charter and contrary to some other provisions, Article 6 (as well as Articles 1, 5, 7, 12, 13, 16, 19 and 20) needs to be accepted as a whole or entirely rejected. There is no third way, cherry-picking some paragraphs of Article 6.[16] For this reason, these paragraphs will not and do not need to operate as communicating vessels. However, as will be shown, in the case of a (legitimate) absence of genuine collective bargaining, the ECSR insists on a system of joint consultation. Furthermore, in the case of a (legitimate) absence of a right to take collective action, the ECSR insists on a system of dispute resolution through arbitration.

In a number of cases, consultation is described as a formal requirement for state intervention (*cf* Articles 3, 10 and 26). Parties to the Charter are requested to adopt specific policies in consultation with employers' and workers' organisations.

[14] A classic example might be the fact of reserving essential trade union rights solely to representative trade unions as opposed to trade unions that have not been recognised as such or reserving these rights to representative trade unions not identified in an objective way or in a way that cannot be challenged in court.

[15] 'The European Social Charter and international Labour Standards' (1961) LXXXIV *International Labour Review* 364, See R094, Co-operation at the Level of the Undertaking Recommendation, 1952 (No 94).

[16] As evidenced by a document published on the Council of Europe website, Austria is the only contracting party that has picked out only part of the paragraphs of Art 6, refusing to accept Art 6§4. www.coe.int/t/dghl/monitoring/socialcharter/Presentation/ProvisionTableRevMarch2015_fr.pdf.

In Articles 21 and 29, a genuine right to information and consultation is mentioned. Both provisions relate to a process of worker involvement at the level of the undertaking.[17] To complicate the picture even further, Article 22 relates to a seemingly stronger level of worker involvement at the level of the undertaking. It refers to the exercise of a right to take part in the determination and improvement of the working conditions and working environment and relates essentially to health and safety issues.[18]

II. CONTENT

In this contribution the four paragraphs of Article 6 are analysed separately, because they deal with four distinct procedures or practices of industrial relations. The linking of the various paragraphs will be analysed, insofar as it sheds light on the interpretation of these paragraphs taken separately. The analysis of these distinct paragraphs will be based primarily on the decisions and conclusions of the European Committee on Social Rights (ECSR), particularly when it expresses an assessment of non-conformity. Furthermore, doctrinal comments, especially of former ECSR members, will be integrated in the analysis.[19]

A. Paragraph 1: Joint Consultation

Article 6§1 focuses on the practices and procedures of joint consultation between workers and employers. The provision can be distinguished from the subsequent provision for two reasons.

Ratione personae, the provision relates to workers and employers, whereas the practice of voluntary negotiations relates to employers or employers' organisations and workers' organisations. In sum, whereas Article 6§1 does not indicate the actor representing the employers and workers concerned, Article 6§2 does identify them. At enterprise level, employers are identified, whereas for the branch and inter-sectoral level, organisations of employers and workers come into play. *Ratione materiae*, neither the outcome nor the object of the procedure has been indicated, whereas voluntary negotiations

[17] See the contribution of Bruno Veneziani in this volume.

[18] See the contribution of Niklas Bruun in this volume.

[19] There is a major difference between the amount of critical observations the ECSR has produced for each of the various paragraphs. Thus, Art 6§4 (*cf* the right to collective action) has given rise to more than 180 statements of non-conformity in conclusions, as opposed to 69 related to Art 6§2, 34 related to Art 6§3 and 23 related to Art 6§1. The doctrinal attention dedicated by former members of the ECSR focuses primarily on the right to take collective action (Art 6§4). These numbers predate the latest series of Conclusions (2014).

are aimed at the conclusion of collective agreements regulating the terms and conditions of employment.

The notion of joint consultation between workers and employers is puzzling for three reasons. The provision does not indicate who needs to consult or to be consulted, nor about what, nor at what level.

Furthermore, as far as personal scope is concerned, joint consultation could be open to other parties than those described in Article 6§2, as long as they are representative of workers and employers.[20] As far as the *material* scope is concerned, whereas negotiations relate to terms and conditions of employment, joint consultations could relate to other issues. The Digest refers in this respect to 'matters of mutual interest, and particularly: productivity, efficiency, industrial health, safety and welfare, and other occupational issues (working conditions, vocational training, etc.), economic problems and social matters (social insurance, social welfare, etc.).' This clarification is in line with a statement of interpretation delivered in 1969.[21] The use of the ideologically connoted notion of a mutual interest warrants the aforementioned thesis that consultation is quite distinct from negotiations amounting to collective agreements.[22] The notion of a 'mutual interest' is reminiscent of the notion of 'mutual concern' that appears in ILO Recommendation No 94 concerning Consultation and Cooperation between Employers and Workers at the level of the Undertaking, which predates the drafting of the Charter (1952). The Committee insists that joint consultation should cover this vast range of matters.[23] Furthermore, joint consultation needs to cover the private as well as the public sector.[24]

As far as territorial scope is concerned, in order to avoid overlap with the more precise provisions of Articles 21, 22 and 29, it seems consistent to restrict the scope of Article 6§1 to other levels than the undertaking (branch level and national level). The Digest supports this thesis solely by referring

[20] C Kollonay Lehoczky, 'The fundamental right of workers to information and consultation under the European Social Charter', in F Dorssemont and T Blanke (eds), *The Recast of the European Works Council Directive* (Antwerp, Intersentia, 2010) 8. The author stresses the distinction between Art 6 as a whole and Art 22 to argue that only the latter would allow transcending the trade union as holders. In my view, there is a distinction already within Art 6 ESC.

[21] ECSR, Conclusions I, 31 May 1969.

[22] *Contra*: C Kollonay Lehoczky, 'The fundamental right of workers to information and consultation under the European Social Charter', in F Dorssemont and T Blanke (eds), *The Recast of the European Works Council Directive* (Antwerp, Intersentia, 2010) 7. The author stresses that Art 6 as a whole is 'based on opposite interests of the employer and workers, whereas workers' participation operates on the basis of the recognition of the managerial power'. Although I agree with this general assessment of Art 6, it is my view that this approach needs to be mitigated with respect to Art 6§1 ESC. The use of the notion 'mutual interest' bears witness to this.

[23] ECSC, Conclusions (XIX), Croatia. ECSR, Conclusions, 22 October 2010, Bulgaria. ECSR, Conclusions, 22 October 2010, Moldova.

[24] ECSR, Conclusions, 22 December 2010, Albania.

to Article 22.[25] Insofar as a state has not accepted ESC provisions with regard to information and consultation at enterprise level, the ECSR examines the situation at length on the basis of Article 6§1. This practice seems to satisfy the needs for a systematic interpretation of the Charter, without leading to undue overlap in the monitoring procedure. Thus, in a critical conclusion concerning Malta, the ECSR disqualifies so-called 'total quality management' as a genuine form of information and consultation.[26]

The role of the state is considered to be complementary to the practices that have developed spontaneously. In a spirit of subsidiarity, the Digest states that the state should refrain from intervening if 'adequate consultation already exists'.[27] Insofar as no adequate consultation exists, the state is required 'to take positive steps to encourage it'. Thus, the Republic of Ireland has been confronted with successive conclusions that were negative, in view of the fact that joint consultation was primarily limited to larger state enterprises and was poorly developed in smaller state enterprises, let alone in the private sector and in agriculture.[28]

According to a statement of interpretation of 1977, the spirit of subsidiarity does not mean that the government should refrain from setting up joint bodies in which a government representative acts as chair.[29] The Digest interprets this statement as implying that consultation can take place within tripartite bodies as long as 'both sides of industry have an equal say in the matter'. Insofar as a chair is acting as a representative of the government, the tripartite character is obvious. A fortiori, joint bodies chaired by a civil servant who does not act as a genuine representative of the government can be considered to be in conformity as well.

Insofar as the state creates a body for joint consultation that is restricted to representative trade unions only, the representativeness criteria should be prescribed by law, objective and reasonable and subject to judicial review offering appropriate protection against arbitrary refusals.[30] If these guarantees are not fulfilled, a violation of Article 5 is imminent as well.

Article 6§1 applies to both the private and the public sector.[31] The provision can compensate the absence of collective bargaining in the public

[25] See, however, ECSR, Conclusions, 22 October 2010, Bulgaria: the ECSR decides not to assess the information related to information and consultation of employers, since this would be covered by Art 21 ESC (which Bulgaria has accepted). Digest 48.

[26] ECSR, Conclusions, XVIII-1, Vol 2, 31 October 2006, Malta.

[27] Digest 48.

[28] ECSR, Conclusions, XI-2, addendum, 31 December 1991, Ireland; ECSR, Conclusions, IX-2, 30 June 1986, Ireland; ECSR, Conclusions, VIII, 31 January 1984, Ireland; ECSR, Conclusions, V, 31 December 1977, Ireland; ECSR, Conclusions, III, 31 July 1973, Ireland.

[29] ECSR, Conclusion V, 31 December 1977.

[30] See ECSR, Conclusions XX-3, Portugal.

[31] See the recent conclusion of non-conformity against Bulgaria for not providing joint consultation in the public sector: ECSR, Conclusions, XX-3, Bulgaria, and also ECSR, Conclusions, XX-3, former Yugoslav Republic of Macedonia.

sector by insisting on joint consultation between employers and workers. In such a scenario, the role of the state in its capacity as a party obliged to promote joint consultation and as a partner of such consultation might coincide. The question arises concerning which power of the state this obligation to promote joint consultation is effectively addressed to. In Collective Complaint No 25/2004, a Belgian public sector trade union complained about a violation of Article 6§1. Under Belgian law, the administration is obliged to submit drafts for basic regulations on employment conditions in the public sector for negotiations in specialised committees where the competent administrative authorities and representative trade unions have a seat. Although Belgian legislation extends this obligation to draft legislation submitted by the government (contrary to proposals submitted by Members of Parliament or to amendments submitted regarding these proposals by the government), no legal remedy was or is available to sanction a violation of that obligation to previous negotiations.[32] The ECSR did not consider the Belgian situation to be contrary to Article 6§1. It did not issue a statement on the absence of legal remedies against a violation of the statutory obligation to negotiate legislative proposals submitted by the government. The absence of any obligation to submit proposals tabled by Members of Parliament or government amendments to joint consultation was considered to be legitimate in order to prevent the legislative process from 'being paralysed'.[33]

B. Paragraph 2: Collective Bargaining

Article 6§2 touches the logical core of Article 6. The provision refers to a conflictual background, namely a background of negotiations. The concept of negotiations presupposes distinct or divergent interests. In 1961, the co-notated use of social partnership was hardly on anybody's lips. These conflicting interests are made more apparent in the subsequent paragraphs of Article 6 referring to 'labour disputes' (Article 6§3) and to 'conflicts of interests'. It is remarkable that the notion of 'collective bargaining' which is traditionally reserved for such a conflictual process amounting to the conclusion of a collective agreement is used at the start of the 'matrix' in a generic meaning, whereas the generic notion of negotiations is used in a specific manner. However, such a critique is applicable also to ILO Convention

[32] The Constitutional Court has refused to assess the constitutionality of statutory legislation in view of its genesis and has pledged to restrict its assessment to the outcome. Furthermore, the Belgian Conseil d'Etat is not competent to annul draft legislation submitted by the government, these acts not being considered administrative in nature.

[33] For a critique of the position adopted by the ECSR in this decision, see J Jacqmain, 'La négociation collective dans les services publics et la Charte sociale européenne' (2006) 7 *Chron DS* 369.

No 98, which refers to collective bargaining in the title of the convention as well as to 'negotiations' in Article 7 ILO Convention No 98. Contrary to Article 6§2, ILO Convention No 98 explicitly provides that it does not deal with the position of public servants engaged in the administration of the state. Hence, the use of the less conflictual concept of 'negotiations' cannot be explained by the distinction between private and public sector. Article 6§2 is applicable to the public sector as well, but the Committee has stressed that states are free to determine that ordinary collective bargaining does not apply to public officials, provided that they 'retain the right to participate in any processes that are directly relevant to the determination of the procedures applicable to them'.[34] Hence, member states need to establish that public officials are entitled to participate in the processes that result in the determination of the regulations applicable to them.[35] The notion of 'public official' needs to be interpreted narrowly. It can only refer to employees exercising public authority. Hence, postal and rail workers not exercising public authority could not be deprived of their right to collective bargaining. The same applies to workers in the telecom sector. In the same vein, as evidenced by the Decision issued after Collective Complaint No 83/2012, legislation and practice need to ensure sufficient access of police representative associations to pay agreement discussions.[36] The mere fact that some of these workers formerly working for public enterprises opted to maintain civil servant status after privatisation does not alter that assessment, since employees cannot waive their rights under Article 6§2.[37]

An important aspect of Article 6§2 is the idea that negotiations should be *voluntary*. The French language version refers at the start of the provision to a *droit de négociation*. The English language version is more ambiguous, insofar as it refers to a right to collective bargaining. In French, the latter formula can be translated in two distinct ways. There is a major difference between *un droit* à la *négociation* and *un droit* de *négociation*. The first approach suggests that there is a right to have access to a bargaining table, whereas the latter approach suggests that the so-called right to bargain collectively is essentially a *freedom*. The emphasis on the voluntary character confirms the latter approach. The word 'voluntary' also appears in the subsequent paragraph of Article 6 in relation to procedures of arbitration. The voluntary character of collective bargaining would logically entail that employers are completely free to refuse to recognise a trade union for the

[34] Digest, 51.

[35] ECSR, Conclusions XIX-3, 3 December 2010, Croatia; ECSR, Conclusions, 22 October 2010, Albania; ECSR, Conclusions, 22 October 2010, Armenia.

[36] ECSR, Conclusions XX-3, Ireland.

[37] The extensive interpretation of 'civil servants' under German law is a recurring issue in conclusions of non-conformity relating to Germany. See *inter alia*: ECSR, Conclusions XVIII-1, ECSR, 28 February 2005; ECSR, Conclusions XVI-1, 30 May 2003.

sake of collective bargaining, provided that the refusal is not discriminatory. However, the ECSR has taken an interest in legislation dealing with the issue of trade union recognition.[38]

In view of the fact that collective bargaining is essentially a freedom, the role of the state in promoting the machinery for these negotiations is a delicate one. For this reason, Article 6§2 indicates that state intervention (namely promotion) should only be contemplated insofar as it is 'necessary *and* appropriate'. If compared with Article 4 of ILO Convention No 98, two differences are apparent. First, even if necessary, the intervention needs to be appropriate, whereas the ILO Convention only indicates that it should be necessary. Furthermore, under the ESC, there is no scope for a more activist stance 'encouraging' such machinery. In sum, promoting and encouraging are two different notions.[39] However, the ECSR does tend to construe the notions of promotion and encouragement as synonymous.[40] It would be consistent to state that such an obligation cannot constitute a commitment to produce a pre-established result. However, the ECSR has considered that if the coverage is extremely weak, a situation of non-conformity does arise.[41] At present no conclusion has been adopted that requires a statutory intervention to ensure that collective autonomy prevails over individual autonomy.

The stance of the ECSR on state intervention reducing or extending the coverage of collective agreements is illustrative in this regard. Statutory restriction of the coverage of collective agreements solely to Danish seamen residents has been considered contrary to Article 6§2.[42] Furthermore, the absence of statutory legislation precluding management by seduction, allowing employers to give financial incentives to workers to exclude themselves from the scope of collective agreements, is contrary to Article 6§2. This critique has been a consistent aspect of the conclusions

[38] See especially Ireland (Conclusions XIV and subsequent Conclusions).

[39] *Contra*:, F-121/10 *M Heath v BCE* (CJEU, 29 September 2011); see also for a comment: F Dorssemont, 'The Constitutional Court of Justice of the European Union and the right of collective bargaining: *Timeo danaos et dona ferentes*. Part II', in *Liber amicorum Bruno Veneziani* (Bari, Cacucci editore, 2012) 113–14.

[40] See the following passus: the Committee recalls that according to Art 6§2, if the spontaneous development of collective bargaining is not sufficient, positive measures should be taken to facilitate and *encourage* the conclusion of collective agreements. ECSR, Conclusions XIX-3, 12 March 2010, Latvia, and ECSR, Conclusions XIX-3, 12 March 2010, Slovak Republic. Conclusions XX-3, Slovakia (coverage of about 30 employees).

[41] ECSR, Conclusions XIX-3, 3 December 2010, Latvia, and Conclusions, XX-3, Latvia; see also ECSR, Conclusions; 22 October 2010, Bulgaria, and ECSR, Conclusions XX-3, Bulgaria, where a situation of a decrease of coverage to 30% is described; ECSR, Conclusions 2010, 22 October 2010, Lithuania (less than 20%); Conclusions XX-3, Lithuania; Conclusions XX-3, Estonia (coverage of 33%); Conclusions XX-3, Hungary (coverage of 33.6%).

[42] ECSR, Conclusions XIX-3, 12 March 2010, Denmark. This has been a recurring issue since ECSR, Conclusions XIV-1. See recently ECSR, Conclusions, XX-3, Denmark.

regarding the United Kingdom, both prior and posterior to the *Wilson and Palmer* case.[43] In this case, the European Court of Human Rights (ECtHR) considered these practices to violate Article 11 ECHR, thus upholding the previous critical comments of the ECSR to which it specifically referred.[44]

Statutory legislation seems to be necessary in order to ensure that an employer bound by a collective agreement is unable to disregard a collective agreement for the benefit of internal labour regulations adopted by that employer.[45] In a critical conclusion addressed to Moldova in 2010, the ECSR asked to what extent the rules on collective bargaining prescribe liabilities incurred by a party not complying with its obligations under a collective agreement.[46]

In the latest conclusions, the ECSR had occasion to examine the issue of the decentralisation of collective bargaining, allowing employers at company level to derogate from sectoral collective agreements.[47] The conclusions related to Spain indicate that a distinction needs to be made between derogations based upon opening clauses and derogations that are the result of government intervention that alters the primacy of sectoral bargaining. In the case of Spain, this intervention was considered to be disproportionate with regard to the aim invoked by the government to justify these austerity measures. A major argument that was decisive for the assessment of non-conformity was the fact that this intervention reforming the framework for collective bargaining was done without prior consultation of the social partners.[48] An example of state intervention not aimed at promoting collective bargaining but at restricting it is administrative measures imposing a wage freeze. The ECSR has indicated that such a restriction needs to be compatible with the conditions fleshed out in Article G. In a critical conclusion regarding Spain, such an intervention of the Spanish government for only one year (1997) was not considered to be compatible with Article G. The intervention at hand is paradoxical, because the government by its decision seems to have breached an agreement that it had itself concluded. The decision was at odds with a collective agreement between the public

[43] ECSR, Conclusions, 22 October 2010, United Kingdom. This conclusion deals with the assessment of the legislation that was at the basis of the judgment in *Wilson, National Union of Journalists v UK* App no 30668/09 (ECtHR, 2 July 2002). The ECSR has criticised the British legislation in a number of Conclusions that predate that judgment. ECSR, Conclusions XVI-1, 30 March 2000, United Kingdom; ECSR, Conclusions XIV-1, 30 March 1998, United Kingdom. The problem has apparently not been solved: ECSR, Conclusions, XX-3, United Kingdom.

[44] See *Wilson, National Union of Journalists v UK* §32.

[45] ECSR, Conclusions, 22 October 2010, Georgia.

[46] ECSR, Conclusions, 22 October 2010, Moldova.

[47] On this issue, see A Jacobs, 'Decentralisation of labour law standard setting and the financial crisis', in N Bruun (ed), *The Economic and Financial Crisis and Collective Labour Law in Europe* (Oxford, Hart Publishing, 2014) 171–92.

[48] ECSR, Conclusions XX-3, Spain.

administration and the trade unions for the period 1995–97, providing for annual wage increases in accordance with specified criteria. The amount of the increase was not stated but according to the agreement was to have been fixed through annual bargaining.[49]

Recent austerity measures aimed at imposing a wage freeze after a consultation of social partners that failed to achieve a consensus have *not* been considered in violation of the freedom of collective bargaining.[50]

A well-known example of state intervention was prompted by the *Laval* judgment of the CJEU, which urged the Swedish legislator to construe collective bargaining as a system setting a ceiling rather than a floor of rights, furthermore limiting the number of subjects who could be the object of collective bargaining in favour of posted workers. The ECSR considered this legislation to constitute a violation of Article 6§2.[51]

One of the most puzzling judicial interventions by the Supreme Court of the Republic of Ireland[52] resulted in declaring that a system to declare collective agreements binding *erga omnes* was considered to violate the constitutional sovereignty of the Irish legislator, stating that there is 'wholesale grant, indeed abdication, of lawmaking power to private persons unidentified and unidentifiable at the time of grant to make law in respect of a broad and important area of human activity and subject only to a limited power of veto by a subordinate body'. The ECSR did not have occasion to scrutinise this judgment because it fell outside the reference period.

Although the restriction of institutionalised collective bargaining to representative trade unions and employers' organisations is not incompatible *in se et per se* with Article 6§2, the representativeness should be based upon objective and reasonable criteria regulated by law, which are subject to judicial review offering appropriate protection against arbitrary refusals. A violation of these principles will entail a violation of Article 5.[53]

C. Paragraph 3: Conciliation and Voluntary Arbitration

Article 6§3 deals with two standard procedures for dealing with labour disputes, namely disputes between management and labour. The most natural

[49] ECSR, Conclusions XV-1, 30 March 2000, Spain.

[50] See ECSR, Conclusions XX-3, Belgium.

[51] *Swedish Trade Union Confederation (LO) and Swedish Confederation of Professional Employees (TCO) v Sweden*, Collective Complaint No 85/2012 and ECSR, Conclusions, XX-3, Sweden. For a recent comment, see M Rocca, 'A clash of kings. The European Committee of Social Rights on the "Lex Laval" ... and on the EU framework for the posting of workers' (2013) 3 *European Journal of Social Law* 217 and N Moizard, 'Le droit d'action collective en droit de l'Union après la décision LO et TCO c Suède du Comité européen des droits sociaux', RTDH 2015 603–22.

[52] *McGowan v Labour Court Ireland* [2013] IESC 21.

[53] See also the contribution of Antoine Jacobs in this volume.

way to deal with such a conflict is joint consultation or voluntary negotiation. Insofar as consultation or negotiation fails to produce a consensual or contractual outcome, conciliation or voluntary arbitration could be helpful to avoid an 'open' conflict between both parties, having recourse to means of collective action protected under Article 6§4. The ESC does not provide a definition of conciliation and of 'voluntary' arbitration. It is mute on mediation. However, the Digest adds 'mediation' to the procedures that should be instituted to facilitate the resolution of collective conflicts (Digest, 51).

Whereas the first and indeed only statement of interpretation indicated that Article 6§3 applied to 'any kind of labour dispute',[54] the Digest states that 'conflicts of interest' are

> conflicts which concern the conclusion of a collective agreement or the modification, through collective bargaining, of conditions of work contained in an existing collective agreement. It does not concern conflicts of rights, ie conflicts related to the application and implementation of a collective agreement or to political dispute.[55]

In her account of the *travaux préparatoires,* T Novitz indicated that the idea of introducing a provision related to conciliation and arbitration emerged during the Tripartite Conference. She explains how this provision was construed as a counterpart of the recognition of the right to strike, forcing the workers' delegation to state that the structure of the draft Article 6 suggested that the right to collective action was a kind of *ultimum remedium,* following a process of consultation, negotiation, conciliation and arbitration.[56] Although such an isolated statement had the virtue of appeasing the employers' delegation at the time, it is extremely hazardous to construe purely 'implicit' restrictions on the basis of the structure of a provision of the Charter, outside Article G. At the time of the drafting of the Charter of 1961, the ILO had already adopted a Recommendation concerning Voluntary Conciliation and Arbitration No 92 (1951).

This recommendation takes a different stance from that adopted during the *travaux préparatoires* of the Charter, by stating that 'no provision of this recommendation may be interpreted as limiting, in any way whatsoever, the right to strike'. The recommendation only states that if a dispute is being submitted to a conciliation procedure or to an arbitration procedure with the consent of all the parties, the latter should be *encouraged* to abstain from strikes and lock-outs during those procedures. The recommendation is mute on mediation. In our view, nothing in Article 6 necessitates use of the

[54] Conclusions I, statement of interpretation on Art 6§3.
[55] ECSR, Conclusions 2010, 22 October 2010, Georgia,
[56] Novitz (n 8) 142.

travaux préparatoires.[57] Neither the structure of Article 6 nor its wording can be taken as enshrining or even suggesting an unwritten principle as if strikes not preceded by mediation or conciliation would fall outside the ambit of Article 6.

In legal doctrine[58] mediation and conciliation is distinguished from arbitration, due to the outcome of the intervention of a third party. Whereas a mediator or a conciliator has no means to impose a settlement of a dispute, an arbiter will do just that. The compulsory character of arbitration needs to be distinguished from the mandatory outcome of the procedure. Arbitration is compulsory when at least one of the parties involved has not agreed on the intervention of the arbiter. Conciliation could be compulsory, but the outcome is never mandatory. Hence, the ECSR examines both aspects in order to assess whether a situation of compulsory arbitration is at stake.[59] The distinction between mediation and conciliation is more subtle. Whereas the mediator will facilitate a solution, he or she will, in contrast to a conciliator, be unable to propose a solution. The ECSR examines whether so-called mediators in fact function as arbitrators. Hence, the notions 'conciliation' and 'arbitration' have independent meanings.[60]

A major difference between Recommendation No 92 and Article 6§3 relates to the fact that the Recommendation stresses the voluntary character of *both* conciliation and arbitration. The ECSR does not object to the mandatory character of conciliation or mediation;[61] it only objects to mandatory arbitration. In both cases, there is an impact on the recourse to strike action. Whereas mandatory arbitration tends to exclude recourse to strike, mandatory conciliation amounts to a kind of cooling-off period, suspending the ability to have recourse to strike action.

For this reason, it can be considered that *mandatory* mediation or conciliation restricting recourse to strike action in such a procedural way requires a justification in light of Article G, although the case law of the ECSR seems mute on the existence of such a requirement.

A system of compulsory arbitration can constitute a restriction of both Article 6§1 and Article 6§2. For obvious reasons, it can also amount to a

[57] See Art 32 VCLT.

[58] See S Dubled and R De Quénaudon, 'Les modes alternatifs de règlement des conflits (collectifs) du travail: Généralités', in M Rigaux and P Humblet, *Conciliation, mediation et arbitrage* (Brussels, Bruylant, 2011) 11–17 and F Valdés-Dal-Ré, 'Synthesis Report on Labour Conciliation, Mediation and Arbitration in the European Union', in F Valdés-Dal-Ré, *Labour Conciliation, Mediation and Arbitration in European Union* (Madrid, Ministerio de Trabajo y Asuntos Sociales, 2003) 51.

[59] See ECSR, Conclusions, 22 October 2010, Malta; ECSR, Conclusions XX-3, Malta.

[60] See the critical conclusions related to Norway: ECSR, Conclusions XV-1, 30 March 2000, Norway.

[61] See, for example: ECSR, Conclusions XV-1, 30 March 2000, Norway. The compulsory character of the mediation concerned did not give rise to an assessment of non-conformity.

violation of Article 6§4.[62] The most natural way to solve a labour dispute is a process of negotiations within the meaning of Article 6§2. Insofar as the object of the dispute falls beyond the realm of negotiations amounting to collective agreements on terms and conditions of employment, joint consultation seems to be the most adequate way to solve a dispute, rather than access to an *obligatory* scheme of conciliation. In the same vein, a form of participation in the determination of employment conditions is a more appropriate means to solve a labour dispute affecting public officials deprived of access to collective bargaining.

Hence, the ECSR is extremely critical of compulsory processes of conciliation that take place prior to the exhaustion of proper means of social dialogue *inter partes*. In other words, states need to facilitate as much as possible a dialogue *inter partes*.

Although a system of compulsory arbitration goes hand in hand with a prohibition on strike action, statutory legislation organising a system of compulsory arbitration has thus come under scrutiny in conclusions related to Article 6§2 ESC. Thus, the statutory legislation of Malta allowing the relevant minister to refer a collective dispute to compulsory arbitration at the request of only one of the parties in the dispute was considered not to be in conformity with Article 6§2.[63]

Article 6§3 applies to both the public as well as the private sector. Absence of a conciliation procedure in the public sector can amount to a conclusion of non-conformity.[64]

Compulsory arbitration can only be justified insofar as it is consistent with Article G.[65] The Committee is reluctant to validate recourse to compulsory arbitration prior to collective action. Such preventive recourse cannot be justified by a rationale to safeguard objectives enshrined in Article G, when these objectives are jeopardised by long strikes.[66]

Furthermore, as is evidenced by the Digest (55), 'arbitration systems must be independent, and the outcome of arbitration may not be predetermined by pre-established criteria'.[67]

[62] ECSR, Conclusions XX-3, Norway; ECSR, Conclusions, XX-3, Portugal; ECSR, Conclusions XX-3, Spain.

[63] ECSR, Conclusions, XV-1, 30 March 2000, Malta; ECRS, Conclusions XIV-1, 30 March 1998, Malta.

[64] ECSR, Conclusion XV-1, 30 March 2000, Malta; ECSR, Conclusions XIV-1, Malta; ECSR, Conclusions XX-3, Bulgaria.

[65] See ECSR, Conclusions 2010, 22 October 2010, Albania; ECSR, Conclusions 2010, 22 October 2010, Moldova; ECSR, Conclusions 2010, 22 October 2010, Portugal; ECSR, 30 March 1998, Conclusions, XIV-1, Norway.

[66] See ECSR, Conclusions 2010, 22 October 2010, Albania; ECSR, Conclusions 2006, 30 June 2006, Moldova; ECSR, Conclusions 2006, 30 June 2006, Albania.

[67] ECSR, Conclusions 2010, 22 October 2010, Georgia.

D. Paragraph 4: The Right to Take Collective Action

(i) *The Right to Take Collective Action, a Quintessence rather than an Accident*

Article 6§4 does not constitute a coda of the catalogue. Strategically, it rather goes to the heart of the right to collective bargaining. Collective bargaining would be pointless if workers and their organisations could have no recourse to collective action. The *travaux préparatoires* indicate that the provision on conciliation and arbitration was the counterpart of the recognition of the right to strike. Article 6§4 constitutes the oldest binding international instrument recognising the right to collective action, including the right to strike. In this respect, it can be considered a codification or reception at the level of the Council of Europe of the position adopted by the CFA (ILO) as early as 1952. However, this reception goes beyond that position, insofar as a notion of collective action is being introduced as a *generic* expression, which is larger than the specific means of collective action known as a 'strike'. As opposed to the Digest of decisions and principles of the Freedom of Association Committee (2006), the Charter explicitly recognises that *employers* have a right to collective action. The CFA is mute on the existence of such a right under ILO Conventions No 87 and No 98. The only statement in the Digest related to lock-outs seeks to protect workers who have participated in a strike against the consequences of a lock-out.[68]

The use of the generic expression 'collective action' opens a window of opportunities to recognise other means of collective action for workers than a strike. It can be useful to avoid a semantic discussion related to the scope of the notion 'strike', which could be a serious inherent or internal limit to the right to take collective action.

In this chapter, the notion 'collective action' will be analysed. It is not defined in the Charter. Subsequently, the issue of holding the right to take collective action will be examined. The main part of the analysis is dedicated to the delicate issue of restrictions on the right to take collective action. The obligation to recognise not only obliges a contracting party to refrain from introducing unjustified restrictions, but also to take positive steps to protect workers participating in collective action against retaliation. These positive obligations will be examined at the end, because they can be seen as an obligation to 'implement' the ESC or as an obligation to provide

[68] See CFA Digest (2006) 853. It is inconsistent with the right to strike for an employer to be permitted to refuse to reinstate some or all of the employees at the conclusion of the strike, lock-out or other industrial action without those employees having the right to challenge the fairness of that dismissal before an independent court or tribunal.

sanctions in case of a violation of the right to take collective action by employers.[69]

It is important to distinguish restrictions that stem from the law of the contracting states from those that stem from the formula of the recognition of the right to take collective action in Article 6§4 ESC.[70] The latter could be qualified as delimitations of recognition under the Charter, rather than as restrictions to the right to collective action. They can also be qualified as internal restrictions, namely, restrictions stemming from the formula of the recognition. The distinction is relevant, insofar as only restrictions need to pass the test of Article G.

The notion of restriction could also be distinguished from the notion of prohibition. Whereas a prohibition prevents or precludes workers and employers from having recourse to collective action, restrictions only affect the exercise of that right. There is no watertight division between prohibitions and restrictions. Some restrictions might in fact deprive recourse to collective action of its useful effect. Furthermore, prohibitions and restrictions need to pass the test of Article G. However, it seems logical that restrictions can more readily be considered necessary in a democratic society than prohibitions.

The ESC makes a distinction between derogations and restrictions. Whereas derogations need to pass the test of Article F, restrictions need to pass the test of Article G.

Article G is an extremely relevant provision for the protection of the right to strike. Contrary to other provisions recognising a right to strike in national constitutions or at international level, it does not refer to national law as a prima facie unconditional limit on the exercise of the right to strike. Thus, the French (1946) and the Italian (1948) constitutions only recognise the right to strike 'dans le cadre des lois qui le réglementent' or 'nell'ambito delle leggi che lo regolanno'. In the same vein, Article 81(d) ICESCR only protects the right to strike 'provided that it is exercised in conformity with the laws of a particular country'. Although it would be problematic not to

[69] The notion of restriction warrants some preliminary observations. It needs to be handled with care. In the Appendix to the ESC, which has been integrated into the appendix of the Charter, the word 'restriction' is used in a statement related to Art 6§4. It says: 'It is understood that each Party may, insofar as it is concerned, regulate the exercise of the right to strike by law, provided that any further restriction that this might place on the right can be justified under the terms of Article G.' This Appendix suggests that rules that regulate the exercise can and need to be distinguished from rules that restrict the exercise. Not every rule that regulates the exercise will constitute a restriction. However, rules that regulate the exercise can constitute a source of restrictions. These restrictions stemming from the law of the contracting states need to comply with Art G.

[70] In the same vein: APCM Jaspers, '*Nederlands stakingsrecht op een nieuw spoor?*' (Deventer, Kluwer, 2006) 61. *Contra:* R Birk, 'Derogations and restrictions on the right to strike under international law', in R Blanpain (ed), *Labour Law, Human Rights and Social Justice* (The Hague, Kluwer International, 2001) 100.

accept that there is a core, or *Kernbereich,* that cannot be restricted, these texts do not offer any tools to assess whether that hard-core is being affected by the restriction. The same critique can be expressed with regard to Article 28 CFREU, which refers to an exercise in accordance with EU law, national laws and practices, although Article 52 CFREU at least seems to point to the existence of a hard-core (the essence).

(ii) Material Scope: Collective Action and Strikes

Hitherto, the ECSR has only recognised three means of collective action. The first of these means is inevitably the right to strike, which is the only means to be explicitly mentioned. In an important statement of interpretation dating back to 1969, the ECSR made it abundantly clear that the right to lock out falls within the ambit of the Charter.

(a) Strikes and Lock-outs

It is clear from the text that this provision relates to both strikes and lock-outs, even though the latter are not explicitly mentioned in the text of Article 6§4 or in the gloss to this provision in the Appendix. The Committee came to this conclusion because the 'lock-out is the principal, if not the only, form of collective action which employers can take in defence of their interests'.[71]

This statement does not clarify whether the protection granted to the right to lock out should be identical to the protection of the right to strike in the legal order of a contracting party. This question is legitimate in view of a deeply rooted idea of equality of arms in the German system of industrial relations. In a statement of interpretation dating back to 1978, the ECSR indicated that the ESC does not at all enshrine an obligation to ensure such a principle in the legal order of the contracting parties. It stated:

> The Charter does not necessarily imply that legislation and case-law should establish full legal equality between the right to strike—which the Charter indeed mentions explicitly and which is recognised as a fundamental right by the Constitution of several member States—and the right to call a lock-out. Consequently, the Committee thought, in the first place, that a State party to the Charter cannot be found at fault for not having passed legislation regulating the exercise of lock-out and, in the second place, that the competent tribunals were entitled to place certain restrictions on the exercise of lock-out in specific cases where it would in particular constitute an abuse of right or where it would be devoid of justification on the ground of 'force majeure' or of the disorganisation of the enterprise caused by the workers' collective action.[72]

[71] ECSR, Statement of Interpretation, Conclusion, 31 May 1969.
[72] ECSR, Statement of Interpretation, Conclusions VIII, 31 January 1984.

The asymmetry[73] between both rights is remarkable, because the ECSR at a later date condemned the reference to the doctrine of the 'abuse of right' in a number of Belgian cases in order to restrict the right to strike. As evidenced below, this refutation of the 'doctrine of abuse' was based upon an important consideration that strikes at the heart of collective autonomy, namely, the prohibition on judges' encroaching on the assessment of the appropriate character of a trade union demand.

(b) Other (Collective) Actions

The question arises of whether the generic notion of a collective action allows for the recognition of collective actions that cannot be qualified as strike action. In many legal orders, strike tends to be defined as a collective stoppage of work. The etymological origin of notions such as *grève* (French), *sciopero* (Italian) or *huelga* (Spanish) strengthens the idea that a strike is essentially an omission to perform a contract of employment. For this reason, an unconventional or counterproductive performance of the employment contract will usually be disqualified as a strike.

The ECSR made the effort during the XIVth and XVth monitoring cycles to ask some contracting parties to indicate whether other means of collective action were protected in their legal orders. The mere fact that the ECSR made such an effort suggests that the notion of collective action includes the right to strike, but cannot be restricted to it. At present, the Conclusions of the ECSR give no guidance on the collective actions of workers falling within the scope of Article 6§4. A recent decision[74] issued upon a collective complaint of the ETUC and the Belgian representative trade unions sheds more light on this troublesome issue. The plaintiffs argued that the right to picket in a way that effectively, though peacefully blocked the entrance to an undertaking fell within the ambit of Article 6§4. They claimed that the judicial orders prohibiting this obstructive picketing (as well as non- or less obstructive picketing) in summary proceedings was an unjustified restriction of the right to take collective action. The complaint urged the ECSR to adopt a position regarding the preliminary question of whether these actions were protected at all under Article 6§4, prior to the assessment of the justified character of that restriction.

[73] See also S Evju, 'The right to take collective action under the European Social Charter' (2011) *European Labour Law Journal* 201.

[74] *CSC, CES, CGSLB, FGTB v Belgium*, Collective Complaint No 59/2009. See F Dorssemont, 'Libres propos sur la légitimité des requêtes unilatérales contre l'exercice du droit à l'action collective à la lumière de la décision du Comité européen des droits sociaux', in I Ficher, PP Van Gehuchten et al (eds), *Actions orphelines et voies de recours en droit social* (Limal, Anthémis, 2012) 129–48 and JF Neven, 'Les piquets de grève, la procédure sur requête unilatérale et les pouvoirs du juge des référés après la décision du comité européen des droits sociaux du 13 septembre (2012)', *Revue de droit social*, 393.

In two crucial paragraphs (§§35 and 36) of the Decision the ECSR seems to draw a line between the kind of actions that fall within Article 6§4 and those that fall outside the ambit of the provision.

In essence, the ECSR draws a line between collective actions that are peaceful and those that are not. The first fall within the ambit of Article 6, the latter do not. In this respect, the approach is not entirely distinct from the approach adopted by the CFA (ILO). More importantly, the ECSR goes at length to define when an action ceases to be peaceful. Strikers should refrain from intimidation or violence against non-strikers. Furthermore, they should 'not violate the right of other workers to choose whether or not to take part in strike action'.[75]

In the case of obstructive pickets, these conditions are fulfilled. Belgian trade unions do not have recourse to intimidation or violence, but they may block access to undertakings through physical blockades. The mere fact that a person who would like to work is prevented from doing so does not entail that they have no choice whether to participate to the strike or not. Indeed, a person who is unable to obtain access and is unable to work will not for that reason be considered a striker. Under Belgian law, a strike is defined as a voluntary stoppage of work. In this case, the stoppage is not voluntary. The latter does not mean that the ECSR does not recognise the existence of a right of employees willing to work to have access to the enterprise, which could in fact restrict the exercise of the right to take collective action. However, a collective action that is at odds with those rights does not for that reason cease to fall within the ambit of Article 6§4.[76]

(iii) Personal Scope of the Right to Take Collective Action

The issue of the personal scope of the right to take collective action raises two major issues.

[75] 'Le recours à des '"'piquets" n'empêche en rien le libre choix des salariés de participer ou non à la grève.'

[76] See also No 119 of ECSR, Decision, 3 July 2013, LO; *TCO v Sweden*, Collective Complaint No 85/2012.

See also the contribution of A Koukiadi in this volume, who rightly raises the right of co-workers to work as an issue of conflicting rights able to restrict the right to take collective action, rather than as an issue of delimitation. The recent conclusions regarding Belgium illustrate that the situation there continues to be problematic. No shift in the case law regarding picketing has been detected. Furthermore, no proper information on the decision towards the judicial authorities has been given, according to the Committee. In fact, the government has communicated the decision to the *Conseil National du Travail*, a body for the consultation of the social partners at intersectoral level. According to one author, the Collège des Procureurs has been informed by the Minister of Justice. He has criticised this communication because the Ministère public has no role to play in the summary proceedings. JF Neven, 'Piquets de grève: les suites de la décision du comité européen des droits sociaux du 13 septembre 2011', in F Krenck (ed), *Droit du grève: actualités et questions choisies* (Brussels, Larcier, 2015) 40.

The first is related to the question of the extent to which civil servants can be precluded from taking collective action. Paradoxically, contrary to Article 5, which merely relates to the right to form and join trade unions, Article 6 is completely mute on this issue. As evidenced by the contribution of Jacobs in this volume, Article 5 allows contracting parties to preclude members of the armed forces from forming and joining trade unions, whereas it solely allows restrictions on the exercise of that right by members of the police force. Article 8 ICESCR allows lawful restrictions on the exercise of the rights granted under that provision (the right to organise, as well as the right to strike) by members of the armed forces or of the police or of the administration of the state.

At first sight, this means that the ESC is more lenient on the margin of appreciation granted to contracting parties to regulate the right to organise than the right to take collective action. In view of the fact that the right to take collective action might generate more far-reaching damage to the public interest, such an assessment amounts to a paradox.

The second issue is related to the question of whether the mere fact that Article 6's right to take collective action is construed as a right of workers and employers precludes contracting parties from considering that a spontaneous collective action by workers is illegal *in se et per se*. In this perspective, the European Social Charter would have ruled out an organic approach to the right to take collective action in favour of a so-called liberal approach In an 'organic' approach, the right to call a collective action is a prerogative of a trade union. Hence, there is no right to participate in a collective action that has not been called by a trade union. In a more liberal approach, the right to collective action is a right that needs to be exercised in a collective manner, namely together with other workers. Hence, it is irrelevant whether a trade union has actually called for a collective action.

A former member of the ECSR, S Evju,[77] has made an extensive analysis of the evolving case law of the ECSR between 1971 and a more or less Copernican conclusion in 2004, related to Sweden. It considers that the reference to 'workers' in Article 6§4 relates to those who are entitled to take part in collective action, but says nothing about those empowered to call a strike. In other words, this provision does not require states to grant any group of workers authority to call a strike, but leaves them the option of deciding which groups shall have this right and thus of restricting the right to call strikes to trade unions.

However, such restrictions are only compatible with Article 6§4 if there is complete freedom to form trade unions and the process is not subject

[77] S Evju, 'The right to take collective action under the European Social Charter' (2011) 3 *European Labour Law Journal* 213.

to excessive formalities that would impede the rapid decisions that strike action sometimes requires.[78]

At present, no interpretative statement has been issued regarding this quintessential issue on who has the right to take collective action. However, the Digest[79] has been adapted in order to take into account this important 'restatement' by the ECSR. It summarises the position by stating that 'the decision to call a strike can be taken only by a trade union provided that forming a trade union is not subject to excessive formalities'. A timeframe of 30 days to establish a trade union under Portuguese law was considered excessive.[80] An evolution has also been identified by an author who has not served as a member of the ECSR. Contrary to Evju, Kovacs[81] asserts that the position adopted by the ECSR does not constitute, as Evju phrased it, a U-turn, but that the 'Committee, rather, seems to accept the individual doctrine and protect the right of all groups of individuals to call a strike'.

The right to call a strike cannot be a prerogative of representative trade unions.[82] In the same vein, the idea of reserving the right to call a strike to trade unions that fulfil the condition of *Soziale Mächtigkeit* ('social power') under German Law was considered problematic as well.[83]

The conclusion from the ECSR seems to take into account the diversity of systems of industrial relations. It offers a margin of appreciation to contracting parties to herald either an organic or a more liberal vision. The ECSR has attempted to reconcile the legitimacy of an organic vision with the wording of the Charter by introducing a scholastic distinction between the right to take part in collective action, on one hand, and a right that is not mentioned in the ESC, namely the right to call a strike. This distinction allows the ECSR to uphold the idea that the right to strike is an individual right, although its legitimacy is dependent upon trade union recognition of such a strike. The distinction can be saluted from a formal point of view, insofar as it challenges the idea that the right to strike as such could be qualified as a collective right, let alone a trade union prerogative. Because a strike is a stoppage of work, it can never be exercised by a trade union that is unable to conclude any contract of employment entailing an obligation to work. However, the idea that citizens can be a holder of a right that can only be exercised insofar as that exercise has been authorised by a collective, comes close to a denial of such a right. The counter-price to

[78] See ECSR, Conclusions, 31 May 2004, Sweden.

[79] Digest, 152.

[80] ECSR, Conclusion XX-3, Portugal.

[81] E Kovacs, 'The right to strike in the European Social Charter' (2004/2005) *Comparative Labour Law and Policy Journal* 454. See also AM Swiatkowski, *Charter of Social Rights of the Council of Europe* 229.

[82] ECSR, Conclusions, XX-3, France; ECSR, Conclusions, XX-3, Romania.

[83] ECSR, Conclusions, XX-3, Germany.

be paid for subjecting the right to collective action to an authorisation by trade unions is a seemingly reinforced freedom for workers to form and join trade unions. *Per analogiam*: it would be hard to imagine how the right to organise or the freedom of expression could not be considered to have been violated if it were made subject to prior authorisation.

Furthermore, the approach of the ECSR is astonishing insofar as it does not take into account an essential distinction between Article 6§2 and Article 6§4 in the identification of the holder of a right. Whereas the right to negotiations is attributed to workers' organisations, the right to strike is being attributed to a worker. The fact that the ECSR allows the right to strike to be linked to the authorisation by trade unions might be called consistent with the approach of the CFA (ILO), which does not object to the prohibition of wildcat strikes. However, there is a major difference. The CFA has recognised the right to strike as a corollary of the right to freedom of association, which cannot be dissociated from it. The Charter juxtaposes both rights. Last but not least, the alleged illegality of wildcat strikes reduces trade unions to the role of peace-keeping actors, rather than upholding their role under the ESC as actors protecting economic and social interests.

(iv) Teleological Restrictions

Teleological restrictions are restrictions that stem from a *telos,* namely the underlying rationale behind the recognition of the right to take collective action. Article 6 seems abundantly clear with regard to the identification of the underlying rationale. It states that the right to take collective action has been recognised with a view to ensuring the effective exercise of the right to bargain collectively. Furthermore, Article 6§4 refers to a context of conflicts of interest. According to a statement of interpretation, the latter need to be opposed to conflicts of rights, 'such as conflicts related to the existence, validity or interpretation of a collective agreement'.[84]

The apparent nexus between a process of collective bargaining and a right to strike has raised the question of whether a well-known teleological restriction under German law, the so-called *Tarifvertragbezogenheit*, hence the restriction of collective action to the objective of concluding a formal collective agreement, could be considered to be in conformity with Article 6§4. The ECS has taken the occasion to clarify that the nexus between the right to take collective action and collective bargaining is in fact much broader. It is sufficient that a collective action take places in 'any context of negotiation between employers and employees in order to settle an industrial dispute'.[85]

[84] ESCR, Conclusions I, 31 May 1969, Statement of Interpretation.
[85] Digest, 53.

The teleological restriction of the right to strike, banning strikes not aimed at the conclusion of a collective agreement under German law, continues to be criticised as incompatible with the ESC.[86] However, the nexus described above in my view excludes from the ambit of Article 6§4 protest strikes—erroneously called 'political strikes'—aimed at criticising government policies that affect genuine socio-economic interests. The mere fact that the ECSR has stated at least implicitly that 'political strikes' fall outside the ambit of Article 6§4 ESC is not decisive, because the notion was not defined by the ECSR. It is not the object of an industrial dispute that constitutes an insurmountable obstacle, but the identification by the ECSR of the parties in the conflict of interest seems to be fatal. It is extremely difficult to argue that such a protest strike will deal with a conflict between employers and employees.

Such an obstacle might be overcome, insofar as a collective action is aimed at criticising a government intervention that restricts the freedom of collective bargaining. Such a collective action might indeed be exercised with a view to ensuring the right to collective bargaining. The Dutch Supreme Court, which considers Article 6§4 to be the cornerstone of the right to collective action under Dutch law, has indicated that collective actions in protest against government policies that concern issues that fall within the realm of collective bargaining are, as a matter of principle, protected under Article 6§4 ESC.[87]

A link between the right to take collective action and the right to organise along the lines of the approach adopted by the CFA (ILO) is able to overcome this hurdle. The right to organise seeks to allow trade unions to further and defend the interests of workers and their employers. These interests need to be safeguarded in the employment relationship, as well as in relations between trade unions and political authorities.

Another issue that has not yet been clarified completely is the legitimacy of a solidarity strike. In some authoritative comments, former members of the ECSR have argued that solidarity strikes fall outside the ESC.[88] In my view, this statement is questionable and is not corroborated by any interpretative statement of even a conclusion or decision from the ECSR. From a formal point of view, solidarity strikes or actions do concern conflicts between employers and employees. The ECSR has never stated that these conflicts need to concern conflicts between workers and *their* employers.

[86] See ECSR, Conclusions, XX-3, Germany. The ECSR has expressed this in successive conclusions ever since Conclusion XV-1 (2001).

[87] See Hoge Raad, 30 May 1986, NS. See also well APCM Jaspers, *Nederlands stakingsrecht op een nieuw spoor* (Deventer, Kluwer, 2004) 55–57.

[88] A Swiatkowski, *Charter of Social Rights of the Council of Europe* (Alphen aan den Rijn, Kluwer International, 2007) 227–28. M Mikkola, *Social Human Rights of Europe* (Porvoo, Bookwell Ltd, 2010) 283.

Hence, there is no reason to assume that the notion of a conflict of interests needs to be interpreted in the narrow meaning of the British TULRCA. In fact, the ECSR has indicated that the provisions of the TULRCA are far too restrictive and violate Article 6§4. The ECSR has indicated that the approach of the British legislator deprives employees of the opportunity to exert pressure against a person who might be distinct from the contractual employer, but is in fact the corporate person who has a major influence over the working conditions and the socio-economic interests of the employees involved.[89]

In a recent landmark judgment the Dutch *Hoge Raad* ruled that a boycott inspired by solidarity does fall within the ambit of Article 6§4. It is sufficient that there be a reasonable nexus between the solidarity strike and a process of collective bargaining within the ambit of Article 6§4. The mere fact that a secondary action could contribute to satisfying the demands put forward in the primary action was deemed sufficient.[90] Contrary to what the Strasbourg Court suggested in the *RMT* judgment, no proof need be given that the trade unions would have won the day provided that they had had recourse to solidarity action.

(a) Procedural Restrictions

For the purposes of this chapter, procedural restrictions are defined as formal requirements that have to be fulfilled prior to having recourse to collective action. Violation of these requirements will affect the legitimacy of a collective action. Contrary to the Digest, so-called peace obligations will not be qualified as procedural restrictions. They affect the *legitimate* objectives of a collective action. Hence, they need to be qualified as teleological restrictions.

Both Article 6§4 and Article G allow for procedural restrictions. Whereas procedural restrictions based upon Article 6§4 stem from 'collective agreements previously entered into', procedural restrictions based upon Article G can be based upon other legal sources. It is sufficient that they be prescribed by law. However, this latitude is restricted by the requirement that procedural restrictions always need to serve the legitimate objectives defined in Article G, and need to be necessary in a democratic society. Apparently, conventional restrictions do not need to pass that test. In fact, Article G deals with substantive restrictions based on the balancing of competing public and private interests. For these reasons, in a strict reading of Article G it is difficult to justify purely abstract procedural restrictions unrelated to

[89] See esp ECSR, Conclusions, XX-3, United Kingdom.

[90] See Hoge Raad, 31 October 2014 (*Enerco*), JAR, 2014/298 with a comment by EM Hoogeveen.

such a balancing exercise. The fact remains that the approach of Article G is substantive rather than procedural.[91] Arguments related to the *travaux préparatoires* or to the 'structure' of Article 6 are far from convincing or compelling.

Collective agreements have a twofold nature. The obligatory part generates obligations between the signatory parties, whereas the so-called normative part will generate obligations for the members of the signatory parties, for example, the employees. The question of whether signatory parties—for example, trade unions—are empowered to restrict or even alienate fundamental workers' rights is intimately linked to the issue of the holding of those rights. It is difficult to accept that the right to take collective action is construed as a workers' right, if a trade union could regulate and indeed restrict its exercise. As already indicated, the ECSR has given some guidance on the issue as far as the 'social peace clause' is concerned. The ECSR has indeed upheld the conformity of these clauses, explicitly or implicitly, with the ESC on the basis of Article 6§4. Hence, there is no reason to assume *per analogiam* that the normative part of a collective agreement could not be a source for procedural restrictions of the right to take collective action as well. Such leeway granted to social partners might be inconsistent with a more public law approach to the right to strike as a constitutional right granted to workers/citizens, which can only be restricted by statutory law. French case law provides evidence of such an approach. The Digest does not provide a lot of guidance on this issue. Harris and Darcy have pointed out in a general way that restrictive conventional obligations 'can only affect the right to take collective action of those workers *subject* to the collective agreement'.[92]

It is reasonable to assert that the fact that the ESC insists that restrictions can only be based upon collective agreements previously entered into constitutes a second and important restriction on the legitimacy of empowering trade unions to restrict the workers' right to collective action. *A contrario*, it seems to warrant the thesis that the normative part can be used as a source of restrictions. The suggestion is in fact that employees cannot be confronted with a retroactive application of the collective agreement.

Procedural restrictions can also be based upon 'law' within the meaning of Article G. Given the broad interpretation of the notion of law, the latter can refer to statutory as well as judge-made restrictions.

[91] See in this respect L Schut, *Internationale normen in het Nederlandse stakingsrecht* (Den Haag, Sdu, 1996) 186. See also M Tilstra, *Grenzen aan het stakingsrecht* (Deventer, Kluwer, 1994) 331.

[92] D Harris and J Darcy, *The European Social Charter* (New York, Transnational Publishers, 2001) 106. (However, this assumption is based upon a Conclusion (Norway) related to the issue of the social peace clause. XIV-1 618.)

A first issue to be treated is related to ballot procedure, which subjects the calling of a strike to a referendum among the workers concerned. Given that any obligation to hold a referendum can only be subject to the observation of rules developed in minute detail (the definition of the workers eligible to vote, the rules on how a referendum needs to be organised, rules related to quorum and majority and so on), the latter will in practice not be judge-made law.

Another issue is the observation of a pre-established and precise cooling off period, often combined with an obligation to respect mediation and conciliation procedures. Such rules will not be judge-made law either; in practice, they are based on rules established either in collective agreements or in statutory instruments.

Last but not least, there is the much less precise judge-made principle that recourse to collective action needs to be construed as a last resort. This principle suggests that collective action can only be undertaken provided that a process of collective bargaining has effectively taken place and has not been interrupted or terminated prematurely.

The Digest makes no attempt to explain how or why these restrictions can be justified at all.

It would be reasonable to suggest that such a justification is far from evident. There is no single element in Article 6§4 that could be used as an argument for procedural restriction. Though the structure of Article 6 as a whole suggests a controversial logic of bargaining, mediation and conciliation preceding a process of collective action, it does not suggest that calling a strike should be made subject to a referendum as well.

The conclusions adopted by the ECSR, especially regarding the United Kingdom and related to Article 6§4, were digested as follows in 2008:

> Subjecting the exercise of the right to strike to prior approval by a certain percentage of workers is in conformity with Article 6§4, provided that the ballot method, the quorum and the majority required are not such that the exercise of the right to strike is excessively limited.

A majority requirement of two-thirds was considered excessive.[93]

The maxim of the Digest is to some extent at odds with more recent conclusions of the ECSR, which are extremely critical of the very existence of a ballot procedure. In a recent conclusion regarding the United Kingdom, the ECSR considered the mere juxtaposition of an obligation to issue notification of a strike, as well as to organise a referendum, to be excessive. This conclusion reiterated an earlier position adopted in 2010.[94]

[93] ECSR, Conclusions XX-33, 2014, Czech Republic (a majority requirement of two-thirds was considered excessive). Conclusions, XX-3, Hungary: the committee insists that the majority concerned needs to consist of trade union members, instead of all employees involved.

[94] ECSR, Conclusions XX-3, 2014.

As far as the obligation to give notice is concerned, the ECSR has never opposed this practice. Insofar as this notice will often go hand in hand with a notice period, a caveat is necessary. The ECSR has indeed insisted that such a notice period should be of a reasonable duration.[95] The same conclusion is warranted for pre-strike conciliation procedures. The latter can be combined with a notice period. As far as the latter are concerned, the issue of their conformity needs to be assessed in light of Articles 6§3 and 6§4.

An obligation to notify not merely a strike action, but the duration of that action was considered to be excessive, despite the fact that it affected so-called essential services in Italy.[96]

The *ultimum remedium* principle was severely criticised by the ECSR when it took notice of the so-called *Douwe Egberts* judgment. In *Douwe Egberts*,[97] the Supreme Court referred to the ESC in order to argue that the right to take collective action was construed as an *ultimum remedium*. For this reason, the Supreme Court argued that a judicial decision prohibiting a strike considered to be premature needed to be upheld. In a subsequent conclusion the ECSR has considered that nothing in the Charter warrants the idea that a right to take collective action could be prohibited because a judge has the feeling that there was still sufficient scope for negotiations. The ECSR has indicated in this respect that the doctrine of collective action as an *ultimum remedium* would inevitably urge judges to assess the appropriate character of a strike instead of restricting their concern to assessing its legality. In the *Amsta* landmark judgment, the Dutch Supreme Court tends to mitigate its previous position regarding the *ultimum remedium* character of the right to take collective action. It states that such a condition cannot be construed any longer as a sufficient or independent reason to outlaw collective action. The Supreme Court does indicate that procedural considerations can come into play in an assessment of a more substantive balancing exercise, based upon Article G.[98]

(b) Substantive Restrictions

Like any right under the ESC, the right to collective action can be made subject to substantive restrictions, namely restrictions based on conflicting private and public interests. The private and public interests that can justify restrictions are enumerated exhaustively in Article G. For the issue of the right to take collective action, substantive restrictions can be extremely

[95] ECSR, Conclusions XX-3, 2014, Czech Republic: a cooling-off period of 30 days was considered to be excessive, starting from the day the mediator was acquainted with the issue (a majority requirement of two-thirds was considered excessive).

[96] ECSR, Conclusions, XX-3, Italy.

[97] Hoge Raad, 28 January 2000, NJ 292.

[98] Hoge Raad, 19 June 2015, JAR 2015/1260.

detrimental to effective recourse to collective action. Collective actions seek to exert pressure against an antagonist in order to influence his conduct and to enforce demands. In the case of a primary action, this will comprise economic damage directly inflicted on this antagonist.

(c) Rights and Freedoms of Others

Hence, the first question will be whether the legitimate justification of the protection of the 'rights and freedoms' of others also cover purely economic damage inflicted on an employer who is a party to the conflict of interests. Two separate arguments could be put forward to claim that such a justification does not meet the test of Article G. First, it could be argued that economic damage and 'rights and freedoms' are two different concepts. Whereas a violation of a right does not always entail economic damage, neither does inflicting economic damage always corresponds to the violation of rights and freedoms. Furthermore, it is unclear whether the 'rights and freedoms' concerned need to be 'rights and freedoms' of a fundamental character or not. Insofar as mere economic damage inflicted on an antagonist allows for a restriction of the right to take collective action, there is a serious risk that 'proportionality' will not be used as a measure to assess the legitimacy of a restriction, but as a condition for the legitimacy of the exercise of the right to take collective action.

The Digest does not provide any guidance on this essential issue. It focuses on restrictions justified by public interests.

In an important conclusion delivered by the Committee following critical observations by the Belgian trade unions (FGTB and CSC) on the Belgian Report, the Committee condemned the application of the doctrine of the *abus de droit* on the following grounds:

> Analysis of this case law also shows that a change is taking place, to the extent that certain decisions forbid strikes themselves, and no longer only certain practices linked to them. In such cases, the proportionality criterion is used by the judge. The Committee observes that use of the concept of abuse of right or the proportionality criterion is leading the courts to act as judges of strikes' appropriateness, and consequently of their lawfulness. Thus, if the judge considers that the harmful effects of a strike are disproportionate or that the strike could be organised at a less damaging time without losing its effectiveness, a ban will be imposed. Urgent applications are also sometimes submitted on a preventive basis. The Committee considers that the judicial practices concerned that restrict the exercise of the right to strike go beyond the restrictions accepted in Article 31 of the Charter.[99]

This conclusion amounts to a clear-cut prohibition of the proportionality principle. Although the German system is much better known for its use

[99] ECSR, XVO, Belgium. See also F Dorssemont, 'La (non)conformité du droit belge relative

of the proportionality test as a condition for the legitimacy of the exercise of the right to strike, the Committee has never taken the opportunity to assess the legitimacy of that criterion. In a separate opinion in a subsequent control cycle, however, Aliprantis seriously questioned the legitimacy of the German case law applying a proportionality test.[100]

(d) Public Interests

The ECSR has provided more guidance on the conflict between the right to strike and 'public interests'. The notion 'public interest' is mirrored by the notion of *ordre public* in the French language version, which clearly warrants a very restrictive reading.[101]

The ECSR has given much more guidance on the scope of the kind of public interests that could justify restrictions than on the relevant private interests. Some of these public interests are listed explicitly, such as 'national security' and 'public health'. In my view, the *moral* ground for restriction is not a relevant reason to restrict the right to strike. It is difficult to understand how demands related to socio-economic interests could be qualified as 'immoral', despite the fact that the ECSR considered, in an old conclusion related to Germany, that the prohibition of immoral strikes was compatible with the ESC.[102]

Thus, the reference to public interest cannot justify a general restriction affecting the entire civil service.[103] It is indeed essential that a prohibition of the strike is necessary to safeguard the public interests at stake. Although the ECSR has argued that some services affect the public interest within the meaning of Article G and can be qualified as essential, the latter does not warrant a generic sectoral prohibition either. Such a generic sectoral prohibition was considered to be excessive in two decisions following a collective complaint procedure. In a Bulgarian case, such a generic sectoral prohibition was at stake in the electricity (production, distribution and supply), communications and health care sectors.[104] The Committee qualified all these

à l'action collective par rapport à la Charte sociale européenne', in P Humblet, *Actualités du dialogue social et du droit de grève* (Waterloo, Kluwer, 2009) 194–96.

[100] See dissenting opinion of Aliprantis ECSR, XVII-1, Germany.

[101] In the same vein: APCM Jaspers, *Nederlands stakingsrecht op een nieuw spoor?* (Deventer, Kluwer, 2004) 95–97.

[102] See in this respect Conclusion II, Germany, Art 6§4 1971 and the comments of A Koukiadaki in this volume. The notion of *Sittenwidrigkeit* (violation of moral principles) is more related to the issue of damages inherent in strike action than to the objectives of the strikes. Nowadays this issue tends to be regulated by the notion of proportionality (*Verhältnismässigkeit*). See W Reinfelder, 'Sonstige Schranken des Streikrecht', in W Däubler (ed), *Arbitskampfrecht* (Baden-Baden, Nomos, 2011) 294.

[103] See ECSR, Conclusions, XX-3, Denmark; ECSR, Conclusions XX-3, Germany.

[104] See ECSR, No 32/2005, *European Trade Union Confederation (ETUC), Confederation of Independent Trade Unions in Bulgaria (CITUB), Confederation of Labour 'Podkrepa'*

services as essential services. This approach is divergent from the approach adopted by the ILO CFA, which does not qualify electricity and communications as essential services. In an Irish case, a generic ban on strikes by the police force was considered to be disproportionate as well.[105] It seems logical to assume that the ECSR is suggesting that a minimum service is a more proportionate way to restrict the right to strike in such a scenario. It has not yet had the opportunity to indicate at length how the legitimacy of the design of this minimum service needs to be assessed. In a recent conclusion regarding Serbia, involvement of workers as such and on the same footing as employers has been put forward as an essential element.[106] The ECHR's recent *Veniamin Tymoshenko and others v Ukraine*[107] might provide proper guidance, insofar as it insists on the importance of sufficient clarity and foreseeability.

(v) Implementing the Obligation to Recognise the Right to Collective Action

The question arises of how such an obligation to recognise the right to collective action needs to be implemented.

The ECSR has never insisted that the recognition of a right to strike should be based on a constitutional or statutory basis.[108] However, a statutory prohibition or criminal law is incompatible with such a duty to recognise.[109] Furthermore, the ECSR has indicated that a duty to recognise implies a positive obligation for states to provide adequate protection against dismissal for workers who have participated in a (legal) strike.[110] In the past, the

(CL 'Podkrepa') v Bulgaria. See also critical conclusions with regard to Iceland concerning a ban on strikes in civil aviation: ECSR, Conclusions, XX-3, Iceland; ECSR, Conclusions, XX-3, Slovak Republic.

[105] *European Confederation of Police (EuroCOP) v Ireland*, Collective Complaint No 83/2012.

[106] ECSR, Conclusions, XX-3, Serbia.

[107] *Veniamin Tymoshenko and others v Ukraine* App no 48408/12 (ECtHR, 2 October 2014).

[108] See in this respect, the observations in *CSC, CES, CGSLB, FGTB v Belgium*, Collective Complaint No 59/2009.

[109] See ECSR, Conclusions, XII-2, Ireland.

[110] See ECSR, Conclusions, I, statement of interpretation, 31 May 1969: 'Lastly, the Committee examined the compatibility with the Charter of a rule according to which a strike terminates the contract of employment. In principle, the Committee takes the view that this is not compatible with respect of the right to strike as envisaged by the Charter. Whether, in a given case, a rule of this kind constitutes a violation of the Charter is, however, a question which should not be answered in the abstract, but in the light of the consequences which the legislation and industrial practice of a given country attaches to the termination and resumption of the employment relationship. If, in practice, those participating in a strike are, after its termination, fully reinstated and if their previously acquired rights, eg as regards pensions, holidays and seniority, in general, are not impaired, the formal termination of the contracts of employment by the strike does not, in the opinion of the Committee, constitute a violation of the Charter.'

ECSR has also indicated that the strike should be protected against recourse by the employer to workers wishing to break a strike. Hence, the German government could not have recourse to civil servants to replace contractual workers.[111]

III. IMPACT ON EUROPEAN HUMAN RIGHTS INSTRUMENTS

The impact of Article 6 will be illustrated primarily through its most contentious issue, namely the right to collective action. The notion of impact is being used in a generic manner. It shall be examined whether the existence of these provisions has been a catalyst for a more progressive interpretation of (aspects of) the right to take collective action based upon other European or national provisions by judicial bodies empowered to apply the latter provisions. The assessment of the impact of the Charter is in line with a more intertextual approach to interpreting human rights standards as heralded by the Grand Chamber of the Strasbourg Court. The question of whether this approach is in line with the Vienna Convention on the Law of Treaties (VCLT) came to the fore in the recent *RMT* judgment.[112] Insofar as Article 6§4 ESC is the oldest, the most explicit and the most fleshed-out provision recognising a right to take collective action, it seems obvious to assume that it has been a catalyst of a more progressive interpretation. However, it might be useful to keep in mind that there is a quintessential difference between, on one hand, anchoring the right to take collective action 'with a view to ensuring the effective exercise of the right to bargain collectively' and, on the other hand, recognising such a right as an important or even essential means to protect workers' interests within the right to organise. In both cases, there are distinct strings attached.

Insofar as there is a divergent approach to protection under the Charter and the ECHR, there is a problem of coherence inside one legal order. In this part of the chapter, divergences or convergences between the RESC and the ILO Conventions will not be dealt with.

Last but not least, it will be assessed whether the extent of recognition and the protection of the right to bargain collectively *sensu lato* under EU law is comparable or at variance with that under Article 6. *In casu*, a case of divergent protection raises the issue of a conflict between two distinct legal orders, which has not been solved by converging constitutional provisions of both legal orders to uphold the most favourable level of protection. Such a conflict might confront an EU member state with two obligations stemming from different legal orders that are incompatible. A potential means

[111] ECSR, Conclusions XIII-2, Germany.

[112] *RMT v United Kingdom* App no 31045/10 (EctHR, 8 April 2014).

to avoid such a conflict, namely Article 351 TFEU, will not be relevant to so-called 'old member states', because the (R)ESC does not pre-date the Rome Treaty.

A. European Convention on Human Rights

The European Convention on Human Rights takes a different stance towards the issue of 'collective bargaining'. Whereas the ESC dissociates the issue of collective bargaining and the right to organise by dedicating two distinct provisions to these issues, the ECHR is mute on the freedom of collective bargaining. It only recognises the right to form and join trade unions. In recent years, the European Court of Human Rights has furthered the path laid down in the Grand Chamber judgment in *National Union of Belgian Police*,[113] recognising that some means are essential for the protection of workers' rights and fall within the scope of Article 11 ECHR. Ever since the *Unison* judgment, even merely important means fall within the scope of Article 11 ECHR. Hence, the question arises of the extent to which recognition of the right to collective bargaining, as well as the right to collective action in Article 6 ESC has served as a catalyst for the recognition of these rights under Article 11 ECHR.

As far as the right to bargain collectively is concerned, the Grand Chamber judgment in *Demir and Baykara*[114] relied very much on the fact that the Charter recognised the right to bargain collectively. Furthermore, it took into account the fact that the ECSR had 'noted the organic link between freedom of association and freedom to bargain collectively'. The mere fact that the Turkish Republic had not accepted Article 6 was not considered to be a decisive element to rule that the right to collective bargaining constituted an essential means to protect workers' rights under Article 11 ECHR.

As far as the right to take collective action is concerned, as highlighted above there is an evolution in the case law of the European Court on Human Rights in recognising the right to collective action as an essential means to protect workers' interests within the meaning of Article 11 ECHR. Though the Court has never explicitly qualified the right to take collective action as such an essential means, it has stated that it is a *corrolaire indissociable*, or even that it is the most powerful means. In the landmark judgment in *Enerji Yapi-Yol Sen,* it did explicitly refer to Article 6§4.[115] Contrary to the concurring opinion of Judge Pinto de Albuquerque, the judgment in

[113] *National Union of Belgian Police* App no 4464/70 (ECtHR, 27 October 1975).

[114] *Demir and Baykara v Turquie* App no 34503/97 (ECtHR, 12 November 2008).

[115] Stating 'Elle rappelle que la Charte sociale européenne reconnaît aussi le droit de grève comme un moyen d'assurer l'exercice effectif du droit de négociation collective'.

Hrvatski Lijecnicki Sindikat (HLS) v Croatia[116] does not refer to any European or international instrument in order to qualify the right to take collective action as the most powerful means.

The recognition of the right to take collective action as a corollary of the right to organise under Article 11 ECHR has added value for a number of reasons. Article 6§4 subjects the recognition of the right to collective action to an important teleological condition. The right to collective action is recognised solely 'with a view to ensuring the effective exercise of the right to bargain collectively'. Teleological conditions are essentially different from the restrictions mentioned in Article G or in Article 11§2. In fact, Article 11 ECHR does not suggest that member states could allow conventional restrictions that do not satisfy the conditions of Article 11§2. Hence, in order for a teleological condition to be legitimate under the ECHR, a substantive justification will always be necessary.

For the purposes of Article 11 ECHR, it is sufficient that collective actions serve to protect workers' interests, irrespective of whether they are related to collective bargaining. The latter restrict the exercise of the right to take collective action, whereas teleological conditions determine whether a collective action falls inside or outside the scope of the recognition.

Furthermore, the restrictions listed in the ESC are twofold. The ESC allows for conventional as well as statutory restrictions. Whereas statutory restrictions need to pass the triple test of proportionality, conventional restrictions just need to be 'conventional'.

In the recent *RMT* case the ECtHR recalled that it considers the ECSR interpretation of the ESC. It highlighted that it assesses 'from a legal standpoint the compliance of national law and practice with the obligations arising from the Charter'.[117] Furthermore, it qualified the ECSR to be a 'particularly qualified body' in this domain.[118]

B. Charter of Fundamental Rights of the European Union and General and Fundamental Principles of EU Law

The CJEU does not have an immaculate track record in upholding fundamental workers' rights enshrined in Article 6.

[116] *Hrvatski Lijecnicki Sindikat v Croatia* App no 36701/09 (ECtHR, 27 November 2014).

[117] *RMT v UK* App no 31045/10 (ECtHR, 8 April 2014) §94.

[118] Despite this lip service, the Court refused to recognise the Committee's systematic critique of the general prohibition of secondary action. It argued that 'the general character of a law justifying an interference is not inherently offensive to the principle of proportionality'. The Court tried to justify its position by pointing out the different nature of the quasi-judicial monitoring by the Committee aimed at assessing whether the law of a state was in conformity with the Charter, compared with a more judicial approach of the Court assessing a given application of those statutory provisions.

This section looks at the way in which the CJEU has recognised the right to collective bargaining and to take collective bargaining as a general or fundamental principle of EU law. For obvious reasons, Article 28 CFREU could have served as a catalyst for such a recognition. Furthermore, the question arises of the extent to which Article 6 has served as a conceptual framework for interpreting Article 28 CFREU, when the CJEU has indeed referred to it.

The record of the CJEU with regard to the freedom of collective bargaining is troublesome. It has consistently refused to take the opportunity to recognise the freedom of collective bargaining as a general principle of EU law. In *Albany* the Court did not take the freedom of collective bargaining into consideration in order to assess the question of whether competition rules could restrict the validity of collective agreements declared universally applicable. Advocate General Jacobs argued that the collective bargaining process, like any other negotiation between economic actors, is 'sufficiently protected by the general principle of freedom of contract'. Such an approach is questionable. It neglects the quintessential difference between individual and collective autonomy.[119]

In *UEAPME*,[120] the General Court did interpret the Maastricht Agreement on Social Policy as precluding an enforceable right to take part in negotiations which could amount to an agreement concluded at Community level. It highlighted the voluntary character of the bargaining process based upon mutual recognition of the social partners. The voluntary nature of the bargaining process is consistent with the case law of the European Court on Human Rights, as well as with the approach of the freedom of collective bargaining under the European Social Charter. Unfortunately, the Court did not refer to this conceptual framework.

In *Commission v Germany*,[121] the CJEU could not avoid the question of whether the right to bargain collectively constitutes a general principle of EU law. The Commission had started an infringement procedure against the Federal Republic of Germany because local authorities and local authority undertakings had awarded service contracts in respect of occupational old-age pensions directly, without a call for tenders at EU level. The Commission argued that this constituted a violation of a series of Council Directives.[122]

[119] Case C-67/96 *Albany International BV v Stichting Bedrijfspensioenfonds Textielindustrie* (CJEU, 21 September 1999).

[120] Case T-135/96 *Ueapme v Council* (CFI, 18 March 1997).

[121] Case C-271/08 *Commission v Germany* (CJEU, 15 July 2010).

[122] Council Directive 92/50/EEC of 18 June 1992 relating to the coordination of procedures for the award of public service contracts [1992] OJ L209 and Directive 2004/18/EC of the European Parliament and of the Council of 31 March 2004 on the coordination of procedures for the award of public works contracts, public supply contracts and public service contracts [2004] OJ L134/114.

The Federal Republic of Germany replied that these decisions were based on collective agreements that, because of their nature and subject matter, fell outside the field of application of the related Directives in view of the so-called '*Albany* immunity' which shields collective agreements from competition rules. The CJEU did not accept this argument and was thus forced to consider whether the application of these Directives had to be balanced against the right to bargain collectively. It did accept that the right to bargain collectively had to be recognised as a general principle of EU law. The CJEU in this respect referred to the fact that this right had been enshrined in Article 6 of the Charter and in the provisions of instruments drawn up by the member states at Community level or in the context of the European Union.

Unfortunately, as was the case in *Viking* and *Laval*, this only prompted the CJEU to suggest a need to balance the fundamental economic freedoms underlying these Directives against the 'general principle' concerned.

In a staff case,[123] the Civil Service Tribunal (CST) had to consider the request of a retired employee of the European Central Bank who challenged the annual adjustment of his retirement benefits for 2010. This case is relevant because the decision was adopted *after* the Lisbon Treaty came into force. The applicant attacked the fact that the annual adjustment of the pension benefits was decided in a unilateral way, rather than as the outcome of a procedure of collective bargaining. The applicant conceded that Article 28 CFREU did not force the ECB to conclude a collective agreement with the representative trade union of the ECB. However, the absence of a procedure for collective bargaining allegedly violated an obligation to promote in an active manner a culture of dialogue and bargaining. Judged otherwise, the *effet utile* of Article 28 CFREU would be violated.

The CST ruled that neither Article 28 CFREU nor Article 11 ECHR provides an obligation to conclude a collective agreement, nor to introduce a bargaining procedure. The Tribunal paid a formal tribute to Article 6§2 Charter, which enshrines an obligation solely 'to promote, where necessary and appropriate, machinery for voluntary negotiations between employers or employers' organisations and workers' organisations, with a view to the regulation of terms and conditions of employment by means of collective agreements'. According to the Tribunal this obligation does not entail an obligation to introduce a bargaining procedure. It was construed as a provision just 'encouraging' such procedures. Neither could such an obligation be deduced from Article 11 ECHR.

As opposed to the ECB, the Tribunal in *Heath v ECB* did not explicitly dispute that the Charter was indeed applicable to employees of the ECB.

[123] F-121/10 *M Heath v BCE* (Civil Service Tribunal, 29 September 2011) §§110–23. (160 'Dès lors, les droits et obligations en cause étaient déjà suffisamment déterminés par la méthodologie prévue à l'article 17, paragraphe 7, de l'annexe III des conditions d'emploi'.)

Neither did it disregard Article 11 of the ECHR, despite the fact that the European Union has not yet acceded to the Treaty. The fact that Article 11 is taken into account does suggest that the Charter needs to be construed in light of the ECHR. In fact, the Court extends this exercise in intertextuality to the ESC, which had not been quoted by the applicant.[124]

In a more recent case, *Petsch v European Commission*,[125] the absence of a system of collective bargaining in order to determine the establishment rather than the application of such a grid in a conventional rather than a unilateral way, was not considered to be a violation of Article 28 CFREU. The CST seems to be satisfied with the existence of a system of mere consultation (*concertation*). Furthermore, the reference to the *Association de Médiation Sociale*[126] case suggests that the CST considers Article 28 CFREU to be deprived of a direct effect. No reference at all was made in the considerations to Article 6 ESC in order to assess whether the absence of a system of genuine collective bargaining for the entire workforce was indeed compatible with the ESC. It is questionable whether people working at a Kindergarten could in fact qualify as public officials and be deprived of a system of collective bargaining in light of Article 6 ESC. As has already been evidenced by the *Defrenne* case,[127] the mere fact that discriminatory measures have been enshrined in collective agreements, will not shield those instruments from provisions prohibiting discrimination. Following the formal recognition of the right to collective bargaining as a fundamental principle in *Commission v Germany*, the Court has paid formal lip service to Article 28 CFREU, stating that this provision cannot be used in order to shield collective agreements from being censured for not respecting provisions prohibiting discrimination, which are indeed legion in EU secondary law. No genuine balancing operation takes place, neither has an attempt been made to refer to Article 6 ESC.[128]

The record of the CJEU in upholding the right to take collective action as a fundamental principle of EU law is infamous.

In *Viking* and *Laval*, the CJEU did recognise a right to have recourse to collective action as a general principle of EU law. The Court construes the right to have recourse to collective action partially by reference to ILO instruments related to the freedom of association and partially by reference

[124] On appeal, the General Court changed that position. It ruled that the issue at stake was actually outside the purview of bargaining, because since the conflict was merely about the application of a pre-established grid. In sum, the principle of collective bargaining was not even supposed to be at stake. T-645/11 *P—Heath v ECB* (CST, 18 June 2013).

[125] F-124/14 *Petsch v European Commission* (CST, 30 June 2015).

[126] Case C-176/12 *Association de mediation sociale* (CJEU, 15 January 2015).

[127] Case C-43/75 *Defrenne v Sabena* (CJEU, 8 April 1975).

[128] Case C-447/09 *Prigge Fromm, Lambach v Deutsche Lufthansa AG* (CJEU, 13 September 2010) §47 and Cases C-279/10 and 298/10 *S Hennings v Eisenbahn-Bundesamt and Land Berlin v Alexander Mai* (CJEU, 8 September 2011) §67.

to the European Social Charter. The *Laval* and *Viking* cases of the CJEU have already been referred to as recognising a right to take collective action as a general principle of EU labour law. Insofar as this recognition is not restricted to one species of collective action, namely strike action, the recognition can be said to have a 'liberal' character. In fact, the collective actions concerned were not strike actions, but were a circular appealing to a boycott (*Viking*) and a blockade of a construction site (*Laval*).

Despite this promising momentum, both cases are infamous for imposing restrictions on recourse to collective action that were hitherto unprecedented in Finnish *(Viking)* and Swedish *(Laval)* law. Furthermore, in a decision issued after a collective complaint against the so-called '*Lex Laval*', which sought to adapt Swedish industrial relations law to the *Laval* judgment, the ECSR severely criticised the balancing operation between fundamental economic freedoms and genuine human rights operated by the CJEU. The decision focuses on the way in which the '*Lex Laval*' restricts the freedom of collective bargaining, as well as the right to take collective action, whereas the preliminary questions in *Laval* are mute on the tension between the freedom to provide services and the right to collective bargaining. The ECSR considered that the '*Lex Laval*' violated the collective autonomy of the Swedish trade unions. More importantly, as far as restrictions on the right to collective action were concerned, the ECSR seems to take the view that there is an incommensurability between economic freedoms and fundamental workers' right. For this reason, it has stated that the economic freedoms cannot be considered to have a greater a priori value than core labour rights. Thus, indirectly the ECSR disqualifies the balancing operation. It suggests that the CJEU asserts a hierarchy instead of balancing. Furthermore, it suggests that that hierarchy is an *Umwertung aller Werte* ('revaluation of all values') that is at odds with the 'system of values, principles and fundamental rights embodied in the Charter'.

C. Domestic Courts

The most well-known example of an impact on domestic recognition of the right to take collective action is undoubtedly the case law which has been developed by the Dutch Supreme Court. In the landmark *NS* judgment,[129] the Supreme Court referred to Article 6 as the legal foundation of a right to collective action in the Netherlands. In subsequent cases, the Charter has remained the central point of reference of the Supreme Court.

The Supreme Court deserves credit for giving guidance on the scope of the notion of collective action, including atypical collective actions under

[129] *NJ* 1986 (Hoge Raad, 30 May 1986) 688.

its protection. Such protection always comes at a price, however, because the Hoge Raad suggested that in the case of atypical performance of the contract of employment, the obligation to pay full remuneration will have to be mitigated.[130]

The Supreme Court has used the Charter to justify restrictions as well as to justify some collective action. In *Douwe Egberts* it referred to the ESC in order to argue that the right to take collective action was construed as an *ultimum remedium.* This judgment was severely criticised by the ECSR.[131] In *Enerco,* the Supreme Court ruled that a boycott of a ship in order to prevent breaking a primary action was protected under Article 6§4, provided that there was a reasonable nexus between such a boycott and an ongoing process of collective bargaining.[132]

[130] ibid 688 §3.6.

[131] ECSR, XVI, The Netherlands, 30 May 2003. See also: F Dorssemont, 'De prullenbak als *locus naturalis* voor het leerstuk van het misbruik van stakingsrecht' (2002) *Nederlands Tijdschrift voor Sociaal Recht* 325.

[132] *Enerco* JAR 2014/298 (Hoge Raad, 31 October 2014) with comment by EM Hoogeveen.

Article 7

The Right of Children and Young Persons to Protection

ISABELLE SCHÖMANN

Article 7—The right of children and young persons to protection

With a view to ensuring the effective exercise of the right of children and young persons to protection, the Parties undertake:

1. to provide that the minimum age of admission to employment shall be 15 years, subject to exceptions for children employed in prescribed light work without harm to their health, morals or education;
2. to provide that the minimum age of admission to employment shall be 18 years with respect to prescribed occupations regarded as dangerous or unhealthy;
3. to provide that persons who are still subject to compulsory education shall not be employed in such work as would deprive them of the full benefit of their education;
4. to provide that the working hours of persons under 18 years of age shall be limited in accordance with the needs of their development, and particularly with their need for vocational training;
5. to recognise the right of young workers and apprentices to a fair wage or other appropriate allowances;
6. to provide that the time spent by young persons in vocational training during the normal working hours with the consent of the employer shall be treated as forming part of the working day;
7. to provide that employed persons of under 18 years of age shall be entitled to a minimum of four weeks' annual holiday with pay;
8. to provide that persons under 18 years of age shall not be employed in night work, with the exception of certain occupations provided for by national laws or regulations;
9. to provide that persons under 18 years of age employed in occupations prescribed by national laws or regulations shall be subject to regular medical control;
10. to provide that persons under 18 years of age employed in occupations prescribed by national laws or regulations shall be subject to regular medical control; to ensure special protection against physical and moral dangers to

which children and young persons are exposed, and particularly against those resulting directly or indirectly from their work.

Article I—Implementation of the undertakings given

1. Compliance with the undertakings deriving from the provisions of ... paragraphs 4, 6 and 7 of Article 7, ... shall be regarded as effective if the provisions are applied, in accordance with paragraph 1 of this article, to the great majority of the workers concerned.

Appendix:

Article 7, paragraph 2

This provision does not prevent Parties from providing in their legislation that young persons not having reached the minimum age laid down may perform work in so far as it is absolutely necessary for their vocational training where such work is carried out in accordance with conditions prescribed by the competent authority and measures are taken to protect the health and safety of these young persons.

Article 7, paragraph 8

It is understood that a Party may give the undertaking required in this paragraph if it fulfils the spirit of the undertaking by providing by law that the great majority of persons under eighteen years of age shall not be employed in night work.

I. INTRODUCTION

A. Context and Main Content

Children and young people are an exceptionally vulnerable and in many cases disadvantaged group in society with a particular potential for being socially excluded, even in the member states of the EU.[1] Children should be protected, in order to secure an 'environment conducive to the full development of their personality and their physical and mental capacities'.[2]

The Charter, as pendant of the European Convention on Human Rights (ECHR) and a ground-breaking instrument with regard to the protection of economic and social rights, is a major international treaty that makes a meaningful contribution to shaping substantive law on children's rights by

[1] UNICEF, *Child Labour Today* (New York, 2005) 32; H Stalford. 'Art 32 Prohibition of child labour and protection of young people at work', in S Peers, T Hervey, J Kenner and A Ward (eds), *Commentary on the Charter of Fundamental Rights of the European Union* (Oxford, Hart Publishing 2014) 281.

[2] Council of Europe, *The rights of the child. A European perspective* (Strasbourg, Council of Europe Publishing 1996) 553.

recognising the need to ensure their general protection, paying particular attention to adolescents and young adults entering the labour market.

The 1996 Charter brought significant improvements in raising the minimum age of entry to employment from 16 to 18 years. Article 7 has been added in its entirety to the hard-core of the Charter, as part of the 'compulsory nucleus' of rights.[3] Article 7 has been further subject to reporting by states every four years since 2006,[4] for the specific thematic group 4 devoted to 'Children, families and migrants'.

In general, Article 7 has been broadly ratified, with the exception of 11 member states.[5] Interestingly, the least often ratified paragraphs are §§5 and 6 which are related, respectively, to the rights to fair wages and to vocational training.

The protection of children and adolescents at work has developed in close relationship with other international instruments but also in relation to other domains, such as forced labour and the abolition of slavery.

B. International Sources

The large range of international[6] and regional sources on the prohibition of child labour[7] recall the long battle for an indispensable defence of children

[3] And as such must be accepted by member states upon ratification of the Charter. Council of Europe (n 2) 551.

[4] Following a decision of the Committee of Ministers at its 963rd meeting on 3 May 2006, the provisions of the Charter have been divided into four thematic groups. States present a report on the provisions related to one of the four thematic groups on an annual basis. As a consequence, each provision of the Charter is reported on once every four years. As of 2014, state parties, having accepted the complaints procedure, have to provide a national report only every two years (Committee of Ministers Decision CM(2006)53 of 3 May 2006 'European Social Charter—Governmental Committee of the European Social Charter—New system for the presentation of reports on the application of the European Social Charter—Proposal of the Governmental Committee'). On the reporting procedure, see also the chapter by S Clauwaert in this volume.

[5] As for the 1996 Charter, Austria did not accept §6; Cyprus did not accept §5 and §9; Estonia did not accept §5 and §6; Finland did not accept §6 and §9; the Former Yugoslav Republic of Macedonia did not accept §5; Hungary only accepted §1; Norway did not accept §4 and §9; the Republic of Moldova did not accept §5 and §6; and Sweden did not accept §5 and §6. As for the 1961 Charter, Denmark and Iceland did not accept Art 7 as a whole; Germany did not accept §1; Poland did not accept §§1, 3 and 5; and the United Kingdom has not accepted §§1, 4, 7 and 8.

[6] Among others the UN Declaration of the Rights of the Child of 1959, building on the 1924 League of Nations Declaration in which protection against neglect, cruelty and exploitation, trafficking, under-age labour and discrimination are foreseen.

[7] Child labour ranges from the involvement of children and adolescents in (generally low-paid) activities such as domestic work, textile manufacturing and agriculture, up to the worst cases of exploitation such as (domestic) slavery, prostitution, trafficking and recruitment to armed and military conflict.

against physical and mental abuse at work.[8] Sources prior to 1961 have clearly influenced the way the Council of Europe has drafted the protection of children and adolescents. However, the 1961 Charter has played a catalysing role: for example, it was the first international instrument to unify the right to a minimum age for working adolescents, independent of the sector of activity, and influenced the ILO when it adopted the Minimum Age Convention No 138[9] in 1973.

In 1989, the Convention on the Rights of the Child (CRC)[10] recognised the right of children and adolescents to be protected from economic exploitation and hazardous work. In the same year, optional protocols were signed in respect of sex trafficking and armed conflict as regards enhanced protection of children from commercial exploitation and performance of hazardous or harmful work. The additional Protocol to the American Convention on Human Rights[11] requires just, equitable and satisfactory conditions of work for persons under 18 years of age, with a special focus on minors under the age of 16, for whom work must not constitute an impediment to compulsory schooling. In 1994, the European Union embarked on setting minimum standards for the protection of young people at work, passing Directive 94/33/EC.

The 1996 Charter encouraged the ILO to revisit the issue and led to the ILO Declaration on Fundamental Principles and Rights at Work adopted in 1998, in which member states commit to respect and promote principles and rights in four categories, whether or not they have ratified the relevant Conventions, including the abolition of child labour.[12] In 1999 the ILO Convention on the Worst Forms of Child Labour was adopted, as was the African Charter on the Rights and Welfare of the Child guaranteeing that

[8] Referring to the technical ILO conventions: the C005 Minimum Age (Industry) Convention 1919, the C007 Minimum Age (Sea) Convention 1920, the C010 Minimum Age (Agriculture) Convention 1921, the Minimum Age (Trimmers and Stokers) Convention 1921, the C015 Minimum Age (Non-Industrial Employment) Convention 1932, the C058 Minimum Age (Sea) Convention (Revised) 1936, the C059 Minimum Age (Industry) Convention (Revised) 1937, the C033 and C060 Minimum Age (Non-Industrial Employment) Convention (Revised) 1937, the C113 Minimum Age (Fishermen) Convention 1959, the C123 and C124 Minimum Age (Underground Work) Conventions 1965, the C079 Night Work Convention of 1946 and, finally, in relation to medical examinations, the C016, C077 and C078 Conventions (the latter were unified in 1973 in ILO C138).

[9] ILO C138 Minimum Age Convention, of 1973—fundamental: 'Considering that the time has come to establish a general instrument on the subject, which would gradually replace the existing ones applicable to limited economic sectors, with a view to achieving the total abolition of child labour', Preamble, 4th recital. Arts 2 and 3 are the bases of the rights of the child and adolescent.

[10] ibid Art 32 ILO C138.

[11] Protocol of San Salvador of 1988 Art 7.

[12] Together with the freedom of association, the right to collective bargaining, the elimination of forced or compulsory labour and the elimination of discrimination in respect of employment and occupation.

children should be protected against economic exploitation in formal and informal employment. Further, it requires the adoption of legislation to secure minimum wages for admission to every form of employment. Both the ILO and the Charter appear to be mutually complementary, whereby the protection developed in the Charter appears broader and much more detailed[13] in its personal and material scope, particularly in relation to children and minors at work.

The Charter appears to be one of the most advanced international treaties, and a necessary complement to the European Conventions[14] and to a large number of international sources focusing largely on the rights of the child, mainly in terms of the care and assistance of infants, the rights to nationality, social protection and education, as well as protection in cases of adoption, abduction and custody.

C. Relationship to Other Provisions of the Charter

The Charter devotes much attention to the protection of children and adolescents inside and outside the workplace. The overarching principle and primary consideration throughout Article 7 is the best interests of the child, within the meaning of Article 3 of the CRC. The rights to vocational training[15] and to a system of apprenticeship for adolescents[16] are further anchored in the Charter. With less connection to the employment relationship, the Charter addresses the right of the child in the context of their family[17] and foresees the right to social, legal and economic protection[18] of mothers and children,[19] to the reunification of the families of migrant workers[20] and the protection of young offenders against physical and moral dangers.[21]

13 L Samuel, *The long way towards more social rights in Europe* (Germany, Nomos Verlagsgesellschaft mbH & Co. KG 2013) 141.

14 J-F Akandji-Kombé, 'L'application de la Charte sociale européenne: la mise en œuvre de la procédure de réclamations collectives' (September/October 2000) *Droit Social* 888.

15 Art 9.

16 Art 10§2.

17 Maternal health protection, Arts 8 and 11.

18 Art 16.

19 Arts 17 and 27.

20 Art 19§6.

21 Such as ill-treatment, alcoholism, drugs, pornography, Aids, etc, to give a few examples; Article 7§10 contains the adjective 'particularly' and therefore allows for a broad definition of 'physical and moral dangers'.

II. CONTENT

The protection of children and minors at work consists of forbidding children's employment under a certain age, while allowing certain forms of (light) work, specifying the appropriate working conditions applicable and the necessary guarantees in terms of working time, wage, vocational training, holidays, night work, medical controls and special protection against physical and moral dangers.

Furthermore, the Charter imposes an unconditional obligation on states to 'ensure the effective exercise of the rights of children and adolescents at work'.[22] The ECSR recalls[23] that the aim and purpose of the Charter, being a human rights protection instrument, is to protect rights not merely theoretically, but also in fact. In its purposive interpretation, the ECSR regularly emphasises that legislation must be effectively applied in practice and rigorously supervised. In this respect, the Labour Inspectorate has a decisive role to play,[24] so that the ECSR concludes a case of non-conformity if it cannot be established that the labour inspectorate supervises work carried out by persons under the age of 18.[25]

A. Paragraph 1: Minimum Age of Admission to Employment

Article 7§1 clarifies the personal scope of the prohibition of child labour, which should be understood extensively. It is commonly defined as work of children under the age of 18 years, as the dominant terminology proposes,[26] whereas Directive 94/33/EC offers more restrictive scope, including young persons aged at least 15 but less than 18 years of age, and no longer subject to compulsory full-time education under national law.[27]

In the same vein, the material scope of Article 7 in respect of employment requires a broad interpretation, as the ECSR ruled on the occasion of the first collective complaint,[28] an interpretation that largely confirms its

[22] See chapter on 'The Charter's supervisory procedures' by S Clauwaert in this volume.

[23] *International Commission of Jurists v Portugal*, Collective Complaint No 1/1998 of 09.09.1999 §32.

[24] Collective Complaint No 1/1998; Conclusions 2011, Cyprus; Conclusions 2011, France.

[25] Conclusions 2011, Republic of Moldova.

[26] See Art 1, Convention of the Right of the Child.

[27] See also Art 32 CFREU, which reads: 'The employment of children is prohibited. The minimum age of admission to employment may not be lower than the minimum school-leaving age, without prejudice to such rules as may be more favourable to young people and except for limited derogations.'

[28] ECSR, *International Commission of Jurists v Portugal*, Collective Complaint No 1/1998 of 09.09.1999.

conclusions elaborated within the framework of the reporting system:[29] the prohibition of the employment of children under the age of 15 applies to all economic sectors, to all places of work, including work within family enterprises and in private households (helping out at home), 'even if such work is not performed for an enterprise in the legal and economic sense of the word and the child is not formally a worker'.[30] It also extends the scope of Article 7 to all forms of economic activity, regardless of the status of the worker (employee, self-employed, unpaid family helper or other), irrespective of the existence of a formal work contract, whether paid or not paid. As domestic staff, children should be covered by labour legislation,[31] as 'they account for a significant part of illegally employed workers'.[32] In this respect, the ECSR stressed that 'the supervision of states must, in such cases, ... concern not just the Labour Inspectorate but also the educational and social services'.[33]

Furthermore, the ECSR addressed the issue of light work. While stressing that not all forms of work are considered to be detrimental to the child's development, the ECSR recalled that Article 7§3 guarantees the right of every child to education by safeguarding its capacity to learn, so that only light work is permissible for schoolchildren under this provision. Therefore, the ECSR interpreted Article 7§3 as providing for an exception in respect of 'prescribed light work', meaning work that does not endanger the child's health, morals or education. Additionally, states should check whether work might be

> unsuitable because of the physical effort involved, working conditions (noise, heat, etc.) or possible psychological repercussions [that] may have harmful consequences not only on the child's health and development, but also on its ability to obtain maximum advantage from schooling and, more generally, its potential for satisfactory integration in society.[34]

Work can be considered 'light' in nature, but ceases to be so if it is performed for an excessive duration.[35] Therefore, the Charter requires national law to either list certain tasks that children are permitted to perform, or to identify the categories of work[36] considered to be light.

29 Akandji-Kombé (n 14) 894.
30 Collective Complaint No 1/1998 §28.
31 ibid.
32 Conclusions 2011, Spain.
33 Collective Complaint No 1/1998 §28.
34 ibid §30; Conclusions 2011, Slovak Republic.
35 Collective Complaint No 1/1998 §31, Conclusions 2011, Slovak Republic. See also Conclusions II and Conclusions IV.
36 Conclusions 2011, Albania.

B. Paragraph 2: Minimum Age for Dangerous or Unhealthy Occupations

The Charter in particular draws attention to dangerous or unhealthy employment situations, and raises the minimum age of admission to employment to 18 years.[37] Article 7§2 should be read in conjunction with Article 3 on the right for all workers to safe and healthy working conditions.

As requested in the Appendix, domestic legislation must provide for an adequate statutory framework to identify potentially hazardous work, which either lists such forms of work or defines the types of risk (physical, chemical, biological) that may arise in the course of work.[38] It should further mention in particular the need for expert supervision, and only for the time necessary.[39] The Appendix to Article 7§2 also permits exceptions in cases where adolescents under the age of 18 have completed their training for performing dangerous tasks and thus have received the necessary information.[40] Furthermore, the ECSR emphasises that domestic legislation should lay down an absolute prohibition for persons under the age of 18 to work in dangerous activities outside the vocational training context or without having had such training beforehand.[41]

C. Paragraph 3: Work cannot deprive young workers of compulsory education

Compulsory education is a priority and should not be hampered by any employment that could deprive young workers of the full benefit of their education.

In 2011,[42] the ECSR reconsidered its statement of interpretation concerning a mandatory period of rest during school holidays for children who are still subject to compulsory education. It believed it necessary to adopt a more specific approach in order to better assess the broadly 'diverging national situations and traditions in a fair and balanced way'. The ECSR therefore examines whether states provide a mandatory and uninterrupted period of rest during school holidays, which shall under no circumstances be less than two weeks, whereby it will assess the adequacy of the length of the mandatory and uninterrupted period free of any work on a case-by-case

[37] It replaces the 1961 formulation that required a 'higher minimum age', thus leaving states to set this 'higher minimum age' by legislation.

[38] Conclusions 2006, France.

[39] Conclusions 2006, Norway.

[40] Conclusions 2006, Sweden.

[41] Conclusions 2011, France.

[42] Conclusions 2011 XIX-4.

basis, taking into account a number of factors, in particular the length and distribution of holidays over the school year and the timing of the uninterrupted period of rest. The ECSR ruled that the mandatory rest period must be granted during the long school holidays, that is, the summer holidays. The ECSR therefore concluded that it would not be in accordance with Article 7§3 where there were provisions allowing pupils over the age of 15 and still in compulsory full-time education to work a maximum of four weeks during the holidays, when the summer holidays last for approximately six weeks.[43]

The ECSR stressed that during a school term, the time during which children may work must be limited so as not to interfere with their attendance, receptiveness and homework. The right to compulsory education must be guaranteed in practice[44] and four hours of light work per day during the school term for children aged 13–15 was ruled excessive and not in conformity with Article 7§3.[45] Finally, concerns have been expressed about the possible resurgence of child labour, partly as a result of growing school drop-out rates in time of economic crisis, in particular in Portugal.[46]

D. Paragraph 4: Working Time

The limitation of working hours applies to 'persons under 18 years of age'.[47] The paragraph concerns adolescents under the age of 18 who are in compulsory education, as well as adolescents no longer in compulsory education, as the reference to vocational training suggests.

The Charter does not set any working time limit. Domestic legislation, regulations, contracts or practice must stipulate the working time limit during which young workers can perform a job.[48] However, the ESCR regards any law that allows persons under 16 years of age to work as many as eight hours a day or 40 hours a week as contrary to this provision.[49] For young workers over 16 years of age a higher limit of eight hours per day and 40 hours per week has been deemed to be in conformity with this provision of the Charter. A question remains whether the working time limitation also applies to overtime.

43 Conclusions XVII 2, Germany.

44 Conclusions 2011, Albania.

45 Conclusions 2011, Cyprus.

46 N Muiznieks, Strategy for the Rights of the Child, speech on the occasion of the first meeting, DH/Speech (2014), 12.

47 This higher age limit replaces the formulation of 1961 in which the limitation applied to 'persons under 16 years of age'.

48 Conclusions 2011, The Former Yugoslav Republic of Macedonia.

49 Conclusions XI-I, Netherlands; Conclusions XIII-3, Finland and Conclusions 2002, Italy.

Furthermore, the ECSR has found that, in principle, no work of any kind should be permitted before going to school in the morning,[50] such as delivering newspapers from 6 am onwards.[51] However, if domestic law allows work before school starts, adequate safeguards must be adopted so that the competent authorities can ensure protection from work that may deprive children of the benefits of education.[52]

With reference to Directive 94/33/EC, the ECSR considered the provision under national legislation for adolescents aged 14 to 16 to work up to 24 hours per week to be excessive. In the case of activities of a cultural, artistic or advertising-related nature, the ECSR also declared as excessive domestic legislation and/or practice allowing children to work far beyond the Directive recommendations of two hours on a school day and 12 hours a week for work performed in term-time outside the hours fixed for school attendance, given that the daily working time should not exceed seven hours.[53]

In relation to light work, although no general limit on the duration of permitted light work has been set, the ECSR considered a situation in which a child under the age of 15 years works for between 20 and 25 hours per week during the school term or three hours per school day and six to eight hours on weekdays when there is no school to be contrary to the Charter.[54]

E. Paragraph 5: Fair Wage

Domestic law must provide for fair wages or other appropriate allowances. The 'fair' nature of pay and the 'appropriateness' of apprentices' allowances are assessed by the ESCR in comparison with the basic or minimum wage paid to a single adult without children after deduction of social security contributions and taxes, given that the adult reference wage must be sufficient to comply with Article 4§1.[55] The aim is to strike a balance between ensuring that young employees are not exploited, and that the rate of pay does not encourage students to leave full-time education.

[50] See Art 7§3.

[51] Conclusions XVII-2, Finland.

[52] Conclusions XII-1, Netherlands.

[53] Conclusions 2011, Portugal. Practices allowing children between the ages of seven and 12 to work three hours per day and nine hours per week, with an additional three hours added to each limit in cases in which the additional activity takes place on a day on which the child has no school activities, as well as children between the ages of 12 and 16 to work four hours per day and 12 hours per week, with an additional 3 hours added to each limit in cases in which the additional activity takes place on a day on which the young person has no school activities, were considered not to be in conformity with the Charter.

[54] Respectively, Conclusions II and Conclusions IV.

[55] Conclusions XII-2, Malta.

As a result, the wages of young workers may be less than the minimum wage of an adult, but the difference must be reasonable and the gap must close quickly. The ECSR recalled that wages of young workers aged 15–16 that are 30 per cent lower than the minimum wage are acceptable, and that a 20 per cent difference is acceptable in the case of young workers aged 16–18.[56] The ECSR emphasised that, where the adult reference wage is very low, the wages of young workers cannot be considered fair.[57] However, if in practice the rate payable to workers under 18 years of age is 30 per cent less than that paid to experienced adult workers, the minimum net wage is manifestly inadequate.[58] Furthermore, adolescents working for close relatives are to be covered by the domestic legislation on minimum wages.[59]

Concerning apprentices, however, allowances must equal at least one-third of the adult minimum wage at the beginning of the apprenticeship, and at least two-thirds at the end.[60] The ECSR has insisted that 'the apprenticeship system must not be deflected from its purpose and be used to underpay young workers'.[61] The ECSR stressed that making a distinction between the period of work, for which wages are paid, and the period of training, during which apprentices and trainees do not receive wages, is not in conformity with Article 7§5.[62]

F. Paragraph 6: Vocational Training during Normal Working Hours and as Part of the Working Day

The Charter strikes a balance between the need to protect young workers at work and the need to provide vocational integration for a better start in the labour market. Vocational training is regarded as an intrinsic part of young workers' rights. In order to avoid any abuse, Article 7§6 stipulates that the time spent on vocational training by young people during normal working hours must be treated as part of the working day[63] and considered normal working time. Training time must therefore be remunerated in the same way as normal working hours[64] and there must be no obligation to make up for

[56] Conclusions 2006, Albania.

[57] Conclusions XII-2, Malta.

[58] Conclusions 2011, Ireland and although the Irish National Minimum Wage Commission recommended that employees under the age of 18 should be entitled to 70% of the national minimum wage.

[59] Conclusions 2011, Ireland.

[60] Conclusions 2006, Portugal.

[61] Conclusions XVII-2, Belgium.

[62] Conclusions 2011, Norway.

[63] Conclusions XV-2, the Netherlands.

[64] Conclusions 2011, Albania.

the time spent in training, as this would effectively increase the number of hours worked. Such training must, in principle, be done with the employer's consent and be related to the young person's work, but not necessarily paid for by the employer.[65]

G. Paragraph 7: Minimum of Four Weeks' Annual Holiday with Pay

The Charter introduces a change in comparison with 1961 and lays down in Article 7§7 that adolescents under 18 years of age should at least have four weeks' annual paid holiday, instead of three. The ECSR found that domestic provisions allowing employed persons under 18 years of age the option of giving up their annual holiday in return for financial compensation[66] or increased remuneration were not in conformity with Article 7§7.[67]

The ECSR recalled that

> employees incapacitated for work by illness or accident during all or part of their annual leave must have the right to take the leave lost at some other time—at least to the extent needed to give them the four weeks' paid annual leave provided for in the Charter. This principle applies in all circumstances, regardless of whether incapacity begins before or during leave, or where a company requires workers to take leave at a specified time.[68]

The ECSR[69] ruled in the case dealing with the introduction of 'special apprenticeship contracts' for individuals aged 15 to 18 that there was a violation of Article 7§7 when apprenticeship contracts are excluded from the scope of the labour legislation and when there is no entitlement to an annual holiday with pay.

H. Paragraph 8: Prohibition of Night Work

Article 7§8 is inspired by, respectively, ILO Convention No 77 Medical examination of young persons (industry) and No 78 Medical examination of young persons (non-industrial occupations). The ECSR rules that domestic laws and regulations must cover all sectors of the economy[70] and be

[65] Conclusions V, Statement of interpretation of Art 7§6; Conclusions 2011, XIX-4, Croatia.

[66] Conclusions 2011, Armenia.

[67] Conclusions 2011, Albania.

[68] See, *mutatis mutandis*, Conclusions XII-2, Art 2§3. See also the chapter on Art 2(3) by K Lörcher in this volume.

[69] *GENOP-DEI and ADEDY v Greece*, Collective Complaint No 66/2011, Decision on the merits, 23 May 2012 §§31 and 32.

[70] Conclusions XIII-2, Cyprus, as well as Conclusions XIII-3, Turkey.

applicable to both (young) men and women.[71] Domestic legislation that prohibits night work for workers under 18 years of age only in industrial undertakings is not in conformity with Article 7§8.[72]

Since 1994[73] the ECSR has requested information on the number of young workers who are exceptionally authorised to work at night, in order to assess whether the statutory prohibition is being applied to the great majority of young workers. Domestic legislation that does not provide for such information is not in conformity with Article 7§8.[74] Furthermore, information on exceptions to the prohibition of night work in some economic sectors should be available and the number of young workers concerned must be low.[75] The ECSR further emphasises that the situation in practice should be regularly monitored and rigorously supervised by the Labour Inspectorate, and the findings should be documented with reference to the applicable sanctions.[76]

I. Paragraph 9: Regular Medical Control

Here again, Article 7§9 was inspired by ILO Conventions No 77 and No 78. It provides that young workers under the age of 18 years shall be subject to regular medical control. The ECSR has stressed that intervals between medical controls must not be too long; an interval of two years in the case of young seamen is considered too long.[77] Furthermore, medical examinations must be geared to young people's specific situations and the particular risks to which they are exposed.[78] The ECSR has also found a breach of Article 7§9 when the right of young workers to regular medical examinations is not guaranteed due to ineffective enforcement of the legislation.[79]

J. Paragraph 10: Special Protection against Physical and Moral Dangers

The intention of Article 7§10 is twofold: to ensure the protection of children against all forms of commercial and economic exploitation, and against

[71] Conclusions XII-2, Malta.
[72] Conclusions 2011, Turkey.
[73] Conclusions XIII-2, Conclusions XIII-4 and Conclusions XV-2.
[74] Conclusions XVII-2.
[75] Conclusions 2011, Malta.
[76] Conclusions 2011, Czech Republic; *International Commission of Jurists v Portugal*, Collective Complaint No 1/1998, decision on the merits of 09.09.1999 §32.
[77] Conclusions X-1 Sweden; Conclusions 2011, Estonia.
[78] Conclusions 2006, Albania.
[79] Conclusions 2011, Bulgaria.

exposure to harmful materials and information technology. However, work-related dangers remain the rationale when interpreting the provision.[80]

The ECSR recently confirmed that the material scope of Article 7§10 should be interpreted broadly. It recalled that states undertake 'to protect children not only against the risks and forms of exploitation that result directly or indirectly from their work, but also against all forms of exploitation'.[81] It underlined in particular that states must prohibit the use of children in forms of exploitation resulting from trafficking or 'being on the street, such as domestic exploitation, begging, pick pocketing, servitude or the removal of organs, and take measures to prevent and assist street children'.[82]

The Charter urges domestic legislators to provide for an adequate statutory framework to identify potentially hazardous work, by either listing such forms of work or defining the types of risk (physical, chemical, biological) that may arise at work. Furthermore, the minimum age required for the performance of any such work should be clearly indicated. In cases in which such work proves essential for vocational training purposes, domestic legislation should specify the conditions under which it may be performed, and mention in particular the need for expert supervision, and the relevant time limits.

III. IMPACT ON EUROPEAN HUMAN RIGHTS INSTRUMENTS

A. European Convention on Human Rights

The Council of Europe managed in 1961 and in 1996 to align the rights of the child and young person in employment with existing political and civil rights and, consequently, to give 'full value to the principles of indivisibility, universality and interdependence of human rights', devoting specific attention to social rights. The Charter and the ECHR, despite differences related to their nature, as well as to the fact that they are quasi-jurisdictional[83] and judicial organs of control, respectively, not to mention the supervisory mechanism of the Charter, have become mutually reinforcing.[84]

[80] M Schlachter, L Leppik, B Nyström and E Machulskaya, Dissenting opinion to the decision on admissibility of 2 July 2013 in *Association for the Protection of all Children (APPROACH) Ltd v Cyprus*, Collective Complaint No 97/2013.

[81] Decision on the merits of 23 October 2012, *Defence for Children International (DCI) v Belgium*, Collective Complaint No 69/2011. See also Decision on admissibility of 2 July 2013, *Association for the Protection of all Children (APPROACH) Ltd v Belgium*, Collective Complaint No 98/2013.

[82] Conclusions 2006, Moldova.

[83] Akandji-Kombé (n 14) 888.

[84] Samuel (n 13) 137.

The ECtHR's landmark jurisprudence of 2008, *Demir and Baykara v Turkey*,[85] offers an important ruling that generalises the active method of the ECtHR in the use of international sources. With this outstanding example of dynamic and progressive interpretation of the Convention, the ECtHR clarifies its methodology: it recalled its role as 'defence mechanism of human rights' (§66) and the 'living' character of the ECHR (§68) that may be the object of an evolutionary interpretation. Furthermore, the ECtHR stresses that when defining 'the meaning of terms and notions in the text of the Convention, [it] can and must take into account elements of international law other than the Convention, the interpretation of such elements by the competent organs and practice of European States reflecting their common values' (§85), even though the respondent states in the proceedings have not ratified such elements of international law.[86] This judgment reveals the voluntarism of the ECtHR with respect to social and economic rights. As the ECtHR affirms its intention to rely on a set of tools and practices outside the conventional system to find—or build—'the existence of a consensus of the contracting states to advance economic and social rights' (§84), and applies this method to justify the extension or consecration of the rights and freedoms protected by the Convention, it is by analogy obvious that Article 7 should also be put in conjunction with Article 8 ECHR on the right to respect for private and family life and the case law of the Court, as covering (many if not most) elements of Article 7.

In the same vein, Article 7 should also be read in conjunction with—among others—Article 4 ECHR on the prohibition of forced labour and slavery. In a series of cases related to modern slavery involving young girls as housemaids, the ECtHR has recalled the duty of the Council of Europe to lead the fight against all forms of slavery and trafficking in human beings,[87] including adolescents and young adults.

B. Charter of Fundamental Rights of the European Union and Further EU Law

The Charter has had a major impact on the recognition of the rights of young people at work in EU primary and secondary law.[88] Notwithstanding

[85] *Demir and Baykara v Turkey* App no 34503/97 (ECtHR, 2009ate).

[86] And, in the case in question, Art 6 of the Charter on the right to bargain collectively.

[87] *Kawogo v UK* App no 56921/09 (ECtHR, 3 September 2013); *Siliadin v France* App no 73316/01 (ECtHR, 25 July 2005).

[88] L Samuel, 'Fundamental social rights in the EU legal order in connection with the European Social Charter' (Seminar, 'Reform of the European Social Charter', Helsinki, 8–9 February 2011) 23.

the existing international body of law, the 1961 Charter first brought the European Union to deal definitively with the issue.[89] Protection of children and adolescents at work has been anchored in the social policy chapter of the 1992 Amsterdam Treaty,[90] on the basis of both the 1961 Charter and the 1989 Community Charter of the Fundamental Social Rights of Workers. Both texts, and subsequently the 1996 Charter, are inspiring sources of EU social policy.[91] Although the European Commission issued a recommendation to address the protection of young workers at work in 1967,[92] it was only in 1987 that the European Parliament adopted a resolution on child labour calling for a directive, as well as for ratification of the respective ILO Convention.[93] In 1989 the Community Charter addressed the issue (§§20 to 23). However, it had and still has no legally binding force. A Directive[94] was adopted on the issue in 1994.

The 1961 and the 1996 Charters have also been the main sources of inspiration for Article 32 CFREU, elaborated in 2000 and adopted as a legally binding Charter in 2007. In light of the new legal environment since the ratification of the Lisbon Treaty, the European Commission has developed a strategy for the implementation of the CFREU, with the objective of ensuring the effective protection and promotion of fundamental rights,[95] and refers to the CFREU as an 'innovative instrument' that 'brings together in one text all the fundamental rights protected in the Union' and stemming from[96] the Social Charters adopted by the Council of Europe. Although Article 32 CFREU sets no minimum age of admission to employment,[97] stating that it 'may not be lower than the minimum school-leaving age, without prejudice to such rules as may be more favourable to young people and except for limited derogations', the Explanations to Article 32 CFREU[98] refer explicitly to

[89] P Koncar, 'Protection of young people at work', in M Schlachter (ed), *EU Labour Law: A Commentary* (The Hague, Wolters Kluwer, Law and Business, 2015) 322.

[90] In particular in Art 136, now to be found in Art 151 TFEU.

[91] Ojeda-Aviles, *Transnational Labour Law* (The Hague, Wolters Kluwer, Law and Business, 2015). J Petman, 'Final remarks and conclusion' (Seminar, 'Reform of the European Social Charter', Helsinki, 8–9 February 2011) 142. See also the chapter on 'The European Social Charter: the Social Constitution of Europe' by O De Schutter in this volume.

[92] Recommendation 67/125/EEC of the Commission of 31 January 1967 to the member states on the protection of young workers [1967] OJ L25.

[93] Koncar (n 89) 322.

[94] Council Directive 94/33/EC of 22 June 1994 on the protection of young people at work [1994] OJ L216.

[95] European Commission, Strategy for the effective implementation of the Charter of Fundamental Rights by the European Union Brussels COM (2010) 573 final 3.

[96] But also the constitutional traditions and international conventions common to the member states, the ECHR, the Social Charters adopted by the Community, and the case law of the CJEU and the ECtHR.

[97] And in comparison with the Charter, the 1989 Community Charter of the fundamental social rights of workers (in §20) and ILO Convention No 138.

[98] Although not specifically referred to in the text of the CFREU. See Samuel (n 88).

Article 7 of the Charter. Therefore, it shall be interpreted with 'due regard to the Explanations and sources mentioned therein'.[99] In the same vein, Stalford points out that the interpretation of the material scope of Article 32 CFREU should be done in light of the jurisprudence of the ECSR and include 'all economic sectors and all types of enterprises, including family businesses, as well as all forms of work, whether paid or not'.[100] Identically, a range of issues that are not addressed by the CFREU[101] have to be interpreted in light of Article 7.

Article 32§2 CFREU stresses the need to fight against economic exploitation and any work likely to harm the safety, health or physical, mental, moral or social development of children or to interfere with their education. This latter point characterises the influence of the Charter, but also of the ILO Conventions No 138 and No 182 on the CFREU.

In contrast to the large jurisprudence of the ECSR, so far only a few cases have been brought to the CJEU in relation to the protection of adolescents at workers, thus not allowing for interpretation of the substance of the rights as stipulated in Directive 94/33/EC.[102]

IV. CONCLUSIONS

The Charter is one of the most significant international treaties that provides for comprehensive protection of the rights of children and adolescents in order to empower them as full bearers of human rights. Article 7 has undeniably become an indispensable complement to other international legal standards devoted to the protection of children.[103] Furthermore, it has received important recognition by and influenced EU law and the CJEU.

Article 7 imposes an unconditional and positive obligation on states to undertake definite actions and to adopt binding measures with a predefined content or to recognise a defined right to effectively guarantee the protection of children at work. Furthermore, the ECSR via its dynamic case law, plays a determining role in formalising such a right, to the extent of operating a shift from obligations of means to obligation of results.[104] Also, the limited

[99] According to Art 6(1)(3) TEU.

[100] H Stalford, 'Art 32 Prohibition of child labour and protection of young people at work', in S Peers, T Hervey, J Kenner and A Ward (eds), *Commentary of the Charter of Fundamental Rights of the European Union* (Oxford, Hart Publishing, 2014) 285–88.

[101] Light work, limitation of working hours, rest and annual vacations, but also vocational training, prohibition of night work, regular medical control.

[102] Two judgments, C-45/99 and C-47/99, dealt with the failure to transpose the Directive into, respectively, French and Luxembourg legislation (CJEU 45/99 of 18 May 2000. OJEU I-3620 and CJEU 47/99 of 16 December 1999 OJEU I-9003).

[103] Samuel (n 88).

[104] Akandji-Kombé (n 14) 895; M Mikkola, '4. Migrants', in M Mikkola (ed), *Social human rights of Europe* (Porvoo, Karelactio Legisactio Ltd, 2010) 27.

derogations are closely monitored and restrictively interpreted by the ECSR, following the fundamental principle that any action should be undertaken with regard to the best interest principle.

In many cases, however, the ECSR has even observed that domestic situations, despite modest or even substantial improvements, still fail to comply in practice with the requirements of Article 7. Indeed, child labour is not yet eradicated, not least in the European Union, and practice shows that a large number of basic children's rights are hampered by legislation and practices that do not sufficiently protect children against economic exploitation. Children's protection at work still relies on NGOs and trade union action in conjunction with the tireless commitment of the ECSR and would certainly be reinforced by accession by the European Union to the Charter, as a consolidation of the rights of the child in the EU, as well as contributing to the uniformity of application of EU law in a single converging legal system.[105]

[105] A O'Neill QC, 'Social rights in the Charter: employment and social security, social protection and the idea(ls) of Europe' 20; O De Schutter, 'The accession of the European Union to the European Social Charter', UCL, Brussels, 8 July 2014). (in French), available at SSRN: http://ssrn.com/abstract=2475754 or http://dx.doi.org/10.2139/ssrn.2475754

Article 8

The Right of Women to Maternity Protection

CSILLA KOLLONAY-LEHOCZKY

Article 8—The right of employed women to protection of maternity

With a view to ensuring the effective exercise of the right of employed women to the protection of maternity, the Parties undertake:

1. to provide either by paid leave, by adequate social security benefits or by benefits from public funds for employed women to take leave before and after childbirth up to a total of at least fourteen weeks;
2. to consider it as unlawful for an employer to give a woman notice of dismissal during the period from the time she notifies her employer that she is pregnant until the end of her maternity leave, or to give her notice of dismissal at such a time that the notice would expire during such a period;
3. to provide that mothers who are nursing their infants shall be entitled to sufficient time off for this purpose;
4. to regulate the employment in night work of pregnant women, women who have recently given birth and women nursing their infants;
5. to prohibit the employment of pregnant women, women who have recently given birth or who are nursing their infants in underground mining and all other work which is unsuitable by reason of its dangerous, unhealthy or arduous nature and to take appropriate measures to protect the employment rights of these women.

Appendix

Article 8, paragraph 2

This provision shall not be interpreted as laying down an absolute prohibition. Exceptions could be made, *for instance* in the following cases:

a. if an employed woman has been guilty of misconduct which justifies breaking off the employment relationship;
b. if the undertaking concerned ceases to operate;
c. if the period prescribed in the employment contract has expired.

I. INTRODUCTION

A. Context and Main Content

Article 8 is one of the provisions[1] that have gone through the most changes with the adoption of the Revised Charter. It has changed in approach, spirit and substance. In fact, it did not just change, but in some respects turned into the opposite of its 1961 Charter version, confronting the Committee occasionally with the demanding task of reconciling opposed requirements and harmonising its assessments. Article 8 of the 1961 Charter was based on a rather paternalistic, protective, restrictive approach to female workers ('benign discrimination')—typical of the first half of the twentieth century and earlier, permeating the relevant international Conventions, although not undisputed even at the time of drafting of the original text of the Charter,[2] and generating opposed views at the time of the first assessment of national reports. It laid down limitations and barred women from certain types of work with reference to the dangerous or unhealthy nature of such jobs, 'unsuitable' for women. It also guaranteed special rights to pregnant and breastfeeding women and these provisions were, again, a mix of entitlements and constraints on the women concerned.

The Revised Charter abolished the restriction on women workers in general and, under its changed heading,[3] grants protection and additional rights for women with respect to maternity, namely for pregnant women, women in the post-natal period and breastfeeding mothers. The shift from protective discrimination to the protection of equal freedom and autonomy is uniquely reflected by the text and case law of Articles 8§4 and 8§5 and has already infiltrated the interpretation of Article 8§1, too, regarding the minimal length of post-natal maternity leave.[4]

Article 8 is an equality provision, but a particular one. Frequently it is not included in the usual list of equality provisions of the Charter, mainly for its 'protective pedigree' inherited from its 1961 predecessor. In addition, Article 8 is permeated with demanding financial obligations, which are far from characteristic of equality provisions that are normally negative, just

[1] Together with Arts 15 and 17. The relationship with Art 15 produces multiple common features that will be mentioned below.

[2] For example, Scandinavian delegations expressed opposition to protecting women in general and wished to limit the protection to expectant and nursing mothers; however, their efforts were rejected by the Consultative Assembly. N Valticos, *International Labour Law* (Dordrecht, Springer-Science & Business Media, 1979) 179.

[3] The original heading, 'The right of employed women to protection', was replaced by 'The right of employed women to protection of maternity', bringing a whole world of change by adding the two words.

[4] See below, section II.A(i).

imposing prohibitions without requiring effort (let alone costly efforts).[5] Nonetheless, Article 8 is one of the most important guarantees of equal opportunities for women in the labour market: it accommodates the difference deriving from the ability of women to become pregnant, to give birth and to breastfeed a child—the only real biological difference between men and women that requires accommodation as a precondition of equal treatment. Consequently, Article 8 is among those provisions[6] that require instant realisation and effective guarantees, laying down an 'obligation of result' and not an 'obligation of conduct' targeting progressive realisation.[7] It has to be guaranteed fully and effectively to everyone covered by the provision.

The wording of the title and the text of Article 8 limit the personal and material scope of the protection to 'employed women'. Article 8 was interpreted by the Committee as applying solely to women in paid employment and not to self-employed women.[8] On the other hand, it must cover all women employees, whatever the type of employment. The ECSR interpretation pays particular attention to the protection of those in atypical employment, such as temporary and fixed-term employees, part-timers, domestic workers, migrant workers and employed family members.

The progress of thinking about gender roles, the growing awareness of the distinction between the biological and social roles of the sexes and the erosion of traditional stereotypes may bring about legal changes that will further impact on the context of Article 8, confronting the ECSR with new interpretation perspectives.[9] The unfavourable demographic changes in Europe may bring positive developments with regard to this Charter provision, motivated by the need of governments to offer incentives and encouragement to have children.[10]

In summary, not only the history, but also the future of Article 8 may entail significant changes in its context and content.

[5] Here Art 8 meets Art 15: the milestone decision on the merits of Collective Complaint No 13/2002 in *International Association of Autisme Europe v France* established that equal treatment—when differences have to be accommodated and equalised—requires positive measures and financial allocation.

[6] That is, the other non-discrimination norms (such as Art 1§2, Art 20), or the one prohibiting forced labour or child labour.

[7] G Quinn, 'The Legal Status of the European Social Charter—Taking Interdependence and Indivisibility of Human Rights Seriously', presentation at the Coimbra conference, 14.

[8] Conclusions I, 49–50.

[9] An indication of future directions of progress is the right of fathers to part of maternity leave, which has already emerged in Spain, see: Conclusions XIX (2011). See also below, under section II.A(i)(a).

[10] See, for example, Conclusions 2011, Portugal, where a prenatal family allowance was also created to provide women with an incentive for having children, increased by 20% in the case of single-parent households, to compensate them for the additional costs they incur during pregnancy.

B. International Sources

All situations and forms of protection covered by Article 8 were regulated by ILO Conventions in part well before the adoption of the 1961 Charter, and most of them have been amended in the course of time. The protection of maternity stems from the 1919 Maternity Protection Convention (C003) preceding the declaration of the principle of protection of motherhood and childhood in the 1948 Universal Declaration of Human Rights.[11] The inspiration of Article 8 comes, however, from the updated provisions of the Maternity Protection Convention, No 103 (1952). Article 8§§1, 2 and 3 mainly reiterate the text of the Convention, but also go beyond, showing the differences between a global and a more demanding regional instrument: C103 required medical cash benefits for maternity leave, the Charter required paid leave, under stricter prohibition of dismissal than C103. The original (1961) Article 8§4 laid down restrictions for all working women in terms of the contemporary approach to the protection of women. Subsection (a) of §4 was based on the C089 Night Work (Women) Convention of 1948, however, unlike the full prohibition in the Convention, the Charter required only the regulation of female night work. Subsection (b), prohibiting underground and other dangerous, unhealthy or arduous work, was based on multiple ILO instruments, following the total prohibition stipulated by them for all women.

The progress in the approach to the equality of women in society and in the labour market, as well as to the equal protection of health and safety of men and women, prompted changes in the international conventions and led to the above-mentioned radical changes in the text and content of Article 8 of the Charter. Later UN Treaties deserve mention, primarily the main treaty in the field, claiming equal rights for women in the area of economic and social life, in particular in labour matters, namely the Convention on the Elimination of Discrimination against Women (CEDAW), adopted in 1967, emphasising in the Preamble that 'the role of women in procreation should not be a basis for discrimination'. The International Convention of Economic, Social and Cultural Rights adopted by the UN General Assembly in 1966 requires special protection to be accorded to mothers during a reasonable period before and after childbirth. These provisions already reflect the impact of Charter Article 8.

The last decades of the twentieth century can be described, in terms of what is at issue here, as an upward spiral as a result of the interplay between the Charter, the UN documents and EU law. Article 8 of the Revised Charter could therefore rely on more developed international background that was, in turn, influenced by the Charter itself.

[11] Art 25§2.

At the level of the European Union the 1992 Pregnant Workers Directive[12] (PWD) can be considered a counterpart of Article 8. Their content and standards are comparable: the Explanatory Report to the Charter explicitly refers to the PWD as a source of the definition of protected women[13] and both the provisions and the progress of the interpretation of Article 8 draw on the PWD. The nature of this directive is also similar to Article 8: while their provisions are indispensable for equal opportunities for women in employment, none are purely 'equality provisions'. Instead, they lay down substantive obligations regarding terms of employment, health and safety rules with due respect to the differences deriving from the reproductive function of women.

C. Relation to Other Provisions

Article 8 is connected to several provisions of the Charter by its content and history. The new text of Article 2§4 and the addition of Article 2§7 resulting, to some extent, from the change of Article 8, move the protection of working women to Article 3, laying down the health and safety protection of women and men equally.[14]

Articles 1§2 and 20 are the general equal treatment provisions, having common attributes with Article 8, a special equality norm, such as the expected uniform consequences in case of breaches of the norm. This specific 'equality' nature and its assessment establish a relationship with further provisions guaranteeing equal treatment and equal opportunities in employment without regard to sex and family obligations, such as Article 4§3 and Articles 26 and 27.

Article 20 is also a counterpoint to Article 8: it is a repudiation of the former text of Article 8§4[15] and, in contrast to Article 8, it is explicitly a non-discrimination provision.

Articles 12 and 13 regulating social security and social assistance are directly connected to the income security of mothers for the period of maternity leave. Under Article 12§1, the existence of the maternity and family branches is taken into consideration, but the scope and level of the benefits are assessed under, respectively, Articles 8 and 16.[16] The amount of the benefit must be 'on a par' with holiday pay, establishing thereby a

[12] Council Directive 92/85/EEC of 19 October 1992 on the introduction of measures to encourage improvements in the safety and health at work of pregnant workers and workers who have recently given birth or are breastfeeding.

[13] Explanatory Report s 50.

[14] See Explanatory Report s 27.

[15] Subparas (a) and (b).

[16] Conclusions XVIII-1 and 2006, all countries.

connection to Article 2 as well (even if the amount of pay for the holiday, its level and relation to the effective amount of the wages has not been scrutinised routinely so far by the Committee).

II. CONTENT

A. Article 8§1: Right to Maternity Leave with Pay

Article 8§1 lays down two basic obligations for the contracting parties:

1. to provide employed women with the right to take at least fourteen weeks of leave before and after childbirth; and
2. to provide women with an income for the period of the leave, either by continuing the payment of wages or by adequate social security benefits or by benefits from public funds.

(i) The Right to a Minimum Maternity Leave of 14 Weeks

(a) The Minimum Length of the Post-Natal Entitlement and its Mandatory Nature

Maternity leave must be at least 14 weeks (a minimum of 12 weeks under the 1961 Charter), it must be guaranteed by law[17] (provision by collective agreements, by established practice or custom alone is insufficient to comply with the obligation) and must be guaranteed to all women with the status of employee.

While the period of the leave is generally observed, the division of the required length to periods before and after childbirth has confronted the Committee with difficulties in balancing between two opposed considerations from the beginning: limiting the possibility of employers' abusive practices, and guaranteeing the greatest possible autonomy for the women concerned.

Employers have an interest in removing pregnant women from the workplace at a relatively early stage of pregnancy, but also to get the employee back to work soon after childbirth. This interest dictates providing the major part of the leave before childbirth and cutting short the post-natal leave.[18] To avoid practices that contravene the purpose of the provision, case law requires national laws to guarantee an entitlement to a minimum

[17] Conclusions III, Statement of Interpretation on Art 8§1, 48.

[18] See, eg, Conclusions 2011, Azerbaijan, granting 126 days in the case of normal childbirth, 70 days before and 56 days after, meeting the minimal requirements and being in conformity with the Charter in that respect, 171.

of six weeks leave in the post-natal period. On the other hand, mothers may have an interest in opting for a shorter period of maternity leave for professional, career or financial reasons.

While the permitted reduction of the minimum length of the post-natal leave by the employer is a breach of the Charter (for example, when the child is stillborn[19] or with reference to the failure of the mother to give three weeks' notice of maternity leave before it begins)[20], the Committee was confronted with the question of what part of post-natal leave could be relinquished at the request of the mother?

The stance of the Committee has changed back and forth over time. In Cycle I, it did not see a problem in permitting mothers 'not to avail themselves of the right over a part of the twelve weeks'.[21] Later (in Cycle IV), however, it considered that this opportunity 'made considerable inroads in the protection provided for by this clause' where it was coupled with a low level of maternity benefits.[22] Similarly, negative experiences in some countries where employers were ready to put pressure on women in order to make them return to work early after childbirth prompted the Committee to give priority to the protective, compulsory aspect of the rule. Thus, in Cycle VIII it interpreted Article 8§1 as meaning that national law may permit women to opt for a shorter period of maternity leave, although a compulsory period of not less than six weeks was not permitted to be further waived by the woman concerned.[23]

This interpretation, even if motivated by unfair practices in only a limited number of state parties, has been applied in an undifferentiated way for all countries, automatically finding a breach of the Charter where the free choice of women was granted, regardless of the surrounding guarantees,

Thus, Denmark, where workers could voluntarily forfeit all or part of the post-natal section of the fairly long (seven months) maternity leave, was not found in keeping with the requirements, even if no cases were known in practice where the woman had been subjected to pressure to return to work.[24] Similarly Sweden where only two weeks were compulsory, leaving the rest to women's discretion, was considered in violation of Article 8§1,[25] without regard to the effective guarantees that make the worker's decision genuinely free, without any undue pressure. From Cycle VIII to 2011 (Cycle XIX), the Committee consistently held, regardless of the dissenting

[19] Greece, XII-1, 148.
[20] Conclusions XIII-2, Malta, 303–04.
[21] C-I, 50.
[22] C-IV, 66, UK (see the problem with the level of benefit under (ii) below).
[23] Conclusions VIII, Statement of Interpretation on Art 8§1, 123.
[24] Cycle XII 1, 97 and Cycle-XIII 1, 165.
[25] See: Cycle 2005, Sweden, 691, dissenting opinion from M Mikkola ibid 738.

opinions,[26] that the six-week period of post-natal leave was compulsory and may not be renounced.

(b) Progressive Change of Case Law—With Further Room to Develop

In 2011 the ECSR changed the disputable former case law, adjusting it to the progress under international and European law.[27] It came to a compromise regarding the alleged 'public interest', namely the health of the mother and child, on one hand, and the right of the mother to decide whether to use all, or only part of the parental leave entitlement, on the other.[28]

Under the new approach, the obligation of the employer to provide a minimum of six weeks' post-natal period is unchanged. At the same time the Committee has not specified the minimum period of the mother's obligation to stop working after confinement. Instead, it emphasised the role of 'adequate legal safeguards' (protection from any undue pressure, sufficient amount of benefit) that fully protect the right of employed women to choose freely when to return to work after childbirth.

The 2011 statement of interpretation went as far as possible in ending the 'mandatory minimum' era and raised further progressive ideas: section 6 closed with the possible future of 'a parental leave system whereby either parents can take paid leave at the end of the maternity leave'.

The text reflects evident progress combined with remaining stereotypes. The reference to the 'more general interest in public health, ie the health of the mother and child' retains the paternalistic approach considering 'public control' necessary over the decision of the mother. The health of the adult mother in the post-natal period is a private matter, no less than the health of any female or male worker. The health of the children is undeniably a matter of public responsibility coupled with that of the parents, however not connected to the biological function of pregnancy and childbirth. Physically either of the parents can take care of the newborn—their decision in this regard must be free.

The acknowledgement of the right of the father to take paid leave is progress, while adding 'at the end of the maternity leave' reflects a mixed mind. Portugal put the issue on the agenda long ago, permitting the mother to waive her leave in favour of the father, which was found to be inconsistent with the Charter.[29] In 2011 compliance was based on the changed law obliging the mother to take six weeks after childbirth.[30] This is similar to the

[26] See the dissenting opinion of Mr Fabricius already in Conclusions VIII, 233, Ms Billum Stegard in Conclusions XII-1, 207.

[27] Under the PWD (Art 8§2) maternity leave must include compulsory maternity leave of at least two weeks allocated before and/or after confinement.

[28] General Introduction, 2011, 5: s 8. Statement of interpretation of Art 8§1.

[29] Conclusions XIII-5, 195.

[30] 2011, Vol 3, 919.

Spanish legal system, where the mother 'can relinquish part of her maternity leave taken after birth to the father, provided that the compulsory six-week postnatal period is taken by the mother'.[31]

(ii) Adequate Maternity Benefits

Contracting parties have a financial obligation accompanying maternity leave: mothers must be entitled to adequate financial benefits during this leave. Dependent on national legislation, this may be the continued payment of the individual's wages, the payment of social security benefits, or benefits from public funds. State parties have the choice to select the method or a combination of methods.

The 'adequacy' of maternity benefits is determined by two factors: (i) the level (amount) of the benefit in relation to the former wages or salary of the employee; (ii) the eligibility requirements entitling women to the payment.

The 'adequacy' of the benefit is governed by the view of the ECSR that maternity leave must not be regulated as sick leave, but must be on a par with holiday pay.[32] It must guarantee the maintenance of the former income level and consequently must be equal or close to the value of the salary.[33] A benefit equal to 70 per cent of the salary is still adequate[34] (as established in earlier cycles, this was adequate when compared with the gross salary).[35] The majority of countries provide more, between 80 and 100 per cent of the former salary. A flat rate benefit, departing from the wages of the woman affected, as well as a lower percentage are in breach of the Charter.[36]

The Committee accepted that as in the case of social security incomes, there might be ceilings and qualification requirements (periods).

For high wages, a significant reduction in pay during maternity leave is not, in itself, contrary to Article 8§1. Various elements are taken into account in order to assess the reasonableness of the reduction, such as the upper limit for calculating benefit, how this compares with overall wage patterns, and the number of women in receipt of a wage/salary above this limit.[37]

[31] Conclusions XIX, Spain, 333.

[32] First CIE Art 22 Report, 19, cited by D J Harris and J Darcy: The European Social Charter, Ardsley, NY, Transnational Publishers, 2001, 2nd ed, 131. This is a higher level than that set by the PDW. It requires, for 'adequacy' of the allowance paid for the period of maternity leave, the payment of 'income at least equivalent to that which the worker concerned would receive in the event of a break in her activities on grounds connected with her state of health, subject to any ceiling laid down under national legislation' (PWD Art 11§3).

[33] Conclusions XV-2, United Kingdom, 594.

[34] Conclusions XVII-2, Latvia, 488.

[35] Conclusions X-2, XIII-1, Ireland.

[36] Conclusions XV-2, UK, 594; XVII-2 Vol 2, 819.

[37] Conclusions XV-2, Belgium, 8

The payment of maternity benefit is financed in most countries by social security and therefore there may be a minimum period of contribution and/or employment as a legitimate precondition; however, such requirements must be reasonable.[38] Periods of unemployment shall be included in the calculation of the qualification period.[39] Qualification requirements are considered too demanding, for example when it requires a 12-month contribution to the social security scheme prior to the pregnancy.[40]

The adequate level of the benefit as well as reasonable eligibility requirements are evident factors that have to be taken into consideration when a departure from the minimum six-week mandatory duration of maternity pay is examined: difficulties qualifying for the benefit, or a low or decreasing payment beyond the six weeks may exert undue pressure on the woman to return to work.

B. Article 8§2: Prohibition of Dismissal during Pregnancy and Maternity Leave

Under Article 8§2 parties undertake to prohibit dismissal of pregnant women and women on maternity leave, subject to limited exceptions. The scope of the prohibition has to apply to all employed women, including public employees and domestic workers, and equally to women on fixed-term and open-ended contracts. The prohibition must be explicit, covering all potentially affected women. The lack of clear and explicit prohibition cannot be explained by the prohibition on hiring pregnant women in the given area (for example, as seafarers).[41]

(i) The Period of the Prohibition

Article 8§2 expects national law to prohibit an employer from giving a woman notice of dismissal during the period from the time she notifies the employer of her pregnancy until the end of her maternity leave, or to give her notice of dismissal at such a time that the notice would expire during such a period.

According to the Explanatory Report this provision of the Charter 'extends the minimum period of protection against dismissal for pregnant women as compared with the corresponding provision of the [1961] Charter' that prohibited giving notice during the absence on maternity

[38] Conclusions XV-2, France, 197.
[39] Conclusions 2005, France, 227, Conclusions 2011, Vol 1.
[40] Conclusions 2011, Albania, 48.
[41] Conclusions XIII-4, Greece, 93–94.

leave or at such a time that the notice would expire during such absence.[42] The second prong of the prohibition—'giving notice at such a time that the notice would expire during such an absence'—had great significance under the 1961 Charter: it extended the protection 'backwards' to the period of pregnancy and helped to prevent discriminatory dismissals.

The Charter now, by changing the phrase from 'during such absence' to 'during such a period' (that is, during the protected period) excludes the possibility of giving notice at any time from the beginning of the pregnancy. This interpretation decreases the significance of the date ('when she notifies') of the notification required: simultaneous or *a posteriori* notification can also block termination. Estonian law provides, for example, that in the event of a notice of dismissal the employee 'has to provide a medical certificate establishing pregnancy at the request of the employer within 14 days after notice of dismissal unless the employer had previously been notified of it'.[43]

Such an interpretation is in line with the view of the Committee expressed from the beginning that it 'would have been better if the prohibition had covered the entire period of pregnancy'.[44]

(ii) Exceptions

Article 8§2, from Cycle I, was interpreted by the Committee as not laying down an absolute prohibition. Because the purpose of the protection is to prevent discriminatory dismissals due to pregnancy, it permitted exceptions in certain cases when the employer had 'good reason' to terminate the employment, such as misconduct that justifies breaking off the employment relationship, if the undertaking ceases to operate or if the period prescribed in the employment contract expires.[45] These reasons have now been put explicitly into the Appendix to Article 8§2.

In view of the increased use of fixed-term employment contracts, which is likely to effectively deprive the prohibition of its effect, and in response to the concern expressed in Article 2§3 of the ILO Convention (C158) on the Termination of Employment, the ECSR asks the state parties to the Revised European Social Charter to supply figures showing the proportion of female workers on insecure contracts whose situation is consequently weakened in terms of the protection of pregnant female workers.[46]

[42] Explanatory Report, s 47.

[43] Conclusions 2011-Vol 1, Estonia, 348.

[44] See the first report on certain provisions of the Charter that have not been accepted, p 23, referred to by L Samuel, *Fundamental Social Rights* (Strasbourg, Council of Europe Publishing 1997) 236; Harris and Darcy (n 32) 133, referring to the First CIE Art 22 Report, 23.

[45] Conclusions I, 51.

[46] Conclusions XV-II, eg Cyprus, Malta, Slovakia.

The prohibition is not merely to protect pregnant women and mothers from discrimination; dismissals 'for objective reasons' are not permitted, either. The Committee found a number of objective reasons going beyond the permitted exceptions. Inclusion of pregnant women in collective dismissals,[47] relocation of all or part of the business where the woman works and she does not follow the company[48] are not good reasons for terminating the employment of the pregnant woman. Termination due to the abolition of the job on economic, market, technological or structural grounds,[49] or when the post she occupies was previously occupied by a person who was illegally dismissed and is required to be reintegrated,[50] were also found by the Committee to exceed the permitted exceptions.

Reasons connected to the person of the employee, such as fault, or unsuitability not reaching the level of misconduct foreseen by the Appendix, such as lack of skill or failure to adapt to technological changes, repeated absence for justified reasons,[51] indecent acts, or the employer's loss of trust in the employee, are also found unacceptable.[52] Connecting the dismissal to the permission of the Labour Inspectorate and its proper scrutiny may legitimise such questionable reasons.[53] On the other hand, the Committee considered 'non-conformity to the instructions of the employer', 'neglected performance of duties' and 'repeated unauthorised absence from work' constituted serious misconduct, and recognised them as valid grounds for dismissal.[54]

The reasons indicated by Ireland, such as the employee's inability to perform adequately the work for which she was employed or to continue to do her work without contravention of a statutory requirement by her employer, provided in both cases that the employer had no other suitable vacancy to offer at the time of the dismissal, or she refused an offer of a suitable alternative job, even if seemingly objective, connected with pregnancy status are suspect of being discriminatory particularly because they may invoke the protection provided by Article 8§§4 and 5. Without detailed guarantees they may contravene the protection granted by the Charter.[55]

The Committee found acceptable the liquidation of the company or bankruptcy of the employer,[56] as well as expiry of the contract on the death of an employer, if the contract was concluded for the purpose of providing

[47] Conclusions 2011 Vol 2 Ireland, 558.
[48] Conclusions XVI-2, Slovakia, XVII-2 or 'XVI-2 (2003)' Czech Republic; Conclusions 2011, Bulgaria.
[49] Conclusions, XIII-3, Portugal, 307.
[50] Conclusions 2011 Vol 1, Bulgaria,
[51] Conclusions XIII-5, Portugal, 197.
[52] Conclusions 2011, Vol 1, Armenia, 128.
[53] Conclusions 2005, Estonia, 144.
[54] The exceptions were illustrated by court decisions. Conclusions XIII-1, Greece, 170.
[55] Conclusions 2011, Vol 2, Ireland, 558.
[56] Conclusions 2011, Vol 1, Armenia, 128.

services specifically to this person.[57] A criminal judgment preventing the employee from continuing her work, and similarly the employee losing through her own fault the necessary certificates to carry out her work, are also considered acceptable exceptions.[58]

In view of the developed case law the exceptions are restricted to situations in which continued employment is impossible to expect from the employer or is de facto impossible.

(iii) Remedies

In cases of dismissal contravening Article 8§2 of the Charter, national legislation must provide for adequate and effective remedies. These remedies are not different from those required under other provisions of the Charter where dismissal takes place in violation of a prohibition of the termination of employment, including discriminatory dismissal.[59]

First, such a remedy requires that employees who consider that their rights in this respect have been violated must be able to take their case before the courts or other independent judicial organs.

Second, if a violation of the prohibition is established, reinstatement of the woman should be the rule.[60] Financial compensation as a substitute for reinstatement is accepted only if reinstatement (continuation of employment) is impossible, for example, where the enterprise closes down, or if the woman concerned does not wish it. Countries where only financial compensation is available are in breach of their obligation.[61] Also, even though an agreement can be struck between employer and employee to consider the dismissal null and void, in the absence of an explicit statutory obligation to reinstate the worker, the situation remains in breach of the Charter.[62]

Third, in the above-mentioned exceptional cases, when financial compensation may substitute for reinstatement, the Committee holds that compensation for unlawful dismissal must be both proportionate to the loss suffered by the victim and sufficiently dissuasive for employers. National rules must not prevent courts (or any other competent authority or judicial organ) from awarding a level of compensation that is sufficient both to deter the employer and fully compensate the victim of dismissal, hence any ceiling on the level of compensation that may be awarded is not in conformity with the Charter.[63]

57 Conclusions 2011, Vol 2, Lithuania, 679.
58 ibid; Conclusions XIX-IV, Poland, 293.
59 See: Art 1§2, Art 20.
60 Conclusions 2005, Cyprus, 73.
61 Conclusions 2011, Albania.
62 Conclusions XIII-4, Finland, 74–75, also 2011, 348–49.
63 Conclusions 2005, Vol 1, Estonia, 144; Conclusions 2011, Czech Republic, 105.

The requirement of the joint guarantee of reinstatement (primary) and adequate level of compensation (for exceptions) has to be underlined: none of them could be a substitute for the other. Thus, for example, both in Bulgaria and Estonia, reinstatement was guaranteed; however, if this was not possible, or the employee opted not to be reinstated, she was entitled to only six months' salary.[64] The Committee found these cases not to be in compliance with the Charter.

Conversely, Finland, while improving its law by abolishing the limits on compensation payable in the event of sex discrimination, has not made any provision in law for the reinstatement of women unlawfully dismissed during pregnancy or maternity leave, and therefore its law remained in breach of the Charter.[65]

The consistent rigour of the Committee with regard to upper limits of compensation that courts may award not only in the context of Article 8, but also in similar cases of discriminatory or retaliatory dismissal under other articles (Articles 1§2, 4§3, 20 and also 27§3) have been accompanied by repeated dissenting opinions.[66]

In its new (2011) case law the Committee slightly relaxed the criteria of compliance, not automatically finding breach of the Charter if there is an upper limit in the law. It further holds that any ceiling on compensation that may preclude damages from being commensurate with the loss suffered and sufficiently dissuasive are proscribed. However, in the event of a ceiling for pecuniary damage, the national system might correspond to the Charter's criteria if the victim is able to seek compensation for non-pecuniary damage through other legal avenues, and the courts competent for awarding compensation for pecuniary and non-pecuniary damage decide within a reasonable time.[67]

C. Article 8§3: Right to Time Off for Nursing

According to Article 8§3, all employed mothers who breastfeed their babies shall be granted time off for this purpose. This entitlement shall be explicitly guaranteed in law.

As to the scope of the coverage, similar to other provisions of Article 8, this provision also requires that this right be guaranteed to all working women with the status of employee, regardless of the type or location of the

[64] Conclusions 2003, Vol 1, Bulgaria, 46; Conclusions 2005, Vol 1, Estonia, 145.

[65] Country Factsheets, Finland, www.coe.int/t/dghl/monitoring/socialcharter/Country-Factsheets/Finland_en.pdf and Conclusions 2011, Vol 1, 394.

[66] On Art 8§2 see Conclusions XIX-4 and 2011: Dissenting opinion by M Schlachter on Art 8§2.

[67] Statement of interpretation, Conclusions XIX-4, 6.

work. Thus, it has to be guaranteed to all employees, in both the private and public sectors. Personal scope cannot be limited with regard to exceptions made when ratifying ILO Convention 103 (amended).[68] The Committee has paid special attention to two areas: public service, and domestic workers and employees working at home. Italy, Romania and Spain were found repeatedly in violation due to their excluding domestic workers and family workers from the right to breaks for breastfeeding.[69]

France has been found in violation of its obligation because in the civil service (traditionally, primarily a male domain) 'it is not possible to grant special authorisations for mothers who breastfeed their child'. Only if the services concerned have childcare facilities or these childcare facilities are sufficiently close to the workplace should mothers be given the possibility of breastfeeding their children, by granting them two 30-minute breaks per working day.[70]

The length of the break varies between countries and is frequently combined with specific solutions (for example, providing part-time work) and therefore a case-by-case assessment is necessary. From the first Cycles, the Committee has found that two 30-minute breaks or a single one-hour rest period during the working day was sufficient to comply with the undertaking,[71] and apparently this is the standard solution across countries.

Time off for nursing must be granted at least in principle until the child reaches the age of nine months.[72] It is also an acceptable solution when either the break is provided for one year, or throughout the period of breastfeeding. Two hours' break for eight months and the entitlement subsequently depending on a medical certificate in Bulgaria has also been accepted.[73]

Each situation is assessed on a case-by-case basis; legislation providing for two daily breaks for a period of one year for breastfeeding, two half-hour breaks where the employer provides a nursery or room for breastfeeding,[74] one-hour daily breaks[75] and an entitlement to begin or leave work earlier have all been found to be in conformity with the Charter.[76]

An important requirement is that the time off for nursing should in principle be granted during working hours and should be treated as normal working time.[77] The Committee has repeatedly found the situation in France,

[68] For example, in respect of 'agricultural undertakings, other than plantations' and 'domestic work for wages in private households', Conclusions XIII-1, Netherlands.

[69] Conclusions 2003, 2005, Romania; Conclusions 2005, 2011, Italy; Conclusions XVII, XIX, Spain.

[70] Conclusions 2011, Vol 2, France, 446.

[71] Conclusions I, Federal Republic of Germany, 191.

[72] Conclusions 2005, Cyprus, 74.

[73] Conclusions 2011, Bulgaria.

[74] Conclusions I, Italy, 51.

[75] Conclusion I, Germany, 191.

[76] Conclusions 2005, France, 228.

[77] Conclusions XIII-4, Netherlands, 102.

where, although the break is provided up to the child's first birthday, this is not treated as working time and remuneration is therefore not mandatory, as not acceptable under Article 8§3. Although in practice breastfeeding women are permitted to begin work half an hour later and finish half an hour earlier than usual without loss of pay, this does not satisfy the purpose of this provision, which is that regulation of payment should be in national law.[78] Similarly, payment being dependent on observance of the obligation to act as 'good employer[s]', as contained in the Civil Code, is not enough.[79]

Provision for part-time work may be considered sufficient where loss of income is compensated by a parental benefit or other allowance.[80]

D. Article 8§§4 and 5: Employment of Pregnant Women or Women after Childbirth in Night Work and in Dangerous, Unhealthy or Arduous Work

(i) General Note on Articles 8§§4 and 5

Paragraphs 4 and 5 of Article 8 in the Revised Charter are replacing sub-paragraphs (a) and (b) of the former Article 4, bringing it into line with the principle of equal treatment of men and women eradicating the protective discrimination implied in the 1961 Charter. They provide protection for pregnant and breastfeeding mothers, while the protection of employed women in general is to be guaranteed along the general norms of health and safety, paying due attention to the equal protection of men and women either in night shifts or performing particularly dangerous, unhealthy or arduous work.

Harris and Darcy rightly phrase the reason behind the change of Article 8§4 and 8§5 'of treating men equally with women where possible'[81] (instead of the standard terminology 'treating women equally with men'). Indeed, the change of these two sub-paragraphs eliminates discrimination in two directions. First, women are not excluded from jobs that, though more demanding, may offer better earnings and career opportunities. Second, men shall enjoy equal—equally better!—protection with women against obvious harms and dangers that previously were considered properly addressed by the exclusion of women from those jobs.[82]

[78] Conclusions 2003, also 2011, France.
[79] Conclusions XIII-1, Netherlands.
[80] Conclusions 2005, Sweden, 689.
[81] Harris and Darcy (n 32) 264.
[82] See the chapter on Art. 2 by K Lörcher, sections II.D and G.

The case law of the Committee reflects a successful effort to reconcile the contradictory requirements, and proceeds towards the real equality intended by the amendment. That is, admitting women to jobs unavailable to them in the past, but also entitled to accommodation of their pregnancy in those areas of work if it is needed with regard to the special risks or dangers of the particular occupation or type of activity. The necessary measures—transfer of the pregnant woman to other jobs or workstations, offering her a different work schedule or, as a last resort if no other suitable solution exists, exemption from work with retention of wage rights. In that sense, the new §§4 and 5 are more burdensome for employers than §4 of the 1961 Charter, which was just a 'negative provision' involving prohibition, without the onus of accommodation requiring positive measures, implying a financial and administrative burden. This feature may impact on the assessment of a country under Article 8§1 (length and division of maternity leave) and Article 8§2 (prohibition of dismissal).[83]

(ii) Regulation of Night Work (Article 8§4)

The Explanatory Report to this provision describes the basic idea behind the amendment of the former provision taken from ILO Convention No 171 (Night Work) of 1990[84] and from the PWD.[85] Because regulation of the night work of employed women is needed only in the case of maternity,[86] the personal scope of the provision is limited, covering only expectant or breastfeeding mothers, instead of women in general, under Article 8§4(a) of the 1961 Charter. The definition of 'pregnant women', 'women who have recently given birth' and 'women who are nursing their infants' is inspired by the PWD, which refers to national legislation and/or practice for the content of the definition.[87] The margin of appreciation given to states by reference to 'national legislation and/or national practice' may not narrow the personal scope, for example, by not extending the protection to women after childbirth who are not breastfeeding.[88] While the personal scope is restricted, the material scope is wider: states have to regulate night work for the women concerned in all segments of the labour market, including public employment and not only in industrial employment, as under the 1961 provision.

[83] See the case of Ireland under Art 8§2 (n 55).

[84] For the few (13) ratifications it has not yet replaced C089 of 1948, however, reflecting the progress, rightly considered as a better model for European standards.

[85] fn 12.

[86] Explanatory Report to the Revised European Social Charter, s 49.

[87] Explanatory report, s 50.

[88] Conclusion 2011, Vol 1, Bosnia-Hercegovina.

The provision requires states to 'regulate' and not to prohibit night work for pregnant or breastfeeding women, but the regulation must safely guarantee the exclusion of any case when the night work performed would carry risks for the health of the mother or the child and to limit any adverse effects. When night work by an affected mother is necessary, regulations must lay down the conditions, for example, prior authorisation by the Labour Inspectorate (when applicable), prescribed working hours, breaks, rest days following periods of night work, the right to be transferred to daytime work in case of health problems linked to night work, and so on.[89]

The expected measures neither include nor exclude the prohibition on night work of women covered by Article 8§2. The case law of the Committee encompasses a broad range of regulations accepted as complying with Article 8§4. Merely stipulating that the employer must evaluate risks to which the women concerned can be exposed and to 'take all measures to avoid them' (that may include assigning them to daytime work) equally are found to be in compliance.[90] Similarly, when there is no special regulation for breastfeeding mothers, they are covered (under Article 2§7) by the general rules on night work, or for workers with family duties who cannot be obliged to undertake night-shifts,[91] are positively assessed, together with national laws in which there is a prohibition for this category of workers.[92]

Regulations whereby the employer is required to transfer the woman to day work if she so requests or where the occupational physician certifies that night work is incompatible with her condition are complying with the requirements of the Charter. If a transfer to day work is not possible, the employment contract can be suspended until the end of the maternity leave[93] without decrease of salary. Regulations vary regarding the entitlement to full salary or without significant decrease, by granting average salary, or a 'balancing allowance' if the salary is reduced due to the transfer.[94]

(iii) Employment of Pregnant Women or Women after Childbirth in Dangerous, Unhealthy or Arduous Work (Article 8§5)

This provision, similarly to §4, accomplishes a shift toward equal treatment of men with women—that is, permitting differences only with respect to pregnancy and motherhood.

[89] Conclusions X-2, Statement of Interpretation on Art 8§4, 97.
[90] Conclusions 2011, Vol 1, Andorra, 87.
[91] Conclusions 2003, Vol 1, France, 125.
[92] Conclusions 2011 Vol 2, Georgia, 516; Hungary.
[93] See above in section (ii).
[94] Conclusions XVI-2, Slovakia.

The personal and material scope of Article 8§5 is identical to that of §4. Prohibiting the employment of the women concerned in underground work in mines, the provision takes over automatically the legal framework from the 1961 Charter and it orders application of the prohibition to extraction work, but not to women who:

— occupy managerial posts and do not perform manual work;
— work in health and welfare services;
— spend brief training periods in underground sections of mines.[95]

Certain other activities, such as those involving exposure to lead, benzene, ionising radiation, high temperatures, vibration or viral agents, must be prohibited or strictly regulated for the group of women concerned, depending on the risks posed by the work. National law must ensure a high level of protection against all known hazards to the health and safety of women who come within the scope of this provision.[96]

Because now under the Charter (but not under the 1961 Charter) compliance with the prohibition may require the suspension or amendment of the former job or work of the pregnant woman, the text adds to the prohibition the obligation of the employer to protect the employment rights of the affected woman by taking appropriate measures. Namely, such workers shall be given the possibility of transfer to suitable work, or to be granted leave from work if a transfer is not feasible, with the payment of salary or other adequate allowance and without loss of status, seniority or access to promotion.[97]

III. IMPACT ON EUROPEAN HUMAN RIGHTS INSTRUMENTS

The development of the protection of women, especially during pregnancy, after childbirth and while breastfeeding under UN (particularly ILO) treaties, in the European Union and under the European Social Charter has developed in a triangular and constant flow of interactions. For this reason, while the Charter has certainly had an impact on the UN and EU norms, Article 8 of the Charter, its interpretation, case law and amendment have themselves been influenced by international developments.

Thus, Article 10§2 of the ICESCR adopted by the UN General Assembly in 1966, and Article 11§2 of the Convention on the Elimination of Discrimination against Women (CEDAW), adopted in 1967, both reiterate, in a slightly more generalised way, the requirements of the first three paragraphs of Article 8. ICESCR Article 10§2, going beyond ILO C103 and

[95] Conclusions X-2, Statement of Interpretation on Art 8§5, 97.
[96] Conclusions 2003, Bulgaria, 46.
[97] Explanatory Report, s 51.

complying with Article 8§1 of the Charter, provides that 'Special protection should be accorded to mothers during a reasonable period before and after childbirth. During such a period working mothers should be accorded paid leave or leave with adequate social security benefits' (Article 10§2). CEDAW Article 11§2 lays down provisions on the Parties' obligation to introduce maternity leave with pay or with comparable benefits, without loss of former employment, seniority or social allowances, prohibition of dismissal on the grounds of pregnancy or maternity leave and also on the prohibition of harmful work during pregnancy. The protection is similar to the protection under Article 8, albeit less specific. The renewed ILO Maternity Protection Convention No 183, adopted in 2000, was based on the updated content of Article 8§§1–3; moreover, it sets more elevated requirements, whereby it also contributes to the development of interpretation. Similar is the impact of ILO Termination of Employment Convention (No 158).[98] This interplay shows the continued reciprocity and synergy between the UN instruments and Article 8 of the Charter.

CFREU 33(2), according to the Explanation, draws on Article 8 (as well as the PDW), regarding the protection of pregnant women against dismissal and their rights to maternity leave. It also declares, corresponding to the explanation above with regard to Article 8§2, that maternity 'covers the period from conception to weaning'.[99]

Due to the inseparable development of the international instruments, their impact on national law development is also hard to distinguish. Although there are examples in which the impact of the Charter (negative conclusions) might be detected,[100] the influence of the Charter and other (mainly EU) instruments works in a 'collaborative' way.

[98] See section II.B(ii) above.

[99] Explanation to the text of the CFREU, [2007] OJ C303/27.

[100] For example, Luxembourg Act of 7 July 1998 on the prohibition of dismissal during maternity leave, and the right of the dismissed woman to reintegration, following a negative conclusion (CXIII-5, 134), Belgium collective labour agreement No 80/2001: paid breastfeeding break following negative conclusions due to the denial of this right to mothers. Bulgarian law SG No 52/2004 amending the Labour Code on mandatory maternity leave, following Conclusions 2005.

Article 15

The Right of Disabled Persons to Vocational Training, Rehabilitation and Resettlement

ISABELLE SCHÖMANN

Article 15—The right of persons with disabilities to independence, social integration and participation in the life of the community[1]

With a view to ensuring to persons with disabilities, irrespective of age and the nature and origin of their disabilities, the effective exercise of the right to independence, social integration and participation in the life of the community, the Parties undertake, in particular:

1. to take the necessary measures to provide persons with disabilities with guidance, education and vocational training in the framework of general schemes wherever possible or, where this is not possible, through specialised bodies, public or private;
2. to promote their access to employment through all measures tending to encourage employers to hire and keep in employment persons with disabilities in the ordinary working environment and to adjust the working conditions to the needs of the disabled or, where this is not possible by reason of the disability, by arranging for or creating sheltered employment according to the level of disability. In certain cases, such measures may require recourse to specialised placement and support services;
3. to promote their full social integration and participation in the life of the community in particular through measures, including technical aids, aiming

[1] Art 15 of the 1961 reads as follows: 'Disabled persons have the right to vocational training, rehabilitation and resettlement, whatever the origin and nature of their disability. With a view to ensuring the effective exercise of the right of the physically or mentally disabled to vocational training, rehabilitation and resettlement, the contracting parties undertake: 1. to take adequate measures for the provision of training facilities, including, where necessary, specialised institutions, public or private; 2. to take adequate measures for the placing of disabled persons in employment, such as specialised placing services, facilities for sheltered employment and measures to encourage employers to admit disabled persons to employment.'

to overcome barriers to communication and mobility and enabling access to transport, housing, cultural activities and leisure.

I. INTRODUCTION

A. Context and Main Content

The specific protection of persons with disability finds its roots in international treaties in the 1950s and has been based since the 1980s on their inclusion in society. Article 15 securing the protection of the disabled, with an emphasis on 'vocational training, rehabilitation and resettlement', dates back to 1961. It was entirely revisited in 1996 to echo progress in disability policies, from 'welfare and segregation towards inclusion and choice'[2] of the disabled to guarantee their independence, social integration and participation in the life of the community with a focus on education and employment, communication and mobility. With the revision, the gap with the European Convention on Human Rights (ECHR) was reduced significantly to secure the equal treatment and access to rights to persons with disabilities[3] on the ground of the non-discrimination principle.[4]

B. International Sources

(i) Content

The protection of persons with disabilities was recognised in the Universal Declaration of Human Rights of 1948 as grounds for additional attention, with the aim of securing 'the right to a standard of living adequate for one's health and well-being and of family … and the right to security in the event of unemployment, sickness, disability, widowhood, old age or other lack of livelihood in circumstances beyond his control'.[5]

[2] L Samuel, *The Long Way Towards More Social Rights in Europe* (Germany, Nomos Verlagsgesellschaft mbH & Co. KG, 2013) 141.

[3] L Loucaides, The European Convention on Human Rights and the rights of persons with disabilities. Kiev; Promeni, 2006.

[4] Art 14 ECHR and in particular since 2000 with Protocol No 12 to the Convention for the Protection of Human Rights and Fundamental Freedoms on the general prohibition of discrimination that stipulates a fully autonomous right to equality in the enjoyment of any rights set forth by law. Protocol No 12 to the Convention for the Protection of Human Rights and Fundamental Freedoms.

[5] Art 25 ECHR.

The approach adopted in the ECHR of 1950 differs, as disability falls under the overarching principle of non-discrimination and is not listed as a ground,[6] but falls under the category of 'other status'.[7,8]

The ILO adopted Recommendation No 99 on Vocational Rehabilitation of the Disabled in 1955,[9] which first defined a person with a disability as 'an individual whose prospects of securing and retaining suitable employment are substantially reduced as a result of physical or mental impairment'. The aim is to provide persons with disabilities with 'continuous and coordinated process of rehabilitation vocational rehabilitation', in the form of 'vocational services, and selective placement, designed to enable a disabled person to secure and retain suitable employment'.[10] Furthermore, ILO Convention No 111 on Discrimination in respect of employment and occupation of 1958 urges states to 'determine special measures designed to meet the particular requirements of persons who, for reasons such as … disablement,[11] are generally recognised to require special protection or assistance'.[12]

The 1961 Charter has followed this path and addressed disablement, independently of its origin and nature, with a focus on vocational training, rehabilitation and resettlement via specialised placement services and sheltered employment.

In the 1970s, a range of international instruments paved the way for a change in disability policies.[13] The 1975 UN Declaration on the Rights of Disabled Persons seems to be the first initiative to propose a holistic and progressive approach including 'any person unable to ensure by himself or herself, wholly or partly, the necessities of a normal individual and/or social life, as a result of deficiency, either congenital or not, in his or her physical or mental capabilities'.[14] In the same vein, the ILO adopted Convention

[6] Such as 'sex, race, colour, language, religion, political or other opinion, national or social origin, association with a national minority, property, birth'.

[7] Art 14 ECHR.

[8] Louciades (n 3); in 2009 the ECtHR expressly recognised for the first time a violation of Art 14 on the grounds of disability: *Glor v Switzerland* App no 13444/04 (ECtHR, 30 April 2009).

[9] It was followed in 1961 by Recommendation No 115 concerning workers' housing, which included in its scope 'physically handicapped persons' (Art 1).

[10] See point 28 of s VII on the 'Methods of Widening Employment Opportunities for Disabled Persons' of ILO Recommendation No 99.

[11] But also such as sex, age, family responsibilities or social or cultural status.

[12] Art 5§2 ECHR.

[13] See the UN Declaration on the Rights of Mentally Retarded Persons of 1971 that specified in its Art 3 that mentally retarded persons have 'a right to economic security and to a decent standard of living'. They have 'a right to perform productive work or to engage in any other meaningful occupation to the fullest possible extent of [their] capabilities'.

[14] Art 1 1975 UN Declaration on the Rights of Disabled Persons. It further specifies that persons with disabilities have the right, according to their capabilities, 'to secure and retain employment or to engage in a useful, productive and remunerative occupation and to join trade unions' in Art 7.

No 142 on Human Resource Development in 1975, providing for a comprehensive set of tools to promote Vocational Guidance and Training in the Development of Human Resources, addressing specifically persons with disabilities.

The turning point occurred in the 1980s. Following the UN action plan elaborated in 1976 on equalisation of opportunities, rehabilitation and prevention of disabilities, in 1981 the UN General Assembly proclaimed the International Year of Disabled Persons, launching a profound shift in the perception of the disabled, moving away from welfare and segregation, to their full participation and equality. The Committee on Economic, Social and Cultural Rights (CESCR)[15] made a landmark contribution to the new approach by stressing the need to adapt the terminology to 'persons with disabilities',[16] so as to better to embrace the situation of disablement and avoid a restrictive interpretation of disability.

In this context, the ILO revised its existing position on disablement[17] and adopted Convention No 159 on Vocational Rehabilitation and Employment (of the Disabled) in 1985. This repositioning had a far-reaching impact, as 'each member shall consider the purpose of vocational rehabilitation as being to enable a disabled person to secure, retain and advance in suitable employment and thereby to further such person's integration or reintegration into society.'[18] It further encourages 'members ... to formulate, implement and periodically review a national policy on vocational rehabilitation and employment of disabled persons'.[19] In 1988 the ILO adopted Convention No 168 concerning Employment Promotion and Protection against Unemployment. This is intended to reinforce the principle of non-discrimination in employment, and specifies that: 'each member shall ensure equality of treatment ... without discrimination on the basis of ... disability.[20]

In the same vein, the Council of Europe Parliamentary Assembly adapted its approach.[21] In 1992, two recommendations were adopted on Rehabilitation Policies for the Disabled[22] and on a Coherent Policy for the

[15] The CESCR is a body of 18 independent experts that monitors implementation of the International Covenant of the same name.

[16] CECSR (1994) Report adopted at the 10th and 11th sessions Annex IV, 110–20. See General Comment No 5 Persons with disabilities.

[17] Vocational Rehabilitation (Disabled) Recommendation 1955; Human Resources Development Recommendation 1975; and Vocational Rehabilitation (Disabled) Recommendation 1955.

[18] Art 1(2).

[19] Art 3.

[20] Art 6, next to race, colour, sex, religion, political opinion, national extraction, nationality, ethnic or social origin and age. Further specific references to disability to be found in Art 5, 8 and 24. It was followed by Recommendation No 168 on Vocational Rehabilitation and Employment (Disabled Persons) of 1988.

[21] Within the framework of the first European Conference of Ministers responsible for policies on people with disabilities.

[22] No 1185.

Rehabilitation of People with Disabilities,[23] resulting in 'prompting new inclusive policy actions plans that have positively benefited people with disabilities both at the national and international level'.[24]

In 1995 the Committee of Ministers adopted a Charter on the Vocational Assessment of People with Disabilities that provides for a common framework and sets out the main ethical and methodological principles.[25] Herewith it broadly defined disability as

> a restriction caused by physical, psychological, sensory, social, cultural, legal or other obstacles that prevents disabled people from becoming integrated and taking part in family life and the community on the same footing as everyone else. Society has a duty to adapt its standards to the specific needs of disabled people in order to ensure that they can lead independent lives.[26]

It further emphasised the need for placement, training services and legislation allowing people with disabilities to obtain ordinary employment.[27] This initiative definitively influenced the revision of Art 15.

While the EU passed Directive 2000/78/EC on equal treatment in employment and occupation,[28] the Council of Europe, celebrating the European Year of People with Disabilities 2003,[29] adopted Recommendation No 1592[30] laying the ground for a 2006–15 Disability Action Plan,

[23] No 92.

[24] Recommendation Rec (2006) 5 of the Committee of Ministers, p 4, point 1.1.1 Mission Statement.

[25] Council of Europe (1995) Resolution AP (95) 3 of the Committee of Ministers on a Charter on the vocational assessment of people with disabilities, adopted on 12 October 1995, at the 545th meeting of ministers' deputies.

[26] Art 3. Art 5 provides a definition of a range of concepts, as defined by the World Health Organization: 'impairment' is any loss or abnormality of psychological, physiological or anatomical structure or functions; 'disability' is any restriction or lack (resulting from an impairment) of ability to perform an activity in the manner of or within the range considered normal for a human being; 'handicap' is a disadvantage, for a given individual, resulting from an impairment or a disability, that limits or prevents the fulfilment of a role that is normal (depending on age, sex and social and cultural factors) for that individual.

[27] Art 6iii(d). Only in the most serious cases can employment in cooperatives and sheltered workshops be envisaged.

[28] With the purpose of laying down a general framework for combating discrimination on the grounds of religion or belief, disability, age or sexual orientation as regards employment and occupation, with a view to putting into effect in the member states the principle of equal treatment.

[29] And following Resolution ResAP (2001) Towards full citizenship of persons with disabilities through inclusive new technologies, as well as Resolution AP (95) 3 on a charter on the vocational assessment of people with disabilities.

[30] Recommendation 1592 urged the Committee of Ministers to instruct the relevant bodies of the Council of Europe: '1) to begin forthwith the preparation of a convention: establishing a minimum recruitment quota for people with a disability in companies employing more than fifty staff, with an obligation for firms which are certified as being unable to attain the quota to contribute to a specific fund for the benefit of all people with disabilities; reserving the posts which suit the types of training given to people with disabilities, in national and local government offices and services; prescribing advantages, particularly in respect of taxation, for

which provided a comprehensive roadmap for policymakers within the non-discrimination and human rights frameworks to enhance the independence, freedom of choice and quality of life of people with disabilities and to acknowledge disability as a part of human diversity.[31] Action line 5 of the Action Plan is devoted to employment, vocational guidance and training with the aim of mainstreaming their employment chances by addressing the barriers to their participation in the workforce and promoting their active integration in the open labour market.[32]

The UN went a step further in 2006, with the adoption of a Convention on the Rights of Persons with Disabilities to ensure 'that societies recognize that all people must be provided with the opportunities to live life to their fullest potential, whatever that may be',[33] with a particular focus on the right of equal treatment at work and the promotion of the 'right to work, including for those who acquire a disability during the course of employment'.[34]

The international approach to persons with disabilities has experienced a fundamental shift towards the acceptance of disablement as a difference on the same footing as sex, nationality, birth and so on that should not lead to any discrimination, in particular at work. Both the UN and the ILO have been the main drivers for such a shift in law, followed by the Council of Europe, with the amendment of Article 15. So far, Article 15 has been broadly ratified. Among the member states of the EU that have not yet ratified the Charter but have ratified the 1961 Charter, only Croatia has not ratified Article 15§§1 and 2, and the Czech Republic Article 15§1.

enterprises and employers who recruit people with a disability, such advantages at all events offsetting the expenditure for conversion of the premises and/or workplace; 2) to introduce a quality seal under the supervision of the competent authorities for goods and services meeting the statutory or regulatory requirements as regards employment of people with a disability; 3) to establish an in-house code of good practice to ensure ... the employment of a higher percentage of people with disabilities' (Art 11 iv).

[31] Recommendation Rec (2006) 5 of the Committee of Ministers, 2006, 4, point 1.1.2 Mission statement.

[32] ibid 18. The action plan covers also support to progress from sheltered and supported employment to open employment and stresses the need to ensure the same rights for employees with a disability as for other employees in respect of consultation of employment conditions and membership and active participation in trade unions, in respect of access to health and safety legislation, but also to internship and traineeships.

[33] www.un.org/disabilities/convention/questions.shtml.

[34] Art 27. A catalogue of the obligations imposed on states ranges, among other things, from the prohibition of discrimination on the basis of disability with regard to all matters concerning all forms of employment and the protection of the rights of persons with disabilities on an equal basis with others, to just and favourable conditions of work and the right to exercise their labour and trade union rights on an equal basis with others. An additional point is made on the obligation for state parties to 'ensure that persons with disabilities are not held in slavery or in servitude, and are protected, on an equal basis with others, from forced or compulsory labour' (Art 27(2)).

C. Relationship with Other Provisions of the Charter

Besides Article 15, some provisions of the Charter are applicable to persons with a handicap with particular relevance to access to appropriate facilities for vocational guidance, *including the handicapped*,[35] with a view to choosing an occupation suited to personal aptitude and interests and for vocational training,[36] as well as the right not to be discriminated against.[37] Article 1§4 guarantees the right to vocational guidance, continuing vocational training for employed and unemployed persons, and specialised guidance and training for persons with disabilities.[38] States must provide such services to all those interested and ensure equality of treatment for persons with disabilities.[39]

II. CONTENT

The ECSR has stressed over the years[40] that Article 15 'reflects and advances the change in disability policies ... towards inclusion and choice',[41] putting the emphasis on the non-discrimination principle.

A. General: The Right to Independence, Social Integration and Participation in the Life of the Community

The notion of disability is perceived as embracing a wide interpretation of situations concerning people's state of health, being mentally, physically and/or psychologically impaired, or suffering from physical, mental and/or psychological disorders, so as to exclude any direct or indirect discrimination at their expense. Persons with a disability should be treated in such

[35] Art 9, author's emphasis.

[36] Art 10.

[37] Art E.

[38] Conclusions 2003, Bulgaria; Digest (2008), 25–26.

[39] As well as for nationals of other state parties to the Charter and Conclusions XII-1, Statement of Interpretation of Art 1§4.

[40] The last national reporting on Art 15 on the protection of the disabled, as part of the thematic Group 1 on employment, training and equal opportunities, took place in 2011 and led to Conclusions XX-1 for the ESC and Conclusions 2012 for the RESC with as reference period 1/1/2007 to 31/12/2010. A next assessment by the Committee will take place in 2016 based on national reports to be submitted by October 2015 and dealing with the reference period 1 January 2011 to 31 December 2014 with a simplified procedure for the countries that have accepted the collective complaint procedure, namely, the Netherlands, Sweden, Croatia, Norway, Slovenia, Cyprus (Group B) to report in 2015 and the Czech Republic and France, Greece, Portugal, Italy, Belgium, Bulgaria, Ireland and Finland (Group A), which reported in 2014.

[41] Conclusions 2003, Statement of Interpretation on Art 15.

a way that ensures effective enjoyment of the rights allocated to every individual.[42]

The notion is a dynamic one: the ECtHR held that 'a person's health status, including HIV infection, should be covered either as a form of or in the same way as disability or by "other status"'.[43]

Recently, the CJEU ruled that obesity constitutes a 'disability', as 'it entails a limitation resulting in particular from long-term physical, mental or psychological impairments which in interaction with various barriers may hinder the full and effective participation of the person concerned in professional life on an equal basis with other workers'.[44]

The ECSR has constantly interpreted disability as extensively as possible. It has clarified the nature of Article 15 as a non-discrimination norm in the disability context.[45] In the same vein, the ECSR has explained that the scope of the protection encompasses 'all persons with disabilities regardless of the nature[46] and origin of their disability and irrespective of their age'.[47] The aim is to ensure that they enjoy on the same footing as non-disabled the 'right of independence, social integration and participation in the life of the community'.[48] This implements a profound shift of values in all European countries 'away from treating persons with disability as objects of pity, towards respecting them as equal citizens'.[49]

B. Paragraph 1: The Right to Education, Vocational Training in the Framework of General Schemes

The equality principle appears as a *leitmotif* throughout Article 15. In 1996 the stress was put on the necessity to provide persons with disabilities with

[42] *X and Y v The Netherlands* App no 8978/80 (ECtHR, 26 March 1985), as interpretation of the scope of Art 8 ECHR. For the ECtHR, this protection ranges from the prohibition of torture and access to adequate care in case of imprisonment, to the right of liberty and security in case of detention in psychiatric institutions, to the right to a fair trial and the respect for private and family life, thus embracing the concept of physical and psychological integrity. See for more details: Factsheet of the ECtHR on 'Persons with disabilities and the European Convention on Human Rights', available on the ECtHR website.

[43] *IB v Greece* App no 552/10, para 73 with reference to Art 14 of the Convention.

[44] Case C-354/13 *Fag og Arbejde (FOA) v Kommunernes Landsforening (KL)* (CJEU, 18 December 2014).

[45] Conclusions 2003, Statement of Interpretation on Art 15. See also the chapter by C Kollonay-Lehoczky on Art 8 in this volume.

[46] In particular to be put in parallel with Art E on non-discrimination including physical and mental handicapped persons: Conclusion I, Statement of Interpretation on Art 15§2.

[47] *Association Internationale Autisme—Europe (AIAE) v France*, Collective Complaint No 13/2002, Decision on the merits of 04.11.2003 §48.

[48] Position driven by Recommendation 6 on a coherent policy for people with a disability adopted by the Committee of Ministers on 9 April 1992 and endorsed in the case law of the Committee.

[49] ibid fn 34.

the necessary means within the framework of general schemes wherever possible.

The ECSR[50] has ruled that the effective inclusion of persons with handicaps, and therefore an effective right to education, should take place within the framework of general or mainstreamed education schemes, in combination, if needed, with a general anti-discrimination approach. It ruled that, as a minimum, national legislation must provide for a compelling justification for recourse to special or segregated education systems and, in case of unjustified exclusion of general or mainstreamed education schemes or abuse of recourse to special or segregated education systems, an effective remedy.[51]

C. Paragraph 2: Promotion of Access to and Maintenance in Employment and Ordinary Working Environment

Article 15§2 stresses that persons with a disability should have access to employment in the ordinary working environment, with adjustment of working conditions if needed. Only where integration in a regular working environment is not possible by reason of the disability, should the state arrange or create sheltered employment. Where recourse to sheltered employment facilities is needed, in firms where production is the main activity, persons with a handicap should enjoy the usual benefits labour law provides for on the open labour market, and in particular the right to fair remuneration and respect for trade union rights.[52] Furthermore, national legislation must place an obligation on the employer to adapt the workplace, within reason, so that persons with disabilities have effective access to employment. Employers should, a fortiori, take the necessary steps to keep a disabled person in employment, in particular when the disablement is the result of an industrial accident or an occupational disease.[53]

The ECSR ruled that non-discrimination legislation is a sine qua non condition for a genuine equality of opportunities in the open labour market, independently of whether the state has ratified the 1996 Charter.[54]

National legislation may but does not have to introduce a quota system, by which an employer has to comply with numerical requirements for hiring and promoting persons with a handicap, as a way of diminishing discrimination towards them. However, when such a system exists, the ECSR reserves the right to ascertain its effectiveness.[55]

[50] *AIAE v France*, Collective Complaint No 13/2002.
[51] Conclusions 2005, Cyprus.
[52] Conclusions XVII-2, Czech Republic.
[53] Conclusions 2007, Statement of Interpretation on Art 15§2.
[54] Conclusions 2003, Slovenia.
[55] Conclusions XIV-2, Belgium.

D. Paragraph 3: Promotion of Social Integration and Participation in Community Life

This new provision[56] aims at promoting the full social integration and participation in the life of the community of persons with a disability with a focus on communication and mobility, access to housing, cultural activities and leisure.

The case law of the ECSR interpreting Article 15§3 has repercussions for employment, stressing the need for a coherent policy, encompassing both the public and private spheres in areas such as transport and telecommunications, in the form of positive actions that should have a clear legal basis.[57] In the same vein, it underlines the necessary consultation of the disabled and their representative organisations in the design and ongoing review of such positive measures.[58]

III. IMPACT ON EUROPEAN HUMAN RIGHTS INSTRUMENTS

A. European Convention on Human Rights

While the impact of the ECHR and the jurisprudence of the ECtHR on the Charter and the case law of the ECSR has been developed above, reciprocity appears less obvious.

Nevertheless, such an influence appears in two ways. In a more general sense, the ECtHR's landmark decision in *Demir and Baykara v Turkey*[59] gave the Court the opportunity to reaffirm its praetorian methodological approach, in which reference to international instruments, such as the Charter, as source of interpretation of the ECHR are given as much weight as the ECHR itself, independently of the ratification or not by the respondent state in the proceedings. More specifically, the ECtHR mentioned Article 15 as 'explicitly guaranteeing people with disabilities the effective exercise of the right to independence, social integration and participation in the life of the community'.[60] However, the ECtHR stressed that the prohibition of discrimination can only be invoked by applicants in combination with another provision of the ECHR.[61]

[56] In comparison with the 1961 Charter.

[57] Conclusions 2007, Slovenia.

[58] Conclusions 2003, Italy.

[59] *Demir and Baykara v Turkey* App no 34503/97 (ECtHR, 12 November 2008).

[60] *Dordevic v Croatia* App no 41526/10 (ECtHR (First Section), 24 October 2012).

[61] See *Mehmet Bayrakci v Turkey* App no 2643/09, in which the applicant, a worker with a disability, complained about the lack of accessible toilets at the workplace. The ECtHR considered that the complaint fell under Art 8 ECHR on the right to respect for private life and family, including the physical and psychological integrity of the person, but that the prohibition

The ECSR has adopted a different approach, relying on the non-discrimination clause in order to affirm the justiciable nature of social rights, while recognising that these are in principle subject to progressive realisation. In *AIAE v France* it concluded that there was a violation of Article 15, whether alone or combined with the non-discrimination requirement, because the state had failed to raise significantly the proportion of children with autism being educated in either general or specialist schools, in comparison with other children.[62] With this decision, the ECSR illustrated how the requirement of non-discrimination may provide a direction for the realisation of socio-economic rights by identifying categories of people who, because of their particular vulnerability, deserve special attention.[63]

B. Charter of Fundamental Rights of the European Union

The Charter is recognised as one of the sources for the determination and interpretation of the EU Charter of Fundamental Rights (CFREU), in particular in its preamble and in the Explanations to Article 26 CFREU on the integration of persons with disabilities with the express assertion that 'the principle set out in this Article is based on Art. 15 of the Charter'.[64]

The CJEU was inspired by the proactive evolution of the definition of disablement. The CJEU clarifies the provisions of Directive 2000/78/EC in reference to the Charter's advanced understanding and jurisprudence on disablement[65] as an instrument[66] of reference for the EU and its member states, as 'they set the objectives of the promotion of employment, improved living and working conditions, so as to make possible their harmonization, an adequate social protection, social dialogue, development of human resources with a view to lasting high employment and combating of exclusion'.[67] Furthermore, the CJEU distinguishes handicap[68] from (long-lasting) illness, as a limitation resulting from physical, mental or psychological impairment and hinders the participation of the person concerned in working life for a long

of discrimination can be invoked only in combination with another provision of the ECHR. The case was rejected for procedural reasons, as the applicant should have exhausted domestic remedies.

[62] Decision on the merits, *AIAE v France*. Collective Complaint No 13/2002.

[63] O De Schutter (2010) The European Social Charter: a social constitution for Europe, Brusels, Bruylant 735–36 and 846–47. In the same vein, Decision relative to *International Commission of Jurists v France*, Collective Complaint No 1/1998 §32.

[64] As well as point 26 of the Community Charter of Fundamental Social Rights.

[65] A Lhoste, 'Evolution de la jurisprudence européenne sur les aménagements raisonnables' (2014) 7 *Chroniques de droit social* 331.

[66] And the Community Charter of Fundamental Social Rights of Workers of 1989.

[67] Case C-13/05 *Sonia Chacón Navas v Eurest Colectividades SA* (CJEU of 11 July 2006) Recital 3, I 6505.

[68] In respect of Directive 2000/78/EC.

period of time. It has furthermore developed the concept of discrimination by association, when an employer has treated an employee with a disabled child less favourably than his or her colleagues with non-disabled children, amounting to harassment because he or she is associated with a disabled person although not him- or herself disabled.[69]

The ECSR has not yet had the opportunity to deal with the concept of 'discrimination by association' and hope may be expressed that the praetorian jurisprudence of the CJEU will inspire the ECSR in the future.

In other cases,[70] the CJEU has preferred to refer to the 2009 UN Convention of the Rights of Persons with Disability and the definition it gives: 'Persons with disabilities include those who have long-term physical, mental, intellectual or sensory impairments which in interaction with various barriers may hinder their full and effective participation in society on an equal basis with others',[71] concluding that an illness that does not include such a limitation cannot be defined as a handicap within the meaning of Directive 2000/78/EC.

In its jurisprudence, the CJEU shows a willingness to develop a modern and holistic understanding of disablement. In doing so, the CJEU takes inspiration from, among other things, Article 15 and the case law of the ECSR.

IV. IMPACT ON NATIONAL CASE LAW

In the same vein, the impact of the Charter on national courts provides evidence of the dialogue between national and European jurisdictions to complement their interpretation. Although it is difficult to trace back such relationships, it is striking that in a case in which the applicant contested the suppression of a compensation benefit for people with a disability when they turn 60,[72] the French Conseil d'Etat[73] quoted Article 15 in its entirety to rule that 'provisions, which require the intervention of additional acts to produce effects in respect of individuals, serve the exclusive aim of governing the relations between States and as a result, cannot be used by the applicant'.

[69] Case C-303/06 *S Coleman v Attridge Law and Steve Law* (CJEU, 2008).

[70] Case C-335/11 *HK Danmark* and Case C-337/11 *Commission v Italy*.

[71] Art 1 UN Convention on the Rights of Persons with Disabilities.

[72] And whose disability meets the criteria defined by decree, in particular taking into account the nature and extent of compensation requirements with regard to his life project.

[73] *Confédération française pour la promotion sociale des aveugles et des amblyopes* App no 341533 (4 July 2012).

V. CONCLUSION

The so-called 'sleeping beauty',[74] as a programmatic right requiring specific actions by the contracting parties, has benefited from the proactive and praetorian interpretation of the ECSR, as well as the interaction and mutual reinforcement between different international and European sources of rights and jurisdictions to operate and implement a radical shift from segregation to the civic, social and economic integration of the disabled, as fully fledged actors in society. Such a dynamic development participates in the conviction that 'social justice and economic growth demand the same thing: as many people as possible who are leading active and productive lives, free of wasteful and damaging prejudice and discrimination and contributing positively to society and communities in which they live. That is the vision which inspired and continues to inspire the Charter'.[75]

[74] But also called 'the paper tiger'.

[75] L Samuel, 'Fundamental Social Rights in the EU Legal Order in Connection with the European Social Charter' (Presentation delivered at the seminar 'Reform of the European Social Charter', 8–9 February 2011, Helsinki) 145.

Article 19§4

The Right of Migrant Workers and Their Families to Protection and Assistance

STEFAN CLAUWAERT

Article 19—The right of migrant workers and their families to protection and assistance

With a view to ensuring the effective exercise of the right of migrant workers and their families to protection and assistance in the territory of any other Party, the Parties undertake: …

4. to secure for such workers lawfully within their territories, insofar as such matters are regulated by law or regulations or are subject to the control of administrative authorities, treatment not less favourable than that of their own nationals in respect of the following matters:
   a. remuneration and other employment and working conditions;
   b. membership of trade unions and enjoyment of the benefits of collective bargaining;
   c. accommodation.

I. INTRODUCTION

A. Context and Main Content

Together with Article 18, Article 19 ensures certain minimum safeguards for migrant workers and their families. From the outset, the basic intention of both articles was to (i) liberalise the conditions of migration, (ii) ensure the rights of migrant workers and their families and (iii) ensure equal treatment of migrants.[1] Whereas Article 18 secures mainly the right to engage in a

[1] M Mikkola, '4. Migrants', in M Mikkola (ed), *Social human rights of Europe* (Porvoo, Karelactio Legisactio, 2010) 567

gainful occupation, Article 19 secures the right of migrant workers and their families to protection and assistance in various areas, such as social services, family reunion, earnings and taxes.

Article 19's importance is underlined by the fact that it belongs to the so-called hard-core provisions of the Charter.[2] Despite this, Article 19 forms, probably due to its (politically) sensitive content, one of the least well ratified articles of the Charter, a feature it seems to have in common with other international instruments dealing with migrant workers' rights (see below, section I.B).[3]

In this chapter, the focus lies on the fourth paragraph of Article 19, and in particular indents a) and b), because, first, according to its wording, this paragraph can be considered the closest to the main starting point of the present publication, namely the employment relation, and second, due to the ECSR's *Laval* decision,[4] leading to a (new) clash between EU law and the Charter, this paragraph (again) came into the centre of attention and controversy.

B. International Sources

At the international level, various instruments deal with the protection of migrant workers and their families. From a general 'UN' perspective, and although several texts have relevance for the protection of migrants' rights,[5]

[2] See also Conclusions XIV-1, General introduction: 'Article 19, and especially paragraphs 4, 5, 6 and 8 have preserved every dimension of their original importance and topicality, and are of fundamental importance for the effective implementation of social rights in modern Europe. The Committee therefore asks states to do their utmost to ensure observance of these provisions'. Confirmed by L Samuel, 'Article 19—the right of migrant workers and their families to protection and assistance', in L Samuel (ed), *Fundamental social rights. Case law of the European Social Charter*, 2nd edn (Strasbourg, Council of Europe Publishing, 2002) 402; and A Swiatkowski, 'Chapter 9 Rights of other States-Parties to the European Social Charter', in A Swiatkowski (ed), *Charter of Social Rights of the Council of Europe* (The Hague, Kluwer Law International, 2007) XXI, 349.

[3] Only 25 out of the 43 contracting parties accepted Art 19§4. According to the reports on non-accepted provisions (see chapter on 'Enforcement and Procedures'), the ECSR considered that, given the situation in practice and law, Andorra, Azerbaijan, Bulgaria, Lithuania, Malta and Moldova are in a situation to ratify Art 19§4a and b.

[4] ECSR, Decision on the merits of 03.07.2013 in *Swedish Trade Union Confederation (LO) and Swedish Confederation of Professional Employees (TCO) v Sweden*, Collective Complaint No 85/2012.

[5] For example, the Universal Declaration of Human Rights (1948), the International Convention on the Elimination of All Forms of Racial Discrimination (1965), the International Covenant for Economic, Social and Cultural Rights (1966). For an interesting comparison between the content of this Convention and the Charter, see G Kolanjec, 'La Charte Sociale européenne et le Pacte international des Nations Unies relative aux droits économiques, sociaux et culturels', in Conseil de l'Europe, *Charte Social européenne. Colloque tenu à l'Université de Grenade à l'occasion du 25e anniversaire de la signature de la Charte sociale européenne, 26–27 octobre 1987* (Strasbourg, Conseil de l'Europe Division des publications et des documents, 1989) 77–90.

only the International Convention on the Protection of the Right of Migrant Workers and Members of their Families of 18 December 1990 directly relates to the rights of migrants and their families.[6]

Also within the ILO, a vast number of texts relate to the protection of migrant workers,[7] the most important being Convention No 97 (1949) on Migration for Employment (Revised) and Convention No 143 (1975) on Migrant Workers (Supplementary Provisions) and their respective Recommendations No 86 (1949) and No 151 (1975).[8] Convention No 97 obliges states to apply a treatment no less favourable than that which applies to their own nationals in respect to a number of matters, including conditions of employment and freedom of association. Several scholars confirm that Article 19 of the Charter is based to a large extent on this ILO Convention, and highlight the particularly close relationship between Article 19§4 of the Charter and Article 6§1a of Convention No 97.[9] Convention No 143, on the other hand, provides mainly for measures to combat clandestine and illegal migration, but also extends the scope of equality

[6] For a summary overview of those rights, in particular those related to the specific rights guaranteed by the Charter, see Council of Europe, *Migrant workers and their families protection with the European Social Charter*, Human Rights Social Charter monographs, No 4 (Strasbourg, Council of Europe, 1996) 111–15. The Convention refers in its general considerations to several ILO conventions albeit not to (Art 19 of) the 1961 Charter at that time already applicable. Adopted on 18 December 1990 it only entered into force on 1 July 2003 and 'from a Charter perspective', only Armenia, Montenegro and Turkey ratified it.

[7] For an overview of the ILO standard-setting activities on migrant workers, see ILO, 'General Survey on the reports on the Migration for Employment Convention (Revised) (No 97), and Recommendation (Revised) (No 86), 1949, and the Migrant Workers (Supplementary Provisions) Conventions (No 143), and Recommendation (No 151), 1975' (Geneva, International Labour Conference, 1999) 17–20.

[8] These four instruments do not permit states to exempt any category of regular-entry migrant workers not specified in the instruments and thus no distinction can be made between migrants for permanent settlement and migrants who do not intend to stay for any significant length of time in the host country, such as seasonal workers. They also do not operate on the basis of reciprocity, that is, migrants do not have to be a national of a state that has ratified the instruments or guarantees equal treatment to the subjects of the ratifying state in order that the provisions apply (ILO (n 7) 43).

[9] H Wiebringhaus, 'The European Social Charter and International Labour Standards: I', (1961) LXXXIV–5 *International Labour Review* 375; H Bartolomei de la Cruz, 'La Charte Sociale européenne et l'Organisation Internationale du Travail: 25 années de collaboration exemplaire', in Conseil de l'Europe, *Charte Social européenne. Colloque tenu à l'Université de Grenade à l'occasion du 25e anniversaire de la signature de la Charte sociale européenne (26-27 octobre 1987)* (Strasbourg, Conseil de l'Europe Division des publications et des documents, 1989) 107; D Harris and J Darcy, 'Article 19: The Right of Migrant Workers and Their Families to Protection and Assistance', in D Harris and J Darcy (eds), *The European Social Charter*, 2nd edn The Procedural Aspects of International Law Book Series, Vol 25 (Ardsley, NY, Transnational Publishers, 2001) 220; and L Samuel, 'Article 19—the right of migrant workers and their families to protection and assistance', in Samuel (n 2) 413. Art 6§1a reads as follows:

> '1. Each Member for which this Convention is in force undertakes to apply, without discrimination in respect of nationality, race, religion or sex, to immigrants lawfully

between legally resident migrant workers and national workers beyond the provisions of Convention No 97. However, the latter Conventions are, like Article 19 of the Charter, rather poorly ratified.[10]

Other Council of Europe instruments relevant for the protection of the rights of migrant workers and their families are the ECHR and its additional protocols (for example, Article 6 ECHR, Article 2§§2 and 4 of Protocol No 4 and Article 1 of Protocol No 7), the European Convention on Establishment of 1955 (in particular Articles 10–14 and 17–18), the European Convention on the Legal Status of Migrant Workers (1977) and the European Code of Social Security. Furthermore, there are some interesting texts from the Committee of Ministers[11] and from the Parliamentary Assembly, which, more recently, adopted some specific recommendations related to migrant (workers) rights in the context of the economic crisis.[12]

Also at European Union level, manifold texts of primary and secondary legislation refer to the Charter.[13] As for EU texts directly related to the content of Article 19§4, the ECSR refers in its working document on the relationship between EU law and the Charter to the following directives (although in none of them is explicit reference made to the Charter):[14] Council Directive 2000/43/EC of 29 June 2000 implementing the principle of equal treatment between persons irrespective of racial or ethnic origin;[15] Council Directive 2000/78/EC of 27 November 2000 establishing

within its territory, treatment no less favourable than that which it applies to its own nationals in respect of the following matters:

(a) in so far as such matters are regulated by law or regulations, or are subject to the control of administrative authorities
   (i) remuneration, including family allowances where these form part of remuneration, hours of work, overtime arrangements, holidays with pay, restrictions on home work, minimum age for employment, apprenticeship and training, women's work and the work of young persons;
   (ii) membership of trade unions and enjoyment of the benefits of collective bargaining;
   (iii) accommodation.'

[10] Convention No 97 and Convention No 43 are, respectively, ratified only by 18 and 13 contracting parties.

[11] CM Recommendation R(91)3E on the social security protection of seconded workers of 14 February 1991.

[12] PACE Recommendation 1187(1992) on relations between migrants and trade unions of 8 May 1992; PACE Recommendation 1211(1993) on clandestine migration, traffickers and employers of clandestine migrants of 11 May 1993; PACE Recommendation 1910(2010) on the impact of the global economic crisis on migration in Europe of 27 April 2010; PACE Recommendation 1917(2010) on Migrants and refugees: a continuing challenge for the Council of Europe of 30 April 2010; and PACE Recommendation 1970(2011) on Protecting migrant women in the labour market of 15 April 2011.

[13] For an overview, see ECSR, 'The relationship between European Union law and the European Social Charter', working document, 15 July 2014, 8–21.

[14] ibid 118–19.

[15] [2000] OJ L180/22–26.

a general framework for equal treatment in employment and occupation;[16] Directive 2002/73/CE of the European Parliament and of the Council of 23 September 2002 amending Council Directive 76/207/EEC on the implementation of the principle of equal treatment for men and women as regards access to employment, vocational training and promotion, and working conditions;[17] and Directive 2004/113/EC of the Council of 13 December 2004 implementing the principle of equal treatment between men and women in the access to and supply of goods and services.[18] In its decision in the *Laval* collective complaint, the ECSR also refers to Directive 96/71/EC of the European Parliament and of the Council of 16 December 1996 concerning the posting of workers in the framework of the provision of services;[19] Directive 2008/104/EC of the European Parliament and of the Council of 19 November 2008 on temporary agency work;[20] and Directive 2006/123/EC of the European Parliament and of the Council of 12 December 2006 on services in the internal market.[21]

C. Relationship to Other Provisions of the Charter

As already mentioned, Article 19 is most closely related to Article 18. However, it is also related to Articles 1 to 17 and 20 to 31 as these articles—although they do not explicitly refer to them—also apply to migrant workers when they are nationals of contracting parties lawfully resident or working regularly within the territory of the contracting party concerned.[22] A kind of dual protection thus applies as certain matters covered by Article 19§4 are also covered by other Charter articles (for example, Articles 2, 3, 4, 5 and 6 of the Charter) and this entails that if a state is found in non-conformity with one of those latter articles because of discrimination between workers on nationality grounds, it might also be found in breach of Article 19§4. Finally, there is of course the connection with the horizontal Article E on non-discrimination.[23]

16 [2000] OJ L303/16–22.
17 [2002] OJ L269/15–20.
18 [2004] OJ L373/37–43.
19 [1997] OJ L18/1–6.
20 [2008] OJ L327/9–14.
21 [2006] OJ L376/36–68.
22 Appendix to the RESC, Introduction, §1: 'Without prejudice to Article 12, paragraph 4, and Article 13, paragraph 4, the persons covered by Articles 1 to 17 and 20 to 31 include foreigners only in so far as they are nationals of other Parties lawfully resident or working regularly within the territory of the Party concerned, subject to the understanding that these articles are to be interpreted in the light of the provisions of Articles 18 and 19. This interpretation would not prejudice the extension of similar facilities to other persons by any of the Parties.' See also Committee of Independent Experts, *Fourth Report on certain provisions of the Charter which have not been accepted* (Strasbourg, Council of Europe Publishing, 1995) 18–19.
23 See the chapter on Art E by C Kollonay-Lehoczky in this volume.

II. CONTENT

A. Personal Scope

(i) General Considerations

In the context of the Charter a 'migrant worker' is a person who is a national of a contracting party to the Charter and who is lawfully resident or working regularly within the territory of another contracting party, but this interpretation does not preclude extension of the rights to other persons by any of the contracting parties.[24] So according to a textual interpretation, to be entitled to the rights under Article 19 two conditions must be satisfied: (i) be a national of one of the Parties to the 1961 or 1996 Charter and (ii) lawfully residing (that is, be authorised to enter and reside in that state's territory) or working regularly (that is, be authorised to enter and work in that state's territory). As the Appendix uses the term 'person' and not 'worker', the rights under Article 19 are thus applicable to all categories of workers, be they jobseekers, cross-border workers, seasonal workers, wage earners or self-employed.[25] Furthermore, no distinction is allowed between permanently or temporarily lawful migrants, and although the wording in Article 19 is masculine, the protection applies equally to women.[26]

According to Mikkola, and in light of the introduction to the Appendix to the Charter, stateless persons and refugees are also covered and must be treated equally and if necessary, positive actions for their inclusion must be taken.[27] According to him, the Charter does not cover migrants from third countries; nor does it apply to tourists or situations of mass exodus.[28]

The changes in migration flows have had an impact on ECSR case law. When Article 19 was drafted in 1961, migrant workers were mainly male

[24] Appendix to the RESC, Introduction §1.

[25] Conclusions I.

[26] Council of Europe, 'Migrant's rights in the European Social Charter', Information document prepared by the Secretariat of the ESC, 22 June 2006, 4.

[27] Appendix to the 1996 Charter, Introduction §§2 and 3. As for the application of the Charter to stateless persons, see also Conclusions 2013, Statement of Interpretation on the rights of stateless persons. As for the application to refugees, see Conclusions XVII-1 (2004), Statement of Interpretation on the personal scope of the Charter. Furthermore, in the wake of the massive migration flows in 2015, the ECSR reiterated the fact that the rights guaranteed by the Charter (including Art 19§4) are to be enjoyed to the fullest extent possible by refugees in its Statement of Interpretation on the rights of refugees under the European Social Charter elaborated during the 28th session of the ECSR, 7–11 September 2015 (Conclusions 2015, Statement of Interpretation on the rights of refugees under the European Social Charter, 30 January 2015). In this Statement of Interpretation the ECSR also extensively elaborates on the very close link between (and application of) the social and economic rights embedded in the 1951 UN Convention relating to the Status of Refugees (and its 1967 Protocol) and the related rights in the Charter.

[28] Mikkola (n 1) 563–64 and 568–69.

blue-collar workers who temporarily left their families behind, but over time migration has come to involve well-educated men and women seeking permanent residence in the host country. The reasons for migration have also become more varied, such as studying, starting a business or family, retirement and so on. Furthermore, there was a shift from collective to individual migration[29] and an increase of irregular migration. Thus, the ECSR increasingly regarded Article 19 as protecting the rights of all migrants and also looked for (more) objective criteria to determine who is a migrant worker or not (such as legality of entry (from the receiving country's point of view), the regularity and permanence of employment and the duration of residence).[30]

(ii) Extension of Application to Non-lawfully Residing or Working Third-country Nationals/Workers?

Some confusion has arisen on this question because of the wording of the Appendix to the Charter, which states that 'persons covered by Articles 1 to 17 include foreigners only in so far as they are nationals of other contracting parties', which could be interpreted, *a sensu contrario*, to mean that by not mentioning Articles 18 and 19 these were applicable to all foreigners. However, this interpretation has been rejected by the ECSR, which considered that it was sufficiently clear from the wording of Articles 18 and 19 that these only applied to nationals of contracting parties.

However, the problem of this 'extension' of scope of application is not yet fully solved. In its Conclusions 2004, the ECSR again addressed the possibility of extending the application to foreign nationals of non-party states. Relying on the Appendix, which stipulates that parties can extend the Charter's application to persons other than those covered by the Appendix, the ECSR stated that:

> the Parties to the Charter (in both its versions) have guaranteed to foreigners not covered by the Charter rights identical to or inseparable from those of the Charter, by ratifying human rights treaties—in particular the European Convention of Human Rights—or by adopting domestic rules whether constitutional, legislative or otherwise without distinguishing between persons referred to explicitly in the Appendix and other non-nationals. In doing so, the Parties have undertaken these obligations.[31]

However, the ECSR added that these obligations: 'did not in principle fall within the ambit of its supervisory functions' and made it clear that it did not rule out 'that the implementation of certain provisions of the Charter

[29] General introduction to Conclusions XIV-1 and Samuel (n 2) 402.
[30] Mikkola (n 1) 561–62.
[31] Conclusions 2004, Statement of Interpretation.

could in certain specific situations require complete equality of treatment between nationals and foreigners, whether or not they are nationals of member states, Party to the Charter'.[32]

The latter extension of the scope has recently created a lot of controversy following an ECSR decision in two collective complaints against the Netherlands, whereby the Dutch government considered that the ECSR was interpreting the Appendix to the Charter even *contra legem* by extending the protection of the rights in the Charter to persons who were not legally residing in the country.[33] During a debate between the Governmental Committee and the ECSR in Turin in October 2014, the ECSR explained that its case law was consistent, as it has always highlighted that 'the European Social Charter was a human rights treaty' and that 'the Appendix to the Charter, if applied literally, would exclude irregular migrants including their children from basic human rights such as the right to physical integrity and the respect for human dignity'. It added that this 'was a case law on which there had been unanimous agreement within the ECSR in recent times'.[34]

As for Article 19§4 in particular, giving its wording and next to the general scope, it applies to workers 'lawfully within their territory', that is if they have entered that territory in accordance with its laws (likely to require

[32] Council of Europe, Digest of the case law of the European Committee of Social Rights, 1 September 2008, 183.

[33] *European Federation of National Organisations working with the Homeless (FEANTSA) v The Netherlands*, Collective Complaint No 86/2012 and *Conference of European Churches (CEC) v The Netherlands*, Collective Complaint No 90/2013.

[34] In the meeting report, reference is also made to a letter of the ECSR President of 13 July 2011 inviting the contracting parties to abandon the provision on personal scope in the Appendix; an invitation which did not receive a favourable response from the contracting parties. The ECSR's case for extending the scope was then that 'such a limitation is hardly consistent with the nature of the Charter, intended as a human rights instrument, and it is also a sort of anomaly: one does not find the same kind of limitation in other international legal instruments aimed at protecting human rights in general, or social rights in particular. Moreover, the limitation of the personal scope provided for in the Appendix appears to be questionable in the light of the meaning and value that state parties to the Charter attach to the dignity and fundamental rights of any human being as such, regardless of her/his nationality. Indeed, state parties seem already inclined, and conscious of their duty, to apply social rights beyond the limited personal scope indicated in the Appendix. In addition, important social changes, which have occurred since the text of the Charter was adopted, make it increasingly urgent to overcome the limitation of the personal scope prescribed by the Appendix, in order to render the Charter system fully consistent with the object and purpose of European and international standards of human rights protection … The fact that under the Charter system only nationals of the state parties can invoke and obtain respect for their social rights, turns out to be a substantial discrimination, making the Charter system at odds with the universal nature of human rights, and with the fundamental values underpinning the Charter' (European Committee of Social Rights and Governmental Committee of the European Social Charter and the European Code of Social Security, Report joint meeting held on 14 October 2014—ILO Training Centre, Turin, Italy, Strasbourg, GC(2014)23 final, Strasbourg, 19 December 2014; for a copy of the main parts of the letter see ECSR, Activity Report 2011, 33–34).

a valid residence and/or work permit), and so long as their continued presence is in accordance with those laws. Finally, and although in general the Charter (and Article 19) requires reciprocity (only protection to nationals of other contracting parties), Article 19§4 cannot be made subject to reciprocity and its protection applies also to migrant workers of a contracting party that has not ratified Article 19§4.[35]

(iii) Application to Posted Workers?

In its *Laval* decision, the ECSR clarified the application of Article 19§4 to posted workers. The ECSR recalled 'that posted workers are workers who, for a limited period, carry out their work in the territory of a State other than the State in which they usually work, which is often their national State' and that it

> is aware that, in terms of length and stability of presence in the territory of the so-called 'host State', as well as of their relationship with such a State, the situation of posted workers is different from that of other categories of migrant workers, and in particular from the situation of those foreign workers who go to another State to seek work and to be permanently embedded there. Nonetheless, the Committee considers that ... they fall within the scope of application of Article 19 of the Charter and they have the right, for the period of their stay and work in the host State to receive treatment not less favourable than that of the national workers of the host State in respect of remuneration, other employment and working conditions, and enjoyment of the benefits of collective bargaining. (Article 19§4a and b)[36]

According to Rocca, and as the ECSR emphasises in its reasoning, the literal version included in the Charter of a 'migrant worker' as being a worker 'coming from another State and lawfully within the territory of the host state', the 'logical conclusion' was to include posted workers in the category of 'migrant workers', which also shows the ECSR's 'perfect awareness about the legal context in which the posting phenomenon takes place'.[37]

[35] Harris and Darcy (n 9) 221 with reference to Conclusions VIII, Spain.

[36] §134 of the ECSR Decision.

[37] M Rocca, *Posting of Workers and Collective Labour Law: There and Back Again. Between Internal Market and Fundamental Rights*, Social Europe Series No 33 (Cambridge, Intersentia, 2015) 267–68. The ECSR thereby overrules the interpretation of BUSINESSEUROPE and IOE, who considered Art 19§4 as being not applicable to posted workers, based on ILO Convention No 143, which indeed excludes from the definition of migrant workers 'employees of organisations or undertakings operating within the territory of a country who have been admitted temporarily to that country at the request of their employer to undertake specific duties or assignments, for a limited and defined period of time, and who are acquired to leave that country on the completion of their duties or assignments.' The ECSR, however, gives precedence to the fact that Art 19§4 is built on Art 6(1) of Convention No 97 and thus considers to be a migrant worker any workers coming from another state and lawfully within the territory of another state.

In the framework of its Conclusions 2015, the ECSR elaborated a further Statement of Interpretation on Article 19§4 particularly dealing with the rights of posted workers. After recalling its decision in Collective Complaint n° 85/2012 (in particular paragraph 134; see above), the ECSR firstly asks contracting parties that ratified Article 19§4 to provide 'information concerning the legal status of posted workers and what legal and practical measures are taken to ensure their equal treatment in matters of employment, trade union membership and collective bargaining', and secondly, and more importantly, the ECSR recalls that 'states must respect the principles of non-discrimination laid down by the Charter in respect of all persons subject to their jurisdiction. It thus considers that in order to conform with the requirements of the Charter, any restrictions on the right to equal treatment for posted workers, which are imposed due to the nature of their sojourn, must be objectively justified by reference to the specific situations and status of posted workers, having regard to the principles of Article G of the Revised Charter (Article 31 of the 1961 Charter)'.[38]

B. Content

Besides §§5 and 7, Article 19§4 in the first instance highlights the principle of equality by requiring contracting parties to secure for migrant workers treatment not less favourable than that of their own nationals, and this in particular in the areas of: (i) remuneration and other employment and working conditions, (ii) trade union membership and the enjoyment of benefits of collective bargaining, and (iii) accommodation. As already mentioned, this paragraph is closely modelled on Article 6(1)a of ILO Convention No 97.[39]

[38] Conclusions 2015, Statement of Interpretation—Article 19§4—rights of posted workers.

[39] See above section I.B. It is worth noting that Art 6§1a refers to conditions of work, but not to access to employment. Art 10 of Convention No 143, however, refers, *inter alia*, to 'employment' and 'occupation'. The latter terms are similar to those used by Convention No 111, of which Art 1(3) provides that the terms 'employment' and 'occupation' include access to vocational training, access to employment and to particular occupations, and terms and conditions of employment. It would appear logical therefore to assign them the same meaning here, especially because the provisions of Recommendation No 111 detailing the content of these various subjects were included in similar terms in Recommendation No 151. The content of conditions of work in Art 6§§1a and 2 of Recommendation No 151 consists essentially of remuneration, hours of work, holidays with pay, minimum age for employment, apprenticeship and training, vocational guidance and placement, advancement, security of employment, etc. Art 6§1a(ii) also has to be read in conjunction with Art 10 of Convention No 143, which binds governments to pursue a policy designed to promote and guarantee equality of opportunity and treatment in relation to 'trade union rights'. The content of these rights is described in greater detail in para 2(g) of Recommendation No 151, which covers membership of trade unions and the exercise of trade union rights. This paragraph also mentions eligibility for office in trade unions and in labour–management relations bodies, including bodies representing workers in the workplace. Furthermore, Art 6§1a does not oblige states to take legislative

(i) General Aspects

As for the principle of equality, the ECSR already in its first supervisory cycle emphasised that Article 19

> goes beyond merely guaranteeing equality of treatment as between foreign and national workers in the sense that, recognizing that migrants are, in fact, handicapped, it provides for the institution by the Contracting Parties of measures which are more favourable and more positive in regard to this category of persons than in regard to the states' own nationals. Such being the case, the Contracting Parties should not limit the fulfilment of their obligations between their own nationals and foreigners but should pursue a positive and continuous course of action.[40]

Furthermore, states are required to guarantee certain minimum standards in the areas mentioned in indents a) to c) with a view to assisting and improving the legal, social and material position of migrant workers and their families. They are also required to prove the absence of discrimination, direct or indirect, in terms of law[41] and practice[42] and should inform the ECSR of any practical measures taken to remedy cases of discrimination.

On the other hand, the introductory sentence of Article 19§4 does not impose on contracting parties an obligation to regulate the matters in question by legislation or regulations or to subject them to the control of administration. What is required is that the laws of a contracting party must not discriminate and that its officials must not do so either in the exercise of any discretion that they may have in law.[43] Also, any discriminatory practice against migrants violates the Charter, irrespective of the number of persons affected.[44] Interesting to note also is that during the drafting of the 1961 Charter, a proposal by the workers' delegates at the Tripartite Conference (December 1958) to replace in the introductory sentence the words 'are subject to the control of administrative authorities' by 'by collective agreements' was opposed by the United Kingdom on the grounds that the

or other measures to redress inequalities in practice. States are under the general obligation when the matters covered by clause (a) in particular are regulated by national legislation, to ensure that the legislation is applied particularly by means of labour inspection services or other supervisory authorities. The wording according to which the state must apply 'treatment no less favourable than that which it applies to its own nationals' allows the application of treatment which, although not identical, would be equivalent in its effects to that enjoyed by nationals. (ILO (n 7) 145; for more information on trade union rights and distinctions based on nationality, see also ibid 150, 158–59, 174–76).

[40] Conclusions I.

[41] Conclusions II, Statement of Interpretation.

[42] Conclusions III, Statement of Interpretation, 31/07/1973.

[43] Conclusions II. According to Harris and Darcy, the prohibition of discrimination by officials can be conducted from ECSR Conclusions III, 92, stating that 'it is not enough for a government to prove that no discrimination exists in law alone but that it is obliged to prove in addition that no discrimination is practiced in fact' (Harris and Darcy (n 9) 221).

[44] For example, Conclusions V, Cyprus.

supervision of such agreements was not a matter for the state and that the words 'are subject to the control of administrative authorities', which are taken from Article 6 of ILO Convention No 97, had been inserted to cover matters such as the allocation of housing by local authorities.[45] A valid argument of course in relation to housing covered by Article 19§4c, but 'less valid' for the issues covered by indents a) and b), which are predominantly regulated by law or via collective agreements! This is an omission that could be rectified in a future revision of the Charter and/or the ECSR case law.

As for the terms 'territory of' in the introductory sentence, they also apply to oil rights situated beyond territorial waters but under the supervision of a contracting party.[46] According to Harris and Darcy, presumably employment on ships or aircrafts registered under the law of a contracting party is also covered by Article 19.[47]

Also interesting, in particular in times of (economic) crisis, is that the ECSR—as early as 1975—stated that the obligations deriving from Article 19§4 are

> increasing in importance and pose particular problems in a period when most Contracting Parties are suffering from economic recession. The countries concerned should take specific action to avoid discrimination to the extent that an increase of the level of unemployment is likely to have a particular impact on this (highly vulnerable) category of workers.[48]

(ii) Remuneration and Other Employment and Working Conditions

States are thus obliged to eliminate all legal and de facto discrimination concerning remuneration and other employment and working conditions, including in-service training and promotion.

As for the term 'employment', the ECSR recalled that this correlates in particular with Article 1 (right to work) and Articles 9, 10 and 15 of the Charter (respectively, on vocational guidance, training and rehabilitation).[49]

[45] Harris and Darcy (n 9) 221; Samuel (n 2) 413.

[46] See eg Conclusions IV; Conclusions VI, Germany and Norway; and Conclusions VIII, Norway.

[47] Harris and Darcy (n 9) 212.

[48] Conclusions IV—Statement of Interpretation (30/11/1975). Also in 2010, the ECSR stressed in an opinion on Recommendations 1910 and 1917 of the Parliamentary Assembly on 'the impact of the global economic crisis on migration in Europe' and on 'Migrants and refugees: a continuing challenge for the Council of Europe' the importance of Arts 18 and 19 in times of crisis. (ECSR, 'ECSR Activity Report 2010' (Strasbourg, European Social Charter, Directorate General of Human Rights and Legal Affairs, Council of Europe, 2011) 33). The importance the ECSR attaches to respect for equal treatment of migrants in times of crisis leads Harris and Darcy to argue that Art 19§4a also applies to redundancy (Harris and Darcy (n 9) 222).

[49] Committee of Independent Experts (n 22) 20.

In relation to access to employment, the ECSR case law seems to have shifted, because to begin with this was considered to be subject to Article 18 of the Charter,[50] whereas more recently the ECSR has found cases of non-conformity under Article 19§4.[51] Article 19§4a also applies to provisions in law guaranteeing the employment of persons who are obliged to return to their own country to perform military service.[52] As for vocational training, the ECSR stated that this also applies to the right of access to institutions offering vocational guidance, training and rehabilitation, and that for instance deciding that young foreigners can only become apprentices on the basis of a work permit[53] or that denial of access to vocational training to migrant workers, even if it only affects only some migrants, is incompatible with the Charter.[54]

As for the terms 'remuneration' and 'working conditions', the ECSR emphasised that this concerns particularly Article 2 (right to just conditions of work), Article 3 (right to safe and healthy working conditions) and Article 4 of the Charter (right to a fair remuneration).[55] In the ECSR's opinion, migrant workers should also enjoy certain advantages granted to national workers when changing jobs or taking up a first job, such as removal or settling-in allowances,[56] the same for receiving wages guaranteed to them after the employer terminated the contract for reasons not associated with the worker.[57] According to Harris and Darcy, further clarification of the scope of these terms can be found in Article 6 of ILO Convention No 97, which requires equal treatment in respect of 'remuneration, including family allowances where these form part of remuneration, hours of work, overtime arrangements, holidays with pay, restrictions on homework, minimum age for employment, apprenticeship and training, women's work and the work of young persons.'[58]

As for the issue of remuneration (in the wider sense), further clarification can be found in two ECSR decisions in relation to collective complaints.

[50] See Harris and Darcy (n 9) 222.

[51] For example, the ECSR considered restrictions on access to occupations for migrants, including that of doctor, dentist, pharmacist, seaman, docker, ophthalmologist and veterinarian not in conformity with the Charter (Conclusions 2011, Turkey). On the possibility of barring nationals of other states from occupying certain jobs, see S Deakin in this volume. A particular problem here is access of migrants to the civil service. See, for example, Conclusions VIII and Conclusions XIII-2.

[52] Conclusions XIII-2, Germany, repeated in—among others—Conclusions XIV-1 and Conclusions XVII-1. See also Swiatkowski (n 2) 350 and Samuel (n 2) 417.

[53] Conclusions XIII-3, Austria.

[54] Conclusions VII, United Kingdom.

[55] Committee of Independent Experts (n 22). For a more extensive analysis on these articles, see the chapters by K Lörcher and S Deakin in this volume.

[56] Conclusions III.

[57] Conclusions IV.

[58] Harris and Darcy (n 9) 222.

First, in its *Laval* decision[59] and although according to law it is admissible, regarding wages and other working conditions, to grant foreign posted workers, irrespective of their age or level of occupational experience and skills, minimum standards equivalent to those enjoyed by national workers under the correspondent central collective agreements (unless employers voluntarily grant more favourable conditions), the ECSR found a violation because

> in Sweden collective agreements do not very often provide for rules concerning minimum wages, and that the minimum wage can be considerably lower than the normal rate of pay generally applied throughout the country to Swedish workers (working in the same professional sector). In addition, minimum wages rules, when they are provided for by collective agreements, are normally applied only to people without occupational experience, such as young people; the collective agreements often oblige the employer to pay a higher rate to workers with professional experience and skills.[60]

On the other hand, the ECSR found no violation of Article E (on non-discrimination) in conjunction with Article 19§4 when the French authorities refused to grant civilian officials of the French military forces working/stationed in Germany a certain benefit in the career structure of public officials for the sole reason that their former contracts were private law contracts under German labour legislation. Using the criterion 'other status' mentioned in Article E, the ECSR considered that although they all were working abroad, there was no discrimination because of the different conditions of their recruitment and the legal status which applied to them.[61]

Finally, what is crystal-clear from the case law is that both in relation to equality of employment and working conditions, any length of residence requirement is contrary to the Charter.[62]

(iii) Membership of Trade Unions and Enjoyment of the Benefits of Collective Bargaining

The requirement in indent b) is identical to that in Article 6 of ILO Convention No 97 and obliges States to eliminate all legal and de facto discrimination concerning trade union membership[63] and as regards the enjoyment of the benefits of collective bargaining, including access to administrative and managerial posts in trade unions.[64] The ECSR stressed in that sense

[59] Collective Complaint No 85/2012.
[60] §§135 and 136 of the ECSR decision.
[61] Collective Complaint No 50/2008, *CFDT v France*.
[62] Council of Europe (n 47) 7.
[63] Conclusions XIII-3, Turkey. Repeated in Conclusions XIV-1 and Conclusions, XV-1.
[64] Conclusions VI, France.

that these issues concern also Article 5 (right to organise) and Article 6 (right to collective bargaining), in particular Article 6§2, and that thus discrimination observed in one of these matters may also give rise to a negative conclusion in respect of Article 19§4.[65]

The ECSR also consistently held that under 'membership of trade unions' Article 19§4b guarantees not only the right to join a trade union, but also to participate in trade union activities, including the right to be a founding member of a trade union.[66] This non-discrimination also extends to eligibility criteria for works councils and other official bodies in which management and labour participate in the State concerned, such as employment tribunals, social security institutions, public bodies representing trade and professions, etc.'[67] As for indent a) also here any length of residence requirement is contrary to the Charter.[68]

As regards enjoyment of the benefits of collective bargaining, the ECSR has clarified this further in its *Laval* decision. The ECSR considered the withdrawal of the requirement for foreign undertakings belonging to EEA countries, carrying out economic activities in Sweden, to appoint a contact person authorised to negotiate and conclude collective agreements with Swedish trade unions, as undermining the possibility for those trade unions to promote collective agreements with foreign employers, and thus violating Article 19§4b. Foreign undertakings should be treated equally by the host state when they provide services by using posted workers.[69] The ECSR also considered that prohibiting collective action if the employer shows that, as regards pay and other working terms, posted workers have conditions that are at least as favourable as the minimum conditions in a collective agreement concluded at central level is a violation of Article 19§4b, in particular

> when there is only a limited scope of working conditions that applies to those posted workers and which could be regulated in a collective agreement. Considering such a prohibition of collective action, it is unlikely that employers will agree to grant posted workers more favourable conditions, since there would be no effective negotiating methods to be used by posted workers to persuade their employer to agree on better conditions during their posting.[70]

[65] Committee of Independent Experts (n 22) 21.

[66] Conclusions 2011 and Conclusions XIX-4—Statement of Interpretation on Article 19§4 (both referring to Conclusions XIV-1, Turkey).

[67] Conclusions XIV-1 Addendum Conclusions XV-1, Luxembourg.

[68] Council of Europe (n 47) 8.

[69] ECSR decision, Collective Complaint No 85/2012 §§137–42.

[70] ibid §§135–36.

C. Remedies and Sanctions

Article 19§4 provides in the introductory sentence that ensuring equal treatment is 'subject to control of administrative authorities', and national governments indeed often report on controls made by inspectorate services to ensure compliance in practice. The ECSR case law does not, however, provide anything particular in relation to remedies and sanctions in the framework of Article 19§4. Given the importance of this article (a hard-core article) and the issue of migration and migrant workers as such (especially in the present situation), it might be worthwhile for the ECSR to elaborate this enforcement aspect in its future case law.

III. IMPACT

A. European Convention on Human Rights (ECHR)

As the ECHR pre-dates the Charter, there was of course no impact from Article 19§4 on the text of the ECHR. Research by Lörcher and Clauwaert on references to the Charter in European and national case law reveals that Article 19§4 has not yet been referred to in ECtHR case law.[71] However, it might be worth looking at how the ECtHR case law, as set forth in the *Gygusuz* judgment, could be further strengthened by using Article 19§4 as a reference.[72] In this case, the ECtHR considered the non-provision of emergency assistance under the Austrian Unemployment Insurance Act to a worker of Turkish origin who had paid contributions to the unemployment insurance fund on the same basis as Austrian workers to be a violation of Article 14 ECHR. The ECtHR considered a difference in treatment solely on the ground of 'national origin' not to be an 'objective and reasonable justification' under the ECHR, and thus discriminatory.

B. Charter of Fundamental Rights of the European Union (CFREU)

According to the explanations to the CFREU, Article 19 and in particular §4 has been a source of inspiration of Article 15(3) CFREU[73] and, according

[71] K Lörcher and S Clauwaert (2015) 'References to the (revised) European Social Charter in European and national case law', (version 02/04/2015—not published) 61.

[72] *Gaygusuz, v Austria* App no 17371/90 (ECtHR, 16 September 1996).

[73] Explanations to the Charter of Fundamental Rights, OJ C 303, 14/12/2007, 23. Art 15(3) CFREU reads: '3. Nationals of third countries who are authorised to work in the territories of the member states are entitled to working conditions equivalent to those of citizens of the Union.'

to Vigneau, Article 15(3) CFREU can be considered 'the consecration at European level of the principle of non-discrimination at work on the basis of nationality'.[74] Article 15(3) CFREU establishes also a principle of equal treatment as regards working conditions between EU citizens and non-EU citizens (thus including Council of Europe contracting parties not members of the EU). However, the scope of Article 15(3) CFREU appears to be narrower compared with Article 19 of the Charter. First, it only refers to 'nationals of third countries who are authorised to work' and thus seems to exclude those who work and/or reside without authorisation.[75] According to Ashiagbor, Article 15(3) as construed now does not change the legal positon of third-country nationals in terms of rights of access to national labour markets or free movement of workers and to do so would have had the effect of extending EU competences, which is contrary to the restriction in Article 51(2) of the CFREU.[76] Second, the horizontal and 'restrictive' Article 52(2) CFREU is also applicable to Article 15(3). Third, Article 15(3) only provides for a protection 'equivalent to those of citizens of the Union', whereby a literal interpretation of 'equivalent' has a narrower meaning than 'identical' or 'equal', and for Ashiagbor Article 15 therefore 'at first sight does not extend the principle of equal treatment to third country nationals with regard to rights *at* work'. A further limitation lies in the fact that according to the explanations, 'working conditions' are to be understood in the sense of Article 156 TFEU (former Article 137(2) TEC) which suggests an exclusion in relation to matters covered by Article 153(5) TFEU, such as pay, freedom of association and the right to strike. And Article 156 TFEU requires unanimity within the Council when acting on matters related to conditions of employment for third-country nationals legally residing in Community territory. Both Vigneau and Ashiagbor are of the opinion, however, that in relation to working conditions, Article 15(3) has to be read in conjunction with other articles of the CFREU as those provide rights to every worker, including third-country nationals (for example, protection against unjustified dismissal (Article 30), health and safety (Article 31(1)) and limits to working hours, rest periods and annual leave (Article 31(2)).[77]

[74] C Vigneau, '7. Freedom to choose an occupation and right to engage in work (Article 15)', in B Bercusson (ed), *European Labour Law and the EU Charter of Fundamental Rights* (Baden-Baden, Nomos Verlag, 2006) 189–90.

[75] According to Vigneau, earlier draft versions of Art 15(3) did refer to 'nationals of third countries who are authorised to reside in the territories of the member states', but it was changed at a late stage of the discussion of the draft CFREU (ibid 189).

[76] D Ashiagbor, 'Article 15', in S Peers, T Hervey, J Kenner and A Ward (eds), *The EU Charter of Fundamental Rights. A Commentary* (Oxford, Hart Publishing, 2014) 432.

[77] Vigneau (n 73) 190–91; Ashiagbor (n 75) 433.

In any case, it appears that Article 19§4, being a source of inspiration of Article 15(3) and given its larger scope, might thus in future offer a basis for a wider interpretation of Article 15(3) CFREU.

C. National Case Law Referring to the Charter

As mentioned before, Article 19§4 is, as far as is known, not yet referred to in national case law.[78]

[78] Lörcher and Clauwaert (n 70).

Article 20

The Right to Equal Opportunities and Equal Treatment in Matters of Employment and Occupation without Discrimination on The Grounds of Sex

CSILLA KOLLONAY-LEHOCZKY

Article 20—The right to equal opportunities and equal treatment in matters of employment and occupation without discrimination on the grounds of sex

With a view to ensuring the effective exercise of the right to equal opportunities and equal treatment in matters of employment and occupation without discrimination on the grounds of sex, the Parties undertake to recognise that right and to take appropriate measures to ensure or promote its application in the following fields:

a. access to employment, protection against dismissal and occupational reintegration;
b. vocational guidance, training, retraining and rehabilitation;
c. terms of employment and working conditions, including remuneration;
d. career development, including promotion.

Appendix:

Article 20

1. It is understood that social security matters, as well as other provisions relating to unemployment benefit, old age benefit and survivor's benefit, may be excluded from the scope of this article.
2. Provisions concerning the protection of women, particularly as regards pregnancy, confinement and the post-natal period, shall not be deemed to be discrimination as referred to in this article.
3. This article shall not prevent the adoption of specific measures aimed at removing de facto inequalities.

4. Occupational activities which, by reason of their nature or the context in which they are carried out, can be entrusted only to persons of a particular sex may be excluded from the scope of this article or some of its provisions. This provision is not to be interpreted as requiring the Parties to embody in laws or regulations a list of occupations which, by reason of their nature or the context in which they are carried out, may be reserved to persons of a particular sex.

I. INTRODUCTION

A. Context and Main Content

Historically, discrimination on grounds such as race, sex or religion has always been based on social hierarchy and dominance, rather than on objective and relevant differences between human beings. We all are different, however dominance is what makes differences qualitative and hierarchical.[1] Attributes of members of the dominant group appear as the (single) 'norm', differences are seen as marks of inferiority and preserve unjust inequality, resulting in manifest and prolonged disadvantages.

Historically in the world of labour, based on the 'male worker' standard, the biological differences between men and women were considered to amount to a qualitative disparity and a natural ground of disparate treatment. Besides such practices, mandatory protection with regard to women's maternal function and weaker physical make-up legally barred women from working and earning under equal conditions with men ('benign discrimination').[2] The role of male supremacy in unequal workplace opportunities remained unregarded until the last third of the twentieth century.[3]

Equality of men and women was not included in the 1961 ESC as a particular human rights principle. Article 1§2—the right to freely choose an occupation—prohibited discrimination on any ground. The only explicit reference to gender equality was the obligation of states to recognise the right of men and women to equal pay for work of equal value under Article 4§3, besides the inclusion of gender in the non-discrimination clause of the Preamble. This approach to equality was similar to the then

[1] See: C MacKinnon, 'Difference and Dominance: On Sex Discrimination' [1984], in KT Bartlett and R Kennedy (eds), *Feminist Legal Theory* (Boulder, Westview Press, 1991) 82–83, 87.

[2] A seminal case of such discrimination was *Muller v Oregon* 208 US 412, 1908 in the United States.

[3] FE Olsen, 'The family and the market: A study of ideology and reform' (1983) 96 *Harvard Law Review* esp 1505–06.

legal framework of the European Community: no general rule on gender equality, only—competition-motivated—pay equality gained acceptance in Article 119 EEC Treaty, now Article 157(1) and 157(2).

The ESC had a broader phrasing already at adoption: the principle of equal pay had to be applied for 'work of equal value', reflecting the guidance of ILO Convention C-100 on Equal Pay, while Article 119 of the Treaty originally guaranteed 'equal pay for equal work' only.[4]

Article 20 was originally added to the Charter by the 1988 Additional Protocol, Article 1 on the right to equal opportunities and equal treatment in matters of employment and occupation without discrimination on the grounds of sex.

This provision can be considered a compromise. On the basis of the Declaration of Human Rights of 27 April 1978,[5] proclaiming the decision of the member states of the Council of Europe to explore 'the possibility of extending the lists of rights of the individual, notably rights in the social, economic and cultural field',[6] various bodies (committees) were instructed 'to consider whether there are any rights which might be suitable for inclusion in the European Convention on Human Rights'. The initiative failed on the lasting perception that only civil and political rights—usually requiring non-interference—were capable of government protection and that social and economic rights could only be gradually and progressively realised, not as individual rights. The result was that, instead of adding new, immediately enforceable social or economic rights to the Convention, the rights under the Charter were extended by the adoption of the 1988 Protocol.[7] The headway of criticism of that one-sided approach and the progress of opposite views was obvious by the early 1990s; nonetheless, the right to equal treatment of men and women in employment and occupation did not attain the status of individually justiciable right when added to the Charter as Article 20.

Article A§1b of the Charter—determining the hard-core provisions—added Article 20 (together with Article 7) to the former list of hard-core articles, with reference to their particular importance.[8]

It is an equality norm by its heading, but still the Committee approached it, when first assessing implementation, as a provision of a dynamic nature and decided to assess the situation at a given moment with regard to the progress achieved and ongoing efforts.[9] This first approach changed over

[4] It was Council Directive 75/117/EEC on the application of the principle of equal pay for men and women that corrected the wording, and later the Amsterdam Treaty (Art 141) took it over.

[5] Committee of Ministers, 62nd Session.

[6] *Yearbook of the European Convention of Human Rights*, s 8, III, 82–83.

[7] V Shrubsall, 'The Additional Protocol to the European Social Charter—Employment Rights' (1989) 18 *Industrial Law Journal*, 40.

[8] Explanatory Report, s 122

[9] Conclusions XIII-3, 419.

time and this provision now requires countries to have obtained 'results': discrimination eliminated in law and practice and adequate sanctions. The dynamic nature is also reflected in the requirement of progress in promoting equal opportunities through 'positive measures'.

B. Relationship to Other International Sources

International acknowledgement of the equality of men and women as a part and principle of human rights started after the Second World War and went through a gradual development from formal equality (coupled questionably with protection) to various ways and forms of equal opportunities in today's developed countries. However, de facto equality and genuine gender diversity at all economic and social levels still have a long way to go.

The UN Charter[10] and the UN Universal Declaration of Human Rights (UDHR)[11] declared respect for and protection of human rights without distinction on any ground, including sex. For more detailed protection the United Nation later adopted two further documents on the protection of universal human rights: the International Covenant on Civil and Political Rights (ICCPR) and the International Covenant on Economic, Social and Cultural Rights (ICESCR).[12] They follow an identical line on equality: in Article 2 of both there is a provision for the equal protection of the rights recognised in the Covenant, and then, in a separate and explicit provision, Article 3 specifically declares the undertaking of the Party States to ensure the equal enjoyment of the right guaranteed in that document by men and women.[13] These provisions are to be applied in conjunction with one or more of the broad range of specific rights guaranteed under the treaty.[14] In contrast, Article 20 is a 'stand-alone' provision on equal treatment of women and men applicable in all situations of employment and occupation.

ILO labour standards have promoted the principle of equality since the foundation of this organisation in 1919. The road has been laced with detours giving priority to (discriminatory) physical protection over equal opportunity. As a result of the evolving idea of equality, resulting from the changing roles of men and women in society, the approach has changed significantly.

[10] Art 1§3

[11] Art 2.

[12] Both were adopted in 1966 and entered into force in 1976. The division between the two groups of rights was mainly a result of the political division of the world then into two 'blocs' or 'camps'.

[13] Arts 3 of both the ICCPR and the ICESCR.

[14] Arts 6–15 in Pt III, of which Arts 6–8 relate to work and employment, and Art 9 to social security.

There are instruments now that refer explicitly to gender equality and non-discrimination between men and women, such as the Convention on equal remuneration between women and men 1951 (No 100), or the UN Declaration on the Elimination of Violence against Women (1994), which extends also to work and educational institutions. Other ILO instruments prohibit discrimination in employment on several grounds, including sex, such as the Discrimination (Employment and Occupation) Convention 1958 (No 111) and the Termination of Employment Convention 1982 (No 158).

In the process of combatting stereotypes, particular significance is to be attributed to ILO conventions that do not mention either discrimination, or men or women, but do address areas that expose predominantly women to unfavourable working conditions. These include the conventions on workers with family responsibilities (1981, No 156), part-time workers (1994, No 175), home workers (1996, No 177) and decent work for domestic workers (2011, No 189). These treaties promote gender equality by the undifferentiated extension of protection to both men and women.

The most important UN instrument comprehensively protecting the right of women to be free from discrimination is the Convention on the Elimination of All Forms of Discrimination against Women (CEDAW), adopted in 1979. It not only covers employment, but prohibits any distinction, exclusion or restriction impairing or nullifying the equal exercise by women of human rights and fundamental freedoms in the political, economic, social, cultural, civil or any other field.

Two further features—distinct from Article 20—have to be mentioned: it has a basically negative approach and a one-way prohibition. It is predominantly a prohibiting instrument; positive measures eliminating social differences resulting from historical discrimination have a limited role under this treaty. Furthermore, taking into account the enormous asymmetry between discrimination occurring against women and against men, it deals with the elimination of discrimination against women only, and not sex-based discrimination in general.

This is significantly different from the European instruments' 'binary' approach in prohibiting discrimination in a symmetric way, against men and women, notwithstanding that EU policy also makes a conscious effort to promote equal opportunity of women in the member states. Article 23 CFREU similarly requires equality for both women and men. Positive measures are not required, just permitted, providing for specific advantages in favour of the 'under-represented' sex.

The European Social Charter reflected the same conceptual development from the unequal perception of equality to a more substantive progress to equality, from pure protection (benevolently limiting the equal opportunities of women) to the equal protection of both men and women with regard to employment and social conditions with regard to their autonomy and dignity.

The text of Article 20 is based on the 'binary' approach: it prohibits discrimination on the ground of sex, male or female. At the same time, it also mandates equal opportunities and equal treatment in employment and occupation. This 'equal opportunity' part of the undertaking, by its reference to 'existing inequalities', focuses distinctly on women. This double nature of Article 20 indicates the differences in the concept of discrimination and corresponding state obligations.

C. Relation to Other Charter Provisions

Article 20 is interconnected with a significant number of other articles of the Charter. Because equal treatment is a principle and a horizontal norm, it is connected to all provisions that, by their material scope, overlap with the scope of Article 20 (areas of employment, occupation, training or social security).

Two groups of provisions that have special relevance for Article 20 can be identified in the Charter. The first group comprises those provisions that also explicitly target non-discrimination. Articles 1§2, 4§3 and 8 already protected equal treatment in the field of employment and occupation under the 1961 Charter. Article 20 'entails greater commitment' than these provisions,[15] increasing the scope of protection, in part by not only prohibiting discrimination but also requiring the promotion of equal treatment by positive measures. Articles 26 and 27 were also added to complement gender equality in specific areas (protecting dignity in the workplace and protection against discrimination with regard to family responsibilities). They not only complete equality protection in an implicit, indirect way, but, especially under Article 27, also in a more far-reaching way by contributing to the dismantling of gender role stereotypes in the long run.[16]

The other group of articles related to Article 20 contain provisions that do not protect against discrimination either explicitly or implicitly, but when implemented without discrimination (following from Article E) they can contribute significantly to increasing the equal opportunities of women in employment. Such provisions are laid down by Articles 1§4, 9, 10 and 15 on vocational guidance, training, retraining and rehabilitation, and also have particular significance with regard to matters of occupational reintegration. All these areas are defined by Article 20a and b as fields in which the Parties are obliged to take measures to ensure and promote the right to

[15] Conclusions Cycle XIII-3, 419.
[16] See the chapter on Art 27 by I Schömann.

equal treatment and equal opportunity.[17] Article 12 on social security and also Article 24 on protection against termination of employment without a valid reason can be added to the list of Charter articles interrelated with Article 20. The connection with Article 12—besides the explicit coverage of equal treatment in social security—extends to the examination of wage equality inasmuch as the sufficiently wide definition of pay may include rights and benefits in an occupational pension scheme.[18]

The overlap with the three 'predecessors'—Articles 1§2, 4§3 and 8—deserves more attention.

Article 1§2 is about the freedom to choose an occupation without discrimination (or force). It prohibits discrimination on any ground, including sex. Thus, it is more general regarding the grounds of the prohibition, while Article 20 is more specific, protecting equal treatment only with regard to sex, but protecting equality in respect of a broader material scope. The material scope of the prohibition of discrimination under Article 1§2 is unclear. The focus of the text is free entry to a chosen occupation; early interpretations extended its scope to further aspects of employment.[19]

Article 20 goes beyond Article 1§2 also in respect of the obligation not only to prohibit discrimination but also to promote equal opportunities and the equal position of women on the labour market by positive measures. Thus, as it is worded in the Digest of the case law, Article 20 is a *lex specialis* for the protection of gender equality; when assessing Article 1§2, issues of sex discrimination are not particularly scrutinised by the Committee for countries that have accepted both Article 1§2 and Article 20.[20]

Article 4§3 on equal pay is fully absorbed by Article 20; there is no element of this provision that is not addressed by Article 20 and also with a more up-to-date approach, paying attention to eliminating barriers by way of achieving equal compensation. For this reason, the interpretation of equal pay under Article 20 applies also to Article 4§3.

Article 8 needs special mention for its radical alteration by the adoption of Article 20. Limiting its personal scope to 'pregnant women and women who have recently given birth and women nursing their infants', it increased the power of this provision to promote genuine equal opportunities for women. An indirect and implied effect of restricting protection to maternity by the adoption of Article 20 is the changed approach to the norms of Articles 2 and 3: the right to fair, healthy and safe working conditions now protect

[17] See also: J Darcy and D J Harris, *The European Social Charter*. Ardsley, NY Transnational Publishers, 2001. 2nd ed. 240.

[18] Conclusion 2008, Netherlands.

[19] See more on the interpretation of Art 1§2 in the chapter by Simon Deakin in this volume.

[20] While Art 1§2 is accepted by all Parties, Germany, Iceland, Luxembourg, Poland and the United Kingdom—each still under the 1961 Charter—are the only exceptions, not yet accepting Art 1 of the 1988 Protocol.

male and female workers equally when working under hard, unusual or strenuous conditions.[21]

II. CONTENT

Article 20 lays down the duty of state parties to recognise and promote the right of all workers to equal opportunities and equal treatment in matters of employment and occupation, without discrimination on the grounds of sex.

A. Personal and Material Scope

The text of Article 20 is silent about the personal scope of the provision.[22] It is indicated by Part I of the Charter and gives a practically unlimited definition: 'all workers' have the right to equal treatment. The principle of equal treatment must be applied to anyone who is a worker.

The personal scope extends to all workers working in the private or public sector. Not only employees, but also independent contractors, the self-employed and anyone performing work for someone else are protected. With regard to equal pay, this overall coverage extending to all areas of the economy and all forms of employment was expressly established by the Committee. The personal scope was further expanded by the Explanatory Report to Article 1 of the 1988 Additional Protocol (the predecessor of Article 20): 'The term "workers" ... shall be taken to include unemployed persons, persons seeking employment, those undergoing vocational training and all other potential workers.'[23]

The broadly defined material scope covers employment and social security.

As regards employment, the text of Article 20 specified four areas encompassing most possible aspects of employment:

a. access to employment, protection against dismissal and occupational reintegration;
b. vocational guidance, training, retraining and rehabilitation;
c. terms of employment and working conditions, including remuneration;
d. career development, including promotion.

(i) Access to Work and Labour Market Services

Non-discrimination in access to employment and protection against discriminatory dismissal is part of Article 1§2, too, while the inclusion

[21] See the chapters on Arts 2 and 3 by K Lörcher in this volume.
[22] In contrast to Art 8, for example, which expressly refers to 'employed women'.
[23] S 18 of the Explanatory Report.

of 'occupational reintegration'[24] in sub-paragraph (a) shows the progress compared with the 1961 approach.

The protection of equal right of access to employment should mean not only the prohibition of the exclusion of women from access to certain types of jobs, but also protection in advertisements and the whole selection process (prohibiting discriminatory tests, interviews, certain questions relating to family burden and so on).

Equal treatment of men and women has to be guaranteed at each stage of employment, including dismissal. Regulatory discrimination on dismissals is scarce; however, when it comes up, the case law of the Committee reflects consistent rigour. For example, it found that Turkish law violated Article 20 by exempting small employers (those with fewer than 30 employees) from observing non-discrimination when dismissing employees with less than six months' employment at the firm.[25]

Article 20 sub-paragraphs (a), (b) and (d) require more than just equality in getting and keeping a job. Equality involves the adoption of programmes that, with regard to the different situation of women in family and social life, help to reinstate or upgrade their position in the labour market after situations of interruption, drop-out or involuntary stepping back from an achieved position. Such possible measures range from regulating the return to the job following maternity leave or parental leave[26] to undertaking training at the request of the employer, which is paid as working time,[27] and the promotion of returning to the labour market not only by gender-neutral means but also by efficient vocational guidance and training.

Labour market services, enumerated in sub-paragraph (b) of Article 20, are also included in the state obligations undertaken by ratifying Article 1§4 and more specifically under Articles 9, 10 and 15, and in principle all these provisions fall under the non-discrimination principle laid down in Article E. Such measures are frequently established not specifically for women, but for all vulnerable groups that have difficulties with professional reintegration (together with young people, persons over a certain age and persons with disabilities). The addition under Article 20 is the special emphasis on the particular promotion of the resumption of employment by women after a voluntary or involuntary break, moving from one job to another without a break, possibly after retraining. The term 'retraining' covers any supplementary training to enable workers to adapt their knowledge and skills to industrial, technological and scientific progress.[28] Specific measures may include

[24] 'Occupational resettlement' in the original wording of the Protocol—a concept that, according to the Explanatory Report (s 21) does not appear as such in the 1961 ESC.

[25] Conclusions 2012, Turkey.

[26] Overlapping here with Art 27§1(a).

[27] Conclusions XV-2, Slovakia.

[28] Explanatory Report to Art 1§2 of the 1988 Protocol, s 21.

those of the kind adopted by Spain, aiming at the professional reintegration of women who have been victims of domestic violence, by providing financial aid for companies recruiting such women,[29] demonstrating a genuine intention on the side of government.

(ii) Terms and Conditions of Employment

The expression 'terms of employment and working conditions' in subparagraph (c) refers to all rights and situations associated with the position of the worker in his or her occupational relations and working environment.

The text expressly includes remuneration, and thereby the principle of 'equal pay for work of equal value' laid down in Article 4§3. This provision is wider in scope than the principle of 'equal pay for work of equal value' under Article 4§3. It extends the concept of pay and requires progress in decreasing the gender pay gap. According to the Explanatory Report to the Protocol, Article 1 (s 23), 'Remuneration' shall mean 'basic or minimum wages or salary plus all other benefits paid directly or indirectly in cash or kind by the employer to the worker by reason of the latter's employment'.[30]

The material scope of Article 20 guarantees equal treatment with regard to social security that implies the absence of any discrimination on grounds of sex, particularly as far as the scope of schemes, conditions of access to schemes, the calculation of benefits and the length of entitlement to benefits are concerned.[31]

According to the Appendix, social security matters, as well as other provisions relating to unemployment benefit, old age benefit and survivor's benefit may be excluded from the scope of Article 20.[32] This power had to be exercised, not necessarily by a declaration, at the time of ratification of the Protocol or later, when accepting further articles; nonetheless, the exclusion has to be indicated explicitly, as requested by the Committee.[33] No country has taken this opportunity of exclusion; no such declaration has been made. Instead, most countries have made a declaration of their intent to observe the principle of equal treatment in matters relating to social security. The right to equal treatment in social security is progressively extended to areas formerly not covered (equalising survivors' benefits, sickness pay,[34] extension of the eligibility to pensions,[35] access to social security benefits).[36]

29 Conclusions XIX-1, Spain.
30 See also Conclusions XIII-5, 257–58.
31 Conclusions 2008, Armenia, Georgia; Conclusions 2012, Russian Federation.
32 Appendix, Protocol Art 1.
33 Cycle XIII-3, 418.
34 Conclusions XV-1, Malta, Art 12§1.
35 Conclusions 2002, Netherlands.
36 Conclusions 2006, Romania.

B. The Concept of Non-discrimination and Equality

Several layers of the concept of non-discrimination, equal treatment and equal opportunity have been developed in the theory and in the various legal regimes. The difference between a negative approach (merely prohibiting discrimination) or a positive one (guaranteeing equality) is identified with the difference of the formal versus substantive concept of equality.[37] This approach prohibits discrimination on the ground of sex, but goes beyond 'blind', formal equal treatment and requires state parties to take steps for genuine equal opportunities and the resulting elimination of social differences between the genders.

(i) Prohibition of Discrimination

The principle of equal treatment of women and men is understood to mean the absence of any discrimination on grounds of sex, whether direct or indirect.[38] The concept of direct discrimination is not specified under Article 20, but instead under Article E. It is defined as a difference in treatment between people in comparable situations that does not pursue a legitimate aim and is not based on objective and reasonable grounds.[39]

Article 20 prohibits differentiation on the ground of sex with regard to access to work of a physically demanding nature. Several countries were even recently (in 2012) found in violation of the principle of equal treatment, for prohibiting the employment of women in underground or underwater work, night work or work of an otherwise labour-intensive or arduous nature (for example, in the construction industry).[40]

While not explicitly required, it is viewed positively by the Committee when national law contains explicit prohibitions against asking about pregnancy, adoption or family plans during the recruitment process.[41]

Pay discrimination takes place when women are paid unequally for the same or equivalent work. Determining the comparability of work must be based on the objective criteria—from multiple aspects—of the job, and not on the personal characteristics of the worker (for example,

[37] In the context of the Charter the idea of 'substantive equality' has particular relevance—addressing social disadvantages as a non-discrimination issue and targeting 'equality of results' instead of 'equality of opportunity' only. See: S Fredman, *Discrimination Law* (Oxford, OUP, 2011) 25–28; S Fredman, 'Positive duties and socio-economic disadvantage: bringing disadvantage onto the equality agenda' (2010) 3 *European Human Rights Law Review* 290.

[38] Conclusions XIII-5, Sweden, Art 1 of the Protocol.

[39] *Syndicat national des Professions du Tourisme v France*, Collective Complaint No 6/1999, Decision on the merits of 10.10.2000 §25.

[40] Conclusions 2012, Cyprus, Moldova, Slovenia, Turkey, Azerbaijan.

[41] Conclusions 2012, Norway.

willingness to work overtime or muscular strength).[42] Any form of variable remuneration—namely task- or output-based pay—must be established on the basis of the same unit of measurement.[43] Remuneration calculated on the basis of working time must be the same.

From the very first assessments under the 1988 Protocol, the Committee expected contracting states to permit comparison of wages beyond the given enterprise or undertaking, because if comparison could only be made with reference to the salary scale of the same enterprise, this amounted to a restrictive application of the principle of equal pay.[44] The Committee especially considered looking outside the enterprise of fundamental importance for a system of objective job evaluation, 'in particular in enterprises where the workforce is largely, or even exclusively, female'.[45]

In 2012 the Committee clarified the expected scope of equal pay comparison. Maintaining that meaningful comparison may require to make pay comparisons across companies, it laid down that, at the very least, legislation should require pay comparisons across companies in one or more of the following situations:

> — cases in which statutory rules apply to the working and pay conditions in more than one company;
> — cases in which several companies are covered by a collective works agreement or regulations governing the terms and conditions of employment;
> — cases in which the terms and conditions of employment are laid down centrally for more than one company within a holding [company] or conglomerate.[46]

It is important to add that this statement on Article 20 has been declared as 'the very least' requirement for going beyond the company, and it was issued as guidance for requirements in individual pay-discrimination litigation, and not as a limit on the implementation of equal pay policy and obligations under the Charter.[47]

In the 2014 Conclusions the Committee established a direct link between its Article 4§3 equal remuneration case law and the 'single source' approach of the CJEU by express reference to the determining *Lawrence* and *Allonby* cases.[48] This idea of looking beyond the company for comparison only if there is a 'single source' and thereby some body responsible for pay equality can be found in the background,[49] rather limits than broadens the scope of

[42] Darcy and Harris (n 17) 81; Conclusions XII-1, Greece; XIII-1, Norway; and XIII-2, Germany.

[43] Conclusions 2014, Portugal.

[44] Conclusions XIII-3, ch 4, Art 1, Finland.

[45] Conclusions XIII-5, 271, reiterated in Conclusions XVI-2, Portugal.

[46] Introduction §14, Statement of Interpretation of Art 20.

[47] See: eg Conclusions 2012, Spain, Georgia.

[48] Conclusions 2014, Andorra, Austria, Bulgaria, Lithuania, Netherlands, Norway, Portugal, Romania.

[49] Case C-320/00 *AG Lawrence v Regent Office Care Ltd*, §§18–19, followed by Case C-256/01 *Debra Allonby v Accrington & Rossendale College and Others* §§ 46, 48.

comparison, and may mean a retreat in the interpretation of Article 20 and Article 4§3 if applied as a general framework for the interpretation of states' obligations in guaranteeing equal payment.

Indirect discrimination occurs when men and women are disproportionately affected by a seemingly neutral provision without legitimate reason (for example, unequal treatment of full-time and part-time employees may amount to indirect discrimination). This formulation is similar to the concept of indirect discrimination under EU law.[50] The Committee particularly examined whether the equal treatment of full-time and part-time workers is fully secured.[51] The examination led the Committee to excessive rigour: whenever differentiation disadvantaging groups of part-timers was reported, it automatically found indirect sex discrimination, presuming a disproportionate presence of women in the affected group. Sweden was repeatedly found in violation of the equality principle with regard to social security, because legislation required a minimum working time (three hours per day or 17 hours per week) in order to be entitled to unemployment insurance. Because part-timers are mainly women, without scrutinising the actual composition and size of the group of people affected, the Committee found that the regulation constituted indirect sex discrimination. Later, having become aware of the real proportion of men and women in the group, the assessment changed.[52] Besides this single case,[53] no violation of gender equality in matters of social security was found.

The concept of 'indirect discrimination' developed by the ECSR has a progressive interpretation, leading from targeting formal to substantive equality. It takes the view that indirect discrimination may arise not only from measures disadvantaging members of protected groups in disproportionate numbers, but also from failing to take due and positive account of all relevant differences[54] or by failing to take adequate steps to ensure that the rights and collective advantages that are open to all are genuinely accessible by and to all.[55]

When state inactivity (insufficient monitoring, weak cooperation between ministries and relevant agencies) is combined with a very low level of female employment,[56] or when simply '[n]o particular steps were taken to promote

[50] Art 2.1(b) of the Recast Directive (Dir 2006/54).

[51] See Conclusions XVII-2.

[52] Conclusions 2012, Sweden.

[53] Ireland might be the next 'candidate' for a similar controversy. See Conclusions 2012, Ireland.

[54] *Autisme-Europe v France*, Collective Complaint No 13/2000, decision on the merits of 04.10.2003 §52.

[55] *ERRC v Italy*, Collective Complaint No 27/2004, decision on the merits of 07.12.2005 §36.

[56] Conclusions 2012, Bosnia and Herzegovina.

women's access to employment',[57] the Committee considered the national situation to violate the equality principle contained in Article 20.

Similarly, states must promote positive measures to narrow the pay gap, including measures to improve the quality and coverage of wage statistics and steps to ensure that more attention is paid to equal pay for women and men in national action plans for employment.[58]

While positive action under EU law[59] is only permitted, under the Charter it is also an obligation. By this duality of the meaning of positive action, Article 20 of the Charter marks out the path for the future development of the concept of equality.

C. Exceptions to the Principle of Equal Treatment

The Appendix to Article 20 establishes three 'exceptions' to the principle of the prohibition of discrimination on the ground of sex.[60] The three situations laid down as exceptions are the following:

- provisions concerning the protection of women, particularly as regards pregnancy, confinement and the post-natal period;
- specific measures aimed at removing de facto inequalities;
- occupational activities which, by reason of their nature or the context in which they are carried out, can be entrusted only to persons of a particular sex.

(i) Protecting Women

The first situation defined as an 'exception' reflects an outdated approach to gender equality when women's differences (reproductive capacity) were considered 'non-standard' attributes of a 'worker' that—to provide them with equal opportunities—needed privileges or 'positive discrimination'. Such a view was becoming outdated as an understanding of gender equality by the time of the drafting of the 1988 Protocol. Reproductive functions are standard workers' attributes that need due respect and accommodation, like any other relevant features (for example, sick pay, extra pay or time off in return for irregular working hours or conditions, longer holidays for senior

[57] See: Conclusions XX-1, Protocol Art 1, Netherlands Aruba, Netherlands Caribbean.

[58] Conclusions 2014, Armenia, Andorra.

[59] Directive 2006/54/EU (Recast), Art 3.

[60] Paras 2–4 of Appendix to Art 20. Under the 1988 Protocol, these provisions were included in separate paragraphs (paras 2–4) of Art 1. The change of the place of the provisions does not affect their nature; under Art N of the Charter these provisions are an integral part of the Charter, with the same obligatory nature.

workers, counting study periods or long distance commuting as working time; none of these things is considered 'positive discrimination'). Related provisions in national laws are not considered 'exemptions' from, but rather inherent in the principle of equal treatment.

The word 'particularly' indicates 'that other kinds of protection, essential in other situations, are admissible',[61] bringing back the idea of protective discrimination under Article 8§4 of the 1961 Charter. In order to observe that the Protocol 'shall not prejudice the provisions of the Charter',[62] the Explanatory Report attempts to reconcile the conflict:

> 25 ... It is understood that where several texts coexist, the provision most favourable to the persons concerned shall prevail. It is, however, acknowledged that in this particular context (equality between the sexes) it will sometimes be difficult to establish which measure is the most favourable to women, as opinions may differ. Account will need to be taken of changing attitudes in this regard.

Taking proper account of changed attitudes, the ECSR has consistently considered such 'other' (non-maternity related) protections (typically, banning night work and certain physically demanding jobs) as a violation of the prohibition of discrimination on grounds of sex. The Committee has consistently emphasised that prohibiting women from performing night work while authorising men to do so is contrary to the principle of equal treatment for night work, which is just as detrimental to men as to women.[63]

(ii) Positive Measures, Promoting Equality

Measures aimed at removing inequalities[64] may be, but are not necessarily 'discrimination'. Applying quotas is a clear form of disparate treatment and—albeit not undisputed—might be permissible to expedite the elimination of continuing de facto inequalities generally affecting women. Such measures—relatively scarce and mainly related to public employment[65]—shall be transitional and repealed gradually once equality has been achieved.[66] The controversial nature of such measures is illustrated by the 2006 French Act establishing quotas for balanced gender representation in professional bodies (boards of public and private companies, work councils, staff committees), which was annulled by the Constitutional Council, on the ground

[61] Explanatory Report s 24.

[62] Art 8 of the 1988 Protocol.

[63] Conclusions XVII-2, Netherlands (Aruba), Art 1 of the Protocol.

[64] Art 1, para 3 of the Appendix to Art 20 of the Charter.

[65] For example, Spain took measures on parity in the composition of selection bodies and tribunals. Likewise, a 5% quota is reserved for women for positions in the armed forces. Conclusions XIX-1.

[66] Explanatory Report, s 26.

that quotas in this field were forbidden. The Committee has not commented on this decision and has repeated its former positive conclusion.[67]

Quotas in the education system are also assessed and accepted when objectively justified by insufficient balance of the sexes among apprentices and limited in time.[68] The Committee follows such measures with increased attention even beyond the area of employment and occupation.[69]

Less direct forms of promoting substantive equality, in contrast to quotas, range from permitted differential treatment to positive measures, and may even be required for compliance.

(iii) Genuine Occupational Requirements

Certain occupational activities—but not whole occupations![70]—which, by reason of their nature or the context in which they are carried out, can be entrusted only to persons of a particular sex[71] may be excluded from the scope of Article 20, and similarly the training required for them. States are not required to adopt laws or regulations containing lists of such activities; however, they have an obligation to report on any such exclusion and the reasons for and criteria governing such reservation.[72] The soft warning, that the 'Parties will bear in mind that the intention is to gradually reduce the number of excluded activities to a strict minimum' raises doubts about the types and scope of exclusions; that is, whether they are too broad and permissive.

The exclusion may be based either on the nature or on the 'context in which [certain occupations] are carried out' as a factor that may warrant their being reserved to workers of a particular sex. Such circumstances should ordinarily be quite exceptional. These terms are accordingly to be construed restrictively.[73] Religious communities may establish exceptions.[74]

In determining whether, because of the conditions in which police activities are conducted, sex constitutes a decisive factor in the police force, the army and so on, states may take account of public order or national security-related requirements, provided that they are prescribed by law, pursue a legitimate aim and are necessary in a democratic society (Article G). Like any measure that derogates from the rights guaranteed by the Charter,

[67] Conclusions 2008, France.

[68] Conclusions XV, Norway.

[69] For example, asking for information on temporary provisions in Italy on reserved quotas for women among candidates for EU Parliament elections (at least one-third—resulting in increased (19%) representation in 2004). Conclusions 2006, Italy.

[70] See the mistaken wording in Explanatory Report, s 27.

[71] Appendix to Art 20§4.

[72] Explanatory Report, s 27.

[73] ibid s 28.

[74] Conclusions 2012, Norway.

the exception must be interpreted restrictively and not exceed the legitimately pursued aim.[75]

D. State Duties

By ratifying Article 20, Parties undertake the obligation to 'ensure' or to 'promote' the application of the right to equal treatment. The obligation in question may be met as much by government action (legislation, regulations and so on) as by action by employers and labour (collective agreements) or individuals (bilateral agreements and contracts).[76]

Thus, the states have the following obligations, which are almost identical to those regarding equal pay and other equal treatment requirements:

— to promulgate the rights in legislation;
— to take legal measures designed to ensure the effectiveness of the right; that is, legal measures must provide for the nullity of clauses in collective agreements and individual contracts which are contrary to the principle, also for adequate appeal procedures where the right has been violated and for the effective protection of workers against any retaliatory measures (dismissal or other measures) taken as a result of their demand to benefit from the right;
— to define an active policy and to take practical measures to implement it.[77]

All of these elements have to be guaranteed in law and in practice in respect of the full range of areas belonging to the material scope of Article 20.

(i) Legal Framework

States have the obligation to enact legislation that guarantees the right of women and men to equality by a sufficiently detailed law,[78] including the express legislative provision of the right of women to equal pay for work of equal value.[79] The mere statement of the principle in the Constitution does not suffice. States 'are obliged to enact legislation explicitly imposing equal

[75] The situation in Greece was found to be incompatible with the Charter on the ground that 'the restrictions on the admission of women to the police college and the corresponding exclusion of women from 85% of police duties constitute direct discrimination based on sex that has not been shown to be necessary in a democratic society to protect the public interest or national security or to be justified by the nature of the activities in question' (Conclusions XVI-2, Greece, Protocol Art 1).

[76] Explanatory Report, 20.

[77] Introduction to Conclusions XIII-3, 418, recalled in Conclusion XIII-5, Sweden.

[78] Conclusions XIII-3, Statement of Interpretation of Art 1 of the Protocol.

[79] Conclusions XV-2 (2001), Addendum, Slovak Republic, Protocol, Art 1.

treatment in all aspects.'[80] The legal regulation must be clear and concrete with regard to each area in which equality has to be regulated, not remain vague or contain only very general terms.[81]

The adequate legal framework requires, furthermore, the adoption of laws, administrative or other measures that positively promote equality in all covered areas, taking into consideration also the role and potential of the parties in industrial relations and collective agreements.

Second, any legislation, regulation or other administrative measure that fails to comply with the equality principle must be repealed or revoked. The non-application of discriminatory legislation is not sufficient for a situation to be considered compatible with the Charter.[82] Furthermore, states are responsible for ensuring that parties withdraw, repeal or amend any provision in collective agreements, employment contracts or firms' internal regulations that is incompatible with the principle of equal treatment.[83]

Under the Charter the mere absence of discrimination would not mean that the state has met all its obligations. The legal measures (legislative, administrative or other measures including collective agreements) are expected not only to abolish all existing discriminatory provisions, but also to adopt sufficiently detailed law explicitly imposing equal treatment.

(ii) Right of Appeal and Adequate Remedies

National legislation must provide for appropriate and effective remedies in the event of violation of the principle of non-discrimination.

Employees who consider that they have suffered discrimination must be able to take their case to a court or tribunal.[84]

The requirements and standards regarding the procedure and remedies deriving from gender discrimination at the workplace, including pay discrimination, are no different from those applicable under Article 1§2. That is, the arrangements and standards for the shift of the burden are consistently examined according to the established requirements, and the lack of such regulation results in finding a violation of Article 20.[85]

Adequate compensation, similar to other discrimination cases, has to be sufficient to make good the damage suffered by the victim and act as a deterrent to the offender. It has to include the reinstatement of employment and

[80] Conclusions XVII-2, Netherlands (Aruba), Protocol, Art 1.

[81] See, for example, Conclusions XV-2, Addendum, Slovak Republic: non-compliance due to the prohibition in only very general terms. Conclusions 2012, Bulgaria: the ECSR's inquiry because of the country's reluctance to enact a special law on gender equality.

[82] Slovak Republic, ibid.

[83] Conclusions XIII-5, Statement of Interpretation of Art 20.

[84] Conclusions XIII-3, Statement of Interpretation of Art 20.

[85] Conclusions 2004, Romania, 495. Conclusions 2012, Azerbaijan.

compensation for any pecuniary damage suffered in the event of unlawful or unfair dismissal.[86]

A number of other legal steps should be taken to make the right of appeal fully effective, such as authorising trade unions and other bodies to take action in employment discrimination cases, including action on behalf of individuals[87] or setting up an independent body to promote equal treatment and provide legal assistance to victims.[88] The ECSR consistently has asked for information on the forms of trade union involvement and on their roles in the prevention and correction of discrimination at the workplace.[89]

The right of appeal, adequate compensation (including the issue of the upper limit) is interpreted by analogy with the case law in relation to Articles 1§2 and 8§2.[90]

Employees who try to enforce their right to equality must be legally protected against any form of reprisals from their employers,[91] including not only dismissal, but also downgrading, changes to working conditions and so on. National legislation must provide for the same consequences where an employee is a victim of reprisal measures, like those described above in the sections on appeal procedures and compensation. The Committee applies, under Article 20, the interpretation it adopted originally under Article 4§3: total compensation of actual damages; in cases of (discriminatory or retaliatory) dismissal, primarily reinstatement has to be available. Financial compensation may be acceptable where reinstatement is not possible or not desired by the worker, but only if it is sufficient to deter the employer and to compensate the worker.[92]

III. IMPACT ON INTERNATIONAL HUMAN RIGHTS INSTRUMENTS

The interaction between international UN, European and other regional instruments,[93] turning attention to the protection of gender equality, resulted from and contributed to the accelerated change of thinking about equality and differences between women and men in the last quarter of the past century. The radical change of approach in the 35 years between

[86] Conclusions 2005, Statement of Interpretation of Art 20; Conclusions XVII-2, Czech Republic, Art 1 of the Protocol.

[87] Conclusions XIII-5, Statement of Interpretation of Art 20.

[88] By analogy with the case law in relation to Art 1§2.

[89] Conclusions 2006, Portugal; Conclusions 2008, Sweden regarding wage bargaining.

[90] For further details see the chapter on Art 8 by C Kollonay-Lehoczky, section II.B(iii).

[91] Conclusions XIII-5, Statement of Interpretation on Art 20.

[92] Conclusions, XIII-5, 258–59.

[93] The Maputo Protocol of 13 September 2000 to the African Charter on Human and Peoples' Rights on the Rights of Women in Africa.

the 1961 and the 1996 Charter vested significant power in Article 20. Its interpretation contributed to the changed approach of the ECHR and the European human rights system.

A. European Convention on Human Rights

In its 1985 judgment in *Abdulaziz, Cabales, Balkandali v UK*[94] the ECtHR added to its argument the developing gender equality issue that was just under way in those days. Subsequently the importance of moving towards the equality of men and women was reiterated in various judgments.[95]

The rise of gender equality, together with the fight against racism and xenophobia, enhanced the desire to strengthen their protection, as well as sharpening the 'human rights edge' of economic and social rights.

This has been attempted from two directions, both targeting the amendment of the ECHR. The first was the effort to achieve individual protection for some economic and social rights, getting them into the Convention; the other was to amend Article 14 and extend its material scope. The first endeavour ended in the adoption of the 1988 Additional Protocol as a compromise,[96] extending the scope of the ESC to gender equality in employment.

The second trial was a proposal to broaden the scope of Article 14, abolishing its restrictive, dependent nature. The Steering Committee for Human Rights (CDDH), commissioned with the preparation of the Protocol, called the attention of the Committee of Ministers to the need to strengthen guarantees of racial and gender equality.[97] The compromise here was the adoption of Protocol 12 to the ECHR. Article 20 and Protocol 12, both resulting from these efforts, may be connected in the future, promoting the rapprochement between the RESC and the ECHR.

References to Article 20, a shift from the former usual reference to Article 1§2, indicate a change of mind,[98] and the judgment in *Emel Boyraz v Turkey*[99] can be considered a milestone. Maintaining that the right of recruitment to the civil service was deliberately omitted from the Convention and a refusal to be appointed cannot be complained against, the fact that the refusal in this case happened because of the sex of the applicant was seen by the Court as admissible[100]—also with reference to Article 20

[94] *Abdulaziz, Cabales, Balkandali v UK* (1985) EHHR 471, §78

[95] For example, *Leyla Sahin v Turkey* (2005) App.no. 4477/98, §115, *Cusan and Fazzo v Italy* (2014) App.no. 77/07, §67.

[96] Section I.A above, nn 5–7.

[97] Explanatory Report to Protocol 12 §9.

[98] See *Luczak v Poland* App no 77782/1 (ECtHR, 2008), esp §25.

[99] *Emel Boyraz v Turkey* App no 61960/08 (ECtHR, 2 December 2014).

[100] ibid §§41–42.

of the Charter—and it found a violation of Article 14 of the Convention in conjunction of Article 8.[101]

B. Charter of Fundamental Rights of the European Union

The changed approach also in Europe with regard to the differences between women and men is reflected in the shift in Article 20 of the Charter to equal dignity, autonomy and freedom from the former attitude of protection, limiting women's right to work. The case law of the ECSR has not only kept pace with developments, but has paved the way for further progress and impacted on EU law. The one and a half decades of the development of the case law of Article 20 has been in parallel with EU gender equality law in the field of employment. The similarity is informal and substantive, without formal references to the other regime. (This differs from the relationship between the RESC and the ECHR, which belong to the same regime.)

The general statement of 'equality' between men and women in Article 23 of the CFREU does not indicate its full material scope beyond work; only employment and pay are covered explicitly. The CFREU mentions Article 3 TEU and Article 8 TFEU as its basis, adding Article 20 as a source. The second unnumbered paragraph of Article 23: 'The principle of equality shall not prevent the maintenance or adoption of measures providing for specific advantages in favour of the under-represented sex' may refer to positive action and thereby contribute to the interpretation of this definition.

C. National Developments

The contribution of the Charter to the development of European non-discrimination law has evolved through the regular monitoring procedure, inducing as well as assisting countries in the adjustment. Examples such as Cyprus, which harmonised its law at the same time to bring it in compliance with the Charter and to transpose into national law Directive 2006/54, are not exceptional.[102]

Two points need special mention, in which development has been achieved by the monitoring procedure, backing and also going before EU gender equality law and policy, with the potential to exert an inductive effect.

One is equal pay. The progress prompted by Article 4§3 even before the adoption of Article 20 has amplified the concept of 'equal pay'—extending

[101] The partial dissent by Judge Spano (ibid §2) confirms the indirect relationship between Art 20 and Protocol 12.

[102] Conclusions 2012, Cyprus, Art 20; also Conclusions XX, Greece, Art 20.

its scope and reach beyond the employer. The positive developments in EU member states may need a closer look, considering that the reference to the 'single source' standard, applied by the CJEU, differs from the broader pay comparison required by the ECSR.[103] While in individual litigation the court might not be able to determine what rate ought to be paid by an external comparator employer, the Charter shall require national rules to ensure the alignment of male and female wages through the broad (sectoral) comparison as from the beginning, especially when women's work is systematically undervalued through occupational segregation.[104] This is indispensable for achieving equality not only in law but also in fact, emphasised by the Committee already in the first Conclusions.[105]

The second point is compensation in case of discriminatory or retaliatory dismissal, or dismissal against prohibition. The validity of this provision goes beyond the scope of Article 20, and must be analysed. Not only Article 20, but all provisions regarding unlawful dismissal connected to discrimination are affected by the growing number of countries that are adjusting their legal systems to the ECSR's consistently required interpretation of 'adequate compensation', meaning both restoration of the terminated employment and full financial compensation of moral and pecuniary damages.[106]

IV. CONCLUSION

The concept of the equality of men and women has undergone radical change in the world in general and in Europe in particular: what was progressive 30 years ago is outdated today. This is conspicuously illustrated by the changes in the ILO Conventions, amended and new norms, withdrawals and changing ratifications.

Article 20 of the Charter—not simply in line with developments but also going ahead of them—demonstrates the advantages and disadvantages of the highly optional nature of the RESC, not only the ratification of articles and parts of articles but also the special relationship between the 1961 and the 1996 'editions'. It might be telling that all states under the Revised Charter accepted Article 20, while five out of the 10 countries remaining under the Old Charter have not ratified Article 1 of the 1988 Protocol.

The Appendix to Article 20, listing exceptions to the principle of equal treatment, forms an integral part of it under Article N. Nonetheless,

[103] Conclusions 2012, Netherlands. See above in section II.B.

[104] See also Opinion of AG Geelhoed in *Lawrence v Regent Office Care* (n 48) §37.

[105] §28; Darcy and Harris (n 17) 81.

[106] Conclusions 2006, Belgium, Finland; Conclusions 2008, Estonia; Conclusions XIX-1, Denmark, Greece.

unchanged from 1988 to the 1996, its underlying considerations, now outdated, necessitate the reinterpretation (in fact, a change) of such appended provisions. §1 of the Appendix—permitting the exclusion of social security from the scope of Article 20—is practically invalidated by 'desuetude'. Rather, the ECtHR considered Poland to have bound itself to Article 12 with the ratification of Article 20.[107]

The text of §2 of the Appendix permits 'protecting provisions' (bans) beyond pregnancy and connected periods. The ECSR, consistently, and in line with current thinking, finds a violation of Article 20 by rules banning female labour (or night work) beyond those periods. The consistency of the ECSR has brought about significant progress in national laws abolishing those general prohibitions.[108] However, strictly taken, this practice is *contra legem*, in the words of Appendix §2.[109]

The progress made by national laws under the Charter in respect of equal treatment and equal opportunities with regard to men and women calls attention to the strong harmonising role of the Charter, on one hand, and to the obvious synergy with the development of EU gender equality law, on the other. This interrelationship may have significance for considering the mutual advantages of eventually merging the two systems in this area of human rights, by the accession of the EU to the Charter, as proposed by significant sources.[110]

[107] *Luczak v Poland* App no 77782/01 (ECtHR, 2007) §25.

[108] For example, Croatia; Conclusions XIX-1, Czech Republic; Conclusions XX, Czech Republic.

[109] See also Collective Complaint 14/2003, Decision on the merits §§26–32.

[110] See O De Schuetter in this volume.

Article 21

The Right to Information and Consultation

BRUNO VENEZIANI

Article 21—The right to information and consultation

With a view to ensuring the effective exercise of the right of workers to be informed and consulted within the undertaking, the Parties undertake to adopt or encourage measures enabling workers or their representatives, in accordance with national legislation and practice:

a. to be informed regularly at appropriate times and in comprehensible ways about the economic and financial situation of the undertaking employing them on the undertaking that the disclosure of certain information which could be prejudicial to the undertaking may be refused or subject to confidentiality; and
b. to be consulted in good time on proposed decisions which could substantially affect the interests of workers, particularly on those decisions which could have an important impact on the employment situation in the undertaking.

Article I—Implementation of the undertakings given

2. Compliance with the undertakings deriving from the provisions of ... Articles 21 ... of Part II of this Charter ... shall be regarded as effective if the provisions are applied, in accordance with paragraph 1 of this article, to the great majority of the workers concerned.

Appendix Part II: Articles 21 and 22

1. For the purpose of the application of these article the term 'workers' representatives' means persons who are recognized as such under national legislation or practice.
2. The term 'national legislation and practice' embraces, as the case may be, in addition to laws and regulations, collective agreements, other agreements between employers and workers' representatives, customs as well as relevant case law.
3. For the purpose of the application of this article, the term 'undertaking' is understood as referring to a set of tangible and intangible components, with

or without legal personality, formed to produce goods or provide services for financial gain with power to determine its own market policy.

4. It is understood that religious communities and their institutions may be excluded from the application of this article, even if these institutions are undertakings within the meaning of paragraph 3. Establishments pursuing activities which are inspired by certain ideals or guided by certain moral concepts, ideals and concepts which are protected by national legislation, may be excluded from the application of this article to such an extent as it is necessary to protect the orientation of the undertaking.
5. It is understood that where in a state the rights set out in this article are exercised in the various establishments of the undertaking, the Party concerned is to be considered as fulfilling the obligations deriving from this provision.
6. The Parties may exclude from the field of application those undertakings employing less than a certain number of workers, to be determined by national legislation or practice.

I. INTRODUCTION

A. Context and Main Content

The main content of the Article is workers' involvement in the undertaking as a model of the ideal type of participatory democracy.

Article 21 is a new provision included in Part II of 1996 Charter and its source of inspiration was the Additional Protocol of the 1961 Charter, adopted in 1988. There has been a deliberate choice to qualify the involvement of workers in the undertaking as a human right, 'whose maintenance and further realization' is essential (i) to 'safeguard and realize' the ideals and principles that are the common heritage of all members of the Council of Europe and (ii) to facilitate their economic and social progress.[1]

In the field of labour relations the Community Charter of Fundamental Social Rights of Workers of 1989 strengthens the philosophy of legal promotion of specific collective labour rights, such as strikes (Article 11), collective bargaining (Article 12), association (Article 13) and information and consultation (Article 17).

B. International Sources and Relationships to Other Provisions of the Charter

It is true that the 1961 Charter provided for a fundamental right to collective bargaining through the promotion of 'joint consultation' (Article 6§1).

[1] Preamble, Considerandum 1.

Some 27 years later, information and consultation within the undertaking is identified as an autonomous and general right to be 'effectively realized'.[2]

The full recognition of the rights to information and consultation of workers' representatives within the EU framework has been dealt with within the framework of various approaches in EU Directives on different topics:

— In the case of transfers of undertakings, information was *in se* an autonomous right of workers' representatives and consultation was important for 'seeking an agreement'.[3]
— A more up-to-date model of industrial democracy was provided by the Collective Redundancy Directive.[4]
— In the case of the health and safety of workers at work, information and consultation are:
  — accurately described in detail (content, use);[5]
  — reciprocally functional;
  — and both aimed eventually at reaching a collective agreement.
— In the case of European Works Councils,[6] information and consultation are available to European institutions in Community-scale undertakings and Community groups and in the text of Recast EWC Directive[7] a different type of industrial democracy is represented, whose aim is to promote more efficient and effective dialogue through information, consultation and institutional participation.

[2] Additional Protocol of 1988, Pt 1§2; C Kollonay-Lehoczky, 'The fundamental right of workers to information and consultation in the European Social Charter' in F Dorssemont and T Blanke (eds), *The recast of the European Works Council Directive* (Antwerp-Oxford, Intersentia, 2010) 9.

[3] Art 6 p 1, Council Directive 77/187/EEC of 14 February 1977 on approximation of the law of the member states relating to the safeguarding of employees' rights in the event of transfer of undertakings, businesses or part of businesses (later amended by Council Directive 98/50/EC of 28 June 1998).

[4] Council Directive 75/129/EEC of February 1975 on the approximation of the laws of the States relative to collective redundancy amended by Council Directive 98/59CE of 20 July 1998.

[5] Art 10 and 11 of Council Directive 89/391/EEC of 12 June 1989 on the introduction of measures to encourage improvements in the safety and health of workers at work; but also Art 2 Sec II of Council Directive 98/59/EC of 20 July 1998 on the approximation of the laws of the member states relating to collective redundancies.

[6] Council Directive 94/45/EC of 22 September 1994 on the establishment of a European Works Council or a procedure in Community-scale undertakings and Community-scale groups of undertakings for the purposes of informing and consulting employees and Council Directive 2001/86/EC of 8 October 2001 supplementing the Statute for a European company with regard to the involvement of employees.

[7] Directive 2009/38/EC of the European Parliament and of the Council of 6 May 2009 on the establishment of a European Works Council or a procedure in Community-scale undertakings and Community-scale groups of undertakings for the purposes of informing and consulting employees (Recast) 7 recital; C Sachs Durand, 'Information and Consultation in the Recast Directive' in F Dorssemont and T Blanke (eds), *The recast of the European Works Council Directive* (Antwerp-Oxford, Intersentia, 2010) 314.

— A full model of industrial democracy, enshrined in a general legal framework dealing with the recognition of a general right to information and consultation at plant level, is proposed in the 2002 Directive.[8]

The expression 'participatory democracy' embraces, as it does in ILO sources, a large series of models whose goals and techniques of workers' involvement represent the legal way to prevent a possible conflict at the level of undertaking with joint cooperative efforts and 'mutual understanding', and 'not within the scope of collective bargaining machinery or not normally dealt with by other machinery concerned with determination of terms and conditions of employment'.[9] This prevention strategy is favourable to the 'dissemination and exchange of information as complete and objective as possible' on various aspects of the life of the undertaking and the workers' social conditions.[10]

II. CONTENT

A. Paragraph 1: The Nature of the Right to Information and Consultation

The right to information and consultation can be qualified as a fundamental human right, as has been affirmed by the ILO Committee, which also emphasises how close at the level of the undertaking are the relationships between freedom of association, the right to organise and a 'free and frank consultation procedure' in accordance with the principle of autonomy of the parties,[11] a statement which goes back to 1994. The 'essential content' of the freedom of expression, according to the ECtHR, is the 'freedom to be heard in order to protect' workers' interests.[12]

In approaching this topic the EU Commission has proposed a comprehensive method of analysis consisting in 'the consolidation of the various provisions on workers' information and consultation'.[13]

[8] Directive 2002/14/EC of the European Parliament and of the Council of 11 March 2002 establishing a general framework for informing and consulting employees in the European Community—Joint declaration of the European Parliament, the Council and the Commission on employee representation.

[9] ILO Cooperation at the level of undertaking Recommendation 1952 No 94 (Art 1).

[10] Communication within the Undertaking Recommendation 1967 No 129 (Art 2).

[11] ILO, General Survey on the fundamental conventions concerning rights at work in light of the ILO Declaration on social justice for a fair globalisation, 2008, 101st Session 2012, Report III (Pt 1B) (Geneva, ILO, 2012) 98.

[12] *Police Trade Union v the Slovak Republic* (ECtHR Third Section, 25 September 2012) and consolidated jurisprudence on linkage between Arts 10 and 11 of the ECHR, points 51, 52, 53.

[13] European Commission 2005, Communication of the Commission on the Social Agenda, COM (2005) 33 final.

At the level of EU primary law, in the Charter of Fundamental Rights (CFREU) the participatory democracy enshrined in Article 27 is placed under the Solidarity title, together with the rights of collective bargaining and action and freedom of association.

Article 152 of the Treaty on the Functioning of the European Union (TFEU) does not refer specifically to the industrial democracy model but it can be considered a form of 'promoting legislation' on the role of social partners, which gives them the right to be 'recognised and promoted'[14] at EU level. Article 151 TFEU is recalled by the European Parliament as it provides that action by the EU, and its members must be consistent with the fundamental rights laid down in the 1996 Charter as antidotes to austerity measures.[15]

B. Paragraph 2: Material Scope, Procedure and Rules

The Charter does not contain any definition of 'information'. The legal obligation of the employer consists in providing workers or their representatives with all data necessary to acquire complete knowledge on some limited and specific matters ('economic and financial situation') in order to make their presence in the undertaking meaningful for the protection of workers' interests and influence company decisions. The relevant information is required to enable employees' representatives to form an opinion.[16]

The rights are restricted in terms of their limited range of subject matter—economic and financial situation—and the exclusion of industrial ownership, manufacturing or trade secrets[17] and matters that could be prejudicial to the undertaking or subject to confidentiality.

Furthermore, restrictions must be prescribed by law and 'necessary in a democratic society for the protection of the rights and freedoms of others or for public interests, national security, public health, or morals subject to provisos about secrecy and confidentiality'.[18] The clause mirrors ECHR

[14] Case T-135/96 *UEAPME v Council and Commission* (1998) ECR II-2335; B Veneziani, 'Austerity measures, democracy and social policy in the EU', in N Bruun, K Lörcher and I Schömann (eds), *The Economic and Financial Crisis and Collective Labour Law in Europe* (Oxford, Hart, 2014) 126.

[15] European Parliament Resolution of 13 March 2014 on employment and social aspects of the rule and operations of the Troika (ECB, Commission, IMF) with regard to euro area programme countries, 2014/2007/(Ini). See also European Committee on Social Rights, 'The relationship between EU Law and the Social Charter', 15 July 2014, Council of Europe.

[16] Recast Directive 2009/38/EC on the establishment of a European Works Council, Art 2(i) Council Directive 2001/86/EC of 8 October 2001 supplementing the Statute for a European company with regard to the involvement of employees and Art 2(f) Framework directive.

[17] Para 39 of Explanatory report to the 1988 Additional Protocol.

[18] Charter 1996, Art G (see chapter on Article G by A Koukiadaki in this volume).

Article 11§2 and according to the ECtHR the exceptions set out in this Article are to be construed strictly in the sense that 'only convincing and compelling reasons can justify restrictions on such parties' freedom of association'.[19]

The Articles of the Charter and the other EU instruments and Directives do not mention the oral or written nature of the information because the duty to disclose is not exhaustively described in the Charter. But there are some indications that support the interpretation in favour of oral *and written* information. This conclusion stems from the quality of legal provisions, the democratic function they must perform, the particular content of information and, especially, the rationale of the rule. In fact, Article 21 underlines how the exercise becomes 'effective' as the employer has a duty of 'cooperation' to provide information 'regularly', 'at appropriate times' and in a 'comprehensible way'.

In this way it will be possible for employee representatives to acquaint themselves with particular subject matters and to examine them carefully, mainly if economic and financial data are explained in a strictly technical way, written in a foreign language and supported by an expert's report.

C. Paragraph 3: The Relationship between Information and Consultation

The heading of Article 21 links information and consultation closely and the sequence of the subparagraphs (a) and (b) is connected with the coordinated conjunction 'and'. The wording of the rule seems to suggest that the matters contained in the decisions taken by the employer are broader than those indicated in sub-paragraph (a).[20] The text is clear and does not restrict the range of the duty to disclose information on economic and financial topics, but rather enlarges it to all relevant fields, preceded by the furnishing of appropriate information, 'which could substantially affect the interests of workers'. The relevance of the employer's obligation to cooperate in democratising the undertaking is stressed *especially* when the measures can have an 'important impact on the employment situation in the undertaking', such as all restructuring of the company and plants, new kinds of employee classification models, transfers of the whole or a branch or unit (contracting out), the merger or split of the company, delocalisation of activity branches and company group units.[21] The 'employment situation' must

[19] *Tum Haber Sen and Cinar v Turkey* App no 28602/95 (ECtHR, 21 February 2006 (No 36)) para 35.

[20] Explanatory report to the Additional Protocol 1988, para 43.

[21] Kollonay-Lehoczky (n 2) 21.

be understood not only in a strictly economic sense but also more generally as all factors affecting the conditions and terms of individual employment contracts (individual dismissals, downgrading of workers, atypical labour relationships).

D. Paragraph 4: The Role of the Law and Collective Agreements

The formula 'in accordance with national legislation and practices' (Article 21) shows that only the states, in their full and free autonomy, can take the relevant decisions on how to specify workers' involvement and the relevant topics, as well as how to set up the model of participation of the social partners. Article 33 of the 1961 Charter already affirmed that many cases envisaged by the provisions of the Charter 'are matters normally left to agreements between employers or employers' organisations and workers' organisations … and compliance with them shall be treated as effective if their provision are applied through such agreements'.[22]

According to Appendix N to the RESC 'which shall form an integral part of it'—for the purposes of Article 21 the terms 'national legislation and practice' encompass 'in addition to law and regulations, collective agreements, other agreements between employers and workers representatives, customs as well relevant case law'.[23]

The statement is relevant because it affirms:

- respect for the autonomy of the Parties' legal system, where different sources of law can be more or less strictly interwoven;
- the idea that in many cases industrial relations models can be characterised by a widespread multilevel system of collective agreements (professional, territorial, plant);
- that the terms 'other agreements' shows that negotiations can taken place not only at national but also at company and more frequently at plant levels;
- that these systems have deliberately and voluntarily chosen the structure of their collective autonomy (collective bargaining, action, representation of workers at all levels);
- that the state can ('may') decide also how to 'combine'[24] the two methods of regulation.

A requirement is conditional on the acceptability of the system; that is, implementation must be 'effective and adequate',[25] otherwise any generic

22 Additional Protocol 1988 Pt I, point 2 and Art 2.
23 P 2 Comment to Art 21 Appendix to the Charter.
24 Pt V, Art 7 of the 1988 Protocol.
25 Para 32 of the Protocol 1988.

information on material scope can be considered by the Committee to be 'not concrete'.[26]

In some cases the states decide to leave the task of determining subject matter 'mainly to collective bargaining'.[27] The range of subject matter varies, and in some cases, in reply to the Committee's request, national reports state that collective agreements lay down specific rules on the 'occupational sphere' and on how consultation should be, or 'on the number and nature of agreements on the subject'.[28] The material scope is broader and more precisely specified because the information deals not only with economic and financial dates and functioning of the undertaking (sales activities, customers' orders, productivity, costs of employment), but also with employment in general, envisaged changes in the structure of the undertaking and its impact on dismissals on economic grounds. Changes in wages, liquidity related to wage payment, number of employees hired and their job titles are also potential contents of information.[29]

In the national reports given to the Committee, sometimes information and consultation seem to be equivalent terms and the reporting state does not necessarily respect the clear-cut distinction outlined by Article 21. Reading national reports, it seems that states do not always distinguish between measures. In fact, consultation should be limited to the matter of employers' strategies 'substantially affecting the interests of the workers' (paragraph (b)) and the disclosure of information is limited 'to the economic and financial situation' (paragraph (a)).

The Committee is particularly rigid in requiring the strict observance of the content of information and it defers its conclusions in all cases in which the State does not comply with paragraph (a) of Article 21.[30]

Thus 'information' concerns the activities and economic conditions of the undertaking or the enterprise,[31] both information and consultation deal with the conditions, structure and likely future development of employment in the undertaking or the enterprise, as well as prevention measures or the organisation of work or employment contracts, especially in the case of a transfer of the undertaking, a business or part of the business.[32]

But consultation also takes place on the probable economic development of the company,[33] changes in work organisation, working conditions, training, collective redundancies[34] and 'the undertaking's financial

[26] Conclusions 2014, Estonia.
[27] Conclusions 2010, Romania; 2010, Norway; and 2010, Portugal.
[28] Conclusions 2010, Albania.
[29] Conclusions 2014, Hungary.
[30] Conclusions 2014, Turkey.
[31] Conclusions 2014, Czech Republic.
[32] Conclusions 2010, Greece.
[33] Conclusions 2014, Czech Republic; and 2014, Slovenia.
[34] Conclusions 2010, Belgium.

situation', which is also the content of a specific obligation 'to [provide] written, adequate and accurate information'.[35]

Nothing prevents legislation from drawing a distinction between information and consultation, moving from the idea that economic or financial choices always have an impact on workers in the workplace. This explains why larger matters can be devolved from the national legal system to the consultation procedure: situation, structure and anticipated developments in employment, planned measures, corporate social policies, changes to work organisation or contractual conditions, reduction or suspension of the activities of the employer or parts thereof, merger, amalgamation, division, or change of the legal form of the employer. Consultation can be activated also when the social partners must discuss 'internal regulations'.[36]

These are matters of an 'economic' nature, with a strong impact on workers' individual contracts. Furthermore, consultation also deals with measures 'to prevent employment actions',[37] accidents, transfer of rights and obligations from the employer, collective dismissals and termination of employment, rest days and training.

E. Paragraph 5: Procedure

This Article requires that information be given 'regularly or at an appropriate time' and in a 'comprehensible way' and the consultation must start 'in good time'. In some cases concerning changes or planned measures information given once or twice a year was not 'appropriate'.[38]

The analysis of more recent reports reveals a higher level of compliance in the national statutes that satisfy and integrate the provisions of the Charter.

In the procedural sequence envisaged by the Charter, information plays the role of the first step to make consultation possible and fruitful.

The written form is a model of a 'comprehensible way' (Article 21§a) of providing information about matters regarding the company's financial situation or changes to its structural units[39] having an impact on jobs. The written form, even though not everywhere envisaged, is imposed by national laws.[40]

Information opens the dialogue, and it must be given in due course[41] and be full and accurate.[42] In some cases it should also be adequate and

35 Conclusions 2010, Estonia.
36 Conclusions 2014, Portugal.
37 ibid.
38 ibid.
39 Conclusions 2010, Lithuania; Conclusions 2010, Ukraine, for safety measures.
40 Conclusions 2010, Albania; Conclusions 2010, Estonia.
41 Conclusions 2010, Belgium.
42 Conclusions 2010, France.

enable the employees' representatives to reply in writing with proposals or notify their intention to enter into consultation within 15 days of receipt of the information. Employers who do not wish to accept the proposals are obliged to provide the reasons for their decisions. If they agree to enter into consultation they must do so within seven days of receiving the employees' representatives' request.[43]

Assessment of the legal category of the appropriateness (Article 21§a) of time, place and content must be evaluated in the perspective of 'making the employees' representatives able to conduct the necessary examination' and 'to present opinions and possibly prepare for consultation'[44] and to enable them to give 'a reasoned response'[45] or 'express their position and make their proposal for the decisions of the employer'.[46]

In the case of an undertaking with several different workplaces, employees are informed and consulted either through the works council or subcommittee in each individual workplace or through a central committee, or through both.[47] The choice depends on the level at which the decision in question was taken and the extent of the powers granted to the managers of each separate workplace. According to the case law of the French *Cours de Cassation,*[48] which can hear complaints about employers' decisions or omissions concerning arrangements for informing and consulting employees, all measures managers take must be sufficiently detailed but should not have been adopted or have become irrevocable.

F. Paragraph 6: The Actors

The right to be informed and consulted can be exercised by workers or their representatives, and that means that the right is *owned* by individual workers, as a part of a group, or representative institutions. In some cases national law clearly defines these rights as 'individual rights'[49] and to receive and propose answers on initiatives related to their jobs, changes in the sphere of work, salaries and wages, and all questions bearing upon the organisation of the work process.[50]

The term 'workers' organisation' is a general expression used in ILO Recommendation Consultation (industrial and national levels) 1960 No 113

[43] Conclusions 2010, Estonia.

[44] Conclusions 2010, Greece; Conclusions 2010, Belgium.

[45] Conclusions 2010, Romania.

[46] Conclusions 2010, Slovak Republic; Conclusions 2014, Slovenia; Conclusions 2014, former Yugoslav Republic of Macedonia.

[47] Conclusions 2014, Portugal.

[48] Cass soc 20.11.2000, No 98-19.594P; Cass soc 25/6/2002, No 00-20.939P.

[49] Conclusions 2014, Belgium.

[50] Conclusions 2014, Slovenia; Conclusions 2014, Serbia.

(Article 2), but in the context of Article 21 the more appropriate expression at undertaking level is 'worker representatives' and it originates in 'trade union representatives or such other person as may, under national law and practice, or under a collective agreement, have the task of representing the interests of the workers at the level of the undertaking'.[51] More precisely, ILO Convention No 135[52] expresses the following principles:

(a) 'procedural' democracy consisting in:
  - the freedom of choice of the workers to elect representatives in the undertaking, in accordance with the provisions of national laws or regulations or of collective agreements (Article 3b);
  - the freedom of trade unions or their members to designate or elect representatives (Article 3a);

and

(b) the freedom of association expressed by the pluralism of different representatives envisaged so that co-existence 'of elected representatives is not used to undermine the position of trade unions concerned or their representatives and to encourage cooperation' (Article 5).

The 'golden formula' used in Articles 21 and 22 RESC—'workers or their representatives', also used in Article 27 of the CFREU—is inspired by those two principles and it means simply that the rights afforded by two provisions may be exercised by workers, or by their representatives, or by both, and the fact that they are conferred upon one group does not mean that they cannot be conferred upon the other. In the international legal context the only condition imposed on the practice of voluntary negotiation is that implementation must be 'effective and adequate'.[53]

The principle of voluntarism means that national states must leave management and labour free to decide:

- whether or not to implement;
- what kind of negotiation;
- what level of involvement (production unit, sector or branch, regional, territorial);
- what kind of procedure and rules for the designation of representation.

Voluntarism seems to be inspired by the idea that, in a context of pluralism of representative institutions or bodies, equilibrium among institutions charged with workers' involvement must be respected. Especially if the aim

[51] Art 9b ILO Recommendation concerning Communication between Management and Workers within the Undertaking 3129 of 28 June 1967.

[52] Concerning the Protection and facilities to be afforded to workers' representatives in the undertaking 1971 No 135, Art 3.

[53] Explanatory report Protocol 1988, points 33/34.

of the rules of international sources such as the ILO Recommendations seem to force the employers and workers 'in their common interest, to recognise the importance of the climate of mutual understanding and confidence within the undertaking that is favourable to the efficiency of the undertaking' (Article 2§1 of ILO Recommendation No 1967).

The Committee has correctly acknowledged the legitimacy of both the trade unions and the non-union forms, paying attention to safeguarding the principle of pluralism and how the states have implemented it. But the Committee has observed that in most countries there is a 'domination' of the trade unions in the area of employee representation.

The pluralism of representative models is a value to be respected, and the Committee has acknowledged that in some cases, works council responsibility regarding such issues as information and consultation of workers is exercised only:

— if there is no trade union functioning in the enterprise;

and

— these issues are not the subject of a collective agreement.

If the trade unions have a monopoly on representing workers for the purpose of information and consultation the undertaking suffers from the dangerous and paradoxical situation in which a majority of non-unionised employees would be deprived of the right to be informed and consulted, while the right would be granted to a trade union representing only a minority of employees. The Committee defers its conclusions because such a system deprives workers of legal protection.[54]

National laws state the principle of continuity of representative function. If a trade union is represented within an enterprise, or the staff has selected an appropriate trade union to represent its workers before the work council's term of office has expired, the works council will continue its activities, and collective bargaining will be conducted by the union and the works council. If the latter cannot agree on the formation of a joint representative body, a decision on the matter will be taken at the staff meeting.[55] In undertakings with more than 20 employees in the absence of a trade union, the general meeting of the staff elects representatives, which ensures that the information and consultation right is complied with, but may not continue their activities if trade union representatives are subsequently appointed.[56]

In some cases, the national report[57] witnesses that, according to case law and collective agreement practice, all workers, even non-union

[54] Conclusions 2010, Greece.
[55] Conclusions 2010, Lithuania.
[56] Conclusions 2010, Romania.
[57] Conclusions 2010, Norway.

members, can be protected if the undertaking is bound by a collective agreement.[58]

The importance of the pluralism and continuity of representative functions is also underlined by the changes introduced by state law within national systems of industrial democracy: the Swedish model of co-determination, revised in 2005, provides for a general obligation to disclose information. Employers not bound by any collective agreement shall keep workers' organisations continuously informed, with members employed within the undertaking and those employee organisations bound to an employer by a collective agreement.[59]

G. Paragraph 7: The Rule of 'Great Majority of Workers'

It is also true that the legal context of the Charter is clear in stating that the sources of implementation are the laws or regulations, collective agreements and 'a combination of the two'.

The Charter has conditioned the principle of the effectiveness of protection of the new model of participatory democracy—in the past excluded from the list of rights contained in Article 33 of the 1961 Charter—on the requirement that it 'be applied to the *great majority* of workers concerned'.[60]

This formula poses some questions about the two essential features describing the majority:

— the intensity of quantity: how 'great' is the majority;
— the kind of quality: which skills or categories are involved;
and
— who are the 'workers concerned'.

H. Paragraph 8: Quantity

It must also be stressed that the Protocol of 1988 admitted the enjoyment of some rights (especially Articles 2 and 3 of the 1961 Charter), even though the same source specified that the 'great majority' rule need 'not necessarily be afforded to all workers' (Article 63 Protocol 1988).

In the first Conclusions,[61] the Committee defined the 'great majority' as at least 80 per cent of the total workforce.[62]

[58] Conclusions 2010, Norway.
[59] Conclusions 2014, Sweden.
[60] Art I, para 2 Charter ECSR.
[61] Conclusions cycle 1 1969.
[62] Kollonay-Lehoczky (n 2) 18.

The rationale of Committee decisions stems[63] from EU rules and the need to fix a minimum framework to adopt for correct implementation of Article 21. The scope of Directive 2002/1/EC of the Parliament and of the Council of 11 March 2002 is restricted to undertakings with at least 50 employees or establishments with at least 20 employees in any EU member state.

The quantitative restriction of the scope of 'participatory democracy' is paradoxical. The 'constitutional' nature of the legal source which envisages the model is at the top of the hierarchy of EU rules. Furthermore, it must be recalled that this limitation cannot be restricted unless they are 'necessary in a democratic society for the protection of the rights and freedom of the others'.[64] This solution stems from the reason of 'efficiency' of the small undertakings where an informal, unregulated system of consultation and information exists 'in fact'.[65]

The criterion of an undertaking's size, mentioned in Article 21, is quantitative (number of employees) but it is not the only one. Other reasons for exclusion depend on the fact that collective agreements or other agreements 'contain no provisions relating to information and consultation'.[66] In this case, 'however, the workers not afforded this right must be a minority'.[67]

A crucial role in determining the average number of workers protected is played by the collective bargaining structure and scope and its interrelations with national law. The Committee considers a national system in conformity with the Charter if all employees in undertakings employing at least 35 people are granted a right to be informed and consulted either by special act or by collective agreements.[68] The percentage of coverage rises to a high level (91 per cent of employees protected by a collective agreement, and 71 per cent of workers members of a trade union) in systems where by virtue of legal amendments employers not bound by collective agreements 'shall keep employee organisations with members who are employees of such an employer informed'.[69]

I. Paragraph 9: Quality

The expression 'workers concerned' refers to a broad definition of 'employee' and it is relevant for the purposes of Article 21, which imposes upon member

63 Conclusions 2007, Albania.
64 Art G Pt III of the Charter.
65 Art 2§2 of Explanatory report to the 1988 Additional protocol.
66 Art 7 of the Protocol.
67 §46 Explanatory report, 1988.
68 Conclusions 2014, Denmark.
69 Conclusions 2010, Sweden.

states the obligation not to exclude from the calculation, in principle, any specific category of persons. The lack of information on this essential aspect of the rule means that the legal system is 'not in conformity' with the Charter.[70] The Charter refers to the implementation of its rules through national legislation and practices (work rules, collective bargaining), but member states must respect the obligation to avoid adopting measures likely to frustrate the objective of 'effective exercise of the rights'.[71]

The Committee, in assessing compliance on this point, considers that all categories of employee—in other words, all employees with an employment contract, whatever their status, length of service or workplace—must be taken into account when calculating the number of employees covered. A number of judgments of the European Court of Justice also run along these lines.[72] In many cases the Committee asks whether or not the personal scope of national legislation corresponds to the 2002 Directive.[73]

The expression 'the workers concerned' seems to refer to the workers employed 'in the undertaking',[74] irrespective of their qualifications, skills, type of contract, length of service or workplace.

First of all, every category is subject to the general principle of non-discrimination. In this respect, in many cases national reports follow the rules laid down in the Charter and include nationals of other states,[75] who can be elected as trade union representatives and participate in the meetings of management bodies.[76]

The expression used in the Explanatory Report, 'in the undertaking', needs to be interpreted in light of the transformation of the economy that has occurred in the era of globalisation and economic crisis, where all the legal institutions inherited from the past have been upset. The 'flexibility' of employment contracts in this context has enlarged the personal and material scope of Article 21. The idea of 'workers ... in the undertaking' is defined clearly as embracing all 'workers who do not actually work in the undertaking but are linked to it with an employment relationship' and the list can be expanded by the social partners.[77] The workers' right to information and consultation has been extended to cases of outsourcing and change in the ownership of the company, and personal scope with regard to compliance

[70] Conclusions 2014, former Yugoslav Republic of Macedonia; Conclusions 2014, Norway; Conclusions 2014, Italy; Conclusions 2014, France.

[71] Art 2 and Art 21 para 1 of the Charter.

[72] Case C-385/05 *Confederation General du Travail CGT and others* (CJEU, 18 January 2007); Case C-176/12 *Association de Mediation Sociale* (CJEU, 15 January 2014).

[73] Conclusions 2014, Finland; Conclusions 2014, Turkey; and Conclusions 2014, Slovak Republic.

[74] Arts 2 and 3 of the Explanatory report to the additional protocol 1988.

[75] Conclusions 2010, Belgium.

[76] Conclusions 2010, Romania; Conclusions 2010, Slovenia.

[77] Conclusions 2014, Netherlands.

with those rights has been extended to workers with flexible forms of contract, such as fixed-term employment and private procurement.[78] Anyway, in some cases hired-in workers can enjoy the right 'if they have worked for more than 24 months and contributed to the undertaking's activities'.[79]

J. Paragraph 10: Undertaking

The word 'undertaking' seems not to be restricted to a single monolithic entity, and its function is clear as it is qualified by 'market policy'.[80] But the Parties have complete freedom in adopting a more functionalist approach to leave managers and labour to determine freely the various levels of information and consultation, which need not coincide with the decision-making level. The principle of the *effectiveness* of rights of consultation and information must also take into account a more articulated structure of undertaking composed of 'various production units', that is, 'establishments' acting as decision-making centres.[81] The general image of an undertaking is a market-oriented body which consists 'of one or more production units linked to a single management centre legally and economically'.[82]

It is clear that the main profile characterising the undertaking is its commercial-financial policy, which the Appendix to the Charter describes in depth as 'a set of tangible and intangible components with or without legal personality formed to produce goods or provide services for financial gain and with power to determine its own market policy'.[83] Furthermore, all Parties are equally considered as fulfilling the obligations by developing the rights of Article 21 at the level 'of various establishments'.[84]

The Appendix to 1996 provides that 'religious communities and their institutions' may be excluded from the application of Article 21. The rationale of the restriction is that such bodies pursue 'activities which are inspired by certain ideals or guided by certain moral concepts' to be protected by national legislation.[85] The corollary seems to give room to some interpretations because it is specified that the exclusion has to be 'to such an extent as is necessary to protect the orientation of the undertaking'.[86]

[78] Conclusions 2005, XVII 2 vol 2, Spain.

[79] Conclusions 2014, Netherlands.

[80] Explanatory report to the 1988 Additional protocol §37.

[81] Art 37, Explanatory report 1988 Protocol.

[82] Art 69 of the Appendix to Explanatory report 1988.

[83] Point 3 of Appendix, Arts 21 and 22 of Charter; see also ECSR, Decision on the merits of 28 September 2008 *EU Council of Police trade union v Portugal*, Collective Complaint No 40/2007, 42.

[84] Appendix point 5, Arts 21 and 22.

[85] Arts 21 and 22 Appendix, p 4.

[86] Appendix to the Protocol 1988, Art 68 explains that such exclusion describes the situation in Germany, where *Tendenzbetriebe* are excluded from the scope of the 1972 ACT on the organisation of undertakings, Art 68 Appendix Protocol 1988.

The *Tendenzschutz* ('ideological protection') argument is another paradox that underlines the evolution of labour law at the individual and collective levels. It constitutes 'a conflict of fundamental rights'.[87] It is true that the Charter does not resolve the problem and asks Member States to intervene freely in this topic. The question is whether or not each restriction meets a minimal test of reasonability and proportionality, taking into account:

— respect for the principle of non-discrimination; and
— the evolution of the *Tendenzbetrieb* ('ideological enterprise') of a religious community which, although in different ways, takes part in a commercial market with restaurants, hospitals, hotels and schools directed by religious management and frequently exempted totally or partially from fiscal burdens by the State.

According to Belgian law, a works council has to be established also in those enterprises not having profit-making purposes, such as those providing social and health services and educational institutions.[88]

K. Paragraph 11: Public Employees

The structure of the Charter obliges the Parties to respect collective social rights when the rule is directed to ensure 'the effective exercise of the right to bargain collectively and to collective action' (Article 6), 'the right to information and consultation' (Article 21) and 'to ensure or promote the right to organise' (Article 5). In this last case, the obligation of the states is rigorously described so that they must apply the provision so as 'to not impair nor shall it be so applied as to impair the freedom protected'.

The only restriction admitted is that of non-applicability to police and members of the armed forces, whose guarantee and consequent extent will be devolved to national law or regulations (Article 5).

Other rights do not suffer from the same kind of restrictions, except those listed in Article G, Part III of the Charter and when 'the competent national authority may, by way of exemption and after consulting organisations of employers and workers, exclude certain categories of workers from the protection … by reason of the legal nature of their employment relationship'.[89]

[87] F Dorssemont, 'Art 27, Comment', in S Peers, T Hervey, J Kenner and A Ward (eds), *The European Charter of Fundamental Rights. A Commentary* (Oxford, Hart, Beck, Nomos, 2014) 766.

[88] Kollonay-Lehoczky (n 2) 12.

[89] Appendix to the Charter, Art 25§1.

The impression is that the web of rules of the two Charters does not contain in principle any criterion of exclusion or restriction *ratione personae* except those explicitly admitted in each individual article. More precisely, the main purpose of the right to consultation and information, as in all articles of the Charter, is that:

— 'rights and principles may be *effectively* realised';[90]
— the dogma of the 'great majority of workers' must be respected.[91]

The only possible exclusion is closely linked to the commercial definition of undertaking as it has been accepted by the Parties. The Committee has chosen a sharp attitude on this subject, assuming that, from the definition of undertaking[92] the corollary derives that 'even though Article 21 (and 22) may apply to workers in state-owned enterprises, public employees are as a whole not covered by those provisions'.[93]

The Committee reiterates its interpretation, indicating in general that Article 21 applies to 'all undertakings, public or private' but with the intention and the perspective to know the exact percentage of workers covered by the protection of this Article.[94] The expression 'public' is misleading as it appears in the report which offers a range of reactions and a variety of terms indicating institutional public or semi-public entities. Public means 'state-sector'[95] public undertaking,[96] public sector[97] or 'state as employer'.[98] In the reports, as well in the wording of the Charter, 'public' normally means all kinds of public employment, 'mostly without distinctions between publicly owned undertakings and other public bodies or public institutions'.[99]

Recent trends emphasised in some reports seem to extend the application of the right to workers' involvement to employees in the 'state-owned enterprise's share capital'[100] or 'in both public and private sector'. Furthermore, the right to consultation is provided by different legal sources for 'civil servants' representatives' (Labour Code) and for 'employee in enterprises managed by public authorities'.[101] In Italy, a special law of 2007

[90] Preamble of the Additional protocol of 1988, Pt 1.
[91] See above.
[92] See above.
[93] European Committee of Social Rights, Decision on the merits of 23 September 2008, *European Council of Police Trade Unions v Portugal*, point 42, Collective Complaint No 40/2007; Conclusions XIII 5, Norway, 284, quoted in Decision, point 42.
[94] Conclusions 2010, Albania; 85% of public sector.
[95] Conclusions 2010, Denmark; Conclusions 2007, Norway.
[96] Conclusions 1997, Finland; Conclusions 2010, Romania.
[97] Conclusions 2010, Slovak Republic.
[98] Conclusions 1997, Finland; Conclusions 2010, Italy.
[99] Kollonay-Lehoczky (n 2) 12.
[100] Conclusions 2007, Romania.
[101] Conclusions 2010, Slovak Republic.

covers all enterprises, both public and private, 'whether or not they are profit making'.[102]

The case of the Netherlands is striking, because 'the Works Council Act of 1971 applies also to the public sector and in 2002 it was extended to such specific service areas as district courts, appeal courts and administrative courts'.[103]

The exclusion of public employees creates an imbalance between the principle of participatory democracy and all other rights of collective autonomy (right to collective action and right to collective bargaining) which do not suffer from any restriction by the Charter (namely Article 6).

It could be paradoxical not to guarantee also to public employees the complete enjoyment of all the rights that compose the mosaic of solidarity in a 'public' context where the disproportionate equilibrium between public power and social private powers exists in all branches and sectors of public administrations. The 'right to be heard' is an 'essential element of trade union freedom' not exclusively attributed to trade unions, but to workers as a group or to each worker.[104]

Since the late 1990s public sector employment has provided a testing ground for interventionist strategies because one of the actors of legal systems—the public authority—has a dual role as employer and guardian of public expenditure. In the early 1990s, the public and private sectors in some European countries began to overlap, or at least to converge because of the spread of collective bargaining as a source of regulation for wages in particular, and terms and conditions of work in general. Policies applied in response to the financial crisis have shown a trend towards 'privatisation' strategies in the public sector which, having embraced collective bargaining and rules of civil code, has come to resemble the private sector.[105]

The ILO Freedom of Association Committee (FAC) has underlined that it 'is a general rule that the public authorities should not exercise their financial competences in such way that the effect of collective agreement is prevented or limited as it is not compatible with the freedom of collective bargaining'.[106]

[102] Conclusions 2010, Italy.

[103] Conclusions cycle XV, vol 2, Addendum, op 569, Cycle WVIII quoted by Kollonay-Lehoczky (n 2) 13, fn 33.

[104] Dorssemont (n 87) 754, and about collective freedom ibid 756.

[105] B Veneziani, 'The intervention of the law to regulate collective bargaining and trade union representation rights in European countries: recent trends and problems' (1999) 5 *Transfer* 111.

[106] ILO FAC Case 2820, 1–6 November 2012, quoted in A Jacobs, 'Decentralisation of labour law standard setting and the financial crisis', in Bruun, Lörcher and Schömann (n 14) 190; see also M Schmitt, 'Evaluation of EU responses to the crisis with reference to primary legislation (European Treaties and Charter of Fundamental Rights)', 195 et seq.

L. Paragraph 12: Remedies: Sanctions and Implementations

According to the Charter, the obligation on Parties is to acknowledge that the aim of their policy must be 'the attainment of conditions in which the [following] rights and principles may be effectively realised'. The Protocol 1988 leaves the freedom to choose not to intervene directly to the state if, according to its legal and institutional system, this is the best way of attaining that aim.[107]

The only requirement is that each system be finalised to attain effective protection. In particular, the Committee recalls that the rights of the Charter must take 'a practical and effective rather than purely theoretical form'.[108]

The principle of appropriateness of sanctions implies different kinds of reactions to the violation of the sources—statutes or collective agreements—implementing the 'constitutional' rights of Article 21. This explains why the Charter imposes the obligation on each Party 'to maintain a system of labour inspection appropriate to national conditions' (Article A, point 4). It also explains why the kinds of sanction imposed by public or private institutions must take into account the different nature of violations: breach of statutes, fines[109] and penalties,[110] and breach of duty to perform an obligation stemming from collective agreements, compensation for damages, frequently overlapping in decisions on the case.

The principle of appropriateness requires that the following be ascertained:

- whether or not the Labour Inspectorate is in charge;[111]
- the 'number' of inspections carried out by the Labour Inspectorate;
- the 'number' of sanctions imposed on the employers;[112]
- the level of fines.[113]

A more articulated procedure in which trade union and elected representatives are authorised to initiate an administrative process requesting the intervention of the a public institution and then to appeal to the courts is also in conformity with the 'appropriate protection'. Furthermore, a special court of arbitration intervenes to take a decision particularly with regard 'to information considered by employers to be confidential'; and in the case of 'infringement of collective agreement' the Committee asks 'what maximum fine the court of arbitration can impose' and whether 'any other types of

107 Art 16 Part I, 1988 Protocol.
108 Conclusions 2010, XIX 3, Slovak Republic.
109 Conclusions 2010, Croatia; Conclusions 2014, Slovenia.
110 Conclusions 2010, Bulgaria.
111 Conclusions 2010, Czech Republic.
112 Conclusions 2010, Denmark.
113 Conclusions 2010, Norway.

sanction or remedy are available in the case of employers' failure to respect Article 21'.[114] A special commission, whose chairman is appointed by the national mediator, can be established before appealing to the court,[115] while the Organisational Structure of the Working Conditions Authority has the task of monitoring and inspecting compliance with provisions of law and collective agreements.[116]

Alternative sanctions according to the nature of (private or public) interests damaged can be imposed, in the public sector, on the employer breaching a cooperation agreement because it fails to comply with its obligation in the prescribed time. Appropriate remedies imposed by a special body (cooperation board) include issuing an order of compliance[117] and imposing a penalty.[118] Breaching the provisions of a statute or collective agreement makes employers liable to pay damages awarded by the court of law, including compensation for both financial detriment and the breach of the Act or collective agreement.[119]

From the perspective of a more radical legal philosophy, cumulative sanctions are imposed on the employer by public institutions (Labour Inspectorate or special centre) when information and consultation deal with the prevention of professional risks. In this case a fine can be awarded and a temporary pause of the operation of the particular procedure for a time interval of up to three days can be imposed. In addition to the decision of the Minister of Employment and Social Affairs, the pause of the operation can be prescribed for a period longer than three days and even be made permanent.[120]

The Committee defers its conclusions in the case of uncertainty about the level of fines and other sanctions[121] or about the rights of workers to seek damages.[122]

III. IMPACT ON EUROPEAN HUMAN RIGHTS INSTRUMENTS

The EU Agency for Fundamental Rights suggests that a 'fundamental rights community' established by EU law should be seen 'in a wider context of a multilevel governance perspective with … Council Europe and EU Member

[114] Conclusions 2010, Albania.
[115] Conclusions 2010, Norway.
[116] Conclusions 2014, Portugal.
[117] Civil sanction, Conclusions 2010, Denmark.
[118] Conclusions 2010, XIX 3, Greece.
[119] Conclusions 2010, Sweden.
[120] Conclusions 2010, XIX 3 2019, Greece.
[121] Conclusions 2010, Norway.
[122] Conclusions 2010, Azerbaijan.

States'.[123] It considers that the principle of effectiveness must be increased through the 'inter-operationality context', adding that when EU member states apply EU law, they 'remain responsible for implementing human rights under Council of Europe treaties' (paragraph 34). In the same perspective the Committee on Employment and Social Affairs has delivered a motion for an EU Parliament resolution 'to have regard to the Social Charter on the implementation of Directive 2002/14/EC' (Preamble point 3).

Regarding information and consultation rights, the Recitals in the Preamble to the 2002 Directive make absolutely no reference to the European Social Charter, despite the fact that it has been ratified by all member states and the TEU explicitly refers to it in several rules and occasions. According to Explanations of CFREU, Article 27[124] 'appears' in the Charter, although in some other articles the Explanation uses the words 'based on' (Articles 22 and 31) or 'draws on' (Articles 25 and 30).

The semantic differences do not weaken the strength of the rights of the Social Charter and their interpretation reveals their quality of 'cross-cutting principles of Community law'.[125]

It has been stated by the ECJ that 'the margin of discretion which the member states enjoy in matters of social policy cannot have the effect of frustrating the implementation of a fundamental principle of Community law or of a provision of that law'.[126]

In the past, just before the revision of the EC in 1996, the lack of a specific rule on the general principle of information and consultation was envisaged in some legal sources, but it was located in an ancillary position in respect of the economic aim of legislative intervention. Although a Recital of the EC law on concentration between undertakings warned that the EEC Regulation 'in no way detracts from collective rights of employees as recognised in the undertaking concerned'—including information and consultation—the aim of the ACT was 'to ensure conditions of effective competition'.[127] This generic statement was the basis of the decision of the European Court of Justice to recognise the need to protect 'legitimate interests' in the event of concentration as a decisive criterion to admit a right to *locus standi* of third parties (as workers' representatives) with a view

[123] 2012 Annual report of the European Agency for Fundamental Rights, section on 'Observing fundamental rights obligation in Art 6 of the TEU', in ECSR, 'The relationships between EU law and ESC', Working document, 15 July 2014, para 33.

[124] Explanations regarding CFREU, [2007] OJ C303/17.

[125] EU Parliament resolution of 27 February 2014 on the situation of fundamental rights in the EU (2012) and ECSR, The relationship between EU law and the ESC (n 123) 19.

[126] Case C-167/97 *Seymour-Smith and Perez* [1999] ECR I-623, para 75 and Case C-187/00 *Kutz-Bauer* [2003] ECR I-2741, para 57.

[127] Art 7, point 4 of Council Regulation (EEC) No 4064/89 of 21 December on the control of concentration between undertakings [1990] OJ L257/0013.

to attaining 'the fundamental objectives set by Article 2 of the Treaty'.[128] In the same perspective the Court explicitly recognised in the case of concentration of enterprises the specific obligation to inform the employees' representative organisation *in good time* deriving from Article 6 of Directive 77/187/EEC.[129] In recent times an increasing number of judgments by the CJEU have dealt with several aspects of Article 21 of the Charter, both indirectly and directly. The European judges, although they do not take into account the Charter provisions, recognise the role of the workers' representatives as 'owners' of a 'general interest' of all employees in relation to contracts of employment and 'the obligation on a public administration to consult them ... before adopting any act ... concerning all service rules'. The Luxembourg Court states that consultation amounts to a right of employees' representatives 'to be heard', which is a rather modest form of participation in a decision-making process 'unless it is to undermine the effectiveness of the obligation to consult and the administration must comply fully with that obligation whenever consultation ... is able to have an influence on the substance of the measure adopted'.[130]

A direct reference to Article 21 is made by the EU judges[131] when it declares that pensions are not included in para 1(b) and that *les agents public* are not within the scope of that provision.

[128] Order of the President of First Instance of 15 December 1992 in Case T-96/92 *Comité d'Entreprise de la Société Générale des Grandes Sources and others v Commission of the EC*, points 28–33, European Law Report 1992, p II-02579.

[129] Case T-12/93 *Comité Centrale d'Entreprises de la societé Anonyme Vittel v EC Commission* (ECJ First Instance, 27 April 1995) point 63.

[130] Case F-26/12 *Cerafogli v ECB* (EU Civil Service Tribunal (Second Chamber), 18 September 2014), quoting literally Case T-63/02 *Cerafogli v ECB* (EU Civil Service Tribunal (III Section), 20 November 2003) paras 22, 23 and 24.

[131] T-645/11 P *Heath v ECB* (EU Tribunal, 18 June 2013).

Article 22

The Right to Take Part in the Determination and Improvement of the Working Conditions and Working Environment

NIKLAS BRUUN

Article 22—The right to take part in the determination and improvement of the working conditions and working environment

With a view to ensuring the effective exercise of the right of workers to take part in the determination and improvement of the working conditions and working environment in the undertaking, the Parties undertake to adopt or encourage measures enabling workers or their representatives, in accordance with national legislation and practice, to contribute:

a. to the determination and the improvement of the working conditions, work organisation and working environment;
b. to the protection of health and safety within the undertaking;
c. to the organisation of social and socio-cultural services and facilities within the undertaking;
d. to the supervision of the observance of regulations on these matters.

Article I—Implementation of the undertakings given

2. Compliance with the undertakings deriving from the provisions of … Articles 22 … of Part II of this Charter … shall be regarded as effective if the provisions are applied, in accordance with paragraph 1 of this article, to the great majority of the workers concerned.

Appendix Part II[1]

1. This provision affects neither the powers and obligations of States as regards the adoption of health and safety regulations for workplaces, nor the powers and responsibilities of the bodies in charge of monitoring their application.

[1] The wording of the Appendix to Art 22 is common to that of Art 21; see B Veneziani on Art 21 in this volume.

2. The terms 'social and socio-cultural services and facilities' are understood as referring to the social and/or cultural facilities for workers provided by some undertakings such as welfare assistance, sports fields, rooms for nursing mothers, libraries, children's holiday camps, etc.

I. INTRODUCTION

A. Context and Main Content

The right to safe and healthy working conditions (see above, Article 3) is an important fundamental right of workers. In order for it to be effective it has to be complemented by procedural guarantees, such as the right to involvement of workers' representatives. The latter right has been enshrined in Article 22, which is a new provision included in Part II of the 1996 Charter and closely linked to Article 21. Several key concepts, such as 'workers' representatives' and 'undertakings' have to be applied in conformity with their application under Article 21 (see above). The material content of Article 22 was already included in the Additional Protocol of 1988 as its Article 3. There are therefore some states that have ratified the Additional Protocol and which are bound to it, although they have not ratified the Revised European Social Charter.[2]

The right of workers' representatives to consultation at the enterprise level in matters of health and safety at the workplace is therefore equally dealt with by Article 3 (1988 Additional Protocol). For the states that have accepted both Articles 3 and 22, this issue is examined only under Article 22.[3]

B. International Sources

The most important international source that has had a clear impact on the content and wording of Article 22 is ILO Convention No C 155.[4] Convention No 187, which was adopted as late as 2006, again builds in part on the RESC because it aims to promote, among other things, workplace-related preventive measures.[5]

[2] Such states include Croatia, Czech Republic, Denmark, Greece and Spain.

[3] There are still several Member States that have not accepted either Art 3 or Art 22: Andorra, Austria, Georgia, Malta, Moldova, Montenegro, Macedonia, Germany, Ireland, Luxembourg, Poland and the United Kingdom.

[4] C-155—Occupational Safety and Health Convention 1981 (No 155).

[5] C-187—Promotional Framework for Occupational Safety and Health Convention 2006 (No 187).

C. Relationship with the Other Provisions of the Charter

Regarding the material content of Article 22, it is not only related to Article 3 regarding the right to safe and healthy working conditions, but also to some extent to Articles 2 and 4 because the scope of application of the Article is not restricted to the working environment in the strict sense, but also applies to working conditions and work organisation.

Article 22 is closely linked to three other Articles in the Charter that deal with different aspects of workers participation, namely Articles 21, 28 and 29. In this context this chapter only refers to the separate chapters regarding these Articles, but it emphasises that the principles enshrined in Articles 21 and 28 also apply to workers' involvement in matters related to working conditions and working environment.

II. CONTENT

The structure of Article 22 cannot be partly accepted by state parties because it forms a whole in its structure of sub-paragraphs (a) to (d). In what follows, the wording of the different sub-paragraphs will be analysed, then some general issues will be discussed.

A. 'To the Determination and Improvement of the Working Conditions, Work Organisation and Working Environment'

The aim of the participation right under Article 22 is for 'the determination and the improvement of the working conditions, work organisation and working environment' and 'the protection of health and safety within the undertaking'. Not surprisingly, most of the Committee's practice concerning Article 22 (Article 3 Additional Protocol) has concerned Article 22b (Article 3§1b, Additional Protocol) on health and safety. This Article may be complied with by providing for the representation of workers on a safety committee within the enterprise.[6] Although health and safety is a focus, the ECSR clearly attaches importance to all three elements in the text: working conditions, work organisation and working environment. The Committee has consistently criticised State Parties when the information provided in the reports under this Article essentially concerns only the protection of health and safety at work rather than working conditions, work organisation and the working environment, and therefore it has asked

[6] D Harris, *The European Social Charter* (Ardsley, New York, Transnational Publishers 2001) 250.

for further information.[7] In the case of Belgium the Committee noted that the Act transposed there had a very broad scope, and concerned measures relating to safety at work, health protection, psychological and social problems caused by work, including violence and moral or sexual harassment, ergonomics, occupational hygiene, the improvement of the working environment and steps taken by the company with regard to the working environment and their influence on the other aspects. Given the wide material scope of the Act, the Committee concluded that the situation was in conformity with the Charter.[8] As indicated above, the material scope of sub-paragraph (a) goes much further than the existing case law. Indeed, the term 'working conditions' is to be understood in a wide sense and covers probably the whole area of at least individual labour law, in particular the rights guaranteed under Articles 2, 3, 4, 24, 26 and 27, thus requiring consultation on those issues (independently of whether those rights also include specific consultation requirements).

B. 'To the Protection of Health and Safety within the Undertaking'

It is important to note that the whole aim of Article 22 is to protect health and safety within the undertaking and that the interpretation of the Article must be done with this aim in mind.

C. 'The Organisation of Social and Socio-Cultural Services and Facilities Within the Undertaking'

The Committee has held that Article 22 of the Charter does not require that employers offer social and socio-cultural services and facilities to their employees, but requires that workers may participate in their organisation, where such 'services and facilities have been established'.

Here we can also recall that this provision affects neither the powers and obligations of states as regards the adoption of health and safety regulations for workplaces, nor the powers and responsibilities of the bodies in charge of monitoring their application.

The term 'social and socio-cultural services and facilities' is understood to refer to the social and/or cultural facilities for workers provided by some undertakings, such as welfare assistance, sports fields, rooms for nursing mothers, libraries, children's holiday camps and so on.

[7] Conclusions 2014, Bulgaria.
[8] Conclusions 2014, Belgium.

D. 'To the Supervision of the Observance of Regulations on these Matters'

The contribution to the 'supervision of the observance' of health and safety regulations is to be effected pursuant to the rules in force in each country and without prejudice to the jurisdiction and responsibilities of the bodies and authorities vested with the necessary powers. The role of workers or their representatives is not to replace the bodies responsible for this supervision, but rather to ensure that supervision is as effective as possible.[9] On the other hand, supervision cannot be exercised without rights to information and access to enforcement mechanisms, courts and labour inspections.

E. 'Effective'

It has consistently been held by the Committee that, in order for the right to be an effective one, it has to be interpreted as requiring that workers or their representatives must be able to 'lodge a complaint' in the case of infringement. The Committee has found that a right of appeal to a labour court complies with this requirement.[10] There must also be sanctions available for employers who fail to fulfil their obligations under Article 22.[11]

F. 'To Take Part in'

The expression 'to take part in' covers all situations in which workers or their representatives are in any way whatsoever associated with the procedures for making decisions or taking certain measures, without, however, enjoying a right of joint decision-making or of veto over decisions still the responsibility of the head of the undertaking.[12] The minimum requirements that partly can be drawn from other regulations on workers' participation apply also in this case. Workers have to have access to adequate information, which has to be provided to them in a timely manner, also taking into account that decision-making regarding working environment often has a preventive dimension and must be taken before other measures (introduction of new machines, equipment and so on).

[9] Explanatory Report to Additional Protocol 1988.
[10] Harris (n 6) 249.
[11] Conclusions 2014, Armenia, 4.
[12] Explanatory Report to the Protocol, para 50; see also Harris (n 6) 249.

G. 'The Undertaking'?

As indicated above regarding Article 21, in the Appendix to the Additional Protocol it is stated: 'For the purpose of the application of these articles, the term "undertaking" is understood as referring to a set of tangible and intangible components, with or without legal personality, formed to produce goods or provide services for financial gain and with power to determine its own market policy.'

States may exclude from the scope of this provision those undertakings employing fewer than a certain number of workers, to be determined by national legislation or practice. The Committee has considered as in conformity with this provision a situation where, in undertakings employing fewer than 10 people, 'employees are in direct contact with the employer'.[13]

There has been some uncertainty whether the concept of an 'undertaking' extends to the public sector. The position in the Committee seems to be that state-owned companies are covered, but the public administration as such is not covered. This was fairly clearly stated in the Conclusions on Norway in 2010.[14] The Committee referred to the Appendix to the Protocol, which in the section relating to Articles 2 and 3 (para 3) contains a definition of the term 'undertaking', according to which it is a 'set of tangible or intangible components, with or without legal personality, formed to produce or provide services for financial gain and with power to determine its own market policy'. As stated by the Committee, employees in the public sector are in principle not covered by this provision; in the public sector it only applies to workers in publicly owned undertakings.

The same position has been taken in two complaints regarding Portugal.[15]

Recently the Committee has reiterated this position: 'The Committee underlines that Article 22 applies to all undertakings, whether private or public.'[16] It therefore seems that the ECSR adheres constantly to a very restricted formal interpretation of the word 'undertaking'.

H. 'Workers or their Representatives, in Accordance with National Legislation and Practice'

Under the Appendix to RESC[17] for the purpose of the application of these Articles, the term 'workers' representatives' means 'persons who are

[13] Conclusions 2005, Estonia, 202–03.

[14] Conclusions 2010, Norway.

[15] Decision on the merits, *European Council of Police Trade Unions v Portugal*, Collective Complaint No 40/2007 and *European Council of Police Trade Unions v Portugal*, Collective Complaint No 60/2010.

[16] Conclusions 2014, Hungary.

[17] Appendix pp 1 and 2, see above under Art 21.

recognised as such under national legislation or practice' and the terms 'national legislation and practice' embrace, as the case may be, in addition to laws and regulations, collective agreements, other agreements between employers and workers' representatives, customs as well as relevant case law.

In light of this position it was slightly surprising that the Committee has found that Article 22 (or the corresponding Article 3 of the 1988 Additional Protocol) and especially §1a does not concern the right to collective bargaining.[18]

The conjunction 'or' used in the expression 'workers or their representatives' is not exclusive. It simply means that the rights afforded by these two provisions may be exercised by workers, or by their representatives, or by both, and the fact that they are conferred upon one group does not mean that they cannot be conferred upon the other, as stipulated in the Articles themselves.[19]

A definition of 'workers' representatives' is given in the Appendix. It is drawn from Article 3 of the ILO Convention No 135 concerning protection and facilities to be afforded to workers' representatives in the undertaking, so as to harmonise the definitions contained in the various international instruments.

III. IMPACT

There is a long tradition of workers' participation in the field of health and safety, and in fact the right to take part in activities in this field has since been adopted for other sectors or as a general right to information and consultation.

Cooperation between management and workers and/or their representatives within the undertaking shall be an essential element of organisational and other measures taken in pursuance of the most important obligations under the ILO Occupational Safety and Health Convention 1981.[20]

Article 27 CFREU states that workers or their representatives must, at the appropriate levels, be guaranteed information and consultation in good time in the cases and under the conditions provided for by EU law and national laws and practices. The EU framework Directive on health and safety[21] clearly indicates that EU law provides for such conditions as are laid

[18] Decision on the merits, *GENOP-DEI and ADEDY v Greece*, Collective Complaint No 65/2011. See, however, the dissenting opinion of Mr Petros Stangos on this issue.

[19] See further regarding Art 21 Bruno Veneziani in this volume.

[20] ILO C-155, Occupational Safety and Health Convention, 1981, Convention concerning Occupational Safety and Health and the Working Environment (Arts 16–19).

[21] Council Directive 89/391/EEC of 12 June 1989 on the introduction of measures to encourage improvements in the safety and health of workers at work.

down in Article 11 of the Directive, where it is stated that employers shall consult workers and/or their representatives and allow them to take part in discussions on all questions relating to safety and health at work. Although not mentioned explicitly in the Explanations to Article 27 CFREU, the content of Article 22 should also be taken into account when interpreting Article 27 CFREU (see, for example, the reference to 'the Charter of the Council of Europe' in the preamble of the CFREU).

Article 24

The Right to Protection in Cases of Termination of Employment

MÉLANIE SCHMITT

Article 24—The right to protection in cases of termination of employment

With a view to ensuring the effective exercise of the right of workers to protection in cases of termination of employment, the Parties undertake to recognise:

a. the right of all workers not to have their employment terminated without valid reasons for such termination connected with their capacity or conduct or based on the operational requirements of the undertaking, establishment or service;
b. the right of workers whose employment is terminated without a valid reason to adequate compensation or other appropriate relief.

To this end the Parties undertake to ensure that a worker who considers that his employment has been terminated without a valid reason shall have the right to appeal to an impartial body.

Appendix Part II

Article 24

1. It is understood that for the purposes of this Article the terms 'termination of employment' and 'terminated' mean termination of employment at the initiative of the employer.
2. It is understood that this Article covers all workers but that a Party may exclude from some or all of its protection the following categories of employed persons:
    a. workers engaged under a contract of employment for a specified period of time or a specified task;
    b. workers undergoing a period of probation or a qualifying period of employment, provided that this is determined in advance and is of a reasonable duration;
    c. workers engaged on a casual basis for a short period.

3. For the purpose of this Article the following, in particular, shall not constitute valid reasons for termination of employment:
   a. trade union membership or participation in union activities outside working hours, or, with the consent of the employer, within working hours;
   b. seeking office as, acting or having acted in the capacity of a workers' representative;
   c. the filing of a complaint or the participation in proceedings against an employer involving alleged violation of laws or regulations or recourse to competent administrative authorities;
   d. race, colour, sex, marital status, family responsibilities, pregnancy, religion, political opinion, national extraction or social origin;
   e. maternity or parental leave;
   f. temporary absence from work due to illness or injury.
4. It is understood that compensation or other appropriate relief in case of termination of employment without valid reasons shall be determined by national laws or regulations, collective agreements or other means appropriate to national conditions.

I. INTRODUCTION

The right to protection in cases of termination of employment 'is the most salient of fundamental social rights because ... it asserts the principle that labour is not a commodity or Article of commerce'.[1] Placing constraints on the most symbolic manifestation of the employer's powers helps to preserve the stability and security of employment relations, which are all the more necessary in times of economic and social crisis.[2]

The specific structure of Article 24 reflects the 'substantive unity' of its provisions and explains that it must be accepted in its entirety by State Parties.[3] Seven states among those that had ratified the revised Charter refused to be bound by Article 24: Andorra, Austria, Belgium, Bosnia, Georgia, Hungary and Sweden. There is no doubt that their refusal is based on the obvious incompatibility of the national situation with Article 24 provisions.[4] Moreover, many state parties, including Denmark, Germany,

[1] J Kenner, *The EU Charter of Fundamental Rights: A commentary* (Oxford, Hart, 2014) 832, about Art 30 CFREU.

[2] See ILO, *Recovering from the Crisis: A Global Jobs Pact* (Geneva, ILO, 2009), para 14.

[3] Explanatory Report, point 84. See D Harris, *The European Social Charter* (Cambridge, Transnational Publishers, 2001) 272.

[4] In this respect, the case of Belgium is significant because Belgian law does not require employers to provide reasons for dismissal. Belgian authorities simply explained to the ECSR that they did not want to change this system (ECSR, Rapport de la réunion avec des représentants du gouvernement belge sur les dispositions non acceptées de la Charte sociale européenne révisée, Strasbourg, 3 February 2009, 3). For the same reason, Belgium has not ratified ILO

Greece, Spain and the United Kingdom, are not bound by Article 24 because they have not yet ratified the revised Charter.[5]

Furthermore, it is worth noting that only a single decision on the merits has been delivered, on 2 July 2013, by the European Committee on Social Rights (ECSR) on the ground of Article 24.[6] But two pending complaints concerning Finnish law[7] are incorporated in the present chapter as they raise important new questions related to dismissal based on business reasons. As a consequence of this situation, interpretation of Article 24 is mainly a result of the ECSR appraisal of national situations within the reporting procedure.

Section I of this chapter aims at briefly introducing the main content of Article 24 in light of its context (I.A) and relevant international sources (I.B) as well as highlighting its established or potential connection with other Charter provisions (I.C). In section II, provisions of Article 24 and their interpretation are analysed in detail. Finally, section III deals with the (potential) impact of Article 24 both at European and national level.

A. Context and Main Content

(i) Context

The idea of including a provision in the Charter on unjustified or unfair dismissal was mooted early on in the revitalisation process, in 1990, and was proposed as an addition to the right to just conditions of work (Article 2).[8] The fact that it was finally enshrined autonomously in Article 24 highlights the specificity of dismissal compared with the other employment conditions, as well as the importance of a general and effective protection against unfair dismissal as a tool for preserving the permanence of employment relations.[9] In the context of the reporting procedure, Article 24 precisely belongs to thematic group 1, 'Employment, training and equal opportunities'[10] (not to group 3, dedicated to 'Labour rights'). Thus, the idea that the right to

Convention 158. This is also the case for Andorran law, which provides for dismissal without reason. See ECSR, Premier rapport sur les dispositions non acceptées Andorre, 21 May 2012, 15–16.

[5] Situation at 26 June 2013. Overall, only 26 state parties must ensure the conformity of their national situation with Art 24 requirements.

[6] *Fellesforbundet for Sjøfolk (FFFS) v Norway*, Collective Complaint No 74/2011, on dismissal on the ground of age.

[7] *Finnish Society of Social Rights v Finland*, Collective Complaints Nos 106/2014 and 107/2014.

[8] See Harris (n 3).

[9] See A Swiatkowski, *Charter of Social Rights of the Council of Europe* (The Hague, Kluwer Law International, 2007) 168.

[10] Arts 1, 9, 10, 15, 18, 20 and 25 also form part of group 1.

protection against unfair dismissal contributes to ensure the effectiveness of the right to work appears to be supported. In that respect and although it is excluded from the Charter 'hard core' provisions, Article 24 is given a very broad interpretation in the Appendix and the ECSR conclusions.[11]

(ii) Brief Presentation of the Content

(a) General Principles

Protection provided by Article 24 is divided into substantive guarantees and the right to appeal. The former result from two general principles: the right not to be dismissed unless there are valid grounds (Article 24§a) and, in case of unfair dismissal, the right to adequate compensation or other appropriate relief (Article 24§b). The effectiveness of that right to relief requires that the right to challenge the dismissal's reason before an impartial body be provided. Substantive guarantees have thus to be understood in view of and in connection with this judicial guarantee.

(b) Appendix

The Appendix provides numerous details on the interpretation of Article 24. First, indications are given on the scope of Article 24. The material scope must be broadly defined and extended to 'termination of employment at the initiative of employer'. But, as to personal scope, it is possible for a state party to exclude application of Article 24 to certain categories of workers. The Appendix then contains a list of non-valid reasons that correspond to discriminatory grounds that are prohibited elsewhere in the Charter.[12] Finally, the Appendix requires that states ensure that compensation or other appropriate relief be determined by national law or by a provision of another nature. This implies that the content of the relief must be fixed and known in advance, namely during the dismissal procedure or at the latest when the employer takes the decision to terminate employment.

B. International Sources

(i) Explicit Source: ILO Convention No 158

Article 24 was explicitly inspired by ILO Convention No 158 (Termination of Employment) of 1982[13] (hereafter C158), some provisions of which

[11] The latest conclusions on group 1 rights (Conclusions 2012) were delivered in January 2013 and cover the period 2007 to 2010.

[12] See below section II.C(i).

[13] Explanatory Report, point 86.

are reproduced verbatim. As a consequence, Article 24 must be interpreted according to the Convention and its accompanying Recommendation No 166, as well as the 'case law' of the Committee of Experts on the Application of Conventions and Recommendations (hereafter the 'ILO CEACR').[14]

Categories of workers who can be excluded from protection, the definition of 'termination of employment', as well as the general requirement of a valid reason and non-valid grounds listed within the Appendix are reproduced almost word for word from Articles 2, 3 and 5 C158. Moreover, the Explanatory Report especially states that 'As to the nature of the impartial body mentioned in the last paragraph of the Article, reference is made to Article 8 of the ILO Convention'.[15]

Convention 158 provisions are much more detailed than Article 24, but certain ILO guarantees are enshrined in other Charter provisions (for instance, the right of all workers to a reasonable period of notice for termination of employment enshrined in Article 4§4).[16]

(ii) Other Relevant International Sources

(a) International Covenant on Economic, Social and Cultural Rights

The right to protection in cases of termination of employment is not enshrined as such in the UN International Covenant on Economic, Social and Cultural Rights of 1966. However, the Committee on Economic, Social and Cultural Rights found that the right to work (Article 6) ensures protection against unfair dismissal. Referring explicitly to ILO Convention No 158, it states that the failure to protect workers against unlawful dismissal constitutes a violation of the obligation to protect the right to work.[17]

(b) European Convention on Human Rights

Several ECHR provisions are intended to apply in cases of termination of employment and provide procedural or substantive guarantees.

Procedural rights. Article 6§1 ECHR (right to a fair trial) applies to work-related disputes according to settled case law, which reinforces the link between the right not to be dismissed without valid reason and the right

[14] ILO, *Protection against unjustified dismissal, General Survey on the Termination of Employment Convention (No 158) and Recommendation (No 166) 1982*, International Labour Conference, 82nd Session 1995, Report III (Pt 4B) (Geneva, ILO, 1995); ILO, *Termination of employment instruments*, Background paper for the Tripartite Meeting of Experts to Examine the Termination of Employment Convention, 1982 (No 158), and the Termination of Employment Recommendation, 1982 (No 166) (Geneva, ILO, 2011).

[15] Explanatory Report §86.

[16] See below section I.C(ii).

[17] CESCR, The Right to Work—General Comment No 18, adopted on 24 November 2005, E/C 12/GC/18 (6.02.2006) §§11 and 35.

to appeal to enforce this right. The ECtHR provides important procedural rights, assessing issues such as the unfairness of proceedings concerning removal from office,[18] or excessive overall length of the dismissal proceedings.[19] In *KMC v Hungary*,[20] the Strasbourg Court referred explicitly to Article 24 and held that the dismissal of a civil servant without giving reasons 'amounts to depriving the impugned right of action of all substance'.

Substantive rights. Substantive rights are also afforded to unlawfully dismissed workers. A dismissal based on the exercise of a ECHR freedom or right logically falls within the ambit of the relevant ECHR provisions. Termination of employment has therefore been assessed from the perspective of Article 8 (right to respect of private life),[21] Article 9 (freedom to hold religious beliefs),[22] Article 10 (freedom of expression)[23] and Article 11 (freedom of association).[24]

More surprisingly, Article 8 ECHR is intended to protect workers, their dismissal being analysed by the ECtHR as a privacy breach.[25] This interpretation derives from the very extensive notion of private life including the professional sphere, as initiated in *Niemietz v Germany*.[26] Several recent judgments confirm that the right to protection in cases of termination of employment is protected by Article 8 ECHR.[27] The Court's reasoning is all the more interesting in that it stresses the dramatic consequences that

[18] *Hrdalo v Croatia* App no 23272/07 (ECtHR, 27 September 2011) and *Lesjak v Croatia* App no 25904/06 (ECtHR, 18 February 2010).

[19] *Mishgjoni v Albania*, App no 18381/05 (ECtHR, 7 December 2010) and *Golenja v Slovenia* App no 76378/01 (ECtHR, 30 March 2006).

[20] *KMC v Hungary* App no 19554/11 (ECtHR, 10 July 2012) §34.

[21] *Lustig-Prean and Beckett v the United Kingdom* and *Smith and Grady v the United Kingdom* (ECtHR, 27 September 1999), *Perkins and R v the United Kingdom* and *Beck, Copp and Bazeley v the United Kingdom* (ECtHR, 22 October 2002) on members of the UK armed forces who had been discharged on the sole ground of their sexual orientation.

[22] *Ivanova v Bulgaria* App no 52435/99 (ECtHR, 12 April 2007) and *Eweida and others v the United Kingdom* App nos 48420/10, 59842/10, 51671/10 and 36516/10 (ECtHR, 15 January 2013).

[23] *Heinisch v Germany* App no 28274/08 (ECtHR, 21 October 2010).

[24] *Redfearn v the United Kingdom* App no 47335/06 (ECtHR, 6 December 2012).

[25] See J-F Akandji-Kombé, 'Un nouvel horizon pour le droit à l'emploi: le droit à la vie privée', in *Droit du travail Emploi Entreprise. Mélanges en l'honneur du Professeur François Gaudu* (Paris, IRJS Éditions, 2014) 301–12.

[26] *Niemietz v Germany* (1992) Series A no 251-B, and *Sidabras and Džiautas v Lithuania* App nos 55480/00 and 59330/00 (ECtHR, 27 July 2004). See J Mouly, 'Vie professionnelle et vie privée. De nouvelles rencontres sous l'égide de l'article 8 de la Convention européenne', in F Sudre (ed), *Le droit au respect de la vie privée au sens de la Convention européenne des droits de l'homme* (Brussels, Bruylant Nemesis, 2005) 279–301 and F Hendrix and A Ven Bever, 'Art 8 ECHR: Judicial Patterns of Employment Privacy Protection', in F Dorssemont, K Lörcher and I Schömann (eds), *The European Convention on Human Rights and the Employment Relation* (Oxford, Hart, 2013) 183.

[27] *Özpinar v Turkey* App no 20999/04 (ECtHR, 19 October 2010); *Fernandez Martinez v Spain* App no 56030/07 (ECtHR, 15 May 2012); *Oleksander Volkov v Ukraine* App no 21722/11 (ECtHR, 9 January 2013).

usually result from a dismissal, not only in financial terms but also regarding the capacity to develop a 'social private life'.[28]

In most of these judgments the ECtHR made a vertical application of the ECHR because the cases concerned civil servants. But the same reasoning is extended to horizontal litigations, as shown in *IB v Greece,* a case opposing a private employer and a worker dismissed on the ground of his HIV-positive status.[29] Moreover, the protection against unfair dismissal is strengthened by the combination of Article 8 and Article 14 ECHR where dismissal is based on the grounds of sex or health.[30]

(c) European Union Law and Case Law

Article 30 CFREU provides that 'Every worker has the right to protection against unjustified dismissal, in accordance with Union law and national laws and practice'. According to the Explanations relating to the EU Charter,[31] this provision draws on Article 24 so that it should be interpreted in light of the ECSR requirements and case law.

The critical issue lies in the limited scope of Article 30 CFREU due to the absence of any general directive regulating the termination of employment, although 'protection of workers where their employment contract is terminated' falls under EU competence by virtue of Article 153 TFEU. However, Member States must respect the Charter 'only when they are implementing Union law',[32] this wording being interpreted restrictively by the CJEU. In *Nagy,*[33] the Court of Luxembourg held that the Hungarian legislation allowing the termination of civil servants' employment relation without any justification and the resulting proceedings did not 'concern the interpretation or application of a rule of the Union other than those contained in the Charter', thus excluding the Court's jurisdiction. As a consequence of

[28] See *Emel Boyraz v Turkey* App no 61960/08 (ECtHR, 2 December 2014) §44; *Sidabras and Džiautas* (n 26) §48; *Oleksandr Volkov* (n 27) §166.

[29] *IB v Greece* App no 552/10 (ECtHR, 3 October 2013).

[30] However, it can be argued that a dismissal might be said to fall within the ambit of Art 8, so as to make the non-discrimination principle (Art 14) applicable, even if it does not violate the right to respect for private life. In this sense, M-T Meulders-Klein, 'L'irrésistible ascension de la "vie privée" au sein des droits de l'homme', in F Sudre (ed), *Le droit au respect de la vie privée au sens de la Convention européenne des droits de l'homme* (Brussels, Bruylant Nemesis, 2005) 305–33; R O'Connel, 'The Right to Work in the European Convention on Human Rights' (2012) Issue 2 *European Human Rights Law Review* 176–90.

[31] Explanations relating to the Charter of Fundamental Rights [2007] OJ C303/17.

[32] Art 51§1 CFREU.

[33] Joined Cases C-488/12, C-489/12, C-490/12, C-491/12 and C-526/12 *Nagy and others* ECLI:EU:C:2013:703. See also Case C-323/08 *Mayor and others* ECLI:EU:C:2009:770: given that the Court found that a situation such as that at issue in the dispute in the main proceedings does not fall within the scope of Directive 98/59, or, accordingly, within that of Community law, it is not necessary to answer the question whether the Spanish legislation on collective redundancies infringes Art 30.

this narrow interpretation of the Charter's scope, the CJEU did not answer the question asked by the referring court on the potential direct effect of Article 30 CFREU. Application of Article 30 is then limited to situations where Member States implement relevant EU legislation: directives quoted in the Explanations[34] but also primary Law and Directives protecting workers from discriminations in their employment and working conditions including dismissal.[35]

C. Relationship to Other Provisions of the Charter

Article 24 is, explicitly or not, connected to several other Charter provisions related to the requirement of a valid reason for every employment termination (1) or complementing the content of the protection (2).

(i) Relevant Provisions with Regard to the Requirement of a Valid Reason

(a) Right to Work

The right to protection in the event of termination of employment is directly linked to the right of work.[36] Such a close connection is highlighted by both the UN Committee on Economic, Social and Cultural Rights[37] and the ILO CEACR, asserting that protection against unjustified dismissal 'favour(s) the promotion of employment security which is an essential aspect of the right to work'.[38]

The ECSR also establishes such a direct linked between the right to work (Article 1) and the employment termination, especially as regards the prohibition of discrimination deriving from Article 1§2 and the obligation 'to protect effectively the right of the worker to earn his living in an occupation freely entered upon'.[39]

[34] Directive 2001/23/EC on the safeguarding of employees' rights in the event of transfers of undertakings, and Directive 80/987/EC on the protection of employees in the event of the insolvency of their employer, as amended by Directive 2002/74/EC.

[35] Art 45 TFEU on freedom of movement for workers and discrimination on grounds of nationality; Directive 2000/43/EC implementing the principle of equal treatment between persons irrespective of racial or ethnic origin; Directive 2000/78/EC establishing a general framework for equal treatment in employment and occupation prohibiting discrimination on the grounds of religion or belief, disability, age, and sexual orientation; Directive 2006/54/EC on the principle of equal opportunities and equal treatment of men and women in matters of employment and occupation (recast).

[36] See the chapter on Art 1 by Simon Deakin in this volume.

[37] See above section II.B(ii)(a).

[38] ILC, 59th Session, 1974, *Record of Proceedings* 527.

[39] See, for instance, Conclusions XVI-1 (2002), Austria; Conclusions 2008, Azerbaijan.

(b) Anti-discrimination Provisions

More generally, 'a series of provisions in the Charter require more rigorous safeguards against dismissal on certain grounds. Among these is Article 1§2 with regard to the safeguards against discrimination in relation to the right to work. Most of these grounds are listed in the Appendix under Article 24 as reasons not justifying dismissal'.[40] Protection against unfair dismissal is thus reinforced when combined with one (or several) of the specific Charter provisions pointed out by the ECSR: discrimination (Articles 1§2, 4§3 and 20); trade union activity (Article 5); participation in a strike (Article 6§4); maternity (Article 8§2); disability (Article 15); family responsibilities (Article 27); workers' representation (Article 28).[41]

Because most of these reasons are listed in the Appendix under Article 24, the ECSR decided to restrict its assessment of the conformity of national situations to reasons that are not referred to elsewhere in the Revised Charter, namely 'the filing of a complaint or the participation in proceedings against an employer involving alleged violation of laws or regulations or recourse to competent administrative authorities'. This statement should apply only if States have accepted all these specific provisions.[42]

(c) Relevant Provisions with Regard to the Content of the Protection

Article 24 can be connected to other Charter provisions establishing substantive or procedural rights for (dismissed) workers. With regard to substantive rights, all workers have the right to a reasonable period of notice for termination of employment, afforded by Article 4§4 as an element of the right to a fair remuneration.[43] It may be noted that, according to the Appendix, 'this provision shall be so understood as not to prohibit immediate dismissal for any serious offence'.

In respect of procedural rights, Article 21 lays down a right for workers or their representatives to be informed and consulted on 'decisions which could have an important impact on the employment situation in the undertaking', thus including projected collective redundancies. This right is precisely applied by Article 29 to collective redundancy procedures. It stems from these provisions that they only cover the collective aspects of dismissals. The ECSR indeed holds that 'the right of individual employees to contest the lawfulness of their being made redundant is examined with reference to Article 24'.[44]

[40] Statement of Interpretation on Art 24, Conclusions 2003.

[41] For an in-depth analysis, see the chapters on these articles in this volume.

[42] Conclusions 2005, Estonia.

[43] The connection between Arts 24 and 4§4 is recognised by the ECSR. See *GENOP-DEI and ADEDY v Greece*, Collective Complaint No 65/2011 §25 ff.

[44] Conclusions 2003, Statement of Interpretation on Art 29.

II. CONTENT

A. Scope

(i) Material Scope

Article 24 deals with all cases of 'termination of employment at the initiative of the employer'.[45] This wording can be construed as vague and broad enough to include termination of work agreement by mutual consent of parties, at least when the termination was initiated by the employer.[46] Constructive dismissals should also be included in the scope of Article 24; termination at the initiative of the employee but provoked by the employer's violation of the employee's rights, must be treated in the same way as termination at the initiative of the employer.

Furthermore, the ECSR infers from the Appendix that 'situations where a mandatory retirement age is set by statute, as a consequence of which the employment relationship automatically ceases by operation of law, do not fall within the scope of this provision'.[47] Protection afforded by Article 24 then only applies where employers can freely exercise their right to dismiss an employee, and not in the event of termination imposed by the law. On the other hand, dismissals on the ground that the employee has reached the normal pensionable age fall within the ambit of Article 24.[48]

(ii) Personal Scope

Limits placed on the personal scope of Article 24 are more problematic. According to the ECSR, it 'applies only to persons working under a contract of employment' ('salariés liés par un contrat de travail').[49] As a consequence of this (too) restrictive approach, 'officials elected or appointed to an office or the staff of an administrative agency'[50] are excluded from the scope of Article 24.

In addition, member states are allowed to exclude from the protection of Article 24, wholly or partially, the following categories of workers: those engaged under a contract of employment for a specified period of time or a specified task; those undergoing a period of probation or a qualifying period of employment, provided that this is determined in advance and is of a reasonable duration; as well as those engaged on a casual basis for a

[45] Appendix to the RESC.
[46] See Swiatowski (n 9) 168.
[47] Conclusions 2012, Statement of interpretation on Art 24, §15.
[48] See section III.A(i)(a).
[49] See Conclusions 2003, Bulgaria; Romania (French version); and Conclusions 2005, Estonia (amended English version).
[50] Conclusions 2005, Estonia.

short period. The ECSR asks that states give details on 'whether employees on fixed-term contracts have equal rights concerning dismissal as those with contracts of an indefinite duration, or whether a trial period or a minimum period must be completed before this protection becomes applicable'.[51] As regards the second category, exclusion from the protection against dismissal during six months is considered unreasonable, as such a probationary period 'does not depend on the qualifications of the employees'.[52]

As the list is exhaustive, exclusion of another category of workers constitutes a violation of Article 24. For instance, 'the non-application in Italian law of the protection against redundancy for household employees, professional athletes and employees over the age of 60 obviously goes beyond the provisions of the appendix'.[53] In the same vein, in the absence of a clear provision, protection against unfair dismissal must be granted irrespective of the size of the company.[54]

B. The Right Not to Be Dismissed without a Valid Reason

The need to base termination of employment on a valid reason is the cornerstone of protection in the event of termination of employment.[55] Its essential aim is to avoid arbitrary dismissals by prohibiting termination without justification. To assess the extent to which reasons that employers in practice regard as justifying dismissals are permitted by Article 24, the ECSR examines legislation and 'leading decisions and judgments'.[56]

The Appendix contains a non-exhaustive list of non-valid reasons drawn from ILO Convention No 158 and Recommendation No 166[57] and related to the worker. Article 24 also mentions economic reasons that can constitute valid grounds for dismissal. The effectiveness of the right to protection in cases of termination of employment, finally, implies concrete procedural guarantees.

(i) Personal Reasons

Pursuant to Article 24, personal reasons are related to the worker's 'capacity' or 'conduct'. The ECSR has not yet been given an opportunity to

[51] Conclusions 2003, Bulgaria.

[52] Conclusions 2003, Italy. See also in the same vein, Conclusions 2005, Cyprus 111, on the exclusion of the protection for employees who have not completed a continuous period of 26 weeks with their employer.

[53] Conclusions 2003, Italy.

[54] Conclusions 2003, Bulgaria.

[55] ILO, *Protection against unjustified dismissal* (n 14) §76, about ILO Convention No 158.

[56] Conclusions 2005, Estonia; Norway.

[57] Harris notes that the Revised Charter is more protective as dismissals on the grounds of 'maternity or parental leave' are explicitly prohibited. See Harris (n 3) 272.

give general guidance on the interpretation of these two notions. It can be argued that it would approve the general requirement of the International Labour Conference: 'for reasons connected with the capacity or conduct of the worker to be considered as valid, they must have a bearing on the work of the worker or the working environment'.[58]

(a) The Worker's Capacity

The worker's capacity or aptitude can be altered for several reasons, which correspond to two types of incapacity: incapacity resulting from a lack of the skills or qualities necessary to perform certain tasks, leading to unsatisfactory performance, and incapacity as a result of illness or injury.[59] The ECSR has already taken a position on several grounds for dismissal that correspond to the second category: worker's health and permanent injury. Special attention must be paid to the ground of age that may also be analysed as a factor of the worker's (in)capacity.

Dismissal on the Ground of Worker's Health

Pursuant to the Appendix, temporary absence from work due to illness is not a valid reason for dismissal. However, for the ECSR, absence constitutes a valid reason if it severely disrupts the smooth running of the undertaking and a genuine, permanent replacement must be provided for the absent employee.[60] Furthermore, it seems that the ECSR would admit illness as a valid reason if it is covered by legislation and has been authorised by the Labour Inspectorate, provided that the criteria taken into account are in conformity with the Charter.[61]

More generally, a time limit can be placed on protection against dismissal in such cases[62] and additional protection must be offered, where necessary, for victims of employment injuries or occupational diseases.[63] For instance, Norwegian legislation is in conformity with these requirements because it

> protects employees from dismissal for the first six months following a period of incapacity and the first twelve months if the employee has been employed by the company for five consecutive years or more. If the incapacity is the result of an employment injury or occupational disease, dismissal may not be justified by absence for illness for twelve months following the period of incapacity.[64]

[58] ILC, 67th Session, 1981, Report VIII(2) 33.
[59] ILO, *Protection against unjustified dismissal* (n 14) §94.
[60] Conclusions 2003, France.
[61] Conclusions 2003, Bulgaria.
[62] Conclusions 2005, Norway.
[63] Conclusions 2003, France.
[64] Conclusions 2005, Norway.

Worker's Permanent Injury

Temporary absence from work due to injury is prohibited by the Appendix as a reason for dismissal. In order to check whether national situations comply with the Charter requirements, the ECSR will consider the answers given by states to the following questions:[65]

- Is immediate dismissal for reasons of permanent injury permitted regardless of the origin of the injury? In particular, may this occur in cases of injuries sustained in the workplace or in cases of occupational diseases?
- Do employers pay compensation for termination in cases of immediate dismissal for reasons of permanent injury?
- If the permanent injury allows the worker to carry out light work, is the employer obliged to offer a different placement? If so, if the employer is unable to do this, what alternatives may be envisaged?

The ECSR does not define the relationship between these different elements. It should be hoped that it would come to a negative conclusion if already one element, or at least two, are missing.

Dismissal on the Ground of Age

Age as a ground of discrimination is not mentioned by the Charter or the Appendix to Article 24 as a non-valid reason for termination of employment. As the Appendix is not exhaustive, the ECSR 'takes note of the provisions protecting employees against dismissal because of their age'.[66] Since 2007, it states that, in principle:

> dismissal on grounds of age will not constitute a valid reason for termination of employment except in accordance with a valid retirement age justified by the operational requirements of the undertaking, establishment or service. States should take adequate measures to ensure protection for all workers against [such] dismissal.[67]

For a dismissal to be valid, it must, then, be 'properly justified with reference to one of the valid grounds expressly established by' Article 24.[68] The ECSR further complements its requirements by adopting the EU approach:

> dismissal on the ground of age will not constitute a valid reason for termination of employment unless a termination is, within the context of national law, objectively and reasonably justified by a legitimate aim such as a legitimate employment policy, labour market objectives or the operational requirements of the

[65] Conclusions 2003, Bulgaria.
[66] Conclusions 2005, Norway.
[67] Conclusions 2007, Statement of interpretation on Art 24.
[68] Conclusions 2012, Statement of interpretation on Art 24.

> undertaking, establishment or service and provided that the means of achieving that aim are appropriate and necessary.[69]

In its single decision on the merits on the basis of Article 24,[70] the ECSR applied these strengthened requirements to Norwegian legal provisions authorising termination of employment of 62-year-old seamen, irrespective of their capacity to perform work or conduct, and whatever the operational requirements of the undertaking. The ECSR is not convinced by the arguments invoked by the Norwegian government on the justifications and the proportionality of that age limit, and shows itself more demanding than the CJEU towards states. Indeed, it is not content with the statements made by the government on the objectives of this legislation, but carries out an in-depth assessment of their consistency and effectiveness. Contrary to the CJEU,[71] the ECSR examines whether the age limit made it possible to attain the desired goals and holds in this case that, the age limit is not based on objective grounds and disproportionately affects the rights of the workers.

(b) The Worker's Conduct

Termination of employment connected with the conduct of the worker can be of a disciplinary nature (based on misconduct) or result from the worker's improper behaviour.[72] The Appendix explicitly prohibits retaliatory dismissal, while the ECSR has given its view on other reasons connected to the worker's conduct.

The Exercise of the Right to Appeal

Pursuant to the Appendix, 'the filing of a complaint or the participation in proceedings against an employer involving alleged violation of laws or regulations or recourse to competent administrative authorities' does not constitute a valid reason for termination of employment. Taking this prohibition very seriously, the ECSR considers that

> national legislation should contain an express safeguard, in law or case law, which protects employees against retaliatory dismissal ... In the absence of any explicit statutory ban, states must be able to show how national legislation conforms to the requirements of the Charter.[73]

69 Conclusions 2008, Lithuania.
70 Complaint No 74/2011 cited above.
71 See M Schmitt, 'Départ à la retraite: l'influence du droit de l'Union européenne' (2013) 9 *Journal de Droit européen* 338 et seq.
72 ILO, *Protection against unjustified dismissal* (n 14) §89.
73 Conclusions 2003, Statement of Interpretation on Art 24; Conclusions 2005, Estonia.

Other Reasons

Because the list of non-valid reasons contained in the Appendix is not exhaustive, the ECSR aims to ensure broader workers' protection, for instance by asking state parties whether 'employees enjoy protection against dismissal concerning their civil liberties (freedom of expression, dignity, etc.)'.[74] Aligning its position with that of the ILO CEACR,[75] the ECSR furthermore considers that a prison sentence delivered in court for employment-related offences can be considered a valid reason for dismissal. This is not the case with prison sentences for offences unrelated to the person's employment, which cannot be considered valid reasons unless the length of the custodial sentence prevents the person from carrying out their work.[76]

(ii) Economic Reasons

Article 24 only imposes a general requirement, that dismissals must be 'based on the operational requirements of the undertaking, establishment or service'. It does not mean that all economic circumstances are valid reasons: Article 24 'only permits economic reasons *under certain conditions* to justify laying-off employees.'[77] However, the ECSR was not yet given the opportunity to specify whether this notion only covers situations of economic difficulties or whether other undertakings' strategies are included. This core issue is precisely at the heart of the pending case No 107/2014 submitted by the Finnish Society of Social Rights which considers that a collective dismissal just to increase the profit of the undertaking, establishment or service, or dismissals justified by outsourcing or subcontracting which has been done without economic necessity, violate Article 24. In the same vein, Finland would not be abiding by Article 24 as temporary workers can be taken to cover the job of the dismissed employees.

The ECSR pays more attention to judicial aspects, asking the states since 2003 'whether in cases of dismissal on economic grounds the courts are empowered to review the facts underlying the economic reasons invoked by the employer'.[78]

[74] Conclusions 2003, vol 1, Romania 424.
[75] ILO, *Protection against unjustified dismissal* (n 14) §92.
[76] Conclusions 2005, Estonia.
[77] ibid.
[78] Conclusions 2003, Bulgaria.

(iii) Procedural Guarantees Derived from Article 24 RESC

(a) The Right for the Worker to be Informed of the Reason for Dismissal and to be Heard by the Employer

The obligation to base dismissal on a valid reason implies that the employer shall be required to provide the employee with this reason. This guarantee is not yet formulated as such in the ECSR conclusions, but the latter examines conformity of national situations to the 'Obligation to provide a valid reason for termination of employment'. As a consequence, workers have the right to be informed, at least upon their request. This analysis is reinforced by both Articles 4 and 7 C158 as interpreted by the ILO CEACR[79] and the ECtHR case law under Article 6 ECHR.[80] In the context of ILO Convention No 158, the right to be informed logically derives from Article 7 which 'establishes the principle that the worker, before his employment is terminated, must have an opportunity to defend himself against the allegations made, which presupposes that the latter should be expressed and brought to his attention before the termination'.[81] Such a guarantee results less obviously from Article 24, which is (more) focused on judicial proceedings. Notification of the reason of dismissal could nevertheless be included in this analysis with a view to enabling the preparation of a defence and thus guaranteeing the fairness of the proceedings.

(b) The Obligation for the Employer to Provide Reasons in Writing

Following ILO Recommendation 166,[82] the ECSR states that 'employers must notify employees of their dismissal in writing'.[83] Such a procedural safeguard is indeed indispensable with regard to an appeal for unfair dismissal in order to ensure the worker's right of defence. For the same reason, it should be complemented by the employer's duty to notify in writing the reason(s) justifying the dismissal.[84]

C. Right to Adequate Compensation or Other Appropriate Relief

To be effective, the right to relief first implies that workers benefit from the right to appeal.

[79] ILO, Protection against unjustified dismissal (n 14) §146.

[80] *KMC v Hungary* App no 19554/11 (ECtHR, 10 July 2012).

[81] ILO, *Protection against unjustified dismissal* (n 14) §146. This right for the worker to defend himself before the dismissal is not afforded by ILO C158 when dismissal is based on economic grounds.

[82] ILO R166 §13.

[83] Digest of ECSR case law 2008.

[84] ILO R166 §13.

(i) The Right to Appeal

Workers are entitled to challenge the legality of their dismissal before an impartial body. This right must be interpreted in light of Article 8 of ILO Convention No 158, which details the identity and powers of that body. The ECSR notes that in all state parties it is possible to appeal to a court or a tribunal.

(a) Identity and Powers of the Impartial Body

Pursuant to Article 8§1 of ILO Convention No 158, an impartial body can be, in particular, 'a court, labour tribunal, arbitration committee or arbitrator'. Moreover, the ILO CEACR considers that the requirement of impartiality

> means, for example, that a hierarchical administrative appeal procedure cannot be considered as the appropriate form of appeal under the provisions of the Convention: where such a procedure exists, provision must be made for a subsequent appeal to an impartial body.[85]

According to Swiatkowski and Harris,[86] a parallel would be drawn by the ECSR with other Charter provisions, which obliges States to supervise the decisions made by administrative authorities.[87] In this context,

> the Committee asks in particular that the report state how its members are appointed, the length of their term of office and what statutory factors ensure the required independence. Should the body not be an independent one, the Committee asks whether its decisions could be subject to subsequent review by a court.[88]

As far as the powers of the body are concerned, the ECSR emphasises 'that the right of appeal to an independent body ... implies that this body is empowered to examine at the very least the facts underlying economic measures'.[89] This statement goes beyond the provisions of Articles 8 and 9 C158, which allow each Member State to determine the extent to which the competent bodies should be authorised to review the employer's judgement as to the sufficiency of reasons based on operational requirements; each country is therefore authorised to restrict the powers of the competent body, when investigating whether termination of employment was justified, to review the employer's judgement in relation to workforce numbers.[90] However, it is also reasonable to suggest that the courts should be empowered to consider the reality of the undertaking's economic situation, as well

[85] ILO, *Protection against unjustified dismissal* (n 14) §178.
[86] See Swiatkowski (n 9) 173–74 and Harris (n 3) 273–74.
[87] See Arts 5 and 13(1) (R)ESC.
[88] Conclusions XIII-4, on the right to social and medical assistance (Art 13§1).
[89] Conclusions 2003, Bulgaria.
[90] ILO, *Protection against unjustified dismissal* (n 14) §214.

as the necessity and proportionality of the dismissal, which means that the link between these two elements should be subject to the court's scrutiny.

(b) Elements of the Proceedings

Limitation Period

Under Article 8(3) of ILO C158, states are allowed to establish limitation periods. But the ECSR does not seem to want to impose thresholds on state parties. It thus concluded to the conformity of Norwegian legislation, according to which an attempt to settle a dispute concerning dismissal without valid reason should first be made by 'negotiation with the employer' (within two weeks of the first negotiating meeting) and, if they fail, the employee has eight weeks to commence legal proceedings. One can argue that such a limitation period is very short, while, as stated by the ILO CEACR, 'short time-limits do not allow workers (in particular those who are not directly assisted by workers' representatives) to ascertain their rights in order to be able to decide on the basis of all the facts whether or not they should appeal'.[91]

Length of Proceedings

The only requirement that can be found in ECSR conclusions is that 'the courts competent for awarding compensation for pecuniary and non-pecuniary damage must decide within a reasonable time'.[92] While ILO Convention No 158 does not contain any provision related to such a standard or other requirement on the necessary speed of the proceedings,[93] ECtHR case law under Article 6§1 ECHR provides very useful details for the purpose of work-related disputes.

The reasonableness of the length of proceedings must be assessed in light of the circumstances of the case and with reference to the following criteria: the complexity of the case, the conduct of the applicant and the relevant authorities and what was at stake for the applicant in the dispute.[94] Following well-established case law, the vulnerability of the worker due to his/her financial situation reinforces this general requirement. The Court indeed ruled that

> an employee who considers that he has been wrongly … dismissed by his employer has an important personal interest in securing a judicial decision on the lawfulness

[91] ibid §188.

[92] Conclusions 2012, Finland.

[93] The ILO Committee of Experts shows itself even less demanding, by only stating that 'When the worker has appealed before an impartial body, it would be advisable that the length of the procedure be reasonable and the costs be minimal, so as not to dissuade the worker to claim his rights' (ILO, *Protection against unjustified dismissal* (n 14) §189).

[94] *Frydlender v France* ECHR 2000-VII, §43.

> of that measure promptly, because employment disputes by their nature call for expeditious decisions, in view of what is at stake for the person concerned, who through dismissal loses his means of subsistence.[95]

'Special diligence' is required in all employment disputes.[96] This requirement is reinforced additionally in respect of States where domestic law provides that such cases must be resolved with particular urgency.[97] This is the case for actions emerging from labour accidents and occupational diseases under Portuguese legislation.[98] As a consequence, a global length of proceedings of five years and three months for three levels of jurisdiction—including a conciliatory procedure of one year and five months—is considered excessive.

Burden of Proof

States must provide details about the burden of proof, but the ECSR statement on this issue is not clear. In 2008, the ECSR decided to apply its 'general stance' related to allegations of discrimination and according to which 'the burden of proof should not rest entirely on the complainant, but should be the subject of an appropriate adjustment'.[99] National legislation that requires the employer 'to establish the facts and circumstances of the case' (Bulgaria, 2003) or 'to prove that termination is based on a proper and substantive reason' so that the burden of proof is reversed (Finland, 2012),[100] are then logically admitted. But a total reversal of the burden of proof is not imposed by the ECSR, which should then provide further guidance on how to interpret 'appropriate adjustment' within the meaning of Article 24.

It is worth noting that the ECSR does not (yet) explicitly apply the model of Article 9§2 C158, which establishes two possibilities 'in order for the worker not to have to bear alone the burden of proving that the termination was not justified':

> (a) the burden of proving the existence of a valid reason for the termination ... shall rest on the employer; (b) the bodies ... shall be empowered to reach a conclusion on the reason for the termination having regard to the evidence provided by the parties and according to procedures provided for by national law and practice.

The first possibility does correspond to a reversal of the burden of proof—although, in my opinion, stating that the employer must prove the existence

[95] *Obermeier v Austria* (1990) Series A no 179, 23–24, §72, and *Caleffi v Italy* (1991) Series A no 206-B, 20, §17.

[96] *Ruotolo v Italy* (1992) Series A no 230-D, §17; *Szabo v Hungary* App no 34254/10 (ECtHR, 22 April 2014) §13.

[97] *Szabo v Hungary* (n 96) §53.

[98] *Mendes v Portugal* App no 49185/13 (ECtHR, 30 October 2014).

[99] Statement of interpretation on Art 24, Conclusions 2008.

[100] Only the French version indicates that 'la charge de la preuve est donc inversée, contrairement à la pratique en matière civile, où elle incombe au plaignant' (Conclusions 2012, Finland).

of a valid reason does not necessarily mean that the worker has no role to play at all (for example, taking part in the proof of the facts)—while the second one

> consists of not placing the burden of proof on either the employer or the worker, but allowing the impartial body to reach a conclusion in the light of the evidence provided by the two parties. This implies that each party, in his own interest, will submit to the body the evidence at his disposal and which he considers as establishing his case, and that the body will use, where appropriate, any power of investigation accorded to it by national law and practice.[101]

Such an adjustment could be considered appropriate, provided that tribunals or courts effectively play their central role with due rigour.

(c) The Right to Relief *Per Se*

By virtue of Article 24(b), states must ensure workers whose dismissal is recognised as unjustified by an impartial body an 'adequate compensation or other appropriate relief'. This guarantee is given a very broad interpretation because the ECSR draws on its interpretation on specific Charter provisions protecting workers against discriminatory dismissals.[102] Two cumulative types of relief are thus required: the possibility of reinstatement, and adequate compensation.

The Possibility of Reinstatement

Taken literally, Article 24§b permits compensation to be the only sanction for unjustified dismissals, but states are authorised to establish other types of relief, provided that these are appropriate. Reinstatement is not even mentioned in Article 24, unlike Article 10 C158, which implicitly expresses a preference for such a sanction by imposing an adequate compensation or other relief only if reinstatement is not possible or practicable. Reinstatement indeed corresponds to the measure affording the highest degree of protection.[103]

The ECSR's opinion on whether reinstatement is mandatory or not in case of a dismissal declared unjustified remains unclear. Initially,[104] the

[101] ILO, *Protection against unjustified dismissal* (n 14) §201.

[102] Art 1, Additional Protocol, Art 4§3 ESC, Arts 1§2, 8§2 and 20 RESC. See the corresponding chapters of this volume.

[103] ILO Experts Committee, *Protection against unjustified dismissal* (n 14) §221: 'While financial compensation compensates for the unjustified loss of employment, annulment of the termination and reinstatement guarantee job security by allowing the worker to take up his job again, and offering him the possibility of retaining the rights he has acquired during his years of service, such as entitlement to old-age benefits'.

[104] See Digest 2008.

ECSR did not impose reinstatement, but it seems to have changed its view in 2012, concluding 'that the situation in Finland is not in conformity with Article 24 of the Charter on the ground that the legislation does not provide for the possibility of reinstatement in case of unlawful dismissal'.[105] The same goes for Albanian legislation, with respect to the private sector.[106] However, it remains to be determined whether legislation must impose reinstatement when desired by the worker or whether reinstatement can be one of the possibilities laid down by legislation and left to the courts' discretion. This second interpretation should be admitted only provided that the courts genuinely allow reinstatement when requested by the worker. To resolve this issue, a parallel can be drawn with the ECSR statement on Article 4§3 according to which, in cases of unlawful dismissal of a worker asking to benefit from the right to equal pay, legislation must 'provide for the reinstatement of the worker. In exceptional cases, where reinstatement is not possible or is not desired by the worker, financial compensation instead may be acceptable, but only if it is sufficient to deter the employer and to compensate the worker'.[107] The ECSR should also pay great attention to the reasons that could legitimately justify the employer's inability to reinstate the employee.

Adequate Compensation

The obligation to provide adequate compensation for workers dismissed without a valid reason is strictly interpreted by the ECSR. It seems that compensation is required in addition to reinstatement and that only the *possibility* of being reinstated is not sufficient with regard to Article 24. According to the Conclusions 2003 on Bulgaria,

> when a dismissal is ruled to be null and void and an employee's reinstatement is ordered, or the employment relationship is held to have been uninterrupted, such decisions must at a minimum be accompanied by an entitlement to receive the wage that would have been payable between the date of the dismissal and that of the court decision or effective reinstatement.[108]

As a consequence, a maximum compensatory payment of six months' wages cannot be considered adequate, practice showing that judicial proceedings last on average two years. Thus delimited, the compensation period might lead, on the contrary, to payment of a reduced amount when the litigation is speedily carried out.[109]

105 Conclusions 2012, Finland.
106 Conclusion 2012, Albania.
107 Conclusions XIII-5.
108 Conclusions 2003, Bulgaria.
109 See Harris (n 3) 173.

In addition, compensation paid in the exceptional case where the worker may not be reinstated should be of a higher amount than the remuneration, calculated from the day the work agreement is illegally terminated to the day of the judgment being passed.[110] Indeed, the ECSR recalls that 'compensation for unlawful dismissal must be both proportionate to the loss suffered by the victim and sufficiently dissuasive for employers.'[111] For this reason, ceilings are in most cases not compatible with Article 24. Though they are not prohibited as such, contrary to compensation limits in the case of unlawful dismissal of a pregnant worker,[112] the ECSR considers that

> any ceiling on compensation that may preclude damages from being commensurate with the loss suffered and sufficiently dissuasive are proscribed. If there is such a ceiling on compensation for pecuniary damage, the victim must be able to seek compensation for non-pecuniary damage through other legal avenues (eg anti-discrimination legislation).[113]

Compensation levels that are subject to an upper limit of one year (Albania, 2012) or 24 months (Finland, 2012) are not in conformity with Article 24. But the ECSR also asked the Finnish government to provide information on cases, if any, where the employee has successfully sought compensation under the Tort Liability Act.[114] Complaint 106/2014 pending before the ECSR is precisely based on these conclusions of 2012 and suggests that such cases cannot be found.

Legal Basis for Compensation or Other Relief

The Appendix to Article 24 states that 'compensation or other appropriate relief in case of termination of employment without valid reasons shall be determined by national laws or regulations, collective agreements or other means appropriate to national conditions'. This statement requires that conditions for the granting of relief measures must be specified and known in advance, while at the same time preserving national systems.

III. IMPACT ON EUROPEAN HUMAN RIGHTS INSTRUMENTS

Article 24 as interpreted by the ECSR can play a crucial role with a view to ensuring the synergy between human rights instruments at European level. At national level, compliance of national legislation and practices with its requirements must be guaranteed, at least by the courts. The French

[110] ibid.
[111] Conclusions 2012, Finland.
[112] Conclusions 2005, Estonia.
[113] Conclusions 2012, Finland.
[114] ibid.

situation represents a good example of both difficulties and the potential of an adequate application of Article 24.

A. Towards a European Consensus on the Right to Protection in Cases of Termination of Employment

The consistency of protection of social rights in Europe must be reinforced.[115] In this perspective, the impact of Article 24 should extend to the interpretation of both the ECHR and CFREU. For Judge Pinto de Albuquerque,[116] a 'significant European consensus' results from Article 24 RESC and ECtHR case law, implying 'a positive obligation for the Contracting Parties to the Convention to implement the principle of justification for termination of employment, ie a legal system of justified termination of employment'. Article 30 CFREU 'reinforced this consensus, by drawing on the above-mentioned provision'. Interpretation of Article 24 by the ECSR can thus deepen the phenomenon of 'crossed fertilisation' between the Charter and the ECHR (i), but also help to give a broad content to Article 30 CFREU (ii).

(i) European Convention on Human Rights (ECHR)

Judge Pinto de Albuquerque considered that

> the right to protection in the event of termination of employment has a minimum content in European human rights law, consisting of four core requirements: a formal written notice of termination of employment given to the employee, a pre-termination opportunity to respond given to the employee, a valid reason for termination, and an appeal to an independent body.[117]

These four core elements correspond to procedural guarantees, except for the requirement of a valid reason for dismissal.

Interpretation of Article 6§1 ECHR essentially consolidates these procedural aspects of Article 24. A reverse movement should be deepened by the ECtHR to increase the scope of the requirement of a valid reason for termination of employment, including the proportionality of the dismissal. Thus, the ECtHR could formalise and even extend its emerging case law under Article 8 ECHR by referring to Article 24 and the corresponding case law of the ECSR. Furthermore, incorporation of Article 24 within the Court's reasoning (and not only in the list of relevant international texts) would

[115] Belgian Chairmanship of the Council of Europe, Brussels' Document on the Future of the Protection of Social Rights in Europe, 12–13 February 2015.

[116] *KMC v Hungary* (n 80), Concurring opinion.

[117] ibid.

reinforce the coherence of its position that the dismissal can interfere with Article 8 where there are serious consequences for private life. From that perspective, it is worth noting that, in *Sibadras and Džiautas v Lithuania* the ECtHR mobilised Article 1§2 in its reasoning by ruling that:

> 47. … having regard in particular to the notions currently prevailing in democratic States, the Court considers that a far-reaching ban on taking up private sector employment does affect 'private life'. *It attaches particular weight in this respect to the text of Article 1§2 of the European Social Charter and the interpretation given by the European Committee of Social Rights.*[118]

In my opinion, incorporation of Article 24 RESC within the reasoning of the ECtHR would reinforce the link between that right and the right to work and thus, more broadly, the close connection between social rights and civil and political rights.

(ii) Charter of Fundamental Rights of the European Union

Interpretation of Article 30 CFREU in light of Article 24, reinforced by interpretation of Articles 6 and 8 ECHR by the Strasbourg Court, could give to Article 30 CFREU a more concrete content, as well as a broader scope.[119] The achievement of this route, where Article 24 has a direct impact on the interpretation of Article 30 CFREU, would involve the CJEU softening its recent case law on the (very limited) scope of Article 30 CFREU.[120]

An indirect but thus more complicated way to realise the synergy between these three European instruments would be to use the ECHR as a kind of 'intermediary tool' between Article 30 CFREU and Article 24, by mobilising the theory of 'corresponding rights' developed within Article 52§3 CFREU.[121] By virtue of this provision, Article 47 CFREU, which lays down the right to a fair trial, should be interpreted in light of Article 6§1 ECHR, the latter being recognised by the Explanations to the EU Charter and by the CJEU as its corresponding right. In the same vein, Article 7 CFREU protecting the right to respect for private life corresponds to Article 8§1 ECHR.[122] In *Volker*,[123] the CJEU precisely relied on the ECtHR case law, adopting its very extensive notion of private life, including professional activities. As already shown in this chapter, both Article 6 and Article 8 ECHR are interpreted

[118] *Sidabras and Džiautas* (n 26). (Our italics.)

[119] On the potential impact of Art 24 on the interpretation of Art 30 CFREU, see Kenner (n 1) 820–24.

[120] See above section II.B(ii)(c).

[121] Art 52§3 CFREU: 'So far as this Charter contains rights which correspond to rights guaranteed by the Convention for the Protection of Human Rights and Fundamental Freedoms, the meaning and scope of those rights shall be the same as those laid down by the said Convention'.

[122] Case C-400/10 PPU *J McB* (CJEU, 5 October 2015) §53.

[123] *Volker* (CJEU, 9 November 2010) §§56–64.

as covering termination of employment in several of its procedural and substantive elements. As a consequence, Articles 7 and 47 of the CFREU, in conjunction with Article 30 CFREU, as well as the case law of the Strasbourg Court, are intended to apply in cases dealing with domestic legislations regulating the termination of employment. It is nevertheless true that the recent CJEU case law is absolutely not in favour of such a comprehensive application of Article 52§3 CFREU, because in *Akerberg Fransson*, the Court of Luxembourg clearly decided not to apply this provision.[124]

B. National Developments: The French Case

Recent developments relating to the French situation with regard to the Charter may appear paradoxical. On one hand, a failure to meet the reporting procedure obligations stems from the French Report of 2012, but also some doubts about the conformity of French law with Article 24§1. On the other hand, the Charter has for the first time been given direct effect in a recent case based on Article 24§2.

(i) Content of the Protection

The French situation with regard to protection in cases of termination of employment has been assessed in 2012. The ECSR decided to defer its conclusion due to the lack of information regarding certain important requirement of Article 24, namely the burden of proof and sanctions.

(a) Burden of Proof

As no information was provided on the French situation relating to this issue, the ECSR asked that the next report specify whether the law provides for an adjustment in accordance with the ECSR general statement.[125] The French Labour Code (Article L 1235-1) stipulates that courts (*conseils de prud'hommes* and courts of appeal) must assess the regularity of the dismissal procedure and whether the dismissal is based on real and serious grounds. To that end, courts shall decide, having regard to the evidence provided by the parties and after having ordered, where appropriate, any measure of investigation. The next French report, if answering the ECSR's request, would give it the opportunity to provide details on how interpret the requirement of 'appropriate adjustment' in the burden of proof system.

[124] D Ritleng, 'De l'articulation des systèmes de protection des droits fondamentaux dans l'Union-Les enseignements des arrêts Akerberg Fransson et Melloni' (2013) *Revue Trimestrielle de Droit Européen* 267.

[125] See above section IV.B(i)(b).

(b) Sanctions

Due to the lack of clear and detailed information, the ECSR was unable to check whether French legislation ensures a general possibility of reinstatement in cases of unjustified dismissals. Information on sanctions applicable in the event of discriminatory dismissals (Article 1§2) is considered insufficient. The lack of detailed information might be explained by French legislation and case law's potential failure to comply with ECSR requirements.

Pursuant to Article L 1235-3 of the Labour Code, if the dismissal is recognised to be unjustified, the judge may propose the worker's reinstatement in the undertaking and, if one of the parties refuses, compensation must be awarded to the worker. In practice, reinstatement is almost never proposed by courts. As to the right to adequate compensation, the payments for unjustified dismissal under Article L 1235-3 have no upper limit, but instead a minimum amount. The employee may indeed be awarded compensation of not less than six months' pay. This provision does not apply to employees with less than two years' service, who nevertheless benefited from compensation calculated in relation to the loss suffered (Article L 1235-5) and thus in principle not subject to ceiling. However, case law shows that compensation amounts afforded are of a very low amount.

Furthermore, without any consideration to Article 24 or ILO Convention No 158, the French government forced the adoption on 10 July 2015[126] of new provisions providing for mandatory minimum and maximum ceilings on compensation, which are determined by reference to the size of the company and the employee's seniority. Only in situations of serious infringement of the employee's rights listed in new Article L 1235-3-2 (discrimination, harassment, violation of a fundamental right or freedom) may the employee obtain compensation above the maximum limit. These provisions were censored by the *Conseil constitutionnel*,[127] but maximum ceilings on compensation were declared valid in principle: they can be provided by the legislator in order to facilitate employment, by removing the bottlenecks that constrain hiring. Upper limits could apply provided that they are determined by criteria in relation to the loss suffered by the employee (the employee's seniority, for instance), which is not the case with the criterion of company size. New provisions on compensation are thus declared in contradiction with the principle of equality before the law. A risk therefore remains that the government will make a new proposal providing for ceilings based only on the employee's seniority. In my view, the position of the *Conseil constitutionnel* is too restrictive, as the seniority criterion is not sufficient to take into account all dimensions of the damages suffered by the employee whose dismissal was recognised as unjustified.

[126] Loi pour la croissance, l'activité et l'égalité des chances économiques, 10 July 2015.
[127] Decision No 2015-715 DC, 5 August 2015.

(ii) Direct Effect of Article 24 RESC

In a decision of 10 February 2014[128] the French *Conseil d'État* recognised the direct effect of Article 24, thus enabling a civil servant to take advantage of its provisions and immediately invoke them against their public employer before administrative courts. According to the *Conseil d'État*, the aim of Article 24 is not only to engender obligations for states; moreover, they are sufficiently precise and do not call for additional measures to produce effects with regard to individuals. Direct effect of Article 24 is therefore enshrined in its vertical dimension. However, it can be argued that the French *Cour de cassation*, and so all ordinary courts, will incorporate this statement in their judgments.[129] Application of Article 24 could hence be ensured by case law, while the changes recently envisaged by the French government reduce workers' protection by imposing ceilings on compensation. Article 24 precisely represents a relevant ground to challenge the validity of these provisions and the position of the Conseil constitutionnel. More generally, the settled case law[130] recognising the direct effect of the provisions of ILO Convention No 158 should help French courts by means of 'cross-fertilisation' to give a comprehensive interpretation of Article 24 provisions.

[128] CE 10 February 2014, MB, req No 358992.

[129] J Mouly, 'L'Article 24 de la Charte sociale européenne sur le droit des salariés à ne pas être licencié sans motif valable est d'effet direct' (2014) *Droit social* 474.

[130] CE 19 October 2005, req Nos 283892, 284472, 284555, 284718; Cass soc 29 March 2006 App no 04-46.499; Cass soc 1 July 2008 App no 7-44.124.

Article 26

The Right to Dignity at Work

CSILLA KOLLONAY-LEHOCZKY

Article 26—The right to dignity at work

With a view to ensuring the effective exercise of the right of all workers to protection of their dignity at work, the Parties undertake, in consultation with employers' and workers' organisations:

1. to promote awareness, information and prevention of sexual harassment in the workplace or in relation to work and to take all appropriate measures to protect workers from such conduct;
2. to promote awareness, information and prevention of recurrent reprehensible or distinctly negative and offensive actions directed against individual workers in the workplace or in relation to work and to take all appropriate measures to protect workers from such conduct.

Appendix

It is understood that this article does not require that legislation be enacted by the Parties.

It is understood that paragraph 2 does not cover sexual harassment.

I. INTRODUCTION

A. Context and Main Content

Article 26 in its two paragraphs combines two different types of human rights violation, linked by the idea of 'dignity'. Article 26§1 is a 'classic' non-discrimination article, prohibiting conduct of unequal treatment on the ground of sex. Sexual harassment is a form of discrimination, originating from the historically lower social position of women as a class, similar to other historical forms of discrimination.

Article 26§2, on the other hand, is the first international provision to establish a fundamental right to protection of human dignity against harassment creating a hostile working environment related to any specific characteristic of a person. It cannot be considered a provision prohibiting discrimination in the same sense as Article 26§1. While sex is a classic 'protected attribute', the specific attribute that serves as a ground of the behaviour towards one or more persons creating a hostile working environment is not indicated in Article 26§2.

The conduct may be, but is not necessarily connected to and based on the membership of the victim of groups traditionally discriminated against: harassment on the grounds of race, ethnicity, religion or disability belongs to the acknowledged forms of discrimination. At the same time this attitude might occur on any other ground that would not qualify as a protected attribute under international non-discrimination law and might not even be contemplated by the interpretation of the so-called 'open-ended' catalogues.[1] It is defined in several jurisdictions and in the literature as 'bullying', and is distinct from discrimination.[2] The Explanatory Report also associates this provision with the concept of bullying, albeit with a slight departure from the concept as used today, identifying it with 'victimisation'.[3]

The combination of these two protected situations in one article entails some risk, but also gains. The risk is that it may blur the anti-discrimination nature of Article 26§1 and thereby weaken or dilute the required protection.[4] The potential gain lies in the approximation between 'status' discrimination (based on sex here) and protection against disparate treatment on the ground of socio-economic disadvantages.[5] Article 26§2 might in the future represent a considerable step on the way towards protecting persons against discriminatory behaviour based on their socially disadvantaged position (such as housing and home neighbourhood, social, cultural or nutritional habits and so on). Furthermore the link may proceed toward stronger protection, possibly on quasi-discriminatory or similar grounds against adverse employers' actions in an era of 're-contractualisation' (flexibilisation) of labour law.

Article 26§1 confronts Charter analysts with the dynamic and development of approaches to gender equality similar to Articles 8 and 20. The tension between the earlier and later phases of development is reflected more sharply and squarely in this provision, influencing interpretation. The ambivalences implied in the text have to be seen in light of the progress of

[1] A special issue is what feature might amount to protected attributes, on the ground of which differential treatment is prohibited, even in the case of an extended interpretation of the phrase 'any other ground'.

[2] See below section II.B(ii).

[3] Explanatory Report to the Revised Charter, s 100.

[4] This effect is expressed in the Appendix as well as the repeatedly expressed dissenting opinion reacting to the interpretation requiring state legislation if not yet in place for prevention and protection. See Conclusions 2003 and 2007, dissenting opinion of Stein Evju.

[5] See: S Fredman, 'Positive duties and socio-economic disadvantage: bringing disadvantage onto the equality agenda' (2010) 3 *European Human Rights Law Review* 290.

the dominant social attitudes regarding the presence of women in the workplace and the social place of women in general.

The construction and phrasing of paragraphs 1 and 2 make the interpretation and clear qualification of sexual harassment even more difficult.

Article 26 reflects a point in time when workplace harassment was no longer considered merely personal misbehaviour, beyond the responsibility of the employer and actionable only as a private lawsuit against the offender. At the same time, the text reflects the underlying ambivalences of 25 years ago. Two points needed clarification from the beginning: (i) the status of harassment among fundamental rights violations: what conduct qualifies as harassment and whether it is a form of discrimination or not; (ii) what obligations of the state are generated by the ratification of this provision. Neither of these questions can be answered on the basis of the ambivalent provision.

The title and text of the Article puts 'dignity' in focus, based on and reflecting the approach described in the literature[6] as European 'dignity harm' (based mainly on the German dignity doctrine)[7] approach, distinguished from the US 'discriminatory approach'. The dignity focus of Article 26 sets a 'weight' requirement, arbitrarily drawing a line between harassment and slight offences—frolics, sexist comment, slight touches—that are expected to be tolerated by the victims or otherwise considered to be petty sensitivities. Such a 'dignity approach', requiring gravity in the act and overlooking 'everyday' instances, fails to address the systemic context of inequalities in the workplace.[8]

On this consideration the text indirectly expresses a negative answer: the drafters did not intend to qualify harassment as a form of discrimination. It reflects the attitude of Commission Recommendation No 92/131/EEC on the protection of the dignity of women and men at work,[9] saying that 'unwanted conduct of a sexual nature... *may, in certain instances*, be contrary to the principle of equal treatment'. The position was based on the perception at that time that harassment might occur in the form of a 'preferential' attitude that is not necessarily a form of discrimination based on gender,[10] even though it may harm the dignity or career of the affected person.

The position of the ECSR is that harassment 'shall be prohibited and repressed in the same way as acts of discrimination, independently of the

[6] See A Numhauser-Henning, 'Executive Summary' in A Numhauser-Henning and S Laulom (eds), *Harassment related to Sex and Sexual Harassment Law in 33 European Countries. Discrimination versus Dignity* (Brussels, European Commission, Justice, 2011) 30–33.

[7] S Baer, 'Dignity, Liberty, Equality: A Fundamental Rights Triangle of Constitutionalism' (2009) Fall *University of Toronto Law Journal* 461.

[8] ibid 459.

[9] [1992] OJ L49.

[10] Conclusions 2003, Introduction, Bulgaria.

fact that not all harassment behaviours are acts of discrimination, except when this is presumed by law'.[11]

The second question confronting the expert body was whether the Charter requires states to provide protection against such conduct. The comparison of the various texts (the *travaux preparatoires*, the adopted text and the Appendix) reflects the clash of different approaches.

The 1993 text-proposal of the Charte-Rel committee clearly required '*protection* of workers against conduct of a sexual nature'.[12] The adopted text puts the emphasis on the promotion of awareness, information and prevention; it also requires taking 'appropriate measures' to protect workers from such conduct. However, according to the Explanatory Report (section 97), Article 26§1 does not require that parties must ensure protection against such conduct. Furthermore, according to the Appendix to this provision, parties do not need to enact legislation.

The fluctuating emphasis between prevention through information and awareness-raising and legislative steps for sanction and remedies can result in a synergy between the two different legal approaches presented by Article 26.

B. International Sources

Harassment has emerged at the international level as an issue of equal treatment and also as an issue of workplace health and safety. The relevant treaties reflect conceptual and geo-cultural differences, on one hand, and dynamic historical development and change on the other. The very short history of treating harassment as an international human rights issue goes back to the late 1980s and early 1990s. The preparatory works of the Revised Charter represented a part of the international efforts.

(i) International Level

Since the entry of women into the labour market, sexual harassment has been present in the workplace. The idea that it is a form of unlawful employers' practice and discrimination has been 'imported' to the rest of the world from North American law since the second half of the 1980s.[13] Title VII of the 1964 US Civil Rights Act prohibits discrimination, among other things on the ground of sex, without mentioning harassment. It was acknowledged

[11] Conclusions 2014, Georgia, Turkey.

[12] Proposal 9, CHARTE-REL (93) 19 11 Aug, 2013, ECR9319.CM, p 2.

[13] See Appendix I to the report of 11 August 1993 of the Charte-Rel Committee on the proposed text of Art 26; R Husbands, 'Sexual harassment law in employment: An international perspective' (1992) 131 *International Labour Review* 6 presenting the US case law.

from the 1980s by the federal courts as actionable unlawful conduct under Title VII, establishing the liability of the employer.[14]

From the second part of the 1980s growing awareness in the world has led to enhanced efforts at various international levels to prevent such phenomena.

CEDAW, in its preamble, emphasises that discrimination against women 'violates the principles of equality of rights and respect for human dignity'. Beyond this mention of dignity, CEDAW does not explicitly cover harassment. Sexual harassment was recognised as violence against women in General Recommendation No 12 of 1989. It was defined by General Recommendation No 19 of 1992 as 'unwelcome sexually determined behaviour', and an exemplification of such conduct that 'can be humiliating and may constitute a health and safety problem'.[15]

ILO Convention No 111 of 1958 prohibits discrimination on any ground, including sex. The Committee of Experts in 1988 took the opinion that Article 2 of the Convention implies harassment. The first and only ILO Convention prohibiting specifically sex discrimination is Convention No 169 of 1989, the Indigenous and Tribal Peoples Convention, prohibiting sexual harassment of indigenous and tribal women. In 2003, the ILO approved a 'Code of Practice on Workplace Violence in Services Sectors and Measures to Combat this Phenomenon'.[16]

(ii) European Level

At European level the Revised Charter was the first binding legal instrument guaranteeing the right to dignity at work, prohibiting sexual harassment and harassment.

At EU level the 2002 amendment of the Directive on the principle of equal treatment of men and women in employment and occupation defined the concept of sexual harassment as a form of discrimination, and clearly separated it from other forms of harassment on any protected ground (including sex).[17] Before the adoption of this Directive, harassment was covered and classified as discrimination on grounds protected by the Race Directive 2000/43/EC and the Employment Framework Directive 78/2000/EC.

The adoption of these Directives was preceded by several 'soft' law measures, most importantly by the already mentioned Commission Recommendation 92/131/EEC of 27 November 1991 on the protection of the dignity

[14] *Meritor Savings Bank, FSB v Mechelle Vinson et al* No 84-1979. Decided 19 June 1986.

[15] *Compilation of general comments and general recommendations adopted by human rights treaty bodies*, UNHCR, HRI/GEN/Rev 2, 29 March 1996, 115.

[16] www.ilo.org/wcmsp5/groups/public/@ed_protect/@protrav/@safework/documents/normativeinstrument/wcms_107705.pdf.

[17] Directive 2002/73/EC [2002] OJ L269/15; now Directive 2006/54/EU (Recast).

of women and men at work, calling on Member States to develop measures to create a proper workplace climate.

At European industrial relations level workplace harassment has resulted in framework agreements, also as a health and a dignity issue. The European social partners signed autonomous Framework Agreements in 2004 on Work-related Stress, and in 2007 on Harassment and Violence at Work.

C. Relationship to Other Provisions of the Charter

Article 26 (both §§1 and 2) prohibits a specific form of discrimination, and this is decisive regarding its relation to other provisions of the Charter with workplace and employment relevance.

It is related to Article E, the horizontal provision prohibiting discrimination in respect of the rights set forth in the Charter. So far this connection has not been examined by the ECSR, with special regard to the application of Article E in collective complaint cases, furthermore (and reasonably) it is applied predominantly with regard to substantive provisions and not equal treatment (and therefore horizontal) provisions.

Similar to Article 1§2, it is aimed at guaranteeing the right of workers to earn their living in an occupation freely entered upon, among other things, without discrimination. The overlap here is narrow, considering that the interpretation of Article 1§2 focuses primarily on entering employment and less on conditions in employment.[18]

Article 26§1 overlaps with Article 20 guaranteeing the right of women to be treated equally at the workplace without discrimination. This is not so open and direct a connection, and the text reflects the drafters' uncertainty about harassment as a form of employment discrimination.

Article 26 also overlaps with Article 3 guaranteeing safe and healthy working conditions. The responsibility of the employer to prevent risks to health and safety at the workplace includes psychological harm; workplace harassment that may lead to physical inability to work.[19]

II. CONTENT

A. Paragraph 1

(i) The Concept of Sexual Harassment

Article 26§1 of the Charter qualifies sexual harassment as a breach of equal treatment, even if—as it is phrased—not necessarily a form of

[18] See section I.B in the chapter on Art 20 by C Kollonay-Lehoczky in this volume.

[19] See chapter on Art 3 by K Lörcher in this volume.

discrimination based on gender. Such conduct is determined by the adoption, towards one or more persons, of preferential or retaliatory conduct, or other forms of insistent behaviour that may undermine their dignity or harm their career.[20] It is conduct of a sexual nature, as distinguished from harassment on the ground of sex that belongs to the type of harassment under Article 26§2.[21]

The ECSR emphasised the broad scale of behaviours that fall under Article 26§1, covering all, apparently preferential conduct, that, if unwanted (rather: unwelcome)[22] qualifies as harassment. Such acts can be physical acts, words or gestures having a sexual connotation, and any display of sexually offensive material.

For example, the Committee found that Georgia was not in conformity with its obligations under Article 26§1, despite the 2010 adoption of a law on gender equality that provides, inter alia, that 'Labour relations shall not allow for ... any adverse verbal, non-verbal or physical behaviour of a sexual nature aimed at or resulting in personal offence or creating intimidating, hostile or humiliating environment'.[23] The narrow phrasing (requiring 'adverse' behaviour) may exclude conducts that are not 'adverse', but nonetheless frequently unacceptable at the workplace and also in the absence of adequate enforcement machinery could not establish the country's compliance with its undertaking.

Another uncertainty—also related to the burden of proof—is consideration of the victim's attitude when qualifying an act. In several national laws the victim is supposed to indicate to the harasser that the expressed attitude is 'unwanted'.[24] In a subordinate relationship, but even among peers, this cannot always be reasonably expected, and the lack of such an expression may block the procedure for remedies. Harassment is always a matter of hierarchy, predominantly affecting women, though in a significantly smaller proportion men also.[25] For this reason the definition of harassment may

[20] Conclusions 2005, Statement of Interpretation of Art 26§1.

[21] The Explanatory Report (s 99) is confusing with respect to the terminology used today, similarly its other sections (such as s 100 on 'victimisation').

[22] See Conclusions 2007, Ireland, 2010, Malta on Art 26§1. See also below, on the burden of proof.

[23] Conclusions 2014, Georgia, Art 26§1, p 28.

[24] See, for example, the critique on the requirement in Finland, according to which the harassed person has prima facie responsibility to clearly indicate to the harasser that his/her conduct is repulsive, unless there are particular grounds for not doing so. European Commission Report on Harassment related to Sex and Sexual Harassment Law in 33 European Countries, http://ec.europa.eu/justice/gender-equality/files/your_rights/final_harassement_en.pdf, p 96.

[25] 'Reverse' harassment might increase with the opportunity of women to get into managerial or top decision-making positions—underlying the true nature of sexual harassment based on hierarchy and dominance, in contrast to the perception just half a century ago that attributed it to natural male 'urges' and individual bad temper, or worse, to the lack of due 'preventive' conduct on the part of the victim.

not be based on the person's rejection of or submission to such conduct. 'Unwelcome'—that is, any conduct lacking the welcome-signal—should be considered an unlawful approach.

The definition in most legislation requires serious, deeply offensive, or even physically violent conduct in order to reach the level of prohibited harassment. It has to have the form of unwanted and insulting verbal, written or physical conduct of a sexual nature toward a person with the purpose or the effect of violating the dignity of that person, in particular when creating an intimidating, hostile, humiliating or offensive environment.[26] When the act, in order to become sanctionable, has to reach the level of violence, namely rape, sexual abuse under violence and coercion into sexual intercourse or other types of sexual coercion, even if the fact of using one's position or authority is an aggravating circumstance, the regulation may not provide a satisfactory level of protection.[27]

(ii) The Scope of Article 26§1

The personal scope of the provision covers three groups of persons: the protected (potential victim), the offender and the employer or other person responsible for prevention and remedies.

Article 26 protects all workers, regardless of the type of their contract and the type of employment, provided that they are working under the guidance and control of another person.

The ECSR has drawn a wide scope of coverage, determining that 'it must be possible for employers to be held liable towards persons employed or not employed by them who have suffered sexual harassment from employees under their responsibility or, on premises under their responsibility, from persons not employed by them, such as independent contractors, self-employed workers, visitors, clients, etc.'[28]

The employer—having control over the worksite—has the primary responsibility for everyone and for the conduct of everyone who performs work at the workplace under the employer's control. The ECSR requires national laws to establish the liability of the employer not only for private law violations, but also for acts under the Criminal Code. Noting, for example, that in Lithuania under the Criminal Code employers can be held liable for acts of sexual harassment committed in the workplace only in the case of their own subordinates, the ECSR's opinion was that this did not suffice for compliance with Article 26§1.[29]

[26] Conclusions 2014, Lithuania.
[27] Conclusions 2014, Georgia.
[28] Conclusions 2003, Italy, 324; Lithuania.
[29] Conclusions 2007, Lithuania.

The employer bears the liability for due conduct in preventing such offences; however, such a liability would not absorb or eliminate the liability of the offender.

(iii) State Obligations under Article 26§1

Article 26§1 guarantees the right to be protected from sexual harassment, a violation of dignity and equal treatment. The text entails two different obligations, of equal importance:

1. Prevention: to prevent sexual harassment by spreading information, raising awareness among potential victims and offenders, employers and law enforcement authorities on the unlawful and prohibited nature of this type of discrimination and not in the second rank with regard to the available sanctions and remedies.
2. Protection: because this conduct is a form of discrimination, state parties have the duty to implement all legal instruments available in cases of discrimination: establishing the liability of the employer, recourse to judicial procedure, the reversal of the burden of proof and adopting adequate sanctions and remedies.

The two kinds of obligation are not independent of each other, and cannot substitute for each other. Instead, their proper function may create a synergy whereby efficient prevention through raising awareness serves as a vehicle to more efficient use of available legal procedures and, on the other hand, law put in practice can operate as a preventive instrument through its deterrent effect.

(a) Prevention

Sexual harassment is a particularly sensitive form of discrimination; the social environment frequently stigmatises the victim more than the offender and therefore victims are, in a large proportion of cases, deterred from resorting to legal remedies.

Thus, a crucial obligation of ratifying parties, regardless of the legal sanctions available to conduct information, awareness-raising and prevention campaigns in the workplace or in relation to work. Such programmes have to reach not only those who might be personally involved, either as victims or responsible persons in sexual harassment cases, but also public authorities and law enforcement agencies and such education programmes may be organised by the authorities and agencies themselves, primarily offices of ombudspersons or equality agencies.[30]

[30] See, for example, the wide variety of programmes in Conclusions 2014, Austria.

Several states reported adopted legislation that makes it compulsory for employers to establish procedures and forums in order to prevent harassment. Workplace representatives may be involved in these measures, bodies and consultations.[31] Developing, implementing and communicating an internal system for preventing harassment, as well as establishing pathways for promptly remedying violations may work as incentives to employees to use the system, as a discouragement for potential harassers and also as a means of information for employers of eventual problems early enough to eliminate them.

(b) Legal Remedies

Victims of sexual harassment must have effective judicial remedies to seek reparations for pecuniary and non-pecuniary damage.[32] Effective remedies should mean: (i) available adequate procedures and (ii) appropriate reparations and compensation.

First, there has to be access to independent judicial bodies and the right to appeal, possibly after available alternative dispute resolution services have been used. Ombudspersons or authorities with similar power may be efficient organs for resolving disputes. For example, in Italy any alleged victim of sexual harassment may first and foremost have recourse to the mediation procedures provided for in the Code of Civil Procedure, or may take the case to the local gender equality counsellor.[33]

The ECSR has ruled that effective protection of employees requires a shift in the burden of proof. In particular, courts should be able to find in favour of the victim on the basis of sufficient prima facie evidence and the personal conviction of the judge or judges.[34]

Furthermore, it considers that victims of sexual harassment must have effective legal remedies to seek compensation for pecuniary and non-pecuniary damages. These remedies must, in particular, allow for appropriate compensation of a sufficient amount to make good the victim's pecuniary and non-pecuniary damages and act as a deterrent to the employer.[35] In addition, the persons concerned must have a right to be reinstated in their post with full compensation, as required in cases of discriminatory dismissal under the Charter when they have been unfairly dismissed or forced to resign for reasons linked to sexual harassment. In the view of the Committee the right to reinstatement has to be available to all victims, including

[31] Conclusions 2014, Belgium.
[32] Conclusions 2005, Moldova, 493–95.
[33] Conclusions 2014, Italy.
[34] Conclusions 2003, Slovenia, 537.
[35] Conclusions 2005, Lithuania, 390.

cases in which the employee has been pressured to resign on account of the sexual harassment.[36]

Most countries have adopted criminal sanctions to punish coercive acts of a sexual character, including fines or corrective work (a form of milder criminal sanction under some legal systems), or similar sanctions. The ECSR takes the view that in particular circumstances, perpetrators of sexual harassment may be prosecuted on charges of assault, coercion, slander and abuse of power, which may all be sanctioned by prison sentences, as well as compensatory damages. In these cases the burden of proof lies with the prosecutor. These procedures contribute to prevention, but 'sexual harassment in the workplace covers a much broader range of discriminatory behaviour and practices than those covered by the Criminal Code alone'[37] and cannot be a 'substitute' for civil law remedies.

(c) Dispute over the Obligation to Adopt Measures

The Appendix to Article 26§1 specifies that states have no obligation to enact laws relating specifically to harassment. This is not intended to encourage inactivity on the part of the state. Under the interpretation of the ECSR there is no obligation to enact laws relating specifically to sexual harassment where workers are afforded effective protection against harassment by existing norms,[38] irrespective of whether this is a general anti-discrimination act or a specific law against harassment. Taking this into consideration, Article 26§1 also requires state parties to take adequate preventive measures against sexual harassment. In particular, they should inform workers about the nature of the behaviour in question and the available remedies.[39] Opposite interpretations argue that under the right interpretation of the Appendix the terms 'promote' or 'taking active measures' would not imply the obligation of states to adopt legislation, even in the absence of such norms.[40]

(iv) Employers and Trade Unions

In order to increase the effectiveness of the change of the rules and to facilitate the establishment of workplace procedures, the text of Article 26 expressly requests governments that changes initiated with the intention of preventing and correcting sexual harassment should take place in consultation with employers' and employees' representative organisations.

[36] Conclusions 2014 Austria.

[37] Conclusions 2014 Georgia.

[38] Conclusions 2005, Statement of Interpretation on Art 26§1.

[39] Conclusions 2003, Bulgaria, Italy. According to the opposite view, the word 'promote' triggered dissenting opinions.

[40] See the dissenting opinion of S Evju, joined by R Birk and K Grillberger. Conclusions 2003, Moldova and Italy.

The ECSR put the question to the reporting countries, but apart from a few positive examples[41] the potential role of social partners is apparently underutilised in the reporting countries.

B. Paragraph 2

(i) The Concept of Harassment

Article 26§2 of the Charter establishes a right to protection of human dignity against harassment creating a hostile working environment related to any specific characteristic of a person. Drawing on French terminology this type of attitude is recurrently labelled 'moral harassment' by the ECSR.

Such an attitude may be, but is not necessarily connected to and based on the fact that the victim belongs to groups traditionally discriminated against, such as a racial, ethnic, religious or sexual minority, it may be connected to the age or any kind of disability of the person (including being overweight, recently acknowledged as a form of disability). When such conduct is related to the sex of a person it also covers sex-related attributes (family status, pregnancy).[42]

Irrespective of the admitted or perceived grounds such conduct is considered harassment by the ECSR, creating a hostile working environment characterised by the adoption towards one or more persons of persistent behaviours that may undermine their dignity or harm their career. Such attitudes shall be prohibited and repressed in the same way as acts of discrimination independent of the fact that not all harassment behaviours are acts of discrimination, except when this is presumed by law.[43]

Article 26§2 comprises and merges two categories of unlawful violation of fundamental rights in a workplace situation: (i) 'harassment', a form of discrimination on enumerated grounds under most jurisdictions;[44] (ii) 'bullying' that may occur on any ground. The two categories are very close to each other; both may consist of acts, requests, spoken words, gestures or the production, display or circulation of written words, pictures or other materials.[45] The only difference is the (limited or unlimited) range of potential grounds.

[41] Conclusions 2003, Italy, Slovenia; Conclusions 2014, Bulgaria, Finland.

[42] This has to be distinguished from sexual harassment.

[43] Conclusions 2007, Statement of Interpretation, 12–13.

[44] Under Directives 2000/43/EC on racial (ethnic) discrimination and 2000/78/EC on the Framework Directive on discrimination in employment on different grounds harassment is defined as one form of discrimination and on this ground harassment in EU Member States is a term reserved for discrimination on the enumerated grounds.

[45] Conclusions 2014, Ireland, Art 26§2.

This difference impacts on compliance with Article 26§2: countries may feel they have to conform with the provision by prohibiting harassment as a form of discrimination on familiar grounds.[46]

Retaliation against employees involved in discrimination complaints (either as a victim, representative of a victim or witness) is also a form of conduct that violates the right of persons to equal dignity and the ECSR requires state parties to treat such conduct similarly to the harassment itself.[47]

Regarding the scope of Article 26§2, there is no notable difference compared with Article 26§1. The liability of the employer covers all persons, regardless of their employment or other status, whether they are the offender or victim of harassment.

(ii) State Obligations

The ECSR recalled in its interpretation that irrespective of admitted or perceived grounds, harassment creating a hostile working environment characterised by the adoption towards one or more persons of persistent behaviours which may undermine their dignity or harm their career shall be prohibited and repressed in the same way as acts of discrimination. And this independent of the fact that not all harassment behaviours are acts of discrimination, except when this is presumed by law.

It also considers, repeating its argumentation in regard to Article 26§1, that there is no requirement for a state's legislation to make express reference to harassment where that state's law encompasses measures that make it possible to afford employees effective protection against these phenomena. This protection must include the right to appeal to an independent body in the event of harassment, the right to obtain adequate compensation and the right not to be retaliated against for upholding these rights. It further considers that, from the procedural standpoint, effective protection of employees may require a shift in the burden of proof to a certain extent, making it possible for a court to find in favour of the victim on the basis of sufficient prima facie evidence and the conviction of the judge or judges.[48]

State parties are required to take all necessary preventive and compensatory measures to protect individual workers against recurrent reprehensible or distinctly negative and offensive actions directed against them at

[46] See, for example, Conclusions 2014, Ireland: impeccably phrased prohibition of harassment on the grounds of marital/family status, sexual orientation, religious belief, age, disability, race or membership of the Traveller community—the ECSR found it in compliance. Harassment on grounds not in the 'catalogue' are not considered.

[47] Conclusions 2014, Lithuania.

[48] Conclusions 2007, Statement of Interpretation on Art 26§2. The Statement of Interpretation triggered the same dissenting opinion as the 2003 conclusions.

the workplace or in relation to their work, because these acts constitute humiliating behaviour.[49]

Apart from the difficulties that need clarification with regard to the broad coverage and less specified grounds[50] the obligations of the state parties are the same as under Article 26§1. This identical treatment is particularly relevant to the guaranteed remedies.

III. IMPACT ON EUROPEAN HUMAN RIGHTS INSTRUMENTS

A. European Convention on Human Rights

Although no case law of the ECtHR appears to be available on this specific issue as yet, the problem of dignity in general and the protection of private life in particular with regard to reputation[51] is potentially an important issue under Article 8 ECHR.

B. Charter of Fundamental Rights of the European Union

Article 31§1 CFREU refers to dignity at the workplace and the Explanations directly refer to Article 26. Therefore the CJEU has a sound basis for taking the case law of the ECSR into account when interpreting the former provision.

IV. CONCLUSIONS

An overview of the case law demonstrates that the international approach to harassment—in particular, sexual harassment—has made significant progress since the beginning of the 1990s. This can be considered the start of development on the European continent, which is far from being completed. Article 26 could be part of this start and the review of the case law shows that the approach has kept pace with developments that consistently lay down what is needed to successfully combat this phenomenon.

The text of Article 26 reflects the initial uncertainties that gave impetus to the progressive development of the case law. Most importantly, the interpretation of state obligations has to be noted, namely its apparent contravention of the Appendix. Apart from the progressive and rational argumentation of the ECSR behind establishing an obligation of states to adopt

[49] Conclusions 2005, General introduction.

[50] For example, the shift of the burden of proof may be understood differently.

[51] See generally, *A v Norway* App no 28070/06 (ECtHR, 9 April 2009) para 63.

measures affording employees effective protection against harassment, the progress of ratifications and the development of national laws contradict the accusation that the ECSR has established a duty that disregards the 'premise on which acceptance of Article 26 relies'.[52]

The Committee has also managed to avoid the risk of watering down the discriminatory nature of sexual harassment, while extending the protection of dignity under Article 26§2 to areas that might become important due to recent developmental trends in labour law.

[52] Of the 23 acceptances of Art 26 as a whole, 13 ratifications of Art 26 took place subsequent to the Committee's statement on the states' obligation in the 2003 Conclusions.

Article 27

The Right of Workers with Family Responsibilities to Equal Opportunities and Equal Treatment

ISABELLE SCHÖMANN

Article 27—The right of workers with family responsibilities to equal opportunities and equal treatment[1]

With a view to ensuring the exercise of the right to equality of opportunity and treatment for men and women workers with family responsibilities and between such workers and other workers, the Parties undertake:

1. to take appropriate measures:
    a. to enable workers with family responsibilities to enter and remain in employment, as well as to re-enter employment after an absence due to those responsibilities, including measures in the field of vocational guidance and training;
    b. to take account of their needs in terms of conditions of employment and social security;
    c. to develop or promote services, public or private, in particular child day care services and other childcare arrangements;
2. to provide a possibility for either parent to obtain, during a period after maternity leave, parental leave to take care of a child, the duration and conditions of which should be determined by national legislation, collective agreements or practice;
3. to ensure that family responsibilities shall not, as such, constitute a valid reason for termination of employment.

Appendix:

It is understood that this article applies to men and women workers with family responsibilities in relation to their dependent children as well as in relation to other members of their immediate family who clearly need their care or support

[1] In Pt I of the 1996 Charter, Art 27 'reads as follows: 'Art. 27—All persons with family responsibilities and who are engaged or wish to engage in employment have a right to do so without being subject to discrimination and as far as possible without conflict between their employment and family responsibilities'.

where such responsibilities restrict their possibilities of preparing for, entering, participating or advancing in economic activity.

The terms 'dependent children' and 'other members of their immediate family who clearly need their care and support' mean persons defined as such by the national legislation of the Party concerned.

I. INTRODUCTION

A. Context and Main Content

The principle of non-discrimination has been anchored in the Charter from the outset: the preamble of the 1961 Charter specified that 'the enjoyment of social rights should be secured without discrimination on grounds of race, colour, sex, religion, political opinion, national extraction or social origin'. The principle has filtered down into many other Articles, such as Article 4§3 on equal pay for work of equal value, but also in terms of special protection, such as in the case of maternity (Article 8). However, the 1961 Charter did not adopt a clear position on the need to reconcile obligations attached to paid work with family responsibilities.[2]

The 1996 Charter pays detailed attention to the principle of non-discrimination, so as to adapt the floor of rights to 'developments in social and economic rights as reflected in other international instruments and in the legislation of the Member States, as well as of social problems not covered yet by international instruments,[3] such as in the case of gender equality',[4] or in case of abusive treatment including sexual harassment and any recurrent reprehensible or distinctly negative and offensive actions[5] within the framework of the right to dignity at work. Additionally, Article E mentions that 'differential treatment based on an objective and reasonable justification shall not be deemed discriminatory'. It consolidates the case law of the ECSR, stating that the principle of non-discrimination applies to all the provisions of the Charter.[6]

In particular, the Charter addresses for the first time[7] the principle of equal treatment for workers with family responsibilities, at the workplace or when (re-)entering the labour market. Article 27 is subject to reporting by states and scrutiny by the ECSR, which has occurred every four years since

[2] I Hoskins, *Combining work and elder care. A challenge for now and the future* (Geneva, ILO, 1996) 11.

[3] Explanatory report to the European Social Charter (Revised) para 7.

[4] In Art 20 ESC; see also the chapter on Art 20 by C Kollonay-Lehoczky in this volume.

[5] In Art 26 ESC; see also the chapter on Art 26 by C Kollonay-Lehoczky in this volume.

[6] Explanatory report to the European Social Charter (Revised) para 135.

[7] ibid para 16.

2006,[8] the last took place in 2011, for the specific thematic group of articles devoted to 'Children, families and migrants' (thematic group 4).

In general, Article 27 has been broadly ratified, but with some exceptions among EU member states. Bulgaria, Cyprus, Hungary and Malta did not accept Article 27§1, and Romania did not ratify Article 27§1 and §3. Additionally, Albania, Andorra, Bosnia Herzegovina and Serbia did not ratify any of the paragraphs of Article 27, whereas the Republic of Moldova did not accept Article 27§1 and §3, and the Former Yugoslav Republic of Macedonia did not ratify Article 27§1 and §2.

B. International Sources

The recognition of the right of workers with family responsibilities to equal opportunities and equal treatment is part of a broader concern that relates, among other things, to intergenerational solidarity and gender equality, as well the more recent trend towards reconciliation of work and family life. The main concern is how best to reconcile child-rearing and elder care with safeguarding the interests of the worker, the family and the workplace, as well as that of the child or elderly people, so as to avoid and limit the negative effects of care responsibilities on workers.

Such a comprehensive approach has taken decades to develop, however. The first approach in 1965 was definitively a gender-oriented one: ILO Recommendation No 123 on the Employment of Women with Family Responsibilities acknowledged that women bore greater responsibility for family care, and that 'special measures were therefore needed to assist them in meeting these responsibilities as well as those arising out of work'.[9] ILO Recommendation No 123 completed ILO Convention No 100 on Equal Remuneration of 1951, as well as ILO Convention No 111 on Discrimination (Employment and Occupation) of 1958.

In the 1970s, perceptions of the role of women in society changed toward a more equal repartition of family responsibilities between men and women. This new approach based on non-discrimination found its anchor in ILO Convention No 156 of 1981 on Equal Opportunities and Equal Treat-

[8] Following a decision of the Committee of Ministers at its 963rd meeting on 3 May 2006, the provisions of the Charter have been divided into four thematic groups. States present a report on the provisions related to one of the four thematic groups on an annual basis. As a consequence, each provision of the Charter is reported on once every four years. As from 2014, states parties that have accepted the complaints procedure have to provide a national report only every two years (Committee of Ministers Decision CM (2006) 53 of 3 May 2006 'European Social Charter—Governmental Committee of the European Social Charter—New system for the presentation of reports on the application of the European Social Charter—Proposal of the Governmental Committee'). On the reporting procedure, see also the chapter by Stefan Clauwaert in this volume.

[9] Hoskins (n 1) 8.

ment for Men and Women Workers: Workers with family responsibilities, as well as ILO Recommendation No 165. The aim of the latter Convention has been to promote equal opportunities at work between men and women carrying family responsibilities, as well as between workers with family responsibilities and workers without such duties. The Convention, however, proposed a fairly restrictive scope with regard to those who should be understood as 'family members'. It distinguishes between dependent children, for whom the Convention is applicable immediately, and other members of the immediate family who need clear support from the workers, for whom Member States may apply the Convention in stages. In its supervisory work, the Committee of Experts (CEACR) has, recurrently, reminded Member States that a broad definition of the 'member of the family' should be adopted, including persons with a disability or the elderly, and should not be limited to dependent children. Furthermore, national legislation on leave entitlements should take into consideration a multitude of caregiving situations and the urgency that workers may face. They should furthermore guarantee equal access to these entitlements for men and women, as well as the effective exercise of the right of workers to request flexible working-time arrangements, reduced working hours or home work in order to better combine work with family responsibilities.[10]

Article 27 was inspired by ILO Convention No 156, as well as the related Recommendation No 165, as mentioned in the Explanatory report to the Charter.[11] In particular, the reference to the requirement on the parties to take appropriate measures so as to take account of the needs of workers in terms of conditions of employment and social security originated from Article 4(b) of the ILO Convention.

C. Relationship to Other Provisions of the Charter

Article 27 is clearly related to other provisions of the Charter, in particular as the guarantee for equal opportunities and treatment of workers with family responsibilities necessitates a manifold approach: on one hand, the acceptance of a gendered division of family responsibilities still requires fundamental adaptations, for example in wage policy: as Hoskins points out 'as long as men will earn more on average than women, there will be strong pressures against their taking time off to attend to family responsibilities'.[12] In this respect, Article 27 should be seen in relation to Article 1§2 on the right to protect workers effectively to earn their living in an occupation

[10] See, for example, the list of CEACR's direct requests to Member States in respect of the application of Convention no. 156.

[11] Council of Europe, 1996, Explanatory Report to the European Social Charter (Revised), para 103.

[12] Hoskins (n 1) 68.

freely entered upon, and also to Article 4§3 on the right of men and women workers to equal pay for work of equal value. On the other hand, Article 27 is embedded in the general principle on non-discrimination, and as such is to be seen in relation to Article 20 on the right to equal opportunities and equal treatment in matters of employment and occupation without discrimination on the grounds of sex.

Furthermore, next to equal pay and non-discrimination for workers with family responsibilities, the recognition and promotion of the reconciliation of work with private life should be such that no direct or indirect discrimination at the workplace or when (re-)entering the labour market could occur on the ground of family responsibilities. In this respect, Article 27 should be seen in relation to Article 8 on the right to special protection in the case of maternity, and also Articles 9 and 10 on the right to appropriate facilities for vocational guidance and training. Furthermore, Article 27 should be read in conjunction with Article 12 on the right of all workers and their dependants to social security, but also to Article 16 on the right of the family as a fundamental unit of society to appropriate social, legal and economic protection to ensure its full development and to Article 24 on the the right to protection in cases of termination of employment.

It goes without saying that Article 27 plays the role of a blueprint for effective policies for a more family-responsive workplace within a more wide-ranging approach to the promotion and implementation of the principle of equal treatment at work.

II. CONTENT

A. Paragraph1: The Right to Equality of Opportunity and Treatment for Men and Women Workers with Family Responsibilities and between Such Workers and Other Workers

The Appendix elaborates on the personal scope of Article 27, which includes men and women workers with family responsibilities. It goes on to delineate the 'family' as dependent children as well as other members of the immediate family of the workers, 'as defined as such by the national legislation of the Party concerned'. However, within the framework of Article 27, it appears that much attention has been devoted to dependent children, and possibly less to other members of the immediate family when it comes to elderly and possibly persons with a disability.

Furthermore, two additional conditions are mentioned: first, those family members should clearly need the care or support of the worker; second, such responsibilities must restrict the worker's ability to prepare for, enter, participate in or advance in economic activity.

Furthermore, the Appendix of the Charter explicitly mentions that the scope of the 1996 Charter, in terms of persons protected and, among others, those covered by Article 27

> include[s] foreigners only in so far as they are nationals of other Parties lawfully resident or working regularly within the territory of the Party concerned, subject to the understanding that these articles are to be interpreted in the light of the provisions of Articles 18 and 19. This interpretation would not prejudice the extension of similar facilities to other persons by any of the Parties.

Concerning material scope, the 'appropriate measures' to be taken are defined in the Explanatory report as suitable to national conditions and possibilities.

(i) The Right to (Re-)enter and Remain in Employment

According to Article 27§1a, states should provide workers with family responsibilities with equal opportunities in respect of entering, remaining in and re-entering employment because these persons may face difficulties on the labour market due to their family responsibilities.

Based on its case law, the ECSR has elaborated on the kind of difficulties workers with family responsibilities may face. In its Conclusions of 2003,[13] it underlined that

> the disadvantage of such people lies within the very nature of family responsibilities, which exclude people not only from an employment relation but, what is most important, from professional life; they often do not have time to monitor labour market developments and take measures in order to stay competitive. To be able to return to professional life, they need special assistance in terms of vocational guidance and training.

While it is well-established case law that actions must be taken to promote training aimed at facilitating the (re)integration of workers with family responsibilities in the employment market, the lack of extra services for those workers cannot, however, be seen as a human rights violation,[14] in particular when the quality of standard employment services is adequate.

(ii) To Take Account of Their Needs in Terms of Conditions of Employment and Social Security

According to Article 27§1(b), which provides for the needs of workers with family responsibilities to be taken into account in terms of conditions of employment and social security, the ECSR has had occasion to specify that

[13] Conclusions 2003, Sweden. See also Conclusions 2005, Statement of Interpretation on Art 27§1a; eg Conclusions 2005, Estonia.

[14] Conclusions 2003, Sweden.

the length and organisation of working time is one of the issues at stake.[15] This sub-paragraph corresponds to Article 4§b of ILO Convention No 156.

In its conclusions, the ECSR recalled that part-time working may be agreed upon by employers and workers with family responsibilities. However, a request for part-time work must be accepted if requested by 'inter alia a pregnant woman, a nursing mother, a woman or single parent raising a child (children) under 14 years of age or a disabled child under 16 years of age, or a person nursing a sick family member'.[16] In the same case law, the ECSR considers that whereas there is no obligation to agree to part-time work for a father who is not single, such a measure constitutes discrimination, and can therefore not be considered to be in conformity with Article 27§1 combined with Article E. The ECSR thereby reiterates the principle of equal treatment of men and women, as workers with family responsibilities. Furthermore, the ECSR stresses that parents should be allowed to reduce or cease work because of the serious illness of a child.[17]

A demand to return to full-time employment may also be agreed by employer and workers with family responsibilities.[18]

As mentioned in the Digest of 2008, this type of measure cannot be defined unilaterally by the employer but should be provided by a binding text (legislation or collective agreement). In the same vein, periods of unemployment due to family responsibilities should be taken into account in the calculation of pension schemes or in the determination of pension rights, as reiterated by the ECSR when it ruled that the Irish Employment Equality Act 1998 was not in conformity, on the ground that periods of parental leave are not taken into account in the calculation of pensions.[19]

(iii) To Develop or Promote Services, Public or Private, in Particular Child Day Care Services and Other Childcare Arrangements

In its Conclusions of 2005 in a case concerning Estonia, the ECSR recalled that the aim of Article 27§1(c) is to develop or promote services, in particular child day care services and other childcare arrangements, available and accessible to workers with family responsibilities.[20]

In this respect, Article 27§1c must be read in conjunction with Article 16 on the right of the family to social, legal and economic protection, as

[15] Conclusions 2005, Statement of Interpretation on Art 27§1(b); eg Conclusions 2005, Estonia.

[16] Conclusions 2005, Lithuania.

[17] Conclusions 2005, Norway.

[18] Conclusions 2005, Statement of Interpretation on Art 27§1(a); eg Conclusions 2005, Estonia.

[19] Conclusions 2011, Ireland.

[20] Conclusions 2005, Statement of Interpretation on Art 27§1(c); eg Conclusions 2005, Estonia.

the ECSR stresses that where a state has accepted Article 16, childcare arrangements are dealt with under that provision.[21]

B. Paragraph 2: The Right to Parental Leave

Following the report on Turkey, from which it appeared that the existing possibilities for leave for women are unpaid, the ECSR recalled the importance of remunerating leave (whether as continuation of pay or via social assistance/social security benefits) as a means of encouraging the take-up of childcare leave. It further stated that legislation that does not provide fathers with a right to parental leave is not in conformity with Article 27§2.[22]

In the case of Ireland, the ECSR has observed[23] that, apart from a loss of wages, an employee's position does not change as a result of having taken parental leave. While on parental leave, the employee should be treated as still working, with regard to employment rights, such as leave entitlement. The employee is entitled to return to his/her job after expiry of the parental leave, unless this is not reasonably practicable for the employer. The ECSR further noted that in this case the employee must be offered a suitable alternative position on terms not less favourable than the previous job, including any improvement in pay or other conditions which occurred when the employee was on parental leave.

C. Paragraph 3: Family Responsibilities shall not, as such, Constitute a Valid Reason for Termination of Employment

The principle that family responsibilities are not a valid ground for dismissal was reiterated in general terms by the ECSR in its 2003 Conclusions concerning Bulgaria,[24] stating that 'the purpose of Article 27§3 is to prevent these obligations from restricting preparation for and access to working life, exercise of an occupation and career advancement'. Workers dismissed on such illegal grounds must be afforded the same level of protection allocated in other cases of discriminatory dismissal under Article 1§2. In particular, the ECSR recalled that courts or other competent bodies should be able to award a level of compensation that is sufficient both to deter the employer, and proportionate to the damage suffered by the victim. Therefore limits on

[21] Digest of 2008.
[22] Conclusions 2011, Turkey.
[23] Conclusions 2007, Ireland.
[24] Conclusions 2003, Statement of Interpretation on Art 27§3; eg Conclusions 2003, Bulgaria.

the levels of compensation that may be awarded are not in conformity with the Charter.[25]

Furthermore, the ECSR concluded to the non-conformity with Article 27§3 of provisions of the Bulgarian Labour Code, stating that 'In cases where dismissal requires prior consent of the labour inspectorate, and no such consent has been asked for or given before the dismissal, the court shall cancel the order of dismissal as unlawful on these grounds only, without considering the merits of the labour dispute'. The ECSR ruled that the Bulgarian legislation did not sufficiently protect workers with family responsibilities against dismissal.[26]

In the same vein, the ECSR concluded that the provision of Armenian legislation preventing the court, in a case of unfair dismissal, from ordering the reinstatement of the employee in the previous job was not in conformity with Article 27§3, on the ground that national legislation made no provision for the reinstatement of workers unlawfully dismissed on account of their family responsibilities.[27] The same applies when courts may only order reinstatement of an unlawfully dismissed employee in cases where the enterprise concerned has more than 20 employees[28] or when legislation makes no provision for the reinstatement of workers unlawfully dismissed on grounds of their family responsibilities.[29]

In 2007,[30] the ECSR concluded non-conformity of the Irish Employment Equality Act 1998 and Equality Act 2004, by which the maximum amount of compensation was fixed as a ceiling. The ECSR recalled that Article 27§3 requires that courts or other competent bodies are able to award a level of compensation that is sufficient both to deter the employer and proportionate to the damage suffered by the victim. In the same vein, it decided that limits on levels of compensation that may be awarded are not in conformity with the Charter.[31]

III. IMPACT ON EUROPEAN HUMAN RIGHTS INSTRUMENTS

A. European Convention of Human Rights

In a recent case, *Constantin Markin v Russia*,[32] the ECtHR had occasion to refer to the Charter and its Article 27, as well as to the resolutions and

[25] Conclusions 2005, Estonia.
[26] Conclusions 2011, Bulgaria.
[27] Conclusions 2011, Armenia.
[28] Conclusion 2011, Cyprus.
[29] Conclusions 2011, Finland.
[30] Conclusions 2007, Ireland.
[31] Conclusions 2005, Estonia.
[32] *Constantin Markin v Russia* App no 30078/06 (ECtHR, 22 March 2012).

recommendations of the Council of Europe's parliamentary assembly and the recommendations of the Committee of Ministers. The case dealt with the refusal of the Russian Constitutional Court to recognise the incompatibility with the equality clause of the Russian Constitution of the provisions of the Military Service Act in which parental leave was only allocated to female civil servants, and consequently had been refused to a male civil servant, being a sole carer for his three children.

The ECtHR referred to Article 27 but also to a large range of references elaborated by the Council of Europe. The ECtHR referred to Resolution 1274 of 2002 of the Parliamentary Assembly in which the need to include men as recipients of parental leave was stressed on one hand to acknowledge the wish of men 'to balance work and family life and ensure their children's well-being' and, on the other hand, to recognise 'the role of men in family life, since it permits a genuine partnership in the sharing of responsibilities between women and men in both the private and public sphere' (point 56).[33] It also stressed the need for member states that do not yet apply parental leave equally to men and women to do so (point 57). Furthermore, the ECtHR quotes Recommendation 1796 of 2006 of the Parliamentary Assembly to request member states to take action in particular so as to make it easier for women and men to reconcile work and family life, including paid paternity leave and 'paid, socially-covered parental leave, which may be used flexibly by the father and the mother, taking special care to ensure that men are actually able to use it' (point 58).

The Court went on with a reference to Recommendation of the Committee of Ministers No R(96)5 on Reconciling Work and Family Life on Parental Leave, as well as its Appendix to strengthen the need for member states to promote equal opportunities and equal treatment so as to enable men and women without discrimination to better reconcile their work and family lives and in particular to have the right to take parental leave.[34] The Recommendation R(2007)17 on Gender Equality Standards and Mechanisms[35] was quoted, as well as Recommendation R(2010)4 on the Human Rights of the Armed Forces,[36] to reiterate the standards to be set in order to guarantee reconciliation of work and private/family life.

[33] Parliamentary Assembly, Resolution 1274(2002) on Parental leave, adopted on 26 March 2002.

[34] Adopted by the Committee of Ministers on 19 June 1996 at the 569th meeting of the Ministers' Deputies.

[35] Adopted by the Committee of Ministers on 21 November 2007 at the 1011th meeting of the Ministers' Deputies.

[36] Adopted by the Committee of Ministers on 24 February 2010 at the 1077th meeting of the Ministers' Deputies.

The comprehensive references to the Council of Europe instances and instruments that deem the effectiveness of the rights laid down in the Charter, and particularly the right of workers with family responsibilities to equal opportunities and equal treatment, indicate the will of the ECtHR to make operational use of the Charter as a most relevant international and comparative instrument on an equal footing with the United Nations Conventions and ILO Conventions, as well as European primary and secondary law.

B. Charter of Fundamental Rights of the European Union[37]

The European Union expressed in the CFREU its general recognition of the rights 'as they result, from ... the Social Charters adopted by the Union and by the Council of Europe',[38] as well as the reference in its Article 53 on the level of protection in which 'nothing in this Charter shall be interpreted as restricting or adversely affecting human rights and fundamental freedoms as recognised, in their respective fields of application, by Union law and international law and by international agreements to which the Union or all the member states are party'.

In particular, the CFREU chapter on solidarity relates to a range of workers' rights, and among them to the protection of family life and professional life. In this respect, explicit reference to the Charter is made on several occasions and in particular in the Explanations[39] on Article 33 CFREU on family and professional life with reference to Article 8 on the right to special protection of employed women in case of maternity, to Article 16 on the right of the family, as a fundamental unit of society, to appropriate social, legal and economic protection to ensure its full development, as well as to Article 27.

However, Article 33 CFREU seems to restrict the right to protection against dismissal from employment to reasons connected with maternity, and the right to paid maternity leave and to parental leave following the birth or adoption of a child. The issue of workers as caregivers of elderly or handicapped family members does not appear clearly in the CFREU in comparison to the Charter.

In the same vein, the EU protection against discrimination on grounds of family responsibilities finds its sources in the Charter. From the

[37] European Committee of Social Rights, 'The relationship between European Union law and the European Social Charter', Working Document. 15.07.2014.

[38] Preamble, para 5, CFREU.

[39] Explanations relating to the Charter of Fundamental Rights (2007/C 303/02) [2007] OJ C-303/17–35.

protection in case of pregnancy[40] to parental leave,[41] a wide range of EU primary[42] and secondary law refers to legislation on equal treatment in employment and occupation on equal pay,[43] equal treatment in access to jobs and training[44] and on self-employment (female self-employed workers and female assisting spouses or life partners),[45] that directly or indirectly refers to the Charter.

Reference to the Charter can be indirectly found in the Directive 2010/18/EU[46] of 8 March 2010 implementing the revised Framework Agreement on parental leave concluded by BUSINESSEUROPE, UEAPME, CEEP and ETUC and repealing Directive 96/34/EC,[47] in recital 3 of which reference is made to Articles 23 and 33 of the CFREU relating to equality between men and women and reconciliation of professional, private and family life.

IV. CONCLUSIONS

Reconciling work with family life is one of the main challenges facing Europe, as it impacts on equality in society, the economy and demographic developments.

Enhancing the work-life balance has developed as one of the crucial features of the European and national labour market to guarantee women's economic independence, and in the same vein, to boost male workers' participation in the care of children or the elderly. The large number of international and European instruments, in particular Article 27, indicates the constant effort of the international and European institutions to set and strengthen the principles and rights that are regarded as essential to guarantee such a balance between work and family responsibilities.

Generally, next to maternity, paternity and parental leave, flexible work arrangements are mainly developed in relation to working time. However, such working time arrangements, like part-time work, still encourage more women than men to take family-related leave, as men usually earn more than women for the same job. Furthermore, as part-time work hardly remains a

[40] Directive 92/85/EEC on pregnant workers, workers who have recently given birth and women who are breastfeeding.

[41] Directive 2010/18/EU based on a revised framework agreement on parental leave concluded by the European Social Partners. The first directive on parental leave dates back to 1996 (Council Directive 96/34/EC of 3 June 1996).

[42] Arts 10 and 158 TFEU.

[43] Directive 2006/54/EC.

[44] Directive 2006/54/EC.

[45] Directive 2010/41/EU.

[46] [2010] OJ L68/13.

[47] Council Directive 96/34/EC of 3 June 1996 on the framework agreement on parental leave concluded by UNICE, CEEP and the ETUC, [1996] OJ L145/4–9.

temporary situation, such schemes often lead to a 'motherhood penalty', which is one of the causes of persistent gender gaps in pay and pensions. Furthermore, neutral tax and benefits systems should be developed so as to make it more attractive for both men and women to care for their children or other dependants.[48]

In parallel, while there is a strong focus in the European Union on developing support for workers in respect of childcare, less seems to be proposed in respect of workers who have to leave the labour market, even for a short period of time, to care for dependants or other family members, in particular when they are not direct family members. The current ageing population, however, requires as much attention to supporting care workers.

[48] K Zellmer et al (2015), Forum on the future of gender equality in Europe, Report: 2. http://ec.europa.eu/justice/events/future-of-gender-equality-2015/files/report_forum_gender_equality_en.pdf. See also 2015 study on maternity, paternity and parental leave in the EU: www.europarl.europa.eu/RegData/etudes/STUD/2015/509999/IPOL_STU(2015)509999_EN.pdf.

Article 28

The Right of Workers' Representatives to Protection in the Undertaking and Facilities to Be Accorded to Them

NIKLAS BRUUN

Article 28—The right of workers' representatives to protection in the undertaking and facilities to be accorded to them

With a view to ensuring the effective exercise of the right of workers' representatives to carry out their functions, the Parties undertake to ensure that in the undertaking:

a. they enjoy effective protection against acts prejudicial to them, including dismissal, based on their status or activities as workers' representatives within the undertaking;
b. they are afforded such facilities as may be appropriate in order to enable them to carry out their functions promptly and efficiently, account being taken of the industrial relations system of the country and the needs, size and capabilities of the undertaking concerned.

Appendix Part II: Articles 28 (and 29)

For the purpose of the application of this article, the term 'workers' representatives' means persons who are recognised as such under national legislation or practice.

I. INTRODUCTION

A. Context and Main Content

Article 28 complements Article 5, which prohibits discrimination [against] trade union representatives. Article 28 guarantees the right of workers' representatives, unionised or non-unionised, to protection in the undertaking and to certain facilities.'[1]

The Explanatory Report to the Revised Charter[2] explicitly stated that the provision was inspired by ILO Convention No 135 (Workers' Representatives) of 1971.

A definition of the term 'workers' representatives' is given in the Appendix to the Article, which describes it as meaning persons who are recognised as such under national legislation or practice. This definition is based on that of the Appendix to Articles 21 and 22. Also, the definition of an undertaking, which has been discussed in relation to Articles 21 and 22, applies here. It is understood that national legislation or practice may provide that workers' representatives be elected representatives or trade union delegates.

Sub-section b of the Article, which corresponds to Article 2 of the ILO Convention, provides that workers' representatives be afforded such facilities as will enable them to carry out their functions. The only limitation in the context of the Revised Charter is that account shall be taken of the industrial relations system of the country and the needs, size and capabilities of the undertaking concerned. According to the Explanatory Report, examples of facilities to be granted to workers' representatives may be found in ILO Recommendation No 143 (Workers' Representatives) of 1971.

It must also be noted that the protection of workers' representatives can also be covered by the Right to Organise and Collective Bargaining Convention No 98 (1951).[3] According to Article 1 of this Convention, 'Workers shall enjoy adequate protection against acts of anti-union discrimination in respect of their employment'. It is clear that such discrimination can often be directed towards trade union representatives, which also is illustrated by a voluminous case law from the Freedom of Association Committee in the ILO.[4]

Several European member states have not ratified the revised Charter, nor accepted Article 8 in it. Among the 47 member states to the Charter, 19 are outside this provision; here we also find countries in which workers' representatives have traditionally had a fairly strong position, such as Denmark, Sweden, Germany and Iceland. One reason for this might be that protection of workers' representatives is provided for by collective agreements, which creates some limitations regarding the coverage of protection to all kinds of workers' representatives.

[1] M Mikkola, *Social Human Rights of Europe* (Porvoo, Bookwell, 2010) 254.

[2] See the Explanatory Report to the Revised Social Charter (ETS 163) regarding Art 28.

[3] Convention No 98 concerning the Application of the Principles of the Right to Organise and to Bargain Collectively, adopted 1949 (entry into force: 18 July 1951).

[4] See the Digest of decisions and principles of the Freedom of Association Committee of the Governing Body of the ILO, fifth (revised) edition (Geneva, ILO, 2006).

B. Relations with Other Provisions of the Charter

The method of systematic interpretation requires that the specific rule of Article 28 must be read in connection with all relevant norms of the Charter dealing with the protection of workers when they act as workers' representatives either through a trade union or based on separate elections. Of special relevance are Articles 5 (the right to organise) and 6 (the right to bargain collectively) as well as Article 21 (the right to information and consultation), Article 22 (the right to take part in the determination and improvement of working conditions and working environment), Article 24 (the right to protection in cases of termination of employment) and Article 29 (the right to information and consultation in collective redundancies).

Compared with Articles 21, 22 and 29, in which certain areas of competence are defined for workers' or trade union representatives, Article 28 sets out the general precondition for them to act or to 'effectively exercise' their rights and 'carry out their functions'. It is therefore a very important Article in the European Social Charter. It also has an impact on the protection of migrant workers under Article 19§4, who should be treated no less favourably than nationals with regard to membership of trade unions.[5]

II. CONTENT

A. Who Are 'Workers' Representatives'?

> According to the Appendix of Article 28, the term 'workers' representatives' means persons who are recognised as such under national legislation or practice. States may therefore establish different kinds of workers' representatives, either trade union representatives or other types of representatives or both. Representation may be exercised, for example, through workers' commissioners, workers' councils or workers' representatives on the enterprise's supervisory board.[6]

Where there exist in the same undertaking both trade union representatives and elected representatives, appropriate measures shall be taken, wherever necessary, to ensure that the existence of elected representatives is not used to undermine the position of the trade unions concerned or their representatives and to encourage cooperation on all relevant matters between the elected representatives and the trade unions concerned and their representatives.[7]

Due to the wording of Article 28 its protection applies to workers 'based on their status or activities as workers' representatives'. This might seem

[5] See S Clauwaert on Art 19§4 in this volume.
[6] Conclusions 2014, Austria, Malta and the Netherlands.
[7] ILO Convention No 135, Art 5.

rather loose; how can we define when some 'activities' might create a status as a representative? Therefore there is reason to recall that the term 'workers' representative' means persons who are recognised as such under national legislation or practice.

Workers' representatives can base their status on law, collective agreements or practice, but it must be recognised at national level. On the other hand, reading Article 28 together with the other Articles in the Social Charter in which competencies are given to workers' representatives, it seems clear that state parties actually have an obligation to accept and, when necessary, introduce systems for workers' representatives, as well as make sure that they are protected and granted resources to carry out their functions.

Both trade unions and groups of employees might be subjects of the right to choose and elect their representatives in full freedom. This is a fundamental principle of freedom of association, which has often been dealt with by the Freedom of Association Committee (CFA) in relation to Conventions No 87 and No 98.[8]

B. Protection against Prejudicial Acts and Dismissals

The wording of Article 28 prescribes that workers' representatives shall enjoy effective protection against acts prejudicial to them, including dismissal.

The ECSR therefore requests state parties to establish protection against prejudicial acts other than dismissal, as well as against dismissal. The Italian protection of unitary trade union representatives (RSU) was regarded as sufficient after the ECSR had noted that the RSU leader benefited from the following protections:

— existence of an urgent protective procedure making it possible to obtain the immediate reinstatement of an RSU leader who has been wrongfully dismissed;
— the transfer of an RSU leader from one production unit to another requires the trade union's prior consent;
— the rules on unlawful transfers and dismissals take effect until the end of the year following that in which an RSU leader's term of office expires.

Lack of protection of employee representatives against prejudicial acts other than dismissal is regarded as non-conformity with Article 28. Typical examples of such acts might be transfer to other tasks or production units, unfavourable treatment in the context of management decisions, or indirect

[8] See, for instance, ILO Digest of decisions and principles of the Freedom of Association Committee of the Governing Body of the ILO (5th edn, 2006): case 434: 'When the authorities intervene during the election proceedings of a union, expressing their opinion of the candidates and the consequences of the election, this seriously challenges the principle that trade union organizations have the right to elect their representatives in full freedom.'

discrimination. Also, refusal to grant time off for necessary handling of tasks related to their position as a representative of the employees might constitute a prejudicial act, especially when there are rules in place regarding such time off.

Effective protection against dismissals implies that the burden of proof in the event of a court procedure regarding a dismissal should not be on the workers' representative; furthermore, unlawfully dismissed workers' representatives should be entitled to seek reinstatement and receive compensation.[9]

The ECSR also consistently requires the state parties to extend the protection for workers' representatives to last for a certain period after the end of their functions, in order to be 'effective'.[10] Furthermore the protection should also be extended to those who are candidates for election, because otherwise some candidates might be strongly discouraged from standing for election.

To this end, the protection afforded to workers' representatives shall be extended for a *reasonable period* after the effective end of their period of office.[11] The Committee has, for example, found the situation to be in conformity with the requirements of Article 28 in countries such as Estonia and Slovenia, where the protection is extended for one year after the end of the mandate of workers' representatives or in Bulgaria, where the protection granted to workers' representatives is extended for six months after the end of their mandate.[12]

In the decision on the merits to Collective Complaint 33/2006 the ECSR stated: 'The Committee considers that the protection afforded to worker representatives should extend for a period beyond the mandate. The Committee recalls that the rights recognised in the Social Charter must take a practical and effective, rather than purely theoretical form.'[13] To this end, the protection afforded to them shall be extended for a reasonable period after the effective end of their period of office.[14]

C. Right to Be Afforded Facilities

In the Explanatory Report to the Revised Charter, some short comments were made to sub-section b of Article 28, which corresponds to Article 2 of the ILO Convention. It provides that workers' representatives shall be

[9] See Conclusions 2014, Finland.

[10] Conclusions 2014, Ireland.

[11] Conclusions 2010, Statement of Interpretation on Art 28.

[12] Conclusions 2010, Estonia, Slovenia and Bulgaria.

[13] *International Movement ATD Fourth World v France*, Collective Complaint No 33/2006, Decision on the merits of 05.12.2007 §59.

[14] Conclusions 2014, eg Austria, Finland, Lithuania, Norway, Portugal, Romania, Turkey.

afforded such facilities as will enable them to carry out their functions. The only limitation in the context of the Revised Charter is, according to this Report, that account shall be taken of the industrial relations system of the country and the needs, size and capabilities of the undertaking concerned. Examples of facilities to be granted to workers' representatives may be found in ILO Recommendation No 143 (Workers' Representatives) of 1971.[15] We can recall that the recommendation is quite detailed on this point:

> 10. (1) Workers' representatives in the undertaking should be afforded the necessary time off from work, without loss of pay or social and fringe benefits, for carrying out their representation functions in the undertaking.
>
> (2) In the absence of appropriate provisions, a workers' representative may be required to obtain permission from his immediate supervisor or another appropriate representative of management designated for this purpose before he takes time off from work, such permission not to be unreasonably withheld.
>
> (3) Reasonable limits may be set on the amount of time off which is granted to workers' representatives under subparagraph (1) of this Paragraph.
>
> 11. (1) In order to enable them to carry out their functions effectively, workers' representatives should be afforded the necessary time off for attending trade union meetings, training courses, seminars, congresses and conferences.
>
> (2) Time off afforded under subparagraph (1) of this Paragraph should be afforded without loss of pay or social and fringe benefits, it being understood that the question of who should bear the resulting costs may be determined by the methods of implementation referred to in Paragraph 1 of this Recommendation.
>
> 12. Workers' representatives in the undertaking should be granted access to all workplaces in the undertaking, where such access is necessary to enable them to carry out their representation functions.
>
> 13. Workers' representatives should be granted without undue delay access to the management of the undertaking and to management representatives empowered to take decisions, as may be necessary for the proper exercise of their functions.
>
> 14. In the absence of other arrangements for the collection of trade union dues, workers' representatives authorised to do so by the trade union should be permitted to collect such dues regularly on the premises of the undertaking.
>
> 15. (1) Workers' representatives acting on behalf of a trade union should be authorised to post trade union notices on the premises of the undertaking in a place or places agreed on with the management and to which the workers have easy access.
>
> (2) The management should permit workers' representatives acting on behalf of a trade union to distribute news sheets, pamphlets, publications and other documents of the union among the workers of the undertaking.

[15] Explanatory Report of Revisited Charter 1996, 108.

(3) The union notices and documents referred to in this Paragraph should relate to normal trade union activities and their posting and distribution should not prejudice the orderly operation and tidiness of the undertaking.

(4) Workers' representatives who are elected representatives in the meaning of clause (b) of Paragraph 2 of this Recommendation should be given similar facilities consistent with their functions.

In its 2014 Conclusions the Committee recalls that facilities may include, for example, those mentioned in ILO Recommendation No 143 concerning protection and facilities to be afforded to workers' representatives within the undertaking adopted by the ILO General Conference of 23 June 1971 (support in terms of benefits and other welfare benefits because of the time off to perform their functions; access for workers' representatives or other elected representatives to all premises, where necessary; access without delay to the undertaking's management board; authorisation to regularly collect subscriptions in the undertaking; authorisation to post bills or notices in one or several places to be determined with the management board, the authorisation to distribute information sheets, factsheets and other documents on general trade unions' activities); as well as other facilities such as a financial contribution to the workers' council and the use of premises and materials for the operation of the workers' council.

Moreover, participation in training courses on economic, social and union issues should not result in a loss of pay. Training costs should not be borne by the workers' representatives.[16]

When workers' representatives are required to travel in order to perform their functions, what arrangements are made for covering their expenses? This general question was posed by the ECSR in 2010, which indicates that compensation for travel expenses is also to be seen as facilities under Article 28 sub-section b.[17]

D. Remedies and Sanctions

It is quite natural that the question of remedies and sanctions in relation to Article 28 has largely been focused on dismissals. Dismissal of a workers' representative not only represents unjustified dismissal, but is in many cases also a serious violation of the principles of freedom of association.

The ECSR often recalls that remedies must be available to workers' representatives to allow them to contest their dismissal. In this regard, the

[16] Conclusions 2014, eg Austria, Bulgaria, Finland, Ireland, Italy. These conclusions of the ECSR follow a consistent pattern. Similar Conclusions were made in 2010, see the Statement of interpretation of Art 28.

[17] Conclusions by year, 2010, General Questions from Committee, Art 28.

Committee often asks the state parties when needed to provide information in their next report on the remedies available to workers' representatives contesting their dismissal. The Committee asks whether the Court's approval can be contested. A primary remedy in cases of unjustifiable dismissals of workers' representatives is reinstatement. It seems, however, that the ECSR does not request member states to introduce reinstatement as a remedy, if they enjoy 'effective protection' through other remedies. The ECSR often asks about other available remedies, and it seems that several member states have shortcomings in this regard.

The ECSR has recalled in some cases that where a dismissal based on trade union membership has occurred, there must be adequate compensation proportionate to the damage suffered by the victim.[18] The compensation must at least correspond to the wage that would have been payable between the date of the dismissal and the date of the court decision or reinstatement.[19] The ECSR regularly asks the state parties to indicate whether an adequate compensation proportionate to the damage suffered by the workers' representative who is dismissed is granted.[20]

The ECSR recalls that protection should cover the prohibition of dismissal on the ground of being a workers' representative and the protection against detriment in employment other than dismissal.[21]

III. IMPACT ON EUROPEAN HUMAN RIGHTS INSTRUMENTS

A. ILO Convention C 135

ILO Workers' Representatives Convention 1971 (No 135)[22] has been the most relevant source and inspiration for Article 28. The most important provisions are laid down in Articles 1 and 2. Article 1 states that workers' representatives in undertakings shall enjoy effective protection against any act prejudicial to them, including dismissal, based on their status or activities as a workers' representative or on union membership or participation in union activities, in so far as they act in conformity with existing laws or collective agreements or other jointly agreed arrangements. Article 2 lays down the principle regarding facilities requiring that such facilities in the undertaking shall be afforded to workers' representatives as may be appropriate in order to enable them to carry out their functions promptly and

[18] Conclusions 2014, Austria.

[19] Conclusions 2007, Bulgaria.

[20] Conclusions 2014, eg Ireland, Malta, Netherlands.

[21] Conclusions 2014, Former Yugoslav Republic of Macedonia.

[22] Protection and Facilities to Be Afforded to Workers' Representatives in the Undertaking, adopted 1971 (entry into force: 30 June 1973).

efficiently. The requirement regarding facilities is not, however, unlimited. It is stated in Article 2§2 and §3 that in this connection account shall be taken of the characteristics of the industrial relations system of the country and the needs, size and capabilities of the undertaking concerned and that the granting of such facilities shall not impair the efficient operation of the undertaking. These aspects are directly imported from ILO Recommendation 143 (1971),[23] which was adopted at the same time as Convention 135, but contains more detailed recommendations on how to protect workers' representatives.

In Article 3 of the Convention the term 'workers' representatives' is expressed as meaning persons who are recognised as such under national law or practice, whether they are:

(a) trade union representatives, namely, representatives designated or elected by trade unions or by members of such unions; or
(b) elected representatives, namely, representatives who are freely elected by the workers of the undertaking in accordance with provisions of national laws or regulations or of collective agreements and whose functions do not include activities which are recognised as the exclusive prerogative of trade unions in the country concerned.

B. European Convention on Human Rights (ECHR)

The main Article regarding freedom of association in the European Convention is without doubt Article 11. It seems clear that at least trade union representatives are protected under Article 11, because acts against trade union activists might also be regarded as a violation of Article 11. Especially when the trade union representatives are defending workers' interests in conflict situations, dismissals or reprisals against trade unionists might ensue.

Article 8 of the ECHR can also be of relevance, especially in cases of dismissals of trade union representatives. The Court has consistently held that unjustified dismissals can also be a violation of the right to private life since it has an impact on relationship with other persons, as well as having tangible consequences for the material wellbeing of an individual and their family.[24]

Finally, Article 14 might be of relevance especially in conjunction with Article 11. Since discrimination on grounds of trade union membership or position as a representative might not only be a violation of Article 11 or 8,

[23] See also Workers' Representatives Recommendation, R 143 (1971) Recommendation concerning Protection and Facilities to be Afforded to Workers' Representatives in the Undertaking.

[24] See, for instance, *Volkov v Ukraine* App no 21722/11 (ECtHR, 9 January 2013).

it might also form discrimination on the ground of Article 14, which states that

> the enjoyment of the rights and freedoms set forth in the Convention shall be secured without discrimination on any ground such as sex, race, colour, language, religion, political or other opinion, national or social origin, association with a national minority, property, birth or other status.

Trade union membership or the status of workers´ representative clearly can constitute such other status.[25]

C. Charter of Fundamental Rights of the European Union (CFREU)

Several Articles in the Charter of Fundamental Rights of the EU (CFREU), namely Articles 21 (non-discrimination), Article 27 (workers' or their representatives' right to information and consultation) and Article 30 (Protection against unjustified dismissals) have to be interpreted in light of Article 28.

Directive 2002/14/EC of the European Parliament and of the Council of 11 March 2002 establishes a general framework for informing and consulting employees in the European Community:

> *Article 7, Protection of employees' representatives*
>
> Member States shall ensure that employees' representatives, when carrying out their functions, enjoy adequate protection and guarantees to enable them to perform properly the duties which have been assigned to them.

There is little case law from the CJEU regarding this provision; in Case C-405/08, however, the Court stated that Article 7 of Directive 2002/14 must be interpreted as not requiring that more extensive protection against dismissal be granted to employees' representatives than to the rest of the employees. However, any measure adopted to transpose that directive, whether provided for by legislation or by collective agreement, must comply with the minimum protection threshold laid down in Article 7.[26]

[25] See further N Bruun, 'The Prohibition of Discrimination under Art 14 ECHR', in F Dorssemont, K Lörcher and I Schömann (eds), *The European Convention on Human Rights and the Employment Relation* (Oxford, Hart Publishing, 2013) 367–80.

[26] Case C-405/08, Judgment of the Court (Third Chamber) of 11 February 2010 (reference for a preliminary ruling from the Vestre Landsret, Denmark; Ingeniørforeningen i Danmark, acting on behalf of Bertram Holst, v Dansk Arbejdsgiverforening, acting on behalf of Babcock & Wilcox Vølund ApS).

Article 29

The Right to Information and Consultation in Collective Redundancy Procedures

BRUNO VENEZIANI

Article 29—The right to information and consultation in collective redundancy procedures

With a view to ensuring the effective exercise of the right of workers to be informed and consulted in situations of collective redundancies, the Parties undertake to ensure that employers shall inform and consult workers' representatives, in good time prior to such collective redundancies, on ways and means of avoiding collective redundancies or limiting their occurrence and mitigating their consequences, for example accompanying social measures aimed, in particular, at aid for the redeployment or retraining of the workers concerned.

Appendix Part II: Articles 28 and 29

For the purpose of the application of this article, the term 'workers' representatives' means persons who are recognised as such under national legislation or practice.

I. INTRODUCTION

A. Context and Main Content

Article 29 is to be found in Part II of the Charter and shares with Article 21 the same conception of human rights. It expresses the reformers' intention to take into account 'both developments in social and economic rights as reflected in other international instruments and in legislation of the member states and also of social problems not covered by the other instruments in force'.[1]

[1] Explanatory report to the Charter, para 7.

B. International Sources

Many sources and documents provide a basis for interpretation of Article 29. The Explanatory Report refers explicitly to two instruments:[2]

(i) Council Directive 75/129/EEC of 1975 on approximation of the laws of the member states relating to collective redundancies amended by Council Directive 92/56/EEC of 1992 and subsequently both replaced by Council Directive 98/59/EC **of 20 July 1998;**
(ii) ILO Convention No 158 on Termination of employment at the initiative of the employer (1982).

The following sources are also relevant:

— ILO Recommendation No 166 replacing its predecessor Recommendation 119 (and supplementing Convention No 158);
— ILO Convention No 135 Workers Representatives Convention (1971) concerning protection and facilities to be afforded to workers' representatives in the undertaking;
— Charter of Fundamental Rights of the EU (CFREU): Articles 21 (non-discrimination), 23 (equality between women and men) and 33 (Family and professional life). Articles 27 (information and consultation within the undertaking) and 30 (protection in the event of unjustified dismissals) may also be used to reinforce the established rights of employees on termination of employment.

In the labour law field individual and collective rights are strictly connected in protecting workers from the substantive and procedural points of view. The effective involvement of employee representatives in managing the termination of employment contracts is of vital importance for individuals or members of a group facing dismissal for all sorts of reasons:

— Articles 9 and 157 TFEU;
— Article 14 of the Recast Directive on equal treatment 2006/54/EC;[3]
— the European Works Council Directive,[4] SE[5] Directives and Framework Directive 2002/14/EC;[6]

[2] Para 109.

[3] Directive 2006/54/EC of the European Parliament and of the Council of 5 July 2006 on the implementation of the principle of equal opportunities and equal treatment of men and women in matters of employment and occupation (recast)

[4] Council Directive 94/45/EC of 22 September 1994 on the establishment of a European Works Council or a procedure in Community-scale undertakings and Community-scale groups of undertakings for the purposes of informing and consulting employees and its recast Directive 2009/38/EC of the European Parliament and of the Council of 6 May 2009.

[5] Council Directive 2001/86/EC of 8 October 2001 supplementing the Statute for a European company with regard to the involvement of employees.

[6] Directive 2002/14/EC of the European Parliament and of the Council of 11 March 2002 establishing a general framework for informing and consulting employees in the European

— Article 10 of the Pregnancy and maternity Directive 92/85/EEC[7] on the introduction of measures on the dismissal of pregnant workers;
— Clause 2(4) of the Revised Framework agreement annexed to the Parental Leave Directive 2010/18/EU.[8]

C. Relationship with Other Provisions of the Charter

Systematic interpretation requires that Article 29 must be read in connection with all relevant norms of the Charter dealing with the protection of workers when they lose their 'social citizenship and human dignity' within and outside the enterprise: Article 10 (right to vocational training), Article 12 (right to social security), Articles 16 and 17 (right of the family and of young persons to social, legal and economic protection), Article 23 (right of elderly persons to social protection), Article 24 (right to protection in the case of termination of employment), Article 25 (right to the protection of claims in the event of insolvency of the employer) and Article 26 (right to dignity at work).

Compared with Article 21, which contains the structural principle of workers' involvement with regard to the right to information and consultation, Articles 29 and 24 comprise a *lex specialis* for all events dramatically affecting the economic and financial situation of undertakings.

II. CONTENT

A. A Model of Participatory Democracy Aimed at a Specific Goal

Compliance with the corpus of rules set forth in the Charter may facilitate implementation of the model of socially responsible economic activity requiring direct involvement of workers as 'social citizens'. This idea is expressed in the Tripartite Declaration of Principles concerning Multinational Enterprises,[9] which states that 'in considering changes of operation

Community—Joint declaration of the European Parliament, the Council and the Commission on employee representation.

[7] Council Directive 92/85/EEC of 19 October 1992 on the introduction of measures to encourage improvements in the safety and health at work of pregnant workers and workers who have recently given birth or are breastfeeding (tenth individual Directive within the meaning of Art 16§1 of Directive 89/391/EEC).

[8] Council Directive 2010/18/EU of 8 March 2010 implementing the revised Framework Agreement on parental leave concluded by BUSINESSEUROPE, UEAPME, CEEP and ETUC and repealing Directive 96/34/EC (text with EEA relevance).

[9] ILO, Tripartite Declaration of Principles concerning Multinational Enterprises and Social Policy, adopted by the Governing Body of the International Labour Office at its 204th Session

(including those resulting from mergers, takeovers or transfer of production), which would have a major effect on employment, multinational enterprises should provide reasonable notice of such changes to the appropriate government authorities and workers' representative'. Social partners share the responsibility to examine any adverse effects on the workforce, expressed in terms of 'collective lay-offs or dismissals'.[10]

B. Substantive Requirements with regard to Employers' Decision-making: Reasons for Collective Dismissals

(i) Qualitative Elements

The Charter does not include any provisions directly related to the case of transfer of undertakings or other structural changes, so interpretation could be sustained with reference to Article 24, which makes clear the idea that dismissals must be supported by valid reasons and operational requirements.[11] Article 24 is a sort of general principle to protect employees from employers' whims.

The term 'redundancy' needs to be clarified. The Charter Committee in drafting the Article was inspired by EC Directive 92/56/EEC of 1992, as well as ILO Convention No 158 on social rights. It states that 'the collective redundancies referred to are redundancies affecting several workers within a period of time laid down by law and decided for reasons that have nothing to do with individual workers, but correspond to a reduction or change of the firm's activity'.[12]

The Statements of Interpretation of the ECSR devolve to each national legal system the task of defining the term 'reduction or change of firm activity', which still hides the real substance of operational requirements. In fact, 'reduction' or 'change' are both consequences of a decision taken unilaterally by the employers in the presence of different circumstances, whether internal (depending on an employer's discretionary choices) or external (resulting from economic difficulties, technological changes or fiscal 'austerity' measures, globalisation or cost of raw materials) outside the firm.

According to the ILO's Committee of Experts on the Application of Conventions and Recommendations (CEACR), reasons of an economic, technological, structural or similar nature—stipulated in Article 13 of ILO Convention No 158—are those 'related to operational requirements of

(Geneva, November 1977) as amended at its 279th (November 2000) and 295th Sessions (March 2006).

[10] ibid para 26.

[11] M Mikkola, *Social Human Rights of Europe* (Porvoo, Bookwell, 2010) 223.

[12] See Explanatory Report to the RESC, para 109 and Conclusions 2003 and 2005 Statement of Interpretation on Art 29.

undertakings, establishments or services' and 'could also be defined in negative terms as those necessitated by economic, technological, structural or similar requirements which are not connected with the capacity or conduct of the workers'.[13] This definition must be linked to the statement made by the ILO in the first discussion at the conference, according to which 'dismissals resulting from these reasons may be individual or collective and may involve reduction of the workforce or closure of the undertaking'.[14]

The legal category of collective redundancies covers a wide range of elements arising from employers' discretionary powers. This encompasses the various forms of 'flexibility' introduced in recent decades, as well as self-employment (genuine and bogus), the black economy, micro-businesses and many family enterprises, which are often organised in networks or industrial districts. The definition of reasons or grounds is indispensable for ascertaining the genuineness of the employer's intentions: this explains why the ECSR 'defers its conclusions' when a national legislation fails to define the grounds of collective redundancy.[15]

National reports present a variety of formulas ranging from fairly vague expressions encompassing one or more grounds at the discretion of the employer and not related to a specific employee[16] to reasons 'required by the necessities of enterprises, establishments and activities'[17] or, more simply, 'economic reasons'.[18]

The term 'economic, technological and structural reasons' has been used as a golden formula in the national sources of law (statutes, labour codes or collective agreements)[19] and have included closure of enterprises[20] or the shutting down of one or more establishments and similar structures, as well as market developments.[21] More extreme 'structural reasons' may include liquidation and change of ownership.[22]

(ii) Quantitative Elements: Number and Time

Quantitative elements include, first of all, the number and categories of workers likely to be affected by the employer's decision, and the period over which contract terminations are intended to be carried out.

[13] ILO, General Survey 1995, para 98 (Note on Convention No 158 and Recommendation No 166 concerning Termination of Employment, ILO, B Norms 2009, 2, 0268,-1-en.doc/v2.

[14] ILO, ILC 67th session, 1981, Report VIII(1), 23.

[15] Conclusions 2010, Netherlands.

[16] Conclusions 2010 and 2014, Bulgaria; Conclusions 2010, Albania; Conclusions 2014, Slovak Republic.

[17] Conclusions 2010, Turkey.

[18] Conclusions 2014, the Netherlands.

[19] Conclusions 2010, Lithuania; Conclusions 2014, Montenegro.

[20] Conclusions 2010, Azerbaijan; Conclusions 2014, Cyprus; Conclusions 2010, Turkey.

[21] Conclusions 2014, Portugal.

[22] Conclusions 2010, Ukraine and Georgia.

The effectiveness of workers' rights to be informed and consulted requires transparency with regard to the relevant data on the workers involved in the enterprise in crisis. Article 2§2 of the Additional Protocol of the ESC (1988) gives states the opportunity to exclude companies from the scope of application of the article if the number of employees is lower than a threshold determined by law or national practices.[23]

The Community Charter of Fundamental Social Rights 1989 and the Charter of Fundamental Rights of the European Union (CFREU) do not take into account the dimension of undertakings in the scope of application of rights. The special quality of the rights provided for in the Charter can explain why Article I§2 stipulates that 'compliance with the undertakings deriving from ... Articles 21 and 22 shall be regarded as effective if the provisions are applied ... to the great majority of the workers concerned'.[24]

The same *ratio* that inspires Article 29 induces the Committee to ask states about the number and qualities (categories) of workers affected by the employer's decision to terminate contracts. National reports have followed, but also lightly modified, the scheme suggested by the Collective Redundancy Directive 98/59/EC, in which the workers dismissed are calculated as a net number or percentage of the total workforce and in terms of a particular period of time (Article 1(a)(i)). Thus a *collective* redundancy requires that the number of dismissals in a 30-day period be at least 10 for enterprises with up to 100 workers, 15 for enterprises with up to 200, 20 for enterprises with up to 300 and 30 for enterprises with above 300.[25] In some other cases based on the same model the figures are a little lower.[26] Some reports present other rules that which implement the alternative rule indicated by the same directive (Article 1(a)(ii)).

The main interest of the Committee is to ensure protection of the workers affected by the process. Directive 98/59/EC authorises the exclusion of workers on fixed-term contracts, public employees in the broad sense and maritime workers (Article 1§2).

[23] See also Additional Protocol to the ESC, paras 44–46; F Dorssemont, 'Worker involvement in secondary EC Law prior to the recast Directive', in F Dorssemont and T Blanke (eds), *The Recast of the European Woks Council Directive* (Oxford, Hart, 2010) 67.

[24] A similar provision has been adopted in Art 7(2) of the Additional Protocol on the implementation of Arts 2 and 3 (now Arts 21 and 22 RESC); see C Kollonay-Lehoczky, 'The fundamental right of workers to information and consultation under the ESC', in Dorssemont and Blanke (eds) (n 23).

[25] Conclusions 2010, Albania; Conclusions 2014, Turkey; Conclusions 2014, Serbia; Conclusions 2010, Bulgaria; Conclusions 2014, Montenegro; Conclusions 2010, Romania; Conclusions 2010, Slovakia.

[26] Conclusions 2010, Lithuania; Conclusions 2010, Malta.

National reports use different criteria and rather ambiguous wording, in response to which (as already mentioned) the ECSR may *defer its conclusions*, when:

— the state does not specify whether there are employees not included in the protection;[27]
— the protection does not apply to enterprises with fewer than 20 workers and a substantial segment of public services and employment;[28] or
— the state does not apply protection to seasonal and campaign workers and does not specify 'categories not falling under the procedure'.[29]

Some concluding remarks on the point concern, first of all, national reports and their interchangeable use of words such as 'undertaking' and 'establishment', both *loci* that are relevant for ascertaining the number of workers, which may vary according to the size of establishments, undertakings or units of production.[30] Directive 98/59/EC uses the term 'establishment', whereas in some reports the term 'undertaking' is used to indicate a locus for the purpose of calculating figures and percentages;[31] elsewhere, vaguer terms are sometimes used, such as 'employees working in the same geographical area'.[32]

The second problem is the term 'categories' of workers, interpretation of which is uncertain (workers, employees, civil servants, managers, public or private employees) and does not qualify the kind of employment contract (typical or atypical) of workers whose dismissal will not count in determining the number or percentage of workers being made redundant and in respect of whom consultation does not apply. There is also the question of the nature of the employer (private or public; single enterprise or group of enterprises), an important issue that may affect the existence, content and effectiveness of rights to inform and consult.

According to the Appendix to the RESC, parties may provide that Article 2§6 shall not apply to workers with a contract or employment relationship with a total duration not exceeding one month and/or with a working week not exceeding eight hours. The exclusion also concerns contracts of employment whose nature is such that non-application is justified by objective reasons.

However, it is supposed for the purposes of the Charter that in the absence of definitions, all issues shall be resolved by the national legislators and courts.

[27] Conclusions 2010, Georgia and Ukraine.
[28] Conclusions 2014, Cyprus, 'all public sectors'.
[29] Conclusions 2014, Turkey.
[30] See B Veneziani on Art 21 in this volume.
[31] Conclusions 2010, Lithuania and Malta.
[32] Conclusions 2014, the Netherlands.

C. Procedural Elements of the Structure of 'Finalised' Participatory Democracy

Unlike Article 21 the model of participatory democracy envisaged in Article 29 is based mainly on clearly identified objects (collective redundancies), purposes (effective exercise) and ways and means of protecting workers' rights.

In general terms, the International Finance Corporation's Good Practice Note 'Managing Retrenchment' stresses the importance of consultation, stating that 'without consultation companies run the risk of not only getting key decisions wrong, but also of breaching legal rules and collective agreements and alienating workers and the community. Workers can often provide important insights and propose alternative ways for carrying out the process to minimize impact on the workforce and the broader community'.[33]

(i) Duty of Information

The first message given by Article 29 recalls Article 21 and describes a specific obligation for the employer to manage its discretionary power in accordance with respect for all the interests involved in a delicate phase of the enterprise's life. In legal terms, the duty to inform is the first passage towards implementation of the principle of effectiveness of rights.

In its 2008 general observation on Convention No 158, the ILO CEACR noted that the principles enshrined therein 'are an important source of law for labour courts and tribunals in countries that have or have not ratified the Convention'.[34]

More precisely, the term 'information' must be intended in a proactive sense, namely as enabling workers' representatives 'to scrutinise the information provided without waiting for the end of the information procedure, if the decision by undertakings has direct implications for workers'.[35]

The expression 'in good time prior to the process of collective redundancy' means, according to the ECSR,[36] that 'effectiveness and integrity

[33] International Finance Corporation of the World Bank Group, Good Practice Note 'Managing Retrenchment', August 2005 (No 4), www.ifc.org/ifcext/enviro.nsf/AttachmentsByTitle/p_retrenchment/$FILE/retrenchment.pdf, ILO, p 12, n 45.

[34] ILO, *General Survey on Fundamental Conventions concerning Rights at Work in light of the ILO Declaration on Social Justice for a Fair Globalization*, 2008 Report of the Committee of Expert on the Application of Conventions and Recommendations, ILO Conference 101st Session 2012 (Geneva, ILO, 2012) p 18 and fn 62.

[35] Motion for a European Parliament Resolution of the Committee on Employment and Social Affairs, report on the implementation of 2002 Directive (point 6 a), 27 January 2009.

[36] Statement of Interpretation 2014.

of protection rights' through information can be assured only if the information:

- precedes the process of collective redundancies;
- is provided to workers' representatives
  - 'prior' to and 'far in advance' of the commencement of the consultation, and also
  - throughout the entire duration of the consultation process.

In some cases, national legislators have autonomously integrated provisions requiring also that information be given 'in writing'.[37] They have also indicated the period of time in which documents should be released to trade unions or workers' representatives (three months before negotiations—one month to individual employees; two months before termination of employees).[38] According to ILO Convention No 158 and Recommendation No 166 the purpose of formal written notice and procedural fairness prior to determination are founded on the general right to protection contained in Article 7 of the ILO Convention.[39]

In the event of failure to observe this core requirement the Committee holds that it is 'not in conformity with the Charter pending receipt of information about preventive measures'.[40] A conclusion of 'not in conformity' is reserved to countries that do not give any information about whether dismissals are decided before starting an information and consultation procedure.[41]

In general, the aim of information and consultation is to make workers aware:

- 'of the reason and scale of planned decisions; [and]
- to ensure that the position of workers is taken into account ... in particular as regards the
  - scope,
  - mode and
  - manner of redundancies and
  - the extent to which their consequences can be avoided, limited and or mitigated'.

In the majority of cases the national law requires:

- the reasons for dismissals;[42]
- the number of employees dismissed;

[37] Conclusions 2010, Ukraine, Albania, Malta.

[38] Conclusions 2010, Azerbaijan and Georgia.

[39] J Kenner, 'Article 30—Comment', in S Peers, T Hervey, J Kenner and A Ward (eds), *The EU Charter of Fundamental Rights—A Commentary* (Oxford, Hart, 2014) 826.

[40] Conclusions 2014, Montenegro and the Netherlands.

[41] Conclusions 2014, Sweden.

[42] Conclusions 2010, Albania and Malta.

— the number of the total workforce;
— the time during which implementation of the dismissals is planned;
— criteria of selection;[43] only in one case is it stated that the criteria must not be in conflict with the provisions of labour law or with protection against discrimination;[44]
— compensation and method of calculation of potential payment,[45] duration of insurance for redundant workers, the jobs the employees are performing, age and programmes for assigning dismissed employees to other activities.[46]

(ii) Duty of Consultation

Consultation is the second step in the process, albeit not exhaustive, and is intended to be the moment, after releasing all data relevant to the employer's decision, where the 'position of workers is taken into account' and the employees and their representatives 'become familiar with the key aspects of the planned redundancies'.[47]

The structural features of the consultation concern first of all the *timing*, as the consultation must be held 'before the stage at which the termination become inevitable'[48] and conducted within a time period sufficient to ensure that the workers' representatives 'have an opportunity to present suitable proposals'.[49]

The second feature deals with the *topics* of dialogue, that is, avoiding, limiting and mitigating the effects of the 'proposed redundancies'.

In other words, the scope of negotiations with the undertaking include refusal (avoidance), modification (limitation of the scope) and reduction (mitigation) of the effects of the employer's decision.[50] The same words are used in Article 13 ILO Convention No 158 and Recommendation No 166, which provide guidance for measures that could be adopted to avert or minimise the termination of contracts within a not exhaustive list.[51]

The entire information and consultation process envisages a rather dynamic strategy comprising, on one hand, the duty of employers to give reasons for its intentions and, on the other, the rights of workers' representatives to have their opinion taken into account and to present 'suitable proposals'[52] to make it possible to reach an agreement.[53]

[43] Conclusions 2010, Bulgaria and Lithuania.
[44] Conclusions 2014, Montenegro.
[45] Conclusions 2014, Cyprus.
[46] Conclusions 2014, Montenegro.
[47] Conclusions Statement of Interpretation, 2014.
[48] ILO, General Survey, Report, 12.
[49] Statement of Interpretation, 2014.
[50] Conclusions, Statement of Interpretation, 2014.
[51] ILO Recommendation No 166, para 22.
[52] Conclusions, Statement of Interpretation, 2014.
[53] Conclusions, Statement of Interpretation, 2003.

The duty to consult implies also that, to foster dialogue, all relevant documents must be supplied by the employer before consultation starts.[54] This second step begins, as indicated in the article, in good time prior to the employer taking the decision to manage a crisis with recourse to collective redundancies.

'Good time' is a fairly vague expression (it is the 'right time' in Article 17 of the Community Charter), and needs to be clarified with regard to the inner 'protective' rationale of Article 29.

National rules present a variety of periods of time focused largely on the attempt to cover the dynamic of the complete procedure: seven, eight or 10 working days[55] and 30 days.[56] A longer period of time seems to be used when national law explicitly—45 days[57] or two to three months[58]—considers consultation to be a step aimed at reaching an agreement whose success is promoted by the obligation on the employer to participate in reaching an agreement.[59]

D. The Actors

Under Article 29 the right to protection against collective redundancies applies to workers in their collective dimension as members of a group and as such they must be 'represented by persons acting on behalf of all workers employed in the workplace'.[60]

(i) Workers and Workers' Representatives

The term 'workers' seems to include all workers and employees without distinction of sex or race, religion, or any of the other grounds of discrimination mentioned in Articles 20 and E. According to the scope of persons protected as defined by the Appendix, the protection of Article 29 includes workers who are 'foreigners only in so far as they are ... resident or working regularly within the territory of the party concerned'.

As regards non-standard workers (casual, agency and so on), the Charter seems to exclude workers with a contract or employment relationship 'with a total duration not exceeding one month and/or with a working week not exceeding eight hours' or 'of a casual and/or specific nature'.[61] The rule

[54] Conclusions Lithuania 2005, p 404; Conclusions 2003, Romania, p 429 in Digest 2008.
[55] Conclusions 2010, Malta and Portugal; Conclusions 2014, Serbia.
[56] Conclusions 2010, Lithuania; Conclusions 2014, Slovakia and FYROM.
[57] Conclusions 2010, Bulgaria.
[58] Conclusions 2010, Georgia and Ukraine.
[59] Conclusions 2014, Portugal.
[60] Conclusions Statement of Interpretation 2014.
[61] Art 2 para 6 of Appendix to the ECSR.

sounds similar to ILO Convention No 158, which excludes from its provisions 'workers engaged on a casual basis for a short period'.[62]

Although Directive 98/59/EC excludes from its scope public employees,[63] some national legislators extend protection to civil servants. They recognise the right of notification one month before starting the procedure[64] or, in the event of closing down or reducing the staff of state bodies, where the law provides for a right of priority of placement in other government institutions guaranteeing previous salary, occupation and position.[65]

The reduction of the scope of the rule still remains striking, compared with the quality and nature of (human) rights stipulated in the Charter as deserving the strongest protection. The Charter suffers from lack of homogeneity, which deepens the contrast between different segments of the labour market. The impression is that all interpretations of Article 29 consider that the Charter addresses the right to information and consultation as applying exclusively to workers' representatives and not individual workers. The CJEU[66] affirmed that the right to information and consultation is 'owned' and exercised by workers' representatives. This perspective is far from the legal culture of some national systems, in which there is a clear distinction between individual legal (constitutional) rights belonging to each worker *per se* and their exercise in a collective fashion, managed by the group. Systematic interpretation of the Charter could prove decisive in this sense. The Statement of Interpretation 2014 recognises the peculiar nature of the rights in question, because workers involved in a redundancy procedure have a choice concerning who is to defend their interests.

The employees should be represented by:

(a) 'persons acting on behalf of all workers employed at the workplace' and such representatives may be bodies operating in the employer's enterprises (trade union or works councils);
(b) 'ad hoc representatives appointed for the purposes of the procedure'; and
(c) representatives—even when the employees are not otherwise represented in the context of a particular workplace, lacking representatives of the kind listed in (a) and (b) above—who should perform their function on behalf of 'all employees who may be potentially subject to collective redundancy and should not suffer any negative consequences' stemming from their activities.[67]

[62] Art 2§2(c).
[63] Public administration and public entities, Art 1§2(b).
[64] Conclusions 2010, Georgia.
[65] Conclusions 2010, Azerbaijan.
[66] Case C-12/08 *Mono Car Styling SA v Dervis Odemis and Others* [2009] ECR I-6653, n 4.
[67] Conclusions, Statement of Interpretation 2014.

(ii) Third Parties: Public Authorities

A legal category of a 'socially responsible economic activity' seems to be foreshadowed in the international web of national and international rules dealing with labour law.

The employer's duty to involve a third party—public authorities at all levels—supports the idea that labour market problems are not a private affair of social partners but concern a public general interest of the social state. All sources are consonant with regard to this approach: 'at multinational level enterprises should provide reasonable notice of such changes to appropriate government authorities'[68] and 'the competent authorities as early as possible'.[69] The ILO CEACR has also emphasised the flexibility inherent in the Convention, having noted that the Convention does not refer to the role that might be played by the competent authority to which notification is made 'because it is up to the country in question to determine the purpose of notification'.[70]

Recommendation No 166 details the role of public intervention, in order to mitigate effects of termination of employment, proposing a plan to promote 'the placement of workers affected in suitable alternative employment as soon as possible, with training and retraining where appropriate, through measures taken by the competent authority, where possible with the collaboration of the employer and the workers' representatives concerned'.[71]

It is clear why the Statement of Interpretation 2014 imposes on employers not only the duty to cooperate with the administrative authorities or public agencies responsible for dealing with unemployment, but also indicates the function and fields of intervention. To meet the criteria of a 'socially responsible company', the employer has a duty:

— 'to notify its intention to reduce its workforce to the public administration';
— 'to include the planned collective redundancies'; and
— 'to cooperate with public agencies in relation to retraining employees made redundant or providing them with other forms of assistance with a view to obtaining a job'.[72]

National legislations have enriched these duties, requiring written notification to the public authorities and also[73] a duty to observe suitable

[68] ILO Tripartite Declaration of Principle 2006 para 26.

[69] Art 14(1) ILO Convention No 158.

[70] ILO, General Survey 1995, para 29; in the same direction Directive 98/59/EC Arts 2(3) and 3.

[71] R166 para 25 (1)

[72] Conclusions, Statement of Interpretation 2014.

[73] Conclusions 2010, Albania.

timing.[74] This legal system envisages in detail the nature of state intervention: the authorities shall evaluate the impact of redundancy on the local labour market, provide for opportunities to mitigate their consequences, organise meetings with workers to inform them about the employment situation and develop an action plan to mitigate all negative effects.

The role of the public authorities is not merely passive, as they are required to give an opinion on the planned redundancies in detail[75] in a short time,[76] with compulsory effect.[77] Breach of the duty to inform and involve territorial labour exchanges could even be sanctioned judicially, obliging the employer to reinstate dismissed workers and to pay compensation.[78]

Employers' duty of cooperation is interpreted in various ways. They should, for example, cooperate with public bodies dealing with unemployment, promote retraining and give redundancy assistance in job-seeking.[79]

The final decision of the third party constitutes a permit to terminate employment contracts,[80] or may be directed towards reaching an agreement.[81] The role of the public authorities is to manage a complex procedure in which the employer has a duty to negotiate with the purpose of reaching an agreement. For example, the public authorities in Portugal take part in the long process because the parties concerned have the possibility of asking the employment services to participate in information sessions on registration with employment services, rights and duties pertaining to unemployment benefits and available vocational training programmes. The Institute of Employment and Vocational Training has promoted projects to support workers made unemployed because of the economic crisis. Incentives and measures vary according to the target group and include requalification, retraining and return to the labour market through active employment measures such as vocational training, support for the self-employed and integration plans.[82]

III. IMPACT ON EUROPEAN HUMAN RIGHTS INSTRUMENTS

On one hand, the ECtHR has not dealt with collective redundancies, although more courage would have induced the judges to infer from Article 11

[74] Conclusions 2010, Lithuania.
[75] Conclusions 2014, Finland.
[76] Conclusions 2014, Montenegro.
[77] Conclusions 2014, Ukraine.
[78] Conclusions 2010, Lithuania.
[79] Conclusions 2010 and 2014, Bulgaria; Conclusions 2014, Turkey and Serbia.
[80] Conclusions 2014, Netherland; Conclusions 2010, Romania.
[81] Conclusions 2010, Albania.
[82] Conclusions 2014, Portugal.

of ECHR the principle of participatory democracy as a functional element of the right of association.

On the other hand, the ECJ (now the Court of Justice of the EU, CJEU) made a clear statement about the nature of the right of information and consultation in case of collective redundancies. The Court refused to accept the idea that information and consultation represent a simple obligation imposed upon employers, as sustained by AG Mengozzi.[83] The consequence of the latter's reasoning is that it is impossible to infer from Article 30 of ECHR an individual right of actions for employees. This reasoning and its corollary are not consistent with either the provisions of Article 29 or with ILO Convention No 158 (Articles 13 and 14).[84] In the case of collective redundancies, the Charter has a clearer legal philosophy, expressed in term of rights and duties aimed at guaranteeing workers their 'effective exercise'; above all, the Committee of Social Rights has underlined that in drafting, Article 29 EC Directive 92/56/EEC 'was taken into account'.[85]

Article 24 was also a source of inspiration in drafting Article 30 CFREU. The EU Commission has expressly recognised that the rights and principles of CFREU stem also from the Charter,[86] and in times of crisis the implementation strategy must be accelerated to ensure the promotion and application of all relevant legal sources 'to provide more extensive protection' of the fundamental rights of the Charter.[87]

'More extensive protection' could stem from a methodological approach based on the progressive integration of all legal sources of EU human rights, the ILO Convention on termination of employment No 158 and Article 24, interpreted by various international bodies implementing the principles of effectiveness of rights and adequacy of protection in the case of illegal collective dismissals. In the great majority of cases, decisions of non-conformity with Article 29 taken by the Committee have concerned a lack of information about sanctions following violation of procedural aspects of collective dismissal.[88] Only in a few cases has the Committee suggested more stringent solutions aimed at 'retraining and re-employment' of the workers

[83] Case C-12/08 *Mono Car Styling* (n 66) and Opinion of AG Mengozzi 43–44.

[84] CEACR Observation, Cameroon, quoted in Kenner (n 39) 823.

[85] ECSR, 'The relationship between European Union law and the ESC', Working Document, 15 July 2014, Council of Europe, p 8.

[86] Commission, 'Communication on the Strategy for Effective Implementation of the CFREU by the EU' COM (2010) 573 final.

[87] European Parliament Resolution of 19 May 2010 on the Institutional Aspects of the Accession of the EU to the EU Convention for the Protection of Human Rights and Fundamental Freedoms, European Parliament Document 2009/2241 (INI) para 30.

[88] Conclusions 2014, Sweden and FYROM.

concerned.[89] In line with this solution is also Article 10 of ILO Convention No 158, which envisages the remedy of reinstatement for individual workers or the payment of adequate compensation. Anyway, the principle of 'job security' can be understood as being in line with the human rights inspiration underlying the Charter.[90]

[89] Conclusions 2014, Romania.

[90] N Bruun, 'Protection against unjustified dismissals—Comment to Article 30', in B Bercusson (ed), *European labour law and the European Charter of Fundamental Rights* (Baden-Baden, Nomos, 2006) 337.

Article E

Non-Discrimination

CSILLA KOLLONAY-LEHOCZKY

Part V

Article E—Non-discrimination

The enjoyment of the rights set forth in this Charter shall be secured without discrimination on any ground such as race, colour, sex, language, religion, political or other opinion, national extraction or social origin, health, association with a national minority, birth or other status.

Appendix, Part V

Article E

A differential treatment based on an objective and reasonable justification shall not be deemed discriminatory.

I. INTRODUCTION

A. Context and Main Content

Part V of the Charter on the implementation and enforcement system of the RESC starts with Article E on non-discrimination, thereby indicating its primary role in securing the effective and equal enjoyment of all rights under the Charter. In order to perform this function it has to have its place among the Charter provisions to regulate and control the implementation of the substantive position.

The principle of non-discrimination was set forth originally in the Preamble to the 1961 Charter, and was incorporated into the main body of the Revised Charter by Article E. These two Charter provisions on non-discrimination reveal two different approaches: a more reserved attitude and a strongly committed one. The reference to non-discrimination in the Preamble of the 1961 Charter signalled a wary attitude on the part of the drafters about the inclusion of such a clause,[1] whereas Article E was adopted in the mid-1990s, a period of intense transformation of thinking in international law regarding human rights in the social and economic field and the 'relaunching' and 'revitalising' the Charter as decided in 1990.[2]

This, together with other factors, was not independent of the successful demolition of the wall in Europe between countries that protected primarily civil and political rights and countries that protected only social-economic rights. Last but not least, this was also the time of a change in the relationship between the Charter and the ECHR.

These changes originated an entirely renewed case law and interpretation of the non-discrimination clause under the Revised Charter. Simplifying somewhat, the non-discrimination clause in the Preamble of the 1961 Charter had no real life prior to the application of Article E in the Charter. Its application did not go beyond Article 1§2,[3] whose text by definition excluded discrimination. (Further provisions were drawn under the Preamble's non-discrimination principle only later, in the period of the 'parallel' life of the 'Old' and the 'Revised' Charter.)[4]

By contrast, the case law under the Charter resorts to Article E with primary emphasis on provisions that lay down substantive obligations without any non-discrimination content. Such application and interpretation is in correspondence with and gives meaning to the function of a horizontal non-discrimination provision.

The insertion of the non-discrimination clause into a separate Article in the Charter indicates the heightened importance the drafters attributed to the principle of non-discrimination with regard to the fundamental rights protected by the Charter. The deep changes in the approach to the value of equality resulted in amendments in the substantive provisions establishing new undertakings for the states to adopt non-discrimination legislation. The

[1] In the *Travaux Preparatoires* it is difficult to find much about non-discrimination, and in Vol 6, (1957), pp 431–32, s 107, one finds a text in which the Secretariat draws the attention of the Committee to a clause (that was included in a 1956 draft of the Charter). The text says that 'The HCP [High Contracting Parties] are opposed to all discrimination on grounds of sex, race, colour, language, property, nationality, national or social origin, political or other opinion'. However, this quote is accompanied by a comment: 'It was decided not to include such a clause, but to mention the question in the report.'

[2] J Darcy and D Harris, *The European Social Charter*, 2nd edn (Ardsley, N.Y. Transnational Publishers, 2001) 12–13; Schutter, *International Human Rights Law. Cases, Materials, Commentary*, 2nd edn (Cambridge, Cambridge University Press, 2014) 1000–01.

[3] For example, according to the Committee of Experts, 'Article 1 para. 2 imposes an obligation upon Contracting Parties to eliminate all forms of discrimination in employment and, in this respect, paragraph 2 must be read in conjunction with Preamble of the Charter': L Samuel, *Fundamental Social Rights. Case law of the European Social Charter* (Strasbourg, Council of Europe Publishing, 1997) 29.

[4] A good example is Art 11§1, access to health care. Its interpretation—with reference to the Preamble in cases of state parties not yet joining the Revised Charter—guarantees the principle of non-discrimination. However this did not come up before 2004.

re-drafted text of Article 15, the radically changed provisions of Article 8, the new Article 23 on the rights of the elderly and Article 27 on the right to equal treatment of workers with family responsibilities must be mentioned. These provisions signal the shift from the former protective approach tinted in the past by pity and a patronising and non-dignifying attitude, to an approach based on the equality of fundamental human rights, dignity, autonomy and freedom.[5]

B. International Sources

While drawing on the spirit of the UN Covenants' anti-discrimination provisions,[6] the text of Article E reiterates Article 14 of the European Convention of Human Rights, also in respect of enumerating the prohibited grounds of discrimination. The conscious duplication of the text is one indicator of the approximation of the two treaties. The intention had been expressed at the time of drafting the 1988 Protocol,[7] as well as when adopting the 1995 Collective Complaint Protocol.[8] The convergence between the two treaties resulted in increasing acknowledgement of their complementary nature, including the increasing mutual reference to the case law of the two bodies, most apparent in areas where equality, human dignity and freedom are at stake.

Proclaiming dignity and equality as a centre of universal human rights goes back to the Second World War or even before,[9] although its role in the kinship between civil and political and social and economic rights became evident only in the last decades of the twentieth century.[10] Protecting human dignity operates, in the view of the ECSR, as the concept of establishing 'partnership' between the two instruments, especially in respect of rights under the Charter considered indispensable for preserving the dignity of a human being, for example, health or minimum of dwelling.[11]

[5] B Hepple, 'The starting point of all equality legislation is the right of individuals to autonomy, dignity and participation', in S. Fredman and S. Spencer (eds), *The Age of Discrimination* (Oxford and Portland Oregon, Hart, 2003) 79.

[6] Arts 2 of ICCPR and ICESCR.

[7] See notes 5 and 6 (and the body text relating to them) in Article 16 of this book.

[8] See ch 5, Pt IV. in this book.

[9] UDHR first sentence; but even before, see: 'The Four Freedoms' speech by US President, FD Roosevelt, 6 January 1941, and also Art 151 of the Weimar Constitution, drafted by H Sinzheimer.

[10] Part of the Marshallian citizenship based on an autonomous, participative and dignifying life. See: Arts 3 of ICCPR and ICESCR. In the human rights literature see B Hepple, Final Paper, presented to the IPPR seminar, 11 December 2001 at the Nuffield Foundation. See also J Waldron, 'Dignity, rank, and rights' with commentaries by Wai Chee Dimock, Don Herzog, Michael Rosen, edited and introduced by Meir Dan-Cohen (Oxford, OUP, 2012).

[11] See Conclusions XVII-2, Vol 1, 2005, General Introduction, s 5 on Art 11 referring to the milestone decision of the Committee in *FIDH v France*, Collective Complaint

This partnership permits progress in the mutual but far from symmetric reliance on the case law under Article E of the Charter and under Article 14 ECHR. The case law of the 'older brother' ECtHR has served as precedent law, while the ECSR case law is a 'source of inspiration', with examples proliferating in the course of the time. While their dependent nature—their application is restricted to the substantive clauses of the treaty concerned—associates the two horizontal provisions, Protocol 12 of the ECHR abandons this limited approach; prohibiting discrimination in any respect not only exceeds Article E, but also narrows the distance between the ECHR and the RESC—opening the way, at least in principle, to assess the observation of the principle of non-discrimination in situations covered by the RESC.[12]

Adoption of the EU non-discrimination directives[13] had a fertilising impact on the clarification of concepts such as 'indirect discrimination'; at the same time, the case law of the ECSR transcends the negative approach of the directives, prohibiting only direct and indirect discrimination, rather than establishing a positive duty to promote equality.[14]

According to the Explanations to Article 21 of the CFREU on non-discrimination, it draws on Article 19 of the TFEU (former Article 13 of EC), ECHR Article 14, and Article 11 of the Convention on Human Rights and biomedicine, as regards genetic heritage. Interestingly, it does not mention Article E, while Articles 20, 23, 24, 26 and 27 of the Charter are mentioned as sources behind corresponding provisions. The text of the CFREU—reflecting the hesitations of the late twentieth century—differentiates between dignity and equality in a specific combination with solidarity and protection.[15] The document has been included almost unchanged in the instrument referred to as mandatory by Article 6§1 TEU. As a result of its 15 years of development drawing on these values the case law of the ECSR has developed an autonomous and up-to-date protection of equality and dignity.

C. Relation to Other Provisions

Article E is a horizontal provision applicable to all rights set forth by the substantive clauses of the RESC. It has no independent existence, as it

No 14/2003, s 31, stating that 'human dignity is the fundamental value and indeed the core of positive European human rights law—whether under the European Social Charter or under the European Convention of Human Rights'.

[12] The 'infiltration' of economic and social rights into the case law of civil rights conventions by vehicle of non-discrimination (or procedural fairness) has precedence; the most noted case is *Brooks v Netherlands* (UN Human Rights Committee, 1987).

[13] Directives 2000/43/EC and 2000/78/EC.

[14] See Hepple (n 10).

[15] See together Arts 21, 25, 26, 31 and 32 preserving the past separation between protection and equality, also separating the concept of dignity from equality.

applies only to 'the enjoyment of the rights' guaranteed by these clauses. That means that there is no room for its application unless the situation and the facts fall within the ambit of one or more of the substantive provisions of the Charter.

At the same time, this requirement of combined application does not mean that it has to be combined with the infringement of the provision(s) referred to. In that sense it has an autonomous meaning as a form of control over the application of the substantive provisions. The significance of this autonomous application is that a situation which in itself is in conformity with the substantive provision concerned may infringe this provision when read in conjunction with Article E, by reason of its discriminatory nature.[16]

This status of Article E extends its protection to all provisions in Part II, but the relation to the various Charter provisions is not uniform. As already mentioned (section I.A) the ECSR shifted, contrary to the pre-Article E period, the protective edge of the equality clause to provisions that set up substantive rights, without reference to equality or non-discrimination. When the very first collective complaint on Article E was submitted due to the violation of Article 1§2, the Committee examined the compliance with the Article referred to alone and not 'in combination' with Article E. It found discrimination, without any reference to the general non-discrimination clause.[17] This differentiation is not applied consistently.[18]

A further differentiating element is the relevance of the right guaranteed for the protection of human dignity. The majority of these provisions—such as Articles 11, 16, 13, 30 and 31, the most frequent 'clients' for the protective services of Article E—are outside the area of employment, the main focus of the present volume.

Article E is used mainly within the complaints procedure and originally was used very seldom in the reporting procedure. However, in the course of the time, decisions establishing violation of the non-discrimination principle—being either in Article E, or in the Preamble for Parties to the 1961 Charter—have gradually appeared in the reporting system, either as a follow-up to the decision,[19] asking only the country concerned, or, more significantly, resulting in a general question on the observation of equal treatment by all countries ratifying the given article. This occurs either on decisions considered of general relevance for states, or regarding cases that open up new areas for the examination of compliance with the undertakings. The Committee asks the countries about their law and practice with regard to the given area and later the issue becomes a standard part of the

[16] In *SAGES v France*, Collective Complaint No 26/2004 §34 the ECSR refers, *mutatis mutandis*, to the ECtHR's *Belgian Linguistics* judgment of 23 July 1968.

[17] See No 6/1999 *Syndicat national des Professions du tourisme v France* §56.

[18] Conclusions 2005, Lithuania Art. 27-1.

[19] For example, Conclusions 2013, Art 30, Italy, Portugal.

reporting system.[20] The significance of this kind of 'spillover effect' cannot be overestimated under the conditions of the low ratification of the CCP.

II. CONTENT

A. Personal Scope

The personal scope of Article E is identical with the personal scope of the Charter as defined by the Appendix (§1 on the Scope), excluding third country nationals from application. This provision has been interpreted by the ECSR as extending to third country nationals in extreme cases 'on a right of fundamental importance to the individual since it is concerned with the right to life itself and goes to the very dignity of the human being'.[21] The interpretation has not been extended to Article E so far,[22] but given the deep interrelationship between the broadly interpreted dignity and non-discrimination, future cases leading to the same approach cannot be excluded.

B. Prohibited Grounds of Discrimination

The grounds of prohibited discrimination in Article E are almost identical to those listed in Article 14 of the ECHR, with two exceptions. The two differences are: health was not mentioned in the Convention,[23] while Article E explicitly includes it; at the same time property has reasonably been dropped from the Charter's catalogue of prohibited grounds of discrimination. Differentiating between persons on the ground of 'property' might even be necessary and a pre-condition (for example, Articles 13, 14) in the context of some provisions either regarding access or in some other cases, the individual financial effort required for access to a certain kind of service.

[20] After the first complaints on the violation of the housing rights of the Roma (No 15/2002 *ERRC v Greece*, Collective Complaint No 31/2005 European Roma Rights Centre (ERRC), Collective Complaint No 27/2004 *ERRC v Italy*), the question was put to countries in the reporting system regarding the housing situation of the Roma and the accommodation of their special housing needs. Similarly, the Statement of Interpretation of Art 11 transmitted the core point of *INTERIGHT v Croatia*, Collective Complaint No 45/2007.

[21] *FIDH v France*, Collective Complaint No 14/2003, 08.09.2004 paras 30–32. See on this also A Kombé, 'L'Applicabilité rationae personae de la Chartre Sociale Européenne: Ombres et Lumières' in O De Schutter (ed), *The European Social Charter: a constitution for Europe* (Brussels, Bruylant, 2010) 87–91.

[22] In Case 47/2008, finding violation of rights of unlawfully residing third country children, Art E was seen to be not applicable, pp 74–75.

[23] In the meantime health (HIV specifically), together with disability has been considered by the Court to be a ground of prohibited discrimination. See, *Glor v Switzerland* App. no. 13444/04, (2009) §§ 51, 80), *Kyutin v Russia* App. no. 2700/10 (2011), §57. *IB v Greece* App. no. 552/10 (2013), §73

Quite likely in relation to Article 14 of the Convention, Article E has an 'open-ended' list of prohibited grounds. It starts with the words 'such as' and ends with the phrase 'or other status', both indicating the non-exhaustive, rather exemplificatory nature of the catalogue, that in principle prohibits discrimination on an unlimited number of grounds.

The catalogue, replicating the text of the ECHR, enumerates the historical grounds of prohibited discrimination. The case law of the Charter, however, reveals a different classification, rearranging the relevance of these classic grounds, and strongly elevates the significance of this 'open-ended nature'.

An overview of the grounds for the application of Article E in practice—the division of the Charter provisions into 'economic' (employment) rights and 'social' rights—becomes conspicuous. Discrimination regarding social protection (predominantly housing, social assistance and health care) based on ethnicity or associated grounds (against the Roma and Travellers) fills the folders of the ECSR; employment discrimination is scarcely referred to as a problem under Article E.

(i) National Extraction, Race or Ethnicity

Discrimination on racial or ethnic grounds is strictly prohibited with regard to all rights guaranteed under the Charter. Ethnic discrimination is given special consideration in the case law of the Charter, for two interrelated reasons. First, such discrimination has special significance with regard to the exclusion and segregation of the Roma community in several European countries, aggravated occasionally by violence against these communities.[24] In the absence of adequate activity on the side of governments and authorities, the discriminatory situation continues.

Second, discrimination against the Roma, immigrants and also Roma immigrants has triggered a large proportion of collective complaints, bringing the issue to the forefront of the implementation and enforcement mechanism. Although emerging outside the employment area, these cases have brought about substantial progress with regard to the non-discrimination law of the Charter, among other things by pointing at the responsibility of governments to resort to positive action. Another progressive by-product of the Roma cases is the increased interplay between the complaints system and the reporting system, filling the gaps of the latter.

National extraction is a prohibited ground that is, by definition, not identical with nationality, namely citizenship of a state. Nonetheless the Explanatory Report expressly confirms this exclusion and also permits

[24] *COHRE v Italy*, Collective Complaint No 58/2009 §37, citing *Timishev v Russia* (ECtHR, 2007) §§56–58.

differential treatment on the ground of citizenship, even in regard to state party citizens, in the defence forces or in the civil service (s 137).

(ii) Sex

Sex, as a prohibited ground of discrimination, is, in principle, examined in the context of all provisions, in particular with regard to those where—in the past—gender discrimination was an evident and 'accepted' part of life. In practice this classic and highly ranked protected attribute has relatively little significance for our analysis here, because of the overall protection granted by Article 20, accepted by all Contracting Parties to the Revised Charter.

Discrimination on the ground of sex in employment and social security is prohibited by the self-standing provision of Article 20 covering all possible issues—training, education, access, promotion, conditions and termination—regardless of whether the issue is regulated or not by one of the specific substantive provisions of the Charter. Nonetheless, the broad scope of Article 20 does not exclude the reference to Article E with regard to provisions regulating employment and social security issues (Articles 1 to 10, 12, 18, 19, 21, 22, 24, 25, 28 and 29), which so far has not proved practical.

Discrimination on the ground of sex outside employment has major relevance for Article 16: equality of spouses in family relations, and protection against domestic violence are examined in the reporting system, although not yet under Article E.[25]

(iii) Health

Health is enumerated as a prohibited ground under Article E. It has been assessed in a few cases in the reporting procedure. The Committee found that guaranteeing equal access to health care and reducing health inequalities is an obligation under the Charter.[26] The Slovak rule that sickness pay is reduced to 50 per cent if the sickness is a consequence of alcohol or drug abuse amounts to discrimination under Article E based on health status, according to the ECSR.[27]

A further advance with regard to developing the content of the Preamble was made in *INTERIGHTS v Croatia*, Collective Complaint 45/2007 on a biology textbook containing discriminatory statements relating to sexual

[25] Cycle XVI-1, UK, indicating that property law in Northern Ireland was not entirely free of sex discrimination, Statement of Interpretation on Art 16, Conclusions 2006 on effective protection from violence against women.

[26] Cycle XVII-2, Art 11§1, The Netherlands.

[27] Conclusion 2013, Art 12, Slovak Republic.

and reproductive health education. The Committee found unanimously that there was a violation of Article 11§2 in light of the non-discrimination clause of the Preamble.

(iv) Disability

Disability[28] together with age is not included in the catalogue of prohibited grounds either in the Charter or in the Convention. However, in the course of time both have become 'accredited' grounds of discrimination—not in the last rank—as a result of the development of EU equality law.[29]

Disability was qualified by the ECSR as 'other status' upon receiving the first collective complaint on the rights of a group of disabled people.[30] It has grown to achieve high importance as the 'seed' of the progressive concept of indirect discrimination under the Charter.[31]

Disability, together with age, have a history of being surrounded by mainly protective measures and social assistance. This assistance approach has given way to a human rights approach guaranteeing non-discrimination and equal treatment, increased autonomy and participation. The new attitude can increase the chances of these groups with regard to labour market participation.

Establishing the special protection of the disabled under Article 15, the Committee added that it is fully consistent with both the letter and the spirit of the Political Declaration adopted by the 2nd European conference of ministers responsible for integration policies for people with disabilities (Malaga, April 2003), which reaffirmed the anti-discriminatory and human rights framework as the appropriate one for the development of European policy in this field.[32]

The new, human rights approach reflected by Article 15 and the social concept of disability transpiring from the CRPD resulted in treating disability as a genuine equality issue, where equal treatment means due respect given to the differences of an individual or a group with special characteristics.

(v) Age

Age, as already mentioned, shares the historical attributes of disability, but it has had a different 'life' under the Charter. The Explanatory Report

[28] See also the chapter by I Schömann on Art 15.

[29] The inclusion of disability and age as a prohibited ground in the Directive on the prohibition of discrimination in employment, 2000/78/EC.

[30] *Autisme Europe v France*, Collective Complaint No 13/2002 §51, repeated in later disability cases. Also Conclusions 2003, Statement of Interpretation on Art 15 §5.

[31] See section II.E below.

[32] See *Autism-Europe* (n 30), *MDAC v Bulgaria*, Collective Complaint No 41/2007 and more recently *AEH v France*, Collective Complaint No 81/2012.

to Article E signalled indirectly that age may be a potential ground of prohibited discrimination.[33]

Age as a protected attribute developed in three different contexts. Article 23—a special provision on the right of elderly persons to social protection—includes the obligation of the state parties to lay down explicit prohibition of discrimination specifically with regard to (older) age. The prohibition of discrimination on the ground of (old) age therefore has not been considered under Article E.[34]

Another context is the protection of employment against termination without a valid reason under Article 24.[35] The interpretation of Article 24 raised the issue of age as a protected attribute excluding age from the possible 'valid reasons' of termination of employment at the initiative of the employer.[36]

Finally, age discrimination emerged in the context of Complaint 66/2007 *GENOP-DEI and ADEDY v Greece*. A special programme was established to hire young workers—below 25 years of age—in order to increase their labour market chances, but on very low, less than minimum wages. Thus, the Committee found the situation in violation of Article 4§1 (right to a decent wage) in combination with the equal treatment principle in the Preamble.[37]

(vi) Further Elements of 'Other Status'

With regard to employment the Committee could not establish a stable further list of 'other status'.[38] The concept is 'floating' and not pinned down as clear ground of discrimination. It is nonetheless notable that the cases in which protected status in employment emerged were connected to atypical forms of employment, and unfavourable treatment of that category has emerged even if outside the non-discrimination context.[39]

Atypical forms of employment are a future candidate for 'other status' in need of the protection of equal treatment, with special regard to health and safety.[40] The increased vulnerability of such workers[41] and the development of the case law may bring this area within the scope of Article E.

[33] S 136 of the Explanatory Memorandum, referring to the possibility of justifying age discrimination in certain cases.

[34] From Conclusions 2003 and onwards states are asked about non-discrimination legislation specifically concerning aged persons. (The general prohibition of discrimination does not satisfy the requirements of the ECSR.) Conclusions 2014, Art 23: Finland, Italy, Norway.

[35] See the chapter on Art 24 by Melanie Schmitt in this volume.

[36] Statement of Interpretation of Art 24. General Conclusions, 2012 s 15.

[37] §69 of the decision.

[38] See n 54 below, §§ 44–48.

[39] See Conclusions 2009, Art 3, Andorra, Italy.

[40] See Chapter on Article 8 in this book, section II.B.

[41] See M Bell, 'Between flexicurity and fundamental social rights: the EU Directives on atypical work' (2012) 37 *European Law Review* 42.

A recent complaint alleging a violation of Article 10 and Article E in conjunction with Article 10, Complaint 105/2014, *La Voce dei Giusti v Italy* (declared admissible, still pending) may bring further clarification on 'other status' connected to employment-related discrimination. The case relates to the situation of support teachers for pupils with disabilities, who suffer disadvantage due to the prevention of temporary teachers from having free access to relevant training courses.

This overview of the grounds suggests that the enumerated traditional grounds have become of secondary importance under the Charter, with regard to the employment area, while other grounds creating employment vulnerability invite the protection of the international treaty. Revealing this may contribute to the progressive revision of the traditional approach to discrimination.[42]

The three cases[43] emerging first in the field of employment concern the special employment status of the members of the disadvantaged group, rather than any of the enumerated grounds under Article E.

The short overview above includes sex, race (ethnicity) and health as 'listed' grounds, as well as the 'other grounds' acknowledged by the ECSR as first members of a surely growing list. As will be revealed, the grounds addressed so far and likely to confront the ECSR in the future (the new challenges that technical, economic, social and political developments bring about) can be summarised as covering any individual or group with particular characteristics and guaranteeing that they can all benefit in practice from the rights enshrined in the Charter.[44]

C. Definition of Discrimination

The definition of discrimination always starts with the Aristotelian formula of 'justice'—treating equally those who are alike and unequally those who are unlike—and continues with the controversies and variations about what alike and unlike mean, and what is equal and unequal treatment. There is no space here to delve into the evolution and multiple layers of meaning of equality analysed broadly by academia and jurisprudence.[45] The subject matter makes it possible to adjust the concept to the role of the Charter in the protection of economic and social rights and the protection of the weak and the vulnerable. The positive approach developed by the ECSR under

[42] S Fredman, 'Positive duties and socio-economic disadvantage: bringing disadvantage onto the equality agenda' (2010) *European Human Rights Law Review* 290.

[43] Collective Complaints Nos 6/1999, 26/2004, 50/2008.

[44] See *ERRC v Bulgaria*, Collective Complaint No 31/2005.

[45] See J Rawls, *A Theory of Justice* (Cambridge, MA, Harvard University Press, 1971); R Dworkin, *Theory and Practice of Equality* (Cambridge, MA, Harvard University Press, 2000).

Article E—relying on, but going beyond the case law of the ECtHR—considers 'unlike' those whose chances are, beyond their intention and choices, low with regard to access to opportunities that are available for others and considers that equal (justly unequal) treatment should mean, in such situations, the equalising of those differences.[46]

Observing that the wording of Article E is almost identical to the wording of Article 14 of the ECHR,[47] the Committee has drawn on the case law of the ECtHR in developing its positive approach to the non-discrimination clause, selecting cases that promote its orientation.[48]

Discrimination is defined as a difference in treatment between persons in comparable situations where it does not pursue a legitimate aim, is not based on objective and reasonable grounds or is not proportionate to the aim pursued.[49] It has to be added: discriminatory treatment is not merely different, but also less favourable than the treatment of the comparator person or group. Treating people in different situations in the same way is also discrimination, when it brings disadvantage for the protected group.

Establishing discriminatory differentiation requires, on one hand, that the situation of the group that claims to have been discriminated against is similar to that of the comparator group and, on the other hand, the differentiation has no reasonable and objective justification.

The first complaints claiming violation of Article E in connection with employment rights submitted by trade unions show similarities with each other and differences from the dominant cases (regarding social rights) of the ECSR. These common features of the employment-related cases are as follows: (i) the group claiming discrimination is not in a socially disadvantaged situation compared with the comparator group; (ii) the rights at issue can be labelled 'fundamental rights' (right to work, trade union rights), but the cases in question did not relate to the core content of these rights; and (iii) there is a slight uncertainty regarding the relevance of Article E.

The very first complaint submitted under Article E (No 6/1999 *Syndicat national des Professions du tourisme v France*) was initiated due to a legal differentiation between two categories of tourist guides with differences in their professional certification and with an unfavourable impact on the working (and earning) opportunities of one group.

The complaint concerned Article 1§2 and Article 10§1 and §3. While the unfavourable impact of the existing regulation on the access to work of the complainant group, and therefore the violation of Article 1§2, was

[46] Very close approach to the influential 'capabilities' theory of A Sen, *Development as Freedom* (Oxford, OUP, 1999).

[47] *Autisme Europe v France* (n 30) §52.

[48] The most quoted case law included primarily *Thlimmenos v Greece*, App no 34369/97 (ECtHR, 2001).

[49] *Syndicat national des Professions du Tourisme v France*, Collective Complaint No 6/1999 §§24–25.

established (without reference to Article E), a breach of Article 10§1 and §3—two provisions of progressive implementation—was not found. The decision implied the questionability of the level of available opportunities and the Committee called the attention of the government to the need to provide, as necessary, adequate and readily available training facilities for adult workers, whereas no violation of the provision itself was found, either alone or in combination with the non-discrimination clause.[50]

In Case 26/2004 *SAGES v France* a violation was claimed of Article 5 and Article E (as well as Article G) in conjunction with Article 5 with regard to the trade union election rights of public high school teachers, which belonged under a different procedural regulation from the claimed comparator, a (private) teachers' group. Not finding a violation of Article 5 alone, the Committee simply dismissed the claim under Article E, without explanation.

The strong reliance on ECtHR rulings in social protection (housing, health care, food, financial assistance) cases cannot be seen in these two employment-related cases.

D. Justification of Direct Discrimination

Establishing discriminatory differentiation requires establishing that the differentiation between the complainant and the comparator groups has no reasonable and objective justification.

The Appendix to Article E provides that differential treatment based on an objective and reasonable justification shall not be deemed to be discriminatory. The Explanatory Report[51] itself mentions two justifications: age or capacity might be a justification for differentiating with regard to access to some forms of education, and specific citizenship (not national extraction!) might be an acceptable requirement under certain circumstances, for example for the right to employment in the defence forces or in the civil service.

Whether a difference in treatment pursues a legitimate aim and is proportionate is assessed in light of Article G of the Charter.[52] There is therefore a connection between Article E and Article G,[53] the right to equal treatment and legitimate restrictions.

[50] §54, §55.

[51] §136.

[52] Conclusions XVI-1, Greece, 279–280. Greece has not yet ratified the Revised Charter and therefore Art E cannot be applied in the case of this country. Nonetheless the principle of equal treatment—and on the basis of the broad interpretation of grounds—is applicable, even if without reference to Art E, or eventually, to the Preamble.

[53] See Ch 4.

In the third complaint claiming violation of Article E in an employment context, *CFDT v France*,[54] the ECSR had to decide whether the distinction between civilian staff with French forces in Germany and staff performing the same duties within France is contrary to Article E. The Committee decided that the situation was covered by Article E: stationing in Germany qualified as 'other status' (§44).

Referring to the Court's judgment,[55] the Committee considered the necessary elements for a discrimination analysis. First, it determined whether the difference in treatment constituted discrimination (different treatment without adequate justification). Second, if this was the case, the Committee decided whether it falls within the scope of the Charter provisions referred to in combination with Article E. Only if both of these conditions were met concurrently could it find a violation of the Charter.

Then, referring to court judgments,[56] the Committee considered that a difference of treatment is discriminatory if it 'has no objective and reasonable justification'. Such justification is satisfied if the differentiation pursues a 'legitimate aim' and has a 'reasonable relationship of proportionality between the means employed and the aim sought to be realised'. It added that while the state parties enjoy a certain 'margin of appreciation' in assessing whether and to what extent differences in otherwise similar situations justify a different treatment in law, it is ultimately for the Committee to decide whether the difference lies within this margin (§§37–39 and 41). In this case the Committee considered that the difference with regard to benefits was connected to a different situation and therefore could not be considered discriminatory treatment.

The possible justifications—the level of scrutiny—follow the 'ranking' of grounds and situations and are not independent of how they impact on the dignity of the person. Two kinds of grouping seem to evolve from the case law. The first grouping is on the basis of the ground of the differentiation, the second is the material scope. As to the ground, when it is not listed in Article E and cannot be assimilated by its inherent, unchangeable nature[57] the differentiation does not need weighty justification, in contrast to discrimination on grounds such as race or disability (listed or assimilated to listed grounds).

In cases of racial discrimination against Roma and Sinti, the Committee emphasised that no difference in treatment that is based exclusively or to

[54] Collective Complaint No 50/2008.

[55] In §42 referring to the judgment in *Abdulaziz, Cabales, Balkandali, v UK* (1985) EHHR 471, §82.

[56] The repeatedly used cases are: the *Belgian linguistics* case of 1968, the *Marckx* case of 1978 and the *Rasmussen* case of 1984.

[57] Such as *Syndicat national des Professions du tourisme v France*, *CFDT v France* mentioned above.

a decisive extent on a person's ethnic origin is capable of being objectively justified in a contemporary democratic society.[58]

The other grouping is according to the material scope, again based on the connection to the dignity of the persons affected. While in employment the scrutiny of justification has not been strict, in connection with the right to housing (under Article 31, and also Article 16 in regard to family housing), which very closely affects people's everyday existence and human dignity, the Committee has emphasised that this right cannot be subject to any discrimination based on any of the grounds set out in Section E of the Revised Charter.[59]

E. Indirect Discrimination—Discrimination in the Form of Not Giving Due Consideration to Existing Differences

Indirect discrimination—apparently neutral regulation with disproportionately unfavourable impact on certain groups of persons—is a well-established and well-known (even if not entirely undisputed) notion of equality law. This term and concept in the case law of the ECSR has an autonomous, outstandingly progressive meaning, specific to the context of the Charter and effectively promoting its function.

In Complaint No 13/2002, *Autisme Europe v France*, the complainant organisation claimed that France was failing satisfactorily to apply its obligations under Articles 15§1 and 17§1 because children and adults with autism were unlikely to effectively exercise, in sufficient numbers and to an adequate standard, their right to education in mainstream schooling or through adequately supported placements in specialised institutions offering education and related services. The government provided figures on general measures with regard to disabled or seriously disabled persons, but these did not concern persons with autism directly (§§24–25).

In the Decision on the merits of the complaint, the committee relied on the decision of the ECtHR in the *Thlimmenos v Greece* case, in which the Court had said that 'The right not to be discriminated against ... is also violated when States without an objective and reasonable justification fail to treat differently persons whose situations are significantly different.'[60]

In other words, 'human difference in a democratic society should not only be viewed positively but should be responded to with discernment

[58] *Centre on Housing Rights and Evictions (COHRE) v Italy*, Collective Complaint No 58/2009, Decision on the merits of 25.06.2010 §§37–38, referring to *Timishev v Russia* (ECtHR 2005) §§56, 58).

[59] Conclusions 2005, Lithuania, Art 31§2.

[60] *Thlimmenos v Greece* (n 48) §44.

in order to ensure real and effective equality.' This statement that human differences—congenital, acquired or developed—are to be treated with due respect indicates the path to a society based on qualitative diversity and genuine equality.

The ECSR laid down that Article E not only prohibits direct discrimination but also all forms of indirect discrimination. This can arise not only by measures having differential impact on the case law, but also by failing to take due and positive account of all relevant differences or by failing to take adequate steps to ensure that the rights and collective advantages that are open to all are genuinely accessible by and to all.[61]

The Committee's analysis already refers to the thin line (or even identity) between indirect discrimination and discrimination by failing to respect a difference. In its consecutive decisions it has paved the way to finding discrimination in cases when failure to act adequately results in disparate treatment of disadvantaged (protected) groups.

In *MDAC v Bulgaria* (41/2007) the complainant claimed explicitly direct discrimination against children with mental disability. The Committee explained again that failure to take appropriate measures to take account of existing differences may amount to, and in the actual case it indeed constituted, discrimination (§§51, 54)—without using the terms 'direct' or 'indirect'.

In a later case of disability discrimination (*AEH v France*, 81/2012) the ECSR found that the policy of the French government, leaving children with autism and their families without a choice other than go to abroad (to Belgium) to receive an education in specialised schools, constituted direct discrimination against them (§136). Again, in a sophisticated way, it separated this policy from the restrictions and limited allocation of social funding that affects everyone concerned, but places persons with a disability, who are more dependent on community care, at a disadvantage that indirectly discriminates against them (§144).

III. IMPACT ON EUROPEAN HUMAN RIGHTS INSTRUMENTS

The European non-discrimination regime has seen significant development in the past 15 years, as a result of the interplay of the three separate, still interconnected systems of the ECHR, the RESC and the fundamental rights law of the EU that started to operate effectively in 2000.[62]

[61] §52.

[62] With the adoption of the first non-discrimination directives on the basis of (that time) Art 13 TEC.

A. European Convention on Human Rights

The history of the two human rights treaties of the Council of Europe shows a particular relationship between them due to their anti-discrimination regimes. The original complementarity is confirmed by approximation in part through a slow diminution of the categorical split between the two types of human rights covered by the two instruments.[63] The adoption of the RESC—putting more emphasis on human rights and dignity—was soon followed by the adoption of Protocol 12 of the ECHR, indicating progress and a future promise of a move towards a socially tinted orientation.

The approximation process has been greatly promoted by the changed approach of the RESC non-discrimination regime. The replacement by Article E of the reserved text in the 1961 Preamble has given way to a dynamic interpretation by the ECSR drawing on and pro-actively adapting the interpretation of Article 14 of the ECHR.

The identical wording of Article E with Article 14 naturally created a 'normative partnership' as labelled by the ECSR,[64] which invites the two relevant bodies (the ECSR and the ECtHR) to pay attention to the other instrument in the protection of equality. The strong reliance of the ECSR on the ECtHR case law shows a particular search for connecting points with regard to the protection of dignity[65] and positive measures (*Thlimmenos v Greece*[66] being the model).

The attention paid by the ECtHR to the RESC is also growing, not only repeatedly acknowledging the Charter and its case law as a 'source of inspiration', but also referring to its statements as a 'relevant international instrument'.[67] The recurring need to interpret Article 8 of the ECHR with regard to the boundary between the scope of the Charter and the Convention, with special regard to Article 14, confirms the relationship. The repeated declaration of the difference[68] confirms the proximity, reaching almost joint coverage in *Emel Boyraz v Turkey*.[69]

[63] Connected, among other things, to the end of the division of Europe into two political blocs. See above section I.A.

[64] Statement of Interpretation on Art 11, Conclusions 2005 manifested in decisions 13/2002 *AUTISME v France*, 15/2003 *ERRC v Greece*, 53/2008 *FEANTSA v Slovenia*, 58/2009 *COHRE v Italy* and 72/2011 *FIDH v Greece*.

[65] With references to respect for dignity as part of the meaning of equality under the ECHR; *FIDH v France* (No 14/2003) §27, *DCI v Netherlands*, 47/2008, §§62–63.

[66] See n 48 above.

[67] *Botta v Italia* (1998) 26 EHRR 241 §28; *Sidabras and Dziautas v Lithuania* App. nos:554480/00 and 593300/00 §31; *Zehnalova and Zehnal v the Czech Republic*, 2002 no. 38621/97 (§67); *Rainys and Gasparavičius v Lithuania* App nos 70665/01 and 74345/017 (ECtHR, April 2005), §29.

[68] *Zehnalova and Zehnal v the Czech Republic*.

[69] *Emel Boyraz v Turkey* App no 61960/2008 (ECtHR, December 2014) §33.

Article 1§2 is more readily quoted when it comes to non-discrimination, although direct reference to Article E has also been made in the Court's[70] as well as the Committee's respective case law,[71] and other articles are mentioned, too.[72]

B. Fundamental Rights in the EU *Acquis Communautaire*

The equality law of the EU, starting from the seed of Article 13 of the Amsterdam Treaty (Article 19 of the TFEU) with the equality directives of 2000, and joined by the CFREU as a mandatory part of the EU legal system in 2009, creates a favourable ground for the development of human rights and non-discrimination. The CFREU, confirming the principle of subsidiarity (Preamble and Article 51), emphasises the national development of these fundamental rights. Although not mentioned in the CFREU Explanations (see above I.B.), Article E can play an important role in interpreting the anti-discrimination content of the provisions in Articles 21–26 CFREU,[73] not all of them worded as an equal treatment rule, and clearly treated as such under the Charter.

IV. IMPACT ON NATIONAL LAWS AND CONCLUSION

The Charter has been part of and an actor in the progress made with regard to the principle of non-discrimination in national laws, although is difficult to distinguish the roles, respectively, of the Charter, the secondary legislation of EU law and the CFREU, and last but not least, the national constitutional traditions, referred to in the CFREU.

While progress has been made in the legislation and jurisprudence of several states, the most important are two achievements resulting from the progress, elaboration and expansion of ECSR interpretation since the adoption of Article E.

One is the contribution to the development of the concepts of equal treatment and non-discrimination within the European as well as other legal regimes. The apex of the discussions is the reconciliation of positive measures with the concept of equal treatment, which is seen by many authorities

[70] Together with Art 1§2 in *Sidabras and Dziautas v Lithuania* (n 67).

[71] *Berger-Krall and others v Slovenia* App no 14717/04 (ECtHR, 12 June 2014) §97; *Yordanova and others v Bulgaria* no 25446/06 (2012) §73.

[72] Art 12 of the Charter: *Rainys and Gasparavičius v Lithuania* App nos 70665/01 and 74345/01 (ECtHR, 7 April 2005) §29.

[73] See, for the relationship between EU law and the Charter, chapter 1 by O de Schutter in this volume.

as rather a violation of the principle. The reasoning in the ECSR discrimination cases is gradually developing and providing convincing arguments that the violation of equal treatment is not connected to 'activity' but also to inactivity and consequently positive measures are not only reconcilable but a requirement of equal treatment.

The second result is the enhancement of the nature of the Charter as a legally enforceable document, by its explanation on the concept of discrimination. The cases (primarily on the education of disabled children and housing with regard to the Roma) are excellent illustrations of the elevated and unique importance of non-discrimination and the progressive interpretation of the obligations under the Charter. While in the latter case the obligation of the states is to guarantee the full exercise of the right (for example, the prohibition of child labour[74] or the free choice of occupation[75] must be fully guaranteed), in case of provisions of 'means', the obligation of the state is to make adequate efforts, with appropriate allocation of resources and supervision of progress. However, they are not obliged to de facto guarantee the full realisation of the goal targeted in the Charter. The discriminatory element in a situation—despite the justification of limited budgetary resources—may amount to a violation of the Charter. Moreover it brings the whole given area under closer scrutiny regarding the genuine efforts of the government and measurable progress to achieve compliance with the goal in the undertaken Charter provision (such as recently in *AEH v France*, n 81/2012).

Thus, the original distinction between provisions of 'means' or 'procedure' as against the so-called provisions of 'result' is slowly fading, in part as a result of the non-discrimination case law of the ECSR.

[74] *ICJ v Portugal*, Collective Complaint No 1/1998 §40.
[75] *QCEA v Greece*, Collective Complaint No 8/2000 §§24–25.

Conclusions—The Potentials for the Charter to be Used

NIKLAS BRUUN, KLAUS LÖRCHER, ISABELLE SCHÖMANN AND STEFAN CLAUWAERT

I. FIFTY YEARS OF CHARTER EXPERIENCE

As 'social counterpart' to the European Convention on Human Rights, the European Social Charter emerged in the aftermath of the Second World War. Its swift adoption was initially hindered by a general scepticism towards social and economic rights, but this scepticism has gradually receded, as indicated by the Executive Secretary of the European Social Charter, Régis Brillat, in his Foreword to this publication. Social and economic rights in both the ILO[1] and the Council of Europe were justified not only by the need for social justice and solidarity, but more or less explicitly by the need to create safeguards for democracy and social inclusion in order to prevent phenomena such as xenophobia, racism and totalitarian ideas from gaining popular support.

The recent experiences during the economic crisis in Europe have shown that social rights have not played their rightful role in accordance with the so-called Limburg principles,[2] under which, in times of austerity, social rights should function as criteria of prioritisation in the allocation of available resources. No references are to be found to either the Charter or the Solidarity Chapter of the CFREU in the abundant documentation regarding austerity policies (produced, for example, at EU and national level in response to the eurozone crisis).[3] Furthermore, in many instances implementation of social rights is lacking.[4] The number of non-conformity cases is also worrying. The situation is alarming, and can only be improved by increased political and legal awareness of the Charter and its content.

Around 50 years of experience with the Charter constitute an adequate period for an analysis of the Charter's background, content and impact—in particular in the present situation of social crisis.

[1] See the Philadelphia Declaration 1944.

[2] The Limburg Principles on the Implementation of the International Covenant on Economic, Social and Cultural Rights (UN doc E/CN4/1987/17), Annex. Also available in (1987) 9 Human Rights Quarterly 122–35, see esp Arts 25–28.

[3] See K Tuori, *European Constitutionalism* (Cambridge, CUP, 2015).

[4] See further N Bruun, K Lörcher and I Schömann, *The Economic and Financial Crisis and Collective Labour Law in Europe* (Oxford, Hart Publishing, 2014).

This publication aims to contribute to the legal analysis of the Charter. Obviously, it does not cover the whole corpus, being limited to employment relations. But this area is at the very heart of the Charter. In quantitative terms, this is shown by the fact that its first six articles deal with workers' and trade union rights (Articles 1–6) and that many provisions in the following articles (Articles 7, 8, 15 and 19) fall within the same category. The Additional Protocol of 1988, whose substantive provisions form Articles 20–23, also contains new (collective) rights (Article 21 and 22), as well as anti-discrimination rights in the employment relation (Article 20). In the same vein, most of the newly introduced Articles 24–31 focus on employment issues. Indeed, only the last two Articles of the Charter, 30 and 31, address social policy questions more generally.

In qualitative terms, nearly all elements of the employment relation are governed by the Charter. This is the case with regard to the individual employment dimension from its very beginning (Article 1) in terms of the terms and conditions of the employment relation, such as working time and remuneration (Articles 2 and 4), but also safety and health (Article 3) up to the termination of employment (Articles 24 and 25). Cross-cutting issues such as anti-discrimination are governed by Articles 1(2), 20, 26, 27 and E. Finally, the protection of several vulnerable groups is guaranteed (Articles 7, 8, 15 and 19). Collective rights are guaranteed for freedom of association and trade union activities (Article 5 and 6). The information and consultation of workers' representatives is also becoming increasingly important (Articles 21, 22, 28 and 29).

This publication analyses these elements in detail and shows the potential of the Charter concerning the employment relation. Among other things, the Charter has proved to be a major guardian of workers' rights, for example by elaborating a dynamic case law, in particular in terms of ensuring the effective exercise of the right to fair remuneration, or the rights to collective bargaining and to strike. The same seems to apply in the case of the rights of persons with disabilities, not to mention the right to non-discrimination.

The question increasingly arises as to why the Charter rights do not play a major role in securing social rights. Several—surely not exhaustive—political and legal reasons can be advanced and have to be evaluated.

First, the Charter is considered by several European states to be mainly a political instrument. The lessons from the 1920s and 1930s that were prominent in the post-war debate seem to have been completely forgotten. Again, this publication clarifies the content and legal value of the fundamental social rights in the context of fundamental European democratic values.

Secondly, the Charter is not well-known to legal experts around Europe. The 'Turin process' aims at overcoming this problem. In particular, the 'Action Plan' elaborated by the General Rapporteur of the

Turin Conference held in October 2014[5] will be an important tool to bring the situation closer to this objective. In the same vein, this publication contributes to the process, in particular concerning the employment relation.

Thirdly, international obligations (and in particular those dealing with social rights) are often considered to be outside the national legal order. Of course, this requires an in-depth analysis of the constitutional order of each State Party. In any event, it is clear that these states are bound to implement the obligations they have entered into in legislation and practice.

These reasons are becoming increasingly relevant and are mutually reinforcing each other at EU level. This is one of the core problems. Nevertheless, it should be recalled that there is a close link between the Charter and EU law and, in particular, the case law of the ECtHR has contributed to more visibility, awareness and even more legal effect.

II. IMPROVEMENTS NECESSARY

Not only must the missing knowledge of the Charter and its supervisory system be made good; the ECSR must also be elevated to an equal footing with the ECHR if social rights are to be applied effectively.

Therefore, the Charter's legal value is to be further developed. One important approach is the elaboration of litigation strategies at European and national level. Here, the contribution on the Charter's supervisory procedures offers the necessary information in respect of the use of the reporting system in general and of the complaints mechanism in particular, with the focus on the development of ECSR case-law on the problems arising in the employment relation and its implementation in the legal systems of the state parties.

At the Council of Europe level a closely related litigation strategy is needed in respect of the ECtHR, taking into account international (labour) standards and the case law of the relevant bodies (ECSR).

Within the scope of EU law, the direct link to the Charter and the indirect link via the ECHR should also be used in cases coming before the CJEU. As these cases very rarely stem from direct actions before the General Court (with the possibility for an appeal to the CJEU), the overwhelming majority of cases deal with preliminary proceedings. As in the case of the ECtHR, this raises the important question of the main proceedings at national level. Besides the complaint mechanism which allows for direct access to the ECSR concerning those states that have ratified the Collective Complaints Procedure Protocol, the proceedings at national level form the very basis of a litigation strategy.

[5] Available at www.coe.int/en/web/turin-process/conference-turin.

This brings us back to the question of the compliance of national law with the Charter. This publication is intended to help to find the respective discrepancies with Charter rights. By using the procedures available (reporting and complaints procedures), the actual legal position can be clarified. The respective results can then be used to start further action with the aim of reaching either the ECtHR or the CJEU. First reflections on this potential influence are provided at the end of the contributions in Part II in this publication. An important and promising field of challenging national legislation and practice will probably still be collective rights, in particular the right to strike. The growing importance of the collective complaints procedure and the synergy between these procedures and the regular reporting procedure might—and indeed should—bring about a new dynamic in the application of the Charter.

All these legal activities will not disguise that there are still important weaknesses. Several proposals to cope with these challenges have been advanced. The Helsinki (2011), Turin I (2014), Brussels (2015) and Turin II (2016) conferences have stimulated or at least contributed to this debate. In this respect, this publication wishes to put academic 'flesh on the bone'. In the present Europe there is an urgent need for the Charter and all its related activities, to contribute to act effectively against regression and, moreover, to enhance the 'social progress' referred to in the Preamble of the Charter in the state parties, and especially in the EU.

Index